Language

THIS EDITION WRITTEN AND RESEARCHED BY

Anthony Haywood

**Marc Bennetts, Greg Bloom, Marc Di Duca, Michael Kohn, Tom Masters,
Leonid Ragozin, Mara Vorhees**

Welcome to the Trans-Siberian Railway

The 'Track of the Camel'

We often talk about the Trans-Siberian as a single railway or even as the 'express'. Perhaps it was closest to being *the* Trans-Siberian at the turn of the 20th century, when this engineering feat was celebrated in a grand opening. In reality, it is several different routes and experiences. And as for 'express' – well, it was never that, not this magnificently slow 'track of the camel'.

Russia. Mongolia. China. Three countries, and plenty of opportunities to alight and explore any or all of them during stopovers. Regardless of which route or routes you choose, it's a magnificently rewarding experience of changing landscapes and cultures, people, and of life on the rails.

Russia's Soul

Today, the track from Russia's capital to Vladivostok is the classic Trans-Siberian route. It offers the chance to explore Russia's regions, and after completing its length, you'll have a lasting insight into its people. Involving a six-day nonstop journey, this route is a rite of passage through the taiga-bristled soul of Russia.

Cultural Contrast

The Trans-Mongolian, taking you through Russia, China and Mongolia, is a different experience altogether. Complete this trip nonstop, as is frequently done, and the experience of travelling on the Chinese trains K3 from Běijīng or K4 from

Endless taiga, crackling or snow-dusted steppe, mountains, the Gobi Desert and the Great Wall – the Trans-Siberian routes across Asia unite landscapes and experiences into the journey of a lifetime.

(left) Trans-Siberian journey through autumnal Russian landscapes
(below) House facade in historic Tobolsk (p160)

Moscow might strike you as a cross between a high-rolling party and a geographical expedition conducted from inside a train carriage. Make stopovers and catch short-hop trains, however, and the route offers the chance to explore deeply three very different countries and cultures.

Mongolia & Manchuria

The Trans-Manchurian is an eclectic and unusual route, traversing much of Siberia and veering south into the grasslands of Inner Mongolia and into Manchuria on the flagship *Vostok*. This is a Russian train staffed by Russians who, incidentally, are among the most personable staff you will find anywhere on the world's rails. A high-light of this route is the Manchurian town of Hā'ĕrbīn (Harbin).

Taiga & Tunnels

And then there's the Baikal-Amur Mainline (Baikalo-Amurskaya Magistral; BAM). The most recent of the great Russian rail projects so far completed, it was hailed as the 'Hero Project of the Century' and may one day form part of a rail link across the Bering Strait. If you like railways, you'll love the BAM: tunnels, mountains, limitless taiga, and the beauty of train travel itself, made simply for the sake of a journey.

› Trans-Siberian Railway

Moscow
Culture and the ancient
Kremlin (p58)

St Petersburg
Grand masters on
the Neva (p93)

Tobolsk
Magnificent kremlin and
atmospheric lower town (p160)

Lake Baikal
Russia's sacred
sea (p176)

Ulaanbaatar
Traditional Mongolian culture
meets the modern (p270)

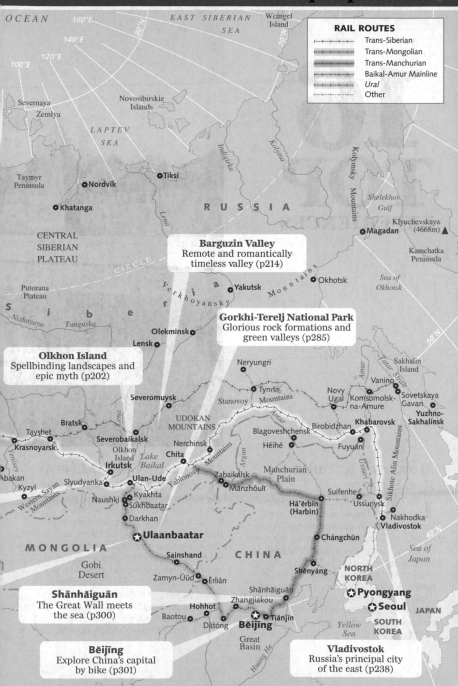

RAIL ROUTES
Trans-Siberian
Trans-Mongolian
Trans-Manchurian
Baikal-Amur Mainline
Ural
Other

Barguzin Valley
Remote and romantically
timeless valley (p214)

Gorkhi-Terelj National Park
Glorious rock formations and
green valleys (p285)

Olkhon Island
Spellbinding landscapes and
epic myth (p202)

Shānhǎiguān
The Great Wall meets
the sea (p300)

Běijīng
Explore China's capital
by bike (p301)

Vladivostok
Russia's principal city
of the east (p238)

16 TOP EXPERIENCES

Moscow's Kremlin & Red Square

1 This ancient fortress (p62) is the founding site of Moscow and the ultimate symbol of political power in Russia. Within its ancient walls you can admire the artistry of Russia's greatest icon painters, gawk at the treasure trove that fuelled a revolution, shed a tear for Russia's great and tragic rulers, and climb the tower for an amazing panorama. Flanking the northeastern wall of the Kremlin, Red Square is dominated by bold towers and the colourful domes of St Basil's Cathedral.

Life in the Caravanserai

2 Daylight gradually fades, electric light illuminates the carriage, and windows turn opaque and reflect life on board. Russia's vast distances make it one of the best places in the world for train travel. The experience is often about the company of strangers, and making your carriage or compartment a home away from home. Perhaps it's in a four-berth compartment across Siberia on Russia's 'track of the camel', or perhaps hurtling through a night in 3rd class to the snores, silences and groans of more than 50 fellow travellers.

Běijīng by Bike

3 In order to get under the skin of Běijīng (p301), hire a bike and cycle like mad all over the city. Navigate twists and turns, thread through alleys, down boulevards and around landscaped parks, and the city will reveal itself as a fascinating mosaic of charming old *hútòng* (narrow alleyway) neighbourhoods and 21st-century architectural wonders. Biking Běijīng puts you at ground level with the locals, and there is a tangible sense of camaraderie as you pull up to an intersection and push off together as if in a massive bike rally.

Russia's Sacred Sea

4 According to the Siberian writer Valentin Rasputin, European Russians who first stumbled upon this 'sea' lacked a language to describe it. Later, the exiled Old Believer Avakuum discovered a bountiful paradise where all was larger than life: mountains and rocky gates that rose into the heavens, and pure waters brimming with fish. Lake Baikal (p197), the world's largest freshwater lake, is a world of virgin taiga, coves and isolated beaches, carved landscapes, cold-flowing rivers, the splendid Great Baikal Trail (p200) – and bears. Watch out for those bears!

Mongolian Landscapes

5 Mongolia is a beautiful country. Get into a Russian 4WD or van and your Mongolian travel mates will be crooning about the blue waters of Lake Khövsgöl, the singing sand dunes of the Gobi Desert and the glaciated peaks of the Altai Mountains. Closer to Ulaanbaatar, it's easy to make day or overnight trips to Gorkhi-Terelj National Park (p285) amid the glorious rock formations and green valleys. For a wonderful experience that combines natural landscapes and wildlife viewing, visit Khustain National Park (p285), where wild *takhi* horses roam across the pristine grasslands of central Mongolia.

Stations & Stopovers

6 The glue between the interior world of the train and the towns and cities along the track is the myriad stations. Some are little more than a ramshackle platform with a telltale name such as '73km' to signify their existence; others are ambitious pieces of architecture befitting one of the world's greatest railway achievements. All along the route at Russia's stations, sellers ply a busy trade – smoked fish, berries, nuts, sausages, anything that will still a traveller's hunger or make a journey more comfortable.

Watching the World Unfurl

7 The swaying of the train as it crosses a subcontinent, the landscapes that unfurl outside the window: steppe, taiga, farmed clearings, fallow land and swamps, and all those Siberian settlements of just a few wooden peasant houses fenced off and staking a dwindling claim in the burlesque proportions of Siberia's landscape. Part of the pleasure of the Trans-Siberian is the ritual of feeding and sleeping, and simply gazing through the glass as time and motion gradually fill the space.

Culture Unleashed in Moscow

8 Moscow is not only Russia's political capital but also a cultural capital, so the performing arts (p83) are a major drawcard. Classical ballet, music and theatre have traditionally been at the heart of Russian culture. Today, exciting and creative artists are experimenting with new forms of theatre, painting, music, sculpture and dance. If you have your heart set on classical opera or ballet at the Bolshoi Theatre, or icons at the State Tretyakov Gallery (p71), you won't be disappointed. But try to catch the experimental cultural scene, too.

St Petersburg's Hermitage

9 Standing proudly at the end of Nevsky pr, Russia's most famous palace houses its most famous museum, the Hermitage (p95). Little can prepare most visitors for the scale and quality of the exhibits, including a staggering number of works by Rembrandt, Rubens, Picasso and Matisse. As well as paintings, there are superb antiquities, sculpture and jewellery on display, and if that's not enough, you can also wander through the private apartments of the Romanovs, for whom the Winter Palace was home until 1917.

Great Wall of China

10 Just as there are two sides to every coin, there are two opinions about the significance of the Great Wall (p321). For the Chinese the Wall represents a marvellous architectural achievement, accomplished with enormous manpower and advanced technical designs. For Mongolians, it represents nomadic strength, power and determination, for only the fiercest of warriors could force another people to construct such a colossal defensive work. For Trans-Siberian travellers, the Wall is a majestic ending (or starting) point to the long cross-continental journey.

KEREN SU / LONELY PLANET IMAGES ©

Culture in Mongolia's Capital

11 You don't have to travel across the Gobi Desert to find Mongolian culture; it's right in Ulaanbaatar (p270). It's a treat to hear the other-worldly *khöömii* (throat singing) and glass-shattering *urtyn-duu* (long songs). Don't miss a rock concert, where young peformers use traditional instruments to fuse Mongolian and Western music. Traditional dance, contortionists and Buddhist *cham* dancing are visual treats. Much of this can be seen at free concerts staged during Naadam, when wrestling, horse-racing and archery contests are in full swing.

11

KRAIG LIEB / LONELY PLANET IMAGES ©

Olkhon Island

12 Sacred of the sacred to the shamanist western Buryats, enchanted Olkhon (p202) sits halfway up Lake Baikal's western shore. It's obvious why the gods and other beings from the Mongol *Geser* epic chose to dwell on this eerily moving island, though today it's more likely to be a bunch of backpackers you meet emerging from a cave. The island's landscapes are spellbinding, Baikal's waters lap balmiest on its western shore and if you're after some Siberia-inspired meditation, there's no better spot.

Vladivostok

13 Vladivostok (p238), capital of Russia's east, has a swagger in its step after being remade for an economic summit in 2012. No longer a remote satellite of Moscow, Vladivostok is Asia's rising star. Golden Horn Bay is its heart and soul. Take it in from one of the city's myriad viewpoints, or join the frenzy of activity with a ferry cruise. Check out the impressive new suspension bridge spanning the bay. Suddenly those San Francisco comparisons don't seem quite so preposterous.

Historical Tobolsk

14 The former capital of Siberia, Tobolsk (p160) is today renowned across Russia for its magnificent kremlin. Crowds are rare, though, and if you come on a weekday you are likely to have its grounds almost to yourself. The kremlin is perched high above the old town, a part of Tobolsk where you lose track of time as you explore the endless wooden buildings and dramatic churches. Tobolsk is off the main Trans-Siberian route, but its charms are well worth the detour.

Tradition in Siberia

15 The villages and depleted small towns of Siberia may be gradually sinking back into the enormous landscape, but Siberians (Sibiryaki) survive and see themselves as the purer essence of Russia – the way Russians elsewhere used to be. Tradition expresses itself in hospitality and acceptance of strangers (and their odd ways). It means Siberian *izby* (wooden houses) clinging to the railway, hugging the rivers and lakeshores, or hiding deep in the forests. Despite the growth of large, loud cities, Siberian tradition and the Siberian identity survive and thrive.

Barguzin Valley

16 The remote and romantically timeless Barguzin Valley (p214) is said to have been the birthplace of Chinggis (Genghis) Khaan's mother. It is one of the Baikal region's most attractive places and, despite the trickle of visitors finding their way into the region these days, remains one of the least visited spots around Lake Baikal. Snow-dusted peaks and curious rock formations gaze down upon a landscape dotted with salt lakes and fairy-tale wooden villages, where horse carts and sleighs are more numerous than cars.

15

16

need to know

Currency

» Yuán (Y; China), tögrög (T; Mongolia), rouble (R; Russia)

Language

» Mandarin, Cantonese (China); Mongolian, Kazakh (Mongolia); Russian (Russia)

When to Go

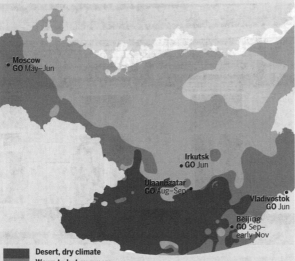

Moscow
GO May–Jun

Irkutsk
GO Jun

Ulaanbaatar
GO Aug–Sep

Vladivostok
GO Jun

Beijing
GO Sep–early Nov

Desert, dry climate
Warm to hot summers
Mild summers, cold winters
Mild summers, very cold winters
Cold climate

High Season
(May–Sep)

» China: accommodation prices peak first week May holiday period

» Mongolia: peak June to August; rain late July to August; book everything early around Naadam

» Russia: peak June to early September

Shoulder
(May & Oct)

» China: shoulder February to April and September to October

» Mongolia: May and September some ger (yurt) camps closed, fewer tourists, weather changeable

» Russia: beautiful but can get chilly

Low Season
(Oct–Apr)

» China: bitterly cold in the north; domestic tourism ebbs (except around Chinese New Year)

» Mongolia: some ger camps and smaller guesthouses closed

» Russia: plan indoor pursuits or winter sports; take saunas

Your Daily Budget

Budget less than

US$50

» Dorm beds and meals in simple restaurants or cafe and street stalls

Midrange

US$50–210

» Eating in decent restaurants and staying in hotels with private facilities; in Mongolia expect a maximum midrange of US$120, in China US$160 and in Russia US$210

Top End over

US$210

» Russia is the most expensive (US$210); in Mongolia you'll find high-end places (starting at US$120) in only a few areas; in China dining and higher comforts begin at US$160

Money

» ATMs plentiful in Russia and in big cities and towns in China, widely available in Ulaanbaatar and regional capitals of Mongolia.

Visas

» Except for US citizens (30 days) in Mongolia, visas required in all countries for most nationalities. Begin organising three months in advance. See p42 for details.

Country Codes

» China ✆86

» Mongolia ✆976

» Russia ✆7

Mobile Phones

» Pre-paid SIM cards readily available in all three countries for unlocked phones. Mongolia has four carriers (two GSM and two CDMA).

Websites

» **Lonely Planet** (www.lonelyplanet.com)

» **Ctrip** (www.english.ctrip.com) Hotel-booking and air ticketing website for China.

» **Danwei** (www.danwei.org) Perspectives into real China; handy links.

» **Mongolia Expat** (www.mongoliaexpat.com)

» **Mongolia National Tourism Centre** (www.mongoliatourism.gov.mn)

» **Moscow Expat Site** (www.expat.ru)

» **Russia Beyond the Headlines** (http://rbth.ru)

» **Way to Russia** (www.waytorussia.net)

Time Zones

Russia has nine time zones. Times are always given in Moscow time at Russian stations and on Russian trains. Ulaanbaatar and Běijīng are in the same time zone, four hours ahead of Moscow and eight hours ahead of GMT/UTC. When it's noon in Moscow it's 8am GMT/UTC and 4pm in Běijīng and Ulaanbaatar. See p46 and p390 for tables.

Exchange Rates

		CHINA	MONGOLIA	RUSSIA
Australia	A$1	Y6.55	T1370	R32
Canada	C$1	Y6.31	T1320	R31
Europe	€1	Y8.55	T1790	R42
Japan	¥100	Y8.19	T1720	R40
New Zealand	NZ$1	Y4.98	T1040	R24
UK	UK£1	Y9.95	T2090	R49
US	US$1	Y6.36	T1340	R31

For current exchange rates see www.xe.com.

Important Numbers

Russia international access code	✆8, wait, then ✆10
China police	✆110
Mongolia police	✆102
Russia police	✆02

Arriving

» **Sheremetyevo Airport, Moscow**

Trains – business R550; half-hourly 5.30am to 12.30am; 35 minutes to Belorussky vokzal.
Taxis – R1000 to R1500. At least an hour; varies wildly with traffic.

» **Domodedovo Airport, Moscow**

Trains – business R550; every half-hour 6am to midnight; 45 minutes to Paveletsky vokzal.
Taxis – R1000 to R1500. At least an hour, often three.

» **Běijīng Capital Airport**

Airport Line light rail – Y25, every 15 minutes.
Taxi – Y85; 30 to 60 minutes to town.

» **Chinggis Khaan Airport, Ulaanbaatar**

Buses inconvenient; private taxis often overcharge (fare should be US$12 to US$20). Organise pick-up through hotels.

what's new

For this new edition of the Trans-Siberian Railway, our authors have hunted down the fresh, the transformed, the hot and the happening. These are some of our favourites. For up-to-the-minute recommendations, see lonelyplanet.com/russia

Contemporary Art Boom

1 Moscow's former Red October chocolate factory has been reincarnated as the city's hottest art and entertainment centre, with the Strelka Institute for Media, Architecture and Design as its focal point (p71). St Petersburg's Erarta Museum of Contemporary Art (p104) and Perm's Museum of Contemporary Art 'PERMM' (p137), in the city's former river station, both serve up the shock of the new.

Ivan the Great Bell Tower

2 The bell tower is almost as old as the Kremlin itself, but now you can enter and climb to the top for incredible views of the city (p66).

Food & Culture in Nizhny Novgorod

3 A new National Centre of Contemporary Art (p134) and several other museums in restored mansions are complemented by a 'Food and Culture' movement, bringing together good grub and alternative culture (p135).

Yekaterinburg

4 The home of Boris Yeltsin has created a monument to its famous son (p156), the boozy Alibi bar opened (p156), and the notorious Gordon's pub... well, it burned to the ground. Shame about that, but ul 8 Marta has now got a Thank God It's Friday restaurant (p154).

Tomsk

5 After a bad write-up from the famous playwright Anton Chekhov, Tomsk gets its own back with a disrespectful statue (p172). Meanwhile, the city has added a hip and tasteful hotel right in the centre – the Toyan (p172).

Lake Baikal

6 Listvyanka now boasts Russia's first purpose-built eco-hostel (p199), while the northeast coast gets a 100km extension to the Great Baikal Trail (p258).

Mongolian Recreation

7 See a 16m-tall standing image of Sakyamuni at Ulaanbaatar's Buddha Park (p273), visit the city's National Amusement Park (p273), or ride a lift up the horse's tail on a 40m-tall equestrian statue of Chinggis (Ghengis) Khaan (p286) that's just out of town.

Vladivostok

8 It's more like what *isn't* new in Vladivostok (p238): new airport, new trains, new hotels, newly developed island, *two* giant new suspension bridges downtown, all built for APEC 2012.

Běijīng Museums

9 The China National Museum (p305) reopened as the world's largest museum, while China's ancient steam locomotives, once on display in Dàtóng, have been moved to the China Train Museum (p310).

if you like...

Majestic Landscapes

The Trans-Siberian, Trans-Mongolian, Trans-Manchurian and Baikal-Amur Mainline (Baikalo-Amurskaya Magistral; BAM) railways weave and wind through magnificent landscapes – grassland or forested steppe, coniferous taiga, soaring peaks and the Gobi Desert.

Tunka Valley Snowcapped peaks send icy streams murmuring into this broad vale where hot springs gush in mineral-hued pools and Buddhist prayer wheels whir in the breeze (p204)

Barguzin Valley Isolated, virtually uninhabited and hemmed by high peaks, this is one of the most stunning Siberian landscapes in which to go astray (p214)

Gobi Desert Where camels slurp water from wells and lone horsemen gallop alongside the train (p267)

Northern Mongolia Gers (yurts) dotting the landscape and rushing streams meandering into the distance (p265)

The Volga River Imbued with history and legend, the Volga's waters loll beneath the main line at Kazan and Nizhny Novgorod (p131)

Views from the Train

Very often, such as when your train passes Lake Baikal, the views are little short of spectacular, yet you may also travel for hours – or even days on some routes – looking into a wall of taiga.

Bratsk Dam The BAM is one long vista feast, but one of the most spectacular moments on the 4200km route comes when the train trundles right across the top of the towering Bratsk Dam (p254)

Lake Baikal No stretch of the Trans-Siberian Railway is more photogenic than the section between Slyudyanka and Posolskaya running tight to the shoreline of Lake Baikal (p179)

Approaching Běijīng Less than one hour outside the Chinese capital the train rolls through a series of 60-odd tunnels, each time emerging with stunning views of mountains, rivers and steep-sided cliffs (p269)

Ulaanbaatar Whichever direction you arrive from, the sprawl, congestion and chaos of Ulaanbaatar make for an engrossing sight (p267)

Iconic Architecture

Moscow and St Petersburg brim with imperial and church architecture. At the other end of the lines in Asia you find architecture of a very different kind.

Peterhof Gape at the Grand Cascade fronting Peter the Great's Gulf of Finland crash pad (p106)

St Basil's Cathedral The most internationally recognised and architecturally exquisite building in the whole of Russia (p68)

Forbidden City China's standout imperial residence, home to two dynasties of emperors and their concubines (p304)

Gandan Monastery Ulaanbaatar's most famous Buddhist monastery is notable for the three-storey-tall Migjid Janraisig Süm. Inside is a towering 26m-high gilt statue of Janraisig, Buddha of Compassion (p272)

Tobolsk A magnificent kremlin looks down upon the city's picturesque old town (p161)

Severobaikalsk train station The architecturally bold station at Severobaikalsk is symbolic of the brave new world in concrete the BAM was meant to represent (p255)

» The kremlin is the focal point of multicultural Kazan (p140)

Strange Places & Experiences

Many would say that spending the better part of a week (or longer!) on a train is a strange experience, and certainly some very strange things have been known to happen. Once you've got over those, check out these places.

Choir This Soviet-era city was once home to thousands of Red Army troops; crumbling statues and mosaic propaganda slogans litter the present (p267)

Wangfujing Snack Street When in Běijīng... Test your mettle by sampling all manner of creepy-crawlies, including scorpions and silk worms (p314)

All-Russia Exhibition Centre A vast 2 sq km in Moscow filled with grandiose pavilions and fabulous fountains glorifying socialism's economic achievements (p69)

Kunstkamera Peter the Great's cabinet of horrors in St Petersburg contains lots of mutant babies in jars, two-headed animals and the like – strange and grotesque (p104)

Traffic-light monument If you overlooked the bombastic opera building, make sure you catch this homage to Novosibirsk's first traffic light (p167)

Multicultural Encounters

Spanning one of the world's most varied regions, the Trans-Siberian routes cross almost as many cultural contours as there are trees in the taiga.

Tartar Kazan For total Tartar immersion, travel the route to Siberia via Kazan, the capital of Tatarstan, where you'll find a thriving Muslim culture (p140)

Nomad hospitality On the vast plains of Mongolia hospitality is a time-honoured tradition. Expect to receive endless bowls of tea, snacks and shots of vodka. (p285)

Carriage liaisons Often the Chinese can be quite reserved, but on the train they loosen up and are usually thrilled to chat with foreigners. Any topic is fair game. On the Russian trains the art of conversation reaches its highest forms.

Ivolginsky Datsan The epicentre of the Russian Buddhist world is contained within an ever-expanding compound of temples, prayer wheels and monks' quarters (p213)

Good Food & Drink

The opportunities along the route are plenty.

Mutton The meat of choice in Mongolia will fill your plate at nearly every meal. Learn to love it if you don't already.

Altai beef and Kalmyk lamb Although the origins of these (the Altai Republic and Kalmykia) aren't on the Trans-Siberian route, never turn down a chance to enjoy them. Perm's Montenegro (p139) serves the latter.

Omul This fish is sold smoked to passengers at Slyudyanka station, and elsewhere around Lake Baikal (p179)

Pozy (Buryat dumplings) Filled with a blend of pork and beef; best enjoyed in the authentic setting of a ger (p211)

Airag (fermented mare's milk) Another Mongolian speciality; ready your intestines for the after-affects

Chinese delights Dumplings are famed in northern China, or try the scorpions on Wángfǔjīng Snack Street (p314)

Haute-Russe cuisine Splurge on a Russian feast amid 18th-century opulence at Café Pushkin (p82)

If you like... combining good food with alternative culture, stop over in Nizhny Novgorod, where there's a flourishing *Eda i Kultura* (Food and Culture) movement, with readings, forums, and music (p135)

Hikes & Walks

Siberian cities can be vast, sprawling beasts, so good walking shoes are useful even on the pavements of the metropolises. Out in the woods they will be especially useful for the spectacular trails.

Great Baikal Trail (GBT) The aim of the organisation behind the GBT is to ring the world's largest freshwater lake with a network of volunteer-built paths and trails (p200)

Frolikha Adventure Coastline Trail A sometimes challenging 100km GBT section on Lake Baikal's northeast coast – worth every mosquito bite and blister (p258)

Great Wall Walk over the mighty ramparts of the Great Wall and get a sense of its long history and significance (p300)

Bogdkhan Mountain Hike from Mandshir Khiid to Ulaanbaatar, taking you through some peaceful forests just south of the Mongolian capital (p284)

Ger-to-ger trek Travel as the Mongols do, horseriding and walking between gers, meeting nomad families on the way (p285)

Shopping

Siberia doesn't tend to be associated with great shopping and there's a very good reason for that – there isn't any, except for the food shopping on the station platforms. That said, a visit to the Grinvich (p155) shopping centre in Yekaterinburg will satisfy any desire for Western fashion labels or last-minute clothing purchases.

Mary & Martha Mongolia Locate this hidden shop on UB's Peace Ave and you'll discover a trove of unique handmade items; good for Kazakh products (p281)

Sanlitun Yashou Clothing Market Bargain like crazy for shirts, pants, hats and other items in this massive clothing emporium (p317)

Udelnaya Fair St Petersburg's vast, sprawling weekend flea market is one of the best in the country (p114)

Izmailovo Market You can buy all kinds of handicrafts, and you can also watch them being made or try your hand at making your own (p88)

River Trips & Rafting

Where would Russia be without its rivers? They were the earliest 'roads' into Siberia, and travelling from west to east you cross some great ones, beginning with the Volga at Yaroslavl, Nizhny Novgorod or Kazan, depending on your route. Almost every town on a large river offers excursions during the navigation season, or go the whole hog on a longer Volga cruise.

Tuul River Paddle a canoe down the Tuul River, just outside Ulaanbaatar, for fun day or overnight trips (p276)

St Petersburg trips Take the *Meteor* hydrofoil from the Hermitage to Peterhof, one of the many river and canal cruises in St Petersburg (p106)

Moscow river cruise Avoid traffic jams and feel the breeze on your face while you get a new perspective on Moscow's most famous sights (p72)

Komsomolsk-na-Amure Choose between mellow multiday floats and one-day white-water whirlwinds in the wilds surrounding this key BAM hub (p262)

month by month

Top Events

1 **Easter** (Russia) Mar or Apr

2 **Lunar New Year** (China, Mongolia) Jan, Feb or early Mar

3 **White Nights** (Russia) Jun-Jul

4 **Naadam** (China, Mongolia) Jul

5 **Sylvester & New Year** (Russia, Mongolia) 31 Dec and 1 Jan

January

Much of Russia, northern China and Mongolia are in deep freeze during this and subsequent months. It's cold outside, but the train will be warm (or stifling hot).

 Russian Orthodox Christmas (Rozhdestvo)

On Christmas Eve (6 January) the religious fast from morning to nightfall, after which they tuck into a feast that includes roast duck and the porridge *kutya*. Special masses are held at midnight.

 Spring Festival/ Lunar New Year

The Chinese New Year is family-focused, with dining and gift-giving of *hóngbāo* (red envelopes stuffed with money) and a week-long holiday. In Mongolia it's a good time to be invited to a family celebration.

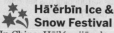 **Hā'ěrbīn Ice & Snow Festival**

In China, Hēilóngjiāng's good-looking capital Hā'ěrbīn is all aglow with rainbow lights refracted through fancifully carved ice statues (p298).

March

Strong winds, sub-zero temperatures, snow and dust storms hit Mongolia. Temperatures are still low in northern China and Russia, but days are significantly longer.

 Pancake Week (Maslenitsa)

Folk shows and games are staged to celebrate the end of winter, with lots of pancake eating before Lent in Russia.

April

Slush in Moscow, and Siberian temperatures are less savage. Northern China remains cold, and in the Mongolia–China border regions April is like March. Gradually the weather improves.

 Easter (Paskha)

Easter Sunday in Russia begins with midnight services. Afterwards, people eat *kulichy* (dome-shaped cakes) and *paskha* (cheesecake), and exchange painted wooden Easter eggs.

May

Everywhere the weather is warming up and the tourist season is getting under way. In Mongolia some ger (yurt) camps open. Snowfall may still occur, especially in the north. All of China is on holiday for the first four days – avoid.

 White Nights

As days lengthen Russia's cultural capital, St Petersburg, hosts a huge party. Events run until late July. (p105)

 Great Wall Marathon

Experience the true meaning of pain while getting your Great Wall sightseeing done. See www.great-wall-marathon.com for more details.

June

Much of China is hot and getting hotter; southern Siberian cities can get sticky; and in Mongolia temperatures are climbing to the pleasant mid- to high 20s (Celsius).

Moscow International Film Festival

Russia's premier film festival runs for a couple of weeks at the end of the month. See www.moscow filmfestival.ru.

Dragon Boat Festival

Find yourself the nearest large river and catch all the waterborne drama of dragon-boat racers in this celebration of one of China's most famous poets.

Roaring Hooves Festival

Often held at a remote location in the Gobi Desert, this international music festival can be staged anywhere in the country. See www .roaringhooves.com.

July

The grasslands of Inner Mongolia turn green; in southern Siberia and elsewhere in Russia temperatures can soar. This is the warmest month in Běijīng. Mongolia gets heat waves, hitting 40°C in the Gobi.

Naadam Festival

Mongolia's premier summer sports festival erupts in July. The date is fixed in Ulaanbaatar (11 to 12 July) but will change from year to year in other cities and towns. In China, the same occurs in Inner Mongolia.

Kamwa Festival

The 'ethno-futuristic' Kamwa Festival (www.kamwa.ru) takes place in late July to early August in Perm and Khokhlova.

Perm White Nights

Inaugurated in 2011, Perm's White Nights (www.perm fest.com) cultural festival runs through most of June.

August

Train prices in Russia can spike during this month as many people take holidays – book ahead if you want to travel on particular services along the Trans-Siberian route. Rain storms in Běijīng; less dusty in Mongolia.

Mongolia Bike Challenge

Mongolia draws serious mountain bikers for this rally. The route of the challenge (www.mongolia bikechallenge.com) varies each year, in an event that covers about 1500km through some of the finest Mongolian landscapes.

Golden Naadam

This late-summer sports festival (usually held 21 August) takes place at Terelj, Mongolia.

September

Come to Běijīng and stay – September is part of the fleetingly lovely tiāngāo qìshuǎng ('the sky is high and the air is fresh') autumnal season – it's an event in itself.

Mid-Autumn Festival

Celebrated in China on the 15th day of the eighth lunar month and also called the Moon Festival. Locals devour cakes stuffed with bean paste, egg yolk, walnuts and more.

Gobi Marathon

Go for a 42km run in one of the world's most inhospitable deserts. See www.gobimarathon.org for information. Try not to die.

December

Short days and long nights keep most people inside for most of this month. If you're prepared it's the best time to see freshly snow-covered landscapes.

December Nights Festival

Moscow's prestigious month-long music event (www.museum.ru/gmii) is hosted at the Pushkin Museum of Fine Arts (p70).

Sylvester & New Year

Russians and Mongolians celebrate New Year's Eve enthusiastically, usually with lots of beer, vodka and fireworks (not necessarily in that order).

Choosing Your Route

Trans-Siberian Railway

Moscow–Vladivostok The classic route between Russia's capital and the Pacific Ocean, crossing the Urals, Siberia and the Far East.

Trans-Mongolian Railway

Moscow–Běijīng via Mongolia Veers south at Ulan-Ude (just beyond Lake Baikal) to Ulaanbaatar and continues to Běijīng.

Trans-Manchurian Railway

Moscow–Běijīng via Hā'ěrbīn (Harbin) From Chita the route crosses the grasslands of Inner Mongolia to Hā'ěrbīn in Manchuria before passing the Great Wall to Běijīng.

Baikal-Amur Mainline (BAM)

Tayshet–Sovetskaya Gavan Curls around the top of Lake Baikal, crosses dense taiga, winds around mountains and burrows through tunnels to the Pacific Ocean.

Alternative Routes

European Russia Travel via Nizhny Novgorod, Kazan or Yaroslavl. Buses and local trains are cheap options to cross borders.

Trans-Siberian: from Moscow to Vladivostok

It's often called the classic Trans-Siberian route and was hailed as the 'fairest jewel in the crown of the Tsars'. This route runs between Moscow and Vladivostok, mostly following the historic path of Russia's first railway across the subcontinent. Trains roll for 9289km across steppe and through taiga on a journey that takes at least 143 hours (around six full days) from Moscow to the Pacific. The experience is one of travelling through a vast Russian heartland, and travellers seeking to widen the cultural or ethnic focus can stop over in Ulan-Ude (Buryatiya) or make side trips to Mongolia.

Because the *Rossiya* (train 1/2) is one of the most expensive on the route, travellers who wish to break the journey along the way are better off using other trains.

Trains

Train 1/2 The *Rossiya* travels via Vladimir and is the prime-choice *firmeny* (higher quality or premium) train on the route, departing Moscow on odd days and, with exceptions, departing Vladivostok on even days (five days, 23½ hours). It's best used for nonstop travel and is among the most expensive (with a children's carriage, kitsch restaurant car and staff carriage with shower).

Train 239/240 Via Yaroslavl, every second day June to September (six days, 16½ hours).

Post train 903/904 A slow, daily train for the masochistic, adventurous or sadly mistaken (10 days).

Sample Prices – Rossiya Train 1/2

The following prices are for the Moscow–Vladivostok journey booked in summer through Russian Railways. Prices vary with season and extra comforts.

TYPE OF TICKET	APPROXIMATE PRICE
Platskart (open compartment with bunks)	R8500 (€210)
Kupe (4-berth compartment)	R21,000 (€510)
Spalny vagon (SV; 2-berth sleeper)	R41,000 (€1000)

See p32 for more detailed train and price information.

Flagship Trains for Shorter Hops

25/26 Moscow–Novosibirsk (*Sibiryak*) Carriage for passengers with disabilities; shower carriage; ironing facilities.

55/56 Moscow–Krasnoyarsk (*Yenisey*) Carriage with shower and ironing facilities.

9/10 St Petersburg–Irkutsk (*Baikal*) Does *not* travel via Moscow. Carriages for children and passengers with disabilities, carriage with shower and ironing facilities.

15/16 Moscow–Yekaterinburg (*Ural*) Via Kazan; few notable extras. The 001Г/002Й (Moscow–Kazan) has a luxury carriage.

Trans-Mongolian: from Moscow to Běijīng via Ulaanbaatar

The Trans-Mongolian route is the most popular one because it takes travellers on a coherent journey across three distinct cultures, landscapes and languages – even if not every traveller on the train is coherent after the 7858km between Moscow and Běijīng. You will need up to three visas (p42).

The major train servicing this route is the weekly Chinese train K3/4 (also appearing on Russian timetables as 33/43), which takes 5½ days between Běijīng and Moscow, travelling via Dàtóng and Èrlián in China, Ulaanbaatar in Mongolia, and Ulan-Ude in Russia. A highlight of the journey is that it traverses part of the Gobi Desert in Mongolia. Many companies offer stopover packages with a night or two in a Mongolian ger (the traditional collapsible yurt dwelling).

Between Ulan-Ude and Moscow the train follows the same route as the Trans-Siberian from Vladivostok, crossing European Russia via Nizhny Novgorod. It's the most comfortable of the regular trains and uses Chinese locomotives, carriages and staff.

Rock-bottom prices on this route with train K3/4 are US$690 through China International Travel Service (CITS) from abroad, or from about US$600 from CITS in Běijīng travelling westwards, and R19,400 (about €485) booking locally in Russia from Intourist on Moscow's Novy Arbat. See p32 for more on prices.

Trans-Manchurian: from Moscow to Běijīng via Manchuria

Two important things to remember about this route are that it uses Russian rolling stock and staff and it does *not* pass through Mongolia. (You will only need visas for Russia and China.) The weekly Trans-Manchurian train 19/20 goes via Chita to Zabaikalsk, the border town on the Russian side where the bogies are changed before the train crosses to Mǎnzhōulǐ in China. The entire journey is 8988km and takes six days and two hours from Moscow to Běijīng, via Nizhny Novgorod in European Russia.

It is a sublime route that can be combined with a stopover in Hā'ěrbīn, a Russian enclave in Manchuria that established itself during construction of the line in the late 19th century. Most of your fellow passengers will be Russians or Chinese doing shorter hops. See p25 for other train and bus options. Eastbound on train 20, Russian Railways prices start from around R31,500/20,500 (€790/515) for a two-/four-berth compartment. Westbound, CITS charges US$1185/762 from abroad, or US$1000/650 from CITS in Běijīng. See p32 for more on buying tickets.

TOP STOPOVERS MOSCOW–VLADIVOSTOK

European Russia & Urals

» **Nizhny Novgorod** Situated on the Volga River, 'Nizhny' has some good museums and a lively food and culture scene. High-speed Sapsan trains from St Petersburg (*kupe* R9948, 8½ hours) and Moscow (seat R1490, four hours) complement conventional services. The nightly premium train 23/24 (*kupe* R2320, 7¼ hours) has super-luxury twin berths with shower and toilet.

» **Yekaterinburg** The unofficial capital of the Urals. Allow three days to explore sights in and around it, or at least a week to explore a chunk of the region. The flagship *Ural* train 15/16 (*kupe* R4520, 27 hours, daily) travels via Kazan.

Siberia – West of Lake Baikal

The most popular Siberian stopovers west of Lake Baikal are **Novosibirsk** and **Krasnoyarsk**. **Tyumen**, the first of the large Siberian cities after you leave Yekaterinburg, has the advantage of being the springboard for an easy side trip off the main line to historic **Tobolsk**, with its magnificent kremlin overlooking the Irtysh River (allow a minimum of three days so you have at least one full day in Tobolsk). **Omsk** is a very Siberian, oft-underrated city. **Novosibirsk** is Russia's 'third city' and the unofficial capital of Siberia. Two to three days will give you a taste of the city. Anyone with a week or more up their sleeve for an extended side trip should consider bussing to the **Altay Republic**, as its Mongol-Turkic heritage offers an interesting cultural contrast on this route. Upstart **Krasnoyarsk** (Siberia's 'secret capital') is situated on the Yenisey River and provides opportunities for extended side trips into **Tuva** – again, offering an ethnic contrast – or north to **Yeniseysk**.

Lake Baikal to the Pacific

» **Irkutsk and Lake Baikal** Irkutsk is easily the most popular of the stopovers, and for one reason: Lake Baikal. If you arrive in Irkutsk during the day and immediately step into a *marshrutka* (collective taxi), you can be sipping a drink on the lapped shores of the world's largest freshwater lake in just over an hour. A three- to four-day stopover is the absolute minimum if you want to at least dip a toe into the Baikal region. Irkutsk is also the base for longer side trips to Olkhon Island or the Tunka Valley. The most popular pastime during a short Baikal stopover, though, is simply lotus eating (more accurately, smoked-fish eating) in Listvyanka or other accessible small towns on Lake Baikal.

» **Ulan-Ude** Travellers have been known to stop here just to see with their own eyes the monumentally oversized bonce of Lenin's memorial. Buryat and Buddhist (with doses of shamanism) culture are also drawcards.

» **Khabarovsk** Stop here for the flavour of a historic and lively Amur town.

» **Blagoveshchensk** A Russia–China border town offering an alternative route into China (see p26).

» **Vladivostok** This is Russia's bustling Far East port and one end of the line.

Baikal-Amur Mainline (BAM)

Obscure, eclectic and a Soviet-era brainchild, the BAM is entirely within Russia, beginning in Tayshet, a rail junction east of Krasnoyarsk (and almost 4800km east of Moscow). It skirts the northern tip of Lake Baikal at Severobaikalsk and terminates 4287km east of Tayshet at Sovetskaya Gavan. Many travellers exit shortly before this, however, at Vanino as there's a ferry here to Sakhalin Island. Getting to and from the eastern railhead of the BAM can be inconvenient, and your best rail hub is Komsomolsk-na-Amure, 13½ hours before the terminus.

Unlike the other routes, the BAM largely passes towns lacking historic character, as most were founded in order to build the line. This is grubby-window and taiga country. The BAM weaves through dramatic mountain landscapes rising to over 3000m, cuts a swath through seemingly endless taiga that fringes the track, and plunges suddenly into the darkness of tunnels up to 15.3km long.

Severobaikalsk is the major stop for relaxing on Lake Baikal, and stops at Bratsk, Tynda and especially Komsomolsk-na-Amure are popular for short breaks from the poetic rattle of rail life.

Invariably, travelling on the BAM involves taking short hops, such as from Tayshet to Komsomolsk-na-Amure, and from Komsomolsk-na-Amure to Sovetskaya Gavan (see p26).

Alternative Routes & Transport

With notable exceptions, such as train 15/16 (*Ural,* which goes via Kazan), the major trains cross European Russia via Nizhny Novgorod. A third route north via Yaroslavl is less commonly used. Unless you decide to make a detour via Petropavlovsk in Kazakhstan (Kazakh visa required), the route from the Ural Mountains into Central Siberia is simple: along the main line from Yekaterinburg through cities such as Tyumen, Omsk, Novosibirsk and Krasnoyarsk. After that, lines begin to fan out again.

Budget & Border Alternatives

There are many ways to cut costs, but border hopping is a good one. Don't forget, however, that you will also need to stay overnight in some places, in which case add up to €50 per night for a midrange hotel.

Russia–Mongolia Border

The Russia–Mongolia border on the Trans-Mongolian route is at Naushki on the Russian side and Sükhbaatar on the Mongolian side. There's also a road border at Kyakhta-Altanbulag which is convenient for the Ulan-Ude–Ulaanbaatar bus. We've covered alternatives, with prices, in detail on p270.

Lake Baikal–Ulaanbaatar

Good options are daily trains (263/264; or 362 on Russian timetables) between Irkutsk and Ulaanbaatar (R4500, 27 hours), and the

PLAN YOUR TRIP CHOOSING YOUR ROUTE

BUYING SEPARATE TICKETS

The only practical way to break a journey is to buy separate tickets. In order to break a Moscow–Běijīng journey in, say, Irkutsk, it's best to take a Russian domestic train and then pick up the twice-weekly train 5/6 at Irkutsk for Ulaanbaatar, and then the once- to twice-weekly K23/24 between Ulaanbaatar and Běijīng. The *Rossiya* (train 1/2) is among the most expensive Russian trains, so if you want to break a journey on the Moscow–Vladivostok route, it's much cheaper to use other trains.

once- to twice-weekly 5/6 (also on timetables as train 63) between Moscow and Ulaanbaatar (from Moscow R15,200, four days five hours), which stops in Irkutsk.

From Ulan-Ude (Russia) you have bus and train options, as well as plane. See p213 for details.

Mongolia–China Border

The border between Mongolia and China crosses at Zamyn-Üüd (Mongolia) and Èrlián (China). This is often a sleepless leg, as most trains cross at night. See p287 for details.

Russia–China Border

The border between Russia and China on the Trans-Manchurian is at Zabaikalsk (Russia) and Mǎnzhōulǐ (China). There are numerous train and bus options here; see p298. The website www.chinatrainguide.com is useful for planning train connections within China.

Other border crossings are in the Amur and Primorye regions of Russia; see p26.

Trans-Manchurian Budget Route

How? Moscow to Irkutsk (*platskart* €120, three days 14 hours). Stopover in Irkutsk. Irkutsk to Zabaikalsk (*platskart* €63, 31 hours). Zabaikalsk to Mǎnzhōulǐ (bus €10). Stopover in Mǎnzhōulǐ. Mǎnzhōulǐ to Běijīng (hard sleeper €50, 32 hours).

Total cost: Approximately €250.

RESEARCHING ALTERNATIVES ONLINE

If you're searching for alternative trains, check out the website www.rzdmsk.ru/home.htm (in Russian) and scroll down to the timetables for stations (Расписание поездов). The information is not always current, but it gives you a starting point of the routes available so you can begin looking for trains on particular days on sites like www.tutu.ru, http://rasp.yandex.ru or the Russian Railways website http://rzd.ru (all in Russian). The German National Railways site, www.bahn.de, is your best English-language option.

On the Chinese side of the border, do an inland search on www.chinatrainguide.com. Also see www.chinahighlights.com/china-trains/erlian-train-schedule.htm.

The most informative and current site for train travel in Russia, Mongolia and China (and other countries) is www.seat61.com/Trans-Siberian.htm. It also has suggestions on getting to the railheads and on ferry services. The LP Thorn Tree forum on www.lonelyplanet.com, and one of its dedicated contributors, Everbrite (Ruth), www.myazcomputerguy.com/everbrite/Page2.html, are also very useful.

Trans-Mongolian Budget Route

How? Moscow to Ulan-Ude (*platskart* €125, three days 16½ hours). Stopover in Ulan-Ude. Ulan-Ude to Ulaanbaatar (bus €25, 12 hours). Stopover in Ulaanbaatar. Ulaanbaatar to Èrlián (hard sleeper €44, 12½ hours). Èrlián to Běijīng (sleeper bus €20, 10 hours).

Total cost: Approximately €225.

Alternatives – Amur & Primorye Regions

Much of the northeastern border between China and Siberia is an often forgotten region along the Amur River. Here it's possible to roam Siberian forests and visit dwindling settlements of northern minorities, such as the Daur, Evenki, Hezhen and Oroqen. One border-crossing option is on ferries plying the river between Khabarovsk (Russia) and Fŭyuǎn (Fuyuan, China; one way R350, 90 minutes).

Blagoveshchensk (Russia)–Hā'ěrbīn (China)

Blagoveshchensk is off the Trans-Siberian main line. This approach involves crossing the Amur River by frequent boat to/from Hēihé (p229) and taking a train to/from Hā'ěrbīn (soft sleeper Y220, 10½ hours), which has good rail links with Běijīng (Y429, eight to 18 hours).

Hā'ěrbīn (China)–Vladivostok (Russia)

Trains between Vladivostok and Hā'ěrbīn go via Ussuriysk and take over 40 hours. The easiest way is by daily bus from Vladivostok's train station; see p248. You can also short-hop to the border on trains from Ussuriysk to Grodekogo (not daily) or by bus. On the China side, there are good connections between Suífēnhé and Hā'ěrbīn (p300).

Vladivostok–Sovetskaya Gavan

A through carriage on the daily train 351 links the Trans-Siberian Railway with the BAM, travelling via Khabarovsk and Komsomolsk-na-Amure between Vladivostok and Sovetskaya Gavan (*kupe* R4400, 41 hours).

Amur-Yakutsk Mainline (AYaM)

At the time of research, this new line into Yakutia had been completed between Tynda on the BAM to just beyond Tommot. Currently most travellers continue to Yakutsk from Neryungri train station by minivan or jeep (p263).

Extending from the Railheads

If you have the time and money, consider taking a train rather than a plane to the railheads. At the Moscow end, the choices lead to many cities of Western and Central Europe, whereas from Běijīng some interesting choices are Vietnam and Hong Kong. Vladivostok has the best choices for taking ferries.

St Petersburg

St Petersburg is gradually starting to be seen as the start of a Trans-Siberian journey.

St Petersburg–Moscow–Yekaterinburg–Chelyabinsk Trains 145 and 40 run on odd and most even days respectively via Moscow and Yekaterinburg to Chelyabinsk (*kupe* R6220, two days). Train 146 does the reverse direction on odd days.

St Petersburg–Moscow–Nizhny Novgorod The high-speed Sapsan (www.poezdsapsan.ru, in Russian) connects St Petersburg with Moscow (seat from R2612, four hours, five daily) and Nizhny Novgorod (seat R5620, eight hours, daily).

St Petersburg–Irkutsk Train 9/10 (*Baikal*). Does *not* go via Moscow. Usually on odd days in both directions (*kupe* R9850, three days 19 hours).

International

See p394 for more international connections.

European Russia

Helsinki–St Petersburg Five daily trains, including four high-speed *Allegro* trains (2nd class €102, 3½ hours). Ferries and buses also do the route.

Helsinki–Moscow via St Petersburg Daily train 31/32 (*Lev Tolstoi; kupe* €133, 13½ hours)

Moscow–Tallinn (*kupe* €155, 16 hours, daily)

St Petersburg–Vilnius–Warsaw (*kupe* €160, 25½ hours) Bypasses Belarus (and Belarus visa formalities), with changes of train in Vilnius and Šeštokai (both in Lithuania).

Amsterdam–Moscow Direct daily train service via Cologne, Berlin, Warsaw and Minsk to Moscow (two-berth compartments €320, 36½ hours).

London–Moscow via Brussels & Cologne Take the *Eurostar* train to Brussels, then a high-speed train to Cologne and change to the train from Amsterdam to Moscow. Expect to pay from €500 for the complete one-way trip in a two-berth sleeper.

Běijīng

Běijīng–Hanoi Four-berth rail sleepers, twice-weekly trains, departing Běijīng Thursday and Sunday, departing Hanoi (Vietnam) Tuesday and Friday (US$175, 40 hours). London to Saigon by rail takes about two weeks (see www.seat61.com/vietnam.htm).

Běijīng–Pyongyang (North Korea; US$175, 26 hours, four per week)

Běijīng–Hong Kong (Y526, 24 hours, every two days)

Vladivostok (By Sea)

Vladivostok–Sakaiminato Via Donghae (Korea; from US$185 one way, 20 hours), continuing to Sakaiminato (Japan; from US$250 one way, 42 hours). See p248.

itineraries

Whether you've got six days or 60, these itineraries provide a starting point for the trip of a lifetime. Want more inspiration? Head online to lonelyplanet .com/thorntree to chat with other travellers.

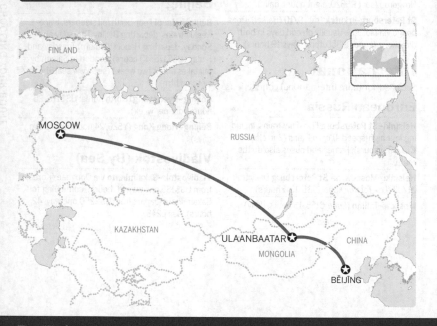

Two Weeks
The Trans-Mongolian Route

This highly popular journey between **Moscow** and **Běijīng** goes via the Mongolian capital of **Ulaanbaatar**, allowing you to compare and contrast the landscapes of three countries. A nonstop itinerary is best suited to travellers who want to see Moscow and Běijīng, enjoy the changes of landscape, and experience life on the train as it rolls across Asia. It can be covered in either direction, but if you wish to spend time in Moscow at the start of the journey, a transit visa will *not* suffice.

The train journey in itself takes almost six days, which allows several days in Moscow and several in Běijīng to explore two of the world's most dynamic capitals. In Moscow, spend three days visiting Red Square and the Kremlin, and taking in at least one large gallery. At the other end of the line, the Forbidden City, the Great Wall, the Summer Palace and Tiananmen Square will each take a day. Between these two very different geographic points, taiga, steppe and desert unfold in a mesmerising landscape panorama, with views of iconic Lake Baikal, the Gobi Desert and the Great Wall of China.

The Trans-Siberian Route

Although this route can be done in either direction, we suggest going against the general flow by starting in **Vladivostok**, at the far eastern end of Russia, so you can finish up with a grand party in either **Moscow** or, better still, **St Petersburg**. The route takes six days without stopovers on the *Rossiya*, the premium train 1/2, which means the absolute minimum required for this itinerary is one week. It is best done, however, with stopovers over three to four weeks, and can easily be tailored to your own schedule.

Vladivostok, situated on a stunning natural harbour, merits several days to enjoy Russia's Pacific seaboard and rest from jetlag if you have flown in from other time zones. It's also worth taking a break of a couple of days or more at **Khabarovsk**, a lively city on the banks of the Amur River that's an overnight hop from Vladivostok. Save another couple of days for **Ulan-Ude**, a fascinating city where Russian and Buryat cultures mingle, and from where you can venture into the steppes to visit Russia's principal Buddhist monastery, **Ivolginsky Datsan**. Just west of Ulan-Ude the railway hugs the southern shores of magnificent **Lake Baikal**. Allow at least five days to see the lake, visit the equally lovely **Olkhon Island** and spend time in **Irkutsk**, one of the Trans-Siberian's most important rail junctions.

Krasnoyarsk, on the Yenisey River, affords the opportunity for scenic cruises along one of Siberia's most pleasant waterways and can easily be visited on a two-day stopover to see the city itself. If you want to visit the Stolby Nature Reserve or take an excursion on the Yenisey River, however, plan on four days to do this comfortably. Crossing the Ural Mountains into European Russia, schedule a stop in **Yekaterinburg**, a bustling historic city stocked with interesting museums and sites connected to the murder of the last tsar and his family. Finally, you have the choice of pausing in cities such as **Nizhny Novgorod**, which has some good museums and restaurants, or stopovers in the tranquil Golden Ring towns of **Vladimir** and/or **Suzdal**, both packed with onion-domed churches, and a million miles away from the pace of the megacities to come.

Four Weeks
The Běijīng Loop

You will want to schedule plenty of time in historic, dynamic **Běijīng** either at the start or end of the trip. A day each is needed to see the Forbidden City and Tiananmen Square, the Great Wall and the Summer Palace.

An excellent overnight service connects the capital with **Hā'ěrbīn**, famous for the ice sculptures of its midwinter Ice & Snow Festival. Russians came here at the end of the 19th century to build the railway, and handsome architectural evidence of their stay lies at the city's heart close to the Songhua River. Take a couple of days to enjoy Hā'ěrbīn's cosmopolitan atmosphere and visit the nearby **Siberian Tiger Park**.

The Chinese–Russian border lies an overnight train ride away at **Mǎnzhōulǐ**. If you're not on one of the weekly Trans-Manchurian services that continue across the border and through to Moscow, it's a process of hopping on a bus across to **Zabaikalsk** on the Russian side, where you can reconnect with trains through to **Chita**. This pleasant city is a great base for exploring a relatively unvisited area of Siberia where you'll discover a couple of beautiful Buddhist monasteries at **Aginskoe**. From **Ulan-Ude** you can immediately branch down towards Mongolia, but since you've come this far it would be a great shame not to first venture further west to see **Lake Baikal**. Apart from Ulan-Ude, possible bases for exploring the lake include **Slyudyanka**, **Irkutsk**, **Listvyanka** and **Olkhon Island**. This part of the journey is where where travellers spend the most time, and it's well worth crossing from Listvyanka to **Port Baikal** to briefly walk along the lakeshore on the Circumbaikal Railway line. While in Listvyanka, also try to fit in a short walk on a section of the Great Baikal Trail, or from Irkutsk spend a couple of days in the **Tunka Valley**.

After that, board one of the trains to **Ulaanbaatar**, which is certainly worth at least a couple of days. Its highlight is the lively and colourful Gandan Khiid monastery. From Ulaanbaatar, it's a two-night journey back to **Běijīng** through the Gobi Desert.

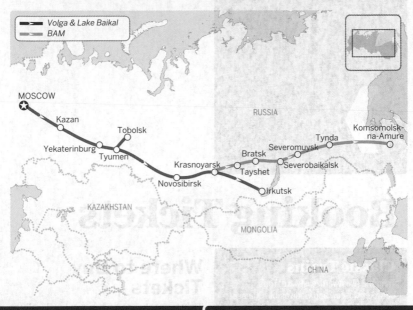

Legend:
- Volga & Lake Baikal
- BAM

Three Weeks
Volga & Lake Baikal

From **Moscow** enjoy an overnight trip to **Kazan**, perhaps taking the premium train with showers and double beds. Spend two to three days exploring the capital of Tatarstan with its splendid kremlin and museums; allow at least a full day for the city and another day for an excursion on the Volga. From Kazan continue to **Yekaterinburg** in the Ural Mountains and spend five days visiting the Romanov sites and Urals attractions. Siberia begins after that, with a night in **Tyumen** and side trip north to **Tobolsk**, which can be completed comfortably in three to four days. The journey continues with two days in **Novosibirsk**, the unofficial capital of Siberia and Russia's third-largest city, situated on the Ob River. **Krasnoyarsk** is closing the gap on Novosibirsk for the title of capital, and is well worth a couple of days in order to explore the city and perhaps visit the Stolby Nature Reserve or take a boat trip on the Yenisey River. From Krasnoyarsk the route continues to **Irkutsk**, where at least five days can be scheduled in for the sights of Lake Baikal.

15 Days
BAM

The 3400km Baikal-Amur Mainline (Baikalo-Amurskaya Magistral, or BAM) travels through some of the most rugged and unforgiving Siberian landscapes. The line officially starts in the drab town of **Tayshet**, but the closest big city, **Krasnoyarsk**, has an airport if you wish to skip all points further west.

At **Bratsk** the train crosses a 1km-long dam. The town also has an excellent open-air ethnographic museum where you can see many of the traditional Siberian buildings that were rescued when the dam was built. **Severobaikalsk**, on the northern tip of Lake Baikal, is the best base for exploring this relatively unvisited end of the lake and it also has a small BAM museum.

En route to **Tynda** the line climbs over and burrows through mountains, the longest tunnel being 15.3km at **Severomuysk**. Home of the BAM construction company's headquarters, Tynda is a must-stop for its comprehensive BAM museum and good *banya* (bathhouse). Continue working your way east to the St Petersburg–styled **Komsomolsk-na-Amure**, the largest city on the line and a great place to ponder the sacrifices and achievements made by hardy Soviet pioneers.

Booking Tickets

Classic Trains

Train 1/2 (westward/eastward) runs between Moscow and Vladivostok. Chinese train K3/4 (Trans-Mongolian) runs between Moscow and Běijīng via Ulaanbaatar. Train 19/20 runs between Moscow and Běijīng via Manchuria.

Russian Firmeny Trains

Russian *firmeny* (private or premium) trains have a higher standard of service but usually cost more. They provide a fast, useful connection, mostly between regional centres and Moscow.

Advance Bookings

Tickets can't be booked more than 45 days ahead in Russia. In China, bookings for C, D, G and Z express trains begin 10 to 20 days before departure, for others it's five to 10 days. From Ulaanbaatar tickets to Moscow or Běijīng are available from a day before departure. Agencies can facilitate earlier bookings in all countries.

Where to Buy Tickets

Tickets are cheapest when you buy locally at the railhead, but this often isn't practical. The alternatives are to use local online booking systems (the best offerings here are for Russian domestic routes) or to go through local or international travel agents and booking offices. Commissions charged by these are higher. Although travel agents are the most expensive, you pay for their networks; they, rather than you, spend time organising often complicated bookings, and they specialise in stitching together a complete itinerary.

Note that unless otherwise stated, the prices given throughout this book are for 2nd-class, four-berth compartments (*kupe*) and don't include meals.

Buying Your Own Tickets Online

Online booking options for Russian trains are very good as you can use the Russian Railways website or the websites of agents to buy an e-ticket. Currently, there are no coordinated online booking systems for the international trains, but many all-purpose websites book these for a fee.

English-Language Booking Websites

Express to Russia www.expresstorussia.com

Hostels.ru www.hostels.ru

Real Russia www.realrussia.co.uk

BOOKINGS

» Bring your passport for all international and distance rail bookings; make a few copies too.

» In order to book in advance on a westward route on the Trans-Mongolian (train K3) and the Trans-Manchurian (train 19), you will need to use China International Travel Service (CITS; p36) or local or international tour and travel agents, and you usually need to board in Běijīng. Agencies in Hǎ'ěrbīn (p300) and Mǎnzhōulǐ (p298) can also arrange tickets on the Trans-Manchurian into Russia.

» From Ulaanbaatar, you can't be certain of an advance reservation on the Trans-Mongolian train 3 or train 4 as they won't know how many places are available.

» Travelling east (from Russia), booking is available through Russian Railways or numerous local and international agents.

» In Russia, avoid using the international trains for domestic routes: they are usually more expensive than nonpremium trains and tickets are difficult to come by outside Moscow.

» Often you can negotiate a berth with the attendants on the platform when a train arrives.

Svezhy Veter www.sv-agency.udm.ru/sv/trains
.htm

Trains Russia www.trainsrussia.com

Visit Russia www.visitrussia.com

Russian-Language Booking Websites

Russian Railways

The Russian Railways website http://rzd.ru allows you to book and pay for Russian domestic train services using a credit card, 45 days or less prior to departure. Currently the site can be difficult for foreigners to use for two reasons. One is that the booking section only works in the Russian-language version. The other is that not every bank credit card works on the site. Theoretically it accepts Visa, Visa Electron and MasterCard, but in practice some foreign credit cards are rejected by the website's security technology.

For English instructions on registering and booking tickets on the website, see www.valigiapronta.altervista.org.

Other Russian-Language Websites

The following accept Visa and MasterCard and issue e-tickets. Again, foreign credit cards don't always work.

eticket Bilet (http://eticket.bilet.ru)

Poezda.net (www.poezda.net) Mostly useful for English-language timetable search function.

Tutu.ru (www.tutu.ru)

UFS (www.ufs-online.ru) A major service used

by the Yandex (http://rasp.yandex.ru) timetable search engine.

Converting E-tickets to Hard-Copy Tickets

When you book online you usually receive an e-ticket. All e-tickets (a booking receipt with a barcode) must be converted to a physical hard-copy ticket before you board. Some stations have machines for this; most don't. More frequently you'll find staffed booths inside the stations or ticket-seller windows with the '@' sign. Failing that, go to any ticket window. Depending on queues and the options available, getting a physical ticket takes anything from one minute to about 30 minutes or longer. An e-registration (available on the most-popular routes) allows you to board without a physical ticket.

Tour & Ticket Agencies

Buying tickets from agents is often the most convenient option. A brief selection of operators follows. For further descriptions and contact details for these companies outside Russia, China and Mongolia, see p396. Many local operators are also equipped to take bookings from abroad; see p36.

USA & Canada

Mir Corporation www.mircorp.com

STA www.statravel.com

Trek Escapes www.trekescapes.com

HOW TO BUY & READ YOUR TICKET

When buying a ticket in Russia, it's a good idea to arrive at the station or travel agency prepared. If you don't speak Russian, have someone who does write down the following information for you in Cyrillic:

» How many tickets you require

» Your destination

» What class of ticket

» The preferred date of travel and time of day for departure, using ordinary (Arabic) numerals for the day and Roman numerals for the month.

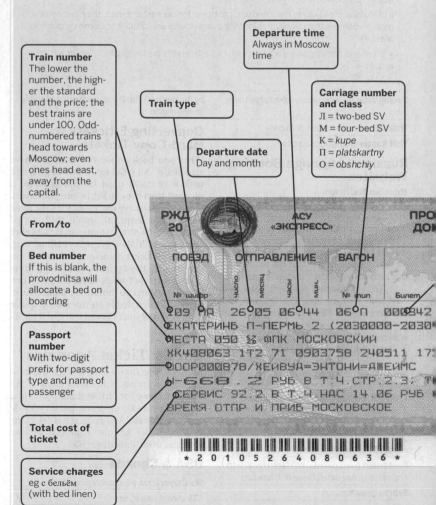

Departure time
Always in Moscow time

Carriage number and class
Л = two-bed SV
М = four-bed SV
К = kupe
П = platskartny
О = obshchiy

Train type

Departure date
Day and month

Train number
The lower the number, the higher the standard and the price; the best trains are under 100. Odd-numbered trains head towards Moscow; even ones head east, away from the capital.

From/to

Bed number
If this is blank, the provodnitsa will allocate a bed on boarding

Passport number
With two-digit prefix for passport type and name of passenger

Total cost of ticket

Service charges
eg с бельём
(with bed linen)

Also bring your passport; you'll be asked for it so that its number and your name can be printed on your ticket. The ticket and passport will be matched up by the *provodnitsa* (carriage attendant) before you're allowed on the train – make sure the ticket-seller gets these details correct.

Tickets are printed by computer and come with a duplicate. Shortly after you've boarded the train the *provodnitsa* will come around and collect the tickets. Sometimes they will take both copies and give you one back just before your final destination; often they will leave you with the copy. It will have been ripped slightly to show it's been used. Hang on to this ticket, especially if you're hopping on and off trains. It provides evidence of how long you've been in a particular place, if you're stopped by police.

Sometimes tickets are also sold with separate chits for insurance in the event of a fatal accident, or for bed linen and meals, but usually these prices appear on the ticket itself. The following is a guide for deciphering your Russian train ticket.

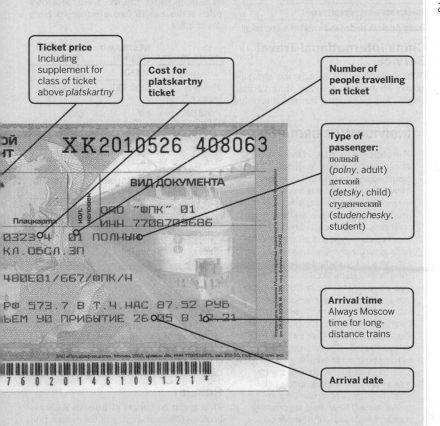

Ticket price
Including supplement for class of ticket above *platskartny*

Cost for platskartny ticket

Number of people travelling on ticket

Type of passenger:
полный (*polny*, adult)
детский (*detsky*, child)
студенческий (*studenchesky*, student)

Arrival time
Always Moscow time for long-distance trains

Arrival date

United Kingdom

GW Travel Ltd www.gwtravel.co.uk

Intourist UK www.intouristuk.com

Real Russia www.realrussia.co.uk

Regent Holidays www.regent-holidays.co.uk

Sundowners www.sundownersoverland.com, www.vodkatrain.com

The Russia Experience www.trans-siberian.co.uk

Australasia

STA www.statravel.com.au

STA www.statravel.co.nz

Travel Centre www.travelcentre.com.au

Germany & Netherlands

Gleisnost www.gleisnost.de

Lernidee Reisen www.lernidee-reisen.de

Pulexpress www.pulexpress.de

Trans-Sputnik Nederland www.trans-sputnik.nl

China International Travel Service

CITS (www.cits.net) is usually the cheapest agency for booking a service from Běijīng. Unless you use one of the recommended

---

INDIVIDUAL OR GROUP?

The choice used to be 'individual or package', but these days tour agencies also create packages for individuals. These range from semi-individual arrangements where you are 'bundled' with several other travellers and a local guide might meet you briefly at a stop, and per-haps even drive you around town for an hour, to fully fledged group tours with a guide to take care of your needs. At the top end of the scale, packages on higher-comfort or luxury trains like the *Tsar's Gold* (higher comfort) and the *Golden Eagle* (luxury) have their own itiner-aries and stops. These often include extras you can't otherwise get, such as tailor-made stopovers with a program for the whole group or a stretch of the spectacular Circum-baikal route. The price is accordingly higher. See p41 for a little more on these trains.

---

agencies, it's pretty much the only way. The following are CITS overseas representatives:

International www.cits.net (go to 'Contact Us' at the bottom and send a request for prices) or www.chinatraveldesigner.com/trans-siberian-trains.

Australia www.travman.com.au

Denmark www.cits.dk

France www.citsfrance.net

Germany www.goldenerdrachen.de

USA www.citsusa.com

Comparative Prices – Asia Trains

Moscow–Běijīng – 2nd Class

In the following tables, the Russian Railways price is a base price without commissions; the CITS price is for tickets bought locally in Běijīng (p319); and the 'Local (Moscow)' price is the walk-in fare at Intourist's Novy Arbat office.

HOW & WHERE?	WESTBOUND (TRAIN 3)	EASTBOUND (TRAIN 4)
CITS (Běijīng)	US$600	n/a
Online or agency	€550-700	€525-650
Local (Moscow)	n/a	€485
Russian Railways	n/a	€440

HOW & WHERE?	WESTBOUND (TRAIN 19)	EASTBOUND (TRAIN 20)
CITS (Běijīng)	US$650	n/a
Online or agency	€550-750	€550-700
Local (Moscow)	n/a	€515
Russian Railways	n/a	€480

Buying Tickets Locally

The international trains, especially the Trans-Mongolian, are popular, so it's often risky to wait and book locally. Generally, it's easier getting tickets if you're going west rather than east, and summer is busier than winter.

Russia

Tickets can be bought at Russian Railways booking offices and many of the private rail-ways booking offices in Russia (ж/д касса). For a list of Russian Railways booking

TRAIN 1/2 (ROSSIYA) MOSCOW–VLADIVOSTOK (SIX DAYS)

Departs odd days from Moscow, even days from Vladivostok. **All times Moscow time** (24-hour clock). The 1/2 does the entire route but is more expensive than short-hop trains.

STATION	Moscow–Vladivostok			Vladivostok–Moscow		
	ARRIVAL	STOP (MIN)	DEPARTURE	ARRIVAL	STOP (MIN)	DEPARTURE
Moscow (Yaroslavsky vokzal)			23:45	17:43		
Vladimir	02:29	23	02:52	14:12	23	14:35
Nizhny Novgorod	05:34	10	05:44	10:50	12	11:02
Kirov (Vyatka)	11:50	15	12:05	04:45	15	05:00
Balezino	15:40	23	16:03	01:08	23	01:31
Perm II	19:48	20	20:08	21:07	20	21:27
Yekaterinburg	01:28	23	01:51	15:22	23	15:45
Tyumen	06:09	20	06:29	10:40	20	11:00
Ishim	10:05	12	10:17	06:56	12	07:08
Omsk	13:47	16	14:03	03:01	16	03:17
Barabinsk	17:59	39	18:38	23:00	24	23:24
Novosibirsk	22:01	19	22:20	19:21	19	19:40
Mariinsk	03:22	25	03:47	13:42	25	14:07
Krasnoyarsk	09:16	20	09:36	07:37	20	07:57
Ilanskaya	13:45	20	14:05	03:03	20	03:23
Tayshet	16:11	2	16:13	00:37	19	00:56
Nizhneudinsk	18:39	12	18:51	21:52	12	22:04
Zima	22:15	25	22:40	17:44	30	18:14
Irkutsk (Sortirovka)	02:06	10	02:16	14:00	10	14:10
Irkutsk (Passenger)	02:30	25	02:55	13:12	35	13:47
Ulan-Ude	09:25	25	09:50	05:56	25	06:21
Khilok	14:24	19	14:43	00:58	15	01:13
Chita	19:04	25	19:29	20:21	25	20:46
Karymskaya	21:18	18	21:36	18:11	18	18:29
Chernyshevsk-Zabaikalskaya	02:21	25	02:46	12:46	30	13:16
Mogocha	08:04	15	08:19	07:09	15	07:24
Amazar	09:51	20	10:11	05:20	20	05:40
Pavlovich (Pavlov)	12:06	21	12:27	03:09	21	03:30
Magdagachi	18:52	15	19:07	20:27	15	20:42
Belogorsk	00:26	30	00:56	14:35	30	15:05
Obluchye	06:00	13	06:13	09:09	15	09:24
Khabarovsk	10:54	30	11:24	03:55	30	04:25
Vyazemskaya	13:17	15	13:32	01:39	15	01:54
Ruzhino	17:28	13	17:41	21:19	15	21:34
Ussuriisk	21:00	18	21:18	17:26	18	17:44
Vladivostok	23:17					15:30

TRAIN K3/4 TRANS-MONGOLIAN ROUTE (5½ DAYS)

Departs Běijīng each Wednesday and departs Moscow each Tuesday. Not all stops are shown. **All times are Moscow time within Russia, local time within Mongolia and China** (24-hour clock). Departure time from Běijīng in some years varies slightly.

STATION	Běijīng–Moscow			Moscow–Běijīng		
	ARRIVAL	STOP (MIN)	DEPARTURE	ARRIVAL	STOP (MIN)	DEPARTURE
Běijīng			07:45	14:04		
Dàtóng	13:51	24	14:15	07:59	12	08:11
Jíníng	16:03	6	16:09	05:47	9	05:56
Èrlián	20:37	202	23:59	21:00	237	00:57
	Bogie change at China–Mongolia border.					
Zamyn-Üüd	00:25	75	01:40	19:10	85	20:35
Ulaanbaatar	13:20	30	13:50	06:30	45	07:15
Sükhbaatar	20:50	75	22:05	21:30	105	23:15
	Mongolia–Russia border. Time-zone change.					
Naushki	19:14	197	22:31	13:08	215	16:43
Ulan-Ude	02:39	30	03:09	07:27	37	08:04
Irkutsk	10:40	25	11:05	23:25	25	23:50
Krasnoyarsk	03:54	20	04:14	06:30	20	06:50
Novosibirsk	15:58	19	16:17	19:13	19	19:32
Omsk	23:28	16	23:44	11:24	16	11:40
Tyumen	06:39	20	06:59	03:54	20	04:14
Yekaterinburg	11:32	23	11:55	23:10	23	23:33
Perm II	17:21	20	17:41	17:30	20	17:50
Nizhny Novgorod	06:55	15	07:10	03:40	12	03:52
Vladimir	10:18	23	10:41	00:30	23	00:53
Moscow (Yaro-slavsky vokzal)	13:58					21:35

TRAIN 5/6 (ALSO 63) IRKUTSK–ULAANBAATAR (25 HOURS)

Starts and terminates in Moscow. Departs Irkutsk Sunday and Monday; departs Ulaanbaatar Friday and Tuesday. Not all stops are shown. **All times are Moscow time within Russia, local time within Mongolia** (24-hour clock). For other trains and departure tables, see Getting There & Away in the Moscow, St Petersburg, Ulaanbaatar and Běijīng chapters.

STATION	Irkutsk–Ulaanbaatar			Ulaanbaatar–Irkutsk		
	ARRIVAL	STOP (MIN)	DEPARTURE	ARRIVAL	STOP (MIN)	DEPARTURE
Irkutsk			23:50 (day 1)	10:40		
Ulan-Ude	07:27	37	08:04 (day 2)	02:39	30	03:09 (day 2)
Naushki	13:08	215	16:43	19:14	197	22:31
Sükhbaatar	21:30	105	23:15	20:50	75	22:05
Ulaanbaatar	06:30 (day 3)					13:50 (day 1)

TRAIN 19/20 TRANS-MANCHURIAN ROUTE (SIX DAYS)

Departs Moscow and Běijīng each Saturday. Not all stops shown. **All times are Moscow time within Russia, local time within Mongolia and China** (24-hour clock).

STATION	Moscow–Běijīng			Běijīng–Moscow		
	ARRIVAL	STOP (MIN)	DEPARTURE	ARRIVAL	STOP (MIN)	DEPARTURE
Moscow (Yaroslavky vokzal)			23:55	17:58		
Vladimir	02:39	23	03:02	14:22	23	14:45
Nizhny Novgorod	05:44	10	05:54	11:00	12	11:12
Kirov (Vyatka)	12:03	15	12:18	04:55	15	05:10
Perm II	19:58	20	20:18	21:17	20	21:37
Yekaterinburg	01:38	23	02:01	15:32	23	15:55
Tyumen	06:19	20	06:39	10:50	20	11:10
Omsk	13:58	16	14:14	03:25	16	03:41
Novosibirsk	21:51	39	22:30	19:11	50	20:01
Krasnoyarsk	09:46	20	10:06	07:27	20	07:47
Irkutsk	02:57	30	03:27	13:52	30	14:22
Ulan-Ude	10:01	25	10:26	06:52	25	07:17
Chita	19:46	25	20:11	21:25	25	21:50
Zabaikalsk	07:17	409	14:06	03:26	391	09:57
	Bogie change at Russia–China border. Time-zone change.					
Mǎnzhōulǐ	18:30	341	00:11	03:27	214	07:01
Hā'ěrbīn	12:23	29	12:52	14:49	21	15:10
Běijīng	05:32					22:56

offices, see the English-language homepage http://eng.rzd.ru and look under 'Passengers' then 'Ticket Offices'. The following local booking agencies are also useful but charge commissions. Bring your passport.

Intourist (📞495-234 9508; www.intouristmp.ru; Novy Arbat 2, Moscow) This very helpful walk-in branch has a railway booking office with low commissions.

Real Russia (📞495-616 8086; www.realrussia.co.uk; ul Bolshaya Mariinskaya 9, office 313, Moscow) Rail tickets, packages, visa services and visa registration.

Ost-West (📞812-327 3416; www.ostwest.com; Nevsky pr 100, St Petersburg) Offers rail bookings and full invitation, visa and package-tour services. Also has a Moscow branch.

China

In addition to the following, also see www.chinatripadvisor.com.

China International Travel Service (CITS; 📞6512 0507; 1st fl, Běijīng International Hotel, 9 Jianguomenwai Dajie, Běijīng; ⏰8.30am–noon & 1.30–5pm; Ⓜ Beijing Train Station) The best place to buy tickets locally. See also p36.

Monkey Business (📞6591 6519; www.monkeyshrine.com; Room 305, Youyi Poachers Inn, 43 Beisanlitun Nan, Běijīng; Ⓜ Dongshishitiao) Arranges all kinds of stopovers and homestay programs, and has a lot of experience in booking international trains for independent travellers. In Hong Kong, it goes under the name **Moonsky Star Ltd** (📞852-2723 1376; www.monkeyshrine.com).

Mongolia

In Ulaanbaatar, you cannot buy tickets in advance for the Běijīng–Moscow or the Moscow–Běijīng trains, because staff in Ulaanbaatar won't know how many people are already on the train. You can only buy a ticket for these trains the day before departure (although you could try asking two days in advance). If you have trouble booking a berth, ask your guesthouse manager or hotel reception desk for assistance. See p282 for local booking details.

siya; Moscow–Vladivostok) and 19/20 (*Vostok;* Trans-Manchurian) use Russian rolling stock and staff. Train K3/4 (Trans-Mongolian) is a Chinese train. The restaurant car is always a local one, even on the Chinese train K3/4.

Classes

For detailed descriptions of trains and classes, see p51. Unless otherwise stated, in this book the price given in each town's Getting There & Away section is for a 2nd-class *kupe* (four-berth compartment) seat, without meals. The major trains 1/2 (*Ros-*

Trans-Mongolian K3/4

» **1st class two-berth** Showers shared by two compartments.

» **1st class four-berth** Soft sleeper, slightly larger than 2nd class.

» **2nd class four-berth** Similar to the Russian *kupe.*

PRICES, DISCOUNTS & SERVICES

Price Comparison by Class

ROUTE	SV	KUPE	PLATSKART
Moscow–Vladivostok (train 1/2)	R41,500 (€1000)	R21,500 (€525)	R8500 (€200)

ROUTE	1ST CLASS (2-BERTH)	1ST CLASS (4-BERTH)	2ND CLASS (4-BERTH)
Běijīng–Ulaanbaatar (UB)–Moscow (train K3)	US$1112 (US$394 to UB)	US$1016 (US$364 to UB)	US$690 (US$253 to UB)
Běijīng–Moscow (train 19)	US$1185	n/a	US$762
Běijīng–Ulaanbaatar (train K23)	US$394	US$364	US$270

The westward prices are those charged by CITS in the US in summer 2011.

Top-Bunk Discounts

In recent years, discounts have been offered on top bunks. It's only on selected routes, on some days and not year-round, but keep an eye out for this locally in Russia.

Services

When you book, you will often see a range of prices. The higher ones are with services, usually meaning meals, often a newspaper and cleaner toilets. These are common symbols you will see online.

CLASS	SERVICES
platskart 3 P (3 П)	not air-conditioned
platskart 3 E (3 Э)	air-conditioned
kupe 2 K (2 К)	not air-conditioned, no services
kupe 2 L (2 Л)	air-conditioned, no services
kupe 2 U (2 У)	not air-conditioned, with services
kupe 2 E (2 Э)	air-conditioned, with services
spalny vagon (1st class) 1 L (1 Л)	air-conditioned, no services
spalny vagon (1st class) 1 B (1 Б)	business class, air-conditioned, with services
additional letters МЖ	male-only carriage

Trans-Siberian & Trans-Manchurian

When booking, you often have the choice of a mixed-sex or women-only *kupe,* although this is not always guaranteed.

» **SV (1st class or soft class)** Two-berth compartments in Russian carriages, built in East Germany (and often refurbished in the Ukraine).

» **Kupe (2nd class)** Four-berth. Berths 33 to 36 are alongside the toilet and can be noisy. The lower the number, the closer you are to the attendant.

» **Platskart (3rd class or hard class)** Carriages sleep 54 passengers in compartments with partitions. Bunks also line the corridors. Not available on the Trans-Manchurian.

Higher-Comfort & Luxury Trains

The *Golden Eagle* (luxury, all-inclusive services) and the *Tsar's Gold* (higher comfort) are the two best-known options. They are used for packages, and the *Golden Eagle* is the last word in luxury Russian rail travel, with prices to match (around US$25,000 for a Gold Class single). Travellers are international and tend to be older than the average train traveller.

For more information on routes and route alternatives, see p22.

Arranging Your Visas

China

A tourist visa is required for all except travellers from Japan, Singapore and Brunei. Visas are most easily obtained from the traveller's country of residence.

Mongolia

A 30-day tourist visa is required by most travellers. US citizens need no visa for up to 90 days. Transit visas are valid for 72 hours, only sufficient for a short stop in Ulaanbaatar.

Russia

The required invitation for a 30-day tourist visa is best organised through a visa agency or travel service. With few exceptions, you can only apply in your country of residence. A nonstop transit visa for a Trans-Siberian Railway journey is valid for 10 days, giving westbound passengers a few days in Moscow; heading east, however, travellers must immediately continue on. Business visas are a more flexible option.

Planning

Depending on your nationality and the Trans-Siberian route you choose, you will need a visa for one to three countries – Russia, Mongolia and China.

» For a Russian visa it is imperative that you apply from your country of residence.

» Except for Chinese visas issued in Hong Kong, more paperwork is involved in getting a visa for China in any place other than your country of residence.

» Mongolian visas can be obtained anywhere but an invitation is sometimes required if you apply outside your country of residence.

» Visas are *not* issued on land borders.

» Visas are valid for entry within three months of issue. Time your applications so they're not too early or too late.

Costs

The following fees don't take into account processing costs by agencies when used.

China UK citizens can expect to pay from £30 for a 30-day tourist visa, US citizens US$140, and other nationalities US$30.

Mongolia Each embassy sets its own price. Sample prices for a single entry/exit visa are £40 in London, Y270 in Běijīng, AU$100 in Sydney, and C$90 in Ottawa.

Russia The minimum charge (excluding processing fees) for a single-entry tourist visa for citizens of Australia is AU$50, most EU countries €35, the UK £50 and the USA US$140. However, count on anything from €150 to around €300 for a full business visa with invitation and processing fees. Note that at present some Russian consulates demand to see proof of funds or regular employment before issuing visas, and many nationalities also need accredited health insurance.

Agencies

The following agencies can arrange visas for all three countries and are especially useful for Russian visas.

Action-visas.com www.action-visas.com

CIBT http://uk.cibt.com

Comet Consular Services www.cometconsular .com

IVDS www.visum-dienst.de

Real Russia www.realrussia.co.uk

VisaHQ.com http://russia.visahq.com

Visalink.com.au http://visalink.com.au

Zierer Visa Services http://zvs.com

Russian invitations can also be arranged with the following:

Express to Russia www.expresstorussia.com

Visa Able www.visaable.com

Way to Russia www.waytorussia.net

Embassy Websites

China www.fmprc.gov.cn/eng/and click on Missions Overseas, or www.chinese-embassy.info

Mongolia www.mongolianembassy.us

Russia www.russianembassy.net

Visas for China

Apart from citizens of Japan, Singapore and Brunei, all visitors to China require a visa, which covers the whole of China, although there are restricted areas that require an additional permit. Hong Kong is a special administrative region and is visa-free for most nationalities (see www.immd.gov.hk/ehtml/hkvisas_4.htm).

A standard 30-day single-entry tourist (L) visa can be issued from most Chinese embassies in three to five working days. Express visas cost twice the usual fee, and in some countries (eg the UK and the US), the visa service has been outsourced from the Chinese embassy to a Chinese Visa Application Service Centre, which levies an extra administration fee. This can double the cost.

A standard 30-day visa is activated on the date you enter China, and must be used within three months of the date of issue. Arranging double-entry visas is fairly straightforward, but 60- and 90-day visas can be harder to obtain.

Having a visa mailed to you will take up to three weeks. In the US and Canada, mailed visa applications have to go via a visa agent, at extra cost. In the US, many people use the **China Visa Service Center** (☑in the USA 800 799 6560; www.mychinavisa.com), taking around 10 to 14 days. China International Travel Service in the US, France and Denmark also handles visas (see p36).

From Hong Kong

Options:

China Travel Service (www.ctshk.com) See the website (under Branch Info) for Hong Kong and international offices.

Visa Office of the People's Republic of China (☑3413 2300; 7th fl, Lower Block, China Resources Centre, 26 Harbour Rd, Wan Chai; ☻9am-noon & 2-5pm Mon-Fri) Single-entry tourist visas processed in one/two/three days cost HK$400/300/150 (American and UK passport holders pay more). Arrive early and queue.

From Mongolia & Russia

It's possible to get a visa for China in Ulaanbaatar, but this takes a week and involves queuing and more paperwork. The website http://mn.china-embassy.org/eng/lsfw lists all fees, opening hours and requirements. When you apply for the visa you must provide one passport photo, proof of departure from China (eg an air or train reservation), proof of a booked hotel stay of three nights and a bank statement. In practice, travellers often obtain all this from any travel agency in Ulaanbaatar and simply cancel afterwards.

In Russia, China has consulates in St Petersburg, Moscow and Khabarovsk. At the very least an invitation letter and/or hotel booking and an onward flight are usually required. In St Petersburg, travellers have successfully organised the invitation and visa through **Milor-Tur** (☑812-982 7489; www.milor -tour.spb.ru, in Russian; ul Bol Konyushennaya 27, office 304). Seven-day processing costs R3000, three-day processing an extra R1000. You will need to be registered in St Petersburg.

Registration & Extensions

There's no individual registration requirement when you enter China. Remember that if you go to Hong Kong or Macau (which are visa-free for many nationalities) you'll need a new visa or a double-entry visa to return to the mainland.

The Foreign Affairs Branch of the local Public Security Bureau (PSB) deals with visa extensions. See p319 for PSB details in Běijīng.

Visas for Mongolia

Currently, a 30-day tourist visa is easily obtained at any Mongolian embassy, consulate, consulate-general or honorary consul (special exit-permit conditions apply for visas from honorary consuls). To stay beyond 30 days, tourist visas can be extended in Ulaanbaatar.

US citizens can stay in Mongolia for up to 90 days without a visa. Israeli and Malaysian citizens can stay visa-free for up to 30 days and Hong Kong and Singaporean citizens can stay visa-free for up to 14 days.

To get a visa for longer than 30 days, you must be invited or sponsored by a Mongolian citizen, foreign resident (expat) or Mongolian company, or be part of an organised tour. It is therefore possible to get a 90-day visa for most nationalities; you just need to pay the inviting agency a fee of around US$30. Most guesthouses can do this. The **Khongor Guesthouse** (www.khongor-expedition.com) in Ulaanbaatar is very reliable.

If you cannot get to a Mongolian consulate, you can pick up a 30-day tourist visa on arrival at the airport in Ulaanbaatar. There is no guarantee, however. You'll need US$93 and two passport photos and you *must* have an invitation from an organisation or company in Mongolia.

A single-entry transit visa costs between US$25 and US$60, depending on where you apply for it, but cannot be extended. You will need to show your train or plane ticket and a visa for the next country (Russia or China). Transit visas are valid for 72 hours from the date of entry, which will only allow you to get off the Trans-Mongolian train in Ulaanbaatar for a very short time before catching another train to Russia or China.

Consulate Websites

International www.immigration.gov.mn
Australia www.mongolianconsulate.com.au
UK www.embassyofmongolia.co.uk
USA www.mongolianembassy.us

From China & Russia

For a list of Mongolian embassies in China and Russia, see p382. Always try to call ahead as hours change frequently. Expect to pay approximately US$40 for normal four-day processing or about US$75 for a same-day rush visa. Invitations are not usually required, but this can be arbitrary and change quickly; it's worth being prepared if you're short of time. See p321 for more.

Registration & Extensions

If you stay less than 30 days, you don't need to register. All visitors who plan to stay more than 30 days *must* be registered within seven days of their arrival. This applies to everyone, including US citizens.

You can extend a 30-day tourist visa by another 30 days. For extensions, registration and exit visas, go to the **Office of Immigration, Naturalization & Foreign Citizens** (INFC; ☎011-1882; ⊙9am-1pm & 2-6pm Mon-Fri), 1.8km east of the airport, an inconvenient 15km trek from central Ulaanbaatar. The office is usually busy, so you should expect to spend an hour or two here. If you've already registered, you should apply for an extension (US$2 per day; minimum extension seven days) about a week before your visa expires. You'll need a passport-size photo and must pay a T5000 processing fee. The extension will be issued on the same day. Bring cash.

Several guesthouses in Ulaanbaatar will take care of visa extensions (and registration) for a small fee. If you don't have a letter of support you can write your own (handwritten is OK); the letter should state the date of your arrival, the date of extension and the reason for travel.

Getting a visa extension outside the capital is difficult, as your passport would need to be sent back to Ulaanbaatar.

Visas for Russia

Everyone entering Russia needs a visa and should apply before leaving home. From Hong Kong, requirements have recently been tightened, but you might try through **Monkey Shrine** (www.monkeyshrine.com). The Russian consulate in Běijīng has been known to issue transit visas (www.russia.org.cn/eng)

and **Legend Tour** (www.legendtour.ru/eng) in Ulaanbaatar is often successful.

Tourist Visa

For most travellers a tourist visa (single or double entry and valid for a maximum of 30 days, nonextendable, from the date of entry) will be sufficient. Travel agents, Russian hotels and specialised visa agencies can provide the invitation; see p42.

Business Visa

If you plan to stay longer than a month, it's advisable to apply for a business visa. These can be issued for three, six or 12 months, and are available as single-entry, double-entry or multiple-entry visas. They are valid for up to 90 days of travel within any 180-day period. You don't need to be on business to get one of these visas (they're great for independent tourists with longer travel itineraries and flexible schedules), but to get one you must have a letter of invitation from a registered Russian company or organisation (arranged via specialist visa agencies).

Transit Visa

For transit by air, this visa is usually good for a maximum of three days. For a nonstop Trans-Siberian Railway journey, it's valid for 10 days, giving westbound passengers a few days in Moscow; those heading east, however, are not allowed to linger in Moscow.

Private Visa

This visa is valid for up to three months and can be issued for single or double entry. To get one you'll need an official invitation certificate from relatives or friends you'll be staying with (this is a big hassle for them to get; applying for a regular tourist or business visa is far simpler).

Application

If the agency is not handling the application as well, you need to lodge it yourself at the consulate. Costs vary from US$50 to US$450 depending on the type of visa applied for and how quickly you need it. Check well in advance what these rules might be; for example, applications in the US and UK must now be made using the online form of the Consular Department of the Ministry for Foreign Affairs of the Russian Federation (available at http://evisa.kdmid.ru).

Immigration Form

Immigration forms are given out on your flight, available in the arrivals hall or produced electronically by passport control (this happens at Moscow airports). Take good care of your half of the completed form as you'll need it for registration and could face problems while travelling in Russia – and certainly will on leaving – if you can't produce it.

Registration

It's crucial that you are registered at least once. Every visitor to Russia must have their visa registered within seven working days of arrival, ie excluding weekends and public holidays. Every time you change cities, you must register again within seven working days.

Once registered, you should receive a slip of paper confirming the dates you'll be staying at that particular hotel. Keep this safe – any police who stop you will need to see it. (Registration used to be required within three days of arrival, and some police are unaware of the change. In any case, it's a good idea to keep your train and bus tickets so you can prove that you didn't need to register.)

Things becomes easier after the first registration as most travellers move on within seven working days, ie before a new registration is required. Travelling the Trans-Siberian routes, you might only be registered once.

If you're staying at a hotel, the receptionist will register you for free (or occasionally for a fee of around €10). Most hotels can do this immediately, which is useful if you're travelling on the next day, but some require a full working day to process it with the Upravleniye Federalnoy Migratsionnoy Slyzhby (UFMS). If you're on a tight schedule, ask how long registration takes. (Note also that the UFMS doesn't process registrations on Wednesday.)

Some inviting agencies (such as Real Russia) can organise registration for the whole period of your stay. This is often worth having if you're travelling to remote regions.

If you're not staying in a hotel, you can register yourself at a post office (see www.waytorussia.net/RussianVisa/Registration.html for the steps), which is difficult at best and nearly impossible in remote places.

Extensions

Extensions are time-consuming and difficult; tourist visas can't be extended at all. Avoid the need for an extension by initially arranging a longer visa than you might need.

Life on the Rails

Internet Resources

Circumbaikal Railway (http://kbzd.trans sib.ru/eng)
CNVOL.com (www.cnvol.com/boarding -china-train.htm) Tips about trains in China.
A Journey on the Trans-Siberian Railway (www.trans-siberian-railway.co.uk) Clive Sampsan's passion for travel, with inspiring photos.
Man in Seat 61 (www.seat61.com) Mark Smith's definitive website.
Meeting of Frontiers (http://international .loc.gov/intldl/mtfhtml/mfhome.html) Online collection about Russians exploring America and vice versa. Under 'Digital Collections' you'll find an original Trans-Siberian guidebook dating from 1900 and rare books and photos, many relating to Siberian and Far East travel and exploration.

Virtual Tours

Google Maps (www.google.ru/intl/ru/ landing/transsib/en.html) A virtual journey on the *Rossiya* from Moscow to Vladivostok, from Google and Russian Railways. Choose the rumble of wheels, Russian radio or between *War and Peace* and several other Russian classics (in Russian).
Russian Railways (http://eng.rzd.ru/vtour/ index.html) A virtual tour inside the *Rossiya*.

Arriving & Boarding

» Allow enough time at the station for formalities and last-minute supplies. Check the name of the station closely on your ticket and arrive 40 minutes to one hour before scheduled departure.

» Wait for the platform (платформ) and track (путь) to be displayed on the departure board.

» Keep your ticket and passport safe but accessible so you can show them for boarding.

Inside the Carriage

Facilities in the carriage will depend on the class of travel. Generally, a 2nd-class *kupe* carriage is as follows. On the left as you enter is one bathroom and alongside that is the attendant's compartment. Opposite this compartment is the all-important samovar with hot water for beverages, and directly opposite this, inset on the wall near the attendant's compartment, is (in theory) potable water. Under no circumstances drink the water in the bathrooms; the best and safest water on the train comes from the samovar.

Each 2nd-class carriage has closed compartments, but during the day the doors are often left open. At the other end of the carriage is a second toilet, and beyond that a smokers' vestibule with an ashtray. The rubbish bin is inside a wooden box opposite the second toilet.

SHE WHO MUST BE OBEYED

On any long-distance Russian train journey you'll soon learn who's in charge: the *provodnitsa*. Though sometimes male (a *provodnik*), carriage attendants are usually women. Some of them sport the most distinctive hairdos you'll come across this side of a drag-queen convention.

Apart from checking your ticket before boarding the train, doling out linen, and shaking you awake in the middle of the night when your train arrives, the *provodnitsa*'s job is to keep her carriage spick and span (most are very diligent about this) and to make sure the samovar is always fired up with hot water. They will have cups, plates and cutlery to borrow, if you need them, and can provide drinks and snacks for a small price. On long journeys the *provodnitsa* works in a team of two; one will be working while the other is resting. Be polite and respectful to your *provodnitsa* and your journey will be all the more pleasant.

Clothes

Loose fitting, comfortable and layered is the motto. Russian train attire often consists of ultra-loud synthetic tracksuit pants, a T-shirt and pullover (or sweatshirt) and thongs or sandals. In contrast to Russian big-city streetwear, this is not high fashion, but it's highly functional. Variations on this theme – such as loose-fitting jeans and using the tracksuit pants as pyjamas – are a good compromise between style and comfort. In winter, a warm jacket or overcoat and a warm hat and gloves, as well as face and lip cream against cold, should be kept close by for station stops.

Be aware of polite signals or requests by others that you should briefly leave the compartment so that the person can get changed – mostly, this happens just before or after departure.

Toilets

The toilets on all major trains are Western type. Unless the train has a closed-system biological toilet (some modern or refitted carriages have these), toilets will be locked before and after arrival at a station. In larger cities, this might be one hour before arrival and one hour after leaving the station, although 10 to 20 minutes on each side of town is more usual. The schedule is attached to the toilet door. There are no showers in passenger carriages except in 1st class on a few top-quality trains, so a flannel is useful for washing at the basin. Most *firmeny* (premium) trains, however, have a staff carriage with shower and ironing facilities. The *provodnitsa* can organise a visit to the rain room for a couple of dollars. Apart from soap and the usual toiletries, pack or buy sufficient toilet paper, although a good attendant will keep the toilets supplied and shipshape. Use the bathroom bin to dispose of sanitary objects. A clothes hook situated in the bathroom is useful for hanging up your day pack or toiletries bag while you go about your ablutions.

Electricity

In the age of manifold hand-held devices and digital cameras, power outlets can be a problem in some carriages, especially on the Russian trains. These have a couple of 110-volt outlets for razors, but often a 2nd-class carriage will have only one 220-volt socket, located halfway along the corridor. Ask politely, however, and you can often use a power outlet inside the attendant's carriage. Modern 1st-class and many newer 2nd-class carriages also have power outlets in the compartments.

Getting to Know

Politely greeting fellow travellers when you first enter the compartment, or greeting new arrivals, is a good icebreaker. Let things develop at a natural pace, though. Offering food, even as a token gesture, used to be de rigueur and remains the best way to cultivate a good travelling relationship.

Russians are masters of the art of conversation, so if you're travelling alone it will be easy to meet people. Chinese travellers are also curious and like talking to foreigners. Sometimes the trolley lady selling drinks and snacks will combine business with pleasure by sitting down for a rest and conversation. If you chat for a long time, it's usual to buy a drink or snack in return. Keep small change for this – snack sellers can disappear into the taiga for several hundred kilometres in order to break the high notes. The more skilled deliver the best vodka and conversation on the train.

If you have difficulties with a fellow passenger (a loud DVD player is a possible one), sort it out locally, but if that fails, the *provodnitsa* can swing into action.

Time Zones

For more on time differences, see p390. Jet-lag is much like the smell of smoked fish in a compartment – it has a habit of lingering. The Trans-Siberian route between Moscow and Vladivostok crosses seven of Russia's nine time zones. Since March 2011 Moscow has kept its clocks permanently on summer time, which is GMT/UTC plus four hours.

WHERE	TIME	GMT/UTC
Moscow	noon (12:00)	+4hr
Běijīng	4pm (16:00)	+8hr
Ulaanbaatar	4pm (16:00)	+8hr
Yekaterinburg & Tyumen	2pm (14:00)	+6hr
Omsk & Novosibirsk	3pm (15:00)	+7hr
Krasnoyarsk	4pm (16:00)	+8hr
Irkutsk & Ulan-Ude	5pm (17:00)	+9hr
Vladivostok	7pm (19:00)	+11hr

Clocks and timetables on trains and at stations show Moscow time (*Moskovskoe vremya*). Local time is known as *mestnoe vremya*.

The best way to cope with the time zones is to drink plenty of bottled water, avoid overdoing the alcohol and shift your meals and bedtime back or forward according to local time. Travellers who take strong medication will need to exercise caution and seek advice from their doctor before setting out (see p403).

Safety & Safekeeping

Russian and Asian trains are safe, but be security conscious, especially if you're travelling alone.

» Keep your valuables and documents with you at all times in a zipped or buttoned-up pocket. Don't flash large amounts of cash or your credit cards around.

» Money belts and ankle stashes are useful, but storing documents and valuables inside your pillowcase while you sleep is the safest stash.

» Ask someone you trust to keep an eye on any bag containing valuable equipment while you are away.

» If you're alone in a compartment, ask the *provodnitsa* to lock it while you go to the restaurant car or get out at long station stops (never leave luggage completely unattended in an unlocked compartment).

» Lock your compartment door from the inside at night and use the additional metal security latch on the door.

Generally, the more alcohol in play, the more safety is an issue. In the rare case that you are molested by a fellow passenger, inform the attendant. If you feel unsafe, a move or swap can be organised.

Luggage

How much to bring will be a compromise between weight and comfort. The baggage allowance per adult on Chinese international

---

I TRAVEL, THEREFORE I AM

One of the most celebrated Trans-Siberian travellers is North Korea's Kim Jong-Il, who in summer 2001 cruised by train across Siberia on a nine-day jaunt to Moscow to meet Vladimir Putin, and then on to Putin's home town of St Petersburg. Unlike lesser mortals, he had the pleasure of a 21-carriage armoured train, which more than did the trick of keeping the media at arm's length. As London's *Independent* put it at the time, 'Mr Kim's trip across Russia has been extraordinarily successful in terms of making Russians and the rest of the world aware that the 59-year-old North Korean leader exists.' This is a good enough reason to take the Trans-Siberian if ever there was one.

A decade later, Kim was back in his train on a trip to Ulan-Ude, where he met Dmitry Medvedev and reportedly told him 'we are having a very fun journey'. Indeed.

TALKING TO THE MAN IN SEAT 61

Mark Smith went from managing London railway stations to running his award-winning website www.seat61.com – the train traveller's definitive compendium. A plane is a 'glorified teleport', he says, that 'detracts from the experience of travel. I think we've almost created a mode of travel that narrows the mind. On a train you can see every blade of grass passing the window; you get a feeling for the distance'.

What got you hooked on train travel in the first place? Anyone who loves travel ought to like journeys as well as destinations. The two go together, like climbing the mountain and being at the summit. And if you like journeys, let's choose a mode of transport where you can see where you're going, where you can meet people, you're not strapped down, you're treated like a human being and can eat in a restaurant, sleep in a bed, and move around freely.

You've travelled a couple of different Trans-Siberian routes. What are the main differences? People talk about the Trans-Siberian as if it's just one experience, but I've had completely different experiences on different routes. When I took the Moscow to Beijing Trans-Mongolian train, almost everyone was going the whole route and it was a party all the way. The scenery changes from four days of Siberia to a day in Mongolia with the total contrast of the Gobi Desert, then it changes again on the final day to the mountains of China and, of course, the Great Wall. On the other hand, travelling from Moscow to Vladivostok was seven solid days of Siberia. Russians tend to use the train for various sections of the route, rather than end to end, and there were no other Westerners except for a couple that got on in Irkutsk. Even I was going a bit stir crazy by the time we reached Vladivostok, and the nicest part of that trip was the ferry from Vladivostok to Japan.

What's the worst experience you've ever had on a train? I don't think I've ever had a really bad experience. If you mean bad experience as an uncomfortable, dirty or late train, paradoxically, some of the experiences on dirty, run-down trains have been the most memorable. There are people who are so scared of having a bad experience that they'd rather have none at all. I think that any experience is worthwhile and better than none. I've travelled on some really run-down trains – for example, in Burma – but it's an experience I will always remember. It's a question of your attitude to travel rather than the train.

What's the most useful item to have with you on a train journey? Well, obviously I never travel without a good book and a corkscrew.

If you could choose one travelling companion for a round-the-world journey by train and boat, who would you choose and why? Good gracious, that's a tough one. I think it could be Michael Palin. I'm a great Monty Python fan, he's a great traveller, and he's gone everywhere I've gone, two years before me, and he hasn't had to pay for his ticket.

trains is 35kg (20kg on domestic trains). On all Russian trains it's 36kg (50kg in 1st class).

Before boarding, stow things needed for the journey in your day pack; the rest can be locked in your baggage and stored either inside the base of one bottom bunk (you can lift up the bunk), beneath the bunk opposite this (less safe), or in the luggage space above the door.

Essential Items

» Pocketknife with corkscrew and openers, plastic or metal mug, plastic or metal cutlery (a metal camping set that fits together is useful)

» Lightweight torch

» Money belt, neck pouch or ankle stash

» Toilet paper, a small medical kit (the attendant also has one) and whatever hygiene articles you need. Buy some from the attendant, or top up at platform kiosks.

» Earplugs or a sleeping mask if white noise or bright light bothers you

» Bottled water

» An electrical plug adaptor if required (see p382)

» Comfortable clothing suitable for the season, and slip-on footwear

Comfort Items

Things that are useful or make life more comfortable are a sense of humour, reading material (audio books and e-books are easiest), a camera, a battery charger and a music-capable device loaded with your favourite tunes. Also bring a notepad and pen to plot random thoughts, and don't forget your mobile-phone plug. A large USB stick, a USB cable for transferring to discs in internet cafes, or even a portable hard drive and replacement memory cards for videos and photos can be useful.

Note that if you're doing a lot of travelling in Mongolia, it's useful to bring along sealable ziplock plastic bags to protect your electronics from dust, and a thin silk or cotton sleeping-bag liner to make threadbare bedding more comfortable.

Smoking

Compartments, carriages and frequently the restaurant car are smoke-free zones, but there's a standing-room vestibule for smokers at the opposite end of the carriage from the attendant's compartment. Hang out there for a long time, however, and you're going to arrive with the complexion of a smoked eel. Also, they're unheated, so in winter you may arrive looking like frost-dusted smoked eel.

Station Stops

Many of the stops along the Trans-Siberian and Asian routes are for two minutes. Halts of 10 to 20 minutes are common at larger towns or junctions, and sometimes extend up to six or seven hours at borders. From some platforms you have enough time to dash into the station, but let the *provodnitsa* know in advance and plan your dash well before you do it. Trains won't wait for you.

» A timetable of station stops (in Cyrillic) hangs in the carriage, but these times are not set in stone. Check the schedule (or take a photo of it), but also double-check with the *provodnitsa* when you get off.

» All train clocks show Moscow time. It's useful to be bi-temporal, eg keeping your watch on Moscow time and a mobile device on local time.

» Take your ticket and passport with you. You might be asked to show them to police on the platform (rare) or to get back on (if you have unremarkable features).

» If you miss your train, inform station staff immediately. They will try to organise alternatives so you can catch up with your luggage. But don't count on it.

Food

Platform Food

Shopping for supplies on station platforms is part of the fun of the Trans-Siberian Railway (note, however, that in Mongolia and China you will find very little food available on platforms). It's a good idea to have plenty of small change on hand, but you'll rarely have to worry about being overcharged.

The choice of items can be excellent, with bread, fresh dairy products, ice cream, grilled chicken, boiled potatoes, home cooking such as *pelmeni* (dumplings) or *pirozhki* (savoury pies), buckets of forest berries and smoked fish all on offer. Through Siberia you'll always find sellers of fresh pine or cedar nuts. Always check the use-by dates on packaged platform food.

Compartment Picnics

Instant noodles have made great inroads into Russia's rail system, but serious eating still tends to involve sliced chunks of cucumber and tomato in summer, more often than not cured sausage, perhaps fish, perhaps a cold dish someone prepared at home, all washed down with beer, tea or, not rarely, vodka. A cloth or newspaper is often spread carefully across the compartment table, then the food is unpacked lovingly and eaten with relish. After that – if it's lunch – everyone usually dozes off. If you buy plentifully on the platforms and have the right travel companions, compartment picnics will be a true highlight of your trip.

Strictly speaking, alcohol cannot be carried onto the train; it can only be bought from the restaurant car or the snack seller. In practice, Russians invariably bring their own. You can currently get beer on platforms, but regulations in Russia about the sale of alcohol at train stations are tightening; no one knows how this will pan out for the platform trade.

Restaurant Cars & Buffets

The restaurant cars are changed at each country's border, so en route to Běijīng you will get Russian, Chinese and possibly Mongolian menus (although it's unlikely there'll be a car attached between the Russian border and Ulaanbaatar).

In restaurant cars, a full meal with accompanying drink typically costs US$20 to US$30, paid in local currency. The cars are open from approximately 9am to 9pm local time, although their hours in Russia are highly unpredictable. With time-zone differences, knowing when to turn up is almost impossible to guess. Generally, Chinese restaurant cars have the best food. On Russian menus, the dishes with prices written alongside them are the ones available that day.

Some trains, especially on the Baikal-Amur Mainline (Baikalo-Amurskaya Magistral; BAM), only have a buffet car with high tables, but these afford good panoramas of the landscape. In the restaurant car there's often a table of pot noodles, chocolate, alcohol, juice and the like.

As well as vendors who go through the carriages with snacks, *provodniki* offer their own drinks and nibbles. Prices are not as cheap as at the kiosks or station halts.

A restaurant or buffet car can be a good place to meet people, or get away from them, depending on the time of day or night and standard of food and service. On some low-grade Russian trains you'll find few signs of edible food or human life, however, except for a few bored staff and the telltale smell of something having been cooked there some time in the distant past. On other trains, the standard isn't too bad.

Classes & Comforts

In theory, all but the cheapest carriages are air-conditioned in summer and heated in winter – that's why the windows are locked shut (though sometimes you'll be able to open them). In practice, air conditioning can break down or a compartment can be stiflingly overheated.

Some Russian 2nd-class compartments are entirely single-sex these days, although this is not available on all trains.

See p399 for specifics about Chinese and Mongolian classes.

Deluxe 1st Class

Deluxe 1st class is available on train K3/4 (Trans-Mongolian). This entails roomy, two-berth compartments with showers shared between two compartments. Train K23/24 between Běijīng and Ulaanbaatar has a similar deluxe 1st class with showers.

1st Class/SV

This class goes by various names: SV (short for *spalny vagon*, or sleeping wagon), *myagky* (soft class) or *lyux*. They are the same size as 2nd-class compartments but have only two berths, so there's more room and more privacy for double the cost. Some 1st-class compartments also have screens for watching DVDs. The *provodnitsa* has DVDs for a small fee (there's nothing to stop you from bringing your own, although they'll need to work on a Russian DVD player, compatible with region 5).

Some premium trains, such as those between Moscow and St Petersburg (train 53/54; http://grandexpress.ru/en), and between Moscow and Kazan, offer luxury SV compartments with double beds and their own shower and toilet.

Chinese 1st Class – Four Berth

A four-berth compartment is available on the Chinese train K3/4. It's a little more spacious than 2nd class, with wider beds, and the carriages have a newer feel.

2nd Class/Kupe

The compartments in a *kupeyny* carriage (2nd class, also called 'compartmentalised' and often shortened to *kupe*) are standard on long-distance trains. These carriages are divided into nine compartments, each with four reasonably comfortable berths, a fold-down table and enough room between bunks to stand and undress.

In every carriage there's one half-sized compartment with just two berths. This is usually occupied by the *provodnitsa*, or reserved for railway employees, but there is a slim chance that you may end up in it, particularly if you do a deal directly with a *provodnitsa* for a train ticket.

3rd Class/Platskart

You either love them or hate them, and it's worth experiencing this at least once to decide for yourself. A reserved-place *platskartny* carriage, sometimes also called *zhyostky* ('hard class', or 3rd class) and usually abbreviated to *platskart*, is essentially

TRAVEL READING ON THE TRAIN

Pack something light, such as a thriller; ploughing through Tolstoy's *War and Peace* is a noble intention, but you will probably be too tired to take it in. If you go for something classic, audio books are a good idea. For other suggestions, see p342. Some recommended travel books:

» **Railway Travel** *The Great Railway Bazaar, Ghost Train to the Eastern Star* or *Riding the Iron Rooster* (Paul Theroux), *The Big Red Train Ride* (Eric Newby), *The Trans-Siberian Railway: a Traveller's Anthology* (Deborah Manly).

» **Russia** *In Siberia* (Colin Thubron), *Travels in Siberia* (Ian Frazier; see p345), *Russia: a Journey to the Heart of a Land and its People* (Jonathan Dimbleby), *A History of the Peoples of Siberia* (James Forsyth), *The Shaman's Coat: A Native History of Siberia* (Anna Reid), *Siberia: a Cultural History* (LP author Anthony Haywood).

» **Mongolia** *Lost Country: Mongolia Revealed* (Jasper Becker), *Wild East* (Jill Lawless), *Dateline Mongolia: an American Journalist in Nomad's Land* (LP author Michael Kohn; see also his 2010 book *Lama of the Gobi*, tracing the life of Mongolian mystic Danzan Ravjaa).

» **China** *China Road* (Rob Gifford), *River Town: Two Years on the Yangtze* (Peter Hessler).

a dorm carriage sleeping 54. The bunks are non-compartmentalised and arranged in blocks of four running down one side of the corridor and in two on the other, with the lower bunk on this side converting to a table and chairs during the day. They're ideal for one-night journeys. In summer the lack of compartment walls means they're not usually as stuffy as a *kupe* can be. Many travellers (women in particular) find *platskart* a better option than being cooped up with three (possibly drunken) Russian men. It's also a great way to meet ordinary Russians.

However, on multiday journeys some *platskart* carriages can begin to resemble a refugee camp, with clothing strung between bunks, a great swapping of bread, fish and jars of tea, and babies sitting on potties while their snot-nosed siblings tear up and down the corridor. Only the hardy would want to do Moscow to Vladivostok or similar nonstop journeys this way.

If you do travel *platskart*, it's worth requesting specific numbered seats when booking your ticket. The ones to avoid are 1 to 4 (next to the attendant and samovar, which means a lot of activity) and 33 to 36 (next to the toilet). Corridor bunks are numbered from 37 (the lower bunk near the toilet and smoking vestibule) to 54 (the upper bunk near the *provodnitsa*). Odd numbers are always lower bunks, even numbers upper. The bottom side berth bunks (ie the odd numbers) are shorter than the rest. Anyone over 180cm (6ft) tall will find the 'pedial overhang' untenable, if not downright uncomfortable.

4th Class/Obshchiy

Also called 4th class, *obshchiy* (general) is unreserved. On long-distance trains the *obshchiy* carriage looks the same as a *platskart*, but when it's full, eight people are squeezed into each unenclosed compartment so there's no room to lie down. Suburban trains normally have only *obshchiy* class, which in this case means bench-type seating. On a few daytime-only intercity trains there are higher-grade *obshchiy* carriages with more comfortable, reserved chairs.

Crossing the Borders

The Trans-Mongolian Railway crosses the Russia–Mongolia border at Naushki-Sükhbaatar, which can take anything from six to 11 hours. Crossing the China–Mongolia border takes about five hours, and the bogies of the carriages are changed to the local gauge here. See p270 and p287 respectively for details about the Russia–Mongolia and Mongolia–China procedures.

The Trans-Manchurian Railway crosses the Russia–China border between Mǎnzhōulǐ (China) and Zabaikalsk (Russia), which takes about half a day. Again, the bogies must be changed. Remember: toilets are always locked at stops and during bogie changes. For more information, see p298.

routes at a glance

The Trans-Siberian Railway is – contrary to popular belief – neither a single route nor one single experience of taking the train across inner Asia. Routes and experiences are as many as the trains, cities and landscapes along the way. In European Russia you can choose from several routes, the main one going via Nizhny Novgorod to Yekaterinburg. From west to east, beyond Yekaterinburg you enter the often remote and unusual landscapes of Siberia, with choices to continue to Vladivostok, take the Baikal-Amur Mainline (Baikalo-Amurskaya Magistral; BAM), or explore more of inner and east Asia along the Trans-Mongolian or Trans-Manchurian routes. Each route has its own attractions, but all are brought together by the rhythms of distance and motion.

Moscow

History ✓✓✓
Culture ✓✓✓
Nightlife ✓✓✓

History
See Russia's earliest roots in the splendour of the Kremlin and the glory of St Basil's Cathedral, while the more recent past is on display at Red Square.

Culture
Classical performing arts and world-class art museums are just part of the cultural scene in Moscow, where artists, musicians and directors are experimenting with new forms.

Nightlife
Night owls enjoy a dynamic scene – not only exclusive clubs, but also bohemian art cafes, underground blues bars, get-down discos and drink-up dives. All are invited to gather in the wee hours to watch the sunrise over Moscow's golden domes and silver skyscrapers.

p58

St Petersburg

Palaces ✓✓✓
History ✓✓✓
Culture ✓✓✓

Palaces
Whether it be the Winter Palace, Marble Palace, Menshikov Palace or Yusupov Palace – each with a tale to tell, from revolution to murder – grandiose architecture on this scale can be found nowhere else in Russia.

History
The city's fascinating, bloody past – from its brutal founding by Peter the Great to the Bolshevik Revolution – can be found on every street corner and is a history buff's dream.

Culture
The Hermitage collection is unrivalled anywhere in the country, if not the entire world, while the Russian Museum groans under the weight of its own collection of Russian paintings from icons to the avant-garde.

p93

Moscow to Yekaterinburg

Scenery ✓
Culture ✓✓✓
Activities ✓✓

Yekaterinburg to Krasnoyarsk

Scenery ✓
Culture ✓✓
Architecture ✓✓

Lake Baikal: Krasnoyarsk to Ulan-Ude

Scenery ✓✓✓
Activities ✓✓✓
History ✓✓✓

Ulan-Ude to Vladivostok

Scenery ✓✓
River Life ✓✓✓
Adventure ✓✓

Scenic Views
Picturesque rather than spectacular, the Ural Mountains form a physical and metaphysical divide between Europe and Asia. The Volga River is a highlight and the scenery is most beautiful just east of Kungur.

Culture
Nizhny Novgorod offers an insight into Volga life and has a thriving food-meets-culture scene. Perm is reinventing itself as an 'art capital', while the lesser-travelled Kazan and Yaroslavl routes offer insight into Islamic (Kazan) and Orthodox (Yaroslavl) cultures.

Activities
Perm offers a base in the Urals for hiking, rafting or horseriding, and beyond this Kungur has easy access to canoeing, cycling and winter cross-country skiing.

p119

Scenic Views
A picture of unchanging taiga and farmland unfurls gradually outside your window as you travel deeper into the heart of Siberia. On a winter journey, a blanket of snow makes the unchanging look utterly dramatic and beautiful.

Culture
For high and low culture head to Tomsk and Novosibirsk. The former, a friendly student town that requires a slight detour off the Trans-Siberian, is home to a lively arts scene.

Architecture
Tomsk is famous throughout Russia for its attractive wooden buildings with intricately carved facades. Other towns with wooden buildings include Tyumen, Omsk and Tobolsk.

p144

Scenic Views
Lake Baikal is the highlight, even viewed through the carriage window. Summer waters lap in shades of blue; winter whiteouts melt the frozen lake into its alpine backdrop.

Outdoor Life
Winter dog sledding and ice fishing on Baikal, ice-trekking or summer hiking along the Great Baikal Trail. Don't forget to take the chilly plunge into Baikal's life-giving waters!

People & History
The peoples of the Baikal region have lent it a colourful and varied history, especially since the 17th-century Russian Cossacks collided with Mongol Buryats. Later came Tibetan Buddhists, aristocratic Decembrists and revolutionaries. Museums explain all.

p176

Scenic Views
The dominant theme is swampy taiga, often denuded by permafrost. The train traces several rivers, and reaches the highest point in the foothills of the Yablonovy Mountains.

River Life
The fortunes of Siberian cities are shaped by rivers, especially the Amur. Lively promenades along the banks are part of the appeal in Blagoveshchensk and Khabarovsk, while Birobidzhan's lifeblood is the Bira River.

Adventure
This section in itself is adventurous, as relatively few travel this far. You'll experience full immersion in Russian culture, especially on short-hop trains. Off the rails, the possibilities are as vast as Siberia itself.

p216

The Baikal-Amur Mainline (BAM)

Scenery ✓✓✓
Activities ✓✓✓
Soviet Relics ✓✓

Scenic Views
Stare into limitless taiga, strain to view the top of a mountain, then plunge into a long, dark tunnel. The BAM bucks and weaves, skirts 3000m-high peaks, rattles over mountain brooks and burrows into earthquake-prone mountainscape.

Outdoor Life
Severobaikalsk makes a superb base from which to explore the surrounding wilds on foot, by bike and on the water. Two sections of the Great Baikal Trail can be accessed from the town, and winter sports flourish around Baikal.

Soviet Relics
Get off the BAM anywhere and it's a step back in Soviet time and space. If you're looking for a bit of nostalgia, you just struck gold.

p250

The Trans-Mongolian Route

Scenery ✓✓✓
History ✓✓
Activities ✓✓✓

Scenic Views
The Siberian forests give way to Mongolia's rolling hills, which ease into grassy steppes. Further south the train travels through the Gobi Desert, and once in China it's back to grasslands. The approach to Běijīng has spectacular mountain scenery.

Historic Sites
Some stunning Buddhist monasteries can be visited in Mongolia, including Amarbayasgalant and Gandan. In China, the Yungang caves, crammed with carved Buddhas, are not to be missed.

Activities
Terelj National Park is an excellent destination for horseriding, mountain biking or hiking. For wildlife viewing, try Khustain National Park, where wild horses roam free.

p265

The Trans-Manchurian Route

Scenery ✓✓
History ✓✓✓
Quirky Sites ✓✓

Scenic Views
The northern section is verdant grassland, but as you head deeper into China there's more evidence of settled life, with vast farmland covering the horizon.

Historic Sites
Make a stop in Shānhǎiguān, where the Great Wall meets the sea, or Chángchūn, home to the Imperial Palace of the Manchu State. Hā'ěrbīn has its own unique history, filled with Russian-built architectural treasures.

Quirky Sites
Mǎnzhōulǐ is a slightly oddball destination, with its hip-hop statues on the streets and gigantic *matryoshka* doll park. In Hā'ěrbīn you can kick back in Stalin Park, one of the last parks to retain the dictator's name.

p290

Běijīng

Shopping ✓✓✓
History ✓✓✓
Food ✓✓✓

Shopping
For a brand new wardrobe on the cheap, bargain at the Sanlitun Yashow Clothing Market. For more traditional items, browse the ancient shops and stalls of Dashilar silk street or Panjiayuan Market.

Historic Sites
The Great Wall, the Forbidden City, Temple of Heaven Park and the Summer Palace – to name just a few. But don't overlook the best of old Běijīng and relaxing bike rides through its winding courtyards and tranquil parks.

Food
Gastronomes will delight at the amazing selection of cuisines in the Chinese capital. Peking duck is the city's signature dish, but head to Wangfujing to try out China's most exotic street snacks.

p301

Every listing is recommended by our authors, and their
favourite places are listed first

Look out for these icons:

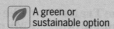 Our author's top
recommendation

A green or
sustainable option

 No payment
required

On the Road

Moscow

Best Places to Eat

» Delicatessen (p81)
» Café Pushkin (p82)
» Stolle (p82)
» Dacha on Pokrovka (p82)
» Barashka (p82)

Best Places to Stay

» Home from Home (p77)
» Golden Apple (p76)
» Artel (p76)
» Basilica Hotel (p77)

Why Go?

Moscow (Москва) is the start or the end point for your train journey across Mother Russia. If you are travelling east to west, you will be relieved – after days (or weeks) on the train – to reach the cultured, cosmopolitan capital, brimming with opportunities to immerse yourself in history; to indulge in world-class music and art; to feast on fabulous food; and to sample the nightlife in a city that never sleeps. If you are travelling west to east, you may be relieved to depart – to escape the overwhelming urbanity, the bumper-to-bumper traffic, the nonstop noise, the panic-inducing prices. Either way, Moscow is an exhilarating and confounding contrast to the rest of Russia.

Soak it up. Examine the art and move to the music; splurge on a ritzy restaurant; stay out till sunrise; get lost in the crowds. Once you get on that train, you may not get to do it again.

When to Go
Moscow

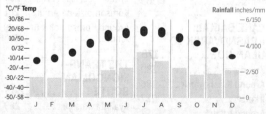

May & Jun Long daylight hours and mild temperatures entice locals to sit at summer terraces.

Sep The capital celebrates City Day, as the foliage turns the city splendid oranges, reds and yellows.

Dec The sparkling snow-covered city hosts its premier cultural event, the December Nights Festival.

Arriving by Air

If you arrive by air, you will fly into one of the city's three airports. The majority of international flights go in and out of Domodedovo and Sheremetyevo International Airports; the third airport is Vnukovo. All three airports are accessible by the convenient **Aeroexpress train** (☎8-800-700 3377; www.aero express.ru; business/standard R550/320) from the city centre.

If you wish to take a taxi from the airport (p92), it is highly recommended you book in advance to take advantage of the fixed rates offered by most companies (R1000 to R1500). Note that driving times vary wildly depending on traffic.

ARRIVING BY RAIL

Rail riders will arrive at one of the central train stations. All trains from St Petersburg arrive at Leningradsky vokzal, while Trans-Siberian trains from the east arrive at Yaroslavsky or Kazansky vokzal. These three railway stations are clustered around Komsomolskaya pl, a bustling square just northeast of the centre. From here, you can hop on the metro (Ⓜ Komsomolskaya) for a quick, easy ride to your destination. Alternatively, most taxi companies offer a fixed rate of R300 to R500 for a train-station transfer, although you will probably get this price only if you book in advance.

Get the Big Picture

Moscow can be overwhelming for the first-time visitor. An introductory tour can provide an overview of the city, as well as useful advice and information for the rest of your trip.

» **Moscow Free Tour** (www.moscowfreetour.com) Offers a free walking tour, led by knowledgeable and extremely enthusiastic guides. Did we mention it's free?

» **Moscow Mania** (p72) Young history scholars offer the informative 'Meet Moscow' tour as an introduction to the city's history and architecture.

» **Capital Tours** (p72) Technically it's a hop-on-hop-off bus service, but it's more useful as a one-off overview of the city.

» **Radisson River Cruises** (p72) and **Capital Shipping Co** (p72) Boats follow the route from Kievsky vokzal or Hotel Ukraina in Dorogomilovo to Novospassky Monastery in Taganka. Again, you can get off and on the boat, but the full 90-minute trip is a pleasant way to get the big picture.

NEED TO KNOW

Most Moscow museums are closed on Monday, but the Kremlin and the Armoury are closed on Thursday instead.

Fast Facts

» Telephone code: ☎495 or ☎499

» Population: 11,514,300

» Time zone: GMT/USC + four hours

New in Moscow

» Red October (p71) Formerly a chocolate factory, now an art and entertainment hotspot.

» Ivan the Great (p66) The bell tower is now open for business.

» Moscow Planetarium (p74) Reopening after 17 years – it was worth the wait.

Resources

» Expat.ru (www.expat.ru) By and for English-speaking expats.

» Moscow Business Telephone Guide (www.mbtg .ru) Bilingual phonebook.

» Art Guide (www.artguide .ru) Galleries and events.

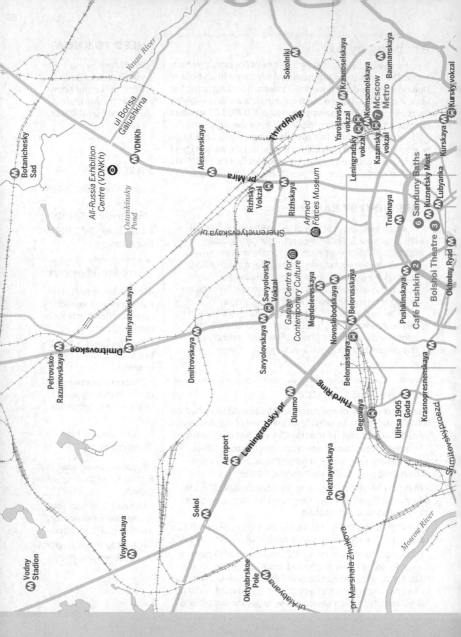

Highlights

1 Being awestruck by the assemblage of tall towers and onion domes on **Red Square** (p62)

2 Splurging on a Russian feast amidst 18th-century opulence at the **Café Pushkin** (p82)

3 Seeing the dancers slide across *Swan Lake* at the **Bolshoi Theatre** (p85)

4 Exploring the former **Red October** (p71) chocolate factory, now filled with art galleries, nightclubs and fashion boutiques

5 Ogling the icons, perusing the Peredvizhniki and contemplating the avant-garde at the **State Tretyakov Gallery** (p71)

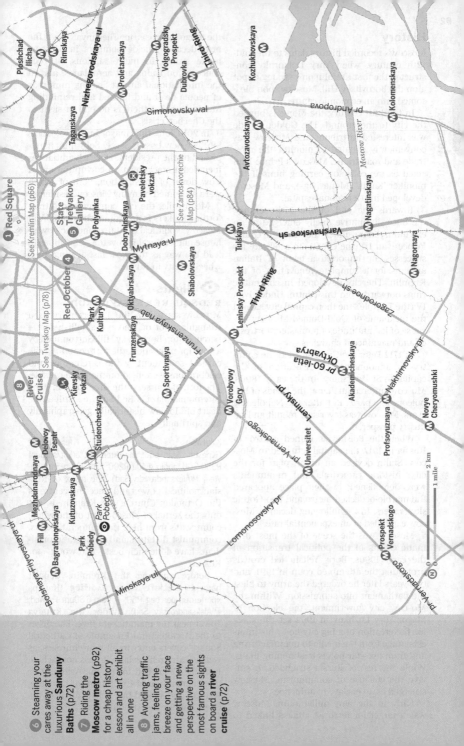

Ploshchad Ilicha

Rimskaya

Nizhegorodskaya ul

Proletarskaya

Volgogradsky Prospekt

Dubrovka

Kozhukhovskaya

Third Ring

Simonovsky val

Taganskaya

Moscow River

pr Andropova

Kolomenskaya

Avtozavodskaya

1 Red Square

See Kremlin Map (p66)

Paveletsky vokzal

See Zamoskvorechie Map (p84)

State 5 Tietyakov Gallery

Polyanka

Dobryninskaya

Nagatinskaya

Nagornaya

Mytnaya ul

Shabolovskaya

Tulskaya

Varshavskoe sh

Red October 4

See Tverskoy Map (p78)

Oktyabrskaya

Park Kultury

Frunzenskaya

Frunzenskaya nab

Leninsky Prospekt

Third Ring

Zagorodnoe sh

Akademicheskaya

Nakhimovsky pr

Sportivnaya

pr-60-letia Oktyabrya

Profsoyuznaya

Nagornaya

River Cruise 8

Kievsky vokzal

Studencheskaya

Vorobyovy Gory

Universitet

pr Vernadskogo

Prospekt Vernadskogo

Novye Cheryomushki

Delovoy Tsentr

Mezhdunarodnaya

Fili

Kutuzovskaya

Bagrationovskaya

Leninsky pr

Lomonosovsky pr

pr Vernadskogo

Park Pobedy

Park Pobedy

Bolshaya Filyovskaya ul

Minskaya ul

1 mile

2 km

6 Steaming your cares away at the luxurious **Sanduny Baths** (p72)

7 Riding the **Moscow metro** (p92) for a cheap history lesson and art exhibit all in one

8 Avoiding traffic jams, feeling the breeze on your face and getting a new perspective on the most famous sights on board a **river cruise** (p72)

History

Moscow's recorded history dates to the mid-12th century, when Yury Dolgoruky constructed the first Kremlin on a strategic spot atop the Borovitsky Hill. Moscow soon blossomed into an economic centre.

In the 13th century, the Mongols burned the city to the ground. The Golden Horde was interested in tribute, and Moscow was conveniently situated to monitor the river trade and road traffic. Moscow's Prince Ivan acted as tax collector, earning himself the moniker 'Kalita' (Moneybags), and Moscow developed into a regional capital.

Towards the end of the 15th century, the once diminutive duchy emerged as an expanding state under the reign of Grand Prince Ivan III (the Great). To celebrate his successes, he imported a team of Italian artisans for a complete renovation of the Kremlin. The city developed in concentric rings outward from this centre. Under Ivan IV (the Terrible), the then capital city earned the nickname of 'Gold-Domed Moscow' because of its multitude of monastery fortresses and magnificent churches.

In 1712 Peter the Great startled the country by announcing the relocation of the capital to St Petersburg. In the early 1800s, Moscow suffered further at the hands of Napoleon Bonaparte. But after the Napoleonic Wars, Moscow was feverishly rebuilt and industry prospered.

When the Bolsheviks gained control of Russia in 1917, the capital returned to Moscow. Stalin devised an urban plan for the city: historic cathedrals and monuments were demolished; in their place appeared the marble-bedecked metro and neo-Gothic skyscrapers. In the following decades, Moscow expanded at an exponential rate.

Moscow was the scene of the most dramatic events of the political transition of the early 1990s. Boris Yeltsin led crowds protesting the attempted coup in 1991, and two years later he ordered the army to blast the parliament into submission. Within the Moscow city government, the election of Mayor Yury Luzhkov in 1992 set the stage for the creation of a big-city boss: his interests range from the media to manufacturing and from five-star hotels to shopping malls. While the rest of Russia struggled to survive the collapse of communism, Moscow emerged as an enclave of affluence.

Early in the new millennium, Moscow was a target for terrorist attacks linked to the ongoing crisis in Chechnya. Over the next decade, suicide bombers in Moscow made strikes in metro stations, at rock concerts, on trains and aeroplanes, and in the international airport, leaving hundreds of people dead and injured and reminding Muscovites that there is no end in sight to the Chechen crisis.

In 2010, long-time mayor Luzhkov lost his job. The new boss is Sergei Sobyanin, hand-picked by the president. His early initiatives included a crackdown on corruption and a slow down of construction, both of which were welcomed by many Moscow residents.

Meanwhile, the city continues to attract fortune-seekers from around the world. And Moscow – political capital, economic powerhouse and cultural innovator – continues to lead the way as the most fast-dealing, free-wheeling city in Russia.

◎ Sights

RED SQUARE & KITAY GOROD

Moscow started in the 12th century as a triangular plot of land – a smallish fort – perched atop Borovitsky Hill. Surrounded by a wall for protection, the fort contained the earliest settlement, while ceremonies and celebrations were held on the plaza outside. The fort, of course, is the Kremlin, while the ceremonial plaza is Red Square – still at the heart of Moscow historically, geographically and spiritually.

Kremlin   HISTORIC SITE
(Кремль; Map p66; www.kreml.ru; adult/student R350/100, audio guide R200; ◎9.30am-5pm Fri-Wed; ⓂAleksandrovsky Sad) The apex of Russian political power and once the centre of the Orthodox Church, the Kremlin is not only the kernel of Moscow but of the whole country. It's from here that autocratic tsars, communist dictators and democratic presidents have done their best – and worst – for Russia.

Before entering the Kremlin, deposit bags at the **left luggage office** (Камера хранения; per bag R60; ◎9am-6.30pm Fri-Wed; ⓂAleksandrovsky Sad), under the Kutafya Tower near the main ticket office. The ticket to the 'Architectural Ensemble of Cathedral Square' covers entry to all four churches, as well as Patriarch's Palace. It does not include Ivan the Great bell tower, the Armoury or the Diamond Fund Exhibition. In any case, you can and should buy tickets for Ivan the Great and for the Armoury here.

MOSCOW IN...

Two Days

Spend a day seeing what makes Moscow famous: **St Basil's Cathedral** (p68), **Lenin's Mausoleum** (p68) and the **Kremlin** (p62). Allow a few hours in the afternoon to gawk at the gold and gems in the **Armoury** (p67). In the evening, attend an opera at the **Bolshoi Theatre** (p85) or dine like a tsar at **Café Pushkin** (p82).

On your second day, admire the art and architecture at **Novodevichy Convent** (p70), then head next door to the eponymous **cemetery**, where many famous political and cultural figures are laid to rest. In the afternoon, make your way across the river to Kievsky vokzal, where you can hop on board a **river cruise** (p72) along the Moscow River.

Four Days

Art lovers should spend their third day at the **State Tretyakov Gallery** (p71), housing a world-class collection of Russian art. In the late afternoon, head to whimsical **Art Muzeon Sculpture Park** (p71) and fun-filled **Gorky Park** (p72), stopping for a drink at **Chaikhona No 1** (p83). In the evening, wander around the former **Red October** factory (p71) for dinner, drinks or other entertainment.

Reserve the next morning for shopping at the **Vernisage Market at Izmailovo** (p88), crammed with souvenir stalls. On your way back into the centre, take a tour around the **Moscow metro** (p92), admiring the architectural achievement and the socialist realist artwork in this marvel of urban design. End up on ul Arbat, where you can take a seat at a pavement cafe and be entertained by portrait painters, street musicians and other passers-by.

Photography is not permitted inside the Armoury or any of the buildings on Sobornaya pl (Cathedral Sq).

Government Buildings

(Map p66) The **Kutafya Tower** (Кутафья башня), which forms the main visitors' entrance today, stands away from the Kremlin's west wall, at the end of a ramp over the Alexander Garden leading up to the **Trinity Gate Tower** (Троицкая башня). On the way to central Sobornaya pl you'll pass a series of buildings that are closed to visitors. On the right is the 17th-century **Poteshny Palace** (Потешный дворец), where Stalin lived, and the bombastic marble, glass and concrete **State Kremlin Palace** (Государственный кремлёвский дворец), built from 1960 to 1961 for Communist Party congresses and now used by the Kremlin Ballet Theatre (p85). On the left is the **Arsenal** (Арсенал), home to the Kremlin guard and ringed by 800 captured Napoleonic cannons; and the yellow, triangular former **Senate** (Сенат) building, now the ultimate seat of power in the modern Kremlin, the offices of the president of Russia. Next to the Senate is the 1930s **Supreme Soviet** (Верховный Совет) building.

Patriarch's Palace

(Патриарший дворец; Map p66) The palace contains an exhibit of 17th-century household items, including jewellery, hunting equipment and furniture. From here you can access the five-domed **Church of the Twelve Apostles** (Церковь двенадцати апостолов), which has a gilded, wooden iconostasis and a collection of icons by leading 17th-century icon painters.

Assumption Cathedral

(Успенский собор; Map p66) On the northern side of Sobornaya pl, with five golden helmet domes and four semicircular gables facing the square, is this cathedral, built between 1475 and 1479. As the focal church of prerevolutionary Russia, it's the burial place of most heads of the Russian Orthodox Church from the 1320s to 1700. The iconostasis dates from 1652 but its lowest level contains some older icons, including the Virgin of Vladimir (Vladimirskaya Bogomater), an early-15th-century Rublyov-school copy of Russia's most revered image, the Vladimir Icon of the Mother of God (Ikona Vladimirskoy Bogomateri).

The delicate little single-domed church beside the west door of the Assumption Cathedral is the **Church of the Deposition of the Robe** (Церковь Ризположения; Map p66),

The Kremlin

A DAY AT THE KREMLIN

Only at the Kremlin can you see 800 years of Russian history and artistry in one day. Enter the ancient fortress through the Trinity Gate Tower and walk past the impressive Arsenal, ringed with cannons. Past the Patriarch's Palace, you'll find yourself surrounded by white-washed walls and golden domes. Your first stop is **Assumption Cathedral 1** with the solemn fresco over the doorway. As the most important church in prerevolutionary Russia, this 15th-century beauty was the burial site of the patriarchs. The **Ivan the Great Bell Tower 2** now contains a nifty multimedia exhibit on the architectural history of the Kremlin. The view from the top is worth the price of admission. The tower is flanked by the massive **Tsar Cannon & Bell 3**.

In the southeast corner, **Archangel Cathedral 4** has an elaborate interior, where three centuries of tsars and tsarinas are laid to rest. Your final stop on Sobornaya pl is **Annunciation Cathedral 5**, rich with frescoes and iconography.

Walk along the Great Kremlin Palace and enter the **Armoury 6** at the time designated on your ticket. After gawking at the goods, exit the Kremlin through Borovitsky Gate and stroll through the Alexander Garden to the **Tomb of the Unknown Soldier 7**.

MARA VORHEES

Tomb of the Unknown Soldier
Visit the Tomb of the Unknown Soldier honouring the heroes of the Great Patriotic War. Come at the top of the hour to see the solemn synchronicity of the changing of the guard.

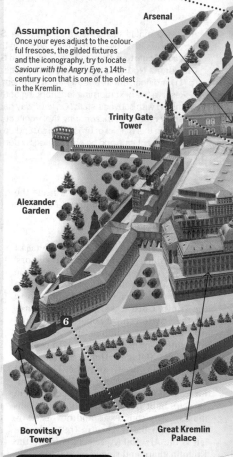

Arsenal

Assumption Cathedral
Once your eyes adjust to the colourful frescoes, the gilded fixtures and the iconography, try to locate *Saviour with the Angry Eye*, a 14th-century icon that is one of the oldest in the Kremlin.

Trinity Gate Tower

Alexander Garden

6

Borovitsky Tower

Great Kremlin Palace

TOP TIPS

» **Lunch** There are no eating options. Plan to eat before you arrive or stash a snack.

» **Lookout** After ogling the sights around Sobornaya pl, take a break in the park across the street, which offers wonderful views of the Moscow River and points south.

KREMLIN PRESS OFFICE

Armoury
Take advantage of the free audio guide to direct you to the most intriguing treasures of the Armoury, which is chock-full of precious metalworks and jewellery, armour and weapons, gowns and crowns, carriages and sledges.

Avoid Confusion

Regular admission to the Kremlin does *not* include Ivan the Great Bell Tower. But admission to the bell tower *does* include the churches on the Kremlin grounds.

Ivan the Great Bell Tower

Check out the artistic electronic renderings of the Kremlin's history, then climb 137 steps to the belfry's upper gallery, where you will be rewarded with super, sweeping vistas of Sobornaya pl and beyond.

Borovitsky Tower

Use the entrance at Borovitsky Tower if you intend to skip the churches and visit only the Armoury or Diamond Fund.

Patriarch's Palace

Tsar Cannon & Bell

Peer down the barrel of the monstrous Tsar Cannon and pose for a picture beside the oversized Tsar Bell, both of which are too big to serve their intended purpose.

Sobornaya pl

Moscow River

Annunciation Cathedral

Admire the artistic mastery of Russia's greatest icon painters– Theophanes the Greek and Andrei Rublyov – who are responsible for many of the icons in the deesis and festival rows of the iconostasis.

Archangel Cathedral

See the final resting place of princes and emperors who ruled Russia for more than 300 years, including the visionary Ivan the Great, the tortured Ivan the Terrible and the tragic Tsarevitch Dmitry.

MOSCOW SIGHTS

Kremlin

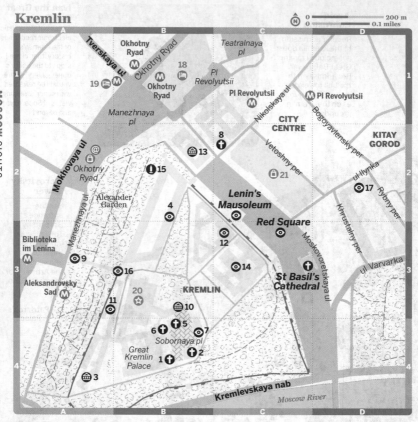

built between 1484 and 1486 by masons from Pskov.

Ivan the Great Bell Tower

(Колокольня Ивана Великого; Map p66; www .belltower.lagutin.ru; admission R500; ⊙10am, 11:15am, 1:30pm, 2:45pm) With its two golden domes rising above the eastern side of Sobornaya pl, the 16th-century bell tower is the Kremlin's tallest structure, visible from 30km away.

Ivan the Great is the site of the Kremlin's newest exhibit, a multimedia presentation of the architectural history of the complex. The 45-minute tour ends with a 137-step climb to the top of the tall tower, yielding an amazing (and unique!) view.

The price of a ticket to Ivan the Great includes admission to the other churches (not the Armoury) so you don't have to buy an additional ticket to the Kremlin grounds.

Beside the bell tower (not inside it) stands the **Tsar Bell** (Царь-колокол), which is the

world's biggest bell. Sadly, this 202-tonne monster never rang. North of the bell tower is the **Tsar Cannon** (Царь-пушка), cast in 1586 for Fyodor I, whose portrait is on the barrel. Shot has never sullied its 89cm bore – and certainly not the cannonballs beside it, which are too big even for this elephantine firearm.

Archangel Cathedral

(Архангельский собор; Map p66) Back on Sobornaya pl, this 1508 cathedral at the square's southeastern corner was for centuries the coronation, wedding and burial church of tsars. The tombs of all of Moscow's rulers from the 1320s to the 1690s (except Boris Godunov, who is buried at Sergiev Posad – see p75) are here. Tsarevich Dmitry (Ivan the Terrible's son, who died mysteriously in 1591) lies beneath a painted stone canopy.

Kremlin

Annunciation Cathedral
(Благовещенский собор; Map p66) Built by Pskov masters in 1489, this cathedral was the royal family's private chapel. Ivan the Terrible's first marriage disqualified him under Orthodox law from entering the church proper, so he had the southern arm of the gallery converted into the **Archangel Gabriel Chapel**, from which he could view services through a grille.

The cathedral contains the celebrated icons of master painter Theophanes the Greek (at the right-hand end of the diesis row, the biggest of the six tiers of the iconostasis). *Archangel Michael* (the third icon from the left on the largest of the six tiers of the iconostasis) is ascribed to Andrei Rublyov.

Armoury
(Оружейная палата; Map p66; adult/student R700/250; ⏰10am, noon, 2.30pm, 4.30pm) The 700-room Great Kremlin Palace is used for official visits and receptions, but isn't open to the public. In the Kremlin's southwestern corner is the Armoury, a numbingly opulent collection of treasures accumulated over time by the Russian State and Church. Tickets specify entry times. Look for royal regalia such as the joint coronation throne of boy tsars Peter (the Great) and his half-brother Ivan V (with a secret compartment from which Regent Sofia would prompt them);

the 800-diamond throne of Tsar Alexey Mikhailovich; and the coronation dresses of 18th-century empresses.

Diamond Fund Exhibition
(Алмазный фонд России; Map p66; www .almazi.net; admission R500; ⏰10am-1pm, 2-5pm Fri-Wed) If the Armoury doesn't sate your diamond lust, there are more in this separate exhibit. The lavish collection shows off the precious stones and jewellery garnered by tsars and empresses over the centuries, including the largest sapphire in the world.

Alexander Garden
(Александровский сад; Map p66) A good place to relax is the pleasant garden along

 STAND ON CEREMONY

Every Saturday at noon on Sobornaya pl (Cathedral Sq), the Presidential Regiment shows up in all its finery for a ceremonial procession, featuring some very official-looking prancing and dancing, both on foot and on horseback. The price of admission to the Kremlin allows access to the demonstration. Otherwise, on the last Saturday of the month, the demonstration is repeated at 2pm for the masses on Red Square.

LENIN UNDER GLASS

Red Square is home to the world's most famous mummy, that of Vladimir Lenin. When he died of a massive stroke (on 22 January 1924, aged 53), a long line of mourners patiently gathered in winter's harshness for weeks to glimpse the body as it lay in state. Inspired by the spectacle, Stalin proposed that the father of Soviet communism should continue to serve the cause as a holy relic. So the decision was made to preserve Lenin's corpse for perpetuity, against the vehement protests of his widow, as well as his own expressed desire to be buried next to his mother in St Petersburg.

Boris Zbarsky, a biochemist, and Vladimir Vorobyov, an anatomist, were issued a political order to put a stop to the natural decomposition of the body. The pair worked frantically in a secret laboratory in search of a long-term chemical solution. In the meantime, the body's dark spots were bleached, and the lips and eyes sewn tight. The brain was removed and taken to another secret laboratory, to be sliced and diced by scientists for the next 40 years in the hope of uncovering its hidden genius.

In July 1924 the scientists hit upon a formula to successfully arrest the decaying process, but their method was kept secret. This necrotic craft was passed on to Zbarsky's son, who ran the Kremlin's covert embalming lab for decades. After the fall of communism, Zbarsky came clean: the body is wiped down every few days, and then, every 18 months, thoroughly examined and submerged in a tub of chemicals, including paraffin wax. The institute has now gone commercial, offering its services and secrets to wannabe immortals for a mere million dollars.

Every so often, politicians express intentions to heed Lenin's request and bury him in St Petersburg, but it usually sets off a furore from the political left as well as more muted objections from Moscow tour operators. It seems that the mausoleum, the most sacred shrine of Soviet communism, and the mummy, the literal embodiment of the Russian revolution, will remain in place for at least several more years.

the Kremlin's western wall. At the garden's northern end is the **Tomb of the Unknown Soldier** (Могила неизвестного солдата), containing the remains of a soldier who died in December 1941 at Km 41 of Leningradskoe sh – the nearest the Nazis came to Moscow. The changing of the guard happens every hour from 10am to 7pm in summer, and to 3pm during winter.

St Basil's Cathedral
CHURCH
(Собор Василия Блаженного; Map p66; www
.saintbasil.ru; adult/student R250/50; ⊙11am-
5pm; ⓜPloshchad Revolyutsii) No picture can prepare you for the crazy confusion of colours and shapes that is St Basil's Cathedral, technically the Intercession Cathedral. This ultimate symbol of Russia was created between 1555 and 1561 (replacing an existing church on the site) to celebrate the capture of Kazan by Ivan the Terrible.

The misnomer 'St Basil's' actually refers only to the northeastern chapel, which was added later. It was built over the grave of the barefoot holy fool Vasily (Basil) the Blessed, who predicted Ivan's damnation.

FREE Lenin's Mausoleum
HISTORIC SITE
(Мавзолей Ленина; Map p66; www.lenin.ru; ⊙10am-1pm Tue-Thu, Sat & Sun; ⓜPloshchad Revolyutsii) Visit this granite tomb while you can, since Vladimir Ilych may eventually end up beside his mum in St Petersburg. For now, the embalmed leader remains as he has been since 1924 (apart from a retreat to Siberia during WWII).

Before joining the queue at the northwestern corner of Red Square, drop your camera at the left-luggage office in the State History Museum, as you will not be allowed to take it with you. After trooping past the embalmed, oddly waxy figure, emerge from his red and black stone tomb and inspect where Josef Stalin, Leonid Brezhnev and many of communism's other heavy hitters are buried along the Kremlin wall.

State History Museum
MUSEUM
(Государственный исторический музей; Map p66; www.shm.ru; Krasnaya pl 1; adult/student R250/80, audio guide R130; ⊙10am-6pm Wed-Sat & Mon, 11am-8pm Sun; ⓜPloshchad Revolyutsii) At the northern end of the square, the State History Museum has an enormous collec-

tion covering the whole Russian empire from the Stone Age on. The building, dating from the late 19th century, is itself an attraction – each room is in the style of a different period or region.

Opposite the museum entrance, tiny **Kazan Cathedral** (Казанский собор; Nikolskaya ul 3; admission free; ⊗8am-7pm; MPloshchad Revolyutsii) is a replica of the original, which was founded in 1636 and demolished 300 years later on Stalin's orders, allegedly because it impeded the flow of parades through Red Square.

Kitay Gorod NEIGHBOURHOOD

(MPloshchad Revolyutsii or Kitay-Gorod) The narrow old streets east of Red Square are known as Kitay Gorod. It translates as 'Chinatown', but the name derives from *kita,* meaning 'wattle', and refers to the palisades that reinforced the earthen ramp erected around this early Kremlin suburb. Kitay Gorod is one of the oldest parts of Moscow, settled in the 13th century as a trade and financial centre.

The busiest street of Kitay Gorod is Nikolskaya ul, once the main road to Vladimir, while the greatest concentration of interesting buildings is along ul Varvarka. See p73 for a walking tour of Kitay Gorod.

TVERSKOY DISTRICT

The streets around Tverskaya ul comprise the vibrant Tverskoy District, characterised by old architecture and new commerce. Small lanes such as **Kamergersky pereulok** and **Stoleshnikov pereulok** are among Moscow's trendiest places to sip a coffee or a beer and watch the big-city bustle.

Moscow Museum of Modern Art MUSEUM

(MMOMA; Московский музей современного искусства; Map p78; www.mmoma.ru; ul Petrovka 25; adult/student R150/100; ⊗noon-8pm; MChekhovskaya) Housed in a classical 18th-century merchant's home, the MMOMA contains 20th-century paintings, sculptures and graphics, including some works by Marc Chagall, Natalia Goncharova, Vasily Kandinsky and Kasimir Malevich. Don't bypass the whimsical sculpture garden in the courtyard.

Gulag History Museum MUSEUM

(Государственный музей истории ГУЛАГа; Map p78; www.museum-gulag.narod.ru; ul Petrovka 16; adult/student R100/20, tour R800; ⊗11am-7pm Tue-Sat; MChekhovskaya) In the midst of all the swanky shops on ul Petrovka, an archway leads to a courtyard strung with barbed wire and hanging with portraits of political prisoners. This is the entrance to the Gulag History Museum. Guides dressed like camp guards describe the vast network of labour camps that existed in the former Soviet Union and recount the horrors of camp life.

PRESNYA & ARBAT

Presnya is Moscow's largest administrative district, encompassing some of the capital's oldest neighbourhoods as well as its newest development at Moscow-City.

Patriarch's Ponds HISTORIC PARK

(Патриаршие пруды; Map p78; Bolshoy Patriarshy per; MMayakovskaya) The peaceful Patriarch's Ponds was immortalised by writer Mikhail Bulgakov, who had the devil appear

MOSCOW SIGHTS

WORTH A TRIP

ALL-RUSSIA EXHIBITION CENTRE

No other place sums up the rise and fall of the Soviet dream like the **All-Russia Exhibition Centre** (Всероссийский Выставочный Центр (ВВЦ); Map p60; www.vvcentre.ru; ⊗pavilions 10am-7pm, grounds 8am-10pm; MVDNKh), north of the centre. The old initials tell the story – VDNKh stands for the Exhibition of Achievements of the National Economy.

VDNKh was originally created in the 1930s to impress upon one and all the success of the Soviet economic system. Two kilometres long and 1km wide, it is composed of wide pedestrian avenues and grandiose pavilions, glorifying every aspect of socialist construction from education and health to agriculture, technology and science. Here you will find the kitschiest socialist realism, the most inspiring of socialist optimism and, now, the tackiest of capitalist consumerism.

The soaring 100m titanium obelisk is a monument to Soviet space flight. In its base is the **Memorial Museum of Cosmonauts** (Мемориальный музей космонавтики; www .space-museum.ru; admission R200; ⊗10am-7pm Tue-Sun), featuring cool space paraphernalia and an inspiring collection of space-themed propaganda posters. Aside from the historical exhibits, there are some excellent displays about the science of space exploration.

DON'T MISS

GARAGE CENTRE FOR CONTEMPORARY CULTURE

Pet project of Dasha Zhukova (supermodel and girlfriend of billionaire Roman Abramovich), the **Garage Centre for Contemporary Culture** (GCCC; Map p60; www.garageccc.com; ul Obratsova 19a; admission R200-300; ⏱11am-9pm Mon-Thu, 11am-10pm Fri-Sun; Ⓜ Novoslobodskaya) is an old bus depot that has been converted into Moscow's largest exhibition hall. It's an incredible space, originally designed in 1926 by constructivist architect Konstantin Melnikov. The GCCC stretches the definition of the word 'exhibit', showcasing interior design, performance art, films and fashion. Two blocks north and two blocks east from Novoslobodskaya or Mendeleevskaya metro station.

here in *The Master and Margarita,* one of the most loved 20th-century Russian novels. The building on the Garden Ring where Bulgakov wrote the novel and lived up until his death now contains the **Bulgakov House** (Дом Булгакова; www.dombulgakova.ru, in Russian; Bolshaya Sadovaya ul 10; admission free; ⏱1-11pm Sun-Thu, 1pm-1am Fri & Sat).

White House   NOTABLE BUILDING

(Белый дом; Map p78; Krasnopresnenskaya nab 2; Ⓜ Krasnopresnenskaya) Scene of two crucial episodes in recent Russian history. It was here that Boris Yeltsin rallied the opposition to confound the 1991 hard-line coup, then two years later sent in tanks and troops to blast out conservative rivals.

Arbat   HISTORIC STREET

(Map p78; Ⓜ Arbatskaya or Smolenskaya) Moscow's most famous street is something of an art market, complete with instant-portrait painters, soapbox poets, jugglers and buskers (and some pickpockets). It makes an interesting walk, dotted with old pastel-coloured merchant houses and tourist-oriented shops and cafes. The statue at the corner of Plotnikov per is of **Bulat Okudzhava,** the 1960s cult poet, singer and songwriter who lived at number 43.

KHAMOVNIKI

The Moscow River surrounds this district on three sides, as it dips down south and loops

back up to the north. Heading southwest from Kropotkinskaya metro, ul Prechistenka is virtually a museum of classical mansions, many of which contain excellent genre-specific art galleries.

Novodevichy Convent & Cemetery   CONVENT

(Новодевичий монастырь и кладбище; off Map p84; convent & church R250, exhibits R200; ⏱grounds 8am-8pm daily, museums 10am-5pm Wed-Mon; Ⓜ Sportivnaya) A cluster of sparkling domes behind turreted walls on the Moscow River, Novodevichy Convent was founded in 1524 to celebrate the taking of Smolensk from Lithuania. The convent is notorious as the place where Peter the Great imprisoned his half-sister Sofia for her part in the Streltsy rebellion. The oldest and most dominant building in the grounds is the white **Smolensk Cathedral**, its sumptuous interior covered in 16th-century frescoes.

Adjacent to the convent, the **cemetery** (⏱9am-5pm) is among Moscow's most prestigious resting places – a veritable 'who's who' of Russian politics and culture. You will find the tombs of Chekhov, Gogol, Mayakovsky, Stanislavsky, Prokofiev, Eisenstein and many other Russian and Soviet notables. The most recent notable addition was former president Boris Yeltsin, who died in 2007.

Pushkin Museum of Fine Arts   MUSEUM

(Музей изобразительный исскуств Пушкина; Map p84; www.artsmuseum.ru; ul Volkhonka 12; adult/student R300/150; ⏱10am-6pm Tue-Sun, 10am-9pm Thu; Ⓜ Kropotkinskaya) Moscow's premier foreign-art museum, the Pushkin shows off a broad selection of European works, mostly appropriated from private collections after the revolution. The highlight is perhaps the Dutch and Flemish masterpieces from the 17th century, including several Rembrandt portraits, and the Ancient Civilisation exhibits, which include the impressive Treasures of Troy.

The Pushkin houses its amazing collection of Impressionist and post-Impressionist paintings next door at the **Gallery of European & American Art of the 19th & 20th Centuries** (Галерея искусства стран Европы и Америки XIX-XX веков; Map p84; www .newpaintart.ru; ul Volkhonka 14; adult/student R300/150; ⏱10am-6pm Tue-Sun, 10am-9pm Thu; Ⓜ Kropotkinskaya). The gallery contains a famed assemblage of French Impressionist works, including Degas, Manet, Renoir and Pissarro, with an entire room dedicated to Monet. Post-Impressionist masterpieces include those by Matisse, Picasso, Rousseau and Van Gogh, as well as an incredible collection of Gauguins.

Cathedral of Christ the Saviour   CHURCH
(Храм Христа Спасителя; Map p84; www.xxc .ru, in Russian; ☺10am-5pm; MKropotkinskaya) Dominating the skyline along the Moscow River, the gargantuan Cathedral of Christ the Saviour sits on the site of an earlier and similar church of the same name, built from 1839 to 1883 to commemorate Russia's victory over Napoleon. The original was destroyed during Stalin's orgy of explosive secularism. Stalin planned to replace the church with a 315m-high 'Palace of Soviets' (including a 100m statue of Lenin) but the project never got off the ground – literally. Instead, for 50 years the site served an important purpose as the world's largest swimming pool.

ZAMOSKVORECHIE
Zamoskvorechie (meaning 'Beyond the Moscow River') stretches south from opposite the Kremlin, inside a big river loop.

State Tretyakov Gallery   MUSEUM
(Третьяковская галерея; Map p84; www.tretya kovgallery.ru, in Russian; Lavrushinsky per 10; adult/ student R360/220; ☺10am-7.30pm Tue-Sun; 📶; MTretyakovskaya) Nothing short of spectacular, the State Tretyakov Gallery holds the world's best collection of Russian icons and an outstanding collection of other prerevolutionary Russian art, particularly the 19th-century Peredvizhniki.

FREE **Red October**   ART CENTRE
(завод Красный Октябрь; Map p84; Berse nevskaya nab; MKropotkinskaya) After more than a century of producing chocolates and other sweets, the famed Krasny Oktyabr factory, opposite the Cathedral of Christ the Saviour, was finally forced to close. The closure happened as part of an effort to remove industry from the historic centre of the capital. In a rare and enlightened move, the historic industrial building has been preserved and converted into Moscow's hottest spot for art and entertainment. The red-brick buildings of this former chocolate factory now host a slew of restaurants, bars, shops and galleries, as well as the centre-piece **Strelka Institute for Media, Architecture & Design** (www.strelkainstitute.ru).

New Tretyakov   MUSEUM
(Третьяковская галерея на Крымском валу; Map p84; ul Krymsky val; adult/student R360/220; ☺10am-7.30pm Tue-Sun; MPark Kultury) The premier venue for 20th-century Russian art is the new building of the State Tretyakov Gallery on Krymsky val, better known as the New Tretyakov. Besides the plethora of socialist realism, the exhibits showcase avant-garde artists such as Kasimir Malevich, Vasily Kandinsky, Marc Chagall, Natalia Goncharova and Lyubov Popova.

Art Muzeon Sculpture Park   SCULPTURE PARK
(Парк искусств Арт-Музеон; Map p84; www .muzeon.ru, in Russian; ul Krymsky val 10; admission R100; ☺10am-9pm; MPark Kultury, Oktyabrskaya) Formerly called the Park of the Fallen Heroes, this open-air sculpture park started as a collection of Soviet statues (Stalin, Dzerzhinsky, a selection of Lenins and Brezhnevs) put out to pasture when they were ripped from their pedestals in the post-1991 wave of anti-Soviet feeling. These discredited icons have now been joined by fascinating and diverse contemporary works. Tsereteli's **Peter the Great** (Памятник Петру Первому) surveys the scene from his post on the embankment

---

WORTH A TRIP

PARK POBEDY AT POKLONNAYA HILL

West of the centre, this huge **memorial complex** (Map p60; MPark Pobedy) celebrates Russia's victory in the Great Patriotic War. The park includes endless fountains and monuments, as well as the memorial **Church of St George**. The dominant monument is a 142m obelisk (each 10cm represents a day of the war).

The centrepiece **Museum of the Great Patriotic War** (Центральный музей Великой Отечественной войны; www.poklonnayagora.ru, in Russian; ul Bratiev Fonchenko 10; adult/child R100/40; ☺10am-5pm Tue-Sun Nov-Mar, to 7pm Apr-Oct) contains two impressive memorial rooms, as well as an exhibit of dioramas of every major WWII battle involving Soviet troops. Exhibits highlight the many heroes of the Soviet Union, as well as show weapons, photographs, documentary films, letters and much other authentic wartime memorabilia.

of the Moscow River. The park can also be entered from Krymskaya nab.

Gorky Park HISTORIC PARK
(Парк Культуры Горького; Map p84; www
.propark.ru, in Russian; ul Krymsky val; ⊗10am-
10pm; ⓂPark Kultury) Amusement park no
longer, Gorky Park is still a perfect way to
escape the hubbub of the city. This place
has undergone a major overhaul: the rides,
games and beer tents have been cleared out,
leaving a pleasant and peaceful green space
to rent bikes or have a picnic. In winter the
ponds are frozen for ice skating and tracks
are made for cross-country skiing. Skis and
skates are also available for rental.

Activities

TOP CHOICE ✔ **Sanduny Baths** BANYA
(Сандуновские бани; Map p78;☎495-628 4633;
www.sanduny.ru; Neglinnaya ul 14; private cabins
per 2hr R3000-6000, general admission per 2hr
R1000-1800; ⊗8am-midnight; ⓂChekhovskaya)
Sanduny is the oldest and most luxurious
banya (bathhouse) in the city. Bookings are
essential for the private cabins.

TOP CHOICE ✔ **Capital Shipping Co** RIVER CRUISE
(Столичная Судоходная Компания; ☎495-
225 6070; www.cck-ship.ru, in Russian; adult/child
R400/150; ⓂKievskaya) Ferries ply the Mos-
cow River from May to September between
Kievsky vokzal and Novospassky Monastery.

Krasnopresnenskie Bani BANYA
(Краснопресненские бани; Map p78; www
.baninapresne.ru; Stolyarny per 7; general admission
per 2hr R850-1000; ⊗8am-10pm; ⓂUlitsa 1905

HAVE YOUR SAY

Found a fantastic restaurant that
you're longing to share with the world?
Disagree with our recommendations?
Or just want to talk about your most
recent trip?

Whatever your reason, head to
lonelyplanet.com, where you can post
a review, ask or answer a question on
the Thorntree forum, comment on a
blog, or share your photos and tips on
Groups. Or you can simply spend time
chatting with like-minded travellers. So
go on, have your say.

Goda) This modern, clean, efficient place provides a first-rate *banya* experience.

Radisson River Cruises RIVER CRUISE
(off Map p78; www.radisson-cruise.ru; adult/children
R800/600; ⓂKievskaya) The Radisson operates big river boats that cart 140 people up
and down the Moscow River from the dock
near the former Hotel Ukraina.

☞ Tours

Capital Tours TOURS
(Map p66; ☎495-232 2442; www.capitaltours
.ru; Gostiny Dvor, ul Ilinka 4; ⓂKitay-Gorod) This
spin-off of Patriarshy Dom offers a **Kremlin tour** (adult/child R1550/775; ⊗2pm Wed),
amongst other walking tours. The company
also operates a **hop-on-hop-off bus** (adult/
child R1000/500; ⊗10.30am, 1.30pm & 3.30pm)
that departs from the Bolshoi, with 13 stops
around the city.

Moscow Mania WALKING TOURS
(☎903-234 9540; www.mosmania.com) Young
and enthusiastic history scholars have
organised more than 50 walking routes
around Moscow, covering the top sights and
many lesser-known destinations.

Patriarshy Dom Tours TOURS
(Map p78; ☎495-795 0927; http://russiatravel-pd
tours.netfirms.com; Vspolny per 6, Moscow school
No 1239; ⓂBarrikadnaya) Provides unique
English-language tours on just about any
specialised subject.

★☆ Festivals & Events

Winter Festival FESTIVAL
Two weeks in December and January. Admire
the elaborate ice sculptures on Red Square,
stand in a crowd of snowmen on ul Arbat and
ride the troika at Izmailovsky Park.

Golden Mask Festival ARTS FESTIVAL
(www.goldenmask.ru) Russia's premier drama,
opera, dance and musical event brightens
up the otherwise dreary March and April.

**Moscow International Film
Festival** FILM FESTIVAL
(www.moscowfilmfestival.ru) This week-long
event attracts film-makers from the US and
Europe, as well as the most promising Russian artists.

City Day FESTIVAL
City Day, or *den goroda* in Russian, celebrates Moscow's birthday on the first weekend in September. The day kicks off with a

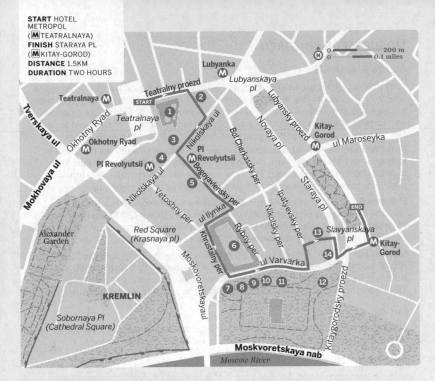

START HOTEL METROPOL
(**M** TEATRALNAYA)
FINISH STARAYA PL
(**M** KITAY-GOROD)
DISTANCE 1.5KM
DURATION TWO HOURS

Walking Tour
Kremlin & Kitay Gorod

❯ Settled in the 13th century, Kitay Gorod is one of the oldest parts of Moscow. Start at the **1** **Hotel Metropol** and walk east down Teatralny proezd to the gated walkway. This historical complex is **2** **Starye Polya**, and includes excavations of the foundations of the 1493 Trinity Church.

Walk down Tretyakovsky proezd to busy Nikolskaya ul and turn right. At No 15, the **3** **Synod Printing House** is where Ivan Fyodorov reputedly produced Russia's first printed book in 1563. The **4** **Zaikonospassky Monastery** at No 7 refers to the busy icon trade that also took place here.

Turn left on Bogoyavlensky per and head south, looking for the 13th-century **5** **Monastery of the Epiphany** on the right-hand side.

Turn right on ul Ilynka and then walk down Khrustalny per. The Old Merchants' Court – **6** **Gostiny Dvor** – has some excellent stops for souvenir hunters.

Take another left on ul Varvarka, crowded with tiny churches. The pink-and-white

7 **St Barbara's Church** dates from 1795 to 1804. The reconstructed 16th-century **8** **Old English Court**, white with peaked wooden roofs, was the residence of England's first emissaries to Russia.

The 1698 **9** **Church of St Maxim the Blessed** at No 4 is now a folk-art exhibition hall. Next along is the pointed bell tower of the 17th-century **10** **Monastery of the Sign**, incorporating a golden-domed cathedral.

The **11** **Romanov Chambers in Zaryadie Museum** is devoted to the lives of these high-ranking nobles. The colourful **12** **St George's Church** at No 12 dates from 1658.

Cross ul Varvarka and walk up Ipatyevsky per. The enchanting 1630s **13** **Church of the Trinity in Nikitniki** is an exquisite example of Russian baroque.

Head east on Ipatyevsky per out to Slavyanskaya pl. Some **14** **remains of the old city wall** can be seen in the underground passage at the corner of ul Varvarka and Staraya pl.

MOSCOW FOR CHILDREN

Sights & Activities

They may not appreciate an age-old icon or a Soviet hero, but Moscow still has plenty to offer the little ones. Among the parks listed in this chapter, Patriarch's Ponds (p69) has a playground and plenty of room to run around; Gorky Park (p72) is good for older kids who can ride bikes. Most of Moscow's art museums have special programs and activities geared toward kids over the age of five (in Russian). Other kid-friendly sights:

Moscow Planetarium (Планетарий Москвы; Map p78; www.planetarium-moscow.ru, in Russian; Sadovaya-Kudrinskaya ul 5; exhibits R350-500; ☉museum 10am-9pm, theatre 10am-midnight Wed-Mon; ⓜBarrikadnaya) The new planetarium incorporates all kinds of high-tech gadgetry and interactive exhibits and educational programs.

Moscow Zoo (Московский зоопарк; Map p78; www.moscowzoo.ru, in Russian; cnr Barrikadnaya & Bolshaya Gruzinskaya uls; adult/child R200/free; ☉10am-7pm Tue-Sun May-Sep, 10am-5pm Tue-Sun Oct-Apr; ⓜBarrikadnaya) Highlights include big cats and polar bears, as well as special exhibits featuring animals from each continent.

Museum of Central Armed Forces (Центральный музей Вооруженных Сил; Map p60; www.cmaf.ru; ul Sovetskoy Armii 2; admission R75; ☉10am-4.30pm Wed-Sun; ⓜNovoslobodskaya) Kids love climbing on the tanks and bombers at the outdoor exhibit. Take trolleybus 69 (or walk) 1.25km east from the Novoslobodskaya metro.

Eating

Many restaurants host 'children's parties' on Saturday and Sunday afternoons, offering toys, games, entertainment and supervision for kids while their parents eat.

Entertainment

Cultural instruction starts at a young age in Moscow, with many companies and performances geared specifically towards young kids. Performances are usually in the afternoons.

Obraztsov Puppet Theatre & Museum (Театр кукол Образцова; Map p78; www.puppet.ru; Sadovaya-Samotechnaya ul 3; adult R300-1000, child R200-600; ☉box office 11am-2.30pm & 3.30-7pm; ⓜTsvetnoy Bulvar) The country's largest puppet theatre performs colourful Russian folk tales and adapted classical plays.

Kuklachev Cat Theatre (Театр кошек Куклачёва; off Map p78; www.kuklachev.ru; Kutuzovsky pr 25; tickets R200-800; ☉noon, 2pm or 4pm Thu-Sun; ⓜKutuzovskaya) At this unusual theatre, acrobatic cats do all kinds of stunts for the audience's delight.

Moscow Children's Musical Theatre (Театр Сац; www.teatr-sats.ru, in Russian; pr Vernadskogo 5; tickets R50-500; ☉times vary Wed, Fri & Sun Sep-Jun; ⓜUniversitet) Performances are entertaining and educational, as actors appear in costume before the show and talk with the children.

Transport

The metro might be fun for kids, but be careful during rush hour, when trains and platforms are packed. Detskoe Taxi (p92) is a taxi company that will look out for your kids, offering smoke-free cars and child seats upon request.

---

festive parade, followed by live music on Red Square and plenty of food, fireworks and fun.

Moscow Biennale of Contemporary Art   ARTS FESTIVAL
(www.moscowbiennale.ru) This month-long festival, held in odd-numbered years, has the aim of establishing the capital as an international centre for contemporary art.

December Nights Festival   ARTS & MUSIC FESTIVAL
(www.museum.ru/gmii) Perhaps Moscow's most prestigious music event, this annual

festival is hosted at the Pushkin Fine Arts Museum.

🛏 Sleeping

For the purposes of this chapter, budget accommodation is less than R3000. Budget accommodation is usually dorm-style, although there are some private rooms available in this range. Prices include coffee and tea, but no breakfast.

Midrange accommodation falls between R3000 and R10,000 per night. This wide-ranging category includes privately owned minihotels, which usually occupy one or two floors in an apartment building. The rooms have been renovated to comfortably accommodate guests, but the hotel itself (which might have a dozen rooms or less) does not usually offer other facilities. Considering the shortage of midrange options, minihotels are some of the best-value accommodation in the city. Top end starts at R10,000 and goes all the way up.

KITAY GOROD

Kitay-Gorod Hotel MINIHOTEL $$
(Отель Китай-Город; Map p78; ☎495-991 9971; www.otel-kg.ru; Lubyansky proezd 25; s R3500-4500, d R5500; ❀❄❀; Ⓜ Kitay-Gorod) Ever since the demolition of the old Hotel Rossiya, it has been impossible for budget-conscious travellers to stay this close to the Kremlin. We're pleased to see that capitalism has brought us full circle, with this privately owned minihotel on the edge of Kitay Gorod. This place has tiny little rooms, but

---

WORTH A TRIP

SERGIEV POSAD

Sergiev Posad (Сергиев Посад) was founded in 1340 by the country's most revered saint. St Sergius of Radonezh was credited with providing mystic support to prince Dmitry Donskoy in his improbable victory over the Tatars in the battle of Kulikovo Pole in 1380. Soon after his death at the age of 78, Sergius was named Russia's patron saint. Since the 14th century, pilgrims have been journeying to this place to pay homage to him.

Sights

The **Trinity Monastery of St Sergius** (Троице-Сергиева Лавра; www.stsl.ru; admission free; ◷10am-6pm) is an active religious centre with a visible population of monks in residence. Visitors should refrain from photographing the monks, female visitors should wear headscarves, and men are required to remove hats before entering the churches.

Built in the 1420s, the squat, dark **Trinity Cathedral** (Троицкий собор) is the heart of the Trinity Monastery. The tomb of St Sergius stands in the southeastern corner, where a memorial service for the saint goes on all day, every day. The icon-festooned interior, lit by oil lamps, is largely the work of the great medieval painter Andrei Rublyov and his students.

The star-spangled **Cathedral of the Assumption** (Успенский собор) was modelled on the cathedral of the same name in the Moscow Kremlin. It was finished in 1585 with money left by Ivan the Terrible in a fit of remorse for killing his son. Outside the west door is the **grave of Boris Godunov** (Могила Бориса Годунова), the only tsar not buried in the Moscow Kremlin or St Petersburg's SS Peter & Paul Cathedral.

Nearby, the resplendent **Chapel-at-the-Well** (Надкладезная часовня) was built over a spring that is said to have appeared during the Polish siege. The five-tier baroque **bell tower** (Колокольня) took 30 years to build in the 18th century, and once had 42 bells, the largest of which weighed 65 tonnes.

Behind the Trinity Cathedral, the **Vestry** (Ризница; adult/student R200/150; ◷10am-5.30pm Wed-Sun) displays the monastery's extraordinarily rich treasury, bulging with 600 years of donations by the rich and powerful – tapestries, jewel-encrusted vestments, solid-gold chalices and more.

Getting There & Away

The fastest way to reach Sergiev Posad is the express train that departs from Moscow's Yaroslavsky vokzal (R320, one hour, at least twice daily) and continues to Yaroslavl (three hours) via Rostov (two hours). Suburban trains also run every half-hour (R130, 1½ hours).

SERVICED APARTMENTS

Entrepreneurial Muscovites have begun renting out apartments on a short-term basis. Flats are equipped with kitchens and laundry facilities and they almost always offer wireless internet access. Apartments are around €100 to €200 per night. Expect to pay more for fully renovated, Western-style apartments.

Cheap Moscow (www.cheap-moscow.com) Heed the disclaimers, but this site has loads of listings for apartments to rent directly from the owner.

Moscow Suites (www.moscowsuites.com) Slick apartments in central locations. Services like airport pick-up and visa support are included in the price, which starts at US$200 per night.

Intermark Serviced Apartments (www.intermarksa.ru) Catering mostly to business travellers, Intermark offers four-star quality accommodations, starting at R5500 per night.

Rick's Apartments (www.enjoymoscow.com) Rick's apartments are off the Garden Ring between Sukharevskaya and Tsvetnoy Bulvar metro stations. Studios start at US$135, with two-bedroom apartments about US$215 per night.

Evans Property Services (www.evans.ru) Caters mainly to long-term renters, but also offers some apartments for US$150 to US$250 per night.

HOFA (www.hofa.ru) Apartments from €62 per night and a variety of homestay programs.

Moscow4rent.com (www.moscow4rent.com) Most flats are centrally located, with internet access, satellite TV and unlimited international phone calls. Prices start at US$150 per night.

---

they are fully and comfortably equipped. The hotel's small size guarantees a warm welcome (unlike at the Rossiya). Half a block from the Kitay-Gorod metro station.

TVERSKOY

TOP CHOICE **Artel** MINIHOTEL **$$**
(Map p78; 495-626 9008; www.artelhotel .ru; Teatralny proezd 3, bldg 3; s/d economy from R2450/2850, s/d standard R3570/4000; ; M Kuznetsky Most) Tucked into an alley behind the Bolshoi, the Artel has an unbeatable location and an awesome, offbeat atmosphere. The economy rooms are minute but the whole place feels very creative and cool. Note the music club Masterskaya (p86) is one floor below, so at times it may *sound* creative and cool too.

TOP CHOICE **Golden Apple** BOUTIQUE HOTEL **$$$**
(Золотое Яблоко; Map p78; 495-980 7000; www.goldenapple.ru; ul Malaya Dmitrovka 11; r from R12,000; ; M Pushkinskaya) 'Moscow's first boutique hotel'. A classical edifice fronts the street, but the interior is sleek and sophisticated. Comfort is also paramount, with no skimping on luxuries such as heated bathroom floors and down-filled duvets.

Check the website for some great promotional discounts.

Hotel Savoy BOUTIQUE HOTEL **$$**
(Отель Савой; Map p78; 495-620 8500; www.savoy.ru; ul Rozhdestvenka 3; r from R8260; ; M Lubyanka) Built in 1912, the Savoy maintains an atmosphere of prerevolutionary privilege for its guests. Unique for its intimate size, it has 70 rooms equipped with marble bathrooms and Italian fittings and furnishings.

Godzillas Hostel HOSTEL **$**
(Map p78; 495-699 4223; www.godzillashostel .com; Bolshoy Karetny per 6; dm R450-780, d/tr R1960/2600; ; M Tsvetnoy Bulvar) Godzillas is the biggest and most professionally run hostel in Moscow, with 90 beds spread out over four floors. To cater to the many guests, there are bathroom facilities on each floor, three kitchens and a big living room with satellite TV. Reminder: don't leave valuables in the luggage storage facility.

Petrovka Loft MINIHOTEL **$$**
(Map p78; 495-626 2210; www.petrovkaloft .com; ul Petrovka 17/2; s & d from R3500; ; M Chekhovskaya) Enter the courtyard and go

straight ahead to find the entrance to this 10-room hotel (note the four-storey climb). None of the rooms are en suite but everything is pretty stylish and clean, and the location is brilliant.

PRESNYA & ARBAT

TOP
CHOICE **Home from Home** HOSTEL & MINIHOTEL **$**
(Map p78; ☎495-229 8018; www.home-fromhome .com; ul Arbat 49, apt 9; dm R450-700, d R2000; ❸@; MSmolenskaya) Original art and mural-painted walls create a bohemian atmosphere, which is enhanced by ceiling medallions and exposed brick. For its excellent private en suite rooms, it goes by the name **Bulgakov Hotel** (www.bulgakovhotel.com). There is also a comfy, cosy common area with kitchen facilities. The building is on the Arbat but you must enter the courtyard from Plotnikov per and look for entrance number 2.

Radisson Royal (Hotel Ukraina) HOTEL **$$$**
(Рэдиссон Ройал Гостиница Украина; off Map p78; ☎495-221 5555; www.ukraina-hotel .ru; Kutuzovsky pr 2/1; r from R10,000; ❸✳☏❄; MKievskaya) This bombastic beauty, occupying one of the Stalinist skyscrapers known as the Seven Sisters, sits majestically on the banks of the Moscow River facing the White House. The place has retained its old-fashioned ostentation, with crystal chandeliers, polished marble and a thematic ceiling fresco in the lobby, while the guestrooms have a similar atmosphere of old aristocracy.

ZAMOSKVORECHIE

TOP
CHOICE **Red Dawn** BOUTIQUE HOTEL **$$**
(Красная Заря; Map p84; ☎495-980 4774; www .red-zarya.ru; Bersenevsky per 3/10, bldg 8; r from R7000; ✳❄; MKropotkinskaya) With a prime waterfront location on the edge of the Red October chocolate factory, this well-placed hotel offers lovely river views and easy access to the capital's hottest nightlife. Prices decrease significantly at the weekend.

Red Arrow HOTEL **$$**
(Красная Стрела; Map p84; ☎985-928 6000; Bolotnaya nab 7, bldg 4; r R2500-4000; ✳❄; MKropotkinskaya) If you can find this teeny-weeny minihotel, you'll enjoy cool, contemporary rooms in Moscow's newest and trendiest area for eating and drinking. Look for a barely marked door in the small courtyard beside Art Akademiya. Note that the place is not protected from the nightlife noise, so you might as well go out and join the party.

Ozerkovskaya Hotel BOUTIQUE HOTEL **$$**
(Озерковская гостиница; Map p84; ☎495-953 7644; www.cct.ru; Ozerkovskaya nab 50; s/d from R5900/6900; ❸☏; MPaveletskaya) This comfy, cosy hotel has only 27 rooms, including three that are tucked up under the mansard roof. Simple rooms, attentive service and a central location (convenient for the express train to Domodedovo airport), make for an excellent-value accommodation option.

Ibis Paveletskaya HOTEL **$$**
(Map p84; ☎495-661 8500; www.ibishotel.com; ul Shchipok 22; r from R3100; ❸✳❄; MPaveletskaya) You know exactly what you're getting when you book a room at the Ibis: affordable, comfortable rooms and professional, reliable service.

BASMANNY

TOP
CHOICE **Basilica Hotel** HOTEL, HOSTEL **$$**
(☎reservations 910-420 3446, front desk 915-462 5575; www.basilicahotel.ru; Serebryanichesky per 1a; s/d from R3000/4000; ❸✳@❄; MKitay-Gorod) On the grounds of the 1781 Church of Silver Trinity, this aptly named hotel offers lovely, light-filled rooms with wood floors and contemporary furnishings. In the same building, the **hostel** (www.sweetmoscow.com; dm R700, s/d with shared bath from R2300/2400) has similarly decorated dorm rooms.

ONCE & FUTURE HOTEL MOSKVA

The story goes that Stalin was shown two possible designs for the **Hotel Moskva** (Гостиница Москва; Map p66) on Manezhnaya pl. Not realising they were alternatives, he approved both. The builders did not dare point out his error, and so built half the hotel in constructivist style and half in Stalinist style. The incongruous result became a familiar and beloved feature of the Moscow landscape, even gracing the label of Stolichnaya vodka bottles. After years of rumours, the infamous Hotel Moskva was finally demolished in 2003, one in a long list of Soviet-era institutions to bite the dust. The site was claimed by Four Seasons, which reconstructed the old building complete with architectural quirks. The new high-class luxury hotel is expected to open in 2012.

Tverskoy

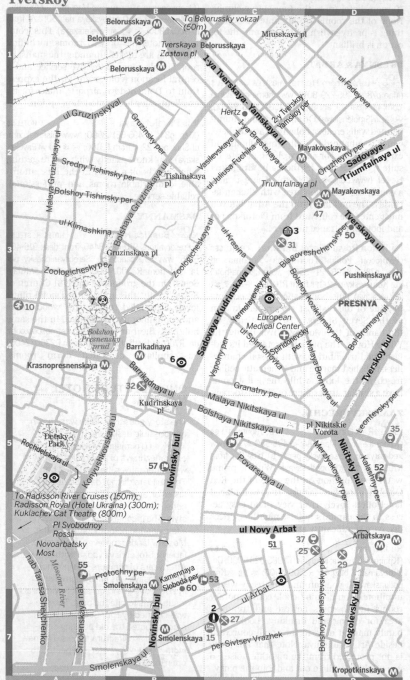

Belorusskaya

To Belorussky vokzal (50m)

Belorusskaya

Miusskaya pl

Tverskaya Zastava pl

Belorusskaya

1-ya Tverskaya-Yamskaya ul

Belorusskaya

ul Fadeyeva

ul Gruzinskyval

2-y Tverskoy-Yamskoy per

Gruzinsky per

Hertz

1-ya Brestskaya ul

Mayakovskaya

Oruzheyny per

Sadovaya-Triumfalnaya ul

Malaya Gruzinskaya ul

Sredny Tishinsky per

Vasilevskaya ul

ul Juliusa Fuchika

Triumfalnaya pl

Mayakovskaya

Tishinsky pl

Bolshoy Tishinsky per

Bolshaya Gruzinskaya ul

Tishinskaya pl

47

Tverskaya ul

ul Klimashkina

ul Krasina

3

50

Gruzinskaya pl

Zoologicheskaya ul

31

Blagoveshchensky per

Pushkinskaya

Zoologichesky per

7

8

Bolshoy Kozikhinsky per

PRESNYA

10

Yermolayevsky per

European Medical Center

Bolshaya Bronnaya ul

Bol Bronnaya ul

Bolshoy Presnensky prud

Barrikadnaya

6

Sadovaya-Kudrinskaya ul

ul Spiridonovka

Spiridonevsky per

Malaya Bronnaya ul

Tverskoy bul

Krasnopresnenskaya

Barrikadnaya ul

Vspolny per

Granatny per

32

Kudrinskaya pl

Malaya Nikitskaya ul

pl Nikitskie Vorota

Leontevsky per

35

Konyushkovskaya ul

Bolshaya Nikitskaya ul

54

Merzlyakovsky per

Nikitsky bul

Detsky Park

Rochdelskaya ul

57

Novinsky bul

Povarskaya ul

Kalashny per

52

9

To Radisson River Cruises (150m);
Radisson Royal (Hotel Ukraina) (300m);
Kuklachev Cat Theatre (800m)

Pl Svobodnoy Rossii

ul Novy Arbat

Arbatskaya

Novoarbatsky Most

51

37

25

Gogolevsky bul

nab Tarasa Shevchenko

Moscow River

55

Protochny per

Smolenskaya

Kamennaya Sloboda per

53

60

29

1

ul Arbat

Bolshoy Afanasyevsky per

Smolenskaya nab

Novinsky bul

Smolenskaya

2

27

Smolenskaya

15

per Sivtsev Vrazhek

Smolenskaya ul

Kropotkinskaya

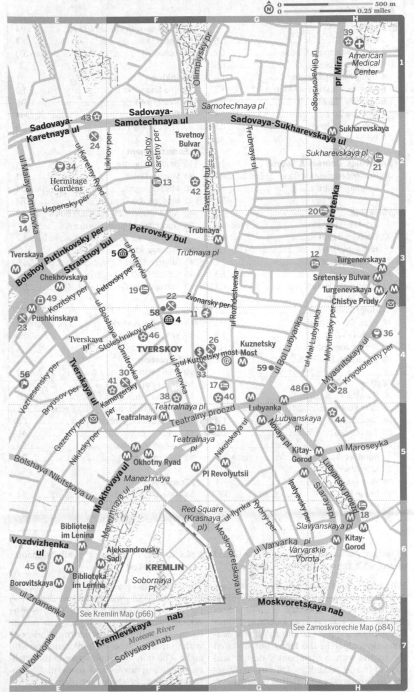

Tverskoy

Breakfast not included. From Kitay-Gorod metro, walk 1km south on ul Solyanka.

Hilton Moscow Leningradskaya HOTEL $$$ (Гостиница Ленинградская; ☏495-627 5550; www.hilton.com; Kalanchevskaya ul 21/40; d from R10,300; ❄❀☏☎; Ⓜ Komsomolskaya) Hilton has maintained the grandiosity of this Stalinist skyscraper in the lobby but updated the rooms with contemporary design and state-of-the-art amenities. Offering easy access to Yaroslavsky vokzal, this beauty overlooks Komsomolskaya pl in all its chaotic, commotion-filled glory.

Trans-Siberian Hostel HOSTEL $ (☏495-916 2030; www.tshostel.com; Barashevsky per 12; dm R630-700, d R2200-3000; ❄@☏; Ⓜ Kitay-Gorod) This tiny hostel has private rooms in addition to two dorm rooms, one with four heavy wooden bunks and one with eight. The only common space is the kitchen, but it's spacious and modern. A train-themed decor brightens the place up.

Boulevard Hotel HOTEL $$

(Отель Бульвар; Map p78; ☎495-776 7276; www
.bulvar-sr.ru; ul Sretenka 1; s R3800-5100, d R4700-
6050; ⊜✿☂; ⓂSretensky Bulvar) On the 2nd
floor of a lovely classical building on the
Blvd Ring Road, this minihotel offers sim-
ple, individually appointed rooms.

Sverchkov-8 HOTEL $$

(Сверчков-8; ☎495-625 4978; www.sverchkov-8
.ru; Sverchkov per 8; s/d R4800/5200; ⊜✿☂;
ⓂChistye Prudy) On a quiet residential lane,
this is a tiny 11-room hotel in a graceful 19th-
century building. Though rooms have old-
style bathrooms and faded furniture, this
place is a rarity for its intimacy and homey
feel. Walk south on the Blvd Ring and turn
right on Arkhangelsky per.

Suharevka Mini-Hotel MINIHOTEL & HOSTEL $

(Сухаревка; Map p78; ☎+7-910-420 3446;
www.suharevkahotel.ru; Bolshaya Sukharevskaya
pl 16/18; dm/r R500/1800; ⓂSukharevskaya;
⊜@☂) This place occupies two side-by-side
flats in a big block on the Garden Ring. The
'hostel side' is cramped and cluttered, with
no real common space. Some travellers will
appreciate the relative spaciousness and
serenity across the hall on the 'hotel side'.
Although the private rooms are also small,
they evoke an atmosphere of old Moscow
with high ceilings and rich fabrics. All bathroom facilities are shared.

Sretenskaya Hotel HOTEL $$$

(Сретенская гостиница; Map p78; ☎495-933
5544; www.hotel-sretenskaya.ru; ul Sretenka 15; d
R12,540; ⓂSukharevskaya; ⊜✿@☂) Special
for its relatively small size and friendly
atmosphere, the Sretenskaya boasts a ro-
mantic, Russian atmosphere. Rooms have
high ceilings and tasteful, traditional decor.
This place is particularly welcoming in win-
ter, when you can warm your bones in the
sauna, or soak up some sun in the tropical
'winter garden'. Discounts are available on
weekends.

Hotel Volga HOTEL $$

(Апарт-Отель Волга; ☎495-783 9109; www
.hotel-volga.ru; Bolshaya Spasskaya ul 4; s/d
R6800/7200; ⓂSukharevskaya; ⊜✿@☂⛶)
This characterless but comfortable hotel
complex, run by Moscow's city government,
is on a quiet corner northeast of the centre. The location is just outside the Garden
Ring and not far from the metro. Most of
the rooms are actually suites with several
rooms or a kitchen, making the Volga ideal

for small groups or families. Hey, kids, this
place also has a playground and a pool table!

✕ Eating

Many restaurants, especially top-end eateries, accept credit cards, and almost all
restaurants have English-language menus.
Discounted 'business lunch' specials are often available weekdays before 4pm. This is a
great way to sample some of the pricier restaurants around town. Most upscale places
require booking a table in advance.

KREMLIN & RED SQUARE
Stolovaya 57 CAFETERIA $

(Столовая 57; Map p66; 3rd fl, GUM, Red Square;
meals R300-400; ⏱10am-10pm; ⓂOkhotny Ryad)
Newly minted, this old-style cafeteria offers
a nostalgic re-creation of dining in post-
Stalinist Russia. The food is good – and
cheap for such a fancy store. Meat cutlets
and cold salads come highly recommended.

TVERSKOY
Delicatessen INTERNATIONAL $$

(Map p78; ☎495-699 3952; www.newdeli.ru;
Savodvaya-Karetnaya ul 20; meals R800-1000;
⏱noon-midnight Tue-Sat; ⊜⌁⑩; ⓂTsvetnoy
Bulvar) 'Thank you for finding us' reads the
sign over the door at this casual but classy
restaurant-bar. It does take some finding,
but it's worth the effort. The menu has an
eclectic array of offerings including salad
Niçoise, shrimp ceviche and steak tartare, as
well as burgers and pasta.

Barashka

AZERI $$$

(Барашка; Map p78; ☑495-625 2895; www.novikovgroup.ru; ul Petrovka 20/1; meals R1500-2000; ☺▣; Ⓜ Teatralnaya) Set in an understated Baku-style courtyard, Barashka offers a menu full of fresh tasty salads, grilled meats and slow-cooked stews, many of which feature the little lamb for which the restaurant is named.

Jagannath

VEGETARIAN $

(Джаганнат; Map p78; Kuznetsky most 11; meals R400-600; ☺10am-11pm; ☺🔊🖉; Ⓜ Kuznetsky Most) If you're in need of vitamins, this is a funky vegetarian cafe, restaurant and shop. Its decor is more New Agey than authentically Indian. Service is slow but sublime, and the food is worth the wait.

PRESNYA & ARBAT

TOP CHOICE Café Pushkin

RUSSIAN $$$

(Кафе Пушкинъ; Map p78; ☑495-739 0033; www.cafe-pushkin.ru; Tverskoy bul 26a; business lunch R750, meals R1500-2000; ☺24hr; Ⓜ Pushkinskaya) The tsarina of *haute-russe* dining, with an exquisite blend of Russian and French cuisines – service and food are done to perfection. The lovely 19th-century building has a different atmosphere on each floor, including a richly decorated library and a pleasant rooftop cafe. Go next door to the Konditerskaya for dessert.

Stolle

RUSSIAN $

(Штолле; Map p78; www.stolle.ru; Bolshaya Sadovaya ul 8/1; meals R200-600; ☺8am-10pm; ☺🔊🖉▣🖐; Ⓜ Mayakovskaya) Don't leave without sampling one of the magnificent *pirogi* (pies). It may be difficult to decide (mushroom or meat, apricot or apple?) but you really can't go wrong.

Tsentralny Restoranny Dom

CAFETERIA $

(Центральный ресторанный дом; Map p78; Kudrinskaya pl 1; meals R200-300; ☺10am-11pm; Ⓜ Barrikadnaya) The 'central restaurant house' is on the ground level of the Stalinist skyscraper at Kudrinskaya pl, and the bombastic Empire-style interior has been preserved. It's an odd setting for a self-service lunch but that's the charm of it. Standard Russian canteen fare for cheap.

Shinok

UKRAINIAN $$

(Шинок; ☑495-651 8101; www.shinok.ru; ul 1905 Goda 2; meals R1000-1200; ☺24hr; Ⓜ Ulitsa 1905 Goda; 🖉▣🖐) In case you didn't think Moscow's themed dining was over the top, this restaurant has recreated a Ukrainian peasant farm in central Moscow. As you dine, you can look out the window at a cheerful babushka while she tends the farmyard animals (very well taken care of, we're assured).

Genatsvale on Arbat

GEORGIAN $$

(Генацвале на Арбате; Map p78; ☑495-697 9453; www.restoran-genatsvale.ru; ul Novy Arbat 11; meals R600-1000; ☺▣🖐; Ⓜ Arbatskaya) Bedecked with fake trees and flowing fountains, this place conjures up the Caucasian countryside – the perfect setting to feast on favourites such as *khachipuri* (cheesy bread) and lamb dishes.

ZAMOSKVORECHIE

Grably

CAFETERIA $

(Грабли; Map p84; www.grably.ru, in Russian; Pyatnitskaya ul 27; meals R200-300; ☺10am-11pm; Ⓜ Novokuznetskaya; ☺🔊🖉🖐) The big buffet features an amazing array of fish, poultry and meat, plus breakfast items, salads, soups and desserts. After you run the gauntlet and pay the bill, take a seat in the elaborate winter-garden seating area.

Sok

VEGETARIAN $$

(Сок; Map p84; www.cafe-cok.ru, in Russian; Lavrushinsky per 15; meals R500-800; ☺11am-11pm; 🖉; Ⓜ Tretyakovskaya) Citrus-coloured walls and delicious fresh-squeezed juices are guaranteed to brighten your day. All the soups, salads, pasta and fabulous desserts are vegetarian, with many vegan options too. The menu even features a few Russian classics such as beef stroganov, made with seitan (a wheat-based meat substitute).

BASMANNY

Dacha on Pokrovka

RUSSIAN $$

(www.dacha-napokrovke.ru; Pokrovsky bul 18/15; meals R500-800; Ⓜ Kitay-Gorod) This ramshackle old mansion offers a welcoming and familiar atmosphere – the perfect place to enjoy delicious and affordable Russian home cooking. From Kitay-Gorod, walk east to the Blvd Ring.

Liudi Kak Liudi   FAST FOOD $
(Люди как люди; www.ludikakludi.ru; Solyansky tupik 1/4; meals R300; ☺11am-10pm Mon-Sat, 11am-8pm Sun; ⓂKitay-Gorod; ☻) This cute cafe has a few things going for it: location, warm welcome, tasty food and low prices. It's the perfect lunch stop for pretty much anyone, which explains why this is such a popular place. It's just around the corner from the Kitay-Gorod metro station.

Avocado   VEGETARIAN $
(Chistoprudny bul 12/2; meals R200-400; ☺10am-11pm; ☻☎✍♿; ⓂChistye Prudy) Meatless versions of soups and salads, pasta and *pelmeni* are all featured (although there is no English-language menu, so bring your phrasebook). One block south of the metro on the Blvd Ring.

🍷 Drinking

TOP CHOICE Bar Strelka   CAFE
(Map p84; www.strelkainstitute.ru; Bersenevskaya nab 14/5; ⓂKropotkinskaya) The focal point of the new development at the Red October chocolate factory. Strelka also promises to give Moscow a healthy dose of contemporary culture, hosting lectures, workshops, film screenings and concerts.

TOP CHOICE Petrovich   BAR
(Map p78; ☑495-923 0082; www.club-petrovich.ru; Myasnitskaya ul 24/1; meals R800-1000; ⓂChistye Prudy) Owned by a local cartoonist this popular place reminisces with Soviet propaganda and pop music. Book in advance and enter through an unmarked door in the courtyard.

Chaikhona No 1   CAFE
(Чайхона No 1; Map p78; www.chaihona.com; Hermitage Gardens; ☺2pm-last guest; ⓂChekhovskaya) This cool outdoor Uzbek lounge and cafe is one of the best chill-out spots in the city. There is another outlet near **Gorky Park** (Map p84; ⓂFrunzenskaya).

Kvartira 44   BAR
(Квартира 44; Map p78; www.kv44.ru, in Russian; Bolshaya Nikitskaya ul 22/2; ☺noon-2am Sun-Thu, noon-6am Fri & Sat; ☻☎; ⓂOkhotny Ryad) This old Moscow apartment has been converted into a crowded, cosy bar. Also in **Zamoskvorechie** (Map p84; ul Malaya Yakimanka 24/8; ⓂPolyanka).

Zhiguli Beer Hall   BREWERY
(Пивной зал Жигули; Map p78; www.zhiguli.net, in Russian; ul Novy Arbat 11; ☺10am-2am Sun-Thu, 10am-4am Fri & Sat; ⓂArbatskaya) It's hard to classify this old-style *stolovaya* (cafeteria) that happens to brew great beer.

☆ Entertainment
Classical Music
Moscow International House of Music   CLASSICAL MUSIC
(Московский международный дом музыки; MMDM; Map p84; www.mmdm.ru; Kosmodamianskaya nab 52/8; tickets R200-2000; ⓂPaveletskaya) This graceful, modern, glass building has three halls, including Svetlanov Hall, which holds the largest organ in Russia.

Tchaikovsky Concert Hall   CLASSICAL MUSIC
(Концертный зал Чайковского; Map p78; ☑box office 495-232 0400; www.classicalmusic

---

FAST FOOD, RUSSIAN STYLE

There's no shortage of fast food in Moscow – and we're not talking about the invasion of McDonalds. If you're short on cash or time, try one of these Russian fast-food chains:

Moo-Moo (Ресторан Му-му; www.moo-moo.ru; meals R200-300; ☺9am-11pm; ♿) Arbat (Map p78; ul Arbat 45/24; ⓂSmolenskaya); Basmanny (Map p78; Myasnitskaya ul 14; ⓂLubyanka) Cafeteria-style service and Holstein-print decor.

Prime Star (Прайм Стар; www.prime-star.ru; meals R200-300; ☺7am-11pm; ✍⬜♿) Tverskoy (Map p78; ul Bolshaya Dmitrovka 7/5; ⓂTeatralnaya); Zamoskvorechie (Map p84; Pyanitskaya ul 5; ⓂNovokuznetskaya); Arbat (Map p78; ul Arbat 9; ⓂArbatskaya) A healthy sandwich shop, also serving soups, salads, sushi and other 'natural food'.

Yolki-Palki (Ёлки Палки; www.elki-palki.ru; meals R300-500; ☻☎⬜♿) Arbat (Map p78; ul Novy Arbat 11; ☺11am-midnight; ⓂArbatskaya); Taganka (off Map p84; Taganskaya pl 2; ☺9am-11pm Mon-Fri; ⓂTaganskaya); Tverskoy (Map p78; Neglinnaya ul 8/10; ☺10am-midnight; ⓂKuznetsky Most); Zamoskvorechie (Map p84; Klimentovsky per 14; ☺10am-9pm; ⓂTretyakovskaya) This Russian chain is beloved for its country-cottage decor and its well-stocked salad bar.

Zamoskvorechie

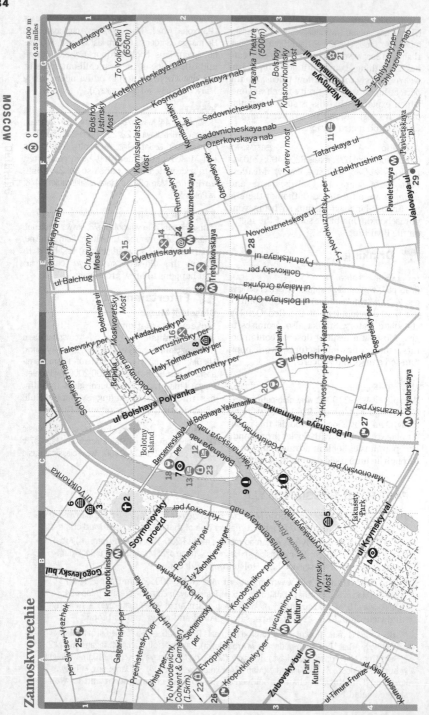

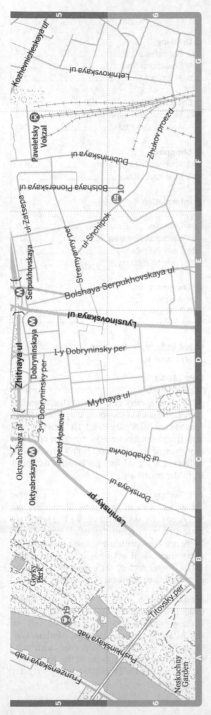

.ru; Triumfalnaya pl 4/31; tickets R100-1000; ; MMayakovskaya) Home to the famous State Philharmonic, the capital's oldest symphony orchestra, the concert hall was established in 1921. It sometimes hosts concerts for children.

Opera & Ballet

TOP CHOICE Bolshoi Theatre OPERA, BALLET
(Большой театр; Map p78; ☎8-800-333 1333; www.bolshoi.ru; Teatralnaya pl 1; tickets R200-2000; MTeatralnaya) The glittering six-tier auditorium has an electric atmosphere, evoking 235 years of premier music and dance. In 2011, the theatre was preparing to reopen the doors of its main stage after several years of work.

Kremlin Ballet Theatre BALLET
(Театр кремлевский балет; Map p66; www.kremlin-gkd.ru; ul Vozdvizhenka 1; ☺box office noon-8pm; MAleksandrovsky Sad) The Kremlin Ballet performs in the State Kremlin Palace (inside the Kremlin).

Folk Music

Russian Ball at Yar CABARET
(Ярь; www.sovietsky.ru; Leningradsky pr 32/2, Sovietsky Hotel; tickets R1000, dinner R800-1200; MDinamo) Everything about Yar is over-the-top, from the vast, gilded interior to the traditional Russian menu to the Moulin Rouge–style dancing girls. About 1km south of Dinamo metro station.

Theatre

Moscow Art Theatre (MKhT) THEATRE
(Московский художественный театр, МХТ; Map p78; http://art.theatre.ru; Kamergersky per 3; ☺box office noon-7pm; MTeatralnaya) Often called the most influential theatre in Europe, this is where method acting was founded over 100 years ago.

Taganka Theatre THEATRE
(off Map p84; www.taganka.org, in Russian; ul Zemlyanoy val 76; MTaganskaya) This legendary theatre is famous for its rebellious director, Yury Lyubimov, and the unruly actor Vladimir Vysotsky. After Lyubimov's sudden retirement in 2011, the theatre is in limbo.

Circus

Nikulin Circus on Tsvetnoy Bulvar CIRCUS
(Цирк Никулина; Map p78; www.circusnikulin.ru; Tsvetnoy bul 13; tickets R400-2500; ☺box office 11am-2pm & 3-7pm; MTsvetnoy Bulvar) Founded in 1880, this circus is now named after beloved actor and clown Yury Nikulin

Zamoskvorechie

(1921–97), who performed at the studio here for many years.

Nightclubs

Krizis Zhanra   NIGHTCLUB

(Кризис Жанра; www.kriziszhanra.ru; ul Pokrovka 16/16; ⊘concerts 9pm Sun-Thu, 11pm Fri & Sat; ⓂChistye Prudy) Good cheap food, copious drinks and rockin' music every night, all of which inspires the gathered to get their groove on. South of Chistye Prudy metro station on the Blvd Ring.

Propaganda   NIGHTCLUB

(Map p78; www.propagandamoscow.com; Bolshoy Zlatoustinsky per 7; ⊘noon-6am; ⓂKitay-Gorod) This long-time favourite looks to be straight from the warehouse district, with exposed brick walls and pipe ceilings. This is a gay-friendly place, especially on Sunday nights.

Simachyov   BAR

(Симачёв Бар & Бутик; Map p78; www.bar nissimachev.com; Stoleshnikov per 12/2; ⊘11am-last guest; ⓂChekhovskaya) By day it's a boutique and cafe, owned and operated by the famed fashion designer of the same name. By night, this place becomes a hip-hop-happening nightclub that combines glamour and humour. You still have to look sharp to get in here, but at least you can be bohemian about it.

Live Music

Masterskaya   LIVE MUSIC

(Мастерская; Map p78; http://mstrsk.livejournal .com, in Russian; Teatralny pro 3, bldg 3; cover R300; ⊘noon-6am; ⓂOkhotny Ryad) The eclectic and arty interior makes a cool place to chill out any time of day. Evening hours give way to a diverse array of live performances. Enter from the courtyard.

Art Garbage   LIVE MUSIC

(Запасник; www.art-garbage.ru; Starosadsky per 5; ⊘noon-6am; ⓂKitay-Gorod; ⧠) The walls are crammed with paintings of all genres, and there are DJs spinning or live music playing every night. Is it art or is it garbage? From Kitay-Gorod metro, walk east on ul Maroseyka and turn right on Starosadsky per.

Madam Galife   LIVE MUSIC

(Map p78; www.madamgalife.ru; Prospect Mira 26/1; ⓂProspekt Mira; ⧠) Looking out to the MGU Botanical Gardens, Madam Galife is like an outdoor cafe. Also adding to the awesome atmosphere is the live music every night– mostly piano and other jazzy ensembles.

Rhythm Blues Cafe   LIVE MUSIC

(Ритм Блюз Кафе; Map p78; ☎499-245 5543; www.blueshouse.ru, in Russian; Starovagankovsky per; ☺noon-midnight Sun-Thu, noon-5am Fri & Sat; ⓜBorovitskaya) If your dog got run over by a pick-up truck, find some comfort at the Rhythm Blues Cafe, with down-and-out live music every night.

🛍 Shopping

TOP CHOICE **Yeliseev Grocery**   FOOD & DRINK

(Елисеевский магазин; Map p78; Tverskaya ul 14; ☺8am-9pm Mon-Sat, 10am-6pm Sun; ⓜPushkinskaya) Peek in here for a glimpse of prerevolutionary grandeur, as the store is set in the former mansion of the successful merchant Yeliseev. It now houses an upscale market selling caviar and other delicacies.

TOP CHOICE **Russkaya Ulitsa**   CLOTHES & ACCESSORIES

(Русская улица; Map p84; www.russian-street.ru; Bersenevskaya nab 8/1; ⓜKropotkinskaya) Showcasing Moscow's burgeoning fashion industry, this little boutique 'Russian street' is crammed with cool clothes and accessories from more than 60 different Russian designers. Located on the grounds of the former Red October chocolate factory.

GUM   SHOPPING MALL

(ГУМ; Map p66; www.gum.ru, in Russian; Krasnaya pl 3; ⓜPloshchad Revolyutsii) In the elaborate 19th-century building on Red Square, the State Department Store – better known as GUM – is a bright and bustling centre filled with shops and cafes.

Russian Gift   HANDICRAFTS

(www.russiangifts.ru; ul Zorge 2; ☺10am-8pm; ⓜPolezhaevskaya) An enormous handicraft centre dedicated to preserving Russian folk traditions. Thousands of handicrafts are on display. There are smaller outlets of this store in GUM and in many of the upscale hotels.

Artefact Gallery Centre   ART GALLERY

(Артефакт; Map p84; ul Prechistenka 30; ⓜKropotkinskaya) Near the Russian Academy of Art, this is a sort of art mall, housing a few dozen galleries under one roof.

Salon Podarkov   SOUVENIRS

(Салоны Подарков; Map p78; Myasnitskaya ul 5; ☺11am-7pm Mon-Sat; ⓜLubyanka) This 'gift salon' is like an indoor souvenir market, with dozens of individual stalls selling all kinds of arts and crafts and more.

ℹ Information

Dangers & Annoyances

As in any big city, be on your guard against pickpockets and muggers. Be particularly careful at or around metro stations, especially at Kurskaya and Partizanskaya, where readers have reported specific incidents. Always be cautious about taking taxis late at night, especially near bars and clubs that are in isolated areas. Never get into a car that already has two or more people in it.

Some police officers can be bothersome, especially to dark-skinned or foreign-looking people. Fortunately, reports of tourists being hassled about their documents and registration have declined. Always carry a photocopy of your passport, visa and registration stamp. If stopped by a member of the police force, do not hand over your passport! It is perfectly acceptable to show a photocopy instead.

Emergency

Russia is in the process of implementing a new **Universal Emergency Number** (☎112), which is supposed to be functional in 2012.

Fire ☎01
Police ☎02
Ambulance ☎03

Internet Access

Almost all hotels and hostels offer wi-fi, as do many bars, restaurants and cafes. If you are not

---

TO MARKET, TO MARKET

Moscow markets (rinok) are busy, bustling places, full of activity and colour. Even if you're not shopping, it's entertaining to peruse the tables piled high with multicoloured produce: homemade cheese and jam; golden honey straight from the hive; vibrantly coloured spices pouring out of plastic bags; slippery silver fish posing on beds of ice; and huge slabs of meat hanging from the ceiling. Many vendors bring their products up from the Caucasus to sell them in the capital. Prices are lower and the quality of product is often higher than in the supermarkets. Bring your own bag and don't be afraid to haggle.

Danilovsky Market (Mytnaya ul 74; ⓜTulskaya)

Dorogomilovsky Market (Mozhaysky val 10; ☺10am-8pm; ⓜKievskaya)

Rizhsky Market (pr Mira 94-96; ⓜRizhskaya)

IZMAILOVO MARKET

The centrepiece of the Kremlin at Izmailovo is the **Vernisage market** (Вернисаж в Измайлово; www .kremlin-izmailovo.com; Izmaylovskoe sh 73; ⊙10am-8pm; MPartizanskaya), packed with art, handmade crafts, antiques, Soviet paraphernalia and just about anything you might want to bring home. Various 'trade rows' are dedicated to icons, carpets, textiles, antiques, paintings and more.

travelling with your own computer, there are plenty of internet cafes around the city:

Cafemax (per hr R100; ⊙24hr; ☎) Dorogomilovo (Bryanskaya ul 5; MKievskaya); Zamoskvorechie (Map p84; Pyatnitskaya ul 25; MNovokuznetskaya) Late-night and early-morning discounts.

Internet Club (Map p78; Kuznetsky most 12; ⊙9am-midnight; MKuznetsky most)

Time Online (Тайм ОнЛайн; www.timeonline .ru; per hr R70-100; ⊙24hr; ☎) Leningradsky vokzal (Komsomolskaya pl 3; MKomsomolskaya); Okhotny Ryad (Map p66; Okhotny Ryad Shopping Centre; MOkhotny Ryad) Copy and photo services; 100 zippy computers.

Media

element (www.elementmoscow.ru) This oversized newsprint magazine comes out weekly with restaurant reviews, concert listings and art exhibits.

Moscow News (www.moscownews.ru) This long-standing Russian news weekly focuses on domestic and international politics and business.

Moscow Times (www.themoscowtimes.com) This first-rate daily is the undisputed king of the hill in locally published English-language

news, covering Russian and international issues, as well as sport and entertainment. The Friday edition is a great source for what's happening at the weekend.

Passport Magazine (www.passportmagazine .ru) An excellent monthly lifestyle magazine

Medical Services

HOSPITALS Both of the international medical facilities listed here accept health insurance from major international providers.

American Medical Centre (Американский Медицинский Центр; Map p78; ☎495-933 7700; www.amcenter.ru; Grokholsky per 1; MProspekt Mira) Offers 24-hour emergency service, as well as an on-site pharmacy with English-speaking staff.

Botkin Hospital (Боткинская больница; ☎495-945 0045; www.botkinmoscow.ru, in Russian; 2-y Botkinsky proezd 5; MBegovaya) The best Russian facility.

European Medical Centre (Европейский Медицинский Центр; Map p78; ☎495-933 6655; www.emcmos.ru; Spirodonevsky per 5; MMayakovskaya) Includes around-the-clock medical and dental facilities.

PHARMACIES

36.6 (Аптека 36.6; ☎495-797 6366; www.366 .ru; ⊙24hr) Arbat (Map p78; ul Novy Arbat 15; MArbatskaya); Basmanny (ul Pokrovka 1/13; MKitay-Gorod); Tverskoy (Map p78; Tverskaya ul 25/9; MTverskaya); Zamoskvorechie (Map p84; Klimentovsky per 12; MTretyakovskaya) A chain of 24-hour pharmacies with many branches all around the city.

Money

Banks, exchange counters and ATMs are ubiquitous in Moscow. Credit cards, especially Visa and MasterCard, are widely accepted. You can also use your credit card to get a cash advance at most major banks.

Alfa-Bank (Альфа-банк; ⊙8.30am-8pm Mon-Sat) Basmanny (Myastnitskaya ul 13/1; MLubyanka); Tverskoy (Map p78; Kuznetsky most

HOW TO DIAL THE TELEPHONE

It's more complicated than you would think. There are now two area codes functioning within Moscow: ☎495 and ☎499. Dialling patterns for the two area codes are different:

» Within the ☎495 area code, dial seven digits, with no area code.

» Within the ☎499 area code, dial 10 digits (including ☎499).

» From ☎495 to ☎499 (or vice versa), dial ☎8 plus 10 digits (including appropriate area code). Although this looks like an intercity call, it is charged as a local call.

The addition of mobile phones also complicates matters, as mobile-phone numbers have a completely different area code (usually ☎915, 916 or 926). To call a mobile phone from a landline (or vice versa) you must dial ☎8 plus 10 digits.

9/10; MKuznetsky Most); Zamoskvorechie (Map p84; ul Bolshaya Ordynka 21/2; MTretya-kovskaya) Has ATMs that offer US dollars and euros in addition to roubles.

Post

Although international service has improved, mail to Europe and the USA can take two to six weeks to arrive.

Central telegraph office (Центральный телеграф; Map p78; Tverskaya ul 7; ☺post 8am-10pm, telephone 24hr; MOkhotny Ryad)

Main post office (Московский главпочтамт; Map p78; Myasnitskaya ul 26; ☺8am-8pm Mon-Fri, 9am-7pm Sat & Sun; MChistye Prudy)

Travel Agencies

Maria Travel Agency (Агентство Мария; Map p78; ☏495-775 8226; www.maria-travel.com; ul Maroseyka 13; MKitay-Gorod) Offers visa support, apartment rental and some local tours.

Unifest Travel (Туристическое Агентство Юнифест Тревел; Map p84; ☏495-234 6555; http://unifest.ru; Komsomolsky pr 13; MPark Kultury) Formerly Infinity Travel, this on-the-ball travel company offers rail and air tickets, visa support, and Trans-Siberian and Central Asian packages. About 1km southeast of Park Kultury metro station.

❶ Getting There & Away

Train

For representative schedules and fares, see p91. For detailed information on timetables and fares, see the Plan Your Trip section.

STATIONS Moscow has nine main stations:

Yaroslavsky vokzal (Ярославский вокзал; Map p60; http://yaroslavsky.dzvr.ru; Komso-molskaya pl; MKomsomolskaya) Serves most Trans-Siberian destinations, including Yaroslavl, the Russian Far East, Mongolia and China, as well as some trains to/from Vladimir, Nizhny Novgorod, Perm, Urals, Siberia; and suburban trains to/from the northeast, including Abramtsevo and Sergiev Posad.

Belorussky vokzal (Белорусский вокзал; off Map p78; www.belorusskiy.info; Tverskaya Zastava pl; MBelorusskaya) Serves trains to/from Smolensk, Kaliningrad, Belarus and northern Europe, as well as suburban trains to/from the west including Borodino, as well as the Aeroexpress to Sheremetyevo.

Kazansky vokzal (Казанский вокзал; Map p60; www.kazansky.info; Komsomolskaya pl; MKomsomolskaya) Serves trains to/from Kazan, as well as some trains to/from Vladimir, Nizhny Novgorod, the Ural Mountains and Siberia.

Kievsky vokzal (Киевский вокзал; Map p60; www.kievskiy.info, in Russian; Kievskaya pl;

KUKUSHKA.RU

Calling all railway buffs! Midway between Sergiev Posad and Rostov-Veliky, the little town of Pereslavl-Zalessky is home to a unique railway museum known as **Kukushka.ru** (www.kukushka.ru, in Russian; adult/child R100/50; ☺10am-6pm Wed-Sun Apr-Oct, to 5pm Sat & Sun Nov-Mar) The collection of locomotives occupies the tracks and depot that were used up until the middle of the 20th century. Don't miss the opportunity to ride on the **hand cart** (adult/child R100/50). Visitors are ferried from the parking lot 1km away from the museum in vintage WWII era cars.

Pereslavl-Zalessky is not on the train line, but buses travel frequently to Moscow (R310, 2½ hours), most arriving at Shchyolkovsky bus station (though some go to Yaroslavsky train station). Not all buses stop at Sergiev Posad (one hour, three daily).

MKievskaya) Serves southeastern Europe, as well as suburban trains to/from the southwest, including Peredelkino and the Aeroexpress to Vnukovo.

Kursky vokzal (Курский вокзал; Map p60; pl Kurskogo vokzala; MKurskaya) Serves towns to the southeast, including the Caucasus, Crimea, Georgia and Azerbaijan. It also has some trains to/from Vladimir, Nizhny Novgorod and Perm; and suburban trains to/from the east and south, including Vladimir and Chekhov.

Leningradsky vokzal (Ленинградский вокзал; Map p60; www.leningradskiy.info; Komsomolskaya pl; MKomsomolskaya) Serves destinations to the northwest including Novgorod, Pskov, St Petersburg, Vyborg, Estonia and Helsinki, as well as suburban trains to/from the northwest including Klin. Note that sometimes this station is referred to on timetables and tickets by its former name, Oktyabrsky.

Paveletsky vokzal (Павелецкий вокзал; Map p84; Paveletskaya pl; MPaveletskaya) Serves southbound trains including the Aeroexpress to Domodedovo airport.

Rizhsky vokzal (Рижский вокзал; Map p60; Rizhskaya pl; MRizhskaya) Serves Latvia, with suburban trains to/from the northwest, including Istra and Novoierusalimskaya.

Savyolovsky vokzal (Савёловский вокзал; Map p60; pl Savyolovskogo vokzala; MSavy-olovskaya) Serves northbound trains.

SAMPLE TRANS-SIBERIAN TRAINS FROM MOSCOW

All fares are for *kupe* (compartmentalised carriages) unless otherwise stated.

DESTINATION	TRAIN NUMBER	DEPARTURE DAY	DEPARTURE TIME	STATION	DURATION	FARE
Irkutsk	06	twice weekly	9.35pm	Yaroslavsky	3 days, 2hr	R9300
Kazan	002 *Tatar-stan*	daily	10.08pm	Kazansky	11½hr	R2900-3000
Krasnoyarsk	056 *Yenisey*	daily	4.20pm	Yaroslavsky	3 days, 15hr	R6800
Nizhny Novgorod	172 *Sapsan*	daily	6.45am	Kursky	4hr	1st/2nd class R4200/1500 (seat)
Omsk	038 *Tomich*	odd dates	10.40pm	Yaroslavsky	42hr	R5500-8000
Novosibirsk	026 *Sibiryak*	even dates	4.20pm	Yaroslavsky	47hr	R5700
Perm	018 *Kama*	daily	12.45pm	Yaroslavsky	21hr	R4500-4800
Tomsk	038 *Tomich*	odd dates	10.40pm	Yaroslavsky	2 days, 8hr	R7400-10,600
Ulaanbaatar	006 *Trans Mongolian Express*	Wed, Thu	9.35pm	Yaroslavsky	4 days, 5hr	R15,200
Vladimir	172 *Sapsan*	daily	6.45am	Kursky	1hr 45min	1st/2nd class R3500/1000
Vladivostok	240	every 2nd day Jun-Sep, via Yaroslavl	12.35am	Yaroslavsky	6 days, 16hr	R13,700
Yaroslavl	016 *Belomorye*	daily	10.05am	Yaroslavsky	4hr	R850-1600
Yekaterinburg	016 *Ural*	daily	4.50pm	Kazansky	25½	R4000-5600

SUBURBAN TRAINS Most Moscow stations have a separate ticket hall for suburban trains, usually called the Prigorodny Zal and often tucked away beside or behind the station building. These trains are usually listed on separate timetables, and may depart from a separate group of platforms.

Air

AIRPORTS Moscow has three main airports servicing international and domestic flights.

Domodedovo (Домодедово; www.domod edovo.ru) Located 48km south of the city, Domodedovo is the city's largest and most efficient international airport.

Sheremetyevo-1 & 2 (Шереметьево; http:// svo.aero) The other main international airport is Sheremetyevo-2, 30km northwest of the city centre, while nearby Sheremetyevo-1 (connected by shuttle bus) services domestic flights.

Vnukovo (Внуково; www.vnukovo-airport.ru) About 30km southwest, Vnukovo serves many domestic flights, including budget airlines such as SkyExpress (see p398).

TICKETS You can buy domestic airline tickets from most travel agents (p89) and at Aeroflot and Transaero offices all over town:

Aeroflot (Аэрофлот; ☑495-223 5555; www .aeroflot.ru; ⊗9am-8.30pm Mon-Sat, to 4.30pm Sun) Tverskoy (Map p78; ul Petrovka 20/1; Ⓜ Chekhovskaya) Kuznetsky Most (Map p78; ul Kuznetsky Most 3; Ⓜ Kuznetsky Most)

Zamoskvorechie (Map p84; Pyatnitskaya ul 37/19; Ⓜ Tretyakovskaya)

Transaero (Трансаэро; ☎ 495-788 8080; www.transaero.com; ☺ 9am-6pm Mon-Sat) Arbat (Map p78; Kamennaya Sloboda per 8; Ⓜ Smolenskaya); Zamoskvorechie (Map p84; Paveletskaya pl 2/3; Ⓜ Paveletskaya)

Bus

Buses run to a number of towns and cities within 700km of Moscow. To book a seat go to the long-distance bus terminal, the **Shchyolkovsky Bus Station** (Ⓜ Shchyolkovskaya), 8km east of the city centre. Buses also depart from outside the various train stations, offering alternative transport to the destinations served by the train.

Car & Motorcycle

See p401 for advice about driving in Russia.

HIRE You might consider hiring a car for trips out of the city. Prices start at R1700 per day.

Avis (Авис-Москва; ☎ 495-578 8425; www .avis.com; Komsomolskaya pl 3; ☺ 10am-8pm; Ⓜ Komsomolskaya) Located at Leningradsky vokzal.

Europcar (☎ 495-926 6373; www.europcar.ru; 4-y Dobryninsky per 8; ☺ 10am-7pm; Ⓜ Oktyabrskaya) Cars prohibited from leaving Moscow Oblast.

Hertz (Map p78; ☎ 495-232 0889; www.hertz .ru, in Russian; 1-ya Brestskaya ul 34; ☺ 9am-9pm; Ⓜ Belorusskaya)

Thrifty (☎ 495-788 6888; www.thrifty.ru) Outer North (Leningradskoe sh 65, bldg 3;

TRAINS FROM MOSCOW

Sample Trains from Moscow to St Petersburg

All trains depart daily from Leningradsky vokzal. Prices are for a *kupe* ticket unless otherwise stated.

TRAIN	NUMBER	DEPARTURE TIME	DURATION	FARE
Krasnaya Strela	02	11.55pm	8hr	R2600-3000
Ekspress	04	11.59pm	8hr	R2600-3000
Grand Express	54	11.40pm	9hr	R2700-3400
Sapsan	152	6.45am	4hr	1st/2nd-class R5056/2612 (seat)
Sapsan	158	1.30pm	4hr	1st/2nd-class R4645/2354 (seat)
Sapsan	162	4.30pm	4hr	1st/2nd-class R5460/2870 (seat)
Sapsan	168	7.45pm	4hr	1st/2nd-class R5530/2870 (seat)

Sample International Trains from Moscow

All trains depart daily. Prices are for a *kupe* ticket.

DESTINATION	TRAIN NUMBER	DEPARTURE TIME	STATION	DURATION	FARE
Helsinki	032 *Lev Tolstoi*	10.50pm	Leningradsky	14hr	R5320
Kyiv	001	11.17pm	Kievsky	8hr 40min	R7800
Minsk	001	10.25pm	Belorussky	10hr	R3450
Rīga	001	6.59pm	Rizhsky	16hr	R6100-6600
Tallinn	034	6.05pm	Leningradsky	15½hr	R6500-7000
Vilnius	005	6.55pm	Belorussky	14hr	R5000-5500

⊙9am-9pm; Ⓜ Rechnoy Vokzal); Outer South (ul Obrucheva 27, Bldg 1; ⊙8am-8pm; Ⓜ Kaluzhskaya) Mileage limited to 200km per day.

❶ Getting Around

To/From the Airports

All three airports are accessible by the convenient **Aeroexpress train** (☏8-800-700 3377; www.aeroexpress.ru; business/standard R550/320) from the city centre.

DOMODEDOVO The Aeroexpress train leaves Paveletsky vokzal every half-hour between 6am and midnight for the 45-minute trip to Domodedovo.

SHEREMETYEVO The slick new Aeroexpress train departs from Belorussky vokzal every half-hour from 5.30am to 12.30am for the 35-minute trip to Sheremetyevo.

VNUKOVO The Aeroexpress train makes the 35-minute run from Kievsky vokzal to Vnukovo airport every hour from 6am to 11pm.

Boat

See p72 for information on ferries that ply the Moscow River.

Metro

The **Moscow metro** (www.mosmetro.ru) is the easiest, quickest and cheapest way of getting around Moscow. Plus, many of the elegant stations are marble-faced, frescoed, gilded works of art.

The 150-plus stations are marked outside by large 'M' signs. Magnetic tickets (R28) are sold at ticket booths. Queues can be long, so it's useful to buy a multiple-ride ticket (10 rides for R265 or 20 rides for R520). The ticket is actually a contactless smart card, which you must tap on the reader before going through the turnstile.

Taxi

TAXI COMPANIES The safest and most reliable way to get a taxi is to order one by phone. Normally, the dispatcher will call you back within a few minutes to provide a description and licence number of the car.

Central Taxi Reservation Office (Центральное бюро заказов такси; ☏495-627 0000; www.6270000.ru; R400 per 30min)

Detskoe Taxi (Детское такси; ☏495-765 1180; www.detskoetaxi.ru; per 10km R500) 'Children's Taxi' has smoke-free cars and car seats for your children.

Diligence Taxi Service (Дилижанс; ☏495-966 5214; www.the-taxi.ru; R500 per 40min)

New Yellow Taxi (Новое жёлтое такси; ☏495-940 8888; www.nyt.ru; R22-30 per km)

UNOFFICIAL TAXIS Many private cars cruise around as unofficial taxis, and other drivers will often take you if they're going in roughly the same direction. Expect to pay R200 to R400 for a ride around the city centre.

Don't hesitate to wave on a car if you don't like the look of its occupants. As a general rule, it's best to avoid riding in cars that already have a passenger. Be particularly careful taking a taxi that is waiting outside a nightclub or bar.

St Petersburg

Best Places to Eat

» Dom Beat (p111)
» Botanika (p111)
» Kompot Café (p111)
» Teplo (p111)
» Makarov (p111)

Best Places to Stay

» Rossi Hotel (p106)
» Casa Leto (p106)
» Andrey & Sasha's Homestay (p106)
» Rachmaninov Hotel (p106)
» Hostel Ligovsky 74 (p111)

Why Go?

Beautiful, complex and imperious, with a hedonistic, creative temperament, St Petersburg (Санкт-Петербург) is the ultimate Russian diva. From its early days as an uninhabited swamp, the 300-year-old city has been nurtured by a succession of rulers, enduring practically everything that history and nature's harsh elements could throw at her. Constantly in need of repair but with a carefree party attitude, Petersburg still seduces all who gaze upon her grand facades, glittering spires and gilded domes.

Even if you don't plan to start or end your train journey in St Petersburg, it would be a shame not to visit the city. The long summer days of the White Nights season are particularly special – the fountains flow and parks and gardens burst into colour. The icy depths of winter have their own magic, and are the perfect time for warming body and soul in all those museums and palaces.

When to Go
St Petersburg

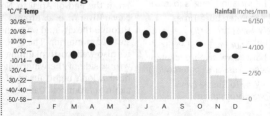

| mid-May–mid-Jul The White Nights, when the sun never sets, is the most popular time to visit. | May & Sep A great time to visit summery St Petersburg without the crowds of the peak months. | Nov–Jan Freezing, dark and blanketed in snow, the winter in St Petersburg is magical. |

NEED TO KNOW

Trains to Irkutsk depart from Ladozhsky vokzal (reached by Ⓜ Ladozhskaya). Trains to Moscow depart from Moskovsky vokzal (reached from Ⓜ Ploshchad Vosstaniya).

Fast Facts

» Telephone code: ☏ 812
» Population: 4,848,000
» Number of metro stations: 65
» Number of bridges: 342

Getting into the City from the Airport

From Pulkovo-1 take bus 39 (R21, every 15 minutes, 5.30am to 12.30am) to Moskovskaya metro. From Pulkovo-2 take bus K-13 (R27, every 10 minutes, 5.30am to 12.30am) to Moskovskaya metro. A taxi from either terminal to the city centre should cost around R700.

Resources

» St Petersburg Tourist Information (eng.ispb.info)
» St Petersburg Times (www.sptimes.ru)
» In Your Pocket St Petersburg (www.inyourpocket.com/russia/st-petersburg)
» Way to Russia (www.waytorussia.net)

Art Attack

St Petersburg, long Russia's artistic engine, has recently seen the opening of several new museums and galleries that are really putting the city on the international art map. As well as the incredible world-class collections at the Hermitage and the Russian Museum, the recent opening of the Erarta Museum of Contemporary Art (p104), Russia's largest private art museum with over 2000 works of modern Russian art, has made St Petersburg about far more than classical art. Add to that two very interesting contemporary galleries, Loft Project ETAGI (p104) and the Rizzordi Art Foundation (p104), and art lovers will find plenty to keep themselves entertained.

PALACES UNDERGROUND

The St Petersburg metro isn't quite as palatial as Moscow's, but you shouldn't miss the stations on the southern half of Line 1 (that's the red line on the official metro map). Some highlights are detailed below.

Avtovo
Check out the Babylonian lavishness of marble and cut-glass clad columns holding up the roof, the relief of soldiers in the ticket hall, and the temple-like entrance.

Narvskaya
A fantastic sculpted relief of Lenin and the rejoicing proletariat hangs over the escalators, and carvings of miners, engineers, sailors and teachers grace the platform columns.

Ploshchad Vosstaniya
Lenin and Stalin are depicted together in the rondels at either end of the platform, as well as Lenin on a tank, Lenin alone, and the Kronshtadt sailors.

Bridges Up!

From the end of April to November all bridges across the Neva River rise at around 1am nightly to let ships pass through the city and on to the rest of the world, or into Russia's deep interior. The spectacle is well worth seeing, but it's also well worth planning for – don't find yourself on the wrong side of the water when the bridges go up, or you'll have a long night ahead of you until they go back down again at around 4.30am. See p117 for more specific times.

History

Starting with the Peter & Paul Fortress, founded on the marshy estuary of the Neva River in 1703, Peter the Great and his successors commissioned a city built to grand design by mainly European architects. By the early 19th century St Petersburg had firmly established itself as Russia's cultural heart. But at the same time as writers, artists and musicians – such as Pushkin, Turgenev and, later, Tchaikovsky and Dostoevsky – lived in and were inspired by the city, political and social problems were on the rise.

Industrialisation brought a flood of poor workers and associated urban squalor to St Petersburg. Revolution against the monarchy was first attempted in the short-lived coup of 14 December 1825. The leaders (who included members of the aristocracy and who became known as the Decembrists) were banished to the outer edges of the empire (see p223).

The next revolution was in 1905, sparked by the 'Bloody Sunday' of 9 January when more than a hundred people were killed and hundreds more were injured after troops fired on a peaceful crowd petitioning the tsar outside the Winter Palace. The tsar's government limped on, until February 1917, when food shortages and miserable social conditions in the newly renamed Petrograd culminated in popular protests that led to the abdication of Tsar Nicholas II. Lenin and his Bolshevik followers took advantage of the weak Provisional Government that held power for the next six months and staged an audacious coup in the Winter Palace in October 1917.

To protect the city during the ensuing Civil War, the seat of government was moved back to Moscow, and, to break with the tsarist past, Petrograd was renamed Leningrad after Lenin's death in 1924. The city – by virtue of its location, three-million-plus population and industry – remained one of Russia's most important, thus putting it on the frontline during WWII. For 872 days the Germans besieged Leningrad, and one million perished from starvation in horrendous conditions.

During the 1960s and 1970s Leningrad's bohemian spirit burned bright, fostering the likes of dissident poet Joseph Brodsky and underground rock groups such as Akvarium, and later on, Kino. As the Soviet Union came tumbling down, the city renamed itself St Petersburg in 1991. Millions of roubles were spent on restoration for the city's tercentenary celebrations and St Petersburg looks better now than probably at any other time in its history.

◉ Sights

While St Petersburg is a huge and sprawling city spread over many different islands, its main sights are fairly well centred in the Historic Heart of the city, the area broadly surrounding the main avenue, Nevsky Prospekt. Other rich pockets of sights include those on Vasilyevsky Island and the Petrograd Side, just across the Neva River from the Historic Heart, and those further down Nevsky pr in the areas around the Smolny and pl Vosstaniya.

HISTORIC HEART

State Hermitage Museum MUSEUM
(Эрмитаж; Map p108; www.hermitagemuseum .org; Dvortsovaya pl; adult/ISIC cardholders & under 17yr R400/free; ⊙10.30am-6pm Tue-Sat, to 5pm Sun; Ⓜ Admiralteyskaya) Mainly set in the magnificent Winter Palace, the Hermitage fully lives up to its sterling reputation. You can be absorbed by its treasures for days and still come out wishing for more. The following are the must-sees:

Room 100 Ancient Egypt

Jordan Staircase Directly ahead when you pass through the main entrance inside the Winter Palace

Rooms 143–146 Hidden Treasures Revealed: French late-19th and early-20th-century paintings taken from private collections in Germany in 1945

Rooms 178–198 Imperial staterooms and apartments including the Malachite Hall, Nicholas Hall, Armorial Hall and Hall of St George

Room 204 The Pavilion Hall

Rooms 207–238 Italian art, 13th to 18th centuries

Rooms 239–240 Spanish art, 16th to 18th centuries

Rooms 245–247 Flemish art, 17th century

Rooms 249–258 Dutch art, 17th century

Room 271 The imperial family's cathedral

Room 298–301 English art

Room 316–320 Impressionist and Post-impressionist art

Room 343–350 20th-century art

St Petersburg Highlights

1 Spending a day (or more!) in the **Hermitage** (p95), one of the world's unrivalled art collections

2 Witnessing the amazing kaleidoscope of colours that is the **Church on Spilled Blood** (p102)

3 Revelling with locals during the ethereal endless daylight of the **White Nights** (p105)

4 Climbing the enormous dome of **St Isaac's Cathedral** (p103) for a bird's-eye view of the imperial city

5 Having the ultimate Russian experience by taking in a ballet at the **Mariinsky Theatre** (p113)

Park 300-Letiya Sankt Peterburg

Staraya Derevnya

Primorsky pr

Hermitage Storage Facility

Bolshaya Nevka

Yelagin Island

Srednyaya Nevka

Kamenny Island

Krutaya Canal

Morskoy pr

Krestovsky Island

Chyornaya Rechka

nab Adm Ushakova

Vyborgskaya nab

pr Engelsa

Circle Baths

Lesnaya

Polyustrovsky pr

pr Marshala Blyuhera

2 km
1 mile

N

VYBORG SIDE

Neva

Vyborgskaya

Sampsonievsky Cathedral

Petrogradskaya nab

PETROGRAD SIDE

Maly pr

rechnaya nab

Aleksandrovsky Park

Neva

Ploshchad Lenina

Finland Station (Finlyandsky vokzal)

Shpalernaya ul

Sverdlovskaya nab

Tulskaya ul

SMOLNY

ul Moiseenko

Shpopskaya nab

Novocherkasskaya

ul Bakunina

Novocherkasskaya

VOSSTANIYA

Kirochnaya ul

Church on Spilled Blood

1 Hermitage

2 Russian Museum

8 Imperial Porcelain

Nevsky pr

4 St Isaac's Cathedral

Zvenigorodskaya

Ligovsky pr

Zagorodny pr

See Historic Heart Map (p108)

5 Mariinsky Theatre

Sadovaya ul

1-ya liniya 1-ya liniya

Maly pr

Sredny pr

Bolshoy pr

VASILYEVSKY ISLAND

Dekabristov Island

Malaya Neva

Korablestroiteley ul

Smolenka River

Morskoy vokzal

Gulf of Finland (Finsky Zaliv)

See Central St Petersburg Map (p100)

Obvodny Canal

Moskovsky vokzal

pr Slavy

Vitebsky pr

ul Titanova

Chesma Church

Monument to the Heroic Defenders of Leningrad

Moskovskaya

Moskovsky pr

Park Pobedy

Park Pobedy

Moskovskie Vorota

Elektrosila

Tekhnologichesky Institut

Baltiyskaya

Frunzenskaya

Ligovsky pr

Museum of Railway Technology

Baltic Station (Baltiysky vokzal)

Rizzordi Art Foundation

Narvskaya

Park Yekateringoff

Gutuyevsky Kovsh

Morskoy kanal

pr Stachek

Kirovsky Zavod

Avtovo

Tallinskoe shosse

6 Cruising the **rivers and canals** (p105) for the best views of this most watery of cities – they don't call it the Venice of the North for nothing!

7 Heading out of town to **Tsarskoe Selo** (p106), Catherine the Great's incredible summer palace, to see the magnificent Amber Room

8 Seeing the sublime collection of art, from icons to the avant-garde, at the **Russian Museum** (p102)

The Hermitage

A HALF-DAY TOUR

Successfully visiting the State Hermitage Museum, with its four vast interconnecting palaces, and some 365 rooms of displays, is an art form in itself. Our half-day tour of the highlights can be easily done in four hours, or can also be extended to a full day.

Once past ticket control, take a right at the end of the Rastrelli Gallery to see Room 101, the fantastic Egyptian collection. Return the way you came and then head up the incredibly grand **Jordan Staircase 1** to the Neva Enfilade and the Great Enfilade for the impressive staterooms, the Romanov's private apartments and the **Palace Church 2**. Head back towards the Jordan Staircase via Rooms 153 and 151 for a full survey of the Romanovs in portrait form. Next visit Hidden Treasures Revealed, a superb survey of late-19th and early-20th-century French art, before proceeding to the Pavilion Hall to see the amazing Peacock Clock. Take in the Renaissance in the Italian rooms, where you shouldn't miss masterpieces by **Da Vinci 3** and **Caravaggio 4**, and should see both the absorbing Spanish and Dutch art collections, the latter culminating in the **Rembrandt 5** orgy of Room 254. Finally, walk through the Great Enfilade, take the staircase to the 3rd floor and end your tour with the modern collection from the impressionists, including a superb room of **Monet 6** and two show-stopping rooms of **Picasso 7**.

THE PRINT COLLECTOR / ALAMY ©

Picasso
The Absinthe Drinker, Room 348
Picasso's blue period is represented in the Hermitage by four paintings, of which this is arguably the most significant. Painted when Picasso was just 22 years old, it is a stunning portrayal of human loneliness.

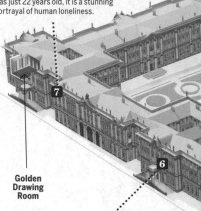

Golden Drawing Room

Monet
Waterloo Bridge, Effect of Mist, Room 319
The Monets in Room 319 make up a sublime ensemble, but no painting is more subtle and delicate than this one, painted from the artist's suite at the Savoy Hotel and depicting the extraordinary light during a foggy morning in London.

THE ART GALLERY COLLECTION / ALAMY ©

Jordan Staircase
Originally designed by Rastrelli, this incredibly lavish staircase is named for the celebration of Christ's baptism in the River Jordan, for which the imperial family would descend the stairs annually to the Neva River.

Rembrandt
Return of the Prodigal Son, Room 254
Perhaps the most famous painting in the Hermitage is this colossal psychological masterpiece. Inspired by the Bible story, the scene of a wayward son returning to his father is a moving portrait of contrition and forgiveness.

St George's Hall

Da Vinci
Madonna and Child (Madonna Litta), Room 214
One of just a handful of paintings known to be the work of Leonardo da Vinci, the *Madonna Litta* makes an interesting counterpart to the Hermitage's other Da Vinci painting, the *Benois Madonna*.

Hermitage Theatre

Palace Church
This stunningly ornate church within the Winter Palace was the Romanovs' private place of worship and saw the marriage of the last tsar, Nicholas II, to Alexandra Fyodorovna in 1895.

Caravaggio
Lute-Player, Room 237
The Hermitage's only Caravaggio is one of three versions of this painting in existence (the other two are in private collections). Caravaggio apparently described the work as the best piece he'd ever painted.

Central St Petersburg

Petrovsky Pond

Petrovsky Park

Sportivnaya

Maly pr

Bolshoy pr

Lizy Chaykinoy

Gorkovskaya

Kamennoostrovskiy pr

Kronverksky Island

Kronverkskaya nab

Troitskaya pl

Sportivnaya

Pr Dobrolyubova

Zverinskaya ul

19

ul Yablochkova

Kronverkskiy pr

10

1

Peter & Paul Fortress

8 7

6

Troitsky most

Malaya Neva

nab Makarova

Tuchkov most

Birzhevoy most

VASILYEVSKY ISLAND

Maly pr

Sredny pr

ul Repina

1-ya liniya

2-ya liniya

3-ya liniya

A-ya i 5-ya linii

Vasileostrovskaya

12-ya liniya

14-ya liniya

16-ya liniya

13-ya liniya

15-ya liniya

17-ya liniya

8-9 linii

nab Makarova

Birzhevoy most

Birzhevaya pl

Suvorovskaya pl

3

Dvortsovaya nab

Dvortsovy most

Dvortsovaya pl (Palace Square)

Nevsky Prospekt

4

Universitetskaya nab

pl Dekabristov

Blagoveshchensky most

Angliyskaya nab

Galernaya ul

Admiralty Gardens

Admiralteyskaya

Nevsky pr

Bolshaya Neva

Konnogvardeysky bulvar

21

Pochtamtskaya ul

Bolshaya Morskaya ul

Gorokhovaya ul

Sadovaya ul

Angliysky pr

nab reki Moyki

13

11

ul Dekabristov

17

Teatralnaya pl

Sadovaya

Sennaya Ploshchad

Sadovaya

16

18

Nikolsky Gardens

See Historic Heart Map (p108)

nab reki Pryazhki

Vitebskaya ul

nab kanala Griboyedova

22

Kanonerskaya ul

Sadovaya ul

Nikolsky Cathedral

nab kanala Kryukova

12

nab reki Fontanki

Obukhovsky most

Pushkinskaya

ul Soyuza Pechatnikov

ul Labutina

Polsky Gardens

SENNAYA

Vitebsk Station (Vitebsky vokzal)

pl Repina

Staro-Kalinkin most

Malo-Kalinkin most

Angliysky most

pr Moskvinoy

nab reki Fontanki

Tekhnologichesky Institut

Lermontovskiy pr

Klimsky pr

Moskovskiy pr

Rizhsky pr

9

Kurlyandskaya ul

Malodetskoselsky pr

Obvodny Canal

nab kanala Obvodnogo

nab kanala Obvodnogo

Maslyany per

Baltic Station (Baltiysky vokzal)

Baltiyskaya

5

Frunzenskaya

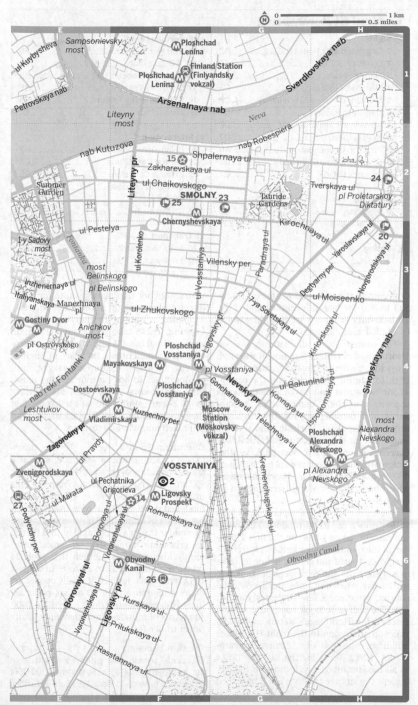

0 — 1 km
0 — 0.5 miles

ul Kuybysheva

Sampsonievsky most

Petrovskaya nab

Ploshchad Lenina

Finland Station (Finlyandsky vokzal)

Ploshchad Lenina

Arsenalnaya nab

Sverdlovskaya nab

Liteyny most

Neva

nab Kutuzova

nab Robespiera

Shpalernaya ul

15

Zakharevskaya ul

Tverskaya ul

ul Chaikovskogo

SMOLNY 23

24

Summer Garden

Liteyny pr

25

Tauride Gardens

pl Proletarskoy Diktatury

Fontanka

Chernyshevskaya

Kirochnaya ul

20

ul Pestelya

ul Korolenko

ul Vosstaniya

Paradnaya ul

Yaroslavskaya ul

Novgorodskaya ul

1-y Sadovy most

Vilensky per

Degtyarny per

ul Moiseenko

Inzhenernaya ul

pl Belinskogo

most Belinskogo

7-ya Sovetskaya ul

Kirochkaya ul

Ispolkomskaya ul

Italiyanskaya ul

Manezhnaya pl

ul Zhukovskogo

Ligovsky pr

Gostiny Dvor

Anichkov most

pl Ostrovskogo

Ploshchad Vosstaniya

Sinopskaya nab

Mayakovskaya

pl Vosstaniya

ul Bakunina

nab reki Fontanki

Dostoevskaya

Ploshchad Vosstaniya

Nevsky pr

Gonchamaya ul

Konnaya ul

Telezhnaya ul

most Alexandra Nevskogo

Leshtukov most

Vladimirskaya

Kuznechny per

Moscow Station (Moskovsky vokzal)

Ploshchad Alexandra Nevskogo

Zagorodny pr

Kremenchugskaya ul

pl Alexandra Nevskogo

ul Pravdy

Zvenigorodskaya

VOSSTANIYA

27

ul Marata

ul Pechatnika Grigorieva

2

14

Ligovsky Prospekt

Podyezdny per

Borovaya ul

Voronezhskaya ul

Romenskaya ul

Borovaya ul

Obvodny Kanal

26

Obvodny Canal

Voronezhskaya ul

Ligovsky pr

Kurskaya ul

Prilukskaya ul

Rasstannaya ul

Central St Petersburg

Concentrate the rest of your time on rooms 333 to 350 for late-19th-century and early-20th-century European art, including works by Matisse and Picasso.

The museum's main entrance is on Dvortsovaya pl (Palace Sq), one of the city's most impressive and historic spaces. Stand back to admire the palace and the central 47.5m **Alexander Column** (Александровская колонна; Map p108), named after Alexander I and commemorating the 1812 victory over Napoleon. Enclosing the square's south side is the **General Staff Building** (Зданиеглавного штаба; Map p108; www.hermitagemuseum.org; Dvortsovaya pl 6-8; admission R60; ☉10am-6pm Tue-Sun; ⓜAdmiralteyskaya), which has a branch of the Hermitage in its east wing.

Queues for tickets, particularly from May to September, can be horrendous. The museum can also be very busy on the first Thursday of the month when admission is free for everyone. Apart from getting in line an hour or so before the museum opens or going late in the day when the lines are likely to be shorter, there are a few strategies you can use. The best is to book your ticket online through the Hermitage's website: US$17.95 gets you admission to the main Hermitage buildings, plus use of a camera or camcorder; US$25.95 is for the two-day ticket to all the Hermitage's collections in the city (except the storage facility). You'll be issued with a voucher that allows you to jump the queue and go straight to the ticket booth.

Joining a tour is another way to avoid queuing. These take you around the main sections in about 1½ hours but at least provide an introduction to the place in English. It's easy to 'lose' the group and stay on until closing time. To book a tour call the museum's **excursions office** (☎571 8446; ☉11am-1pm & 2-4pm); staff there will tell you when they are running tours in English, German or French and when to turn up.

Church on Spilled Blood   CHURCH
(Храм Спаса на Крови; Map p108; www.cathedral.ru; Konyushennaya pl; adult/student R250/150; ☉10am-6pm Thu-Tue; ⓜNevsky Prospekt) This multidomed dazzler of a church, partly modelled on St Basil's in Moscow, was built between 1883 and 1907 on the spot where Alexander II was assassinated in 1881 (hence its gruesome name). It's now most commonly known as the church that took 24 years to build and 27 to restore. In August 1997, with much fanfare, it finally opened its doors after more than 30 artists painstakingly restored the interior's incredible 7000 sq metres of mosaics – and they fully justify the entrance fee.

Russian Museum   MUSEUM
(Русский музей; Map p108; www.rusmuseum.ru; Inzhenernaya ul 4; adult/student R300/150; ☉10am-5pm Mon, to 6pm Wed-Sun; ⓜGostiny Dvor) Facing onto the elegant pl Iskusstv

(Arts Sq) is the former Mikhailovsky Palace, now the Russian Museum, housing one of the country's finest collections of Russian art. After the Hermitage you may feel you have had your fill of art, but try your utmost to make some time for this excellent museum.

The museum owns three other city palaces – all worth visiting if you have time – where permanent and temporary exhibitions are held: the **Marble Palace** (Мраморный дворец; Map p100; www.rusmuseum.ru; Millionnaya ul 5/1; adult/student R300/150; ☺10am-5pm Wed-Mon; ⓂNevsky Prospekt); **Mikhailovsky Castle** (Михайловский замок; Map p108; www.rusmuseum.ru; Sadovaya ul 2; adult/student R300/150; ☺10am-5pm Wed-Mon; ⓂGostiny Dvor); and the **Stroganov Palace** (Строгановский дворец; Map p108; www.rusmuseum.ru; Nevsky pr 17; adult/student R300/150; ☺10am-5pm Wed-Mon; ⓂNevsky Prospekt). A ticket for R600 (R300 for students), available at each palace, covers entrance to them all within a 24-hour period.

St Isaac's Cathedral   CHURCH
(Исаакиевский собор; Map p108; www.cathedral.ru; Isaakievskaya pl; cathedral adult/student R250/150, colonnade R150; ☺10am-6pm Thu-Tue; ⓂAdmiralteyskaya) The golden dome of this cathedral dominates the city skyline. Its lavish interior is open as a museum, but many visitors just buy the separate ticket to climb the 262 steps up to the colonnade around the dome's drum to take in the panoramic views. The French architect Auguste de Montferrand won a competition organised by Alexander I to design the cathedral in 1818. It took so long to build – until 1858 – that Alexander's successor Nicholas I was able to insist on a more grandiose structure than Montferrand had planned. Special ships and a railway had to be built to carry the granite from Finland for the huge pillars. There's a statue of Montferrand holding a model of the cathedral on the west facade.

Yusupov Palace   PALACE
(Юсуповский дворец; Map p100; www.yusupov-palace.ru; nab reki Moyki 94; adult/student/child R500/380/280; ☺11am-5pm; ⓂSpasskaya) In a city of glittering palaces, the extravagant interiors of the Yusupov Palace more than hold their own. A series of sumptuously decorated rooms, each more spectacular than the last, culminate in a gilded jewel box of a theatre, where classical music, ballet and

opera performances are still held; check the website for details.

The palace is certainly one of St Petersburg's finest, but it's very overpriced for foreigners (Russians get a far better deal) and if you want to see the room where Rasputin's murder began, you have to pay for an extra tour (adult/student R300/180), which takes place at 1.45pm daily except Sunday. There are only 20 tickets available each day, so come in good time to secure a place. The admission price to the palace includes an audio tour in English and a number of other languages, but you'll need to leave a R1000 deposit per audio guide.

Sheremetyev Palace   MUSEUM
Facing the Fontanka Canal, the splendid Sheremetyev Palace (Шереметьевский дворец; built 1750–55) houses two lovely museums. The **Museum of Music** (Музей музыки; Map p108; www.theatremuseum.ru; nab reki Fontanki 34; admission R250; ☺noon-7pm Wed-Sun; ⓂGostiny Dvor) contains a lovely collection of beautifully decorated instruments. Upstairs the palace rooms have been wonderfully restored; you get a great sense of how cultured life must have been here.

In a separate wing of the palace, reached from Liteyny pr, is the charming **Anna Akhmatova Museum at the Fountain House** (Музей Анны Ахматовой в Фонтанном Доме; Map p108; www.akhmatova.spb.ru; Liteyny pr 53; admission R100, audio tour R100; ☺10.30am-6.30pm Tue-Sun, 1-9pm Wed; ⓂMayakovskaya), filled with mementoes of the poet and her family, all persecuted during Soviet times. Admission also includes the Joseph Brodsky 'American Study'. The poet did not live here, but his connection with Akhmatova was strong. His office has been re-created, complete with furniture and other 'artefacts' from his adopted home in Massachusetts.

Railway Museums   MUSEUM
Every child's and railway enthusiast's dream will be realised at the **Museum of Railway Transport** (Музей железнодорожного транспорта; Map p108; www.railroad.ru/cmrt; Sadovaya ul 50; adult/student/child R100/50/30; ☺11am-5.30pm Sun-Thu; ⓂSadovaya), which holds a fascinating collection of scale locomotives and model railway bridges, often made by the engineers who built the real ones. As the oldest such collection in the world (the museum was established in 1809, 28 years before Russia had its first working

HISTORIC RAILWAY STATIONS

St Petersburg's oldest and most elegant station is **Vitebsky vokzal** (Vitebsk Station; Map p100; Ⓜ Pushkinskaya), originally built in 1837 to serve the line to Tsarskoe Selo. The current building dates from 1904 and is partly graced with gorgeous Style Moderne (Russian art nouveau) interior decoration.

While at **Moskovsky vokzal** (Moscow Station; Map p108; Ⓜ Ploshchad Vosstaniya) look up at the expansive ceiling mural in the main entrance hall. There's a striking giant bust of Peter the Great in the hall leading to the platforms.

Finlyandsky vokzal (Finland Station; Map p100; Ⓜ Ploshchad Lenina), rebuilt after WWII, is famous as the place where, in April 1917, Lenin arrived from exile and gave his legendary speech atop an armoured car. Lenin's statue, pointing across the Neva towards the old KGB headquarters, stands outside the station.

train!), it includes models of Krasnoyarsk's *Yenisey Bridge,* the ship that once carried passengers and trains across Lake Baikal. It also has a sumptuous 1903 Trans-Siberian wagon complete with a piano salon and a bathtub.

Train spotters should also hasten to view the impressive collection of full-sized locomotives at the **Museum of Railway Technology** (Центральный музей Октябрьской железной дорогой; Map p100; nab kanala Obvodnogo 118; adult/child R200/100; ☺11am-5.30pm Tue-Sun; Ⓜ Baltiyskaya) behind the old Warsaw Station. Around 75 nicely painted and buffed engines and carriages are on display, some dating back to the late 19th century.

Contemporary Art Galleries   ART GALLERY

St Petersburg has a small but thriving contemporary art scene and some of the best places to see contemporary work include **Loft Project ETAGI** (Лофт проект ЭТАЖИ; Map p100; www.loftprojecttetagi.ru; Ligovsky pr 74; ☺noon-10pm; Ⓜ Ligovsky Prospekt), a former bread factory that contains three galleries and two exhibition spaces; **Rizzordi Art Foundation** (Map p100; www.rizzordi.org; Kurlyandskaya ul 49; admission free; ☺2-8pm Tue-Sun;

Ⓜ Baltiiskaya), a beautiful converted brewery; and the well-established group of galleries that collectively make up **Pushkinskaya 10** (Пушкинская 10; Map p108; http://en.p-10.ru; Ligovsky pr 53; admission free; ☺3-7pm Wed-Sun; Ⓜ Ploshchad Vosstaniya).

VASILYEVSKY ISLAND

Some of the best views of St Petersburg can be had from Vasilyevsky Island's eastern 'nose' known as the **Strelka**. The two **Rostral Columns** (Ростральные колонны; Map p108) on the point, studded with ships' prows, were oil-fired navigation beacons in the 1800s; on some holidays, such as Victory Day, gas torches are still lit on them.

The best of many museums on Vasilyevsky Island is the riverside **Menshikov Palace** (Меншиковский дворец; Map p100; www.hermitagemuseum.org; Universitetskaya nab 15; admission adult/student R60/free, free admission first Thu of the month, audio tour R150; ☺10.30am-6pm Tue-Sat, until 5pm Sun; Ⓜ Vasileostrovskaya), built in 1707 for Peter the Great's confidant Alexander Menshikov. Now a branch of the Hermitage, the palace's impressively restored interiors are filled with period art and furniture.

The **Kunstkamera** (Кунсткамера; Map p100; www.kunstkamera.ru; Universitetskaya nab 3; adult/student R200/50; ☺11am-6pm Tue-Sun, closed last Tue of the month; Ⓜ Admiralteyskaya) was established in 1714 by Peter the Great, who used it to display his ghoulish collection of monstrosities, notably preserved freaks, two-headed mutant foetuses and odd body parts. They still draw the crowds today.

Nearby, the **Museum of Zoology** (Зоологический музей; Map p108; www.zin.ru; Universitetskaya nab 1/3; adult/student R200/70, free last Thu each month; ☺11am-6pm Wed-Mon; Ⓜ Admiralteyskaya) has some amazing exhibits, including a complete woolly mammoth, thawed out of the Siberian ice in 1902, and a live insect zoo.

For the intrepid, the new and rather farflung **Erarta Museum of Contemporary Art** (Музей Эрарта; www.erarta.com; 29-aya liniya 2; adult/under 21 R300/150; ☺10am-10pm Thu-Tue; Ⓜ Vasileostrovskaya, then bus 6 from across the road from the metro) is highly recommended. Opened in 2010 and housed in a superbly converted Stalinist building, the museum houses a permanent collection of some 2000 works of Russian art produced between the 1950s and the present day, as well as a wide range of temporary exhibits where the work is normally for sale.

PETROGRAD SIDE

Peter & Paul Fortress FORTRESS

(Петропавловская крепость; Map p100; www
.spbmuseum.ru; ⊘grounds 6am-10pm, exhibitions 11am-6pm Thu-Tue; ⓂGorkovskaya) There's
plenty to see and do at this fortress, dating
from the city's founding in 1703. The oldest
building in St Petersburg, planned by Peter
the Great as a defence against the Swedes,
never saw action, and its main use up to
1917 was as a political prison. To get a sense
of its scale, and for river views, walk the
Nevskaya Panorama (Map p100; adult/stu-
dent R150/120) along part of the battlements,
then enter the **SS Peter & Paul Cathedral**
(Петропавловский собор; Map p100; adult/stu-
dent R200/90), whose 122m-tall, needle-thin
gilded spire is one of the city's defining landmarks. Its baroque interior is the last resting
place of all Russia's prerevolutionary rulers
from Peter the Great onward, except Peter
II and Ivan VI. It's also possible to climb
the **bell tower** (adult/student R130/70; ⊘tours
11.30am, 1pm, 2.30pm & 4pm May-Sep) on an
hour-long guided tour.

At noon every day a cannon is fired
from **Naryshkin Bastion** (Нарышкинский
бастион; Map p100). In the south wall is
Nevsky Gate (Невские ворота; Map p100),
where prisoners were loaded onto boats for
execution. Notice the plaques showing water
levels of famous floods.

Another highlight is the fascinating History of St Petersburg exhibition inside the
Commandant's House (Комендантский
дом; Map p100; adult/student R100/60). Covering up to the 1917 revolution, there are some
very good displays here, including a vivid
painting of the great flood of 1824 that all
but swept the city away, and a model showing how the Alexander Column in Palace
Sq was erected. Outside the house look for
Mikhail Shemyakin's controversial **Peter
the Great statue** with its out-of-proportion
head and hands: local lore has it that it's
good luck to touch his right forefinger.

Individual tickets are needed for each of
the fortress' attractions so the best deal is
the **combined entry ticket** (adult/student
R350/170), which allows access to all the
exhibitions on the island (except the bell
tower) and is valid for 48 hours.

☞ Tours

The following operations can arrange city
tours on foot and Anglo Tourismo can also
organise tours by boat. For something more

private than Anglo Tourismo's cruises, there
are many small boats that can be hired as
private water taxis. You'll have to haggle
over rates: expect to pay around R2500 an
hour for a group of up to six people.

Peter's Walking Tours WALKING TOURS
(☑943 1229; www.peterswalk.com; per person from
R650) Established in 1996, Peter Kozyrev's
innovative and passionately led tours are
highly recommended as a way to see the city
with knowledgeable locals. The daily Original Peter's Walk is one of the favourites and
functions as a do-it-yourself introduction to
the city: you tell your guide what aspects of
the city you're interested in and they impro-
vise a tour for you then and there. Other
tours include a Friday night pub crawl, a
Rasputin Walk and a WWII and the Siege of
Leningrad tour.

Anglo Tourismo BOAT TOURS
(Map p108; ☑325 9906; www.anglotourismo.com;
Nab Reki Fontanki 27; day/night R500/700) While
there is no shortage of boat tours on the canals and rivers of St Petersburg, Anglo Tourismo is the only operator to run all its tours
in English, and you'll pay the same rate per
tour as you would for a Russian-language
one. Boat tours last an hour and leave every
two hours on the hour from 11am until 7pm.
Night boat tours are also available.

VB Excursions WALKING TOURS
(☑380 4596; www.vb-excursions.com; per person
R800-1400) Offers excellent walking tours
with clued-up students on themes including
Dostoevsky and revolutionary St Petersburg.
Its 'Back in the USSR' tour (R1150 per person) includes a visit to a typical Soviet apartment for tea and bliny.

✪ Festivals & Events

The city's biggest event is the **Stars of the
White Nights Festival**, which includes
numerous events ranging from folk to ballet. The official festival dates are the last
10 days of June, but all kinds of arts events
and performances take place across the city
throughout June and often into July, with
the Mariinsky Theatre taking the lead.

🛏 Sleeping

The rates below are for the high season and
include breakfast.

As an alternative to hotel or hostel accommodation, **City Realty** (www.cityrealtyrus
sia.com), **Travel Russia** (www.travelrussia.su)

DETOUR: PETERHOF & TSARSKOE SELO

Among the several palace estates that the tsars built around St Petersburg as country retreats, the ones not to miss are **Peterhof** (Петергоф; www.peterhofmuseum.ru; ul Razvodnaya 2), 29km west of St Petersburg, and **Tsarskoe Selo** (Царское Село; www.tzar.ru; Sadovaya ul 7), 25km south of the city in the town of Pushkin.

If time is limited, Peterhof (also known as Petrodvorets) with its breezy Gulf of Finland location is the one to opt for, mainly because of its **Grand Cascade & Water Avenue**, a symphony of over 140 fountains and canals. To see them you are required to pay to enter the **Lower** (Нижний парк; www.peterhofmuseum.ru; adult/student R400/200; ◷park 9am-8pm, fountains 10am-6pm). They only work from mid-May to early October, but the gilded ensemble still looks marvellous at any time of the year.

Tsarskoe Selo (also known as Pushkin) is a wonderful park, and its highlight is the vast baroque **Catherine Palace** (Екатерининский дворец; adult/student R320/160; ◷10am-5pm Wed-Mon, individuals noon-2pm & 4-5pm), built between 1752 and 1756, but almost destroyed in WWII. The exterior and 20-odd rooms have been expertly restored; the Great Hall and the Amber Room are particularly dazzling.

GETTING THERE & AWAY

From May to September, the *Meteor* hydrofoil (one way/return R500/800, 30 minutes) goes every 20 to 30 minutes from 9.30am until at least 7pm from the jetty in front of St Petersburg's Hermitage to Peterhof.

A far cheaper option is to take a *marshrutka* to Peterhof (R30, 30 minutes). These run frequently from outside the Avtovo (300, 424) and Leninsky Prospekt (103) metro stations.

Marshrutky 286, 299, 342 or K545 regularly shuttle to Pushkin (R30, 30 minutes) from outside metro Moskovskaya. Infrequent suburban trains run from St Petersburg's Vitebsky vokzal. For Tsarskoe Selo (R42) get off at Detskoe Selo station, from where *marshrutky* (R20) frequently run to the estate.

and **Intro by Irina** (www.introbyirina.com) can arrange apartment rentals.

NEVSKY PROSPEKT & AROUND

TOP CHOICE **Rossi Hotel**   BOUTIQUE HOTEL €€
(Map p108; ☎635 6333; www.rossihotels.com; nab reki Fontanki 55; s/d/ste from R5000/9000/10,500; ❄☎; ⓂGostiny Dvor) This fantastic new addition to the local hotel scene is a beautifully restored building on one of St Petersburg's prettiest squares. The 46 rooms are all differently designed, but their brightness and moulded ceilings are uniform, with the very best rooms having superb views over the Fontanka River.

TOP CHOICE **Casa Leto**   BOUTIQUE HOTEL €€€
(Map p108; ☎314 6622; www.casaleto.com; Bolshaya Morskaya ul 34; r R9500-12,000; ❄☎; ⓂAdmiralteyskaya) A dramatically lit stone stairwell sets the scene for this discreet and stylish boutique hotel. With soft pastel shades and plenty of antiques, the spacious, high-ceilinged quarters are full of five-star perks, such as king-size beds, Molton Brown

toiletries, heated floors and free international phone calls.

TOP CHOICE **Andrey & Sasha's Homestay**   HOMESTAY €
(У Андрея и Саши; Map p108; ☎315 3330, 921 409 6701; asamatuga@mail.ru; nab kanala Griboyedova 49; s/d R2400/2800; ⓂSadovaya) Legendary hosts on the St Petersburg homestay and apartment scene, photographer Andrey and doctor Sasha have a couple of apartments they rent rooms in, including this one, which is also their delightfully decorated home.

Rachmaninov Hotel   BOUTIQUE HOTEL €€
(Антик-Отель Рахманинов; Map p108; ☎571 7618; www.hotelrachmaninov.com; Kazanskaya ul 5; r from R6900; ☎; ⓂNevsky Prospekt) Perfectly located and run by friendly staff, the Rachmaninov Hotel is one for those in the know. Stuffed full of antiques, the rooms have been recently renovated and feel pleasantly old world with their hardwood floors and attractive Russian furnishings.

Friends Hostel
HOSTEL €

(Map p108; ☎571 0151; www.friendsplace.ru; nab kanala Griboyedova 20; dm/d R500/2500; 🛜; MNevsky Prospekt) This new chain of hostels is one of the best things to have happened to St Petersburg's budget travellers for ages. All four locations are great, but our favourite is this one, just next to the Kazan Cathedral in a quiet courtyard. The newly done dorms are spotless, all have lockers and share good bathrooms and a kitchen.

Guest House Nevsky 3
MINIHOTEL €€

(Map p108; ☎710 6776; www.nevsky3.ru; Nevsky pr 3; s/d R4700/5300; 🛜; MAdmiralteyskaya) This tiny place has just four individually decorated rooms and gets rave reviews from guests. Each room has a fridge, TV, safe and a fan, and overlooks a surprisingly quiet courtyard just moments from the Hermitage.

Life Hostel
HOSTEL €

(Map p108; ☎318 1808; www.hostel-life.ru; Nevsky pr 47; dm R800-1000, s/d R2200/2600; 🛜; MMayakovskaya) The 15 brand new rooms at Life Hostel range from doubles to dorms sleeping eight. There's a big kitchen, clean bathrooms, free laundry and professional English-speaking staff – all in all, a great option.

Petro Palace Hotel
HOTEL €€

(Map p108; ☎571 2880; www.petropalacehotel.com; ul Malaya Morskaya 14; r from R5500; ❋🛜🏊; MAdmiralteyskaya) This large, superbly located midrange hotel between St Isaac's Cathedral and the Hermitage has 194 rooms and excellent facilities, including a great basement fitness centre with a decent pool, Finnish sauna and full gym. Standard rooms are spacious and furnished in an anonymously tasteful way.

3MostA
BOUTIQUE HOTEL €€

(Map p108; ☎332 3470; www.3mosta.com; nab reki Moyki 3A; s/d from R3000/5000; ❋🛜; MNevsky Prospekt) This brand new property, whose name means 'Three Bridges' in Russian, is surprisingly uncramped given its wonderful location. There are 24 rooms here, and even the standards are a good size with tasteful furniture, minibars and TVs.

ST PETERSBURG SLEEPING

REIMAGINING THE CITY

Ever since Peter the Great, the St Petersburg powers that be have traditionally deferred to foreign architects for major construction projects, something that hasn't changed much in three centuries. Today firms such as Foster & Partners, RMJM and Diamond & Schmitt are influencing how St Petersburg transitions architecturally into the 21st century.

Canadian firm Diamond & Schmitt are the designers of the **New Mariinsky Theatre** (see Map p100), currently under construction behind the present theatre. The project to construct much-needed modern premises for the Mariinsky began a decade ago when an extraordinary original design by Dominique Perrault was accepted, scandalising and exciting locals in equal measure. Perrault's proposed black marble building was to be wrapped in a vast, irregular golden glass dome, and would have totally broken with St Petersburg's architectural tradition, but it fell foul of local building codes and – crucially – the Kremlin, which objected to the project's spiralling costs. After a new competition in 2009, Canadian architects Diamond & Schmitt won the €295 million tender to build a very different structure, which can at best be described as a fairly unexciting modern building – too bland to excite but too modern to fit in. Originally slated to be open by late 2011, at the time of writing there was still some confusion as to when the project would be completed: don't hold your breath, although officially an opening date of 2012 is envisaged.

Even more controversial is the now notorious **Okhta Centre**, originally to have been called Gazprom City, but now on its third name, the Lakhta Centre, following years of local opposition to St Petersburg's first high-rise building.

The name and location may have changed, but the beast has not. The Lakhta Centre will be Europe's tallest building, towering almost 400m over the Neva (that's three time higher than the spire of the SS Peter & Paul Cathedral). The project was originally planned to occupy the site of an abandoned factory on the Vyborg Side, just opposite Smolny Cathedral. But such was the (rare) public and international outcry at the plan that in 2010 City Hall backed down and cancelled the project, to the joy of many locals. It was later announced that the building would still be constructed at a new location in Lakhta, a good distance from the Historic Heart beyond the Kirovsky Islands.

Historic Heart

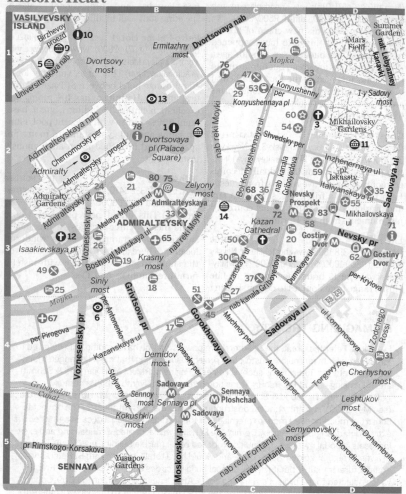

Pushka Inn
BOUTIQUE HOTEL €€

(Map p108; ☎312 0913; www.pushkainn.ru; nab reki Moyki 14; s/d from R4500/6700, apt R10,000-15,000; ❄🛜🛗; MAdmiralteyskaya) On a particularly picturesque stretch of the Moyka River, this charming inn is housed in a historic 18th-century building. The rooms are decorated in dusky pinks and caramel tones, with wide floorboards and – if you're willing to pay more – lovely views of the Moyka.

Location Hostel
HOSTEL €

(Map p108; ☎490 6429; www.location-hostel.ru; Admiralteysky pr; dm/d R600/1500; 🛜; MAdmiralteyskaya) With a brilliant location virtu-

ally on the doorstep of the Hermitage, this arty but small hostel is definitely a good choice for budget travellers. Dorms are quite crowded, with six to eight bunks in them, but there are also some double rooms if you need more space. There's a communal kitchen, rather tatty-looking shared bathrooms and plenty of cool art in the staircase.

Pio on Griboyedov
MINIHOTEL €€

(Пио на Грибоедова; Map p108; ☎571 9476; www.hotelpio.ru; nab kanala Griboyedova 35, apt 5; s/d/tr/q R3400/3800/4800/5400; 🛜; MNevsky Prospekt) This excellent place overlooks the

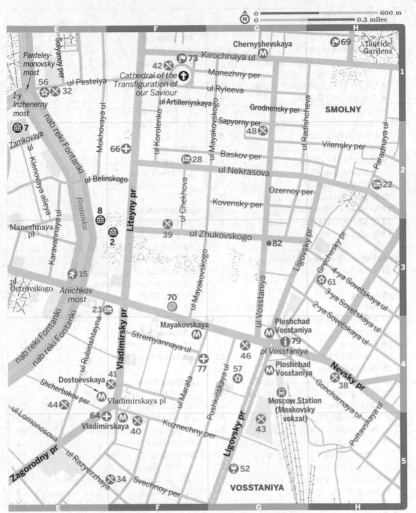

Griboyedov Canal and has six rooms, all of which share three bathrooms and toilets. It's not as hostel-like as it sounds though, much more like staying in a large apartment with friends. The communal areas are very pleasant and the rooms are comfortable and clean.

Hotel Vera
HOTEL €€
(Map p108; ☎702 6190; www.hotelvera.ru; Suvorovsky pr 25/16; s/d from R3600/4990; ❄️🛜; ⓜPloshchad Vosstaniya) Housed in a fabulous building built in 1903, this well-run hotel has slanted ceilings, stained-glass windows, ceramic tile stoves and ornate mouldings that hark back to its art deco origins. It's not all stuck in the past, however – there's satellite TV and fridges in all rooms and the bathrooms are thoroughly modern.

Puppet Hostel
HOSTEL €
(Map p108; ☎272 5401; www.hostel-puppet.ru; ul Nekrasova 12; dm/d R600/800; 🛜; ⓜMayakovskaya) Offering pretty basic dorms and doubles, it's also an ideal choice if you're travelling with kids because staying here includes free tickets to the puppet theatre next door.

Historic Heart

ELSEWHERE IN ST PETERSBURG

Alexander House BOUTIQUE HOTEL €€
(Дом Александра; Map p100; ℡334 3540; www.a-house.ru; nab kanala Kryukova 27; r/ste from R9500/11,000, apt from R15,000; ❄🌐; ⓂSennaya Ploshchad) Owners Alexander and Natalya have converted this historic building opposite Nikolsky Cathedral, styling each of the 14 spacious rooms after their favourite international cities. Lovely common areas include a fireplace-warmed lounge and a vine-laden courtyard containing a guests-only restaurant.

Hostel Ligovsky 74 HOSTEL €
(Map p108; ℡329 1274; www.hostel74.ru; Ligovsky pr 74; dm/r R600/1500, design rooms R2500; 🌐; ⓂLigovsky Prospekt) The 3rd floor of Loft Project ETAGI (see p104) is given over to this super-friendly hostel. Some of the dorms here are enormous (one has 20 beds in it!) but the facilities are spotless, including washing machines and a small kitchen.

Arkadia BOUTIQUE HOTEL €€
(Map p108; ℡571 6173; www.arkadiahotel.ru; nab reki Moyki 58; s/d from R4100/5100; ❄🌐🚇; ⓂAdmiralteyskaya) Hidden away inside a quiet flower-filled courtyard, this bright yellow hotel provides a welcome respite from the city's crowds. Warm hues, wood floors and natural lighting characterise the guest rooms.

Northern Lights MINIHOTEL €€
(Map p108; ℡571 9199; www.nlightsrussia.com; ul Bolshaya Morskaya 50; r without bathroom R3000, s/d with bathroom R4000/4300; ❄🌐; ⓂAdmiralteyskaya) Opposite the childhood home of Vladimir Nabokov is this very pleasant and friendly minihotel at the end of an impressive old staircase. There are just five rooms here: three have their own bathrooms and air-con, while two share facilities and are fan-cooled.

🍴 Eating
Restaurants

Botanika VEGETARIAN €
(Ботаника; Map p108; www.cafebotanika.ru; ul Pestelya 7; mains R200-450; 🚇🌐🚽; ⓂGostiny Dvor) Enjoying perhaps the friendliest and most laid-back atmosphere of any restaurant in St Petersburg, this vegetarian charmer wins on all counts. The menu takes in Russian, Indian, Italian and Japanese dishes, all of which are good, and service is friendly.

Teplo INTERNATIONAL €€
(Тепло; Map p108; ℡570 1974; www.v-teple.ru; ul Bolshaya Morskaya 45; mains R250-650; ⏰9am-11pm, from 11am Sat, from 1pm Sun; 🌐🚇; ⓂAdmiralteyskaya) This much-fêted, eclectic and original restaurant has it all just right. Service is friendly and fast (when it's not too busy) and the peppy, inventive menu will have something for everyone – there's a heavy Italian presence, but dishes come from all over the world. Reservations are usually essential, so call ahead.

Kompot Café INTERNATIONAL €€
(Первое, второе и компот; Map p108; www.kompotcafe.ru; ul Zhukovskogo 10; mains R200-600; 🌐🚽🚇; ⓂPloshchad Vosstaniya) This stylish new restaurant has three rooms decked out in different decors and there's a menu stretching from breakfasts served all day to soups, sandwiches, pies and 'funky tomato bouillabaisse'.

Dom Beat INTERNATIONAL €
(Дом Бита; Map p108; www.dombeat.ru; ul Razyezzhaya 12; mains R300-500; 🌐🚽🚇; ⓂLigovsky Prospekt) The sleek, retro-humorous interior, sumptuous menu and great atmosphere add up to make this one of the best eating choices in town. As well as great breakfasts (served until 7pm!), there's a wide choice of dishes ranging from top-notch Asian cuisine to modern takes on Russian meals and international bar food.

Makarov RUSSIAN €€
(Макаров; Map p108; ℡327 0053; Manezhny per 2; mains R500-800; ⏰9am-11pm Tue-Fri, 11am-11pm Sat-Mon; 🚽🚇; ⓂChernyshevskaya) A charming place, overlooking the Cathedral of the Transfiguration of our Saviour, Makarov serves up traditional Russian dishes with a twist in a relaxed setting. Good breakfasts are served daily until noon, and until 2pm on weekends (reservations are essential).

Fartuk INTERNATIONAL €
(Фартук; Map p108; ul Rubinshteyna 15/17; mains R200-300; 🌐🚽🚇; ⓂDostoevskaya) Despite its unfortunate name, Fartuk is a beautifully designed place with tiled floors and old-world-meets-industrial fittings. The crowd here is cool and the menu is interesting: wok-cooked chicken with ginger and coriander sits next to freshly made bruschetta, soups and steaks.

Schastye

ITALIAN €€

(Счастье; Map p108; www.schaste-est.com; ul Rubinshteyna 15/17; mains R200-700; ⊗8am-midnight, to 6am Fri & Sat; 🖥️📶🚭; Ⓜ️Dostoevskaya) 'Happiness' comes in several forms here: a multi-roomed venue full of cosy nooks and crannies to huddle up in, an expansive and interesting Italian menu, delicious pastries and sweets piled up on plates around the place, and a lavish and thoroughly warm, if somewhat random, decor.

Terrassa

FUSION €€

(Терасса; Map p108; 🚋937 6837; www.terrassa.ru; Kazanskaya ul 3a; mains R450-1000; ⊗11am-1am Mon-Fri, from noon Sat & Sun; 🖥️📶🚭; Ⓜ️Nevsky Prospekt) Atop the Vanity shopping centre, this cool bistro boasts unbelievable views towards Kazan Cathedral. In the open kitchen, chefs busily prepare fusion cuisine, exhibiting influences from Italy, Asia and beyond.

Café King Pong

ASIAN €€

(Map p108; www.kingpong.ru; Bolshaya Morskaya ul 16; mains R300-600; 🖥️📶🚭; Ⓜ️Admiralteyskaya) From the team that brings you the excellent Soup Vino comes this innovative and fun pan-Asian diner, occupying sleek and luminous premises with a retro-glamorous feel just off Nevsky. The large menu is very good quality and takes in dim sum, noodles, soups and rice dishes.

Cafes & Quick Eats

Soup Vino

ITALIAN €

(Суп вино; Map p108; www.supvino.ru; Kazanskaya ul 24; mains R200-500; 📶🚭; Ⓜ️Nevsky Prospekt) This cute, tiny place does exactly what it says on the label. The menu features Mediterranean-influenced soups, pasta and salads, perfect washed down with glasses of wine.

TOP CHOICE Stolle

BAKERY €

(Столле; Map p108; www.stolle.ru; Konyushenny per 1/6; pies R50-200; ⊗8am-10pm; 📶; Ⓜ️Nevsky Prospekt) The delicious, freshly baked Saxon-style pies ('stolle') at this cool and atmospheric bakery are legendary in St Petersburg, and a selection of sweet and savoury offerings sits on the counter, fresh from the oven any time of day. Takeaway is available. Other central outlets include ul Vosstaniya (Map p108; ul Vosstaniya 32; Ⓜ️Chernyshevskaya) and ul Dekabristov (Map p100; ul Dekabristov 19 Ⓜ️Sadovaya).

Garçon

FRENCH €

(Map p108; www.garcon.ru; sandwiches R200; ⊗9am-9pm; 📶) off Nevsky pr (nab kanala Griboye-dova 25; Ⓜ️Nevsky Prospekt); Nevsky pr (Nevsky pr 103; Ⓜ️Ploshchad Vosstaniya) Finding a decent sandwich in this town can be a Herculean feat, so this *boulangerie* chain's outlet just off Nevsky pr is a very welcome discovery. Freshly made sandwiches in freshly baked baguettes – not to mention a great range of cakes and other treats – are all available to stay or go. There's also a branch near Moscow Station.

Dve Palochki

ASIAN €€

(Две палочки; Map p108; www.dvepalochki .ru; mains R200-600; ⊗11am-6am; Ⓜ️Nevsky Prospekt) Nevsky pr (Nevsky pr 22); Italianskaya ul (Italianskaya ul 6) This local chain is one of the most sophisticated of the ubiquitous sushi bars in the city. These central branches are always packed with a trendy crowd.

Zoom Café

EUROPEAN €

(Map p108; www.cafezoom.ru; Gorokhovaya ul 22; meals R100-400; ⊗9am-midnight Mon-Sat, 1pm-midnight Sun; 🖥️📶🚭; Ⓜ️Sennaya Ploshchad) Perennially popular cafe with a funky feel and an interesting menu, Zoom does everything from Japanese-style chicken in teriyaki sauce to potato pancakes with salmon and cream cheese. A great lunch spot.

Self-Catering

Kuznechny Market

MARKET

(Кузнечный рынок; Map p108; Kuznechny per; ⊗8am-8pm; Ⓜ️Vladimirskaya) The best fresh-produce market in town.

Stockmann

SUPERMARKET

(Map p108; Nevsky Centre Shopping Centre, Nevsky pr 112; ⊗10am-11pm; Ⓜ️Ploshchad Vosstaniya)

Okey

SUPERMARKET

(Map p108; Galeria Shopping Centre, Ligovsky pr 30A; ⊗10am-11pm; Ⓜ️Ploshchad Vosstaniya)

Lend

SUPERMARKET

(Лэнд; Map p108; Vladimirsky Passazh, Vladimirsky pr 19; ⊗24hr; Ⓜ️Dostoevskaya)

🍷 Drinking

TOP CHOICE Dyuni

BAR

(Дюны; Map p108; Ligovsky pr 50; ⊗24hr; Ⓜ️Ploshchad Vosstaniya) St Petersburg's hippest bar is this hipster sandpit at the back of the large warehouse complex in the courtyard of Ligovsky 50. There's a cosy indoor bar and a sprawling sand-covered outside area with table football and ping pong. To find it, simply continue in a straight line from the entrance to the courtyard.

Terminal Bar BAR

(Терминал; Map p108; ul Rubinshteyna 13A; ☺4pm-6am; MDostoevskaya) A slice of New York bohemia on one of St Petersburg's most happening streets, Terminal is a great place for a relaxed drink with friends, who can spread out along the length of the enormous bar, while live piano from anyone who can play fills the long, arched room.

The Other Side PUB

(Другая сторона; Map p108; www.theotherside .ru; Bolshaya Konyushennaya ul 1; ☎✈📷; MNevsky Prospekt) There's live music most nights at this fun and funky bar as well as decent food (mains R200 to R400), but most people turn up to enjoy the seven beers on tap and other alcoholic libations.

☆ Entertainment

Check the weekly *St Petersburg Times* for up-to-date listings.

Classical Music, Ballet & Opera

Mariinsky Theatre BALLET, OPERA

(Мариинский театр оперы и балета; Map p100; www.mariinsky.ru; Teatralnaya pl 1; ☺box office 11am-7pm, performances 7pm; MSennaya Ploshchad) Home to the world-famous Mariinsky Ballet and Opera company, a visit here is a must, if only to delight in the sparkling glory of the interior. Use the website to book and pay for tickets in advance of your visit to the theatre or to the acoustically splendid new concert hall (Концертный зал Мариинского театра; ul Pisareva 20), which is nearby. Don't miss (how can you?) the **New Mariinsky Theatre** (ul Dekabristov 34), being completed across the Kryukov Canal.

Shostakovich Philharmonia Bolshoy Zal CLASSICAL MUSIC

(Большой зал филармонии Шостаковича; Map p108 www.philharmonia.spb.ru; MNevsky Prospekt) Under the artistic direction of world-famous conductor Yury Temirkanov, the St Petersburg Philharmonic Orchestra represents the finest in orchestral music. The **Bolshoy Zal** (Большой зал; Grand Hall; Mikhailovskaya ul 2) on pl Iskusstv is the venue for a full program of symphonic performances, while the nearby **Maly Zal** (Малый зал Глинки; Small Hall; Nevsky pr 30) hosts smaller ensembles.

Mikhailovsky Theatre BALLET, OPERA

(p108; www.mikhailovsky.ru; pl Iskusstv 1; MNevsky Prospekt) Challenging the Mariinsky in terms of the standards and range of its perform-

ances is this equally historic and beautifully restored theatre.

Live Music

St Petersburg is a great place to see live bands.

Chinese Pilot Dzhao Da LIVE MUSIC

(Китайский лётчик Джао Да; Map p108; www. spb.jao-da.com; ul Pestelya 7; cover R100-200 for concerts; ☺noon-midnight; MGostiny Dvor) This is one of the very best places to see live music in the city. The premises are charming – the main bar area is bathed in light and there's plenty of seating and a genial buzz all day; there's a stage and more seating for nightly gigs in the back room.

Fish Fabrique LIVE MUSIC

(Map p108; www.fishfabrique.spb.ru; Ligovsky pr 53, ground level; ☺3pm-6am, concerts from 8pm Thu-Sun; MPloshchad Vosstaniya) Here in this museum of boho life, artists, musicians and wannabes of all ages meet to drink beer and listen to music. Live bands kick up a storm from 8pm nightly.

Zoccolo LIVE MUSIC

(Цоколь; Map p108; www.zoccolo.ru, in Russian; 3-ya Sovetskaya ul 2/3; cover R100; ☺noon-midnight Sun-Thu, noon-6am Fri & Sat, concerts 8pm; MPloshchad Vosstaniya) Zoccolo, in its urgently orange and green underground space near pl Vosstaniya, has slowly become another institution in St Petersburg's music scene. Entry is free before 5pm, when the venue functions as an arty cafe.

JFC Jazz Club JAZZ CLUB

(Map p100; ☎272 9850; www.jfc-club.spb.ru; Shpalernaya ul 33; cover R100-500; ☺7-11pm; MChernyshevskaya) Very small and very New York, this cool club is the best place in the city to hear modern, innovative jazz music, as well as the occasional blues, bluegrass and various other styles (see the website for a list of what's on). Table reservations are a good idea.

WANT MORE?

For in-depth information, reviews and recommendations at your fingertips, head to the Apple App Store to purchase Lonely Planet's St Petersburg City Guide iPhone app.

ST PETERSBURG ENTERTAINMENT

Nightclubs

Griboyedov
NIGHTCLUB

(Грибоедов; Map p100; www.griboedovclub.ru; Voronezhskaya ul 2a; cover R200-400; ⊙noon-6am, concerts 10pm; 🛜; Ⓜ Ligovsky Prospekt) Griboyedov is the longest-standing and most respected music club in the city. Another club in a bomb shelter, this one was founded by local ska collective Dva Samolyota. It's a low-key bar in the early evening, gradually morphing into a dance club later in the night. Excellent music acts and international DJs play electronic, rock and dubstep.

Mod Club
NIGHTCLUB

(Map p108; www.modclub.info; nab kanala Griboyedova 7; cover Fri & Sat R100-300; ⊙6pm-6am; Ⓜ Nevsky Prospekt) A popular spot for students and other indie types who appreciate the fun and friendly atmosphere, the groovy mix of music (live and spun) and added entertainment such as *novus* tables (a billiard-like game that is increasingly popular in Russia). Laid-back and great fun, this is a solid choice for a night out.

Tunnel Club
NIGHTCLUB

(Map p100; www.tunnelclub.ru; cnr Zverinskaya ul & Lybansky per; cover R100-230; ⊙midnight-6am Thu-Sat, midnight-3am Sun-Wed; Ⓜ Sportivnaya) Closed for several years, this military-themed club reopened in the bomb shelter where it was first born. The setting is still spooky but somehow appropriate for the techno and dubstep that goes down here.

Barakobamabar
NIGHTCLUB

(Map p108; www.barakobamabar.ru; Konyushennaya pl 2; ⊙6pm-6am; Ⓜ Nevsky Prospekt) In the summer months there's a great outdoor bar and dance floor, while inside there are a couple of cosy bars and a hookah lounge spread over two floors, both always full of beautiful young things. It's right at the back through the complex at Konyushennaya pl 2.

🛍 Shopping

TOP CHOICE Udelnaya Fair
MARKET

(Удельная ярмарка; Vyborg Side; ⊙8am-5pm Sat & Sun; Ⓜ Udelnaya) St Petersburg's only well-established flea market is one shopping experience that's truly worth travelling for. Exit the Udelnaya metro station to the right and follow the crowds across the train tracks.

Souvenir Market
SOUVENIRS

(Рынок сувениров; Map p108; nab kanala Griboyedova 1; ⊙sunrise-sunset; Ⓜ Nevsky Prospekt) You're unlikely to find any incredible bargains at this market behind the Church on Spilled Blood, but you will find a great selection of handicrafts and other souvenirs. Haggle with the vendors – they speak enough English to barter back.

Gostiny Dvor
SHOPPING CENTRE

(Гостиный двор; Map p108; www.bgd.ru; Nevsky pr 35; ⊙10am-10pm; Ⓜ Gostiny Dvor) Despite a renovation for the city's tercentennial celebrations, the exterior of Russia's oldest shopping mall is already looking like it needs a serious repaint. The interior retains a largely Soviet, if quaint, feel.

ℹ️ Information

Dangers & Annoyances

Watch out for pickpockets, particularly along Nevsky pr and in crowded places such as theatres and cinemas. It's also wise to avoid crossing directly in front of Moskovsky vokzal unless you have to, since police there have been known to shake down foreigners for supposed infringements of visa registration rules.

From May to September mosquitoes are a nightmare. The plug-ins that slowly heat repellent-saturated cardboard pads are available everywhere in the city and are very effective. Alternatively bring repellent or cover up.

Tiny traces of *Giardia lamblia*, a nasty parasite that causes stomach cramps and diarrhoea, have been found in St Petersburg's water. There's no preventative drug so the best advice is not to drink straight from the tap. To be absolutely safe, drink only bottled water.

Emergency

All of the following numbers have Russian-speaking operators. If you need to make a police report and don't speak Russian, first contact the Tourist Information Centre (p115). Emergency numbers are as follows:

Ambulance 📞03
Fire 📞01
Gas leak 📞04
Police 📞02

Internet Access

Wireless access is increasingly ubiquitous across the city's hotels and restaurants. In nearly all cases it's free, but you'll have to ask for the password. If you don't have a smart phone or a laptop, the following internet cafes are centrally located.

Café Max (Map p108; www.cafemax.ru; Nevsky pr 90; per hr R120; ⊙24hr; Ⓜ Mayakovskaya) A big fancy place with 150 computers, a game zone and a comfy cafe and beer bar. It's located on the 2nd floor. There's a second branch inside the Hermitage.

Internet Cafe (Map p108; Nevsky pr 11; per hr R80; ☺24hr; ⓜAdmiralteyskaya) Above Subway.

Media

The following English-language publications are available free at many hotels, hostels, restaurants and bars across the city.

In Your Pocket (www.inyourpocket.com/city/st_petersburg) Monthly listings booklet with useful up-to-date information and short features.

Pulse (www.pulse.ru) Fairly substance-free monthly magazine with features and reviews.

St Petersburg Times (www.sptimes.ru) Published every Wednesday, this plucky little newspaper has been fearlessly telling it like it really is for over 15 years. The column Chernov's Choice, a rundown of what's going on in the city from veteran music journalist Sergey Chernov, is especially useful.

Medical Services

CLINICS

The clinics listed below are open 24 hours and have English-speaking staff.

American Medical Clinic (Map p108; ✆740 2090; www.amclinic.ru; nab reki Moyki 78; ⓜSadovaya)

Medem International Clinic & Hospital (Map p108; ✆336 3333; www.medem.ru; 6 ul Marata; ⓜMayakovskaya)

PHARMACIES

Look for the sign *apteka,* or the usual green cross to find a pharmacy.

36.6 Pharmacy (Аптека 36,6; http://spb.366.ru) A chain of 24-hour pharmacies around the city.

Apteka Petrofarm (Map p108; Nevsky pr 22; ☺24 hr; ⓜNevsky Prospekt)

Money

ATMs are ubiquitous and there are currency-exchange offices all the way along and around Nevsky pr, many of which are open 24 hours a day.

Post

Post office branches are scattered throughout the city. All the major air-courier services are available in St Petersburg.

Central post office (Почтамт; Map p100; Pochtamtskaya ul 9; ☺24hr; ⓜAdmiralteyskaya) Worth visiting just to admire its recently renovated, elegant Style Moderne interior. The express mail service EMS Garantpost is available here.

Telephone

You can buy a local SIM card at any mobile-phone shop for as little as R150, including R100 credit. See p388 for information on the main mobile providers.

Tourist Information

The English-speaking staff at the **City Tourist Information Centre** (Городской туристический информационный центр; Map p108; ✆310 2822; www.ispb.info; Sadovaya ul 14/52; ☺10am-7pm Mon-Fri, noon-6pm Sat; ⓜNevsky Prospekt) do their best to help with advice and information. There are also kiosks outside the **Hermitage** (Map p108; Dvortsovaya pl 12; ☺10am-7pm; ⓜAdmiralteyskaya), on **Pl Vosstaniya** (Map p108; Pl Vosstaniya; ☺10am-7pm; ⓜPloshchad Vosstaniya) and desks at the **Pulkovo-1** and **Pulkovo-2** airports (☺10am-7pm Mon-Fri).

Travel Agencies

All the following agencies have English-speaking staff.

City Realty (Сити Риалти; www.cityrealty.ru) Can arrange all types of visas (tourist visas from US$25) including business ones, as well as accommodation and transport tickets. Very reliable.

Ost-West Kontaktservice (www.ostwest.com) The multilingual staff here can find you an apartment to rent and organise tours, train tickets and visa invites.

Sindbad Travel (www.sindbad.ru) A genuine Western-style discount air-ticket office, staffed by friendly, knowledgeable people. It also sells train tickets and ISIC/ITIC/IYTC cards and can book youth hostel accommodation.

Travel Russia (www.travelrussia.su) A small and very well-run company, Travel Russia organises apartments, visas, transfers and registration.

ⓘ Getting There & Away

Train
LONG-DISTANCE TRAINS

There are four major long-distance train stations in St Petersburg. Those taking Train 10И to Irkutsk will depart from **Ladozhsky vokzal** (Ладожский вокзал; ✆768 5304; Zanevsky pr 73; ⓜLadozhskaya), which also receives services to/from Helsinki, the far north of Russia and the Urals.

Most commonly used is **Moskovsky vokzal** (Московский вокзал; Map p108; ✆768 4597; pl Vosstaniya; ⓜPloshchad Vosstaniya), which mainly serves Moscow, but also the rest of western Russia, Crimea and the Caucasus.

Other stations include **Finlyandsky vokzal** Финляндский вокзал; Map p100; ✆768 7687;

pl Lenina 6; Ⓜ Ploshchad Lenina) for services to/ from Helsinki, and **Vitebsky vokzal** (Витебский вокзал; Map p100; ☑ 768 5807; Zagorodny pr 52; Ⓜ Pushkinskaya) for the Baltic states, Eastern Europe, Ukraine and Belarus. Suburban services also run from these stations, as they do from **Baltiysky vokzal** (Балтийский вокзал; Map p100; ☑ 768 2859; Obvodny Kanal 120; Ⓜ Baltiyskaya).

Tickets can be purchased at the train stations, the **Central Train Ticket Office** (Центральные железнодорожные кассы; Map p108; ☑ 762 33 44; nab kanala Griboyedova 24; ☺ 8am-8pm Mon-Sat, 8am-4pm Sun; Ⓜ Nevsky Prospekt), the **Central Airline Ticket Office** (p116) and many travel agencies around town.

TRANS-SIBERIAN ROUTES

Most travellers continuing to Siberia will travel via Moscow from where they will have a far wider choice of trains continuing east. However, it is possible to take the Train 10И, the Irkutsk, from Ladozhsky vokzal to Irkutsk. Train 10И leaves at 4.22pm on uneven dates, arriving three days and 14 hours later in Irkutsk. Tickets start at R9000. Note that the train does not go via Moscow.

MOSCOW

There are about 10 daily trains to Moscow, all departing from Moskovsky vokzal: see p116 for a table that lists the most popular services. Most depart between 10pm and midnight, arriving in the capital the following morning between 6am and 8am. On the more comfortable *firmeny* (premium) trains, a first-class *lyux* ticket runs R5200 to R6000, while a *kupe* is R2000 to R3000. The overnight sleepers will save a night's accommodation costs, while if you really want to save money, some services have *platskart* (open dorm) carriages with very cheap tickets.

There are also high-speed Sapsan day trains that travel at 200km/h and reach Moscow in four hours or less. Trains depart throughout the day. Comfortable 2nd-class seats are R2300 to

R2800, while super-spacious 1st-class seats run R5000 to R5600.

INTERNATIONAL DESTINATIONS

From Helsinki there are four daily Allegro express trains that take you from the Finnish capital to St Petersburg in an impressive 3½ hours. See www.vr.fi for prices and timetables. Services in both directions stop at Vyborg, so you can save yourself some money if you take a bus or local train there and then catch the train to Helsinki. The *Lev Tolstoi* (train 32) departs St Petersburg Ladozhsky for Helsinki daily from June to August (R3224, 6¾ hours). See p394 for more international connections.

St Petersburg is well connected by train to lots of cities throughout Eastern Europe, including Berlin, Budapest, Kaliningrad, Kyiv, Prague and Warsaw, but most trains pass through Belarus, for which you're required to hold a transit visa.

Air

Pulkovo-1 and **Pulkovo-2** (☑ Pulkovo-1 704 3822, Pulkovo-2 704 3444; www.pulkovoairport .ru/eng) are, respectively, the domestic and international terminals that serve St Petersburg. Pulkovo-2 is the main international terminal, while Pulkovo-1 handles all internal flights and those to Commonwealth of Independent States (CIS) countries.

St Petersburg has direct air links with all major European capitals and the many larger Russian cities. Tickets for all airlines can be purchased from travel agencies (p115) and from the **Central Airline Ticket Office** (Центральные авиакассы; Map p108; Nevsky pr 7; ☺ 8am-8pm Mon-Fri, 8am-6pm Sat & Sun; Ⓜ Admiralteyskaya), which also has counters for train and international bus tickets.

Boat

Between early April and late September, international passenger ferries connect Stockholm,

POPULAR TRAINS FROM ST PETERSBURG TO MOSCOW

TRAIN NUMBER & NAME	DEPARTURE TIME	DURATION	FARE
1 *Krasnya Strela*	11.55pm	8hr	R2600-3000
3 *Express*	11.59pm	8hr	R2380
5 *Nikolaevsky Express*	11.30pm	8hr	R2750
53 *Grand Express*	11.40pm	9hr	R5000-6000
151A Sapsan	6.45am	4hr	R2612
157A Sapsan	1.30pm	4hr	R2354
161A Sapsan	3.15pm	4hr	R2870
165A Sapsan	7.45pm	4hr	R2870

Helsinki and Tallinn with **Morskoy vokzal** (Морской вокзал; Map p96; pl Morskoy Slavy 1). It's a long way from the metro, so either take bus 7 or trolley bus 10 from outside the Hermitage.

In the summer, regular river cruises depart from the **River Passenger Terminal** (Речной вокзал; pr Obukhovskoy Oborony 195; MPro- letarskaya) and float along the Neva to inland Russia, including cruises to Valaam, Kizhi and Moscow. Tours can be booked through most travel agents, or through the **Ferry Centre** (Паромный центр; Map p108; ul Vosstaniya 19; MPloshchad Vosstaniya).

Bus

St Petersburg's main bus station, **Avtovokzal No 2** (Автовокзал No 2; Map p100; www .avokzal.ru; nab kanala Obvodnogo 36; MOb- vodny Kanal) – there isn't a No 1 – has both international and European Russia services. The website has current timetables and routes. The single cheapest way to get to Helsinki is to take a *marshrutka* from pl Vosstaniya (R500); they leave all day when full from the corner of Nevsky pr and Ligovsky pr, opposite the metro station.

Other international buses are offered by a number of companies:

Ecolines (Map p100; www.ecolines.ru; Po- dyezdny per 3; MPushkinskaya) Daily buses from Vitebsky vokzal to Tallinn (R980), Rīga (R1250), Kyiv (R1880) and Odesa (R2320).

Lux Express (www.luxexpress.eu; Admiral Business Centre, Mitrofanievskoe sh 2; ☺9am- 9pm; MBaltiyskaya) Runs buses from both Avtovokzal No 2 (above) and from outside the Baltiysky vokzal. Its buses run very regularly to Tallinn (from R850, 12 daily) and Rīga (from R1000, three daily).

Sovavto (Map p108; www.sovavto.ru; Grand Hotel Europe, Mikhailovskaya ul 1; MGostiny Dvor) Daily departures in very comfortable, air- conditioned buses from the Grand Hotel Europe to Helsinki (R1600, eight hours) and Turku (R2320, 11 hours).

❶ Getting Around

St Petersburg can be a frustrating place to get around for visitors: the metro, while an excellent system, actually has relatively few stations in the centre of the city, and distances from sta- tions to nearby sights can be long. Many visitors find buses and *marshrutka* a little daunting, as all the signage is in Russian only and you need to know where you're going, so many people just walk: bring comfortable shoes!

To/From the Airport

St Petersburg's airport is at Pulkovo, about 17km south of the centre. Domestic and CIS flights arrive at Pulkovo-1, from where you can take bus

---

RAISING THE BRIDGES

From the end of April to November all major bridges rise at the following times nightly to let seagoing ships through. The following schedule (which every year changes by five minutes here or there) governs the lives of the city's motorists and nighthawks trying to get from one area to another.

Most Alexandra Nevskogo 2.20– 5.10am

Birzhevoy most 2–4.55am

Bolsheokhtinsky most 2–5am

Dvortsovy most 1.25–4.50am

Blagoveshchensky most 1.25–2.45am & 3.10–5am

Liteyny most 1.40–4.45am

Troitsky most 1.35–4.45am

Tuchkov most 2–2.55am & 3.35–4.55am

---

39 (R21, every 15 minutes, 5.30am to 12.30am) from outside the terminal building. It connects you to Moskovskaya metro, from where you can get to anywhere in the city. Buy your ticket on the bus. Alternatively jump into any *marshrutka*, and check with the driver that it goes to Mosko- vskaya metro (nearly all do).

International flights arrive at Pulkovo-2, from where bus K-13 shuttles you to Moskovskaya metro (R27, every 10 minutes, 5.30am to 12.30am). Turn left when you leave the arrivals area and the bus stop is between departures and arrivals. The bus terminates at Moskovskaya metro, so you don't need to worry about where to get off.

If you'd prefer to take a taxi from either terminal, there are now taxi booking stands in the arrivals area of both terminals where staff speak English. State your destination and you'll be given a slip of paper with the price on it and be taken to a taxi outside. Expect to pay R600 to R800 for a trip to the centre, depending on where exactly you're heading.

Bus, Marshrutka, Trolleybus & Tram

Tickets (R21 to R25 depending on the service) are bought inside the vehicle. Bus stops are marked by roadside 'A' signs (for *avtobus*), trol- leybus stops by 'm' (representing a handwritten Russian 'T'), tram stops by a 'T'; all usually indi- cate the line numbers, too. Stops may also have roadside signs with little pictures of a bus, trol- leybus or tram. *Marshrutky* stop anywhere you hail them (except on Nevsky pr, where they're banned from operating). Most transport runs from 6am to 1am.

The following are some useful routes across the city:

Along Nevsky pr between Admiralty and Moskovsky vokzal Buses 7 and 22; trolleybuses 1, 5, 7, 10 and 22. Trolleybuses 1 and 22 continue out to pl Alexandra Nevskogo. Trolleybuses 5 and 7 continue to Smolny.

From Ligovsky pr via Troitsky most to Peter & Paul Fortress and Petrograd Side *Marshrutka* K76.

From Vitebsky vokzal via Sennaya pl and Mariinsky Theatre to Vasilyevsky Island *Marshrutka* K124.

From the Hermitage to the far side of Vasilyevsky Island Bus 7; trolleybus 10.

To the Kirovsky Islands Bus 10 from the corner of Bolshaya Morskaya ul and Nevsky pr.

Metro

The St Petersburg **metro** (www.metro.spb.ru; flat fare R25; ☺6am-midnight) is a very efficient five-lined system. The network of some 65 stations is best used for travelling long distances, especially connecting the suburbs to the city centre.

Zhetony (tokens), valid for one ride, can be bought from the booths in the stations. You're supposed to buy an extra ticket if you're carrying a large amount of luggage. If you are staying more than a day or two, however, it's worth buying a smart card (R30), which is good for loading multiple journeys over a fixed time period. The more trips you buy, the more you save – though note, you can't share a card with a friend.

Moscow to Yekaterinburg

Includes »

Route Info

» Distance: 1814km

» Duration: 26 hours

» Time zones: Moscow, Moscow +2

Best Places to Stay & Eat

» Jouk-Jacques hotel (p134)

» Hotel Giuseppe (p140)

» Hotel Edem (p139)

» Bezukhov bar & restaurant (p135)

» Grill Taverna Montenegro (p139)

» Vkus Stranstvy *stolovaya* (p139)

Why Go?

For travellers, this section of the journey across European Russia will often be accompanied by the excitement of departure from the capital. It is a relatively densely populated section that has three main routes. One veers northeast via Yaroslavl and a second (used by Yekaterinburg's flagship *Ural* train 16) goes southeast via multicultural Kazan. The most common route, however, passes through the ancient town of Vladimir and at Nizhny Novgorod crosses the Volga – a geographic highlight of this leg – before continuing to Perm, a city that is reinventing itself as a modern cultural capital. Kungur, set in rolling hills, has a spectacular ice cave, and finally the train rattles sublimely across the Europe–Asia border and into Yekaterinburg.

When to Go
Nizhny Novgorod

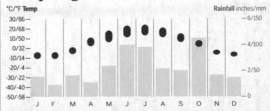

Feb Much of the Volga River will be frozen over and draped in a winter landscape.

late Apr–late May A spring sun warms the air and life moves onto the streets.

late Jul–Sep The navigation season is in full swing on the Volga and hiking is excellent in the Urals.

Moscow to Yekaterinburg Highlights

① Exploring the **museums** (p134) of Nizhny Novgorod

② Focusing on the lively **eating and drinking** (p135) scene in Nizhny Novgorod

③ Strolling through the ice cave of **Kungur** (p142) and enjoying a moment of pitch darkness

④ Sailing the **Volga** on a short excursion in Nizhny

Novgorod (p131) or Kazan (p140)

⑤ Strolling through multicultural **Kazan** (p140), one of Russia's most

dynamic cities and home to a picturesque kremlin

⑥ Checking out the shock of the new at **PERMM** (p137), Perm's museum of modern and contemporary art

⑦ Taking a tour through **Perm-36** (p142), the haunting Gulag camp memorial

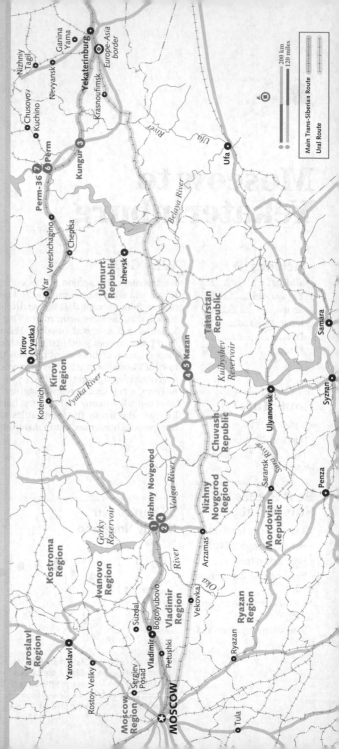

The Route
Moscow to Nizhny Novgorod

0KM FROM MOSCOW For travellers leaving from Moscow and taking the train eastwards, departure will mean finding the right station (check your ticket carefully) and leaving plenty of time (about an hour is good) to pass through security, stocking up on last-minute snacks and waiting for the platform and track to be shown on the departure board. Once the doors have closed and the train slowly crawls away from the railhead, the *provodnitsa* (carriage attendant) will walk around the carriage to tear the silver seal on the tickets and give you bedding if this is not already in the compartment.

Gradually the train leaves behind the platforms and station and sets a course between the streets, backyards and apartment buildings of the capital towards provincial Russia. Most likely you will see comic signs warning Muscovites against taking shortcuts across the tracks. Everywhere, Muscovites will be taking shortcuts across the tracks, some of them carrying plastic shopping bags or rushing to work.

13KM A short distance beyond **Los** the train crosses the Moscow Ring Road. This stretch of track through outer Moscow has been immortalised by the Soviet underground writer Venedikt Yerofeyev in his novel *Moscow to the End of the Line*. The main character travels to **Petushki** on a whistle-stop *elektrichka* (suburban train) at the time of Gorbachev's liquor ban, philosophising on the virtues of alcohol and the evils of the Soviet lifestyle while toasting every station. He consumes mind-boggling cocktails, such as the 'Tear of a Young Communist League Girl', which consists of three brands of cheap Soviet eau de toilette, mouth rinse, nail polish and lemonade. Don't try to repeat this fictional (!) experience, or you'll never get anywhere, let alone to Siberia.

190KM (210KM) About three hours after departing, the train reaches **Vladimir** (p123), where most trains pause for about 20 minutes. Approaching the city, look for the golden spires and domes of the Assumption Cathedral high on the embankment to the north. Vladimir has some of the oldest churches in Russia and it was here that in 1157 Prince Andrei Bogolyubsky established his capital and shaped the town with architecture based on Kyivan and Western traditions. The dark side of the glitter is that our man met a sticky end: almost 20 years later a plot was hatched to get rid of him and on one fateful night his flunkies, bursting into the chamber while he slept, finished him off with an axe.

200KM (220KM) Just beyond Vladimir you pass the small town of **Bogolyubovo** (p125), another of the historic highlights of the region and the place where Prince Andrei built his palace. Today it is largely a monastery complex dating from the 18th century. You can glimpse this if you look north as the train approaches, and east of it is the Church of the Intercession – the paragon of Russian church architecture, sitting in splendid isolation at the confluence of the Nerl and Klyazma Rivers.

254KM (274KM) Tracing the valleys of the Klyazma and Oka Rivers, the train passes several other ancient towns. One of these is **Kovrov**, mostly known as the centre of the peculiar sport of motoball – football on motorcycles. This is followed by the pretty **Gorokhovets** at 363km (382km), home of the popular ski resort of **Puzhalova Gora** (www.puzhalova.ru, in Russian).

441KM (460KM) The train slows and arrives at **Nizhny Novgorod** (p131), one of the most interesting cities in the region. Most trains stop for about 10 minutes, which is another chance to step onto the platform and engage in some serious hunting and gathering of supplies.

Nizhny Novgorod to Perm

442KM (461KM) If you have done the Moscow to Nizhny stretch of the route overnight, one of the first things you will see on waking is the Volga River – a fine way to start a day at any time of year. In spring, however, it's impressive because the river is coated with a crust of ice broken by bluish waters. The Volga flows roughly north–south for 3530km – that's the equivalent of the distance by rail from Moscow to the city of Tayga in Siberia – and culminates in a beautiful wetland at its delta on the Caspian Sea.

In the 13th century, the entire Volga region was conquered by the heirs of Chinggis (Genghis) Khaan, the Mongol-led Golden Horde. Challenged by the marauder armies of Timur

---

MOSCOW TO YEKATERINBURG ROUTE PLANNER

The following is a suggested itinerary for covering the main sites of this chapter:

Day 1: Leave Moscow; 2½-hour train to Vladimir; stay Suzdal

Day 2: Tour Suzdal; return to Vladimir; train to Nizhny Novgorod

Day 3: Explore Nizhny Novgorod

Day 4: Continue exploring Nizhny Novgorod or excursion to Gorodets; night train (14½ hours) from Nizhny Novgorod to Perm

Day 5: Look around Perm

Day 6: Visit Perm-36 Gulag camp or do a day trip to Kungur

Day 7: Train (six hours) to Yekaterinburg

Moscow to Yekaterinburg

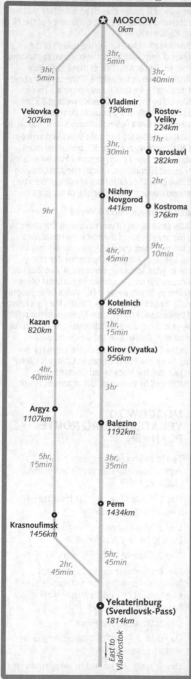

MOSCOW
0km

3hr,
5min

3hr,
5min

3hr,
40min

Vladimir
190km

Vekovka
207km

**Rostov-
Veliky**
224km

1hr

3hr,
30min

Yaroslavl
282km

2hr

**Nizhny
Novgorod**
441km

9hr

Kostroma
376km

4hr,
45min

9hr,
10min

Kotelnich
869km

Kazan
820km

1hr,
15min

Kirov (Vyatka)
956km

4hr,
40min

3hr

Argyz
1107km

Balezino
1192km

5hr,
15min

3hr,
35min

Perm
1434km

Krasnoufimsk
1456km

5hr,
45min

2hr,
45min

**Yekaterinburg
(Sverdlovsk-Pass)**
1814km

*East to
Vladivostok*

(Tamerlane) in the south and upstart Muscovite princes in the north, the Golden Horde eventually fragmented into separate khanates: Kazan, Astrakhan, Crimea and Sibir. In the 1550s Ivan the Terrible razed Kazan and Astrakhan, and claimed the Middle and Lower Volga for Muscovy (modern-day Moscow), the capital of the new Russian state. This was a critical juncture in Russian history as the collapse of Kazan allowed Slavic Russians to move into the Urals region around Perm, a stepping stone into Siberia.

The landscape after Nizhny Novgorod is a typical blend of farmland, forest clearings and forest itself that is not yet the true taiga of conifer we associate with Russia.

510-956KM (530-956KM) After passing **Semenov** (510km), which is home of the Khokhloma folk-art style, the train reaches **Kotelnich** (869km), the junction with the old Trans-Siberian route from Yaroslavl. See p127 for more on this route. Kotelnich is famous as a dinosaurs' playground – numerous Permian-period giant-lizard fossils have been discovered here. Just outside Kotelnich the train crosses the Vyatka River, a meandering 1367km waterway that accompanies the railway route to **Kirov** (956km), which is better known by its old name: Vyatka, same as the river. Most trains stop here for about 15 minutes. Not a lot of meaningful activity can be fit into the stopover at Vyatka, but one is perhaps to buy some beer and clink glasses on the occasion of reaching the northernmost point of your whole Trans-Siberian journey.

1126KM Yar is the first town you'll pass through in the Udmurt Republic, home to the Udmurts, one of Russia's four major groups of Finno-Ugric people. Around here the countryside becomes picturesque, with plenty of pretty painted log cabins.

1192KM At **Balezino** there's a change of locomotive during the roughly 20-minute halt.

1221-1314KM After crossing the **Cheptsa River**, the train enters the town of the same name. **Cheptsa** (1223km) is the junction with the line that runs between Perm and Kazan. About 40km further east, you'll cross into Perm Region and reach the foothills of the **Ural Mountains**, which stretch about 2000km from Kazakhstan to the Arctic Kara Sea. However, the Urals rarely break 500m above sea level in these parts, prompting the Russian academician Peter Pallas to drily note in 1770 on one of his journeys that the middle section of the Urals were particularly inconspicuous. Nevertheless, as the landscape unfolds you will have glimpses of verdant rolling hills and pine and birch forests, and this is one of the more attractive sections of the route before Kungur. In Perm Region (by the time you reach **Vereshchagino**; 1314km), local time is two hours ahead of Moscow time.

Perm to Yekaterinburg

1434KM The train rolls across the wide **Kama River** into the industrial city of **Perm** (p137), where most trains stop for 20 minutes. On the northern side of the train is a steam locomotive, and the station itself has a small railway museum on the 2nd floor.

1535KM The railway turns southeast after Perm and reaches **Kungur** (p142), the centre of the Stroganov patrimony. This industrial family virtually ruled the Urals from the time of Ivan the Terrible to the reign of Peter the Great, and with the implicit agreement of Ivan the Terrible it also financed Yermak's campaign across the Urals into Siberia (p349). From Kungur, the railway follows the meandering course of the Sylva River, which on a fine day is dotted with anglers casting lines into the shallows, behind them a picturesque backdrop of low mountains. This stretch, in fact, offers the entertaining contrast of scenery and anglers beyond the window, the creaking of fittings inside the train as it struggles around the curves, and – if you are in *platskart* (3rd class) – the likely interior scenario of weary travellers huddling over crosswords on their bunks, mentally ticking off the kilometres.

1777KM The landscape recedes to unremarkable upland once the train leaves the valley of the Sylva River, and the next major point is the one-dog station of **Vershina** (6km after Pervouralsk) at the **border between Europe and Asia**, marked by a white monument. You will need to have your wits about you to catch it, located on the south side of the line.

1814KM The train travels along the Chusovaya River as it approaches **Yekaterinburg**, through a valley that was long the heart of the mining industry in the Urals. The first major station in Asian Russia – but still 260km short of the official beginning of Siberia – is **Yekaterinburg** (p148), where you can expect a 15- to 20-minute stop.

Vladimir   Владимир

📱4922 / POP 340,000 / ⊘MOSCOW

Vladimir may look like another Soviet Gotham City, until you pass the medieval Golden Gate and stop by the cluster of exquisite churches and cathedrals, some of the oldest in Russia. Hiding behind them is an abrupt bluff with spectacular views of the Oka Valley. Prince Andrei Bogolyubsky chose Vladimir as his capital in 1157 after a stint in the Holy Land where he befriended European crusader kings, such as Friedrich Barbarossa. They sent him their best architects, who designed the town's landmarks, fusing Western and Kyivan traditions. Vladimir flourished for less than a century

---

KILOMETRE POSTS

Use kilometre markings as approximations, as variances are inevitable. Over the years, the route of the Trans-Siberian has changed, making many of the kilometre markings inaccurate. For example, several different lines lead out of Moscow, each with their own markers from the railhead. Two join to form one line near Fryazevo, whereafter markers show the distance from Kursk Station. Further down the track, at the junction of this line and a former mainline route via the town of Yaroslavl, the distances are measured from Moscow via the old Yaroslavl route. On this first leg, the figures in bold brackets are the actual distance you've travelled from Moscow's Yaroslavl Station via Vladimir up to Kotelnich.

---

under Andrei's successor Vsevolov III, until a series of devastating Tatar-Mongol raids led to its decline and dependence on Moscow. The last, a 1408 siege, is vividly if gruesomely reenacted in Andrei Tarkovsky's film *Andrei Rublyov*.

⊙ Sights

Assumption Cathedral   CHURCH
(Успенский собор; Sobornaya pl; admission adult/under 15 R70/30; ⊘7am-8pm Tue-Sun, tourist time 1-4.45pm) Construction on this white-stone version of Kyiv's brick Byzantine churches began in 1158, its simple but majestic form adorned with fine carving, innovative for the time. The cathedral gained the four outer domes when it was extended on all sides after a fire in the 1180s.

Inside the working church, a few restored 12th-century murals of peacocks and prophets can be deciphered about halfway up the inner wall of the outer north aisle; this was originally an outside wall. The real treasures though are the Last Judgment frescoes by Andrei Rublyov and Daniil Chyorny, painted in 1408 in the central nave and inner south aisle, under the choir gallery towards the west end.

The church also contains the original coffin of Alexander Nevsky of Novgorod, the 13th-century military leader who was also Prince of Vladimir. He was buried in the former **Nativity Monastery** (Рождественский монастырь) east of the cathedral, but his remains were moved to St Petersburg in 1724 when Peter the Great awarded him Russian hero status.

Adjoining the cathedral on the northern side are an 1810 **bell tower** and the 1862 **St George's Chapel**. It is presumed that outside the allocated tourist time, you can only visit the cathedral for prayer.

Cathedral of St Dmitry
CHURCH

(Дмитриевский собор; Bolshaya Moskovskaya ul 60; admission adult/under 15 R50/20) A quick stroll to the east of the Assumption Cathedral is the smaller Cathedral of St Dmitry, built between 1193 and 1197, where the art of Vladimir-Suzdal stone carving reached its pinnacle.

The attraction here is the cathedral's exterior walls, covered in an amazing profusion of images. The top centre of the north, south and west walls all show King David bewitching the birds and beasts with music. The Kyivan prince Vsevolod III, who had this church built as part of his palace, appears at the top left of the north wall, with a baby son on his knee and other sons kneeling on each side. Above the right-hand window of the south wall, Alexander the Great ascends into heaven, a symbol of princely might; on the west wall appear the labours of Hercules.

Chambers
MUSEUM

(Палаты; Bolshaya Moskovskaya ul 58; admission adult/under 15 R150/70; ⊙10am-5pm Tue-Sun) The grand 18th-century court building between the two cathedrals is known as Palaty – the Chambers. It contains a children's museum, art gallery and historical exhibition. The former is a welcome diversion for little ones, who may well be suffering from old-church fatigue. The art gallery features art since the 18th century, with wonderful depictions of the Golden Ring towns.

History Museum
MUSEUM

(Исторический музей; Bolshaya Moskovskaya ul 64; admission adult/under 15 R50/20; ⊙10am-5pm Wed-Mon) Across the small street from the Palaty, this museum displays many remains and reproductions of the ornamentation from Vladimir's two cathedrals. Reminiscent of Moscow's History Museum, the red-brick edifice was purpose-built in 1902.

Golden Gate
TOWN GATE

(Золотые ворота) Vladimir's Golden Gate, part defensive tower, part triumphal arch, was modelled on the very similar structure in Kyiv. Originally built by Andrei Bogoly-

ubsky to guard the western entrance to his city, it was later restored under Catherine the Great. You can climb the narrow stone staircase to check out the **Military Museum** (Военный музей; admission adult/under 15 R40/20; ⊙10am-6pm Fri-Wed) inside. It's a small exhibit, the centrepiece of which is a diorama of old Vladimir being ravaged by nomadic raiders in 1238 and 1293. Across the street to the south you can see a remnant of the **old city wall** (Старая стена города) that protected the city.

Crystal, Lacquer Miniatures and Embroidery Museum
MUSEUM

(Выставка хрусталя, лаковой миниатюры и вышивки; Bolshaya Moskovskaya ul 2; admission R60; ⊙10am-4pm Wed-Mon) Housed in the former Old Believers' Trinity Church, this museum features the crafts of nearby towns, including Gus-Khrustalny. The shop in the basement has a decent selection of crystal for sale.

🛏 Sleeping

All hotel prices include breakfast.

Voznesenskaya Sloboda
HOTEL €€€

(Вознесенская слобода; ☎325 494; www.vsl oboda.ru; ul Voznesenskaya 14b; d R4600; ▣) Perched on a bluff with tremendous views of the valley, this hotel might have the most scenic location in the whole of the Golden Ring area. Outside is a quiet neighbourhood of old wooden cottages and new villas dominated by the elegant Ascension church. The interior of the new building is tastefully designed to resemble art nouveau style c 1900. The popular restaurant Krucha is on the premises.

Hotel Vladimir
HOTEL €€

(Гостиница Владимир; ☎324 447; www.vladimir -hotel.ru; Bolshaya Moskovskaya ul 74; s/d from R2300/2800; @) This hotel near the train station used to be a state-run establishment, but it has successfully survived the transition to a privately owned, efficiently run hotel. All the rooms have been renovated with new bathrooms and furniture, but retain a hint of old-fashioned Soviet charm in the choice of wallpaper and draperies. It is a big place with a slew of services.

Monomakh Hotel
HOTEL €€

(Гостиница Мономах; ☎440 444; www.mono mahhotel.ru; ul Gogolya 20; s R2300-2800, d R3500; ⊝▣@🖥) Off the main drag, this newish hotel has 16 rooms that are simply decorated but fully equipped.

🍴 Eating & Drinking

Salmon & Coffee
EUROPEAN, ASIAN €

(Лосось и кофе; www.losos-coffee.ru; Bolshaya Moskovskaya ul 19a; meals R200-400) Salmon is yet to be found in the Oka, while coffee is not exactly what medieval princes had for breakfast. But instead of hinting at the city's past, this DJ cafe is here to give a cosmopolitan touch to the ancient town. Lots of dark wood, dim lights and magenta-coloured metal railings create a cool, intriguing atmosphere. The menu is divided in half between European and Japanese. One can only admire the chef's sense of experimentation, but some dishes seemed way too funky to our tastes.

Traktir
RUSSIAN €

(Трактир; ☑324 162; Letneperevozinskaya ul 1a; meals R300-500; ☉11am-last guest) This wooden mega-cottage, serving a simple menu of Russian food, is about the liveliest place in town. In summer, the terrace opens up for cold beer and grilled shashlyk. With live music on weekends (8pm to 11.30pm, Thursday to Saturday), it's a popular spot for people to congregate and celebrate.

Guinness Pub
SPORTS BAR

(Bolshaya Moskovskaya ul 67; beer R100) Here is a friendly, cheapish and blissfully unauthentic pseudo-Irish pub, its walls adorned with insignia of obscure teams from obscure leagues. Plasma screens show football or hockey non-stop, but a surprising number of regulars come here to play chess.

ℹ️ Information

Coffee Bean (Bolshaya Moskovskaya ul 19a, inside Torgovye Ryady shopping mall) This outlet of the best Moscow coffee chain is mostly useful for free wi-fi. Ask baristas for the key.

Post & telephone office (Почтамт и переговорный пункт; ul Podbelskogo; ☉8am-8pm Mon-Fri)

ℹ️ Getting There & Away

Vladimir is on the main Trans-Siberian line between Moscow and Nizhny Novgorod.

TRAIN The cheapest train from Moscow is the high-speed *elektrichka* that departs from Kursky vokzal around 6pm (R600, 2½ hours). Sapsan high-speed train calls twice daily on the way to Moscow (R1200, two hours) and Nizhny Novgorod (R1300, two hours). Another useful Moscow–Nizhny train is *Burevestnik* (2½ hours in both directions). About 10 slower trains daily stop on the way to/from the Urals and beyond (*platskart* R800 to R1000, *kupe* from R1700, three hours), notably Perm-bound *Kama* and Novosibirsk-bound *Sibiryak*.

BUS Buses going to Kursky vokzal in Moscow depart from outside the train station hourly (R300, 3½ hours). For other destinations use the main bus station across the square. Suzdal buses leave every 30 minutes (R70, one hour).

TAXI Drivers charge R700 for Suzdal.

ℹ️ Getting Around

The train station is located about 500m southeast of the centre. Trolleybus 5 from the train and bus stations runs up and along Bolshaya Moskovskaya ul, passing the main sights and hotels.

Bogolyubovo   Боголюбово

☑4922 / POP 3900 / ☉MOSCOW

According to legend, when Andrei Bogolyubsky was returning north from Kyiv in the late 1150s, his horses stopped where Bogolyubovo now stands, 11km east of Vladimir. Apparently, they wouldn't go another step, so Andrei was forced to establish his capital in Vladimir and not his father's old base of Suzdal.

Whatever the reasoning, between 1158 and 1165, Andrei built a stone-fortified palace at this strategic spot near the confluence of the Nerl and Klyazma Rivers. Nearby, he built the most perfect of all old Russian buildings, the Church of the Intercession on the Nerl. Bogolyubovo is accessed most easily from Vladimir.

◎ Sights

Palace & Monastery
HISTORICAL BUILDINGS

Fragments from Andrei Bogolyubsky's palace survive amid a renovated and reopened 18th-century monastery. Travelling along the Vladimir–Nizhny Novgorod route, you can't miss the monastery in the middle of Bogolyubovo.

The dominant buildings today are the monastery's 1841 **bell tower** beside the road and its 1866 **Assumption Cathedral**. Just east of the cathedral there is the arch and tower, on whose stairs – according to one chronicle – Andrei was assassinated by hostile *boyars* (nobles). The arch abuts the 18th-century **Church of the Virgin's Nativity**.

Church of the Intercession on the Nerl
CHURCH

(Церковь Покрова на Нерли; ☺10am-6pm Tue-Sun) The church's beauty lies in its simple but perfect proportions, a brilliantly chosen waterside site (floods aside) and the sparing use of delicate carving. Legend has it that Andrei had the church built in memory of his favourite son, Izyaslav, who was killed in battle against the Bulgars. As with the Cathedral of St Dmitry in Vladimir, King David sits at the top of three facades, the birds and beasts entranced by his music. The interior has more carvings, including 20 pairs of lions. If the church is closed (from October to April the hours are more sporadic), try asking at the house behind.

To reach this famous church, walk down Vokzalnaya ul, immediately east of the monastery. At the end of the street, cross the railroad tracks and follow the cobblestone path across the field. You can catch a ride in the horse-drawn carriage for R150 per person, two people minimum.

❶ Getting There & Away

To get to Bogolyubovo from Vladimir, take trolleybus 1 to any stop beyond the railway station turn, then catch *marshrutka* 53, 153 or 18 (R12; 15 minutes).

Suzdal Суздаль

☑49231 / POP 12,000 / ☺MOSCOW

The Golden Ring comes with a diamond and that's Suzdal. If you have only one place to visit near Moscow, come here – even though everyone else will do the same. In 1864, local merchants failed to coerce the government into building the Trans-Siberian Railway through their town. Instead it went through Vladimir, 35km away. As result Suzdal was bypassed not only by trains, but by the 20th century altogether. This is why the place remains largely the same as ages ago – its cute wooden cottages mingling with golden cupolas that reflect in the river, which meanders sleepily through gentle hills and flower-filled meadows.

As it happens, Suzdal served as a royal capital when Moscow was a mere cluster of sheds. It transformed into a major monastic centre in the times of Ivan the Terrible and an important commercial hub later on. But nowadays, it seems perfectly content in its retirement from both business and politics.

Sights

Kremlin
HISTORIC SITE

(Кремль; exhibits R30-70, joint ticket adult/child R400/100; ☺10am-6pm Tue-Sun) The 1.4km-long earth rampart of Suzdal's kremlin, founded in the 11th century, encloses a few streets of houses and a handful of churches, as well as the main cathedral group on Kremlyovskaya ul.

Nativity of the Virgin Cathedral

(Рождественский собор) The Nativity of the Virgin Cathedral, its blue domes spangled with gold, was founded in the 1220s. Only its richly carved lower section is original white stone though, the rest being 16th-century brick. The inside is sumptuous, with 13th- and 17th-century frescoes and 13th-century damascene (gold on copper) on the west and south doors.

Archbishop's Chambers

(Архиерейские палаты) The Archbishop's Chambers houses the **Suzdal History Exhibition** (admission R70; ☺10am-5pm Wed-Mon). The exhibition includes the original 13th-century door from the cathedral, photos of its interior and a visit to the 18th-century **Cross Hall** (Krestovaya palata), which was used for receptions. The tent-roofed 1635 **kremlin bell tower** (Соборная колокольня) on the east side of the yard contains additional exhibits.

Torgovaya ploshchad
CENTRAL SQUARE

Suzdal's Torgovaya pl (Market Sq) is dominated by the pillared **Trading Arcades** (Торговые ряды; 1806–11) along its western side. There are four churches in the immediate vicinity, including the **Resurrection Church** (Воскресенская церковь; admission R50). Make the precarious climb to the top of the bell tower and be rewarded with wonderful views of Suzdal's gold-domed skyline. The five-domed 1707 **Emperor Constantine Church** (Царево-Константиновская церковь) in the square's northeastern corner is a working church with an ornate interior. Next to it is the smaller 1787 **Virgin of All Sorrows Church** (Скорбященская церковь).

Saviour Monastery of St Euthymius
MONASTERY

(admission R20-80 each, all-inclusive ticket R300, under 15 R150; ☺10am-6pm Tue-Sun) Founded in the 14th century to protect the town's northern entrance, Suzdal's biggest monastery grew mighty in the 16th and 17th centuries after Vasily III, Ivan the Terrible and the

AROUND BEAR'S CORNER

Back in Soviet times, most Trans-Siberian trains used to go via Yaroslavl, northeast of Moscow, rather than via Vladimir and Nizhny Novgorod, as they do today. This is still a viable alternative to the usual itinerary, which allows you to reunite with the main route shortly before the Urals.

The most practical train to use on this route is the Moscow–Yaroslavl high-speed *elektrichka* (R760, 3¾ hours, twice daily), which leaves the capital around 8am and calls at Sergiev Posad (p75) and Rostov-Veliky (R430, three hours, twice daily) en route.

Rostov-Veliky Ростов-Великий

Rostov is ideal for recovering from Moscow's chaos. Coloured in the same shade of pink as the sunsets they have been watching for hundreds of years, the impregnable walls and perfectly proportioned towers of its **kremlin** (www.rostmuseum.ru; grounds R50, joint ticket to exhibitions R450; ☺10am-5pm) rise magnificently above the shimmering Lake Nero. Frowning upon Moscow for its relatively young age, Rostov (first chronicled in 862) was the original capital of Kyivan princes who moved into the land, which would become known as Muscovy and Russia. Today it is a sleepy village-like town which wakes you up with the sound of cockerels and gets eerily quiet when darkness falls, especially in winter. Rostov is about 220km northeast of Moscow. The train and bus stations are together in the drab modern part of the town, 1.5km north of the kremlin.

If you like it cheap and funky, consider staying at **Khors** (Хорс; ☎62 483, +7903 163 05 94; www.khors.org; r weekdays R500-1200, weekends R1000-2400; @) – an art gallery–hotel with Soviet furniture and shared bathroom. A more upmarket option is **Usadba Pleshanova** (Усадьба Плешанова; ☎76 440; www.hotelvrostove.ru; Pokrovskaya ul 34; r from R2000-2300; ❄), which occupies a 19th-century manor house, once the residence of a merchant and philanthropist family.

Yaroslavl Ярославль

Yaroslavl is just one hour further down the line. It was founded by its namesake Kyivan prince, who – as legend goes – came to the place then known as Bear's Corner and axed the local tribe's totem bear, which now appears on the city's coat of arms.

Embraced by two rivers, the mighty Volga and the smaller Kotorosl, Yaroslavl's centre is dotted with onion domes like no other place in Russia. It indeed boasts a record-breaking 15-dome **Church of John the Baptist at Tolchkovo** (Церковь Иоанна Крестителя в Толчково; 2-ya Zakotoroslnaya nab 69; admission R50; ☺10am-5pm Sat-Thu). The city's best attraction is the riverside promenade passing most churches and museums of note, such as the unique **Music & Time museum** (Музыка и время; ☎328 637; Volzhskaya nab 33a; admission R150; ☺10am-7pm), which contains ex-conjuror John Mostoslavsky's impressive collection of clocks, musical instruments, bells and old vinyl records. Guides, including the owner himself, turn each tour into a bit of a concert.

The most atmospheric place to stay in Yaroslavl is the floating **Vozlshkaya Zhemchuzhina** (Волжская жемчужина; ☎731 273; www.riverhotel-vp.ru, in Russian; Volzhskaya nab; s R2700-3300, d R4300-5200; ❄✿☎), located in a converted 'river station' – dozens of floating hubs like this one lined the Volga when boat travel was still in vogue. Cheap accommodation is scarce. To save money, you may rent an apartment from the **Uyut agency** (☎+7903 690 1879, +7920 659 3233; www.yar-nasutki.ru; apt R1300-2000; ☎).

No Yaroslavl visit will be complete without a bash at **Dudki Bar** (☎330 933; ul Sobinova 33; meals R200-400) – a two-storey affair which is good both for eating during the day and partying with local hipsters all night.

The main station is Yaroslavl Glavny, on ul Svobody, 3km west of the centre. There are several eastbound trains daily that will get you back on the main Trans-Siberian line at Perm (R1500 to R3500, 20 hours, four daily).

The Golden Ring chapter of Lonely Planet's *Russia* guidebook covers this region in detail and can be purchased through www.lonelyplanet.com.

Suzdal

N

0 ____ 500 m
0 ____ 0.2 miles

To GTK Suzdal
(100m)

To Goryachie
Klyuchi (1km)

ul Spasskaya

ul Shakhovskogo

ul Pozharskogo

12
5
3
4
8
7
1

**Saviour
Monastery
of St Euthymius**

10

9

ul Lenina

21

Alexandrovsky
Convent

Pokrovskaya ul

25

ul Stromynka

ul Gasteva

ul Slobodskaya

ul Engelsa

per Engelsa

22

Monastery
of the Deposition
of the Holy Robe

Krasnaya pl

ul Lounskaya

24

ul Krupskoy

Naberezhnaya ul
Kamenka River

19

18
6

17 16

15

Vasilievskaya ul

To Bus Station
(2km)

ul Kremlyovskaya

ul Lebedeva

ul Lenina

14

2   11

Kremlin

ul Tolstogo

20

Pushkarskaya ul

13

Kamenka River

23

Suzdal

Inside, the **Annunciation Gate-Church** (Благовещенская надвратная церковь) houses an interesting exhibit on Dmitry Pozharsky (1578–1642), leader of the Russian army that drove the Polish invaders from Moscow in 1612.

A tall 16th- to 17th-century **cathedral bell tower** (Звонница) stands before the seven-domed **Cathedral of the Transfiguration of the Saviour** (Спасо-Преображенский собор). Every hour on the hour from 11am to 5pm, a short concert of chimes is given on the bell tower's bells. The cathedral was built in the 1590s in 12th- to 13th-century Vladimir-Suzdal style. Inside, restoration has uncovered some bright 1689 frescoes by the school of Gury Nikitin from Kostroma. The tomb of Prince Dmitry Pozharsky is by the cathedral's east wall.

The 1525 **Assumption Refectory Church** (Успенская церковь), facing the bell tower, adjoins the old **Father Superior's chambers** (Палаты отца-игумена), which houses a display of Russian icons and the excellent naïve art exhibition showcasing works by Soviet-era amateur painters from local villages.

The old **monastery prison** (Монастырская тюрьма), set up in 1764 for religious dissidents, is at the north end of the complex. It now houses a fascinating exhibit on the monastery's prison history, including displays of some of the better-known prisoners who stayed here. The combined **hospital** and **St Nicholas Church** (Больничные кельи и Никольская церковь; 1669) features a rich museum of church gold treasures.

FREE **Intercession Convent** CONVENT
(Покровский монастырь; Pokrovskaya ul; admission free; ☉9.30am-4.30pm Thu-Mon) This convent was founded in 1364, originally as a place of exile for the unwanted wives of tsars. Among them was Solomonia Saburova, the first wife of Vasily III, who was sent here in the 1520s because of her supposed infertility. The story goes that she finally became pregnant, but she was too late to avoid being divorced. A baby boy was born in Suzdal. Fearing he would be seen as a dangerous rival to any sons produced by Vasily's new wife, Solomonia secretly had him adopted, pretended he had died and staged a mock burial. This was probably just as well for the boy since Vasily's second wife did indeed produce a son – Ivan the Terrible.

noble Pozharsky family funded impressive new stone buildings and big land and property acquisitions. It was girded with its great brick walls and towers in the 17th century.

The legend received dramatic corroboration in 1934 when researchers opened a small 16th-century tomb beside Solomonia's in the crypt underneath the **Intercession Cathedral** (Покровский собор). They found a silk-and-pearl shirt stuffed with rags, but no bones. The crypt is closed to visitors.

Museum of Wooden Architecture & Peasant Life
MUSEUM

(Музей деревянного зодчества и крестьянского быта; Pushkarskaya ul; adult/under 15 R150/60; ☺9.30am-7pm Wed-Mon May-Oct) This open-air museum, illustrating old peasant life in this region, is a short walk across the river, south of the kremlin. Besides log houses, windmills, a barn and lots of tools and handicrafts, its highlights are the 1756 **Transfiguration Church** (Preobrazhenskaya tserkov) and the simpler 1776 **Resurrection Church** (Voskresenskaya tserkov).

🏃 Activities
The rolling hills and attractive countryside around Suzdal are ideal for outdoor adventures, including horse riding and mountain biking.

GTK Suzdal
CYCLING, HORSE RIDING

(GTK; ☎23 380, 20 908; ul Korovniki 45; ☺10am-6pm) The Hotel Tourist Complex rents bikes, snowmobiles and skis, as well as offering horse-riding tours.

Goryachie Klyuchi
BANYA

(Горячие ключи; ☎24 000; www.parilka.com; ☺11am-1am) Rural Suzdal is a great place to cleanse body and soul in a Russian *banya* (bathhouse). Beautiful, lakeside *bani* are available for rent at Goryachie Klyuchi starting at R1000 per hour for up to four people. Rooms start at single/double R2100/2500.

Dva Kolesa
CYCLING

(Two Wheels; ☎8-910-186 0252; www.dvakolesa.ru; ul Tolstogo 5) This little guesthouse rents bicycles at R500 per day to those who didn't come on their own, unlike most of their guests. Owners lead bicycle excursions through villages surrounding Suzdal. Rooms go for R2000 during the week and R3000 on weekends.

🛏 Sleeping
Suzdal is experiencing a tourist boom, which means there is plenty of choice in the midrange and high-end bracket – from quaint two- to three-room guesthouses to vast holiday resorts. You may save up to R1000 per night if you avoid coming to Suzdal during weekends or holidays. Breakfast is included in all prices, unless otherwise stated.

Pushkarskaya Sloboda
RESORT €€

(Пушкарская слобода; ☎23 303; www.sloboda-gk.ru; ul Lenina 45; d in inn from R2900, d in village from R3700; ☺✳☒) This holiday village has everything you might want from your Disney vacation – accommodation in the log-cabin 'Russian inn' or the reproduction 19th-century 'Gunner's Village'; three restaurants, ranging from the rustic country tavern to a formal dining room; and every service you might dream up. It's an attractive, family-friendly, good-value option, though it might be too well-manicured for some tastes.

🏆 TOP CHOICE Petrov Dom
GUESTHOUSE €€

(☎23 326, 8-919-025 8884; www.petrovdom.ru; per Engelsa 18; r weekdays R1500, weekends R2000, holidays R2500; ☺🖭) Vlad and Lena offer three nicely furnished and strictly non-smoking rooms in their wooden dacha-style house with a lovely garden on a quiet street (not to be confused with ul Engelsa), which makes it a great option for travellers with children. A sumptuous breakfast is included. Self-caterers are welcome to use the kitchen and garden grill.

Godzillas Suzdal
HOSTEL €

(☎in Moscow 495-699 4223; www.godzillashostel.com/suzdal; Naberezhnaya ul 12; per person R650-750; 🖭) An affiliate of the namesake hostel in Moscow, this big log cabin facility overlooking the river opened just a few years ago, but has already undergone a thorough renovation. Each dorm room has its own bathroom and balcony. Guests can also enjoy the blooming garden and Russian *banya*, as well as the chill-out lounge and the bar in the basement. Breakfast not included.

Stromynka 2
HOTEL €€

(☎25 155; www.stromynka2.ru; ul Stromynka 2; s/d from R2300/2500; ☺) A cross between a Russian gingerbread cottage and a Swiss chalet, this medium-sized hotel prides itself in having used only natural materials in the construction. Large and airy rooms are well-equipped, smell like untreated wood and offer nice views of the Kamenka River Valley. Bikes available for hire; breakfast not included.

Nikolayevsky Posad
RESORT €€

(☎23 585; www.nposad.ru; ul Lenina 138; r from R3200; ☺✳☒@) Another large manicured resort near St Euthymius Monastery.

Accommodation is in two-storey buildings styled as merchants' mansion houses. There is a nice restaurant and a 'hangover' cafe in the premises.

Kremlyovsky Hotel
HOTEL €€

(Кремлёвский Отель; ☎25 055; www.kremlinhotel.ru; ul Tolstogo 5; s/d weekdays from R2700/2900, weekends R3700/3900; ❄✷@) This white stone hotel mirrors the tall towers of the kremlin on the opposite bank of the river. The rooms are contemporary and comfortable and they offer lovely views of the winding waterway and the rustic wooden architecture in the vicinity.

Rizopolozhenskaya Hotel
HOTEL €

(☎24 314; ul Lenina; s/d/q R1200/2100/3000) Housed in the decrepit Monastery of the Deposition and destined to be grabbed by the church sooner or later, this cheapie has no intention to upgrade. Instead, it keeps its Soviet-furnished rooms clean, if poorly lit, and prices low enough to attract a steady flow of guests. Breakfast not included.

GTK Suzdal
HOTEL €€

(☎21 530; www.suzdaltour.ru; r hotel/motel from R2500/3300; ✷@✷) A former Intourist flagship, this place is low on charm but high on facilities. Accommodation is in a large hotel or in terraced houses with garage in the first floor and rooms in the second. The complex includes a fitness centre, a bowling alley, several restaurants and a slightly more expensive hotel with upgraded rooms.

✗ Eating

In addition to the places listed below, all of the hotels have restaurants.

Salmon & Coffee
EUROPEAN €€

(Лосось и кофе; Trading Arcades, ul Lenina 63a; mains R200-450) Like its sister in Vladimir, Suzdal's S&C is about the best place for an unhurried lunch or a cup of coffee. It is, however, much quainter, with lots of aged whitewashed wood to evoke the 'Cherry Orchard' dacha ambience. Despite the name, salmon is not really prominent on the menu, which includes inventive fusion European dishes and sushi.

Graf Suvorov & Mead-Tasting Hall
RUSSIAN €€

(Граф Суворов и зал дегустаций; Trading Arcades, ul Lenina 63a; tasting menu R130-350, mains R150-300) With vaulted ceilings and kitschy wall paintings depicting Russian military

hero Count Suvorov's exploits in the Alps, this place serves standard Russian food and a few dozen varieties of locally produced *medovukha* (mead), a mildly alcoholic honey ale that was drunk by princes of old. Go for tasting sets, which include 10 samples each. Apart from the regular one, there are separate sets of berry- and herb-flavoured *medovukha*.

Kremlin Trapeznaya
RUSSIAN €

(Кремлевская трапезная; meals R300-500; ☺11am-11pm) The attraction here is the choice location in an old dining hall inside the Archbishop's Chambers. The menu features filling Russian favourites.

ℹ Information

Post & telephone office (Почтамт и переговорный пункт; Krasnaya pl; ☺8am-8pm) Open 24 hours for phone calls.
Sberbank (Сбербанк; ul Lenina 73a; ☺8am-4.30pm Mon-Fri) Exchange office & ATM.

ℹ Getting There & Away

Suzdal is not on the Trans-Siberian line but can be accessed from Vladimir (see p125). The bus station is 2km east of the centre on Vasilievskaya ul. Some long-distance buses pass the central square on the way. Buses run every half-hour to/from Vladimir (R50, one hour). Otherwise, most of the buses originate elsewhere. A daily bus goes directly to/from Moscow's Shchyolkovsky bus station (R365, 4½ hours).

Nizhny Novgorod
Нижний Новгород

☎831 / POP 1.25 MILLION / ☺MOSCOW

A glorious setting is not something most Russian cities can boast, but Nizhny (as it is usually called) is a lucky exception. The mighty cliff-top kremlin overlooking the confluence of two wide rivers – the Volga and the Oka – is the place where merchant Kuzma Minin and Count Dmitry Pozharsky (men commemorated in a monument in front of St Basil's Cathedral, Moscow) rallied a popular army to repel the Polish intervention in 1612.

Nizhny has been a major trading centre since its foundation in 1221. In the 19th century when the lower bank of the Oka housed the country's main fair – *yarmarka* – it was said that 'St Petersburg is Russia's head; Moscow its heart; and Nizhny Novgorod its wallet'. During Soviet times the city was named Gorky, after the writer Maxim Gorky,

Nizhny Novgorod

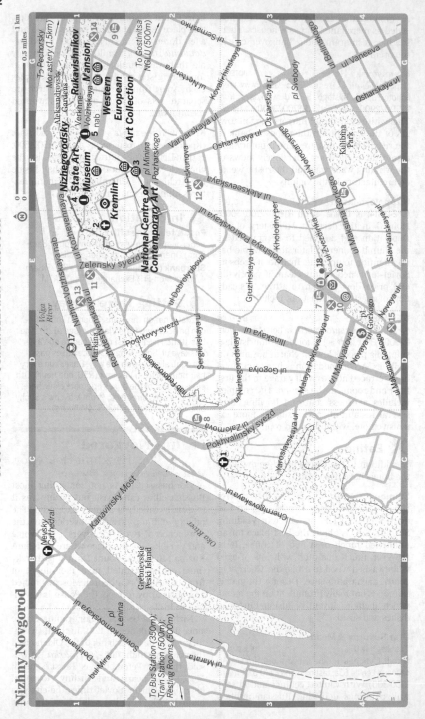

Volga River

Oka River

To Pechorsky
Monastery (1.5km)

Aleksandrovsky
Gardens

**Rukavishnikov
Mansion**

**Western
European
Art Collection**

Verkhne
Volzhskaya
nab

**Nizhegorodsky
State Art
Museum**

Kremlin

**National Centre of
Contemporary Art**

pl Minina
i Pozharskogo

Varvarskaya ul

Osharskaya ul

Osharskaya ul

Osharskaya ul

pl Svobody

ul Belinskogo

ul Vaneeva

Osharskaya ul

Kulibina
Park

ul Volodarskogo

ul Piskunova

ul Alekseevskaya

Bolshaya Pokrovskaya ul

Kholodny per

ul Zvezdinka

ul Maksima Gorkogo

Slavyanskaya ul

Novaya ul

pl
Gorkogo

Novaya ul

ul Maslyakova

Malaya Pokrovskaya ul

ul Nizhegorodskaya

ul Gogolya

Ilinskaya ul

Gruzinskaya ul

ul Dobrolyubova

Sergievskaya ul

Pochtovy syezd

pl
Markina

Nizhne-Volzhskaya nab

ul Kozhevennaya

Zelensky syezd

Rozhdestvenskaya ul

nab Fedorovskogo

Pokhvalinsky syezd

ul Zalomova

Yaroslavskaya ul

Chernigovskaya ul

Kanavinsky Most

Grebnevskie
Peski Island

**Nevsky
Cathedral**

pl
Lenina

Sovnarkomovskaya ul

bul Mira

Dolzhanskaya ul

ul Marata

To Bus Station (350m);
Train Station (500m);
Resting Rooms (500m)

To Gostinitsa
NGLU (500m)

ul Nesterova

ul Kovalikhinskaya

ul Minina

To Gostinitsa
NGLU (500m)

1 km
0.5 miles
0

Nizhny Novgorod

born here in 1868. Closed to foreigners by the Soviets, Gorky was chosen as a place of exile for the dissident physicist Andrei Sakharov.

Nizhny is often called Russia's 'third capital', but it is markedly quieter than the other two, with a laid-back ambience characteristic of the Volga cities downstream. Walking along riverside promenades, drinking beer in an outdoor cafe by the kremlin or taking a boat ride to the painters' town of Gorodets are all excellent cures for nerves damaged by Moscow's crowds and traffic.

◉ **Sights**

The shop on the 2nd floor of the Nizhegorodsky State Art Museum sells an excellent *Walk Around Nizhny Novgorod* book (R170) in English, German and Russian with 10 illustrated routes.

Kremlin HISTORICAL BUILDING
(Кремль; www.ngiamz.ru) Built upon remnants of an earlier settlement, Nizhny Novgorod's magnificent kremlin dates back to 1500–15 when the Italian architect Pyotr Fryazin began work on its 13 towers and 12m-high walls. Even before the kremlin was finished the Khan of Kazan made his first attempt to take it and failed. Inside, most of the buildings are government offices. The small 17th-century **Cathedral of the Archangel Michael** (Собор Михаила Архангела) is a functioning church. Behind it, an eternal flame burns near a striking **monument** (Памятник героям Отечественной войны) to the heroes of WWII. The main entrance to the kremlin is at the **Dmitry Tower** (Дмитриевская башня; admission R70; ☉10am–5pm, closed Mon), which has changing exhibitions on local history.

Annunciation Monastery MONASTERY
(Благовещенский монастырь; ul Garshina) The proliferation of onion domes and golden spires is a ubiquitous reminder of the city's rich history. The 13th-century Annunciation Monastery, above Chernigovskaya ul, is located among the city's oldest buildings.

Pechorsky Monastery MONASTERY
(Печерский Вознесенский монастырь; Privolzhkaya sloboda 108) The 17th-century Pechorsky Monastery, overlooking the Volga, houses a small **Museum of the Nizhny Novgorod Diocese** (Музей Нижнего Новгородского епархий; admission R20; ☉10am–5pm), which includes a moving exhibition on Bolshevik repressions against the church. Beneath the monastery is the **Rowing Canal**, with sandy banks that have become the city's main beach, sprinkled with beach restaurants. Take any *marshrutka* or bus from pl Minina i Pozharskogo to pl Sennaya.

Museum of Volga People's Architecture & Culture MUSEUM
(Музей архитектуры и быта народов Нижегородского Поволжья; www.ngiamz.ru; Gorbatovskaya ul 41; admission R40; ☉10am–5pm Sat-Thu, closed mid-Oct–mid-May) The open-air Museum of Volga People's Architecture & Culture has a pleasant woodland

NIZHNY NOVGOROD'S STATE MUSEUMS

Nizhny Novgorod has an excellent ensemble of museums inside and around the kremlin. Inside the kremlin, the **Nizhegorodsky State Art Museum** (Нижегородский государственный художественный музей; www.museum.nnov.ru/art; admission R100; ☺11am-6pm Wed-Mon) focuses on Russian artists, beginning (on the left after you enter) with 16th-century icons. The entire collection is chronological, so you can see by Room 6 how rudimentary landscape perspectives creep into 17th-century icons. After the icons comes the large collection of mostly oil-on-canvas paintings by Russian masters, including Vasily Surikov and lots by Nikolai Rerikh (aka Nicholas Roerich; Room 20), culminating in Soviet art. The English descriptions are excellent.

Situated in the former arsenal located on the right after you enter the main gate, the new **National Centre of Contemporary Art** (Государственный центр современного искусства; www.ncca.ru; admission R100; ☺noon-8pm Tue-Sun) has changing exhibitions of international and Russian contemporary artists.

Outside the kremlin and just a short walk along the attractive Verkhne-Volzhskaya nab, lined with restored 19th-century buildings, you find the **Western European Art Collection** (Собрание Западноевропейское искусство; Verkhne-Volzhskaya nab 3; admission R120; ☺11am-6pm Wed & Fri-Mon, noon-8pm Thu), with its collection of mostly anonymous or lesser-known European painters who, despite their modest credentials, produced some remarkable works.

A few houses along, inside a 19th-century mansion once belonging to the Rukavishnikov merchant family, is the **Rukavishnikov Mansion** (Усадьба Рукавишникова; Verkhne-Volzhskaya nab 7; tours R300; ☺10am-5pm Tue-Fri, noon-7pm Sat & Sun). This is visited on 40-minute tours in Russian and English leaving every 1½ hours from 10am to 4pm weekdays and half-hourly weekends from noon to 6pm. Furniture and the illustrious interior of the unusual mansion are the threads running through all excursions in this museum, and these are complemented by changing exhibitions – often with a focus on household furnishing and objects.

setting and a collection of traditional wooden buildings from Russian and Mordva (a Finno-Ugric people) villages. The museum is located in the remote Shchelokovsky Khutor Park, which is the final stop of bus 28 (30 minutes, every hour), which passes ul Belinskogo in the centre. *Marshrutka 62* also stops close.

Sakharov Museum   MUSEUM
(Музей Сахарова; ☎466 8623; pr Gagarina 214; admission R50; ☺9am-5pm Sat-Thu) A reminder of more repressive times, the Sakharov Museum is located in the flat where the dissident scientist spent six years in exile. The Nobel laureate was held incommunicado until 1986, when a KGB officer came to install a telephone. When it rang, it was Mikhail Gorbachev at the other end, informing Sakharov of his release. The phone is a highlight of the exhibition. To get there take bus 1 from pl Minina i Pozharskogo or *marshrutka* 3 or 19 from pl Gorkogo to the stop Muzey Akademika Sakharova.

☞ Tours

Team Gorky   TOURS
(☎278 9404; www.teamgorky.ru; ul 40 let Oktyabrya 1a) Canoe and bicycle tours in the Nizhny Novgorod region and beyond. Three-day adventure canoe trips start at R6300.

🛏 Sleeping

TOP
CHOICE **Jouk-Jacques**   BOUTIQUE HOTEL €€€
(Жук-Жак; ☎433 0462; www.jak-hotel.ru; Bolshaya Pokrovskaya ul 57; s R3750-6825, d R6825, ste R9375; ✳️🅿️) This cosy boutique hotel is one of the best in town. The cheapest rooms are a bit cramped, but they're neat and breakfasts are superb by Russian standards.

Nizhegorodsky Hotel Complex   HOTEL €€
(Нижегородский Гостиничный Комплекс; ☎430 5387; www.hotel-nn.ru; ul Zalomova 2; s R2660-4250, d R3200-4250; ➖🅿️) This ugly concrete eyesore has good refurbished rooms, and the embankment underneath has been converted into a lovely terraced park. The more expensive rooms have fabu-

lous river views. Steps just to the left as you exit lead directly to the Rozhdestvenskaya bus stop.

Ibis Hotel
HOTEL €€

(Ибис Отель; ☏233 1120; www.ibishotel.com; ul Maksima Gorkogo 115; r without breakfast from R3100) Nizhny's Ibis is a relative newcomer and offers a high standard of rooms and comforts, with the advantage that it is large enough to cope with busy periods.

October Hotel
HOTEL €€€

(Гостиница Октябрьская; ☏432 8080; www.oktyabrskaya.ru; Verkhne-Volzhskaya nab 9a; s R4000-5000, d R6100, ste R10,000-14,000; ❀@☞) The rooms here have been renovated but overall it retains a hint of post-Soviet kitsch.

Gostinitsa NGLU
HOTEL €

(Гостиница НГЛУ; ☏436 5945; Bolshaya Pecherskaya ul 36; dm R480, s/d R880/1440 without bathroom, tw apt with bathroom R2520; ❀) This is part of the Linguistic University dormitory; it doesn't register visas.

Resting rooms
HOSTEL €

(Железнодорожные комнаты отдыха, komnaty otdykha; ☏244 2110; dm R750, s/d without breakfast R1550/3300) Located in a separate building on your right as you *exit* the train station.

Eating & Drinking

The cheap and cheerful summer cafes by the city's main hang-out near the **Pilot Valery Chkalov monument** (Памятник летчику Чкалову) are a great place to mingle with locals. Rozhdestvennskaya ul east of the river station also has clusters of places to eat and drink.

TOP CHOICE **Bezukhov**
RUSSIAN, INTERNATIONAL €

(Безухов; www.bezuhov.ru; Rozhdestvenskaya ul 6; mains R375; ☻24hr; ☞☊) This literary cafe with antique furnishings, stucco ceiling and the feel of a living room is part of a project in Nizhny Novgorod called *Eda i Kultura* (Food and Culture), which brings food and culture together into a delicious whole. The menu is overflowing with salads, pastas and

---

VOLGA-URALS SIDE TRIP

The Volga, one of Europe's great rivers, winds for some 3530km through Russia's heartland and has been a part of the continent's longest 'highway' for time immemorial. Travelling along or alongside the Volga you encounter spectacular hilltop kremlins in Nizhny Novgorod, Kazan and Astrakhan, bombastic architecture in Volgograd, numerous lively provincial capitals, as well as picturesque stretches such as the Samara Bend.

Trains cross the Volga at Yaroslavl (the northern route in European Russia), Nizhny Novgorod (the major route) and Kazan (a southern route through Tatarstan). Each of these is worth a stopover, but for longer Volga trips Nizhny Novgorod and Kazan are the best starting points. From Nizhny Novgorod it's possible to take day trips on hydrofoils to the artists' town of Gorodets (see p136). Chapters of Lonely Planet's *Russia* guidebook covering the Volga and Urals regions in detail can be purchased online from www.lonelyplanet.com.

Prices and times for the following Volga-Urals side trip are from the previous stop:

» **South to the Volga delta** Leave the Trans-Sib at **Nizhny Novgorod** (p131) and head south by train to **Kazan** (p140; *platskart* R822, nine hours, daily), continuing on to **Ulyanovsk** (*platskart* R550, six hours, frequent). From Ulyanovsk the easiest way to **Samara** (R370, five hours) is by bus. From there, get back on the rails again to continue to **Volgograd** (*kupe* R1760, 19 hours), **Astrakhan** (*platskart* R685, 10½ hours) and the **Volga Delta**.

» **Northeast return leg** The nicest way to rejoin the Trans-Sib is to return from the lower Volga by rail via **Ufa** (Bashkortostan) and **Chelyabinsk**, then head north to rejoin the Trans-Siberian route at **Yekaterinburg** (p148; from Volgograd: *kupe* R5010, 39 hours).

» **How long and how much?** Plan a minimum of two weeks and about €100 per day in all-up costs, including transport, for this side trip with a couple of stopovers plus time in the delta and on one of the Urals lakes.

fish, poultry and red-meat dishes, and augmented by good breakfasts and sushi rolls.

Restoratsia Pyatkin
RUSSIAN €€

(Ресторация Пяткин; Rozhdestvenskaya ul 23; mains R350; ⊙noon-midnight) This place makes you feel like a merchant back in his mansion after a great trading day at the fair. The menu is full of Volga fish specialities; it also brews the unusual apple *kvas* and has a children's menu.

Moloko
RUSSIAN, BAR €€

(Молоко; ul Alekseevskaya 15; mains R200-300, coffee R100; ⊙noon-2am; ☎🍴) Also part of the Food and Culture project – more upmarket in style but with very similar food to Bezukov – 'Milk' exudes a sleek lounge feel beyond its sofas and aged wooden panelling. Pl Minina i Pozharskogo is your best transport stop.

Angliiskoe Posolstvo
PUB €€

(Английское Посольство; ul Zvezdinka 12; mains R500; ⊙8am-midnight Mon-Fri, 8am-2am Sat & Sun; 🍴) Set on two levels, the 'English Consulate' is a convivial place for that familiar pub atmosphere (or Russian interpretation of it). A selection of English beers is available and fish and chips costs R260.

Tiffani
INTERNATIONAL, CAFE €€€

(Тиффани; ☎436 3542; Verkhne-Volzhskaya nab 8; mains R370-950; ⊙breakfast-late; ☎🍴) This upmarket all-rounder is a restaurant during the day and evening, a cafe at any time and has well-known DJs some nights. The views across the Volga to the forest are spectacular and kids love it because they can loll on plush sofas beneath the black marble ceiling. Dress up in the evening.

Vesyolaya Kuma
UKRAINIAN €€

(ul Kostina 3; mains R400; ⊙noon-midnight; 🍴🍴) Set among a row of lesser restaurants, the 'Happy Godmother' merrily serves hearty borsch and other Ukrainian fare.

Biblioteka
ITALIAN €

(Библиотека; Bolshaya Pokrovskaya ul 46; dishes R180-300; ⊙11am-10pm; 🍴🍴🍴) Upstairs from the Dirizhabl bookshop with generic but tasty Italian dishes in an informal, quirky atmosphere.

🛍 Shopping

Dirizhabl
BOOKSTORE

(Дирижабль; Bolshaya Pokrovskaya ul 46; ⊙10am-9pm Mon-Sat, 11am-8pm Sun) A good selection of maps and local guidebooks, and some books in foreign languages.

ℹ Information

Central post office (Центральный почтамт; pl Gorkogo; internet per hr R40; ⊙8am-8pm)

Ellips Bank (Эллипс Банк; pl Maksima Gorkogo 4/2) ATM, accepts major cards.

Volga Telecom (Волга Телеком; pl Gorkogo; per 30 min R40; ⊙24hr) Internet terminals.

ℹ Getting There & Away

Train

Nizhny Novgorod train station still goes by its old name of Gorky-Moskovsky vokzal (station), so 'Gorky' appears on some timetables. It is on the western bank of the Oka River, at pl Revolyutsii. The **service centre** at the train station is helpful for buying rail tickets, and also has internet access. Go to the blue booth for converting your e-ticket to hard copy. There are *komnaty otdykha* (rest rooms), but you'll need an onward ticket to stay there.

The daily Volga *firmeny* train (a premium, long-distance train; 59) connects St Petersburg's Moskovsky vokzal with Nizhny Novgorod (R5042, 15¼ hours), and numerous cheaper services go to/from St Petersburg and Moscow. Train 24 is a good overnight service from Moscow's Kazansky vokzal (R2183, 6½ hours).

WESTBOUND The high-speed Sapsan (seat R1490, four hours, two daily) runs to Moscow's Kursky vokzal. One service continues to St Petersburg (seat R4200, 8½ hours, daily). Over a dozen other trains (*platskart* R1123, seven hours) also serve Moscow, via Vladimir (*platskart* R872, three hours).

EASTBOUND For Perm the flagship No 18 *Kama* (*platskart* R1716, *kupe* R3184, 14½ hours, daily) or for Kazan the No 41 (*platskart* R822, nine hours, daily) are good services. Other trains go to Yekaterinburg (R3800, 21 hours, six daily) and beyond.

Air

Nizhny Novgorod International Airport is 15km southwest of the city centre. S7 flies six times a week from Moscow (from R4000, one hour) and **Lufthansa** (☎275 9085) flies directly to/from Frankfurt five times a week (return €600, 3½ hours). Airline tickets are available at agencies around the city, including the **Turbyuro** (☎439 3260; ul Zvezdinka 10b; ⊙8am-8pm, closed Sun).

Boat

The **river station** is on Nizhne-Volzhskaya nab, below the kremlin. A **Volga-Flot Tour** (☎461 8030; www.vftour.ru, in Russian; ⊙9am-7pm Mon-Fri, 10am-4pm Sat, 10am-3pm Sun) office inside the station building and the cash office on the embankment sell mostly weekend day trips departing 9am to the ancient **Makaryev** monastery (R1440) at the village of Makaryevo, 60km to the east. Book ahead. Food and an excursion are included. Several hydrofoils daily go to Gorodets (R150, one hour), leaving from their own pier.

Bus

Buses to Vladimir (R400, 4½ hours, eight daily), Kostroma (R750, eight hours, daily) and Gorodets (R120, 1½ hours, almost every half-hour) depart from the small Kanavinskaya bus station. Private operators run minibuses to Moscow, which depart across the road from the train station (R600, six hours, at least six times daily); others start from the bus station.

❶ Getting Around

The train station (Московский вокзал) is located across the river from the kremlin and is connected to the centre by buses and minibuses. The two transport hubs in the centre are pl Minina i Pozharskogo (пл Минина и Пожарского) near the kremlin and pl Gorkogo (пл Горкого) south of this. If you need to, you can change at the stop on the city side of the bridge, Kanavinsky Most. At pl Minina i Pozharskogo, transport heading back to the train station picks up from the kremlin side of the road.

The city's metro might be extended across the river in the lifetime of this book, providing a useful link between pl Gorkogo and the train station (Московский вокзал).

Perm   Пермь

📲342 / POP 1 MILLION / ⊕MOSCOW +2HR

The word 'Perm' once meant a mysterious Finno-Ugric land encompassing most of the northwestern Ural Mountains that was slowly colonised by Russians since the early medieval ages. But the city is relatively new, founded by the lieutenants of Peter I in 1723.

It is believed that Chekhov used Perm as the inspiration for the town his Three Sisters were desperate to leave, and Boris Pasternak sent his Doctor Zhivago to a city clearly resembling Perm. It would be hard for these characters to recognise their city today. The neat provincial architecture has been critically diluted by Soviet concrete blocks and post-Soviet glassy structures. Huge military plants were moved here during WWII when the town was called Molotov after the Soviet minister of Molotov cocktail fame.

Today the city is in the throes of reinventing itself as a cultural centre outside Moscow and St Petersburg, having long had a famous ballet school, augmented by some interesting museums. It is also the base from which

to visit one of the best wooden architecture museums in Russia, located in Khokhlovka; the famous ice cave in Kungur; and a grim reminder of Soviet-era political persecution – the Perm-36 labour camp.

◉ Sights

A green line runs through the central district connecting the major sights, complemented by signs in Russian and English explaining the history. Perm Tourist has a free, multilingual *Green Line* booklet for self-guided city walks. This is complemented by a red line, focusing on local love stories.

TOP CHOICE **Museum of Contemporary Art 'PERMM'**   ART GALLERY
(Музей современного искусства PERMM; www.permm.ru; ul Ordzhonikidze 2; admission R100; ⊙noon-9pm) The brainchild of Marat Gelman, a prime mover and shaker on Russia's gallery scene, this museum of modern and contemporary art is housed inside the former river station hall on the banks of the Kama River. It forms the centrepiece of Gelman's vision to transform Perm into a cultural hub. The exhibitions are often controversial locally, which probably means the museum fulfils its role as a contemporary art space very successfully. Check out the website for what's on. Trolleybus 1 and bus 3 take you there.

Perm State Art Gallery   ART GALLERY
(Художественная галерея; www.sculpture.perm online.ru; Komsomolsky pr 4; Russian/foreigner R120/210; ⊙11am-6pm Tue-Sun) Housed in the grand Cathedral of Christ Transfiguration on the banks of the Kama, the Perm State Art Gallery is renowned for its collection of Permian wooden sculpture. These brightly coloured figures are a product of an uneasy compromise between Christian missionaries and the native Finno-Ugric population. The latter, having been converted, closely identified the Christian saints these sculptures depict with their ancient gods and treated them as such by smearing their lips with the blood of sacrificed animals. There are plans to house the museum in a new building, but the location is yet to be decided; Perm Tourist can tell you more. Take trolleybus 1 to the stop Galereya or trams 3, 4, 7, 12 or 13 to the stop Tsum.

Perm Regional Museum   MUSEUM
(Пермский краевой музей; ul Ordzhonikidze 11; admission R100; ⊙10am-6pm Tue-Sun) Located

Perm

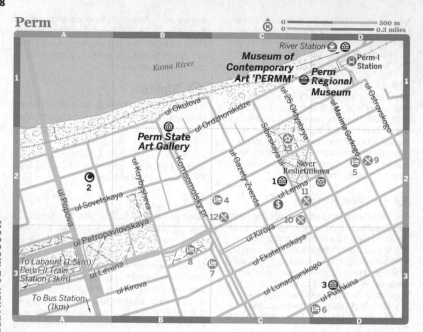

inside the imposing Meshkov House, the regional museum has a moderately interesting collection of household objects, weapons and other cultural relics of the region. It only gets really interesting when you see the small collection of intricate metal castings of the 'Perm animal style' used in the shamanistic practices of ancient Finno-Ugric Permians. More of these metal castings may be on display in the museum branch known as the **Archaeological Collection** (Sibirskaya ul 15; admission R100; ⊙10am-6pm Mon-Fri).

Sergei Diaghilev Museum MUSEUM
(Дом Дягилева; Sibirskaya ul 33; admission by donation; ⊙9am-6pm Mon-Fri, closed 31 May-1 Sep) The Sergei Diaghilev Museum is a small, lovingly curated school museum dedicated to the impresario (1872–1929) who turned Russian ballet into a world-famous brand. Children speaking foreign languages, including English, serve as guides.

Mosque MOSQUE
(Мечеть; ul Osinskaya 5) A lovely mosque that has served local Tatar Muslims since 1902.

☞ Tours

Krasnov TOURS
(Краснов; ☑238 3520; www.uraltourism.ru; ul Borchaninova 4; ⊙10am-6.30pm Mon-Fri, 11am-

5pm Sat) Offers active and adventure tourism such as 19 days of rafting (R22,800) or cross-country skiing in the Urals, beginner Russian courses, river cruises and many more activities. The Russian version of the website has a wider and sometimes less expensive choice.

Perm Tourist Travel Agency TOURS
(Пермь Турист туристическое агентство; ☑218 6999; www.hotel-ural.com/tourist; ul Lenina 58, office 209; ⊙10am-7pm Mon-Fri, 11am-4pm Sat) Inside the Hotel Ural, organises excursions such as to Kungur and Perm-36 (each from R5800), as well as city tours in Perm and Volga river cruises.

✺ Festivals & Events

White Nights CULTURAL
(www.permfest.com) Inaugurated in 2011, the White Nights festival runs through most of June, presenting a month of contemporary music, street art, theatre, readings and interesting side-festival events.

Kamwa Festival CULTURAL
(www.kamwa.ru) The annual 'ethno-futuristic' Kamwa Festival held in late July to early August in Perm and Khokhlovka brings together ancient ethno-Ugric traditions and modern art, music and fashion.

Perm

🛏 Sleeping

Hotel Edem HOTEL €€
(📞212 0036; ul Maxima Gorkogo 21b; r R2000-2500; 🛜) The six large rooms with double beds in this excellent minihotel are named by their colour scheme – the 'Pink Room', and so on. As with some minihotels, service is friendly but patchy; here you get a kettle, coffee, plates and cutlery as well as a fridge in order to make good use of the 24-hour supermarket across the road if you're on a tight budget.

Hotel Ural HOTEL €€
(Гостиница Урал; 📞218 6262; www.hotel-ural .com; ul Lenina 58; s R2000-2700; d R3500-4300; 🖥@🛜) This one-time Soviet monolith rising up in the heart of the city has shed virtually all of its cheap, unrenovated rooms and

boasts a shimmering, high-tech lobby and mostly modern rooms at reasonable prices.

Hotel Astor HOTEL €€
(Гостиница Астор; 📞212 2212; www.astor hotel.ru; ul Petropavlovskaya 40; s R2900-5000, d R3400-5500, tr R6000; 🖥🌐🛜) Spotless white dominates this hotel's colour scheme. Its reputation among business travellers is high, and rooms are low-allergy.

Hotel Prikamye HOTEL €€
(Гостиница Прикамье; 📞219 8353; www .prikamie-hotel.ru; Komsomolsky pr 27; s R2300-3200, d R3300-3850, ste R4600-4900; 🛜) Nicely spruced-up rooms in this former Soviet eyesore make Prikamye a very decent option. Deals are better if you book on the web. Wi-fi is available but expensive.

Hotel New Star HOTEL €€
(📞220 6801; www.newstar-hotel.ru; ul Gazety Zvezda 38b; s/d R3500/5000; 🌐@🛜) Modern well-equipped rooms. The R1900 'economy class' singles are most attractive for solo travellers but can be noisy. Kids get significant discounts here.

🍴 Eating & Drinking

TOP CHOICE **Grill Taverna Montenegro** BALKAN €€
(Гриль-Таверна Монтенегро; ul Maxima Gorkogo 28; meals R700; ⏰noon-midnight; 🍴) The trompe l'oeil village fresco downstairs, upstairs pseudo-portico and outdoor terrace lend nice touches to this excellent restaurant. The Kalmyk lamb kebab is superbly grilled.

Vkus Stranstvy CAFETERIA €
(Вкус странствий; Sibirskaya ul 8; meals R300; ⏰10am-10pm; 🛜) With the feel of a midpriced restaurant, the cheerful 'Taste for Travel' neo-*stolovaya* (canteen) serves some of the best cafeteria food in the Ural Mountains.

Zhivago RUSSIAN €€
(Живаго; 📞235 1716; ul Lenina 37; mains R350-600; ⏰9am-midnight) This restaurant for the well-heeled and the literary inclined is actually two-in-one. Pasternak downstairs has a lounge-like, post-modernist cafe feel, while Zhivago upstairs is a fully fledged formal restaurant. Steaks and several more-expensive dishes cost over R1000.

Kama BREWERY €€
(Кама; www.pivzavodkama.ru; Sibirskaya ul 25; mains R300-600; ⏰noon-2am; 🍴) This micro-brewery brews several tasty varieties of

ALTERNATIVE ROUTE TO YEKATERINBURG VIA KAZAN

The route across European Russia to Yekaterinburg via Kazan is the least travelled of the three major lines on this leg, but it is a fascinating one because it allows you to stop over in Kazan (Казань), an attractive city situated on the Volga River. Kazan is the capital of the Tatarstan Republic – the land of the Volga Tatars, a Turkic people commonly associated with Chinggis Khaan's hordes, although they prefer to identify themselves with the ancient state of Volga Bulgaria, which was devastated by the Mongols. The independent Kazan khanate was created in 1438. It was ravaged in 1552 by Ivan the Terrible's troops and Tatar allies, and the collapse of Kazan caused such unease further east in the surviving khanate of Sibir (in Western Siberia) that Sibir nominally began paying tribute to Ivan. Kazan's collapse also cleared the way for Slavic Russian farmers to pour into the Urals region around Perm.

As well as time spent taking in the sights, allow time to walk around and soak up the multicultural atmosphere of the city. Tatar autonomy is strong here and not just about bilingual street signs. It also ensures that Tatarstan benefits greatly from vast oil reserves in this booming republic. The post-Soviet cultural revival, manifested by the popularity of modern Muslim fashions and Tatar-language literature, characterises its self-confidence.

Football (soccer) fans might be familiar with the city because of its popular club **Rubin Kazan** (http://rubin-kazan.ru/en/main). A highlight in the more traditional sense is the **kremlin** (кремль). After you enter the main gate, an alley leads past the enormous **Kul Sharif Mosque** (Мечеть Кул Шариф), completed in 2005, which is named after the imam who died defending the city against the troops of Ivan the Terrible in 1552. In front of this is the former cadet school building, which today houses the **Hermitage Centre** (Эрмитаж-Казань; admission R120; ⏲10am-5pm, closed Mon) and runs rotating exhibitions from the collection of St Petersburg's Hermitage. Also check out the **National Museum of the Republic of Tatarstan** (Kremlyovskaya ul 2; admission R100; ⏲10am-6pm Tue-Sun), which is located opposite the kremlin's main entrance, occupying an ornate 1770 building. It has a large archaeology collection as well as jewellery, weapons and exhibits on the history of the Tatar people and its literary figures.

If you decide to travel on this route, plan a couple of nights in Kazan. **Hotel Volga** (☎231 6349; www.volga-hotel.ru; ul Said-Galeeva 1; s from R1400, r R1600-4900) is 10 minutes by foot from the station (turn left on the busy street). **Hotel Giuseppe** (☎292 6934; www.giuseppe.ru; Kremlyovskaya ul 15/25; s R3100-5500, d R4030-7150, ste R8000-23,000; ❄📶), above Giuseppe pizzeria, has hints of a Venetian villa (and good eating options). For good food and drinks, drop into **Priyut kholostyaka** (☎292 0771; ul Chernyshevskogo 27a; mains R350-600; ⏲11am-midnight Mon-Fri, to 2am Sat & Sun), the 'Bachelor's Shelter' – a spotlessly white oasis of style. An inexpensive place to try local Tatar food is **Kazan Askhane-Chai Yorty** (ul Baumana 64; mains R80, pastry R30; ⏲9am-7pm).

Kazan's excellent **tourist information centre** (☎292 3010; http://gokazan.com; Kremlyovskaya ul 15/25; ⏲9.30am-6.30pm Mon-Fri, to 3.30pm Sat) has a good sheet map of town (also available in many hotels).

Kazan is the unchallenged highlight of this route, and after it you can doze for about five hours until the Kama River crossing at around 1150km (after Agryz). The overnight *Ural* (16) departs Moscow's Kazansky station late afternoon and arrives at 4.20am, before the night is over (*platskart/kupe* R1254/2123, 11½ hours). Better in all senses is the premium 002Й from Moscow (not to be confused with train 2, the *Rossiya*), towing carriages ranging from *platskart* (R1254) through *kupe* (R3093) to a grand deluxe carriage (peaking at around R30,000 for a double suite with private facilities).

The beautifully restored original train station on ul Said Galeeva now serves as a waiting room for the main train station in a separate building. Buses and *marshrutky* run to the kremlin.

The Volga chapter of Lonely Planet's *Russia* guidebook has further information on this region and can be purchased through www.lonelyplanet.com.

own-brew. The food, including its vegetarian borsch, is reasonably priced by Russian microbrewery standards. Sometimes good bands perform live here; other times it's a guitar soloist with canned backing.

☆ Entertainment

Labarint KARAOKE
(Лабаринт; 3rd fl; ul Lenina 88; cover Thu-Sat R300-400, Sun-Wed free; ☺6pm-6am) This club has 50,000 tunes and everything from Russia's best- and least-known to Western rock of all types (just write down the title and artist's name if it's not on the list).

**Tchaikovsky Theatre of
Opera & Ballet** THEATRE
(Театр оперы и балета Чайковского; ☑212 5416; www.opera.permonline.ru; ul Petropavlovskaya 25) One of Russia's top ballet schools.

ⓘ Information

Main post office (Главпочтамт; ul Lenina 29; internet per hr R45; ☺8am-10pm Mon-Fri, 9am-6pm Sat & Sun)
Perm Tourist (Пермь Турист; ☑218 6021; www.visitperm.ru; ul Lenina 58; ☺9am-8pm Mon-Fri, from 10am Sat & Sun; ☎) City and regional information, including the free multilingual *Green Line* booklet explaining sights on a city walk. Hires city bikes (24 hours R550) and has a list of tour operators. It's inside the Hotel Ural; use side entrance.

ⓘ Getting There & Away

Inside the Hotel Ural you will find a **railways booking office** (☑233 02 03; ☺8am-7.30pm Mon-Sat, to 6pm Sun) and an **Aviakassa** (☑233 2509; ☺8.30am-8pm Mon-Fri, 10am-5pm Sat & Sun).

Train

Perm-II, the city's major train station, 3km southwest of the centre, is on the Trans-Siberian route. Many trains travel the route from Moscow, including the *firmeny* train called the *Kama* (R4370, 20 hours). When the *Kama* leaves Perm for Moscow the station loudspeakers blare out the rousing tune 'Proshchanie Slavyanki' (Slavic Farewell). Heading east, the next major stop on the Trans-Siberian route is Yekaterinburg (*platskart/kupe* R700/1450, six hours), serviced by all the major *firmeny* trains except the 15/16 (*Ural*), which goes via Kazan, not Perm. There were no direct trains to Kazan at the time of research. Note that some trains depart from the *gorny trakt* (mountain track) on the north side of Perm-II, as opposed to the *glavny trakt* (main track). The station has resting rooms (*komnaty otdykha*) on the 3rd floor. The station website (www.perm2.net/r_pass.htm, in Russian) has useful information on trains and how long they usually stop here.

The disused and crumbling Perm-I station, 1km northeast of the centre, is currently being restored.

Air

Several airlines fly to Moscow (about R5000, two hours, nine daily). **Lufthansa** flies to/from Frankfurt four times a week.

Boat

The **river station pier** is at the eastern end of ul Ordzhonikidze, in front of Perm-I station. Boats do short tours of the Kama in the navigation season. Fully fledged seven- to 14-day cruises down the Kama to the Volga and continuing to the major towns between Kazan and Astrakhan cost anything from R11,000 for the cheapest class to R58,000 for the most expensive. The Perm Tourist Travel Agency and Krasnov (see p141) handle bookings.

Bus

From the **bus station** (ul Revolyutsii 68) numerous buses go to or via Kungur (see p143); there are three buses a day to Khokhlovka (R84, 1½ hours) and two daily buses to Ufa (R569, 11½ hours). Buses to Kazan depart Friday and Saturday (R1300, 12 hours, two weekly).

ⓘ Getting Around

The train station is situated about 3km from the Hotel Ural in the centre, connected by tram 4. Tram 11 connects ul Maxima Gorkogo with the central market (about 400m from the bus station) via ul Kommunisticheskaya and ul Lenina. *Marshrutka* 1t links the bus station, the Perm-II train station and the airport. Bus 42 goes between the bus station and the airport.

Around Perm

KHOKHLOVKA ХОХЛОВКА
☑342
The **Architecture-Ethnography Museum** (☑299 7181; admission R100; ☺10am-6pm) is set in the rolling countryside near the village of Khokhlovka, about 45km north of Perm. Its impressive collection of wooden buildings includes two churches dating from the turn of the 18th century. Most of the structures are from the 19th or early 20th centuries, including an old firehouse, a salt-production facility and a Khanty *izba* (traditional wooden cottage). A few buses a day serve Khokhlovka from Perm (R84, one hour), the best ones departing Perm at 9.55am and returning from Khokhlovka at 4.25pm.

PERM-36: EVEN WALLS HAVE EARS *YAKOV L KLOTS*

'Even walls have ears', goes the Russian saying. At Perm-36, the former camp for political prisoners, the walls have survived...unlike most of those who were kept behind them. Dissidents, poets, intelligentsia. Ordinary people whose lives had been taken away and silenced. Concrete floors, barred windows, plank beds, aluminium bowls, spoons and mugs, and the barbed wire coiling along the borders of the restricted areas: all outlived the inmates.

Nowadays, representing the camp's daily routine with an existential accuracy, the walls keep the memory of bygone times – of prisoners who were not fated to see their place of detention become a museum, of halls walked by prison guards instead of high-school students.

Before the first prisoners were brought to Perm-36, all of the trees around the grounds were destroyed. The purpose was to prevent convicts from determining in which part of our vast country they had landed. Prisoners were not allowed to leave their cells, so they could not hear the gush of the Chusovaya River, which flowed a few hundred metres from the camp's gate. And the rich local landscape that they might spy through narrow window slits was wiped out.

But the guards were powerless to prevent local birds from flying and singing above the camp barracks. So an inmate – a biologist sentenced to 25 years of 'special regime imprisonment' – identified the bird species by their songs, and determined he was in the Urals.

One can never know for sure what tomorrow is going to be like. Perhaps the darkest side of life in imprisonment is the constant awareness that tomorrow is *not* going to be different from yesterday. The deathly silence that resounds in the damp, dark cells at Perm-36 reminds us of what this place was like yesterday.

PERM-36   ПЕРМЬ-36

Once an ominous island in the Gulag Archipelago, **Perm-36** (www.perm36.ru; admission R50, tours in Russian R500; ◷10am-5pm Tue-Sun) is now a haunting memorial and museum dedicated to the victims of political repression. The buildings have been preserved in their original condition, with the interior of some re-created to illustrate the conditions under which prisoners lived.

Kungur   Кунгур

☑34271 / POP 68,000 / ◷MOSCOW + 2HR

Between the two regional capitals Perm and Yekaterinburg, Kungur is like cream in a biscuit. Despite the city's rundown appearance, its skyline is graced by a multitude of pretty church cupolas, including the 18th-century **Tikhvinskaya Church** in the centre and the **Transfiguration Church** on the other bank of the Sylva, while the frozen magic of its ice cave draws a steady stream of visitors.

Founded in 1663 on the banks of the meandering river, Kungur was a copper-smelting centre during the 17th and 18th centuries. This topic is covered in the **Regional Local Studies Museum** (ul Gogolya 36; admission R20; ◷10am-5pm Wed-Sun).

The **Kungur Ice Cave** (guided tour R500-600; ◷10am-4pm) is about 5km out of town. The network of caves stretches for more than 5km, although only about 1.5km are open to explore. The ancient Finno-Ugric inhabitants of the Perm region believed the cave to be the home of a fiery underground creature, and the grottos are adorned with unique ice formations, frozen waterfalls and underground lakes. You can enter only with one of the guided tours that depart every two hours. Tickets are sold at the box office outside; the number of participants on each tour is limited to 20, so tickets may not be available for the next departure. The cost of the excursion includes admission to a small museum on the site with displays of rocks and fossils. Take enough warm clothes to withstand subzero temperatures in the initial grottos.

If the cave is your reason for visiting Kungur, you can stay at the popular **Stalagmit Tourist Complex** (☑62 610; www.kungurcave .ru; with breakfast s R800-1500, d R1400-2500; ◈), close to the cave entrance, which has excellent rooms, all with their own bathrooms (the cheaper ones don't have fridges and TV). The beautiful countryside surrounding Kungur is great for outdoor sports, and bicycles as well as rafts, canoes and cross-country skis can be hired inexpensively at Stalagmit.

In the centre of town, **Hotel Iren** (☑32 270; ul Lenina 30; without bathroom s R500-1400, d R1000, with bathroom s R1300-2500, d R2100) is good value, though it doesn't have a lift. Even the rooms without bathrooms are pleasant enough, and the shared toilets and showers are very clean. Prices include breakfast.

Across the bridge, the riverside cafe-disco **Tri Medvedya** (ul Vorovskaya 5; mains R150; ⊘24hr) is a good place to eat. Helpful staff can order a taxi for you back to the bus and train stations.

In Kungur the bus and train stations are located alongside each other. To get to Hotel Iren, take bus 9 from the train station into the centre. By foot it's at least 20 minutes.

Located on the Trans-Siberian route, Kungur is served from Perm by frequent intercity (R472, 1½ hours) and suburban trains (R110, 2¼ hours, four daily) and by distance trains to/from Yekaterinburg (*platskart* R872, four hours). From Perm, bus is the best option, however, with departures every one to two hours, the most convenient being from Perm at 8.25am or 9.25am and returning from Kungur at 6.40pm or 7.55pm (R181, 2½ hours). Bus 9 (R11, every one to two hours) plies the route between Hotel Iren, the train and bus stations and the Stalagmit Tourist Complex.

Yekaterinburg to Krasnoyarsk

Includes »

Route Info

» Distance: 2287km

» Duration: 35 hours

» Time zones: Moscow +2, Moscow +3

Best Places to Stay & Eat

» Hotel Sibir (p162)

» Avenue hotel (p167)

» Toyan hotel (p172)

» Yermolaev bar-restaurant (p160)

» Perchini pasta restaurant (p168)

» Slavyansky Bazar restaurant (p173)

Why Go?

This leg of the journey isn't the most visually exciting, with little more to see than endless miles of semi-taiga and farm-land. Perhaps the best way to make the journey, then, is on a seriews of night trains – you won't miss much in the way of scenery and you'll save on hotels. If you do take day trains, there is admittedly a certain pleasure to be gained from the unchanging countryside and the opportunity it provides to reflect on Russia, life, or whatever takes your fancy. After the historically important city of Yekaterinburg, your journey takes you into Siberia and eventually on to its capital, Novo-sibirsk. But the main attractions on this leg both require detours off the Trans-Siberian route. From oil-rich Tyumen, consider a trip to picturesque Tobolsk. Further on, branch lines will take you to the friendly student town of Tomsk.

When to Go

Novosibirsk

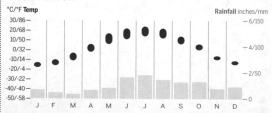

May & Jun Grand WWII Victory Day celebrations in Novosibirsk.

Jul–Sep Travel across Siberia in glorious sun-shine!

Dec & Jan Tramp through Tomsk's winter wonder-land and greet the New Year, Russian style.

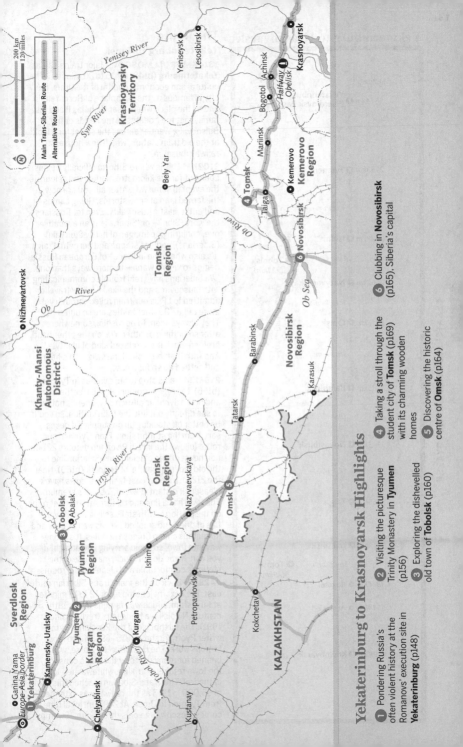

Yekaterinburg to Krasnoyarsk Highlights

1 Pondering Russia's often violent history at the Romanov's execution site in **Yekaterinburg** (p148)

2 Visiting the picturesque Trinity Monastery in **Tyumen** (p156)

3 Exploring the dishevelled old town of **Tobolsk** (p160)

4 Taking a stroll through the student city of **Tomsk** (p169) with its charming wooden homes

5 Discovering the historic centre of **Omsk** (p164)

6 Clubbing in **Novosibirsk** (p165), Siberia's capital

Yekaterinburg to Krasnoyarsk

West to
Moscow

1814km Yekaterinburg
(Sverdlovsk Pass)

4hr, 10min

2138km Tyumen

3hr,
30min

2428km Ishim

1hr, 45min

Tobolsk
(221km)

2562km Nazyvaevskaya

1hr, 30min

To Nizhnevartovsk,
Purpe &
Novy Urengoy

2716km Omsk

3hr, 40min

3035km Barabinsk

3hr, 30min

3343km Novosibirsk

3hr, 35min

3565km Taiga

2hr

3713km Mariinsk

1hr, 50min

Tomsk
(79km)

3846km Bogotol
1hr

3914km Achinsk-1

3hr

4098km Krasnoyarsk

East to
Vladivostok

The Route

Yekaterinburg to Omsk

1814KM FROM MOSCOW Major trains halt at **Yekaterinburg** (p148) for 15 to 30 minutes. The cultural and economic capital of the Urals, the city is famous as the birthplace of Boris Yeltsin and as the place where Tsar Nicholas II and his family met their deaths at the hands of the Bolsheviks. Wander across the street for a look at the old train station, which now houses a railway museum.

2102KM This is where **Siberia** officially begins. Look out for the kilometre marker and celebrate the event in some way. After all, you are now in the famed land of snowstorms, Gulag camps and enthusiastic hospitality. Even for Russians, the word 'Sibir' – or 'Siberia' – is an evocative one, conjuring up images of hardy Sibiryaki (Siberians), endless steppe and perpetual taiga. It's also where the influence of European Russia begins to visibly wane – in more ways than one. 'We Siberians have real trouble communicating with Muscovites and the like,' a fellow traveller admitted to LP as our train rolled through yet more taiga. 'Our mentalities are so different. They always seem to be rushing somewhere after something or other. We, on the other hand, prefer a much more relaxed kind of lifestyle.' And with that, he took a long swig on his beer and settled down for a nap.

2138KM Trains stop for 15 minutes in **Tyumen** (p156), the region's oldest Russian settlement, and now a dynamic oil-rich city. There's not much to see directly outside the train station, so you'd be better off stocking up on supplies if necessary from the station shop. From Tyumen our route follows the Irtysh River and detours 221km northeast off the official Trans-Siberian line to the old Siberian capital of **Tobolsk** (p160). Near the 212km marker, east-facing windows have pleasant if distant views of Tobolsk's kremlin. The town has a fine and picturesque market right on the platform, with stalls selling mainly varieties of dried and smoked fish, as well as beer and ubiquitous cheap Chinese noodles. It's a long way into town, so avoid arriving late at night if you can. If you do get stuck, make use of the station's comfortable and clean resting rooms.

2428KM Back on the main Trans-Siberian route east, the next major stop is for 12 to 15 minutes at tiny **Ishim**, which was famous for its 19th-century Nikolskaya trade fairs (revived since 1991). The birthplace of the Russian fairytale writer Pyotr Yershov (1815–69), whose most famous work, *The Humpbacked-Horse*, was banned for many years by the tsar's censors, the town retains a striking, whitewashed 1793 cathedral. The Trans-Siberian reached this town of 65,000 in 1913 as the railway was extended from Tyumen to Omsk. At 2497km, local time becomes Moscow time plus three hours. Swampy land provides opportunities for birdwatchers, in warmer seasons at least.

2562KM Depending on what train you are on, there's a five- to 15-minute halt at agricultural-processing town **Nazyvaevskaya**. The name of the town is derived from the Russian for 'to name' and while tough to directly translate, it sounds most unimaginative to Russian ears. If you're coming straight from Moscow you'll now be into day three of your journey. It's at this point that many travellers on Trans-Siberian trips lasting a week or more report that disorientation sets in. If you feel like something other than this guidebook to read, papers and magazines (in Russian) are continually offered by salespeople on the trains. There's usually a fair selection of sudoku puzzle books as well, if that's your thing. Most of the salespeople are deaf, but we've never been able to figure out why this is so.

2716KM After the impressive six-span Irtysh River bridge, trains pause for 25 minutes in **Omsk** (p164), where Fyodor Dostoevsky was exiled in 1849. If you are quick, you should have time to nip out and have a look at the fine Lenin statue right outside the station. If you are really fast and urgently need to send an email, you could pop into the internet cafe on the ground level of the station. It's to the left of the entrance.

Omsk to Krasnoyarsk

If you notice an increase in passing trains after Omsk, blame it on coal from the Kuzbas Basin east of Novosibirsk going to the smelting works of the Urals. In freight terms this is the world's busiest section of railway.

3035KM Barabinsk was once a place of exile for Polish Jews. The surrounding Barabinsk Steppe is a boggy expanse of grassland and lakes that was formerly the homeland of the Kirghiz people. Many train engines and carriages that service the Trans-Siberian put in here for repairs at some point or other. The shop on the platform has been full of drunken local teens dancing to disco music around plastic tables on LP's last two visits. If you're in the mood to join in, you'll have time to down a beer and strut your stuff to at least a couple of tracks in the 17-minute stop here.

3330KM Get ready for the seven-span, 870m-long bridge across the **Ob**, one of the world's longest rivers. It's also extremely busy, with all manner of barges and cargo ships going about their business.

3343KM There is a 20-minute stop at **Novosibirsk** (p165), which is just about enough time to inspect the grand station interior, a real temple of the Trans-Siberian. Also try to have a quick look at the two WWII memorial statues on platform 1 depicting a family waving off soldiers to the front. The Nazis never got this far, but lots of Siberians left for the war from this station.

YEKATERINBURG TO KRASNOYARSK ROUTE PLANNER

The following is a suggested itinerary for covering the main Trans-Sib stops in this chapter:

Day 1: Leave Yekaterinburg early morning; arrive in Tyumen around 9am

Day 2: Leave Tyumen for Tobolsk; arrive in Tobolsk around noon; night train to Omsk (14 hours)

Day 3: Briefly explore Omsk; night train to Tomsk (14 to 19 hours)

Day 4: Explore Tomsk

Day 5: Second day in Tomsk

Day 6: Take morning train to Novosibirsk; arrive early afternoon

Day 7: Take evening train from Novosibirsk to Krasnoyarsk (12 to 14 hours)

3565KM The 25-minute halt at the intriguingly named but entirely unspectacular town of **Taiga** provides plenty of time to wish you were heading 79km north up the branch line to **Tomsk** (p169). This is not a Womble (as Brits of a certain age may expect, from the kids' TV program) but a charming old Siberian city that lost much of its regional importance when it was bypassed by the Trans-Siberian Railway. Myth says that the city fathers, fearing the dirt and pollution it would bring, declined the offer to have the town connected to the railway. However, the truth is rather more prosaic – swampland made the construction of a bridge over the river Ob problematic, and a decision was taken not to lay lines to the city. Its beautiful wooden buildings and lively cafe scene are well worth the short detour.

3713KM Spot another engine-repair yard to the south as you approach the station at **Mariinsk**, a 20-minute stop along the banks of the Kiya River. Originally named Kiysk, the town grew wealthy as the focus of a Siberian gold rush. It was renamed in 1857 to honour Tsar Alexander II's wife, Maria. Fifty years later, the town finally got round to unveiling a statue in her honour. Many of the furniture and metal factories that operated here in Soviet times are closed now, leaving few employment opportunities. Do your bit to help the local economy by buying a beer or *kvas* and some dried fish from the women who meet the trains here to offer all manner of goods. We were tempted by a large fluffy toy, but common sense eventually prevailed.

3820KM The line enters vast **Krasnoyarsky Territory**, with enormous mineral and forest wealth. It covers 2.5 million sq km, stretching all the way to the Arctic coast. A journey through this stretch of the Trans-Siberian is particularly memorable around sunset, with sunlight flickering hypnotically through the branches of endless rows of trees. Time, perhaps, to get out that dried fish and reflect once more on Russia and her colossal territory.

3846KM The train makes a very brief stop at **Bogotol**, another example of a town being formed around the Trans-Siberian. A train station was opened here in 1893, but it was another 18 years before the subsequent settlement was awarded town status. Bogotol is today home to a locomotive-production factory, hence the tiny model train perched on top of the welcome-to-town sign.

3914KM Next up is **Achinsk**. This small town, built around an alumina refinery, has its origins in the founding of a fortress in the area in 1683. In the 19th century, soap made in Achinsk was famous all over Russia. The train stops here for a few minutes before twisting through woodlands and over hills with yet more cinematic landscapes to enjoy.

3932KM A small, easily missed white obelisk south of the train line marks the halfway point between Moscow and Běijīng (via Ulaanbaatar).

4098KM Major services stop for 20 minutes at **Krasnoyarsk** (p180). That's just long enough to nip out and see a fine communist-era mural in red mosaics decorating a wall on the station square outside before heading on.

Yekaterinburg
Екатеринбург

📞343 / POP 1.35 MILLION / ⊘MOSCOW +2HR

Gem rush, miners' mythology, the execution of the Romanovs, the rise of Yeltsin and gangster feuds of the 1990s – Yekaterinburg is like a piece of conceptual art in which the subtext is perhaps more startling than surface appearances.

Bland on the outside, the political capital of the Ural Mountains is overflowing with history and culture, while its economic growth is manifested in a thriving restaurant scene and, as in many other regional capitals, in atrociously trafficked avenues.

With one of the best international airports in Russia and a couple of agencies experienced in dealing with foreign travellers, Yekaterinburg is a good base camp for exploring the Ural Mountains.

History

Yekaterinburg was founded as a factory-fort in 1723 as part of Peter the Great's push to exploit the Ural region's mineral riches. The city was named after two Catherines: Peter's wife (later Empress Catherine I), and the Russian patron saint of mining.

The city is notorious, however, for being the place where the Bolsheviks murdered Tsar Nicholas II and his family in July 1918. Six years later, the town was renamed Sverdlovsk, after Yakov Sverdlov, a leading Bolshevik who was Vladimir Lenin's right-hand man until his death in the flu epidemic of 1919. The region still bears Sverdlovsk's name.

WWII turned Sverdlovsk into a major industrial centre, as hundreds of factories were transferred here from vulnerable areas west of the Ural Mountains. The city was closed to foreigners until 1990 because of its many defence plants.

During the late 1970s a civil engineering graduate of the local university, Boris Yeltsin, began to make his political mark,

---

SIBERIA – THE GRAPHIC NOVEL

Graphic novels have never taken off in Russia, with even the genre's best works largely dismissed as being fit purely for children. This lack of a comic-book tradition makes Nikolai Maslov's *Siberia*, released by the US-based Soft Skull Press, all the more astonishing. Drawn entirely in pencil on paper, Maslov's tale of a Soviet youth (the book's original title) spent in Siberia is bleak, bitter and beautiful.

Portraying with almost unbearable honesty the faces of the drunks and bullies he grew up with, Maslov had reportedly never actually read a graphic novel before he approached the French publisher of *Asterix* in Russia with the first pages of the book and asked him to finance the rest. The publisher agreed, allowing Maslov to quit his job as a night watchman and devote himself to his work. Maslov tells the story of his often brutal life with a complete lack of sentimentality, using matter-of-fact, almost crude frames to portray characters and everyday scenes in Western Siberian villages and towns. One of the few works of art to portray everyday life in Soviet Siberia, as opposed to Solzhenitsyn-type Gulag camp tales, Maslov's book has yet to find a publisher in his native Russia.

rising to become regional Communist Party boss before being promoted to Moscow in 1985. Several years later he was standing on a tank in Moscow as the leading figure in defending the country against a putsch by old-guard communists. He became the Russian Federation's first president in June 1991.

That year Yekaterinburg took back its original name. After suffering economic depression and Mafia lawlessness in the early 1990s, the city has boomed in recent years and weathered the various crises well.

◉ Sights

TOP CHOICE **Romanov Death Site** CHURCH, MEMORIAL (Место убийства Романовых; ul Karla Libknekhta & ul Tolmachyova 34; ⊗dawn-dusk) On the night of 16 July 1918, Tsar Nicholas II, his wife and children were murdered in the basement of a local engineer's house, known as Dom Ipatyeva (named for its owner, Nikolay Ipatyev). During the Soviet period, the building housed a local museum of atheism, but it was demolished in 1977 by then governor Boris Yeltsin, who feared it would attract monarchist sympathisers.

Today the massive Byzantine-style **Church upon the Blood** (Храм на Крови) dominates this site and is easily the most celebrated of memorials to the Romanovs. Nearby, the pretty wooden **Chapel of the Revered Martyr Grand Princess Yelizaveta Fyodorovna** (⊗9am-5.30pm) honours the imperial family's great-aunt and faithful friend. After her relatives' murders, this pious nun met an even worse end when she was thrown down a mineshaft, poisoned with gas and buried.

Opposite the site are the historic **Rastorguev-Kharitonov mansion** (Усадьба Расторгуев-Харитонова) and the restored **Ascension Church** (Вознесенская церковь; ul Klary Tsetkin 11).

Istorichesky skver PARK
The prettiest and most lively part of Yekaterinburg in summer is the landscaped parkland alongside the City Pond (Gorodskoy prud), where pr Lenina crosses a small dam. This was where Yekaterinburg began back in 1723. The **Monument to the Founders of Yekaterinburg** (Памятник основателям Екатеринбурга) standing nearby depicts founders Vasily Tatishchev and George Wilhelm de Gennin.

Literary Quarter NEIGHBOURHOOD
Situated north of skver Popova, the Literary Quarter features restored wooden houses. Some of them now house museums about celebrated Ural Mountains writers such as Dmitry Mamina-Sibiryak and Pavel Bazhov; a full list of museums is on the website www.ompu.ur.ru. The **Literary-Memorial House-Museum Reshetnikov** (Литературно-мемориальный дом-музей Решетникова; ul Proletarskaya 6; admission R70; ⊗11am-5pm Mon-Sat) is interesting for its museum section about the postal system – the method of transport across Russia before the advent of the railway.

Museum of Architecture & Industrial Technology INDUSTRIAL MUSEUM
(Музей истории архитектуры города и промышленной техники Урала; ul Gorkogo 4a) Istorichesky skver (Historical Sq) is also the location of the city's major museums. Peek into the old **water tower** (Водонапорная башня), one of the city's oldest structures, then head over to the old mining-equipment factory and mint buildings. These contain the Museum of Architecture & Industrial Technology, which displays the machinery used in the mining industry from the 18th and 19th centuries and through WWII.

Urals Mineralogical Museum MUSEUM
(Уральский минералогический музей; ul Krasnoarmeyskaya 1a; admission R50; ⊗10am-7pm Mon-Fri, to 5pm Sat & Sun) A private collection offering a stunning introduction to the region's semiprecious stones, located in the Bolshoy Ural Hotel.

Museum of Fine Arts ART GALLERY
(Музей изобразительных искусств; ul Voevodina 5; admission R150; ⊗11am-7pm Tue-Sun) The star exhibit of the Museum of Fine Arts is the elaborate Kasli Iron Pavilion that won prizes in the 1900 Paris Expo.

Ural Geology Museum MUSEUM
(Уральский геологический музей; ul Kuybysheva 39; admission R50; ⊗11am-5pm Mon-Fri) Over 500 minerals from the Ural Mountains region and a collection of meteorites. Enter from ul Khokhryakova inside Urals State Mining University.

Military History Museum MUSEUM
(Военно-исторический музей; ul Pervomayskaya 27; Russian/foreigner R50/100; ⊗9am-4pm Tue-Sat) Well worthwhile for buffs and anyone with a general interest. Has a small

Yekaterinburg

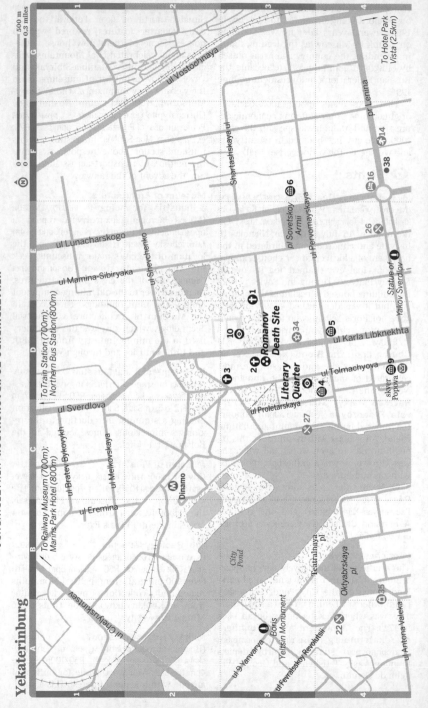

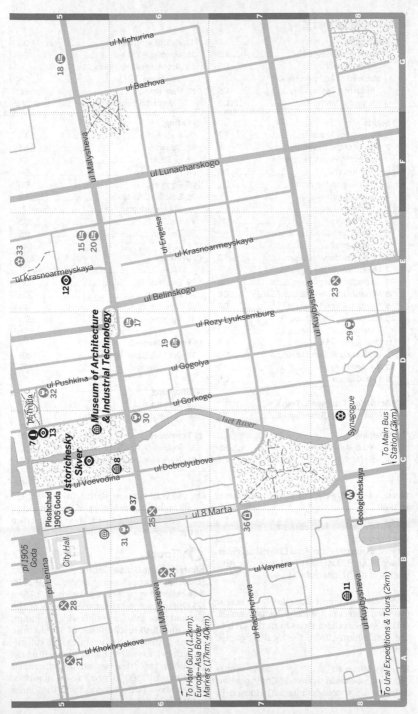

ul Michurina

ul Bazhova

ul Malysheva

ul Lunacharskogo

18

33

15 20

ul Krasnoarmeyskaya

ul Engelsa

ul Krasnoarmeyskaya

12

ul Belinskogo

ul Kuybysheva

23

ul Rozy Lyuksemburg

17

29

19

ul Gogolya

32

ul Pushkina

Museum of Architecture & Industrial Technology

ul Gorkogo

30

Iset River

Synagogue

pl Truda

7 13

Istoricheskiy Skver

8

ul Voevodina

ul Dobrolyubova

To Main Bus
Station (3km)

37

Ploshchad
1905 Goda

ul 8 Marta

25

36

Geologicheskaya

City Hall

31

24

ul Vaynera

pl 1905
Goda

pr Lenina

28

ul Malysheva

11

ul Khokhryakova

ul Radishcheva

ul Kuybysheva

21

To Hotel Guru (1.2km);
Europe–Asia Border
Markers (17km; 40km)

To Ural Expeditions & Tours (2km)

Yekaterinburg

piece of Gary Powers' spy plane, shot down in 1960.

Metenkov House-Museum of Photography   MUSEUM
(Музей Фотографии; ul Karla Libknekhta 36; admission R100; ☺10am-6pm) Features evocative photos of old Yekaterinburg.

FREE Nevyansk Icon Museum   MUSEUM
(Музей Невянская икона; ul Tolmachyova 21; ☺11am-7pm) Excellent icons from the 17th to the 20th century, from the local Nevyansk school.

Railway Museum   RAILWAY MUSEUM
(Железнодорожный музей; ul Chelyuskintsev; admission R75; ☺noon-5pm Tue-Sat) Housed in

the old train station, dating from 1881. Exhibits highlight the history of the railroad in the Urals, including a recreation of the office of the Soviet-era railway director.

☞ Tours

Ekaterinburg Guide Centre   TOURS
(Екатеринбургский центр гидов; ☎359 3708; www.ekaterinburgguide.com; pr Lenina 52/1, office 12) Organises English-language tours of the city and trips into the countryside, including the difficult-to-reach village of Verkhoturie (where Grigory Rasputin started his spiritual journey), as well as hiking and rafting expeditions. Day trips cost anything between R1300 and R7300, depending on numbers. It also books budget dorms from R1150 in a central minihotel.

Ural Expeditions & Tours TOURS
([📞]356 5282; http://welcome-ural.ru; ul Posadskaya 23; [🕐]9am-6pm Mon-Fri) This group of geologists from the Sverdlovsk Mining Institute leads trekking, rafting and horse-riding trips to all parts of the Ural Mountains, including Taganay and Zyuratkul National Parks. English-speaking guides.

🛏 Sleeping

TOP
CHOICE **Hotel Tsentralny** HOTEL €€
(Отель Центральный; [📞]350 0505; www.hotel centr.ru; ul Malysheva 74; s R3150-3780, d R4050-5900; [❄][📶]) This historical hotel is housed in a grand art nouveau building in the heart of town, with excellent business-class and standard rooms. Eating and nightlife are never far away from here. Trolleybuses 1 and 9 are among the many going there from the train station.

Marins Park Hotel HOTEL €€
(Маринс Парк Отель; [📞]214 3000; www.sv-hotel .ru; ul Chelyuskintsev 106; s R1600-2900, d R2300-3900, ste R4400-5100; [📶]) Formerly known as the Sverdlovsk, a Soviet disaster zone when it came to hotels, this place has been renovated and is gradually reinventing itself as a modern congress hotel; it retains its chief advantage of being right across the road from the train station.

Hotel Iset HOTEL €€
(Гостиница Исеть; [📞]350 0110; www.hoteliset .ru; pr Lenina 69/1; s R3400, d R3800-4800, ste R4500; [❄][📶]) If it looks funky from the street, it's because it's shaped like a hammer and sickle when seen from the sky. Inside, curving corridors lead to nicely furnished rooms, though they aren't large. Take any tram going south down ul Lunacharskogo from the station.

Hotel Guru HOTEL €€
([📞]228 5070; www.guruhotel.ru; ul Repina 22; s/d R2800/3500; [❄][✳][@][📶]) This is an intriguing option located inside the new building of a dance school of the same name. But before you check in at a weekend, find out if the disco downstairs is operating (which can be annoying). Trolleybuses 3 and 17 from the train station stop nearby at Institut Svyazi.

Hotel Park Vista HOTEL €€
([📞]216 4244; http://parkvista.ru; ul Vostochnaya 45; s/d R2000/3000; [❄][📶]) Rooms are large and the only downsides of this excellent-value minihotel owned by a local metals-cutting company are the minimal service and that breakfast is a couple of wearily fried eggs and a cup of tea in the 24-hour Azeri eatery downstairs. Bring your own coffee. Take tram 21 from the train station to TsPKiO (ЦПКиО).

Novotel Yekaterinburg Centre HOTEL €€€
([📞]253 5383; http://novotel-ekaterinburg.ru; ul Engelsa 7; s R7000-8000, d R8000-9000; [❄][✳][📶]) This excellent new chain hotel in the centre is 20% cheaper weekdays and offers good deals online through www.hotel.com. The easiest way from the station is *marshrutka* 56 to ul Rozy Lyuksemburg.

Resting rooms HOSTEL €
(комнаты отдыха, komnaty otdykha; [📞]358 5783; train station 4th fl; per bed 6hr 2-/4-bed room R600/350) Onward tickets are not essential if demand is low for beds in the resting rooms at the train station. Prices for 12 hours are R1000/600.

Park Inn HOTEL €€€
([📞]216 6000; www.parkinn.com/hotel-ekaterin burg; ul Mamina-Sibiryaka 98; r R6800-7650; [✳][📶]) Offers rooms with cheering colour schemes and all amenities you would expect for the price. Trolleybuses 18 and 19 from the station stop at Dom Kino close by.

Bolshoy Ural Hotel HOTEL €€
(Гостиница Большой Урал; [📞]350 0143; www .b-ural.ru; ul Krasnoarmeyskaya 1; r without bathroom from R1050, r with bathroom R2300-3500, ste R3800-4200) Occupies an entire city block. The somewhat dour atmosphere is buffered by the prime location. Trolleybus 18 from the station to Dom Kino takes you close.

Transhotel Yekaterinburg HOTEL €€€
([📞]355 1211; www.transhotel.su; ul Gogolya 15; s R3500-4100, d R4100-5900, ste R6200-6900; [✳][📶]) A small and friendly modern hotel behind Novotel.

Minigostonitsa Vesta APARTMENT €€
([📞]219 5488; www.hhotel.ru; apt from R2500) Very centrally located apartments in new buildings for short stays of a couple of days or more.

Meeting Point HOSTEL €
([📞]8-953-604 1941; www.meetingpoint.hostel.com; ul Malysheva 87, apt 73; 8-bed dm €16; [@]) Small hostel in the centre of town with registration that's free for guests staying three days or more. Trolleybus 18 from the train station runs to the Transagenstvo stop nearby.

See **Ekaterinburg Guide Centre** (Екатеринбургский центр гидов; ☑359 3708; www.ekaterinburgguide.com; ul Lenina 52/1, office 12) for another cheap hostel.

Eating

Ulitsa 8 Marta between pr Lenina and ul Malysheva has several popular chain and Western-style places such as Thank God It's Friday and Traveller's Coffee, and ul Vaynera has a moderate choice of eateries.

TOP CHOICE Dacha   INTERNATIONAL, RUSSIAN €€€
(Дача; ☑379 3569; pr Lenina 20a; mains R500-800, business lunch R300; ☺noon-midnight) Each room in this quality restaurant is decorated like a Russian country house, from the casual garden to the more formal dining room. It's a great place to enjoy unbeatable cuisine and hospitality.

TOP CHOICE Zhili Byli   RUSSIAN €
(ul Vaynera 8; mains R250-350; ☺11am-11pm; ☺☎📶) Decorated in the traditional village style of this chain, Zhili Byli serves Russian dishes to the wheeze of saxophones and tinkling lounge music, all totally out of keeping with the fake oak tree, coloured glass windows and peasant costumes that hang around.

La Rond   FRENCH, RUSSIAN €€€
(☑359 6222; http://atriumhotel.ru; ul Kuybysheva 44; mains R1000-1600; ☺lunch & dinner) Located inside the Atrium Palace Hotel, this is an upmarket gourmet act especially popular among its business guests.

Shoko Kofeyniya   CAFE €€
(www.restoraciya.ru; ul Malysheva 74; mains R400; ☺8am-2am Mon-Fri, from 6am Sat, 6am-midnight Sun) This upmarket cafe is the pick of the crop among the cluster of bars and eateries located in and alongside the Hotel Tsentralny building. The hours are useful for chilling out late at night.

Paul Bakery   BAKERY €
(ul Malysheva 36; light meals R250-350; ☺8am-1pm Mon-Fri) This cafe, entered from ul Vaynera, is great for a quick snack and coffee, ordered from the counter.

Demidov   RUSSIAN €€€
(☑371 7344; ul Fevralsskoy Revolutsii 9; mains R350-700; ☺11am-2am) 'Museum' restaurant located in the house where the White Russian leader Kolchak stayed in 1919. With an outdoor grill.

Pozharka   PUB €€
(ul Malysheva 44; mains R350-500; ☺noon-midnight Sun-Thu, to 2am Fri & Sat) About 40 different beers and food (that gets expensive if you don't choose carefully) as an accompaniment.

Serbian Courtyard   SERBIAN €€
(Сербский дворик; ☑350 3457; http://serbskiy-dvorik.blizko.ru; pr Lenina 53; meals R700; ☺noon-midnight) Best Balkan in town.

🍷 Drinking

TOP CHOICE Rosy Jane   PUB
(pr Lenina 34; mains R600-900; ☺6am-4am) This English-style pub aims at the New Russian drinking and eating crowd, who grace the bar (with or without cigars) and perch at polished wood tables gourmandising on steak and other very well prepared Russian and international dishes.

Dr Scotch   PUB
(ul Malysheva 56a; ☺noon-2am) Less expensive and more popular than Rosy Jane.

Ben Hall   PUB
(☑251 6368; ul Narodnoy Voli 65; mains R350-600; ☺noon-2am Sun-Thu, to 4am Fri & Sat; 📶) This popular pub hosts local rock bands at weekends, its owner being a well-known musician. Trams 15 and 27 from Operny Teatr or along pr Lenina to Tsirk (Цирк) drop you close by.

New Bar   BAR
(ul 8 Marta 8; ☺10am-2am Mon-Thu & Sun, to 6am Fri & Sat) Art-scene cafe and cocktail bar on the top floor of Mytny Dvor mall.

☆ Entertainment

Philharmonic   CLASSICAL MUSIC
(Филармония; ☑371 4682; www.filarmonia.e-burg.ru; ul Karla Libknekhta 38) Yekaterinburg's top venue for the classical performing arts often hosts visiting directors and soloists, as well as regular performances of the acclaimed Ural Mountains academic orchestra.

Opera & Ballet Theatre   OPERA, BALLET
(Театр оперы и балета; ☑350 8057; www.uralopera.ru; pr Lenina 45a; tickets from R100) The level of professionalism is not quite on a par with the Philharmonic, but the ornate baroque

theatre is still a lovely place to see the Russian classics.

🛍 Shopping

Grinvich   SHOPPING MALL
(ul 8 Marta 46; ⊙10am-10pm) This enormous shopping complex near the ul Vaynera pedestrian zone is an oasis away from the traffic.

Dom Knigi   BOOKSTORE
(Дом книги; ul Antona Valeka 12; ⊙10am-8pm)

ℹ Information

Main post office (Почтамт; pr Lenina 39; ⊙8am-10pm Mon-Fri, 9am-6pm Sat & Sun) With internet.
Traveller's Coffee (ul 8 Marta 8; ⊙8am-midnight) Free internet on borrowed laptops.

ℹ Getting There & Away

Train

Yekaterinburg – sometimes still 'Sverdlovsk' on timetables – is a major rail junction with connections to all stops on the Trans-Siberian route. The station has resting rooms (see p153), and the closest toilets to the platforms (24 hours) are on the right as you exit the tunnel.

All trains to Moscow stop at either Perm (*platskart/kupe* R700/1450, six hours) or Kazan (*platskart/kupe* R2670/1730, 15 hours). Frequent trains to/from Moscow include the *firmeny* (premium) *Ural* (R4520, 27 hours, daily) via Kazan, but many non-*firmeny* trains will be cheaper. Heading east, the next major stops are Tyumen (*platskart/kupe* R568/1280, 4¾ hours), Omsk (R2580, 14 hours) and Novosibirsk (R4087, 22 hours). If you want to travel direct to Tobolsk (*platskart/kupe* R750/1750) without stopping in Tyumen, the Novy Urengoy service and others do this.

You can buy tickets at outlets throughout the city, including the convenient **Railway and Air Kassa** (☑371 0400; ul Malysheva 31D; ⊙7am-8.30pm).

Air

The main airport is **Koltsovo** (☑224 2367; www .koltsovo.ru), 15km southeast of the city centre. Frequent inland services include Moscow, Novosibirsk, Krasnoyarsk, Irkutsk, Khabarovsk, Ufa, St Petersburg, Samara and a host of Black Sea hubs. International services include Frankfurt am Main (Germany), Běijīng (China), Prague (Czech Republic) and Almaty and Astana (Kazakhstan). **Transaero Tours Centre** (☑365 9165; pr Lenina 50), located inside the City Centre shopping mall, handles bookings for all airlines.

Bus

The main **bus station** (ul 8 Marta 145) is 3km south of the city centre, but most buses pass the northern bus station (Severny avtovokzal), conveniently located by the train station. There's a bus station at the Koltsovo airport serving destinations in Sverdlovsk region and Chelyabinsk (R400, 3½ hours, five daily).

ℹ Getting Around

The train station is located 2km from the centre at the top of ul Sverdlova/Karla Libknekhta. Many trolleybuses and *marshrutky* (pay on board) connect the train station with pr Lenina, where trams 13, 15 and 18 cover long stretches of this main east–west axis. *Marshrutka* 24 runs along ul 8 Marta to the train station and *marshrutka* 57 connects Grinvich shopping centre via ul 8 Marta with the train station.

Bus 1 links the Sverdlovsk-Passazhirskaya train station and Koltsovo airport (one hour) from 6.30am to 11.30pm. *Marshrutka* 26 goes from the airport to metro pl 1905 goda. *Marshrutka* 39 goes to metro Geologicheskaya.

A single metro line runs between the northeastern suburbs and the city centre, with stops at the train station (Uralskaya), pl 1905 goda and ul Kuybysheva near the synagogue (Geologicheskaya).

Around Yekaterinburg

GANINA YAMA   ГАНИНА ЯМА
After the Romanov family was shot in the cellar of Dom Ipatyeva, their bodies were discarded in the depths of the forests of Ganina Yama, 16km northeast of Yekaterinburg. In their honour, the Orthodox Church has built the exquisite **Monastery of the Holy Martyrs** (☑343-217 9146; www.g-ya.ru) at this pilgrimage site. In 2010 one of the seven chapels burned down but is earmarked for reconstruction. According to the Orthodox Church, this is the final resting place of the Romanov family and is therefore sacred ground.

The nearest train station to Ganina Yama is Shuvakish, served by *elektrichka* (suburban train) from the central station. The monastery owns a bus that runs six times a day between the central station, Shuvakish station and Ganina Yama. Ekaterinburg Guide Centre offers three-hour tours for R1300 to R3500, depending on the number of people.

NEVYANSK & AROUND   НЕВЬЯНСК
The small town of Nevyansk is in the heart of the former patrimony of the Demidovs, a

LUBA SUSLYAKOVA'S PLACES

The Yekaterinburg journalist and blogger Luba Suslyakova works on the English-language newspaper *Your Yekaterinburg* and blogs on **Ask Urals** (http://askural.com).

The Romanov Memorial

It's popular with locals, who go there for wedding photos. Russian tourists also like it. Some strong Orthodox believers say they prefer to go to the older churches. Foreigners like it because of the small museum on the ground level, which gives you a picture of what happened there.

For Russian Pies

Stolle (Штолле, Shtolle; ul Maxima Gorkogo 7a; pirozhki from R200; ◷10am-midnight) – we have three in Yekaterinburg. The atmosphere is good and they usually play jazz music.

Boris Yeltsin Statue and Memorial Centre

The sculptor **Georgy Frangulyan** is known for his unusual views. He says he saw Yeltsin as a huge piece of stone moving forward, leaving debris behind him. The 'presidential centre' behind it will have a library and a small museum about Yeltsin.

Drinking Spots

Dr Scotch (p154). There's also a new place called **Alibi** (www.alibibar.ru; ul Malysheva 74; ◷noon-3am Sun-Thu, to 5am Fri & Sat).

Bird's-Eye View

I'd definitely go to the **viewing platform** in the **Antey Shopping Centre** (Смотравая площадка; ul Krasnoarmeyskaya 10; R50; ◷noon-11.30pm; enter through door on far right).

Somewhere Peaceful

Lake Shartash (Озеро Шарташ), a piece of nature right within the city. It's easy to get there by tram. It's peaceful, you can picnic there, walk around the lake, rent a bicycle.

(To get to Lake Shartash, take tram 8, 13, 15, 23, 32 or A from pr Lenina to stop Kamennie palatki. Follow the sign to Shartashsky Lesopark (Шарташский Лесопарк) and climb the stone steps.)

family of industrialists who effectively controlled much of the Ural Mountains and who received Peter I's blessing to develop the region. At their most decadent stage, they bought the Italian feudal title of Count San-Donato. The main highlight here is the **Nevyansk Leaning Tower**, an impressive structure flanked by an equally impressive **Saviour-Transfiguration Cathedral**, which would have graced any large city.

The **Nevyansk History and Architecture Museum** (http://museum-nev.ru; pl Revolyutsii 2; museum R60, Nevyansk tower excursion per group of 1-5 people R1200; ◷9am-5pm Tue-Sun) is where you buy tickets for worthwhile excursions into the tower. This is the only way to access it and get great views over the landscape.

Seven kilometres from Nevyansk is the lovely Old Believers' village of **Byngi**, where an entrepreneurial German and his Russian wife have converted an *izba* (traditional wooden cottage) into a **guesthouse** (www.semken.eu) in the building itself and erected three yurts in the yard. Excursions, including rides on vintage Ural motorcycles, are available. Ekaterinburg Guide Centre runs seven-hour tours to Nevyansk and the nearby old potters' village of **Tavolgi**. Ask to stop on the way at the village of **Kunary**, where a local blacksmith has turned his *izba* into a masterpiece of naive art.

Elektrichki (R104, 2½ hours, 12 daily) – some of them express trains (R154, 1¾ hours) – run to Nevyansk, most bound for Nizhny Tagil.

Tyumen   Тюмень

☎3452 / POP 507,000 / ◷MOSCOW +2HR

Founded in 1586, Tyumen was the first Russian settlement in Siberia. These days the city is the capital of a vast, oil-rich *oblast* (region) stretching all the way to the Arctic Circle. Tyumen has a businesslike drive and youthful bustle, best experienced by strolling through the City Park when the weather is good. There's more than enough here to keep you (mildly) entertained for a day or so, but if you have limited time you'd be much better off seeing Tobolsk instead.

From the fine Trinity Monastery to well beyond the bus station, the main thoroughfare is ul Respubliki. The train station lies around 1km south of ul Respubliki at the end of ul Pervomayskaya.

City maps and bus-route plans are sold at **Knizhny Magazin** (Книжный магазин; Poliklinika Bldg, Privokzalnaya ul 28a; ⊗8.30am-6pm Mon-Sat, 9am-4pm Sun) near the train station and more expensively at **Knizhnaya Stolitsa** (Книжная Столица; ul Respubliki 58; ⊗10am-7pm). They can also be found at newspaper kiosks throughout the city.

◉ Sights

Trinity Monastery
MONASTERY

(Троицкий монастырь; ul Kommunisticheskaya 10) Riverside Trinity Monastery is undoubtedly Tyumen's most appealing architectural complex. Its kremlin-style crenellated outer wall is pierced by a single gate tower. Behind, black and gold domes top the striking 1727 Peter & Paul Church, whose soaring interior is emphasised by a giant, seven-level candelabra and decorated with murals.

To get to the monastery, walk west out of the city to the end of ul Respubliki or take buses 14 or 30 from the city centre. Both also

stop at the nearby 1791 **Krestovozdvizhenskaya Church** (Крестовоздвиженская церковь; ul Lunacharskogo 1). This attractive church is even more photogenic seen across the ferric-brown river from tree-lined Bergovaya ul with its sprinkling of curiously twisted **old wooden houses** (старые деревянные дома), notably numbers 73 and 53. If the weather is good, it's a pleasant 40-minute walk back into the centre of town from the monastery.

City Park
PARK

Take a stroll in the pedestrianised City Park (Svetnoi Bulvar) with all the students, new mums and roller skaters. If you get peckish, grab a snack from one of the many fast-food stalls and cafes. The park also contains a big wheel and other fairground attractions.

Znamensky Cathedral
CHURCH

(Знаменский собор; ul Semakova 13) With its voluptuously curved baroque towers, the 1786 Znamensky Cathedral is the most memorable of a dozen 'old' churches which have recently come back to life following years of neglect.

Saviour's Church
CHURCH

(Спасская церков; ul Lenina 41) Saviour's Church is structurally similar to Znamensky, but unfortunately lacks the quiet backstreet location.

Archangel Mikhail Church
CHURCH

(Храм Михаила Архангела; ul Turgeneva) The attractive Archangel Mikhail Church sits at the top of a hill leading down to streets full of even more old wooden houses.

STRADDLING THE CONTINENTS

The Ural Mountains have numerous monuments marking the border between Europe and Asia. Interestingly, the border was thought to be the Don River by the Ancient Greeks, but Yekaterinburg's founder Vasily Tatishchev drew it at the Ural Mountains in the mid-18th century, based on ideas of the day.

One of the more historic monuments is located 40km west of Yekaterinburg near Pervouralsk. It was erected in 1837 to commemorate a visit by Tsar Alexander II, who drank wine there and inadvertently began a favourite pastime of locals – drinking a glass in Europe and another glass in Asia (as if you needed an excuse!). To reach the monument, take a taxi (about R1000 if you order in advance) to Pervouralsk or one of the very frequent buses 150 or 180 from the Severny bus station (R60). They also stop at the Institut Svyazi at ul Repina 15.

In an attempt to make this geographic landmark more accessible to intercontinental travellers, the city has erected a new border marker, more conveniently located just 17km out of Yekaterinburg and looking a little like a mini Eiffel Tower. This one is more kitsch, but a taxi will take you out there for about R500. Ekaterinburg Guide Centre can organise a trip for R1050 to R2950 per person, depending on the number of people.

Tyumen

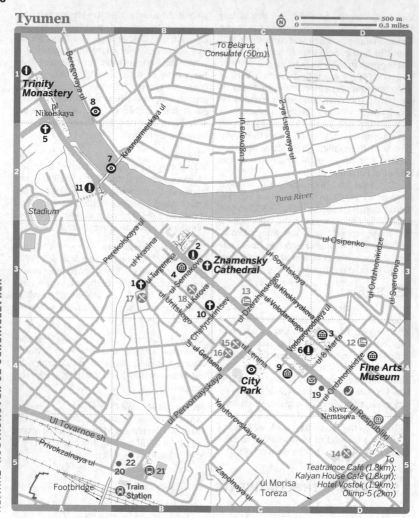

YEKATERINBURG TO KRASNOYARSK TYUMEN

Fine Arts Museum
MUSEUM

(Музей изобразительного искусства; ul Ordzhonikidze 47; admission R270; ☺10am-6pm Tue-Sun) The Fine Arts Museum has an impressive and eclectic collection, ranging from ornate window frames saved from the city's old wooden houses to tiny, intricately carved bone figures produced by Siberian artists. Also puts on some impressive one-off exhibitions.

Lovers Bridge
BRIDGE

(Мост влюблённых; ul Kommunisticheskaya) A short walk from the monastery on the way back into town, Lovers Bridge is a local landmark covered in appropriately romantic graffiti. Some guy called Sasha had just declared his everlasting love for a certain Katya when we were in town (the paint was still wet!).

WWII Monument
MONUMENT

(ul Kommunisticheskaya) Opposite Lovers Bridge, this unusual WWII monument features a Soviet woman piercing the heart of a winged reptilian creature. The embodiment of evil, we assume.

Tyumen

Top Sights

Civil War Monument MONUMENT
(Монумент в честь Гражданской войны; ul Respubliki) To the right of Selskhoz Academy (Сельсхоз Академия), this monument is dedicated to locals who died during battles against the Western-backed White Army immediately after the 1917 Bolshevik Revolution.

Lenin Statue MONUMENT
(Памятник Ленину; Tsentralnaya pl) Flanked by the sturdy buildings of the Tyumen Oblast **Parliament** (Дом Советов) and the **former House of Soviets** (Бывший Дом Советов), now a local government administrative building, Lenin gazes down on skateboarders in the summer months.

House-Museum of 19th- & 20th-Century History MUSEUM
(Музей истории дома XIX-XX вв; ul Respubliki 18; admission R100; ⏲9.30am-4.30pm Tue-Sun) This museum contains artefacts from Tyumen's past and is housed in the city's finest carved cottage. For more examples of wooden houses, take a walk along ul Turgeneva.

Sleeping

Many hotels in Tyumen will only accept foreigners if they have booked in advance via an officially recognised travel agency. The hotels listed below are willing to accept independent, foreign travellers, and all offer complimentary breakfasts.

TOP CHOICE **Hotel Vostok** HOTEL €€
(Гостиница Восток; ☎205 350; www.vostok-tmn.ru; ul Respubliki 159; s/tw R3150/3350; 📶) This former Soviet monstrosity has seen a massive facelift (inside, at least) and now boasts modern, plush rooms with friendly, helpful staff. Within walking distance of the centre.

Hotel Tura HOTEL €€
(Гостиница Тура; ☎/fax 282 209; www.hotel-tura.ru; ul Melnikayte 103a; s/tw/d R2400/2950/3600) This compact hotel near the Vostok has pleasant, if slightly anonymous, rooms with shower booths. Also has a small sports bar (beer R70 to R110).

Hotel Tyumen LUXURY HOTEL €€€
(Гостиница Тюмень; ☎494 040; www.hoteltyumen.ru/en; ul Ordzhonikidze 46; s/d R6500/8700; ❄📶) Tyumen's top hotel offers everything you would expect at a price to match. The complimentary breakfast is one you'll want to linger over.

Prezident Hotel HOTEL €€€
(Президент Отель; ☎/fax 494 747; ul Respubliki 33; s/d/ste R3200/4000/5500; ❄📶) Central and sleek, the Prezident's rooms are fully equipped, but lack a certain charm. If you want to splash out on a hotel, you'd be much better off staying at Hotel Tyumen.

Olimp-5 HOTEL €€
(Олимп-5; ☎273 667; www.olimp5.info/en; ul Respubliki 204; s/d R2300/2900; 📶) This heavily advertised hotel is some way from the centre. Rooms are modest but sufficient and there is free wi-fi in the 1st-floor cafe. Take bus 15 (25 minutes) from the **central**

market to the Воровского bus stop near a red-and-white Lukoil filling station. From here, it's an obvious five-minute walk down a side street. Or take a taxi for R250.

Resting rooms
HOSTEL €

(комнаты отдыха, komnaty otdykha; s/d from R300/500) Some way from the centre, Tyumen's clean and functional resting rooms are not ideal for the sights.

✖ Eating & Drinking

TOP CHOICE Yermolaev
RUSSIAN €€

(Ермолаев; www.ermolaev72.ru; ul Kirova 37; meals R450-950; ☺noon-1am) This spacious bar-restaurant is done up in a wooden, rustic style and serves filling traditional Russian meals. The Siberian mushroom soup (R165) is recommended, as is the *kvas* (a drink of fermented rye bread water). Also has a large selection of beers (R100 to R190), including some home-brewed options, plus genuine Cuban cigars (from R1100). Check out the summer garden if the weather is good.

Malina Bar
BAR €€

(Малина Бар; ul Pervomayskaya 18; meals R400-800; ☺24hr; 🛜) Opposite the City Park, the trendy Malina Bar is popular with a young crowd and their laptops. The eclectic menu runs from Italian food to sushi to pancakes. Also offers a good range of teas, wines and beers (R120 to R250).

Cherry Orchard
CAFE €€

(Вишневый Сад; ul Lenina 46; meals R400-800) The flowery Cherry Orchard offers pastries, Italian food and sushi along with real English ales (R120 to R250) in a cosy building just down from City Park.

Kalyan House Café
CAFE €

(Кальян Хаус; ul Respubliki 155а; meals R300-500; ☺24hr; 🛜) Near the Vostok hotel, this spacious cafe does great breakfasts (R99) and has free wi-fi round the clock. Specialises in flavoured water pipes (from R700).

Teatralnoe Café
CAFE €

(Театральное Кафе; ul Respubliki 36/1; meals R350-550) This refined theatre-themed cafe features tasty cakes, warming soups and a wide selection of teas and coffee.

Yerevan
RUSSIAN, CAUCASIAN €€

(Ереван; ul Turgeneva 19; meals R500-800; 🍴) Opposite the Archangel Mikhail Church, the Yerevan restaurant is located in a cosy, renovated cellar and offers a choice of Russian,

European and south Caucasus food. Worth popping into if you get peckish while walking back into town from Trinity Monastery.

❶ Information

Main post office (Почтамт; ul Respubliki 56; ☺8am-8pm Mon-Sat, 9am-6pm Sun)

Telephone office (Тюмень Телеком; ul Respubliki 51; internet per 30min R40; ☺24hr)

Tyumen.ru (www.tyumen.ru) Has air and railway timetables plus information on local weather, cinema listings etc.

Web Khauz (Хауз; ul Respubliki 61; internet per hr R70; ☺11am-8pm) Down the stairs to the left; follow the blue signs.

❶ Getting There & Away

Train

Trains depart from Tyumen to all Trans-Siberian destinations. There are around eight trains a day to Novosibirsk, with the first and last leaving just after and before midnight (*platskart/kupe* from R1680/3680). There is a useful overnight rail connection to Omsk (*platskart/kupe* R880/1824, 8½ hours, 10.19pm). Seven daily trains (4½ hours) serve Tobolsk. The most convenient leaves at 7.10am (R1127/569). There is one train a day to Tomsk (R3200/2100, 22 hours) at 8am.

The ticket offices are just inside the entrance to the recently renovated station, on the right.

Air

There are four daily flights to Moscow (R4300 to R7000, three hours) and two direct flights a week to St Petersburg (R8021, 3½ hours, Thursday and Sunday).

❶ Getting Around

Tyumen's relatively shiny train station is located some 1.5km southwest of the centre. Bus 25 serves Hotel Vostok and passes near the bus station – to get here, hop off at the Neptun/Stroitel stop, then walk a block east, crossing the big clover-leaf junction of uls Permyakova and Respubliki. Taxis between the bus and train stations cost R100.

Bus 13 from the train station loops around to Hotel Neftyanik; switch to frequent buses 30 or 14 in front of the Prezident Hotel for the Trinity Monastery. These follow ul Respubliki westbound but return along ul Lenina.

Tobolsk   Тобольск

📍3456 / POP 101,000 / ☺MOSCOW +2HR

Once Siberia's capital, Tobolsk is one of the region's most historic cities, sporting a magnificent kremlin and a charmingly decrepit old town. The city is off the Trans-Siberian main line but direct overnight trains to both Yekaterinburg and Omsk make getting here straightforward. Tobolsk can also be reached easily from Tyumen.

The centre of the Russian colonisation of Siberia, the city was founded in 1587. Its strategic importance started to wane in the 1760s, when it was bypassed by the new Great Siberian Trakt (post road). However, until the early 20th century it remained significant as a centre for both learning and exile. Involuntary guests included Fyodor Dostoevsky en route to exile in Omsk, and deposed Tsar Nicholas II, who spent several doomed months here in 1917.

Buses from the inconvenient train station (some 10km north) give visitors a dismal first impression. Concrete drabness reaches a glum centre around the Hotel Slavyanskaya, but don't be put off. Tobolsk's glories begin 3km further south around the splendid kremlin. Immediately beyond and below the kremlin, the old town sinks into the Irtysh's boggy flood plain. The initial view of the old town has been spoiled slightly in recent years by the construction of new office and apartment buildings, but it's still well worth a wander for the views of the kremlin alone.

◉ Sights

Kremlin
HISTORIC BUILDING

(◉grounds 8am-8pm) Within the 18th-century tower-studded walls of the kremlin are the intriguing but disused **Trading Arches** (Гостиный двор) and the glorious 1686 **St Sofia Cathedral** (Софийский собор). Less eye-catching from the outside, but with splendid arched ceiling murals, is the 1746 **Intercession Cathedral** (Покровский собор). Between the two is a 1799 **bell tower**, built for the Uglich bell, which famously signalled a revolt against Tsar Boris Godunov. The revolt failed; in a mad fury, Godunov ordered the bell to be publicly flogged, detongued and banished to Tobolsk for its treacherous tolling. A tatty copy of the bell is displayed in the **Museum of the Spiritual Cultures of Western Siberia** (Архиерейский дом; admission R50; ◉10am-4pm Wed-Sun), an otherwise entertaining museum within the elegant Arkhiereysky mansion.

Deputy's Palace
MUSEUM

(Дворец Наместника; admission R150; ◉10am-6pm Tue-Sun) Just to the right of the kremlin, this 18th-century former administration building houses a museum detailing Tobolsk's

time as the capital of Siberia. Features historical artefacts, paintings and documents. Some English language info, but you'll get much more out of it with some Russian.

Fine Art Museum
MUSEUM

(Музей изобразительного искусства; ul Oktyabrskaya 1; admission R100, video cameras R200; ◉10am-6pm Wed-Sun) Built in 1887 for the 300th anniversary of the founding of Tobolsk, the Fine Art Museum has a celebrated collection of WWI-era Russian avant-garde canvases. It also has a newly acquired mammoth skeleton and a display of bone carvings.

FREE Minsalim Folk Trade
ART GALLERY

(✆240 909; raznoe72@bk.ru; ul Oktyabrskaya 2; ◉9am-5pm) Minsalim will happily demonstrate how he turns antler fragments into a range of detailed figures, as well as give visitors the low-down on Tobolsk's history and culture. His son and some members of staff speak English.

Tobolsk Rayon Administration Building
HISTORICAL BUILDING

(Административный районный центр Тобольска; ul Mira 10) The less-eye-catching Tobolsk Rayon Administration Building was the home in exile of the last tsar, and where he was reportedly tortured, before his fateful journey to execution in Yekaterinburg.

Pryamskoy Vzvoz
LANDMARK

(Прямской Взвоз) Wooden stairs lead beneath the kremlin's Pryamskoy Vzvoz (gatehouse) to the wonderfully dilapidated old town full of weather-beaten churches and angled wooden homes sinking between muddy lanes.

Mendeleyev Mansion
HISTORICAL BUILDING

(Дом Менделеева; ul Mira 9) Near the little 1918 **Victory Chapel** (Часовня Победы), where uls Mira and Kirova meet at a small square, is the grand Mendeleyev mansion, which once housed the family of the famous scientist.

Archangel Mikhail Church
CHURCH

(Церковь Архангела Михаила; ul Lenina 24) The attractive Archangel Mikhail Church has a colourfully restored interior. The character of Tatiana Larina in Pushkin's epic *Eugene Onegin* is said to have been modelled on Natalya Fonvizina, a Decembrist wife who prayed here.

Zachary & Elisabeth Church
CHURCH

(Церков Захария и Елизаветы; ul Bazarnaya pl) The 1759 Zachary & Elisabeth Church, with

Tobolsk

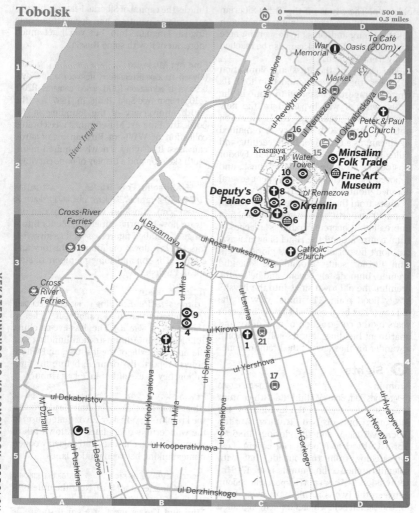

N
0 ————————————— 500 m
0 ————————————— 0.3 miles

To Café
Oasis (200m)

War
Memorial

Market
18

13

14

ul Sverdlova

ul Revolutsionnaya

ul Remezova

ul Oktyabrskaya

Peter & Paul
Church

16

15

20

Krasnaya
pl

Water
Tower

**Minsalim
Folk Trade**

10

8

**Fine Art
Museum**

**Deputy's
Palace**

2

pl Remezova

7

3

Kremlin

6

River Irtysh

Cross-River
Ferries

ul Bazarnaya
pl

ul Rosa Lyuksemborg

Catholic
Church

19

12

Cross-
River
Ferries

ul Mira

ul Lenina

9

4

ul Kirova

1

21

11

ul Yershova

17

ul Semakova

ul Dekabristov

ul
M.Dzhalil

ul Khokhryakova

ul Mira

ul Semakova

ul Gorkogo

ul Alyabyeva

ul Novaya

5

ul Pushkina

ul Basova

ul Kooperativnaya

ul Derzhinskogo

its soaring black-tipped spires, is extremely photogenic.

🛏 Sleeping & Eating

Tobolsk has seen something of a tourist boom in recent years and now has a number of new or refurbished hotels. All of the hotels listed here – with the exception of the Slavyanskaya and the resting rooms – are perfectly located for the kremlin and offer complimentary breakfasts. Despite increased tourism, there is still no restaurant scene to speak of.

TOP CHOICE **Hotel Sibir**   HOTEL €€

(Гостиница Сибирь; ☎222 390; pl Remezova 1; s/tw/ste R2000/2400/3800) Right across from the kremlin, the Sibir's rooms are comfortable and spacious. Rates include a good breakfast and the cosy 24-hour restaurant (meals R350 to R600, beer R90 to R130) does a mean fish soup (*pokhlebnaya ribnaya;* R120).

Hotel Georgievskaya   HOTEL €€

(Гостиница Георгиевская; ☎246 614; www.hotel -georgievskaya.ru; ul Lenekaya 35; s/d R2600/3500; ❄🤖) Right behind a Dostoyevsky statue, the Hotel Georgievskaya has stylish and plush

Tobolsk

◎ **Top Sights**

◎ **Sights**

◎ **Sleeping**

◎ **Transport**

rooms, as well as a sumptuous restaurant (meals R500 to R850, beer R100 to R175).

Hotel Novy Tobol   HOTEL €€

(Гостиница Новый Тобол; ☑246 614; ul Oktyabrskaya 20; s/d R1500/2000) The badly signposted Tobol has sparse but functional rooms with mostly uninspiring views. It's to the left of the Hotel Georgievskaya. There's a bowling alley and a disco on the ground level if you get bored.

Resting rooms   HOSTEL €

(комнаты отдыха, komnaty otdykha; ☑495 222; train station; 12/24hr from R125/250) Clean and friendly, the location is utterly impractical for visiting the city, but ideal if you're arriving late or waiting for an early-morning connection. Cheaper singles are without their own toilet.

Hotel Slavyanskaya   HOTEL €€€

(Гостиница Славянская; ☑399 101; www.slavjanskaya.ru; 9-iy Mikro-Rayon, pr Mendeleeva; s/tw/d from R2200/4400/6000; ❈⊛❂) Astonishingly well appointed for rural Siberia, the big, modern Slavyanskaya has fully Western-standard comforts. Its only disadvantage is the uninspiring new-town location. Offers internet access for R50 an hour in the lobby.

TOP CHOICE **Romanov Restaurant**   RUSSIAN €€€

(Ресторан Романов; ☑399 104; meals R1000-1500; ⊙noon-11pm) Housed in Hotel Slavyanskaya, the Romanov restaurant features succulent 19th-century Russian dishes and is furnished with mock period furniture. Also has a family portrait of Russia's last tsar and his family on the ceiling. Dmitry Medvedev visited here shortly after winning Russia's 2008 presidential elections.

Café Oasis   CAFE €

(Кафе Оазис; ul Oktyabrskaya 44; meals R150-250; ⊙9am-5am) The dark and murky Café Oasis does cheap shashlyk and beers (R60 to R90). Attracts some shady characters as the evening drags on.

❶ Information

Nashtobolsk.ru (http://Nashtobolsk.ru) Handy info on Tobolsk.

Post office (Почта; Komsomolsky pr 42; ⊙8am-6pm) Has an attached telephone office.

❶ Getting There & Away

Train

From Tobolsk there are trains at 9.55am and 11.51pm on odd dates to Novosibirsk (platskart/kupe R3750/R1400 for morning train, R5210/2300 for evening train, both 24 hours). The same train goes to Omsk (R2145/1010, 14 hours). More than 10 trains a day make the short journey to Tyumen (R700/1600). The good resting rooms are up a flight of stairs in the right-hand corner of the 2nd floor, if you are facing the platform. There are also left-luggage facilities on the 1st floor. The station's remoteness and random drunks mean it is not the nicest place to hang around in late at night.

❶ Getting Around

Bus 4 and marshrutka 20 link the isolated train station, new town and kremlin. Buses 1, 3 and 10 travel past the kremlin and loop around the old town. Bus 1 passes the mosque. Taxis from/to the station cost around R200. Eight buses per day to various destinations pass Abalak.

WORTH A TRIP

DETOUR: ABALAK MONASTERY

From Tobolsk, a quiet road skirts the border of the ancient Tatar kingdom of Isker, continuing 25km to Abalak. Here the region's holiest **monastery** was built on the site of a miraculous materialising icon, which was bought up and last spotted in Australia long after the Soviets had turned the church into a tractor barn. There are charming views over the bend in the Irtysh River, with 249 steps leading down to the riverbank. Today the monastery is working again, with a copy of the icon over the door. The monastery, like many remote holy places in Russia, is home to recovering alcoholics and drug addicts, hence the guys and girls wandering around with scars and alcohol-ravaged faces.

A short walk from the Abalak monastery is the **Abalak Holiday Centre**, which offers 'relaxation for not only the body, but also the soul'. The centre, set in pristine countryside, is based around the charming and tiny **Hotel Belaya Sova** (☑331 279; www.abalak.su; R5000-R7000). The rooms, of which there are only three, are cosy beyond belief and have fine views of the nearby river. The hotel **restaurant** (meals R500-950, beer R100-150) serves hearty and tasty traditional Russian food. Animal sculptures and an on-site playground mean kids won't be bored either. Worth a visit even if you don't plan to stay.

Omsk Омск

☑3812 / POP 1.145 MILLION / ⊘MOSCOW +3HR

With its modest sights hidden behind busy roads, this big industrial city is not worth a special detour. You may find it a convenient stopover to break up long journeys.

The trendiest street is ul Lenina (улица Ленина), home to several witty statues including an odd Soviet 1963 'slacker' brass workman emerging from a manhole, and Luba's bench, featuring the wife of a 19th-century city governor reading Pushkin.

If you're looking to kill more time, the **Art Museum** (Омский областной музей изобразительных искусств Врубеля; ☑313 677; ul Lenina 23; admission R100; ⊘10am-6pm Tue-Sun) displays a lot of fussy decorative arts. The rectilinear 1862 building, a historical curiosity in itself, was built as the Siberian governor's mansion and hosted passing tsars. In 1918–19, however, the building was home to Admiral Kolchak's counter-revolutionary government. In the gardens behind the museum there is a **war memorial** (Памятник Великой Отечественной войны) and a **Lenin statue** (Памятник Ленину).

Other attractive buildings include the ornate **Drama Theatre** (Омский академический театр драмы; ☑244 065; www.omskdrama.ru; ul Lenina; ⊘cash desk 10am-7pm) and the **Assumption Cathedral** (Успенский собор; pl Lenina), rebuilt after the collapse of the USSR. The Lenin statue that stood nearby was removed in the 2000s – rumour has it a pious official decided the great

atheist had no business being anywhere near a house of God.

🛏 Sleeping

Hotel Mayak HOTEL €€€

(Гостиница Маяк; ☑/fax 315 431; www.hotel-mayak.ru; ul Lermontova 2; s/tw R2860/4125) In the rounded end of the vaguely ship-shaped art-deco river station, the Mayak has small, stylish rooms with artistic lines and good bathrooms. Popular with Western business travellers. Friendly staff and good complimentary breakfast.

Hotel Turist HOTEL €€

(Отель Турист; ☑316 419; www.tourist-omsk.ru; ul Broz Tito 2; s/d from R2500/3500) A fairly central address with decent, bright rooms and fine views of the river from upper floors. Complimentary buffet breakfast.

Resting rooms HOSTEL €

(комнаты отдыха, komnaty otdykha; train station; s/d R1200/1700) While slightly impractical for the sights, the clean and secure resting rooms should suffice as a base if your time in Omsk is limited. Exit the main station, turn left and find the door before the baggage *kassa* (ticket office).

🍴 Eating

TOP CHOICE **Tamada** GEORGIAN €€

(Тамада; ul Gagarina 3; meals R450-800; ⊘10am-midnight; ☑) This extremely friendly, spacious cellar restaurant serves fine Georgian food amid a setting of fake ponds and vibrant oil paintings. The *khachapuri* (bread baked with cheese filling; R140) and *lobiyo* (spicy red beans stewed in vegetables; R90) are recommended. Just off ul Lenina in a courtyard. They'll even call a taxi for you when you are ready to – probably reluctantly – leave.

Chashka INTERNATIONAL €€
(Чашка; www.hollcup.ru; 3rd fl, Pyat Zvyozd shopping mall, ul Karla Libknekhta; meals R400-650; 🛜) Cosy and professional, Chashka offers a range of dishes from traditional Russian home cooking to reasonably spicy Asian.

ℹ️ Information

Internet Available in the train-terminal lobby for R100 per 30 minutes.

Post office (Почтамт; ul Gertsena 1; ⊗8am-7pm Mon-Sat, 10am-5pm Sun)

ℹ️ Getting There & Away
Train

There are two trains a day for Tobolsk at 5.54am and 1.24pm (*platskart/kupe* R1300/3100, 13¾ hours), and one a day for Tomsk at 5.42pm (R1450/3900, 14 hours). There are over 15 trains a day to Novosibirsk (R950/2010, 9½ hours). There are eight trains a day to Krasnoyarsk, departing from 6.30am to 11.10pm (from R1290/2260, around 22 hours).

Omsk's impressively grand train station is at the southern end of lengthy pr Marksa, some way from the main sights. Ticket offices are to the right of the entrance to the station. The **internet cafe** is to the left. There are handy left-luggage facilities in the basement (take the stairs to the left of the entrance).

Numerous air-ticket agencies at the **river station** (pl Bukhgoltsa) sell rail tickets (R150 commission).

Air

Flight destinations include Moscow (R6500 to R8000, six daily) and St Petersburg (R9400, direct flights on Wednesday).

Boat

On a green barge behind the river station is the **Rechflot** (Речфлот; ☎398 563; ⊗9am-7pm) ticket office. Also here is the jetty for hydrofoils to Tevriz via Tara and for ferries cruising the Irtysh River to Salekhard (1st/2nd/3rd class R3750/1750/1300, six days) via Tobolsk (R2100/1000/950, two days) roughly three times monthly.

ℹ️ Getting Around

From the train station, trolleybus 4 and *marshrutka* 335 run along pr Marksa to pl Lenina, past the main post office. Ul Lenina runs

parallel to pr Marksa – it's on the left if you are heading into the city. Bus 60 crosses the Irtysh to the **airport** (☎517 570; Inzhenernaya ul 1) while trolleybus 7 or the faster *marshrutka* 366 head for the bus station. Construction began on Omsk's metro system back in 1985, but its opening has been delayed and rescheduled for years.

Novosibirsk Новосибирск
☎383 / POP 1.5 MILLION / ⊗MOSCOW +3HR

It may be the capital of Siberia and Russia's third-biggest city by population size, but there isn't actually very much to see in Novosibirsk. As compensation of sorts, there are a lot of nightclubs and restaurants, and the city has a fairly lively music scene.

Novosibirsk grew up in the 1890s around the Ob River bridge built for the Trans-Siberian Railway. Named Novo-Nikolaevsk until 1925 for the last tsar, it grew rapidly into Siberia's biggest metropolis, a key industrial and transport centre exploiting coalfields to the east and mineral deposits in the Urals.

Despite its daunting scale, Novosibirsk has a manageably simple centre focused on pl Lenina. The city's main axis, Krasny pr, runs through this square linking most points of interest. **Dom Knigi** (Дом книги; Krasny pr 51; ⊗10am-8pm Mon-Sat, to 7pm Sun) has maps.

👁 Sights

Opera & Ballet Theatre THEATRE
(Театр оперы и балета) Novosibirsk's pl Lenina is dominated by this huge, silver-domed theatre. Bigger than Moscow's Bolshoi, its grand interior alone makes performances one of the city's highlights. In front, the dashing **Lenin statue** (Памятник Ленину) is flanked by waving partisans vainly trying to direct the chaotic traffic.

Local Studies Museum MUSEUM
(Краеведческий музей; Krasny pr 23; admission R250; ⊗10am-5.30pm Tue-Sun) In an elegant mansion, the Local Studies Museum has Altai shaman coats, cutaway pioneer houses and some splendid religious artefacts.

State Art Museum MUSEUM
(Художественный музей; Krasny pr 5; adult/student R180/100; ⊗10am-5.20pm Tue-Fri, from 11am Sat & Sun) The State Art Museum has an extensive collection including icons, Siberian art and works by celebrated spiritual Russian painter Nikolai Rerikh (known in English as Nicholas Roerich).

Novosibirsk

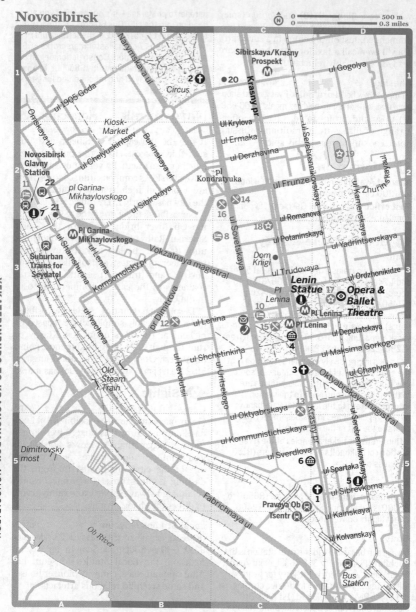

WWII 'Family' Statues   MONUMENTS
Platform 1 at the main train station boasts two WWII 'family' statues depicting a mother and her small daughter and a father and his small son waving off relatives to WWII –

it was from this station that many Siberians went directly to the front.

Chapel of St Nicholas   CHURCH
(Часовня Святителя Николая; Krasny pr) The pretty little Chapel of St Nicholas was said

Novosibirsk

to mark the geographical centre of Russia when it was built in 1915. Demolished in the 1930s, it was rebuilt in 1993 for Novosibirsk's centenary. Today it is an oasis of calm in the bustling city centre.

Cathedral of the Ascension   CHURCH
(Вознесенский собор; ul Sovetskaya 91) The gold-domed 1914 Cathedral of the Ascension has a wonderful, colourful interior with a soaring central space that's unexpected from its fairly squat exterior appearance.

Alexander Nevsky Cathedral   CHURCH
(Собор Александра Невского; Krasny pr 1a) The 1898 Alexander Nevsky Cathedral is a red-brick Byzantine-style building with gilded domes and colourful murals.

Monument to First Traffic Light MONUMENT
(cnr ul Serebrennikovskaya & ul Sibrevkoma) This humorous monument is based at the rumoured site of the city's first ever traffic light.

🛏 Sleeping

The majority of Novosibirsk hotels are poor value by Siberian standards. On top of this, many will only accept foreigners when booked through a tour agency (incurring booking fees and commission).

TOP CHOICE ⟩ **Avenue**   MINIHOTEL €€
(Авеню; ☎227 0534; www.avenu.vipngs.ru; ul Sovetskaya 57; s/d R3400/3600; ☎) Set in a quiet, leafy residential courtyard, this mini-hotel is by far the best place to stay in Novosibirsk. Just a 10-minute walk away from the centre, all the great-value rooms are spacious, stylish and comfortable. Also has free wi-fi, a sauna for rent (R600 per hour) and a good complimentary breakfast. And staff are friendly to boot!

Hotel Novosibirsk   HOTEL €€€
(Гостиница Новосибирск; ☎220 1120; www.hotel-novosibirsk.ru; Vokzalnaya magistral 1; s/tw/ste R3960/4410/8100) Boasting awesome views of the city centre from its upper floors, this formerly glum Soviet-era tower has been transformed in recent years into a plush modern hotel. Odd pricing scheme means it's possible (we managed it) to get two nights for the price of one if you arrive after midnight for the first night. The complimentary breakfast is tasty and filling.

Resting rooms   HOSTEL €
(Комнаты отдыха, komnaty otdykha; ☎229 2376; 2nd fl, Novosibirsk Glavny station; 12/24hr from R550/1100) As clean and pleasant as you could reasonably expect. It's frequently full.

Hotel Tsentralnaya   HOTEL €
(Гостиница Центральная; ☎222 3638; fax 227 660; ul Lenina 3; s/tw without bathroom R1300/1600) The cheapest rooms here are depressing cupboard-like hovels, while the more expensive options are no less welcoming. No complimentary breakfast, either. That said, it is centrally located. And relatively cheap. For Novosibirsk, at least.

YEKATERINBURG TO KRASNOYARSK NOVOSIBIRSK

✕ Eating & Drinking

TOP CHOICE **Perchini** ITALIAN €
(Перчини; www.perchini.ru; Krasny pr 25/1; meals R350-400; ☺10am-1am; 🛜🍴) If all the *pelmeni* (Russian ravioli) and pancakes are getting you down, visit Perchini. With a choice of seven freshly made pastas to choose from and a range of imaginative sauces, this simple yet effective restaurant is popular with a young, hip crowd. Just behind the Ploshchad Lenina metro station, on the 4th floor.

Tiflis CAUCASIAN €€
(Тифлис; www.tiflisnsk.ru; ul Sovetskaya 65; meals R400-800; 🍴) This atmospheric tavern-cavern offers the most authentic Georgian cuisine in town. The filling and delicious *khachapuri po-adzharski* (Georgian cheese bread with a raw egg swimming in the middle) is well worth a try.

Pechki-Lavochki RUSSIAN €
(Печки-Лавочки; ul Frunze 2; meals R250-450) Rustic interior and traditional Russian food at great prices. Try the *kvas*. Can get smoky and noisy in the evenings (beer from R75).

Café Bliss BREAKFAST €
(ul Lenina 20) This modestly named cafe does great pancakes (from R50) and fresh juices as well as good breakfast deals (R150). A nice way – and place – to start the day.

5Nizza BAR €
(5Ницца; ul Lenina 3; beer R90-150, snacks R70-130; ☺noon-2am) Sharing its name with a popular Moscow reggae group, this lively bar is on the 1st floor of the Hotel Tsentralnaya.

Nikolaevskaya Pelmennaya RUSSIAN €
(Николаевская Пельменная; Krasny pr 13; meals R150-210; ☺10am-11pm) Cheap and simple *pelmeni* with meat and fish fillings in an equally modest cafe located beneath a sex shop.

☆ Entertainment

Opera & Ballet Theatre THEATRE
(Новосибирский государственный академический театр оперы и балета; ☎227 1537; www.opera-novosibirsk.ru; Krasny pr 36; admission R200-4000; ☺Oct-Jun) For classical culture don't miss an evening at this gigantic theatre. Ticket prices depend on seats and performances. Morning shows are a lot cheaper.

Spartak Stadium FOOTBALL STADIUM
(Стадион Спартак; ☎217 0474; www.fc-sibir.ru; ul Frunze 15) This 12,500-capacity venue is the home of local football team, Sibir. Games are usually played on Saturday, and tickets cost from R200 to R700. Matches are advertised on posters around the city.

Rock City NIGHTCLUB
(Рок Сити; ☎227 0108; www.rockcity.ru; 3rd fl, Krasny pr 37; tickets from R350; ☺from noon) Novosibirsk's top spot for everything from Latin dancing to heavy-rock concerts. It's above the Old Irish pub.

ℹ Information

Main post office (Главпочтамт; ul Lenina 5; ☺8am-9pm Mon-Fri, to 7pm Sat & Sun)

Telephone office (Междугородный телефонный пункт; ul Sovetskaya 33; ☺24hr)

ℹ Getting There & Away

Train

The city's huge 19th-century train station, **Novosibirsk Glavny** (ul Shamshurina 43), has 14 platforms and sees the departure of numerous daily long-distance trains. There are great views of the station from the upper floors of Hotel Novosibirsk.

For Moscow (48 to 55 hours via Omsk, Tyumen and Yekaterinburg), comfortable flagship train 25 – the *Sibiryak* – (*platskart/kupe* R5400/10,500, 6.40am, on even-numbered dates) is also one of the fastest. The journey from Moscow to Novosibirsk also leaves on even dates and departs at 4.20pm. The much cheaper 239 (R4600/8410, 5.17am, odd-numbered dates) follows the same route but takes six hours longer and isn't quite as comfortable. For Krasnoyarsk, train 12 (R1750/3680, 10.20pm, 11 hours, odd-numbered dates) is well timed. For Tomsk, consider train 38, which leaves at 12.56am (R800/1350, 5½ hours).

Air

Novosibirsk's **Tolmachyovo airport** (☎216 9841; http://en.tolmachevo.ru) is 30km west of the city, off the Omsk road. The website gives timetables. There are a number of direct daily flights to Moscow (from R6000 to R10,000), as well as five direct flights a week to St Petersburg (from R9000). There are also flights to Vladivostok, as well as Bangkok and Běijīng.

Bus

From the **bus station** (Krasny pr 4) around 20 daily buses serve Tomsk (R420, five hours). For roughly double the price, shared taxis shave an hour or more off those times.

ℹ Getting Around

From the centrally located train station, take trolleybus 2 to Severny airport, *marshrutka* 1122

DETOUR: SEYATEL – RAILWAY LOCOMOTIVE MUSEUM

To get to the Seyatel – Railway Locomotive Museum (admission R80; ⊙11am-5pm Sat-Thu) take *marshrutka* 1015 (R30, 30 minutes) from Novosibirsk Glavny train station to Seyatel train station. The museum has over 100 exhibits, ranging from Soviet steam engines to pre-revolution carriages. You can return to central Novosibirsk the same way or jump on an hourly *elektrichka* (suburban train; R50).

---

to Tolmachyovo airport or *marshrutka* 1212 to the bus station via pl Lenina. The metro (trip ticket R12) has a major north–south line running beneath Krasny pr and across the river to Studencheskaya and pl Karla Marksa. For the main train station you'll need metro stop pl Garina-Mikhaylovskogo, which is on a second three-stop line that intersects with the major line at Sibirskaya/Krasny pr. Generally *marshrutky* are handier within the centre. A **taxi** (⊡299 4646) to the airport can be ordered by phone and costs around R500. The journey from the centre takes about 30 to 40 minutes, depending on traffic.

Tomsk　　　　　　Томск

⊡3822 / POP 524,000 / ⊙MOSCOW +3HR

Well worth a short detour off the main Trans-Siberian route, hip and friendly Tomsk is the kind of town where it's no surprise to come across a gigantic and unexplainable Tom Waits poster on the main street (pr Lenina). A university city with half a dozen major academic establishments – around one in every five residents of Tomsk is a student – it has a youthful, intellectual atmosphere.

One of Siberia's oldest cities, Tomsk was founded in 1604 and was a major trade outpost before the founding of Novosibirsk (then Novonikolaevsk) and the subsequent relocation of the Trans-Siberian Railway line.

Magnificent in snow, but pleasant at any time of the year, Tomsk also boasts endless examples of fine wooden buildings and an animated cafe and art scene. The city has enjoyed a reputation as the 'cultural capital of Siberia' since the 1960s, when artists, writers and theatre and film directors were invited to take up residence here.

Tomsk is also excellent for semi-aimless strolls: try exploring the numerous side streets that branch off the central pr Lenina to discover some truly memorable buildings and river views.

The bus station and Tomsk 1 (main) train station sit together about 2km southeast of the centre.

⊙ Sights

Ploshchad Lenina　　　　HISTORICAL SITE

Central pl Lenina isn't really a square so much as a jumbled collection of beautifully restored historic buildings interspersed with banal Soviet concrete lumps. The frustrated **Lenin statue** (Памятник Ленину), now relegated to a traffic circle, points at the ugly concrete of the Drama Theatre, apparently demanding 'build more like that one'. Fortunately, nobody's listening. The theatre is flanked instead by the splendid 1784 **Epiphany Cathedral** (Богоявленский собор), the **former trading arches** (Бывший Гостиный двор) and the elegant 1802 Hotel Magistrat. Topped with a golden angel, in a second circle beside Lenin, is the recently rebuilt **Iverskaya Chapel** (Иверская часовня; ⊙10am-6pm), whose celebrated icon is dubbed 'Tomsk's Spiritual Gateway'.

TOP CHOICE Oppression Museum　　　MUSEUM

(Музей НКВД; ⊡516 133; rear entrance, pr Lenina 44; admission R30; ⊙9am-6pm Mon-Fri) A former NKVD (proto-KGB) prison, this gloomy building is now a memorable Oppression Museum. Tours are recommended, but are only in Russian. Failing that you can just wander round yourself. Look out for the stunning Gulag map, the system of Soviet labour camps depicted as an uncountable mass of red dots across the territory of the former USSR. Outside the museum there are two **monuments to victims of Stalinist repression** – the larger to local victims, the second to Poles slaughtered by Uncle Joe and his cronies.

TOP CHOICE Chekhov Statue　　　MONUMENT

On the riverbank, opposite Slavyansky Bazar restaurant, this cheeky Chekhov statue was sculpted in bronze for the 400th anniversary of the city's founding.

WWII Memorial　　　MONUMENT

(Лагерный сад) A Tomsk landmark, this moving mother and son monument is at the very southern end of pr Lenina. The beautiful birch-tree park here is a local favourite for strolls, not least for its fine views across the Tom River.

Tomsk

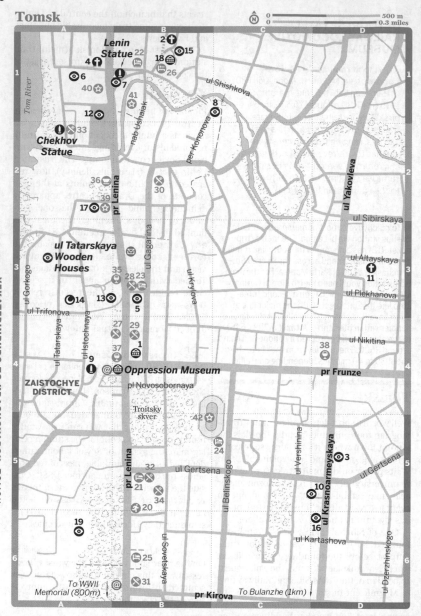

University HISTORICAL BUILDING
(Томский Государственный Университет)
The classically colonnaded main buildings
of the university lie in resplendently leafy
grounds, giving Tomsk the soubriquet 'Ox-
ford of Siberia'. There's not much open to the
public, but there's nothing to stop you taking
a walk around the grounds.

Tomsk Art Gallery ART GALLERY
(Художественный музей; www.artmuseum
.tomsk.ru; per Nakhanovicha 5; admission R60;

Tomsk

⊘10am-7.30pm Tue-Sun) Features a wide range of exhibits, from modern art to religious icons.

Atashev Palace HISTORICAL BUILDING
(Краеведческий музей; pr Lenina 75) Built for gold-mining entrepreneur Ivan Atashev in 1842, the Atashev Palace was once used as a church, hence the incongruous steeple tower and wonderful organ hall where concerts are held.

Ulitsa Tatarskaya HISTORICAL AREA
(улица Татарская) Contains some fine examples of Tomsk's famed 'wooden-lace' architecture – the carved windows and tracery on old log and timber houses. The street is reached via the steps beside a lovely old house at **prospekt Lenina 56** that contains shops selling DVDs, seeds and secondhand clothes in its basement.

Ulitsa Gagarina HISTORICAL AREA
Also well worth strolling along – look out for the picturesque **former 'hunter's house'** (Бывший дом охотника) at number 42.

Ulitsa Krasnoarmeyskaya HISTORICAL AREA
Home to some great examples of wooden mansions, including the spired, bright-turquoise **Russian-German House** (Российско-Немецкий дом; ul Krasnoarmeyskaya 71); the **Dragon House** (Дом Дракона; ul Krasnoarmeyskaya 68), which is home to a clinic; and the fan-gabled **Peacock House** (Дом Павлина; ul Krasnoarmeyskaya 67a). Ul Dzerzhinskogo is worth a look too.

Kirov's House HISTORICAL BUILDING
(Дом Кирова; per Kononova 2) This is where the doomed communist mastermind Sergei Kirov lodged in 1905.

CHEKHOV ON TOMSK – 'BORING CITY, DULL PEOPLE'

Not everyone falls in love with Tomsk. Playwright Anton Chekhov who visited the city on his way to Russia's Far East – certainly didn't. 'Tomsk isn't worth a damn,' he wrote in his diary. 'A boring city...with dull people.' He also described it as 'a drunken city' where there were 'no beautiful women at all'. He also complained that a waitress had wiped a spoon 'against her backside' before handing it to him. But then, as legend has it, he did almost drown while crossing the Tom River, so maybe he was feeling grumpy. The city had its revenge though. In 2004, on Tomsk's 400th anniversary, a caricature of the famous writer was unveiled, in the form of a bronze statue entitled 'Anton Pavlovich [the writer's patronymic] through the eyes of a drunk lying in a ditch'.

Znameniye bozhyey materi Church CHURCH
(Храм знамение Божьей матери; ul Voykova 14) This attractive church is all the more photogenic for the wooden house that stands alongside it.

Resurrection Hill HISTORICAL AREA
This was the location of Tomsk's original fortress, and the replica of its 'Golden Gate' that stands on it today was built in 2004 for the city's 400th anniversary celebrations.

Tomsk History Museum MUSEUM
(Исторический музей Томска; admission R40; ⊙11am-5pm Tue-Sun) This well-presented museum has resprouted its wooden **lookout tower** (Смотровая башня; admission R35): try to spot the seven historic churches from the top. The stone just outside the museum entrance marks the founding of the city.

Ascension Church CHURCH
(Вознесенская церковь; ul Oktyabrsky Vzvoz) This Gothic edifice with five gold-tipped black spires has great potential as a Dracula movie set. A truly massive bell hangs in its lurid-pink belfry.

Ozero Beloye POND
(Озеро Белое; ul Bakunina) Popular with mums and kids, students and the odd very optimistic fisherman, this sizeable pond is a good place to chill with a drink and a pie

from one of the nearby food stands. On the same street, named after the 19th-century 'father of anarchy' and one-time student in the city, is a **Catholic church** (Католическая церковь) dating from 1833.

Old Believers' Wooden Church CHURCH
(Деревянная церковь старообрядцев; ul Yakovleva) This cute church is worth a look if you've got any energy left, though its surroundings are relatively uninteresting.

Peter & Paul Cathedral CHURCH
(Петропавловский собор; ul Altayskaya 47) A Byzantine-style brick cathedral that dates from 1911.

Red Mosque MOSQUE
(Красная мечеть; ul Tatarskaya 22) This modest mosque, dating from 1904, was used as a vodka factory by the atheist Soviets, but was reopened to worshippers in 1997. The friendly imam is always up for a chat with foreigners.

Tours

Tomskturist WALKING TOURS
(Томсктурист; ☎528 179; pr Lenina 59; ⊙9am-7pm Mon-Fri, 11am-4pm Sat) Tomskturist can arrange individual walking tours of the city, with English-, French- and German-speaking guides. It also sells air and train tickets for a small commission. It's based in a lovely wooden house opposite the university.

Sleeping

TOP CHOICE **Toyan** BOUTIQUE HOTEL €€€
(Тоян; ☎/fax 510 151; www.toyan.ru; ul Obrub 2; s/tw/ste from R3900/5900/6900; ☎) Toyan, built in 2008, is both intensely elegant and laid-back – and well worth splashing out on if your budget will run to it. Rooms are tastefully decorated, somehow managing to be both stylish and homely. The more expensive have great views of central Tomsk. All rooms have wi-fi. The complimentary breakfast isn't bad either!

Bon Apart HOTEL €€€
(Бон Апарт; ☎534 650; www.bon-apart.ru; ul Gertsena 1a; s/tw/ste R3400/4500/5700; ✳) The quiet and professional Bon Apart offers small but plush rooms for reasonable prices. It's centrally located, and the complimentary breakfast in the next-door family restaurant is tasty and satisfying.

Hotel TGU HOSTEL €
(Гостиница ТГУ; ☎534 352; 5th fl, pr Lenina 49; dm/s/tw R600/1000/1500) Uniquely good

value, these clean, bright rooms have kettle, fridge and fully equipped new bathrooms (except in the dorms, which share facilities between two triples). Staff are very friendly, to boot. In term-time, reservations are essential (R150 booking fee), but dropping in might work in midsummer. Enter from the rear of the building and climb the stairs to the 5th floor. No lift and no breakfast either. Midnight curfew.

Hotel Siberia　　　　　　　　HOTEL €€
(Гостиница Сибирь; ✆/fax 527 225; www .hotelsibir.tomsk.ru; pr Lenina 91; s/d/ste R2800/3100/5000) This centrally located old hotel is extremely popular, despite its largely unimaginative singles and doubles. It does, however, offer great suites with real fireplaces for R5500, if you are feeling wealthy. Dinner is available on top of complimentary breakfast for R300 extra, but you'd be better off eating elsewhere.

Hotel Sputnik　　　　　　　　HOTEL €€
(Гостиница Спутник; ✆526 660; www.sput nik.tomskturist.ru; ul Belinskogo 15; s/d/tw/tr R850/1700/1900/2400; @ 🛜) The winner of Tomsk's first hotel competition in the 1990s, the Sputnik today remains a decent place to stay, let down only by its dodgy plumbing (there was brown sludge coming out of the taps when we stayed) and doors so flimsy that cheers from the nearby stadium could probably knock them down. Complimentary breakfast is hardly worth getting up for. The cheapest singles and doubles have shared toilets. Wi-fi in every room.

Hotel Magistrat　　　　　　　HOTEL €€€
(Гостиница Магистрат; ✆511 111; www .magistrathotel.com; pl Lenina 15; s/d/ste R5500/6500/9500; ❄ 🛜) Behind the palatial 1802 facade, the luxurious rooms are brand new in a comfortable international style though, sadly, without historical idiosyncrasies. English is spoken and the restaurant is lavish.

Resting rooms　　　　　　　　HOSTEL €
(комнаты отдыха, komnaty otdykha; Tomsk I train station; 3hr s/tw R400/R700) Perfectly clean rooms with shared toilets, and shower and televisions. Curfew 1am to 5am.

✕ Eating

Slavyansky Bazar　　　RUSSIAN €€€
(Славянский Базар; pr Lenina 10; meals R800-1200; 🛜) On the bank of the Tom River, Slavyansky Bazar is one of the most upmarket restaurants in the city, housed in a 19th century building. Black caviar dishes start at R800. Chekhov ate at an earlier incarnation of the present-day establishment in 1890. The food was one of the few things he liked about the city.

Coffee House Leto Café　　　CAFE €
(Кофейная Лето; ul Gagarina 2; meals R300-500; 🛜) One half of a bright-yellow building that also contains a decent sushi restaurant, Bamboo (Бамбук). Sunny and bright and features food with hard-to-get ingredients such as pumpkin, pesto and real feta cheese. Also does real coffee.

Café Fondue　　　　　　　　　CAFE €
(Кафе Фондю; ul Belentsa 14; meals R300-500; ⊙noon-1am Sun-Thu, to 2am Fri & Sat) This small and welcoming cafe was conceived of during the unlikely fondue craze that swept Russia in the mid-2000s. Serves cheese and chocolate fondue options, as well as more traditional Russian and European dishes. Just off pr Lenina 97.

Café Modern　　　　　　　EUROPEAN €
(Кафе Модернь; pr Lenina 83; meals R400-600; 🛜) An atmospheric cafe with painstakingly restored plasterwork tracery on the high ceilings and Gustav Klimt prints on the walls. European menu, with large selections of salads, pastries, desserts, teas, wines (from R75 a glass) and beer (R75 to R120).

Vechny Zov　　　　　　　　RUSSIAN €€
(Вечный Зов; www.vechzov.tomsk.ru; ul Sovet-skaya 47; meals R550-900; ⊙noon-4am) Named after a popular Soviet TV serial, this is one of Tomsk's top dining options and boasts a mock Siberian ranch outside and a cosy antique-filled-home feel inside.

Obzhorni Ryad　　　　　　　RUSSIAN €
(Обжорний Ряд; ul Gertsena 1; meals R250-400; ⊙11am-11pm) Next to the Bon Apart hotel, this good-value family restaurant's name translates as Guzzler's Row. The indoor adventure playground means it's great for those with kids, but anyone else might find all the noise distracts from the simple but tasty Russian dishes.

Korchma u Tarasa　　　　　UKRAINIAN €
(Корчма у Тараса; pr Lenina 51; meals R250-450; ⊙noon-1am) This cheap and friendly cafe specialises in Ukrainian favourites such as salo (salted pig fat; R95 a plate) and borsch

(R70). It's a pick-and-mix kind of place, but there's not much for vegetarians.

Inzhir
ASIAN €€

(Инжир; pr Kirova 66; meals R400-750) Right opposite the train station, Inzhir (Fig) offers a variety of eastern food, from Uzbek dumplings to Turkish kebabs. It's often full in the evening.

Babulini Pelmeshki
RUSSIAN €

(Бабулини Пельмешки; pr Lenina 54; ☉10am-8pm) The cheap and satisfying *pelmeni* and *vareniki* (dumplings; R50 to R130) in this basement cafe come with a range of fillings, from lamb and fish to cheese and cherry. Look out for the cardboard cut-out of a babushka on the street.

🍷 Drinking

TOP CHOICE **Jazz Café**
CAFE, BAR

(Кафе Джаз; www.jazz-cafe.tomsk.ru; pr Lenina 46; beer R100-250; ☉11am-midnight Sun-Thu, noon-2am Fri & Sat; 🖉) A hip and literally underground basement hang-out with an extensive drinks and food menu (meals R500 to R700). We liked the vegetarian borsch (R90) and the screenings of old black-and-white films. There's live jazz, including frequent US guests, most weekends (cover R250 to R400).

Sibirsky Pub
PUB

(Сибирский Паб; www.siberian-pub.ru; pl Novosobornaya 2; Guinness per pint R240; ☉noon-3am) Siberia's first British pub was founded over a century ago by a certain Mr Crawley, an Anglo-Egyptian albino who'd got stuck in Tomsk after touring with a circus freak show. Today's pub is no relation. Bands play live at weekends (cover charge).

Bar House City
BAR

(Бар Хаус Сити; pr Lenina 64; beers R80-120; ☉noon-2am) This popular student hang-out gets extremely lively in term time. Check out the summer garden if the weather is good.

Bulanzhe
CAFE

(Буланже; 2nd fl, pr Lenina 80; espresso R40; ☉8am-midnight) Tomsk's answer to Starbucks serves great coffee and stuffed bliny (from R60). There is another branch at ul Krasnoarmeyskaya 107.

People's Bar & Grill
BAR

(pr Lenina 54; beer from R90; ☉noon-2am) Beer, pizza and thumping dance music in a central location. Can get crowded at weekends. Enter from the rear of pr Lenina.

☆ Entertainment

TOP CHOICE **Tom Tomsk FC**
STADIUM

(Томь Томск ФК; 🖉527 967; www.football.tomsk.ru; ul Belinskogo 15/1) The home of Siberia's top football club. If you're lucky you might catch a game against 2008 UEFA Cup champions Zenit, or one of the big Moscow sides. Tickets cost from R300 upwards. There is also a shop selling Tomsk scarves, T-shirts – and even slippers – attached to the stadium. It's open 11am to 7pm Monday to Friday, and on weekends on home match days.

TOP CHOICE **Human Puppets Theatre**
2+ku
PUPPET THEATRE

(Театр живых кукол 2+ку; www.2ky.tomsk.ru; Yuzhny Per 29; admission from R200) Housed in a quaint log cabin near the WWII memorial (take ul Savinikh all the way down until you can't go any further), this one-man, homey 'robotic puppet' theatre is a real experience, and one you don't need to understand Russian to appreciate.

Aelita Theatre
THEATRE

(Театр Аэлита; 🖉516 131; www.aelita.tsk.ru; pr Lenina 78) Eclectic offerings from rock concerts to Indian dance to experimental plays. An adaption of *Clockwork Orange* was on when we visited.

Philharmonia
CONCERT HALL

(Филармония; 🖉515 965; pl Lenina 1) Classical music and great big-band jazz.

Drama Theatre
THEATRE

(Драматический театр; 🖉512 223; pl Lenina 4)

❶ Information

Afisha (www.afisha.westsib.ru) Has concert and cinema details.

Main post office (Почтамт; pr Lenina 95; ☉9am-7.30pm Mon-Fri, 8am-5pm Sat, 9am-5pm Sun) Stamps, but no postcards of Tomsk!

Netcafe (Неткафе; pr Lenina 44; from per hr R19; ☉24hr) All-night internet access costs R110. Other branches at pr Lenina 32 and pr Frunze 57 open 10am to 8pm.

Sent to Siberia (www.senttosiberia.wordpress.com) An American Fulbright scholar's humorous and affectionate account of life in Tomsk.

Tomsk (www.tomsk.ru09.ru) Interactive maps, photos and general info.

TOM TOMSK FOREVER! *MARC BENNETTS*

It's tough being a supporter of FC Tom Tomsk, Europe's most easterly top-flight football team. The side's nearest Premier League opponents are based in Perm, over 2000km away, and a trip to Moscow means either a four-and-a-half-hour flight or just over two days on a train.

'It's a hobby, I guess, just like anything else,' Tomsk fan Sergei told me during a visit to the team's 15,000-capacity Trud stadium. 'We all go off together – a group of up to 30 of us usually travel…I gave the recent trip to Chechnya a miss though, only two lads supported the team that day.'

Tomsk almost went under in 2009 after cash-strapped regional authorities cut funding. It took the personal intervention of Vladimir Putin to keep the side afloat. Look out for the billboard featuring the ex-KGB man at the stadium. The words on it read: 'There must be football in Tomsk.'

The side has never seriously challenged for honours, but has been a regular fixture in the Premier League since promotion in 2004. Go along and give it your support if you are in town. It managed a creditable 1-1 draw with 2004 UEFA Cup champions CSKA Moscow when I went along.

ⓘ Getting There & Away

Train

If you are taking a detour off the Trans-Siberian line to Tomsk, two trains a day, at 2.01am and 6.48am, pass through the tiny town of Taiga (*platskart/kupe* R390/800, two hours). From Tomsk there are services on odd-numbered dates at 8.20am to Moscow's Yaroslavsky vokzal (R5491/10,061, 56½ hours). For Omsk, there are two trains on odd-numbered dates. The first leaves at 4.10am (R1276/3288, 15 hours) while the second departs at a more convenient 8.20am (R1868/2968). A train to Irkutsk leaves on even-numbered dates at 4.28pm (R1800/3165, 34 hours).

Tomsk's two-storey-high station was opened in 1896 and has two platforms. Ticket offices are to the right of the entrance. Resting rooms are up the stairs from the central hallway.

Air

Bogashevo Airport (☑270 084), 22km southeast of Tomsk, has three flights a day to Moscow (R10,700, 8.40am, 9am, 9.30am), plus some local regional services on **Tomskavia** (☑412 466; www.tomskavia.ru, in Russian; ul Yelizarovkh).

The choice is much wider from Novosibirsk's Tolmachyovo Airport, to which there are five direct buses a day (R320, five hours) from Tomsk bus station.

Bus

For Novosibirsk, shared taxis (from R750, 3½ hours) are much faster than buses from the central bus station (R415, 5½ hours, over 15 daily). Buses to Kemerovo leave five times a day (R310, two hours). There are also useful buses to Novokuznetsk (R500, seven hours, four daily) and Barnaul (R530, nine hours, two daily).

ⓘ Getting Around

Handy bus 7 runs from near the somewhat inconveniently located train station, along pr Frunze, up pr Lenina, then east again on ul Pushkina. *Marshrutka* 11 shows you the wooden houses along ul Krasnoarmeyskaya, 29 does the same for ul Tatarskaya via pl Yuzhny, while bus 4 goes west from the train station and then runs north the length of pr Lenina. Hop on and off buses 9, 12 and 17, which all also go along pr Lenina.

Lake Baikal: Krasnoyarsk to Ulan-Ude

Route Info

» Distance: 1544km
» Duration: 24 to 26½ hours
» Time zones: Moscow +4, Moscow +5

Best Places to Stay & Eat

» Baikaler Eco-Hostel (p199)
» Hotel Sayen (p192)
» Derevenka (p200)
» Nikita's Homestead (p204)
» Kochevnik restaurant (p193)
» Baatarai Urgöö restaurant (p211)

Why Go?

If you've made it this far from Moscow or Běijīng, this 1500km ribbon of rail and sleeper is where things get interesting. Arguably the most varied stretch of the line, bid farewell to your *provodnitsa* (carriage attendant) along its length for some of the most memorable experiences Siberia has to offer.

Most making a single halt on their Trans-Sib odyssey do so in Irkutsk, surely Siberia's most engaging city. Only 350 years old in 2011, this grande dame packs in heaps of history, and when you tire of ornate facades, stuccoed palaces and streets of traditional timber dwellings, glorious Lake Baikal, the unrivalled highlight of any rail trip across Russia, is just a short bus ride away.

When the tracks finally peel away from Baikal's mind-boggling vistas, Trans-Sibbers find themselves in the Republic of Buryatia, an exotically Asian retreat of Buddhist temples and shamanist traditions, increasingly coming under the gravitational pull of southern neighbour Mongolia.

When to Go
Irkutsk

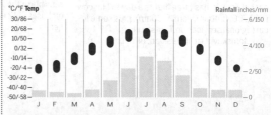

Nov–Mar Snuggle into a Russian Railways blanket and watch the snowbound Siberian landscapes.

Mar Take a stroll on Lake Baikal when Siberia's harsh winter turns its surface hard as steel.

Jul & Aug Join holidaying Russians on the sandy beaches of Lake Baikal's eastern shore.

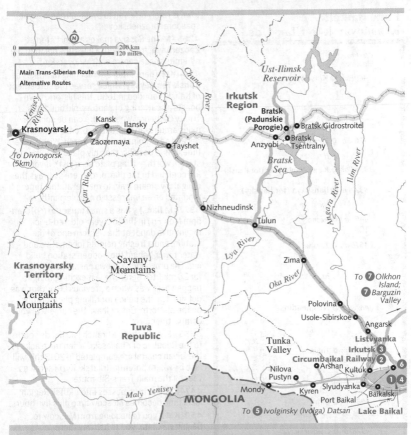

Krasnoyarsk to Ulan-Ude Highlights

1 Gazing out across the **southern shores of Lake Baikal** from a slow train between Irkutsk and Ulan-Ude (p179), possibly the most attractive section of the entire Trans-Sib line

2 Taking the ultimate Trans-Sib branch line trip on the **Circumbaikal Railway** (p203) for some stunning Baikal vistas

3 Admiring the ostentatious 19th-century architecture of **Irkutsk** (p187), once known as the 'Paris of Siberia'

4 Walking, cycling or hitching a lift across frozen **Lake Baikal** (p197)

5 Mooching with the monks at Buddhist temple **Ivolginsky (Ivolga) Datsan** (p213)

6 Navigating a section of the **Great Baikal Trail** between Listvyanka (p197) and Bolshie Koty (p202)

7 Enjoying a couple of meditative days on wonderful **Olkhon Island** (p202) or getting away from it all in the often overlooked **Barguzin Valley** (p214)

The Route

Krasnoyarsk to Tayshet

4098KM FROM MOSCOW Heading east out of Krasnoyarsk your fellow travellers will not have even fathomed there's a foreigner in their midst before the train crosses the 1km-long **Yenisey River bridge**, whose 1898 original won a gold

medal at the 1900 Paris Expo (along with the Eiffel Tower). The Yenisey traditionally marks the unofficial border between Eastern and Western Siberia.

4229KM There's no stop for the *Rossiya*, but most other trains do shudder to a halt at **Uyar**, where you can admire the dinky cream and green art nouveau–style station. Understandably the

Lake Baikal:
Krasnoyarsk to Ulan-Ude

LAKE BAIKAL: KRASNOYARSK TO ULAN-UDE

West to Moscow

4098km	**Krasnoyarsk**
	2hr, 30min
4265km	**Zaozernaya**
	1hr, 10min
4344km	**Kansk-Yeniseysky (for Kansk)**
	30min
4377km	**Ilanskaya (for Ilansky)**
	1hr, 10min
4453km	**Reshoty**
	1hr
4515km	**Tayshet**
	2hr, 20min
4678km	**Nizhneudinsk**
	1hr, 40min
4795km	**Tulun**
	2hr
4934km	**Zima**
	1hr
4978km	**Golovinskaya**
5022km	**Cheremkhovo**
5118km	**Usole-Sibirskoe**
5145km	**Angarsk**
5178km	**Irkutsk Sort.**
5185km	**Irkutsk**
	2hr, 30min
5311km	**Slyudyanka**
	2hr, 20min
5477km	**Babushkin**
	2hr, 10min
5640km	**Ulan-Ude**

To Severobaikalsk (1064km – 17hr)

3hr, 15min

East to Vladivostok

town is rarely referred to by its full name, Uyar-spasopreobrazhenskoye.

4265KM The *Rossiya* makes a short stop at **Zaozernaya**, from where a line runs north to the off-limits space centre of Krasnoyarsk-45.

4344KM There's more screeching of brakes at **Kansk-Yeniseysky**, which serves the settlement of Kansk. Founded in 1636, this historic town boasts a scattering of century-old buildings, a Trinity Cathedral whose spire can be seen for miles around, an impressive bronze war memorial and an illuminated victory arch. With ample time, this is possibly the only place on this entire stretch worth getting off to see (just). If you are confined to the platform, there's always the obligatory steam train to marvel at, this time mounted on an impressive marble plinth.

4377KM **Ilansky** has a small **museum** (⊙10am-5pm Mon-Fri) in the 100-year-old, red-brick locomotive depot at the western end of the station, and a freshly painted locomotive and water tower behind the wooden station building. The *provodnitsa* allows passengers to roam for 20 minutes here. The last exciting thing to happen here was when a previous LP author was detained by the police for taking photographs on the platform. Better leave the camera in your compartment.

4453KM At Reshoty a branch line heads south to the Republic of Khakassia. When the tracks to the Tuvan capital are completed in 2013 this will also be where potential Irkutsk–Kyzyl services veer off the main Trans-Sib route.

4474KM The train passes into Irkutsk Region; local time becomes Moscow time plus five hours.

4501KM If you're heading from Moscow to Běijīng via Chita, you're halfway there.

4515KM The *Rossiya* stops for just two minutes at **Tayshet**, long enough for most people. Other trains can loiter here for 20 minutes, giving you time to photograph yet another beached steam loco and its large, newly renovated station building. This is the Trans-Siberian's westernmost junction with the BAM, but most travellers change at Krasnoyarsk for through services to Severobaikalsk and Tynda. Tayshet was once an infamous transit point for Gulag camp prisoners. The town even gets a less-than-complimentary mention in Aleksander Solzhenitsyn's *The Gulag Archipelago* (not recommended reading on a trip to Russia, believe us).

Tayshet to Irkutsk

4515KM TO 4600KM If riding straight through from Moscow, you're now on day three but only halfway to the Pacific. As the railway skirts the foothills of the **Sayany Mountains**, endless taiga and a real sense of wilderness set in.

4644KM Around about now you can crack open a celebratory tub of instant porridge or sachet of three-in-one coffee – you've made it halfway from Moscow to Vladivostok.

4678KM There's a 12-minute stop at mildly historical **Nizhneudinsk**, but as this comes after 11pm on the *Rossiya*, few are distracted from their vodka and bedtime instant noodles. Cossacks first built a small fortress here in 1649 and for over two centuries the town served as an important centre for gold and fur traders. The St Nicholas Church and the regional **museum** (ul Lenina 27; ⊙8am-5pm) entice few off the rails, but an 18km hike along the Uda River to the 20m-high **Ukovsky waterfalls** could make for an adventurous side trip. Further east the landscape flattens out and the forests have been extensively logged.

4795KM The next stop is timber **Tulun**, where you'll have just two minutes to contemplate the merits of the architecturally confident station building. From here a road heads 225km north to **Bratsk** (p254) on the BAM. The town has a far-flung Decembrist Museum but very few visitors.

4934KM There's an overgenerous 30-minute break in proceedings at the former exile town of **Zima**, which translates ominously as 'winter'.

5087KM (No stop for the *Rossiya*.) More translation is required at **Polovina**, whose name means roughly 'halfway' (between Moscow and Vladivostok), which it was in the early 20th century before the line was rerouted in many places.

5118KM From Polovina the train heads southeast and is joined by the Angara River around **Usole-Sibirskoe**, where a shuddering stop may jolt you from your slumber but hopefully not from your bunk altogether. The town supplies much of Russia's salt and many of its matches.

5145KM By the time you reach oil-rich **Angarsk**, where there's a clock museum and a couple of good restaurants if you really want to get off, it's probably time to start collecting your belongings scattered around the compartment if you're alighting at Irkutsk.

5171KM Around the 5171km marker, look north through the trees; 50m beyond the tracks behind two barbed-wire fences are neat rows of decommissioned old tanks and rocket-launcher trucks (without rockets) rusting away thinking of their Cold War heyday.

5178KM Heading west on some services originating in Irkutsk, you may rejoice at having a compartment all to yourself – that is until hordes of locals board at **Irkutsk Sortirovka**, a marshalling yard on the city's western outskirts.

5185KM The train crosses the Irkut River 3km before **Irkutsk** (p187) station. Once nicknamed the 'Paris of Siberia', Irkutsk is the most popular Siberian stop for most transcontinental travellers, notably as a launching point to reach Lake Baikal, 70km further southeast.

KRASNOYARSK TO ULAN-UDE ROUTE PLANNER

Here's a suggested itinerary for continuing from Krasnoyarsk to Ulan-Ude:

Day 1: Take an overnight train from Krasnoyarsk to Irkutsk (18 hours)

Day 2: Arrive Irkutsk, then head out for a tour of the city

Day 3: Bus to Taltsy Museum of Wooden Architecture then on to lakeside Listvyanka for one night

Day 4: Return to Irkutsk; catch train for short hop to Slyudyanka for more lake views and perhaps a ride on the Circumbaikal Railway to Port Baikal

Day 5: Skirt around the picturesque southern shore of Lake Baikal on a day train to Ulan-Ude

Irkutsk to Ulan-Ude

5185KM TO 5321KM Moving on from Irkutsk, the line takes a sharp right where the tracks once continued along the Angara River to Port Baikal, a stretch flooded by the Angara Dam project. The early 1950s rerouting includes the tightest twists and the steepest descent on the entire line (providing great opportunities for photos of the train) just before **Kultuk**, where passengers get their first tantalising glimpse of **Lake Baikal**.

5311KM At **Slyudyanka** (p204) the lake is so close it's tempting to dash down for a quick dip. However, the scheduled stop here – usually no longer than three minutes for the *Rossiya* – means that you could run the very real risk of being stranded in Siberia as the train chugs off without you. If that prospect doesn't appeal, stay on the platform and snap up a snack of smoked *omul* (a fish native to Lake Baikal) from the countless hawkers instead. If the *provodnitsa* won't let you off, perform the transaction through a window (if one will open). For the next 200km or so the stuffy carriages fill with a fishy aroma, especially on hot days. If you've not bought any *omul*, fellow travellers are certain to offer you some.

5352KM There's no stop for the *Rossiya* between Slyudyanka and Ulan-Ude as it races through the late morning and early afternoon around the southern shores of Lake Baikal. You may be glad the train doesn't hang around in **Baikalsk**, where the smell of boiled rotten cabbage is emitted by the Baikalsk cellulose plant, the biggest polluter of Lake Baikal. Despite the wretched pong, many come to ski at the resort just above the town.

5352KM TO 5561KM Bag a left-facing window for this stretch (right-facing if you're travelling west), considered by most seasoned Trans-Sibbers as the most scenic on the entire line. The tracks run just metres from the lake at some points, at others delving into thick forest. The views across Baikal are superb at any time of year, but especially on crisp sunny days in late winter when the entire lake freezes into one mammoth block of white ice. If you're stuck on the 'wrong' side of the train, don't despair – the views of the Khamar Daban Mountains are equally impressive. Imagine the 18th- and 19th-century tea caravans from China emerging over the ridges to catch their first glimpse of Lake Baikal below.

5391KM Some trains such as the 340 and 362 make a two-minute halt at the lakeside fishing village of **Vydrino**. You've now entered the fascinating Republic of Buryatiya, which is in the same time zone as Irkutsk Region. On this stretch of the Trans-Siberian this is possibly the most worthwhile place to leave the comfort of your compartment. Some 5km to the south lie the Teplye Lakes, wonderful bodies of water cupped by steep wooded hills. The name 'Teplye' means warm and comes from the fact that the water is kept above freezing year round by thermal springs. There's a cheap *turbaza* (holiday camp) nearby.

5420KM Just after another Baikal fishing settlement called **Tankhoi** the train rumbles over a bridge spanning the fast-flowing Pereyomnaya River, one of 300 rivers feeding Lake Baikal. The village is home to the headquarters of the Baikal Biosphere Reserve in which you now find yourself.

5477KM The village of **Babushkin** (for Mysovaya) is a blur from the *Rossiya*, but in the early 20th century, before the line around the south of Lake Baikal was built (and occasionally afterwards), this was where the icebreakers *Angara* and *Baikal* carrying their cargoes of wagons and passengers from Port Baikal would dock. Both of the ships were built in Newcastle-upon-Tyne and the *Angara* (p189) survives as a museum in Irkutsk. The *Baikal* went to the bottom of Lake Baikal during the Russian Civil War, though no one is sure exactly where it lies.

5530KM The Trans-Sib waves farewell to Lake Baikal's bluer-than-blue waters just before the village of **Posolskaya**. A road from here heads to Lake Baikal and the village of Posolskoe, where a recently renovated and very picturesque monastery looks out across the water.

5561KM Around half an hour after Posolskaya the *Rossiya* zips through **Selenga** (for Selenginsk), the nearest stop to the incredible **Selenga Delta** (p215).

5561KM TO 5641KM At Selenga the Trans-Sib joins up with the Selenga River carrying its load of silt (and Mongolian pollution) to Lake Baikal.

The line hugs the left riverbank as far as Tataurovo, after which it crosses to the right bank, just in time to arrive at **Ulan-Ude** (p206).

Krasnoyarsk Красноярск

☑ 391 / POP 974,000 / ⊙MOSCOW +4HR

Bustling, affluent and backed by attractively jagged foothills, Krasnoyarsk enjoys a more appealing setting than most typically flat Siberian cities. While its architecture isn't particularly inspiring, amid the predominantly unaesthetic concrete of post-WWII industrialisation rise a few outstandingly well-embellished timber mansions and a sprinkling of art nouveau curves. Pleasant river trips, the nearby Stolby Nature Reserve and the region's best concert halls, theatres and museums make Krasnoyarsk an agreeable place to break the long journey between Tomsk (612km west) and Lake Baikal.

The city centre's grid layout is easy to navigate, but there's no central square. The zoo and Stolby Reserve are over 10km west along the Yenisey's south bank.

◉ Sights

Dotted about Krasnoyarsk are some very fine wooden houses, notably ul Lenina 88 and 67 and ul Karla Marksa 118. There are also many art nouveau facades such as pr Mira 76, ul Lenina 62 and ul Parizhskoy Kommuny 13.

TOP CHOICE **Stolby Nature Reserve** NATURE RESERVE
Arguably Krasnoyarsk's greatest attractions are the fingers and towers of volcanic rock called **stolby**. These poke above the woods in the 17,000-hectare Stolby Nature Reserve (Zapovednik Stolby) south of the Yenisey River. To reach the main concentration of rock formations, you could try to find the track (7km long) near Turbaza Yenisey (bus 50), but there is much easier access via a year-round **chairlift** (Фуникулёр; R160; ⊙Tue-Sun) belonging to the ski resort. From the top, walk for two minutes to a great viewpoint or around 40 minutes to reach the impressive **Takmak Stolby**. Better still is to take a tour with SibTourGuide (p186; priced according to itinerary). Infected ticks are dangerous between May and July and tick protection or predeparture encephalitis jabs are essential at this time.

Regional Museum MUSEUM
(Краеведческий музей; www.kkkm.ru; ul Dubrovinskogo 84; admission R100; ⊙11am-7pm Tue-

Sun) Housed in an incongruously attractive 1912 art nouveau Egyptian temple, this is one of Siberia's better museums. Arranged around a Cossack explorer's ship, surprisingly well presented exhibitions across the two floors examine every facet of the region's past, from Cossacks and gentlemen explorers to the Tunguska explosion and local fauna, pre-revolution institutions to religious art. Highlights include the 20th-century 'nostalgia' section on the upper level and the 4m-tall mammoth skeleton looking like something straight off a Hollywood museum movie set. There are touch-screen games for kids throughout and a decent cafe to look forward to at the end.

Surikov Museum-Estate
MUSEUM

(Музей-усадьба Сурикова; ul Lenina 98; admission R59; ⊙10am-5.30pm Tue-Sat) The Surikov Museum-Estate preserves the house, sheds and vegetable patch of 19th-century painter Vasily Surikov (1848–1916). The heavy-gated garden forms a refreshing oasis of rural Siberia right in the city centre. More of Surikov's work is on show at the old-school **Surikov Art Museum** (Художественный музей Сурикова; ul Parizhskoy Kommuny 20; admission R50; ⊙10am-6pm Tue-Sun).

Bobrovy Log Ski Resort
SKI RESORT

(Лыжный курорт Бобровый Лог; www.bobrovy log.ru; ul Sibirskaya 92) Below the stolby the slap and swish of skis and snowboards can be heard at the Bobrovy Log ski resort. Snow canons keep the slopes going well into May, and in the summer months the Roedelbahn (a kind of downhill forest roller coaster), a pool and regular sports events keep the fun level high. Ask at the English-speaking year-round **information centre** about ski hire, lift passes and other tickets. Bus 37 runs from the train station direct to the resort.

Roev Ruchey Zoo
ZOO

(Зоопарк Роев Ручей; www.roev.ru; adult/child R160/30; ⊙9am-9pm) Take bus 50 or 50A to this expanding, relatively humane zoo near the Bobrovy Log ski resort to see numerous Siberian species.

Rezanov Statue
MONUMENT

(pr Mira) A statue of Nikolai Rezanov, an 18th-century Russian diplomat and nobleman who died in the city in 1807, gazes towards a slightly temporary-looking arch raised in 2003 to mark the site of the first Cossack stronghold.

Resurrection Church
CHURCH

(Благовещенская церковь; ul 9 Yanvarya) The top-heavy but elegant Resurrection Church (1804–22) was decapitated in the 1930s but given a new tower in 1998–99. Its icon-filled interior billows with incense.

Literature Museum
MUSEUM

(Литературный музей; ul Lenina 66; admission R30; ⊙10am-6pm Tue-Sun) This quaint museum within a glorious 1911 merchant's mansion occasionally hosts classical-music performances.

Chasovnya Chapel
HISTORICAL BUILDING

(Часовня; top of Karaulnaya Hill) For wonderful views climb Karaulnaya Hill to the little chapel which features on the Russian 10-rouble banknote (now slowly being replaced with a coin). At midday there's a deafening one-gun salute here.

SV Nikolai
MUSEUM

(СВ Николай; admission R50; ⊙10am-8pm) Permanently docked below an ugly brown-concrete exhibition centre (formerly the Lenin Museum) is the SV *Nikolai*, the ship that transported Vladimir to exile in Shushenskoe.

Intercession Cathedral
CHURCH

(Покровский собор; ul Surikova) This pleasingly small old church dating from 1795 has an interior of unusually glossed and intricately moulded stucco framing haloed saints.

🛏 Sleeping

There are plenty of accommodation options in Krasnoyarsk, including a couple of budget choices. Though way out of the centre, there are a couple of small peaceful hotels in the Stolby area (south of the river), relatively handy for skiing and trips to the Stolby Nature Reserve. Use bus 50.

For a great insight into local life take an English-speaking homestay organised by SibTourGuide (p186). Most such homestays are in the high-rise Vyetluzhanka area, which is 20 minutes' drive west of the centre but well served by city buses 91, 49 and 43. Prices include a free station pick-up.

CITY CENTRE
Dom Hotel
HOTEL €€€

(📞290 6666; www.dom-hotel24.ru; ul Krasnoy Armii 16a; s/d from R4000/4800; @🛜) Centred around a rather characterless courtyard, the 74 light-filled rooms at Krasnoyarsk's newest hotel are immaculately maintained

Central Krasnoyarsk

and have become a firm favourite among foreigners looking for Western comforts. Staff are courteous and there is an inexpensive restaurant on site. Breakfast costs extra.

Hotel Krasnoyarsk
HOTEL €€€

(Гостиница Красноярск; ☏274 9400; www.hotel krs.ru; ul Uritskogo 94; s/tw from R3860/5320; ✳🛜) Every Soviet metropolis has one: a concrete lumpen hotel celebrating the city's name in metre-high lettering. But unlike many of these stale relics, the sprawling eight-storey Krasnoyarsk is well kept with bright corridors, totally rebuilt full-service rooms and English-speaking receptionists. Rates are also decidedly 'post-Soviet' but at least breakfast is included.

Hotel Metelitsa
HOTEL €€€

(Гостиница Метелица; ☏227 6060; www.hotel -metelica.ru; pr Mira 14; s/d from R3900/R4900; ✳🛜🍽) Intimate, exclusive minihotel of the type favoured by Russia's oil-stained busi-

ness elite and the ugliest gallery of pop stars you're ever likely to see. Every room is done out differently, some with design-mag flair, and bathrooms are far from bog-standard. Staff speak reluctant English and there's a pool where you can pretend you are by an alpine lake. Breakfast included.

Hotel Sever
HOTEL €€

(Гостиница Север; ☏662 266; hotel-sever@mail .ru; ul Lenina 121; s R750-1800, tw R1200-2200) Krasnoyarsk's most central budget option is cheap and friendly with cosmetically improved but loyally Soviet rooms. Pricing has been kept refreshingly straightforward and staff are polite. Breakfast is included in room rates.

Hotel Oktyabrskaya
HOTEL €€€

(Гостиница Октябрьская; ☏227 1926; www.hotel october.ru; pr Mira 15; s R4000-5300, d R5200-6300) Comfortable and professionally run with rooms approximating Western stand-

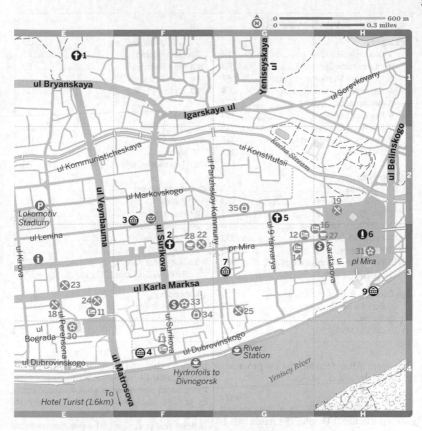

ards, albeit without air-conditioning. Satellite TV includes CNN and some English is spoken. The trendy lobby area has a stylish juice bar. Includes breakfast.

Hotel Ogni Yeniseyya
HOTEL €€

(Гостиница Огни Енисея; ☑227 5262; ul Dubrovinskogo 80; s R750-4600, tw R1350-4350; @🛜) One of the last budget options left, there's a vast selection of rooms here, but whatever you plump for, make sure it has Yenisey views.

Krasnoyarskstroystrategiya
HOTEL €€

(Гостиница Красноярскстройстратегия; ☑227 6911; pr Mira 12; s R630-2100, tw R1260-2960) The only good thing about this place is the dirt-cheap singles. Otherwise, it's unfriendly with, it must be said, smelly, renovated Soviet rooms in need of rehab. Enter from ul Karatanova, if you dare.

Resting Rooms
HOSTEL €

(комнаты отдыха, komnaty otdykha; ☑248 3820; train station; 12/24hr from R320/640) Clean dorm rooms in the train station.

SOUTH OF THE YENISEY
Hotel Turist
HOTEL €€

(Гостиница Турист; ☑276 1900; ul Matrasova 2; s R2280, tw R2640) On a busy roundabout directly across the long Yenisey Bridge from the city centre, this 16-storey Soviet monolith has a variety of rooms with toilet and shower. Some are pleasantly renovated.

STOLBY AREA
Snezhnaya Dolina
HOTEL €€

(Гостиница Снежная Долина; ☑269 8110; www.sneg-dolina.ru; per cottage from R5300, s R700-3200, d R1400-3700; 🏊) This accommodation complex has a hotel, a minimotel and rows of cosy cottages meaning lots to choose from. There's a swimming pool, a tennis court and a decent restaurant, but the main

Central Krasnoyarsk

draw here is the clean air and the proximity to the Stolby and ski slopes.

Turbaza Yenisey   HOTEL €
(Турбаза Енисей; ☎698 110; ul Sverdlovskaya 140/7; d & tw R700) Despite the name this is a two-storey hotel, not a camp. Good-value renovated rooms are simple but neat and share sparkling-clean showers. Some of the pricier doubles have private facilities. There's a glimpse of the river from the small communal terrace but no cafe.

✖ Eating

Krasnoyarsk has the highest concentration of eateries of any Eastern Siberian city with new places springing up all the time. However, most newcomers aim to serve the city's moneyed elite with prices and interiors to match. At the other end of the food chain, self-service canteens abound. For more cheap snacks and picnic supplies head for the extensive **central market** (Центральный Рынок; ul Kerchinskogo; ⊙8am-6pm).

⌂ English School Café   CAFE €€
(www.esc24.ru; ul Lenina 116; mains R70-300; ⊙10am-11pm; @☎▯) With its English-

teacher, expat and traveller clientele, wired castle-themed cellar setting and suitably international menu, every visitor should drop in at this Anglophone sanctuary while in town. The globalised beer menu, inventive coffees, real porridge and top-notch cooking provide good enough reason to come, but it's the five-minute free (yes free!) call to any number in the world from your table, plus free wi-fi, that might have you looking for Lenina 116 sooner rather than later.

Buddha Bar & Lounge   TIBETAN, EUROPEAN €
(ul Karla Marksa 127; mains R100-160; ⊙noon-midnight; ☎▱▯) This low-lit, incense-infused vegetarian cellar eatery and lounge is a calming place to escape the city-centre blare. Order a plate of exotic Tibetan food (*tsampa, momo* and other dishes you won't know) from the English-speaking waitress, then give the bar-top prayer wheel a lazy spin before retreating with a hookah pipe (R400) to the cushioned chill-out lounge where nightly DJs drift chill-out music to a chilled crowd. As if Siberia wasn't chilly enough.

Burzhuy   CAFE €
(Буржуй; 2nd fl, Metropol bldg, pr Mira 10; pelmeni R52, other mains R40-70; ⊙8am-7pm Mon-Sat,

9am-6pm Sun) Cheap and very popular self-service lunch spot where office workers swap chitchat over plates of *pelmeni* (meat ravioli) at formica tables. The 'ear bread' comes with several fillings and sauces, or choose from other hot dishes and salads.

Mama Roma
ITALIAN €€

(pr Mira 50a; pizzas R200-470, pasta R165-465; ⊙11am-1am; ✴🖵) Herb-infused air wafts temptingly out of one of the best Italian eateries in town, where chequered tablecloths and admirable attempts at pasta, risotto and pizza may make you feel you're in Rome or Naples – but only if you've never been there.

Sem Slona
CANTEEN €

(ul Karla Marksa 95; mains R30-70; ⊙24hr) Got a sudden craving for buckwheat at 3am? Then brave the darkened streets and make your way to this all-hours, no-nonsense canteen plating up solid Russian favourites with a growl. The name translates as 'I could eat an elephant' – this being Siberia, a horse just won't do.

Krasnaya Palatka
FAST FOOD €

(Красная Поляна; Bobrovy Log ski resort; meals R150; ⊙10am-10pm) Watch skiers slither down the slopes from the huge circular windows at this film-themed self-service cafeteria. The decor is trendy, but the Russian and international dishes are unexciting and perhaps appreciated more after a long hike or climb in the Stolby.

Miks Patio
FAST FOOD €

(Микс Патио; ul Perensona 20; mains R15-42; ⊙10am-10pm) With budget-airline decor, a menu heavy with Slavic comfort food and prompt service, this is the *stolovaya* (canteen) dragged into the 21st century.

Stolovaya OK
CANTEEN €

(Столовая OK; ul Uritskogo 33; mains R25-40; ⊙10am-6pm Mon-Fri) Well signposted from ul Parizhskoy Komunity, this super-cheap and ultra-basic student canteen keeps both stomachs and wallets happy. Enter from the rear of the building.

🍷 Drinking

Traveller's Coffee
CAFE

(pr Mira 54; ⊙8am-midnight) The tempting aroma of newly milled beans lures you into this trendy coffee house where the circular brown-cream leather tub seats give the impression you're sitting in a cuppa. Smiley

service and sensibly priced milkshakes, muffins and pancakes.

Krem
CAFE

(pr Mira 10; ⊙24hr) Krasnoyarsk's classiest coffee house has black-and-white photography, dark-wood furniture, a belt-stretching dessert menu and reasonably priced lattes and espressos.

Bar Chemodan
PUB

(Бар Чемодан; ul Lenina 116; ⊙noon-midnight Mon-Sat, from 1pm Sun) A wonderfully atmospheric, if fiercely expensive, 1920s-themed pub-restaurant stocking dozens of whiskies. The stair lift outside is for both the disabled and the inebriated.

Kofemolka
CAFE

(Кофемолка; pr Mira 114; ⊙10am-midnight; 🛜) Sip roasts from every corner of the bean-growing world amid faux mahogany as dark as the roasts and geometrically patterned screens that divide things up into intimate gossip booths. Long dessert menu.

☆ Entertainment

Opera-Ballet Theatre
THEATRE

(Театр оперы и балета; 🎫227 8697; www.opera.krasnoyarsk.ru; ul Perensona 2) This architecturally nondescript theatre has two shows a day (11am and 7pm) from October to June.

Philharmonia
LIVE MUSIC

(Филармония; 🎫227 4930; www.krasfil.ru; pl Mira 2b) The Philharmonia has three concert halls showcasing folk, jazz and classical music.

Puppet Theatre
THEATRE

(🎫211 3162; www.puppet24.ru; ul Lenina 119) Classic Russian puppet shows for both children and adults.

Bellini
COCKTAIL BAR

(www.bellini.bar10.ru; ul Mira 10) Pass the monster Mona Lisa to enter this strikingly white cocktail and sushi bar where DJs spin most nights.

Tri Dnya Dozhdya
NIGHTCLUB

(www.3dd.bar10.ru; ul Mira 10) Where Krasnoyarsk's rich, young and beautiful head to pose, drink and dance to top acts.

Havana Club
NIGHTCLUB

(Гавана Клуб; ul Bograda 134; ⊙8pm-1am Mon-Thu, to 3am Fri & Sat) A big nightclub with three dance floors and Moscow DJs.

Rock-Jazz Kafe
LIVE MUSIC

(Рок-Джазз Кафе; ul Surikova 12; ⊙4pm-6am Tue-Sun) Entered through a small bar beside the Dublin Irish Pub, this dark venue showcases live bands around an upturned motorcycle from 6pm most days.

🔒 Shopping

Ekspeditsiya
OUTDOOR GEAR

(Экспедиция; ul Uritskogo; ⊙10am-7pm) Source all the equipment you need for a trek into the Siberian wilderness or replace lost or broken camping gear at this small shop.

Russkoe Slovo
BOOKSHOP

(Русское Слово; ul Lenina 28; ⊙10am-7pm Mon-Fri, to 3pm Sat) A good central bookstore selling useful public transport plans as well as city and regional maps.

ℹ Information

Post office (ul Lenina 62; internet per hr R38; ⊙8.30am-5.30pm Mon-Fri, to 4.15pm Sat)

ROSBank (pr Mira 7; ⊙9am-6pm Mon-Thu, 9am-4.45pm Fri) Currency exchange and 24-hour indoor ATM.

Sayan Ring (☑223 1231; www.sayanring.com; ul 3-ya Krasnodarskaya 14a; ⊙10am-8pm Mon-Fri, 11am-5pm Sat) Specialist agency for Tuva and Khakassia tours.

Sberbank (Сбербанк; ul Surikova 15; ⊙10am-7pm Mon-Sat) Currency-exchange window and ATM.

SibTourGuide (☑2512 654; www.sibtourguide .com) Experienced tour guide Anatoly Brewhanov offers personalised hiking trips into the Stolby, imaginative tours around Krasnoyarsk and general travel assistance. He also runs a mini-hostel, provides authentic 'rural experiences' at his dacha, organises cruises along the Yenisey and leads trips to the site of the Tunguska Event, all while maintaining an info-packed website.

Yergaki tourist office (☑227 8637; www .visitsiberia.info; pr Mira 86; ⊙9am-1pm & 2-6pm) Bona fide but little advertised tourist office with English-speaking staff armed with limited visitor info. Ring the bell to be buzzed in then head to the back of the building, up the stairs and through a grey metal door.

ℹ Getting There & Away

Train

TSAVS (ЦАВС; www.krascavs.ru; ul Lenina 115; ⊙8am-8pm) is the most central booking office, though the station itself is relatively central and often queue-free.

There are up to five overnight trains to Irkutsk, but with a journey time of 18 hours you can't avoid travelling for at least some part of the first or second days. Heading west to Tomsk, trains 11 and 91 only run every other day and neither are overnight services. Otherwise Krasnoyarsk has the following rail connections:

Irkutsk platskart/kupe R1400/3500, 18 hours, up to nine daily

Lesosibirsk (for Yeniseysk) platskart R810, 9½ hours, every other day

Moscow platskart R3110, kupe R6600 to R11,200, two days 16 hours, up to seven daily

Novosibirsk platskart R1360 to R2700, kupe R800 to R1250, 12 hours, up to 13 daily

Severobaikalsk platskart R1660 to R1800, kupe R2600 to R4860, 26 to 36½ hours, three daily

Tomsk platskart/kupe R2170/1020, 14 hours, every other day

Air

From Krasnoyarsk's Yemelyanovo Airport you can fly to almost anywhere in Russia. A handful of flights leave from nearby Cheremshanka Airport – check yours isn't one of them.

Moscow from R5500, up to 10 daily

Novosibirsk from R1400, daily

Kyzyl from R3300, three daily

Irkutsk from R7000, four weekly

Boat

Summer hydrofoils to Divnogorsk depart up to five times a day, returning an hour later. Buy tickets on board.

ℹ Getting Around

Krasnoyarsk's grandly modern train station is located in the southwest tip of the city centre. Frequent, if slow, trolleybus 7 trundles from there through the city centre via ul Karla Marksa.

Within the city centre, almost all public transport runs eastbound along ul Karla Marksa or pr Mira, returning westbound on ul Lenina.

Bus 135 (1¼ hours, hourly) runs from the bus station to Yemelyanovo Airport, 46km northwest of the city. It passes Cheremshanka Airport en route.

Useful bus 50 starts beyond the zoo, passes the Turbaza Yenisey and comes through the centre of town, winding on to the bus station.

From June to September cycle hire is available near the Rezanov Statue (R150 per hour).

Around Krasnoyarsk

DIVNOGORSK
ДИВНОГОРСК

☑39144 / POP 30,000 / ⊙MOSCOW +4HR

From Krasnoyarsk, a popular day trip by bus or summer hydrofoil follows the Yenisey River 27km to Divnogorsk town through

YENISEYSK

Using Lesosibirsk overnight trains, historic Yeniseysk (Енисейск) makes an engaging two-night, one-day excursion from Krasnoyarsk, 340km away. Founded in 1619, this was once Russia's great fur-trading capital, with world-famous 18th-century August trade fairs (recently revived for tourists), and 10 grand churches punctuating its skyline. Eclipsed by Krasnoyarsk despite a burst of gold-rush prosperity in the 1860s, the town is now a peaceful backwater with an unexpectedly good **Regional Museum** (ul Lenina 106; admission R50; ☺9am-5pm Mon-Sat), some faded commercial grandeur along ul Lenina and many old houses; over 70 are considered architectural monuments. Most appealing of the surviving churches are the walled 1731 **Spaso-Pereobrazhensky Monastery** (ul Raboche-Krestyanskaya 105) and the **Assumption Church** (Uspenskaya tserkov; ul Raboche-Krestyanskaya 116) with its unusual metal floor and splendid antique icons.

To reach Yeniseysk, take the overnight train from Krasnoyarsk to Lesosibirsk (*platskart* R810, 9½ hours). A bus meets the train and takes passengers to Lesosibirsk bus station where they must alight, queue up to buy a ticket and reboard. After that there are at least hourly departures to Yeniseysk throughout the day (R90, 45 minutes). If you don't want to travel back overnight, buses run back to Krasnoyarsk day and night (R519, seven hours, 10 daily).

Further North along the Yenisey

From mid-June to early October, passenger ships slip along the Yenisey River from Krasnoyarsk to Dudinka in the Arctic Circle (4½ days) via Yeniseysk (17 hours) and Igarka (three days, two to seven hours). There are three to four sailings per week, most departing early morning. Returning upstream, journeys take 50% longer so most independent travellers choose to fly back to Krasnoyarsk. Foreigners are not allowed beyond Igarka as Dudinka and nearby Norilsk are 'closed' towns. Contact SibTourGuide in Krasnoyarsk for timetables, tickets and round-trip tours. Novosibirsk-based **Acris** (www.acris.ru) can also arrange trips.

a wide, wooded canyon. Some 5km beyond Divnogorsk's jetty is a vast 90m-high **dam**. Turbine-room visits are not permitted, but if you're lucky you might see ships being lifted by a technologically impressive inclined plane to the huge Krasnoyarsk Sea behind. A few kilometres beyond you can observe ice fishing from December to March or, in the summer, boats and yachts can be hired.

The Krasnoyarsk–Divnogorsk road has a panoramic overlook point at km23 and passes quaint **Ovsyanka** village. From the main road walk 100m (crossing the train tracks) to Ovsyanka's cute wooden **St Innocent Chapel** (ul Shchetinkina) then 50m right to find the **house-museum** (ul Shchetinkina 26; admission R50; ☺10am-6pm Tue-Sun) of famous local writer Victor Astafiev, who died in 2001. Directly opposite in Astafiev's grandma's cottage-compound is the more interesting **Last Bow Museum** (ul Shchetinkina 35; ticket valid for both; ☺10am-6pm Tue-Sun), giving a taste of rural Siberian life.

Hydrofoils (R250, 45 minutes, up to five daily) depart from Krasnoyarsk's river station and regular *marshrutky* (R54) leave from Krasnoyarsk's bus station. Taxis meet boats on arrival in Divnogorsk and want at least R700 return to shuttle you to a point overlooking the dam. However, it's potentially cheaper, safer and more fun to hire a mountain bike from a stand 200m downstream from the quay. SibTourGuide in Krasnoyarsk offers various tailored excursions in English or will include the Divnogorsk loop as part of its 'Ten-Rouble Tour'.

Irkutsk Иркутск

☏3952 / POP 587,000 / ☺MOSCOW +5HR

The de facto capital of Eastern Siberia, pleasantly historic Irkutsk is by far the most popular stop on the Trans-Siberian Railway between Moscow and all points east. With Lake Baikal a mere 70km away, the city is the best base from which to strike out for the western shoreline. Amid the 19th-century architecture, revived churches, classy eateries and numerous apartment hostels, plentiful English-speaking agencies can help you plan anything from a winter trek across the lake's ice to a short walking tour through the city.

Irkutsk

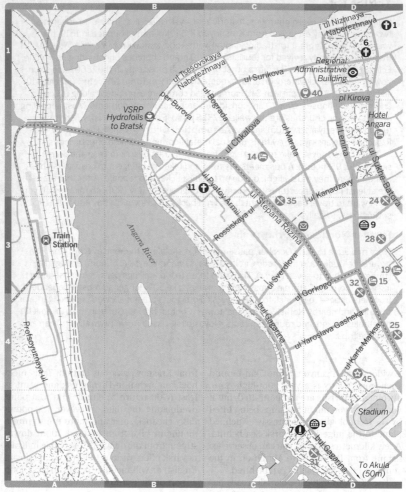

Irkutsk spent the summer of 2011 celebrating its 350th birthday, an event which seems to have triggered something of a mini-revival in civic pride and a recognition that the city may hold some interest for visitors. A new municipally funded information centre, detailed city maps planted at strategic points and a handful of freshly conceived museums may have improved the visitor experience only slightly, but it's a welcome start.

History

Founded in 1661 as a Cossack garrison to extract the fur tax from the indigenous Buryats, Irkutsk was the springboard for 18th-century expeditions to the far north and east, including Alaska – then known as 'Irkutsk's American district'.

As Eastern Siberia's trading and administrative centre, Irkutsk dispatched Siberian furs and ivory to Mongolia, Tibet and China in exchange for silk and tea. Constructed mostly of local timber, three-quarters of the city burnt down in the disastrous blaze of 1879. However, profits from the 1880s Lena Basin gold rush swiftly rebuilt the city's most important edifices in brick and stone.

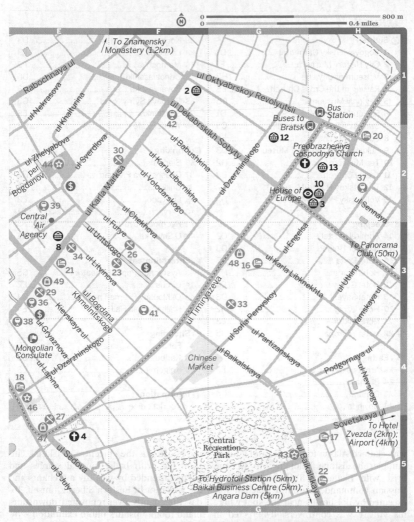

Known as the 'Paris of Siberia', Irkutsk did not welcome news of the October Revolution. The city's well-to-do merchants only succumbed to the Red tide in 1920, with the capture and execution of White army commander Admiral Kolchak, whose controversial statue was re-erected in 2004. Soviet-era planning saw Irkutsk develop as the sprawling industrial and scientific centre that it remains today.

Sights

Irkutsk's centre can be easily explored on foot – you'll only need to hop aboard a bus or *marshrutka* to see the Angara Dam and the Znamensky Monastery.

Znamensky Monastery   HISTORICAL BUILDING
Set in a leafy garden behind a noisy roundabout, the 1762 Znamensky Monastery is 1.5km northeast of the Bogoyavlensky Cathedral. Echoing with mellifluous plainsong, the interior has splendidly muralled vaulting, a towering iconostasis and a gold sarcophagus holding the miraculous relics of Siberian missionary St Innocent. Celebrity graves outside include the nautically themed tomb of Grigory Shelekhov, the man

Irkutsk

who claimed Alaska for Russia, and a much humbler headstone belonging to Decembrist wife Ekaterina Trubetskaya. White Russian commander Admiral Kolchak was executed by Bolsheviks near the spot where his **statue** was controversially erected in November 2004 at the entrance to the monastery grounds; the plinth is exaggeratedly high enough to prevent die-hard communists from committing acts of vandalism.

Volkonsky House-Museum MUSEUM
(Дом-музей Волконского; per Volkonskogo 10; admission R200; ⊙10am-6pm Tue-Sun) The well-preserved home of Decembrist Count Sergei Volkonsky, whose wife Maria Volkonskaya cuts the main figure in Christine Sutherland's unputdownable book *The Princess of Siberia,* is a small mansion set in a scruffy courtyard with stables, a barn and servant quarters. In the decade leading up to the Volkonsky's return to St Petersburg in 1856,

the house was the epicentre of Irkutsk cultural life, with balls, musical soirées and parties attended by wealthy merchants and the governor of Eastern Siberia himself. Today the slightly over-renovated downstairs piano room, upstairs photo exhibition – including portraits of Maria and other women who romantically followed their husbands and lovers into exile – and other displays of everyday objects used by the family tell the story of their time in Irkutsk.

Regional Museum MUSEUM
(Краеведческий музей; www.museum.irkutsk.ru; ul Karla Marksa 2; admission R200; ⊙10am-7pm) Irkutsk's rapidly ageing Regional Museum is within a fancy 1870s brick building that formerly housed the Siberian Geographical Society, a club of Victorian-style gentlemen explorers. The highlights here are the downstairs ethnographical exhibitions and the nostalgic display of 20th-

century junk upstairs, as well as the small gift shop selling birch-bark boxes, jewellery made from Baikal minerals and other interesting souvenirs.

City History Museum
MUSEUM

(www.history.irk.ru; ul Frank-Kamenetskogo 16a; admission R150; ⊘10am-6pm Thu-Tue) Relocated in 2011 from its former far-flung location to the interior of one of Irkutsk's most impressive central edifices, the City History Museum is the greatest symbol of the authorities' efforts to perk up the visitor experience. Painstakingly renovated in time for Irkutsk's 350th birthday, this palatial 19th-century school building now houses a comprehensive overview of the city's three and a half centuries, focusing on trade, life of the merchant classes, education, churches and the Trans-Sib.

Museum of City Life
MUSEUM

(ul Dekabrskikh Sobyty 77; admission R100; ⊘10am-6pm Wed-Mon) This brand-new museum filling six rooms of a former merchant's house illustrates just why 19th-century Irkutsk was nicknamed the 'Paris of Siberia'. Changing exhibitions of everyday and decorative items such as lamps, dolls, tableware and porcelain are donated free of charge by the people of Irkutsk and are displayed against a background of period wallpaper, elegant double doors and high ceilings. The new **Tea Museum** opposite (in the same building as the tourist office) was set to open in late 2011.

Sukachev Regional Art Museum
ART GALLERY

(Художественный музей; ul Lenina 5; admission R100; ⊘10am-5.30pm Tue-Sun) The grand old Art Gallery has a valuable though poorly lit collection ranging from Mongolian *thangkas* (Tibetan Buddhist religious paintings) to Russian Impressionist canvases. Behind a photogenic 1909 facade its **sub-gallery** (ul Karla Marksa 23; admission R100; ⊘10am-6pm Tue-Sun) is strong on Siberian landscapes and petroglyph rubbings and has some superb 17th-century icons.

Raising of the Cross Church
CHURCH

(Крестовоздвиженская церковь; Krestovozdvizhenskaya tserkov; ul Sedova 1) The 1758 baroque Raising of the Cross Church has a fine interior of gilt-edged icons and examples of intricate brickwork in a rounded style that's unique to Irkutsk and the Selenga Delta village of Posolskoe.

Kazansky Church
CHURCH

(ul Barrikad) The gigantic Kazansky Church is a theme-park-esque confection of salmon-pink walls and fluoro turquoise domes topped with gold baubled crosses. Get off tram 4 two stops northeast of the bus station.

Angara Dam
LANDMARK

Some 6km southeast of the centre, the 1956 Angara Dam is 2km long. Its construction raised Lake Baikal by up to 1m and caused environmental problems, most notably the silencing of the so-called singing sands on Baikal's eastern shore. The dam itself is hardly an attraction but moored nearby is the **Angara icebreaker** (admission R150; ⊘10am-8pm). Originally imported in kit form from Newcastle-upon-Tyne to carry Trans-Siberian Railway passengers across Lake Baikal (the trains went on her bigger sister ship *Baikal*, sunk during the Civil War), it's now a less-than-inspiring museum reached by a permanent gangway.

Trubetskoy House-Museum
MUSEUM

(Дом-музей Трубецкого; ul Dzerzhinskogo) Dismantled and carted off for renovation in late 2007, Irkutsk's second Decembrist house-museum was expected to make a comeback in late 2011 or 2012. From the outside the restorers seem to have done a cracking job on the pleasingly symmetrical minimansion.

Trinity Church
CHURCH

(Троицкий храм; Troitsky khram; ul 5 Armii 8) Restoration work remains half-finished on the 18th-century Trinity Church where Admiral Kolchak was christened and married.

Statue of Tsar Alexander III
MONUMENT

(Памятник Александру III) Across the road from the Regional Museum, a recast statue of Tsar Alexander III (a copy of the 1904 original) looks as though he's holding an invisible balloon on a string.

Saviour's Church
CHURCH

(Спасская церковь; Spasskaya tserkov; ⊘8am-8pm) Under heavy renovation at the time of research, this 1706 church has remnants of murals on its facade and until a decade ago housed a museum.

Bogoyavlensky Cathedral
CHURCH

(Богоявленский собор; ul Nizhnaya Naberezhnaya) Much more eye-catching than the Saviour's Church is this fairy-tale ensemble of mini onion domes atop restored salmon, white and green towers. The interior is a fragrant riot of aureoled Byzantine saints with no surface left plain.

Tours

Local tour companies are useful not only for organising excursions but also for booking hotels and most kinds of tickets. All of Irkutsk's hostels can arrange Baikal tours.

Cheap Travel TOUR COMPANY
(✆668 335; www.cheapandtrip.ru) English-speaking travel fanatic Maxim books plane and train tickets for R200 commission, can help out with Mongolian visas and Russian visa registration (R400) and will even find you a bed for the night. The company currently has no base, but is set to operate from 2012 in a new hostel (location to be decided).

Baikaler TOUR COMPANY
(✆336 240; www.baikaler.com) Imaginative Jack Sheremetoff speaks very good English and is well tuned to budget-traveller needs. Original personalised tours, two great hostels and a friendly welcome.

BaikalComplex TOUR COMPANY
(✆461 557; www.baikalcomplex.com) Busy, well-organised operation offering homestays and trips tailored for international travellers.

Baikalinfo TOUR COMPANY
(✆707 012; www.baikalinfo.ru; ul Krasnykh Madiyar 50) Commercial tour company that arranges Baikal tours as well as trips on the Circum-baikal Railway.

Green Express TOUR COMPANY
(✆734 400; www.greenexpress.ru; ul Karla Lib-knekhta 48) Professional outfit specialising in outdoor activities.

Baikal Discovery TOUR COMPANY
(✆200 550; www.baikal-discovery.com) Adventure tours in the Baikal region and beyond.

BaikalExplorer TOUR COMPANY
(✆8-902-560 2440; www.baikalex.com) Baikal cruises, fishing and diving trips.

🛏 Sleeping

Although options are constantly expanding, Irkutsk's accommodation still gets very full in summer. Bookings are generally a very good idea.

The newest swanky places to catch some Zs in Irkutsk will be the Marriot and the Park Inn by Radisson, both under construction at the time of research.

Hostels have sprouted like mushrooms after a rainfall, but lifespans can be short and some are open only in high season. To save you some research time, we've only included a list of the most established backpacker quarters. As across the former USSR, they are ideal for finding English-speaking assistance, arranging tours and meeting fellow travellers.

TOP CHOICE Baikaler Hostel HOSTEL €
(✆336 240; www.baikaler.com; apt 11, ul Lenina 9; dm R700; ❄@🖻) Run by experienced tour guide Jack Sheremetoff, the super-central Baikaler apartment hostel is Irkutsk's original backpacker haven and still *the* place to meet fellow travellers and organise trips. The spotless, air-conditioned dorms are spacious, but beds are limited and booking ahead from June to September is essential. The entrance is from the rear of the building. It also runs the Baikaler Eco-Hostel in Listvyanka.

Hotel Sayen HOTEL €€€
(✆500 000; www.sayen.ru; ul Karla Marksa 13b; r R7700-13,800; ❄🖻) Described by some as the finest luxury sleep east of the Urals, this very central Japanese hotel gets rave reviews and deservedly so. The 24 rooms enjoy design-mag decor, big baths and gadgets galore, going beyond the standards of many Western hotels. The 24-hour room service is a given, there are two top-hole restaurants and a spa is on hand should you feel the urge to have hot stones placed on your back. Possibly about as smart as things will ever get in Irkutsk.

Hotel Viktoria HOTEL €€€
(✆792 879; www.victoryhotel.ru; ul Bogdana Khmel-nitskogo 1; s R3500-3800, d R3800-4300; ❄@🖻) Just a few steps off ul Karla Marksa, the 30 rooms at this relative newcomer remain stylish and unfrumpy despite the antique-style furniture and flowery wall coverings. If you've been in Russia a while, the courteous staff, baths in every room and online booking could feel almost eccentric.

Admiral Hostel HOSTEL €
(✆742 440; apt 1, ul Cheremkhovsky 6; dm R550; @🖻) With its Kolchak-inspired name, this cosy 13-bed apartment hostel has become well-established digs for Trans-Siberian wanderers. The lower bunks sport privacy curtains, staff sell bus tickets to Olkhon Island, there's a free (light) breakfast and you

can even get your washing done. Enter from the rear of the building.

Baikal Business Centre
HOTEL €€€

(☏259 120; www.bbc.ru; ul Baikalskaya 279; s R3900-6100, tw R5100-6100; 🖳🛜) If you're in Irkutsk on business, this white and blue-glass tower is where you'll want to unsheathe the company credit card. Rooms are just about international standard, there's a business centre and rates are slashed at weekends – on a winter Saturday you can pay as little as R1800 for a single, a real bargain for this standard.

Baikalhostel
HOSTEL €

(☏525 742; www.baikalhostels.com; apt 1, ul Lermontova 136; dm R650; 🛜) This German-owned hostel receives rave reviews from travellers, despite the very inconvenient and insalubrious location several kilometres south of the train station; take *marshrutka* 72 from the station to the Mikrochirurgia Glaza stop.

Hotel Yevropa
HOTEL €€

(Гостиница Европа; ☏291 515; www.europehotel .ru; ul Baikalskaya 69; s/d from R2900/3700; 🖳🛜) Behind nine Doric columns immaculate rooms are realistically priced at this gleaming four-star favourite. Reception staff speak English and the Western-style breakfast is reportedly the best in town.

Hotel Zvezda
HOTEL €€€

(☏540 000; www.zvezdahotel.ru; ul Yadrintseva 1ж; s/tw R4000/4300, ste R6000-18000; 🖳🛜) Within a Swiss chalet–style building, rooms here are modern and comfortable, service is pleasant and English is spoken, though you'd expect little less for these room rates. Its atmospheric restaurant specialises in game and exotic meats.

Hotel Gloria
HOTEL €€€

(Отель Глория; ☏540 664; www.gloriahotel .org; Sovetskaya ul 58a; s R3500, d R4500-6500; 🖳🛜) This pastel-beige tower is home to nine international-class rooms and two bigger suites that have both a bath and shower. English is spoken and there's a decent, if pricey, on-site restaurant.

Hotel Uzory
HOTEL €

(Узоры Гостиница; ☏209 239; ul Oktyabrskoy Revolyutsii 17; s/tw R650/1000) Clean, unpretentious rooms with leopard-skin-patterned blankets but communal bathrooms and toilets. It's popular with independent travellers but maintains a tradition of employing Irkutsk's sourest receptionists.

Hotel Delta
HOTEL €€

(Отель Дельта; ☏794 090; www.deltairkutsk.ru; ul Karla Libknekhta 58; s R2950-3850, d R4820-6000; 🛜) Bog-standard rooms with little panache, aimed primarily at low-budget business travellers.

Hotel Gornyak
HOTEL €€

(Гостиница Горняк; ☏243 754; ul Lenina 24; s R1500-2700, tw R2200-3300) As a last resort you could try this reasonably presentable if overpriced central hotel, but at the time of research foreigners were being turned away due to visa registration issues. Enter from ul Dzerzhinskogo.

✖ Eating

🏆 TOP CHOICE Kochevnik
MONGOLIAN €€

(Кочевник; ul Gorkogo 19; mains R200-650; ⊙11.30am-midnight; 🖐) Take your taste buds to the Mongolian steppe for some yurt-size portions of mutton, lamb and steak as well as filling soups and *buuzy* (dumplings), sluiced down with a bottle from the decent foreign wine list. Smiley service, a picture menu, low prices and an exotically curtained summer terrace make this the most agreeable place to eat in town.

Mamochka
CAFE €

(ul Karla Marksa 41; mains R80-100, coffee R70-140; ⊙10am-9pm; 🖐) With its menu of imaginative salads, filling soups and (almost) healthy mains, this is no ordinary point-and-eat canteen. Swab the decks with a Czech, Slovak or German lager then sit back and admire the interior, a mishmash of old newspapers and Soviet bric-a-brac. Great.

Govinda
VEGETARIAN €

(2nd fl, ul Furye 4; mains R30-80; ⊙11am-8pm; 🖳🖐) Irkutsk's only vegie restaurant is a small self-service affair with a half-hearted Indian theme and a menu of soya sausages, basmati rice, spicy soups, mild curries, quorn chilli con carne, imaginative desserts and whole plantations of tea. Extra heat can be added from the chilli bowl on the counter.

Wiener Café
CAFE €€

(Венское Кафе; ul Stepana Razina 19; mains R80-400; ⊙10am-11pm) Marble-top tables, Parisian bar chairs and a Tyrolean folk ensemble of waitresses make this an entertaining nosh stop. A good mid-morning breakfast option with tempting pastries, real oat porridge and ranks of mouth-watering desserts.

Snezhinka
CAFE €€

(Снежинка; opposite ul Karla Marksa 25; mains R200-500; ⊙9am-midnight) This cosy belle époque–style cafe has attentive English-speaking service and regularly wins local awards for its food. It's been around since 1957, making it the city's longest-serving eatery.

Blinnaya
RUSSIAN €

(ul Sukhe-Batora 8; mains R25-70; ⊙10am-6pm Mon-Fri, to 4pm Sat) The city centre's cheapest eat is this unrepentantly Soviet canteen where befrilled dinner ladies dispatch plates of filling pancakes, buckwheat *kasha* (porridge), meatballs and pasta, all washed down with plastic cupfuls of over-diluted *kompot* (fruit squash).

Odnoklassniki
RUSSIAN €€

(bul Gagarina 13a; mains R150-450; ⊙noon-last customer) The name of this contemporary, purpose-built eatery is a rip-off of the Russian-language equivalent of the Friends Reunited website, but this is still an enjoyable place to pig out on grilled meat, salads and generous helpings of Slavic stodge. The nostalgic Soviet-schooldays theme may be a bit lost on foreigners, but who cares with such a vast drinks menu to peruse on the terrace.

Kafe Elen
CAFE €

(ul Timiryazeva; meals R180-350; ⊙9am-11pm Mon-Sat, from 10am Sun; ⊝✲) Bubbling aquariums, rattan furniture, raffia-threaded blinds and lots of potted plants make this a tranquil breakfast and lunch spot as you watch the trams trundle past the church opposite.

Arbatski Dvorik
RUSSIAN €€€

(Арбатский Дворик; ul Uritskogo; mains R350-1500; ⊙noon-last customer; ☎◙) This upmarket restaurant is all inside out, the walls lined with imitation facades, doorways and street lamps. However there's nothing topsy-turvy about the impeccable service and well-crafted menu. Oddly, it's accessed via the gaudy Fiesta fast-food place below.

Lancelot
RUSSIAN €€

(Kievskaya ul 2; mains R200-400; ⊙noon-midnight Sun-Wed, to 2am Thu-Sat; ◙) Flaming torches lead down through a portcullis into an amusing neomedieval castle interior. Arthurian-named dishes can be enjoyed at the round table and there's live music at weekends.

Povaryoshka
FAST FOOD €

(ul Lenina 32; mains R45-100; ⊙9am-10pm) This new self-service canteen has rural knick-

knackery kept high out of clients' reach and a menu of Eurasian standards and half-decent pizzas.

Poznaya Sytny Ryad
CAFE €

(Позная Сытный Ряд; ul Partizanskaya 9a; pozi R30, other mains R60-180; ⊙10am-11pm) Irkutsk's most appealing cheap *pozi* (dumpling) joint is in a primly faux-rural timber house surrounded by the disarray of the market area.

Domino
FAST FOOD €

(Домино; ul Lenina 13a; pizza slices R70; ⊙24hr) Domino has Russian-flavour pizza and vastly superior *bliny* available round the clock.

🍷 Drinking

TOP CHOICE **Liverpool**
PUB

(Паб Ливерпуль; ul Sverdlova 28; ⊙noon-3am; ☎) You'll never walk (or drink) alone at Irkutsk's most popular theme pub. The crowds enter through a mocked-up red telephone box to find an interior tiled in Beatles photos and old vinyl LPs and strewn with reminders of northwest England's erstwhile musical prowess. The beer menu is a global affair, the service laid-back and mimicky local rock bands regularly thump and strum for drinkers.

U Shveyka
PUB

(У Швейка; ul Karla Marksa 34; ⊙noon-midnight; ✲) This beamed cellar pub serves old-style glass tankards of Czech Pilsner Urquell beer made under licence in Irkutsk. The adjacent beer garden is possibly the city's best and is busy with drinkers from May to late September.

Chili
BAR

(Чили; ul Karla Marksa 26; cocktails from R200; ⊙24hr) Aztec-themed nightspot and all-day bar where you can join Irkutsk's moneyed youth on beige couches bathed in flamingo neon for a flashy cocktail or overpriced meals (R250 to R600).

Bierhaus
PUB

(ul Gryaznova 1; ⊙noon-2am Mon-Thu, until 4am Fri & Sat, until midnight Sun; ◙) Upmarket Bavarian-style *bierstube* (beer hall) serving Newcastle Brown and Guinness as well as German beers and sausages. Enter from ul Karla Marksa.

Cheshskaya Pivovarnya
PUB

(Чешская Пивоварная; ul Krasnogvardeyskaya 29; ⊙noon-2am Tue-Sat, to midnight Sun & Mon)

You'll smell this place before you see it as Irkutsk's unpretentious microbrewery-pub creates its own Pilsner Urquell lager, pumping out a pungent hop aroma in the process.

Pervach PUB
(Первач; ul Chkalova 33; ☺noon-1am) Pervach is a cosy, stone-and-brick cellar pub, heated by real fires in winter.

Ryumochnaya BAR
(Рюмочная; ul Litvinova 16; ☺24hr) If low-cost inebriation is your aim, this no-frills bar is your place.

☆ Entertainment

Okhlopkov Drama Theatre THEATRE
(Драматический театр Охлопкова; ☎200 477; ul Karla Marksa 14) Shakespeare, Russian classics and local playwright Vampilov staged regularly (in Russian) from September to June.

Circus CIRCUS
(Цирк; ☎336 139; ul Zhelyabova; ☺ticket office 10am-7pm) Permanent big top with most performances at weekends.

Aystyonok Puppet Theatre PUPPET THEATRE
(Театр Кукол Аистёнок; ☎205 825; ul Baikalskaya 32) Marionette shows for the kiddies.

Philharmonic Hall LIVE MUSIC
(Филармония; ☎242 968; www.filarmoniya.irk.ru; ul Dzerzhinskogo 2) Historic building staging regular children's shows and musical programs from jazz to classical.

Akula NIGHTCLUB
(www.akula-club.ru; bul Gagarina 9) Nothing subtle about this place – expect top DJs, litres of ethanol-based beverages and public nudity at some point.

Panorama Club NIGHTCLUB
(www.clubpanorama.ru; ul Dekabrskikh Sobyty 102) Four dance floors pounding to different music styles and an international DJ guest list.

🛍 Shopping

Fanat OUTDOOR GEAR
(Фанат; ul Timiryazeva; ☺10am-7pm) Sells Western-brand camping, fishing and skiing equipment, hiking boots and mountain bikes.

Knigomir BOOKSTORE
(Книгомир; ul Karla Marksa 28; ☺9am-7pm Mon-Sat, 10am-5pm Sun) Best place to source maps of Irkutsk and many other Baikal towns as well as Russian guides, atlases and large souvenir wall maps of Lake Baikal.

Karibu CLOTHING
(ul Timiryazeva 34; ☺10am-7pm Mon-Sat, noon-5pm Sun) Tiny shop selling beautifully furry *unty* (traditional deerskin cowboy boots) made on site and typically costing around R10,000. Some English spoken.

ℹ Information

IrkutskOut (www.irkutskout.ru) A wealth of practical details including cafe and restaurant listings.

Irk.ru (www.irk.ru) Where locals go for city info.

Moy Bank (Мой Банк; ul Gryaznova 1; ☺9am-8pm Mon-Fri, 10am-4pm Sat) Exchanges Chinese yuán.

Post office (ul Stepana Razina 23; internet access per hr R50; ☺8am-10pm Mon-Fri, 9am-6pm Sat & Sun) Internet access.

Sberbank (Сбербанк; ul Uritskogo 19; ☺9am-7pm Mon-Thu, until 6pm Fri, 10am-5pm Sat & Sun) Currency-exchange window and 24-hour indoor ATM.

Tourist office (☎205 018; www.itsirkutsk.com; ul Dekabrskikh Sobyty 77; ☺9am-6pm; ☎) Municipally funded tourist office with English-speaking staff, free wi-fi, free city maps and lots of well-produced brochures and booklets on Irkutsk and Lake Baikal. Located behind the elaborately carved House of Europe.

Travelling to Baikal (www.travellingtobaikal .com) English-language website promoting tourism in Irkutsk and the Baikal area. Lots of listings.

VTB Bank (ВТБ Банк; ul Sverdlova 36; ☺9.30am-5.30pm Mon-Thu, to 4.30pm Fri) Currency exchange and 24-hour indoor ATMs.

WWW Irkutsk (www.irkutsk.org) Bags of information on every aspect of the city.

ℹ Getting There & Away

Train

Train tickets can be bought from Cheap Travel, the Bratsk bus-ticket booth and many upmarket hotels. Some of the city's hostels can also help out. It's well worth paying the commission these agents charge as you won't waste time making the tram trip to the station and standing in the queues there.

There are up to six overnight trains to Krasnoyarsk, though ones to avoid are the 903 and 929 that take almost 30 hours to do the 18-hour run. Definitely consider doing the Irkutsk–Ulan-Ude journey during the day; otherwise you'll miss the most scenic section of the entire Trans-Siberian Railway around the southern shores of Lake

Baikal. Irkutsk has a connecting service to the BAM (p250), with trains 71 and 87 taking turns on alternate days to make the sometimes gruelling trip to Severobaikalsk via Bratsk. Otherwise Irkutsk has the following rail connections:

Beijing *kupe* R11,000, two days 22 hours, twice weekly

Chita *platskart/kupe* R1400/3100, 16 to 19 hours, up to six daily

Khabarovsk *platskart/kupe* R3600/8400, two days 13 hours, three daily

Krasnoyarsk *platskart/kupe* R1400/3500, 18 hours, up to nine daily

Moscow *platskart* R3500 to R4800, *kupe* R7700 to R12,500, three days three to 15 hours, three daily

Severobaikalsk *platskart* R2100, *kupe* R3300 to R4700, 37 hours, daily

Slyudyanka *elektrichka* (suburban train) R70, four hours, four daily

Ulaanbaatar *kupe* R4500, 27 hours, daily

Ulan-Ude *platskart* R875, *kupe* R1300 to R2300, 6½ to 8½ hours, up to nine daily

Vladivostok *platskart/kupe* R4400/10,100, two days 22 hours, three daily

Air

Irkutsk's antiquated little 'international' **airport** (www.iktport.ru) is handily placed near the city centre. Foreign destinations include Tashkent (€250 to €400), Dushanbe (R20,000), Bangkok (R20,000) and Beijing (R10,000 to R20,000). **Aeromongolia** (www.aeromongolia.mn) operates twice-weekly flights to Ulaanbaatar, while **Yakutia** (www.yakutia.aero) has started useful flights to Munich (R17,400, twice weekly).

For Moscow Domodedovo there are direct flights with S7 Airlines (from R7900 daily) and at least two other companies. Irkutsk also enjoys direct air links to many other domestic

destinations, with tickets for all services sold through the convenient **Central Air Agency** (☑201 517; ul Gorkogo 29; ⊗8am-8.30pm, to 7pm winter).

Boat

In summer hydrofoils buzz along the Angara to Listvyanka (June to September, three daily) and up Lake Baikal to Bolshie Koty (June to September, three daily), Olkhon Island (July and August, three weekly), Ust-Barguzin (July and August, weekly) and Nizhneangarsk (July and August, twice weekly). Departures are from the Raketa hydrofoil station beyond the Angara Dam in Solnechny Mikro-Rayon, two minutes' walk from bus 16 stop 'Raketa'. Timetables are posted by the quay. Services in the other direction to Bratsk leave from a separate jetty in the city centre.

All services are operated by **VSRP** (☑356 726; www.vsrp.ru). Check the website for times and prices.

Bus

From the slowly renovating **bus station** (ul Oktyabrskoy Revolyutsii) book tickets at least a day ahead in summer for Arshan (R250, four daily), and Listvyanka (R100, 1¼ hours, 11 daily) via Taltsy (R60).

Comfortable coaches for Bratsk (R900, 8pm) leave from a special ticket booth opposite the main bus station. Minibuses to Ulan-Ude (R700, seven hours) depart throughout the day but more frequently in late evening from the train-station forecourt.

ⓘ Getting Around

Irkutsk's grand train station is located across the Angara River from the city centre. Trams 1, 2 and 4A run from outside to uls Lenina and Timiryazeva, 4A continuing on to the bus station.

FLIGHTS WITHIN RUSSIA FROM IRKUTSK

DESTINATION	COST	FREQUENCY
Bratsk	R3000-4000	3 per week
Chita	R4500-7000	5 per week
Khabarovsk	R7000-10,000	daily
Magadan	R12,000-20,000	3 per week
Novosibirsk	R6000-15,000	daily
St Petersburg	R15,000	5 per week
Ulan-Ude	R2000	3 per week
Vladivostok	R8000-12,000	8 per week
Yekaterinburg	R8000-12,000	daily

Within the central area, walking is usually the best idea as one-way systems make bus routes confusing.

Frequent trolleybus 4 and bus/*marshrutka* 20, 80, 90 and countless other services connect the city centre with the airport. A taxi costs around R150 to R200.

Tram 4 links the central market with the bus station.

Around Irkutsk

TALTSY MUSEUM OF ARCHITECTURE & ETHNOGRAPHY

About 47km east of Irkutsk, 23km before Listvyanka, **Taltsy** (Архитектурно-этнографический музей Тальцы; www.talci.ru; admission R150; ⊙10am-5pm) is an impressive outdoor collection of old Siberian buildings set in a delightful riverside forest. Amid the renovated farmsteads are two chapels, a church, a watermill, some Evenki graves and the eye-catching 17th-century Iliminsk Ostrog watchtower. Listvyanka–Irkutsk buses and *marshrutky* stop on request at Taltsy's entrance (look out for the roadside 'Музей' sign), and the ticket booth is a minute's walk through the forest.

Western Lake Baikal

Lake Baikal (Озеро Байкал), the 'Pearl of Siberia', is a crystal-clear body of the bluest water. It's drinkably pure, surrounded by rocky, tree-covered cliffs and so vast that you can sail for hours without the mountain backdrops becoming appreciably closer.

Shaped like a banana, Lake Baikal – 636km from north to south, but only 60km wide – was formed by rifting tectonic plates. Though nearly 8km of the rift is filled with sediment, it is gradually getting deeper as the plates separate. It will eventually become the Earth's fifth ocean, splitting the Asian continent. In the meantime it's the world's deepest lake: 1637m near the western shore. As such, it contains nearly one-fifth of the world's fresh, unfrozen water – more than North America's five Great Lakes combined.

Swimmers brave enough to face Baikal's icy waters (never warmer than about 15°C) risk vertigo, as it is possible to see down as far as 40m. In February and March you can drive right across on the 1m-thick ice, though this is safest in the north and most practical between Severobaikalsk (p255) and Ust-Barguzin (p214).

ℹ️ **THE EASY WAY TO OLKHON ISLAND**

To Khuzhir on Olkhon Island convenient door-to-door transfers (R700) can be arranged through any of Irkutsk's hostels. Minibuses pick up from any hostel in the morning and drop off passengers at any guesthouse in Khuzhir mid-afternoon. Hostels sell tickets even to nonguests.

The lake itself is a living museum of flora and fauna, 80% of which is found nowhere else on the planet, most famously the loveable black-eyed *nerpa* (freshwater seals) and salmonlike *omul* fish, which are delicious smoked. Don't worry if you're not getting off the train around Baikal as they're sold on the station platforms, most notably in Slyudyanka.

Listvyanka   Листвянка

📞3952 / POP 1830 / ⊙MOSCOW +5HR

As the closest lakeside village to Irkutsk, Listvyanka – aka the 'Baikal Riviera' – is the touristy spot to which most travellers are funnelled to dunk their toes in Baikal's pure waters. Having picked at *omul,* admired the hazy views of the Khamar Daban mountains on the opposite shore and huffed their way from one end of the village to the other, most are on a *marshrutka* back to Irkutsk late afternoon. But there's more to Listvyanka than this; others stay longer to hike the Great Baikal Trail, discover more about the lake at the Baikal Museum and chill out at one of Siberia's most eco-friendly sleeps.

If you're looking for beach fun, you're at the wrong address – the eastern shore (Buryatiya) is the place to build sandcastles. However, what the Buryat shore doesn't have is Listvyanka's range of activities: anything from short boat trips to diving and jet skiing in the summer and ice mountain biking to lake treks and ice sculpting in the winter.

The village extends 4.5km from Rogatka at the mouth of the Angara to the market area. A single road skirts the shore with three valleys running inland where most of Listvyanka's characterful timber dwellings and accommodation options are located. There's no public transport which can mean some very long walks.

Baikal

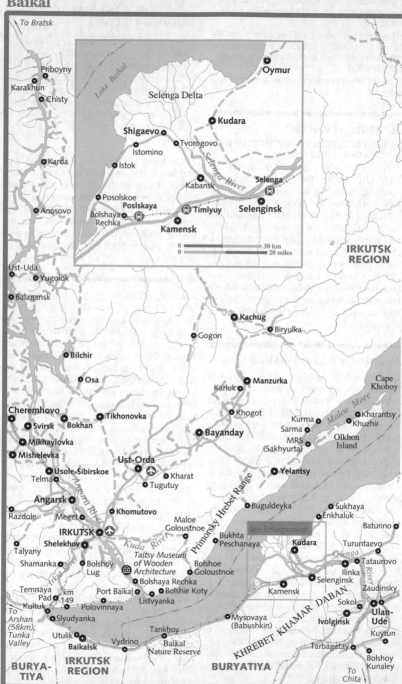

To Bratsk
Priboyny
Karakhun
Chisty
Karda
Anosovo
Ust-Uda
Yugolok
Balagansk

Lake Baikal
Selenga Delta
Oymur
Kudara
Shigaevo
Tvorogovo
Istomino
Istok
Kabansk
Selenga River
Selenga
Posolskoe
Poslskaya
Bolshaya
Rechka
Timlyuy
Selenginsk
Kamensk

0   30 km
0   20 miles

IRKUTSK REGION

Kachug
Gogon
Biryulka
Bilchir
Osa
Manzurka
Karluk
Cape Khoboy
Cheremhovo
Svirsk
Bokhan
Tikhonovka
Khogot
Kurma
Maloe More
Kharantsy
Khuzhir
Sarma
Mikhaylovka
Bayanday
MRS (Sakhyurta)
Olkhon Island
Mishelevka
Usole-Sibirskoe
Telma
Ust-Orda
Kharat
Tugutuy
Yelantsy
Angarsk
Khomutovo
Buguldeyka
Sukhaya
Enkhaluk
Razdole
Meget
Maloe Goloustnoe
Baturino
IRKUTSK
Shelekhov
Talyany
Bukhta Peschanaya
Kudara
Turuntaevo
See Enlargement
Shamanka
Bolshoy Lug
Taltsy Museum of Wooden Architecture
Bolshoe Goloustnoe
Tataurovo
Ilinka
Selenginsk
Zaudinsky
Temnaya Pad
km 149
Port Baikal
Bolshaya Rechka
Bolshie Koty
Kamensk
Sokol
Ulan-Ude
Kultuk
Polovinnaya
Listvyanka
To Arshan (58km); Tunka Valley
Slyudyanka
Mysovaya (Babushkin)
Ivolginsk
Kuytun
Utulik
Tankhoy
Baikal Nature Reserve
Tarbagatay
Baikalsk
Vydrino
Bolshoy Kunaley
BURYA-TIYA
IRKUTSK REGION
BURYATIYA
To Chita
KHREBET KHAMAR DABAN
Primorsky Hrebet Range
Kuda River
Angara River
Irkut River
Selenga River

Sights & Activities

Sourcing a map at Irkutsk's tourist office before you set off will save a lot of hunting.

Baikal Museum MUSEUM
(ul Akademicheskaya 1, Rogatka; admission R150; ⊙9am-5pm Oct-May, to 7pm Jun-Sep) One of only three museums in the world dedicated solely to a lake, this sometimes overly scientific institution examines the science of Baikal from all angles. Pass quickly by the gruesomely discoloured fish samples and seal embryos in formaldehyde to the tanks containing two frolicsome nerpa seals and the various Baikal fish that you may later encounter on restaurant menus. A new attraction is a minisub simulator which takes you deep down into Baikal's nippy waters; adjoining the building is a park containing over 400 species of plants, some rare or endangered.

Baikal Dog Sledding Centre DOG SLEDDING
(☑8-908-660 5098; www.baikalsled.ru; ul Kulikova 136a) From December to March the centre offers thrilling dog sledding on forest tracks. All kinds of tours are available, from 5km tasters for R1500 per person to multiday trans-Baikal ice expeditions costing over R70,000. Some English spoken.

St Nicholaas Church CHURCH
(Krestovka) Listvyanka's small mid-19th-century timber church is dedicated to St Nicholas who supposedly saved its merchant sponsor from a Baikal shipwreck.

Retro Park ART GALLERY
(Krestovka) This garden near the St Nicholas Church is full of wacky sculpture pieces fashioned from old Soviet-era cars and motorbikes.

Nerpinarium AQUARIUM
(www.baikalnerpa.ru; ul Gorkogo 101A; admission R400; ⊙11am-5pm Tue-Fri, to 6pm Sat & Sun) Thirty-minute seal shows in a silver building resembling an upturned ship next to the Priboy Hotel.

Sleeping

Many Irkutsk tour agents and even some hostels and hotels have their own guesthouse or homestay in Listvyanka. For turn-up-and-hope homestays the best street to try first is ul Chapaeva.

TOP CHOICE **Baikaler Eco-Hostel** HOSTEL €
(☑8-924-839 6520; www.baikaler.com/eco-hostel; ul Chapaeva 77A; dm R300-700, tw R1500-1700;

THE GREAT BAIKAL TRAIL

Inspired largely by the Tahoe Rim Trail (a hiking path encircling Lake Tahoe in California and Nevada), in summer 2003 a small band of enthusiasts began work on the first section of what was grandly named the Great Baikal Trail (GBT; in Russian, Bolshaya Baikalskaya Tropa, BBT). Every summer since has seen hundreds of volunteers flock to Lake Baikal's pebbly shores to bring the GBT organisation's stated aim – the creation of a 2000km-long network of trails encircling the whole of Lake Baikal – closer to fruition. This lofty ambition may still be a far-off dream, but the GBT is nonetheless the first such trail system in all Russia.

These rudimentary bits of infrastructure, the GBT organisation hopes, will attract more low-impact tourists to the region, thus encouraging ecofriendly businesses to flourish and providing an alternative to industrial and mass tourism development. Volunteers and local activists are also involved in raising awareness of environmental issues among local people, visiting schools and fundraising. Nomination as a finalist in National Geographic's 2008 Geotourism Challenge is arguably the GBT's greatest achievement to date and greatly raised its profile in the world of ecotourism.

Many Baikal explorers simply enjoy trekking the 540km of trails created thus far, but every year young and old from around the world join work crews for a few enjoyable weeks of clearing pathways, cutting steps, creating markers and cobbling together footbridges. Those eager to volunteer should visit the **GBT website** (www.greatbaikaltrail.org), or contact Evgenia Nekrasova, GBT's International Volunteer Coordinator (gbt.volunteers@gmail.com).

@⊠) Located at the far end of ul Chapaeva, this purpose-built hostel provides top-notch digs for backpacker prices, leaving Listvyanka's other flat-footed accommodation in its green wake. From the energy-saving light bulbs and basalt-foam insulation to the solar-heated water and solar-generated electricity, owner Jack Sheremetoff has crafted a low-impact haven with lots of personal touches. Start the day with a bit of sun worship on the yoga deck and breakfast on the forest-facing chill-out area; end it with a scramble up the mini climbing wall and a scrub down in the *banya* (bathhouse) before snuggling up in a hand-made timber bed (no bunks) in an en suite dorm. Guest kitchen, 24-hour reception and many other features you won't find anywhere else. Booking well ahead is essential.

Derevenka
HOTEL €€
(☑8-914-877 5599; www.baikal-derevenka.ru; ul Gornaya 1; s/d R2000/3000, camping pitch R350) On a ridge behind the shore road, cute little wooden huts (named after Baikal's winds) with stove-heaters, private toilets and hot water (but shared showers) offer Listvyanka's most appealing semi-budget choice. Behind the complex is Listvyanka's only official campsite. Rates include breakfast.

U Ozera
HOTEL €€
(У Озера; ☑496 777; Irkutsk Hwy km3; d R2500-4000, cottages R3500-5000; ⊠) Just 10m from the shoreline, it's not surprising that all nine rooms (doubles only) at this small hotel have wonderful lake views. Rooms are a little too intimate but have balconies where you can stretch out. The cottages sleeping two lack the views but offer more space. Located between Krestovka and Rogatka.

Baikal Dream
GUESTHOUSE €€
(☑496 758; ul Chapaeva 69; s R1100-1300, d R1500-2000) Brick-built Baikal Dream offers big bright comfortable rooms with underfloor heated bathrooms but minimalist decor. There's also a common room with leather sofas and TV and a guest kitchen. Eager-to-please owner Nikolai will pick you up from the bus stop and cook you delicious meals. He also guarantees you won't forget his '*banya* experience'. Breakfast included.

Devyaty Val
GUESTHOUSE €€
(☑496 814; www.9val.irk.ru; ul Chapaeva 24; d R1800-2200; @⊠) Friendly, family-run guesthouse where the huge, good-value *lyux* rooms with big beds, TV and private shower and toilet in a long timber extension are a big step up from the *polo-lyux*. There's a small indoor pool (R1000 per hour) and rates include breakfast.

Hotel Mayak
HOTEL €€€
(496 911; www.mayakhotel.ru; ul Gorkogo 85; s/tw R4300/4900; 🐾) There were once (now mothballed) plans to transform Listvyanka and other villages on the shores of Lake Baikal into purpose-built resorts with plasticky upmarket hotels like the 'Lighthouse'. The village's most in-your-face hotel has Western-standard rooms, a good restaurant and an unbeatable location near the hydrofoil quay.

Baikal Chalet
GUESTHOUSE €€
(3952-461 557; www.baikalcomplex.com; ul Gudina 75; tw R2000) The 13 comfortable twin rooms in this timber guesthouse around 800m back from the lake are a good deal. Sister guesthouse in Bolshie Koty offers similar rates and standards. Breakfast included.

Priboy
HOTEL €€
(496 725; upper fl, ul Gorkogo 101; dm R500, r R2500) Spitting distance from the lake in the port area, this glass-and-steel block of incongruity has cheap, if unappealing, dorms and some basic rooms with shared toilet, shower and dubious taste in wallpaper. A Chinese restaurant occupies the ground level.

Krestovaya Pad
HOTEL €€€
(496 863; www.baikalvip.ru; ul Gornaya 14a; d R3000-6000) Big, brash and quite pricey, this upmarket complex housing very comfortable, international-standard pine-clad rooms dominates the hillside above Krestovka.

Green House
HOSTEL €
(496 707; ul Shtorkmana 3; dm R700) Located right by the market, this one-time guesthouse now touts itself as a hostel. It has a TV room and guest kitchen but ageing communal bathrooms. Bookable through Hostelworld.

✖ Eating
Near the port, the large fish and souvenir market is the best place to buy smoked *omul* and is surrounded by greasy spoons offering cheap *plov* and shashlyk.

Proshly Vek
RUSSIAN €€
(ul Lazlo 1; meals R160-520; ⊗noon-midnight; 🖬) Listvyanka's most characterful eatery has a nautical theme, a fish-heavy menu and Baikal views. The upper floor is filled with fascinating old junk which you can admire while tucking into *omul* done any which way you please.

Pyaty Okean
CAFE €€
(ul Gorkogo 59A; mains R150-320; ⊗11am-10pm) The speciality at this lakeside place is Baikal Abyss – fish and potatoes baked in sour cream. Eat indoors or out by the gurgling Cheremshanka stream.

Café Podlemore
CAFE €
(ul Gorkogo 31; mains R120-160; ⊗9am-midnight; 🖬) The Podlemore has porridge and oven-fresh pastries, but rather flummoxed serving staff. Early opening makes it a popular breakfast halt.

Shury Mury
CAFE €€
(meals R130-400; ⊗10am-11pm) This handy but overpriced cafe next to the tourist centre boasts a lakeside summer terrace.

❶ Information
ATMs can be found in the Mayak and Baikal hotels.

Post office (ul Gorkogo 49; internet per hr R50; ⊗8am-1pm & 2-8pm Mon-Fri, 9am-6pm Sat) Internet access.

Tourist office (656 099; hydrofoil quay; ⊗10am-1pm & 2-6pm) Surprisingly useful office handing out free maps as well as providing bus, ferry and hydrofoil timetables and offering imaginative Baikal boat trips. Bike rental available (per hour/day R150/800); some staff speak English.

❶ Getting There & Away
Hourly *marshrutka* 524 (R100, 1¼ hours) leaves for Irkutsk from outside the information centre (where tickets are bought). The last service departs at 9pm.

From mid-May to late September, hydrofoils stop at Listvyanka between Irkutsk (R320, one hour) and Bolshie Koty (R250, 30 minutes) three times a day.

Year-round a tiny, battered car ferry lumbers across the never-frozen Angara River mouth to Port Baikal from Rogatka.

Port Baikal   Порт Байкал
3952 / POP 425 / ⊗MOSCOW +5HR
You'd be excused for dismissing Port Baikal as a rusty semi-industrial eyesore when seen from Listvyanka across the unbridged mouth of the Angara River. But the view is misleading. A kilometre southwest of Stanitsa (the port area), Baranchiki is a ramshackle 'real' village with lots of unkempt but authentic Siberian cottages and a couple of handy accommodation options. Awkward

ferry connections mean that Port Baikal remains largely uncommercialised, lacking Listvyanka's attractions but also its crowds. It's thus popular with more meditative visitors, but the main draw is that it's both the beginning and terminus of the Circumbaikal Railway.

From 1900 to 1904 the Trans-Siberian Railway tracks from Irkutsk came to an abrupt halt at Port Baikal. They continued on Lake Baikal's far eastern shore at Mysovaya (Babushkin), and the watery gap was plugged by ice-breaking steamships, including the *Angara,* now restored and on view in Irkutsk. Later, the tracks were pushed south and around the lake. This Circumbaikal line required so many impressive tunnels and bridges that it earned the nickname 'The Tsar's Jewelled Buckle'. With the damming of the Angara River in the 1950s, the original Irkutsk–Port Baikal section was submerged and replaced with an Irkutsk–Kultuk shortcut (today's Trans-Siberian). That left poor little Port Baikal to wither away at the dead end of a rarely used but incredibly scenic branch line.

Sleeping & Eating

If the last ferry back to Listvyanka has just left, the B&B is full and the Yakhont seems too expensive, it's always possible to fall back on several basic homestays in Baranchiki. Ask around or look out for 'сдаются комнаты' signs. Apart from the Yakhont restaurant, a couple of poorly stocked grocery kiosks are the only sources of sustenance. Both accommodation options listed here offer meals, and homestays often have a kitchen guests can use.

Yakhont
HOTEL €€

(☏250 496; www.baikalrest.ru; ul Naberezhnaya 3; s/tw R3000/3100) Port Baikal's top digs could be the Siberian boutique hotel you've been dreaming of. It's a traditionally designed log house decorated with eclectic good taste by the well-travelled English-speaking owners. Guests congregate in the stylish communal kitchen-dining room, above which rooms have perfect Western bathrooms. The large restaurant below the hotel is the village's sole eatery. Advance bookings are essential.

Gostevoy Dom Paradis
GUESTHOUSE €

(☏607 450; www.baikal.tk; ul Baikalskaya 12; full board R1450) Cheaper than the Yakhont, this timber guesthouse is set 400m back from the lakeside. Various pine-clad but rather spartan rooms share two Western-style toilets and a shower.

ⓘ Getting There & Away

The ferry (R70, 20 minutes) to Rogatka near Listvyanka's Baikal Museum runs year-round, four times daily at 8.15am, 11.15am, 4.15pm and 6.15pm (departures at 6.50am, 10.30am, 3.50pm and 5.50pm from Rogatka), but check the schedule beforehand. From mid-June to August there are direct hydrofoils to/from Irkutsk (one hour 10 minutes). All services are operated by **VSRP** (www.vsrp.ru).

Very infrequent trains come via the slow Circumbaikal route from Slyudyanka.

Bolshie Koty
Большие Коты

POP 50 / ⊙MOSCOW +5HR

Tiny and roadless, this serene Baikal village is what the great Siberian escape is all about. But things weren't always this quiet; in the 19th century Koty experienced a mini gold rush and boasted soap and candle factories, a glassworks, churches and a school. Today all that's long since over, leaving Irkutsk's nouveau riche to assemble their lakeside dachas in peace.

A section of the Great Baikal Trail runs between Koty and Listvyanka, a fabulous full- or half-day hike (around 20km). Take plenty of food (drink from the lake) as there's none en route.

Three minutes' walk from the hydrofoil quay, the **Lesnaya 7 Hostel** (☏8-904-118 7275; www.lesnaya7.com; ul Lesnaya 7; dm R600-700; ⊙Mar & May–mid-Oct; @) fills a traditional timber house where showers run hot and the 12 beds are all in double rooms. Booking ahead is essential.

The only way to reach Bolshie Koty (unless you hike from Listvyanka) is aboard one of the three hydrofoils a day from Irkutsk (via Listvyanka). Check **VSRP** (www.vsrp.ru) for times and ticket prices. Winter ice roads briefly unite the village with the outside world.

Olkhon Island
Остров Ольхон

POP 1500 / ⊙MOSCOW +5HR

Halfway up Lake Baikal's western shore and reached by a short ferry journey from Sakhyurta (aka MRS), the serenely beautiful Olkhon Island is a wonderful place from

CIRCUMBAIKAL RAILWAY

Excruciatingly slow or a great social event? Opinions are mixed, but taking one of the four-per-week Slyudyanka–Port Baikal trains along the scenic, lake-hugging Circumbaikal Railway (Кругобайкальская Железная Дорога) remains a very popular tourist activity. The most picturesque sections of the route are the valley, pebble beach and headland at Polovinnaya (around halfway), and the bridge area at km149. Views are best if you can persuade the driver to let you ride on the front of the locomotive – possible on certain tour packages. Note that most trains *from* Port Baikal travel by night and so are useless for sightseeing.

The old stone tunnels, cliff cuttings and bridges are an attraction even for non-train buffs who might drive alongside sections of the route on winter ice roads from **Kultuk**. Hiking the entire route or just sections of the peaceful track is also popular and walking a couple of kilometres from Port Baikal leads to some pleasant, if litter-marred, beaches. Or get off an Irkutsk–Slyudyanka *elektrichka* (suburban train) at Temnaya Pad three hours into the journey and hike down the stream valley for about an hour. You should emerge at km149 on the **Circumbaikal track**, from where you can continue by train to Port Baikal if you time things well.

At the time of research, short wooden-seated Matanya trains departed from a side platform at Slyudyanka I station at 1.30pm, four times per week – check timetables carefully. In summer an additional tourist train direct from Irkutsk departs at 7.42am on Saturday. Wonderfully detailed website **Circumbaikal Railway** (http://kbzd.irk.ru/Eng/) has regularly updated timetables plus photographs of virtually every inch of the route.

Irkutsk agencies such as **Krugobaikalsky Ekspress** (☑3952-202 973; www.krugo baikalka.ru) run organised Circumbaikal tours (R1900 including lunch), though some travellers grumble about the rather superfluous 'guides' who tag along for the entire nine-hour trip.

which to view the lake and relax during a tour of Siberia. Considered one of five global poles of shamanic energy by the Buryat people, the 72km-long island's 'capital' is the unlovely village of **Khuzhir** (Хужир), which has seen something of an unlikely tourist boom over the last decade, mainly thanks to the efforts of Nikita's Homestead.

Escaping Khuzhir's dusty, dung-splattered streets is the key to enjoying Olkhon. Every morning, tours leave from Khuzhir's guesthouses to the north and south of the island, the most popular a seven-hour bounce in a UAZ minivan to dramatic **Cape Khoboy** at Olkhon's very northern tip where Baikal seals sometimes bask. Driver-guides cook fish soup for lunch over an open fire, but few speak any English. See the Nikita's Homestead website (www.olkhon.info) for details of this and other excursions. Otherwise, rent a bike and strike out on your own. Maps are available from Nikita's but take all food and water with you as there's none outside Khuzhir.

◉ Sights & Activities

The following sights provide minor distraction in Khuzhir.

Museum MUSEUM
(ul Pervomayskaya 24; admission R100; ⊘2-8pm Sun-Fri) Khuzhir's small museum displays a random mix of stuffed animals, Soviet-era junk, local art and the personal possessions of its founder, Nikolai Revyakin, a teacher for five decades at the school next door.

Shaman Rocks LANDMARK
A short walk north of Nikita's, the unmistakable Shaman Rocks are neither huge nor spectacular, but they have become the archetypal Baikal vista found on postcards and travel-guide covers. A long strip of sandy beach lines the Maloe More east of the rocks.

🛏 Sleeping & Eating

Khuzhir has an ever-growing range of places to stay, though the vast majority of independent travellers bunk down at Nikita's Homestead. If all 50 rooms at Nikita's are full staff can arrange homestays costing around R850 with meals taken at the Homestead canteen (R400 without meals). Booking ahead anywhere in Khuzhir is only necessary during July and August. There's no ATM on the island, so you'll need to bring enough cash to cover your stay.

CASH FOR TRASH

At time of research a small environmental tax (R25) was being levied on all visitors arriving on Olkhon to fund desperately needed refuse collection across the island. Rest assured, this is not a scam.

TOP CHOICE **Nikita's Homestead** GUESTHOUSE €
(www.olkhon.info; ul Kirpichnaya 8; full board per person R900-1150; ⏲reception 8am-11pm) Occupying a sizeable chunk of Khuzhir, this intricately carved timber complex has grown (and continues to grow) into one of Siberia's top traveller hang-outs. The basic rooms in myriad shapes and sizes are attractively decorated with petroglyphs and other ethnic finery and heated by wood-burning stoves – but only a select few have showers (put your name down for the *banya*). The vastly improved organic meals are served three times a day in the large canteen near reception and two other (paid) eateries (French and Uzbek) stand behind. There's a small cycle-hire centre and a packed schedule of excursions and activities, plus staff can register your visa (R350).

U Olgi GUESTHOUSE €
(☎8-908-661 9015; ul Lesnaya 3-1; full board per person R750, without meals R350) This well-liked option has nine rooms, three in a typical village house and six in a purpose-built, pine-fragrant building opposite. New showers and flushing toilets plus scrumptious Siberian fare cooked by Olga herself make this a winner every time. Book through Baikaler in Irkutsk.

Camping Hotel Olkhon HOTEL €€
(Кемпинг-Отель Ольхон; ☎708 885; www.alphatour.ru; Baikalskaya 64; summer huts s R900-2100, d R1300-2100, hotel s R2200-3000, d R2700-3500, economy rooms s R300-600, d R600-800, tent pitches R100) This hotel with an enclosure of timber Monopoly houses out back has four standards of accommodation – comfortable hotel rooms, basic cottages, spartan crash-pad cubicles and tent pitches. Full board is an extra R650 and receptionists speak English. It's 200m beyond the shop (to the left) at the top end of the main street (ul Baikalskaya).

Solnechnaya GUESTHOUSE €
(Солнечная; ☎3952-683 216; www.olkhon.com; ul Solnechnaya 14; full board per person R1100-1450; @) No happening scene like at Nikita's, but it's still a pleasant place to stay offering a good range of activities. Accommodation is in two-storey cabins and tiny single-room shacks with verandas. Enter from ul Solnechnaya or from near the relay station at the top of the hill.

ℹ Getting There & Away

The simplest way to reach Olkhon is aboard the morning *marshrutka* that leaves Irkutsk's hostels around 8.30am. Many other services run in July and August but can be impossible to track down in Irkutsk.

With a little warning, agencies or hostels can usually find you a ride in a private car to/from Irkutsk (5½ hours) for R1250 per seat, R5000 for the whole car. Prices include the short ferry ride to/from MRS – from mid-January to March an ice road replaces the ferry. When ice is partly formed or partly melted, the island is completely cut off for motor vehicles, though an ad hoc minihovercraft service is sometimes operated by locals.

In summer a hydrofoil service operates from Irkutsk to Olkhon, dropping passengers near the ferry terminal, from where it's possible to hitch a paid lift into Khuzhir. See **VSRP** (www.vsrp.ru) for times and prices.

South Baikal & the Tunka Valley

The windows of Trans-Siberian trains passing between Irkutsk and Ulan-Ude frame attractive lake vistas along much of Baikal's south coast. Few Westerners are actually tempted off the train along this stretch but if they are, it's usually at Slyudyanka, the best place to start Circumbaikal train rides and a launch pad into the remotely scenic Tunka Valley.

SLYUDYANKA СЛЮДЯНКА

☎39544 / POP 18,500 / ⏲MOSCOW +5HR

Slyudyanka's glittering marble **train station** is a mere five-minute walk from Lake Baikal's scrappy shore. En route you pass a multicoloured timber **church** and, across the tracks, former locomotive workshops host an interesting **museum** (ul Zheleznodorozhnaya 22; admission R50; ⏲11am-5pm Wed-Sun) with archaeological finds, old railway switching boxes and an identification guide to 47 locomotive types. Unfortunately, there is no English. Geology buffs should consider heading to the privately run **Baikal Mineral Museum** (ul Slyudyanaya 36; admission R100;

⊘8am-9pm), which claims to exhibit every mineral known to man. Take any *marshrutka* heading from the bus station up ul Slyudyanskikh Krasnogvardeytsev and ask to be dropped off at the museum.

A popular picnic excursion is to **Cape Shaman**, an easy 4km stroll north towards Kultuk along Baikal's gravelly shore.

With moulting lino, very basic rooms and shared showers, the friendly **Hotel Chayka** (☑54 073; ul Frunze 8a; d R600) charges R300 for 12-hour stays. To get there from the train station, cross the long footbridge and walk two blocks further to a little **bus station** (ul Lenina); from here the hotel is 4km west by very frequent *marshrutky*. A taxi should cost no more than R70. The **Mineral Museum homestay** (☑53 440; ul Slyudyanaya 36; dm R700) is little more than a two-bed garden cottage which the museum curator rents out in the summer months.

At the time of research Slyudyanka had no cafe or restaurant. The only source of public nourishment was the **Bonus Supermarket** (ul Lenina 116; ⊘9am-10pm) where you can stock up on enough noodles, cheese, bread and instant porridge to keep you going all the way to the Urals.

Elektrichki (R70, four daily) from Irkutsk take four hours to reach Slyudyanka 1 station; express trains (*platskart* R540, up to eight daily) take just two to 2½ hours. Slyudyanka is also the usual starting point for the Circumbaikal Railway trip. *Marshrutky* run to Arshan (R170, two hours, at least eight daily) from the bus station.

ARSHAN АРШАН
☑30156 / POP 3600 / ⊘MOSCOW +5HR

Backed by the dramatic, cloud-wreathed peaks of the Eastern Sayan Mountains, the once drowsy Buryat spa village of Arshan has been rudely awoken from its slumber in recent years. The fast-flowing River Kyngarga still murmurs with ice-cold water from elevated valleys above the village, the prayer wheels still twirl at the tranquil little Buddhist temples and cows still blunder through the streets, but Russian-style tourism has intruded into the idyllic scene, bringing 24-hour *banya*, cut-price vodka, pounding stereos and grisly service in its wake. But despite this Arshan is still the best base in the Tunka Valley from which to strike out into the mountains, with some superb hikes accessible on foot from the village.

Arshan in Buryat means 'natural spring' and it's the pleasantly sweet, health-giving mineral water that most Russians come for. The huge **Sayany Spa** stands at the entrance to the village on the main street (ul Traktovaya), which then fires itself 2km straight towards the mountains.

Opposite the spa grounds, the **Dechen Ravzhalin Datsan** has two sparkling new prayer wheels, a miniature stupa and a dazzlingly colourful interior. From here ul Traktovaya then climbs in a parade of shops, derelict Soviet architecture and plasticky cafes and guesthouses towards the bus station, after which it swerves west to the sprawling **Kurort Arshan** resort where you can sample the water for free (pass through the turnstile near the souvenir kiosks). Head up the stream from here to access the mountain footpaths or cross the river and walk 20 minutes through the forest to the dinky little **Bodkhi Dkharma Datsan**, set in an idyllic mountain-backed glade.

🛏 Sleeping

Even late at night locals line the bottom end of ul Traktovaya like hitchhikers, brandishing their 'Жильё' (rooms) signs in hope. These usually turn out to be very basic homestays from R300 per bed – check standards before committing. Even if you turn up unannounced you'll have few problems getting a room, even at busy times (July and August). This is probably the way to go in Arshan. Otherwise, try to book ahead at the places listed below.

Yasnaya Polyana GUESTHOUSE €
(Ясная Поляна; ☑8-904-114 7808; ul Traktovaya 109; s/d R350/700) A friendly local English teacher runs this compound of 10 pine cottages, each containing two beds, a table, a stove ring and sometimes a kettle. Otherwise, things are pretty basic with a sun-heated shower (best in the evenings) and outdoor washing facilities. To find it, take the second left on entering the village (at ul Traktovaya 99) and keep going until you see a large unmarked green gate on your left.

Priyut Alpinista GUESTHOUSE
(www.iwf.ru; ul Bratev Domshevikh 8) Long a favourite with backpackers, trekkers and climbers, the 'Mountaineer's Refuge' sadly burnt down in 2008. However, there are plans to rebuild it on the same site, three minutes' walk along ul Pavlova from the bus station. In the meantime, contact the owners of the Arshansky Bor for details of the trips into the mountains that used to run from the Priyut Alpinista.

Arshansky Bor
GUESTHOUSE €

(☑8-950-050 6481; ul Bratev Domshevikh 44; dm R350-450) This unmarked pink building is the best budget place to overnight until the Priyut Alpinista is rebuilt. Rooms are dim and spartan, and facilities display the pressures of mass occupation, but there's a large kitchen, a common room and a barbecue area.

Pensionat Vershina
GUESTHOUSE €

(☑8-950-388 7590; ul Mikrorayon 22/1; s/d R350/700) Located near the Sayany Spa, this purpose-built two-storey guesthouse has cosy timber rooms with shared showers, free *banya* and a small cafe.

Monetny Dvor
GUESTHOUSE €

(☑8-904-115 6390; www.arshan-md.ru; ul Traktovaya 89; d from R1000) Brand-new timber-built guesthouse with rooms in a main building and three two-storey cottages. Cycle hire available.

✖ Eating

Eateries are thin on the ground as most Russians prebook full board at the spas. Some of the new cafes at the top of ul Traktovaya are truly dire.

Novy Vek
RUSSIAN €€

(Новый Век; ul Traktovaya 4; ⊘10am-2am) For a proper sit-down meal try this restaurant near the Arshan Spa that has recently sprouted a nightclub, entertainment centre and *stolovaya* (canteen).

Zakusochnaya Khamar Daban
CANTEEN €

(Закусочная Хамар Дабан; ul Traktovaya; ⊘10am-1am; ✱) Located opposite the Sayan Sanatorium, this pleasant canteen serves up a large menu of Buryat and Russian comfort food and cheap beers.

❶ Getting There & Away

The miniature **bus station** (⊘7.30am-6pm) near the top of ul Traktovaya has the village's only ATM, plus left-luggage lockers. Arshan has the following bus and *marshrutka* connections:

Irkutsk R270 to R350, 11 daily

Slyudyanka R170, two hours, eight daily

Ulan-Ude R610, 11 hours, five daily

Ulan-Ude
Улан-Удэ

☑3012 / POP 404,000 / ⊘MOSCOW +5HR

With its smiley Asian features, cosy city centre and fascinating Mongol-Buddhist culture, the Buryat capital is one of Eastern Siberia's most likeable cities. Quietly busy, welcoming and, after Siberia's Russian cities, refreshingly exotic, it's a pleasant place to base yourself for day trips to Buddhist temples and flits to eastern Lake Baikal's gently shelving beaches, easily reachable by bus. For some travellers UU is also a taster for what's to come in Mongolia, to which there are now much-improved transport links.

Founded as a Cossack *ostrog* (fort) called Udinsk (later Verchneudinsk) in 1666, the city prospered as a major stop on the tea-caravan route from China via Troitskosavsk (now Kyakhta). Renamed Ulan-Ude in 1934, it was a closed city until the 1980s due to its secret military plants.

UU's small city centre is easily explored on foot. It's divided into two districts: the communist-era upper city is centred around pl Sovetov and the Lenin Head; descend ul Lenina to the partially pedestrianised lower city, the former merchant quarter, half of which still serves as the commercial hub extending from the 19th-century trading rows (pl Revolutsii). Dust streets of crooked timber dwellings make up the other half.

◎ Sights

Lenin Head
MONUMENT

(Голова Ленина; pl Sovetov) Ulan-Ude's main square is awesomely dominated by the world's largest Lenin head, which some maintain looks comically cross-eyed. The 7.7m-high bronze bonce (head) was installed in 1970 to celebrate Lenin's 100th birthday. Oddly, UU's bird population never seem to streak Lenin's bald scalp with their offerings – out of respect for the great man's achievements, claim die-hard communists (but perhaps due to the barely visible anti-bird spikes, groan the rest).

Khangalov Museum of Buryat History
MUSEUM

(Исторический музей; Profsoyuznaya ul 29; admission per fl R80, for all floors R180; ⊘11am-7pm Tue-Sun) The historical museum charges per single-room floor and the best of these is Buddiyskoe Iskustvo (3rd floor), displaying *thangkas,* Buddhas and icons salvaged from Buryatiya's monasteries before their Soviet destruction. Note sheets in English fail to explain the fascinating, gaudy papier-mâché models of deities and bodhisattvas rescued from Buryatiya's many prewar *datsany* (temples). Note the home shrine table and the sometimes gory Tibetan medical charts. The less-interesting 2nd floor traces Buryat history in maps, documents and artefacts. Spy it for free from the balcony above.

Ethnographic Museum   MUSEUM
(Verkhnyaya Berezovka; admission R150; ⊘9.30am-6pm Tue-Fri, 10am-7pm Sat & Sun) In a forest clearing 6km from central Ulan-Ude, this outdoor collection of local architecture plus some reconstructed burial mounds and the odd stone totem is worth the trip. It's divided into seven areas, each devoted to a different nationality, tribe or ethnic group. There are Hun-era standing stones, Evenki *chumy,* traditional Buryat yurts, timber European townhouses and a whole strip of Old Believers' homesteads, all brimming with period furniture and inhabited by costumed 'locals' giving craft demonstrations. *Marshrutka* 37 from outside the Hotel Baikal Plaza on pl Sovetov passes within 1km and drivers are used to detouring to drop off tourists.

Opera & Ballet Theatre   THEATRE
(Театр оперы и балета Бурятии; ☑213 600; www .uuopera.ru; ul Lenina 51; ⊘ticket office 11am-7pm) UU's striking Stalinist-era theatre reopened after lengthy renovation in June 2011 (the first performance was for a group of foreign tourists from the luxury *Golden Eagle* train). Visitors cannot fail to be impressed by the level of craftsmanship inside, though some might be slightly surprised at the new lick of paint and rub of polish given to all the Soviet symbols, including a couple of smirking Stalins. Next to the building is the 2006 replica of an 1891 **triumphal arch** (Триумфальная арка) honouring the then imperial heir, Nicholas II, the only tsar ever to set foot in Siberia.

Rinpoche Bagsha Datsan   BUDDHIST TEMPLE
(ul Dzerzhinskogo) Roosting high above the city's far north, the inside of this new and unexpectedly modern Tibetan temple looks like a kind of Buddhist-themed bus terminal, though the 6m-high gilt Buddha is pretty impressive and if you catch the monks doing their thing with drums, cymbals and chanting the atmosphere can be electric. The real show-stealer here is the panoramic views, the smog-hazed city ringed by rumpled dust-bare peaks. Take *marshrutka* 97 from outside the Hotel Baikal Plaza on pl Sovetov to the last stop (right by the temple entrance).

Ulan-Ude City Museum   MUSEUM
(ul Lenina 26; admission R50; ⊘10am-6pm) Occupying the merchant's house where imperial heir Nicholas II stayed in 1891, this small museum has exhibits examining Verkhneud-

---

NATIONAL MUSEUM OF BURYATIYA

Still at the planning stage, the aim of the new National Museum project will be to gather together many of Ulan-Ude's museums and galleries in one purpose-built complex located near the hippodrome in the Verkhnyaya Berezovka suburb. This will create a spectacular repository of the nation's past, and, it must be said, free up some pretty valuable city-centre plots for development. City officials claim it'll all be done and dusted by 2014 – locals are sceptical.

---

insk's role in the tea and fur trades, the huge fairs that took place at the trading arches and several other aspects of the city's past.

Odigitria Cathedral   CHURCH
(ul Lenina 2) Built between 1741 and 1785, UU's largest church was also the first stone structure to appear in the city. Used as a museum store from 1929 until the fall of communism, the exterior has been renovated in a chalky white and the domes once again tipped with gold, but the interiors are plain whitewash, awaiting their Byzantine decoration.

Hippodrome   HIPPODROME
(Barguzinsky Trakt) This site near the Ethnographic Museum is the venue for major festivals including the Surkharban in early June, the biggest Buryat sporting event of the year featuring archery, wrestling and exhilarating feats of horsemanship. While the hippodrome lies dormant for most of the year, nearby you'll find a pair of attractive *datsany* backed by stupas and trees aflutter with prayer flags. Take *marshrutka* 37 from pl Sovetov.

Nature Museum   MUSEUM
(Музей природы Бурятии; ul Lenina 46; admission R100; ⊘10am-6.30pm Wed-Sun) The Nature Museum has taxidermically stuffed animals and a scale model of Lake Baikal showing just how deep it is.

FREE Geological Museum   MUSEUM
(Геологический музей Бурятии; ul Lenina 59; ⊘11am-5pm Mon-Fri) This museum displays rocks, crystals and ores from the shores of Lake Baikal as well as art (for sale) made using multi-hued grit, sand and pebbles.

Ulan-Ude

N

0 _____ 200 m
0 _____ 0.1 miles

To Samovar
(100m)

ul Tsivleva

ul Gagarina

31
14

ul Revolyutsii 1905

20
27

Train
Station

Sagaan
Morin
Market

12

Market

ul Borsoeva

Sagaan Morin
Shopping
Mall

11

ul Lesnaya

15

pr 50-let Oktyabrya

ul Sukhe-Batora

ul Ranzhurova

ul Kommunisticheskaya

pl
Sovetov

2

4

19

32 33 9

21

6

16

22

23

25

17

30

Mongolian
Consulate

7

3

Profsoyuznaya ul

10

13

24

Profsoyuznaya ul

ul Lenina

18

5

28

Sovetskaya ul

pr Pobedy

To Former
Main Bus
Station (50m)

ul Smolina

ul Baltakhinova

Vostochnaya ul

ul Kalandarishvili

8

ul Frunze

ul Kommunisticheskaya

29

ul Kirova

ul Shmidta

Chapel

Trading
Arcades

1

26

ul Kuybysheva

To Banzarova Station (100m);
Odigitria Cathedral (150m)

To Chingiskhan (1km);
Hotel Ayan (3.5km)

Ulan-Ude

◉ Sights
1 Fine Arts Museum C7
2 Geological Museum B3
3 Khangalov Museum of Buryat
   History C4
4 Lenin Head B3
5 Nature Museum B5
6 Opera & Ballet Theatre B4
7 Triumphal Arch B4
8 Ulan-Ude City Museum B6

◉ Activities, Courses & Tours
Baikal Naran Tur .... (see 10)
Morin Tur .... (see 12)

◉ Sleeping
9 Hotel Baikal Plaza B4
10 Hotel Buryatiya B5
11 Hotel Geser A2
12 Hotel Sagaan Morin D2
13 Hotel Sibir B5
14 Resting Rooms B1
15 Ulan-Ude Travellers House B3

◉ Eating
16 Happyland B4
17 King Food C4
18 Marusya B5

19 Modern Nomads A4
20 Nikolayevsky Supermarket A1
21 Sputnik Supermarket C4
22 Yurt Café B4

◉ Drinking
23 Beer Mug C4
24 Bochka C5
25 Kofeynya Marco Polo C4
26 Sky Bar D7

◉ Shopping
Baikal Naran Tour Souvenir
   Kiosk .... (see 10)
27 Ekspeditsiya A1
28 Ochir B5

◉ Information
29 Buryat-Intour C7

◉ Transport
30 Akbes Tur C4
31 Buses & Marshrutky to Arshan,
   Irkutsk and Chita B1
32 Central Ticket Office B4
33 Marshrutka 37 to Ethnographic
   Museum B4
S7 Airlines .... (see 15)

Fine Arts Museum   MUSEUM
(Художественный музей; ul Kuybysheva 29; admission R200; ◷10am-7pm Tue-Sun) Come here for regularly changing exhibitions as well as permanent displays of Buryat and Russian art.

☞ Tours

Ulan-Ude has many agencies happy to sell you Buryatiya and Baikal tours. The following companies and individuals all speak English and are tuned in to the needs of Western travellers.

TOP CHOICE **Baikal Naran Tour**   TOUR COMPANY
(☎215 097; www.baikalnaran.com; info@baikalnaran.com; room 105, Hotel Buryatiya, ul Kommunisticheskaya 47a) There's nothing director Sesegma (aka Svetlana) and charming daughter Naran can't arrange for travellers in Buryatiya. They run an award-winning tour company and are by far the best folks to approach if you want to see the republic's more remote corners, Old Believer villages, the Selenga Delta, the Barguzin

Valley and the region's Buddhist and Shamanist heritage.

Denis Sobnakov   TOUR GUIDE
(☎8-950-391 6325; www.uuhostel.com; ul Lenina 63) English-speaking Denis runs the city's best hostel as well as fun-packed walking tours of UU and many other Buryatiya-wide trips.

MorinTur   TOUR COMPANY
(☎443 647; www.morintour.com; Hotel Sagaan Morin, ul Gagarina 25) Focuses on east Baikal, offering various ice and fishing adventures, a horse-sledge trip, seal watching, rafting in the Barguzin Valley and climbing on Svyatoy Nos (Holy Nose) Peninsula.

Buryat-Intour   TOUR COMPANY
(☎216 954; www.buryatintour.ru; ul Kirova 28a) Can arrange birdwatching in the Selenga Delta, monastery visits and city tours. Also sells air tickets.

Firn Travel   TOUR COMPANY
(☎555 055; www.firntravel.ru; ul Babushkina 13a) Eastern Baikal tours and activities.

Solongo TOUR COMPANY

(☎8-902-564 7060) Baseless tour company arranging Old Believer tours and city walks.

🛏 Sleeping

For years Ulan-Ude has been crying out for a hostel – now it has two excellent budget options, where common rooms buzz with traveller talk and Trans-Sib banter.

Showers can run very cold when the city's central hot-water system is turned off for several days (or even weeks) in early summer and autumn for maintenance.

TOP **Ulan-Ude Travellers House** HOSTEL €
CHOICE

(☎8-950-391 6325; www.uuhostel.com; ul Lenina 63, apt 18; dm R600; 🗟) So central is this brand-new, high-ceilinged apartment hostel, you might even catch a glimpse of Lenin's conk from one of the windows. The 14 beds are divided between two spacious, ethnically themed dorms (Russian and Buryat), there's a small kitchen where a free light breakfast is laid out daily, there's heaps of UU information pasted on the walls and there's a washing machine for guests to use. Exceptionally friendly owner Denis is a professional tour guide, fluent English-speaker and guitar demon – bring your six-string for a common-room jam session. Booking ahead advised.

Hotel Ayan HOTEL €€

(Аян Отель; ☎415 141; www.ayanhotel.ru; ul Babushkina 164; s R1500-2000, tw R1800-4000; ✱🗟) The inconvenient location 2km south of the city centre is more than recompensed by pristine international-standard rooms, some with air-conditioning. The cheapest singles are a good deal and every room has its own water heater. There's also a tiny cafe should you get peckish from all the stair climbing you'll do here – incredibly, this six-storey new-build has no lift.

Hotel Sagaan Morin HOTEL €€€

(Отель Сагаан Морин; ☎444 019; www.sagaan -morin.ru; ul Gagarina 25; s/tw R3000/4200; 🗟) The gleaming new 17-storey, 89-room 'White Horse' opened in 2009, replacing its predecessor next door. The switch has promoted the hotel to UU's accommodation premier league with spacious, crisply designed, almost understated rooms, lots of amenities and a 14th-floor restaurant with look-while-you-eat city vistas.

GBT Hostel HOSTEL €

(☎553 470; per Nakhimova 9-2; dm R550, d R1300) A totally different scene from the Travellers House, this homely, freshly fitted-out hostel occupies a suburban house built by Japanese prisoners of war, 2.5km northeast of the city centre. Two dorms sleep 10 and there's one double as well as a fully equipped kitchen. As the name suggests, the owners are heavily involved in the Great Baikal Trail project and this is one of the best places to get trekking info. Book ahead and arrange a free station pick-up as it's almost impossible to find on your own.

Hotel Baikal Plaza HOTEL €€€

(Гостиница Байкал; ☎210 070; www.baikalplaza .com; ul Erbanova 12; s R3600, tw R4600) The 68 modern, if slightly cramped, rooms were arguably UU's finest offering when first renovated a few years ago, and the central location overlooking the Lenin Head is unrivalled. However, huge price rises in recent years mean this is not the attractive deal it once was.

Hotel Geser HOTEL €€

(Гостиница Гэсэр; ☎216 151; www.geser-hotel .ru; ul Ranzhurova 11; s/tw R2500/3100) Modernisation and realistic prices have made this former Party hang-out a popular option – the only Soviet features remaining are clacking parquet floors and the odd clunky fridge. Secondhand tobacco pong spoils some rooms but most are decent enough, especially those with rare baths. Rates include breakfast and one or two staff members speak English.

Hotel Sibir HOTEL €€€

(Гостиница Сибирь; ☎297 257; www.hoteltrk.ru; ul Pochtamtskaya 1; s R3000, d R4000; ✱) This futuristic metallic cube stands in stark contrast to the ageing Buryatiya opposite. Welcoming doubles have dark wood furniture, impeccable bathrooms and flat-screen TVs, but singles are a touch too austere.

Hotel Buryatiya HOTEL €€

(Гостиница Бурятия; ☎211 505; ul Kommunis-ticheskaya 47a; s & d R1600-4600; @) The mammoth Buryatiya, the former Intourist hotel, has 220 rooms of wildly differing sizes and standards: some are Soviet-era broom cupboards with dodgy plumbing, others are almost palatial with sparkling European bathrooms. One advantage to staying here is the convenience of extra services (internet room, tour companies, souvenir kiosks, ATMs) on the 1st floor – there's even a Buddhist temple!

Resting rooms
HOSTEL €

(комнаты отдыха, komnaty otdykha; ☑282 696; Ulan-Ude train station; 12/24hr R600/1200) Well-maintained crash pad at the train station.

✕ Eating

For a fascinating insight into traditional Buryat life, Baikal Naran Tour can arrange dinner in a yurt with a local family out in the suburbs of Ulan-Ude.

Baatarai Urgöö
BURYAT €€

(Barguzinsky Trakt, Verkhnyaya Berezovka; mains R250-400; ☺noon-11pm) This large yurt restaurant in the suburb of Verkhnyaya Berezovka is a great lunch spot after a visit to the nearby Ethnographical Museum. Take a seat in the main tent and give your taste buds the Buryat treatment in the form of *buuzy* (aka *pozi*, meat-filled dumplings), *bukhuler* (meat broth), *salamat* (creamy sour porridge) and a mug of milky green tea. Take *marshrutka* 37 from pl Sovetov to the yurt stop.

Chingiskhan
ASIAN FUSION €€

(Sun Tower, Karla Marksa 25a; mains R250-500; ☺11am-11.30pm) A huge carved portrait of Chinggis himself offers a stern welcome to this upmarket restaurant, crafted in the shape of a traditional circular yurt. The steppe's bon vivant and conqueror of half the world would no doubt approve of the eclectic Eurasian menu of expertly fused Russian, Buryat and Chinese dishes and the finely tuned feng shui. The restaurant is situated in the Sun Tower, south of the river Uda. Take any tram heading south from the market and alight at the Sayany stop.

Yurt Café
BURYAT €

(behind the Hotel Baikal Plaza; mains R20-60; ☺8am-11pm) Three unmarked and interconnecting yurts behind an anonymous grey fence contain the city's liveliest and cheapest nosh spot. A very to-the-point menu lists Buryat dumplings, *shulen* soup, *sharbin* (oily mutton-filled pancakes), bliny, salads, tea and beer – that's it. Stoop through the door, order your food, make a note of your order number and sit down. Waitresses bring out trays in around five minutes. Gets hot in summer and watch out for the wasps!

Samovar
UKRAINIAN €€

(Самовар; ul Gagarina 41; mains R90-360; ☺10am-11pm) Cute basement restaurant with a rural peasant theme (think rag-rug seat covers, spinning wheels and upside-down pots on rickety fences). The menu has a firmly Ukrainian bent, heavy with *salo* (pork fat), *vareniki* (sweet dumplings), *holubtsi* (meat-filled cabbage rolls) and *zapekanka* (cheese cake) but there's plenty of Russian fare in there, too. Filling and tasty lunch menu (R120 to R200).

Marusya
RUSSIAN €€

(Маруся; ul Lenina 46; mains R100-280; ☺10am-10pm) This coy 19th-century dining room with polished samovars, *matryoshka* dolls and waitresses trussed up in pseudo folk costume occupies a corner of the Ulger Theatre. Enjoy inexpensive Russian meals at tightly packed tables to the sound of dreamy 1970s Russian chansons on CD, or flee the Chekhovian pleasantries for the shady terrace.

Modern Nomads
MONGOLIAN €€

(ul Ranzhurova 1; mains R70-1000; ☺11am-11pm Mon-Fri, from noon Sat & Sun; ⓐ) Clean-cut and very popular Mongolian place, good for a quick snack and a beer or for a full-blown dinner splurge costing thousands. Meat features heavily on the menu, but there are lots of salads with a contemporary twist to choose from, too.

King Food
FAST FOOD €

(basement, ul Kommunisticheskaya 43; meals R100-150; ☺11am-11pm) So-so food, striking pillar-box red-and-jet-black decor and crass Russian MTV; on hot days use the cutlery to slice a hole in the air. On the plus side, it's cheap, clean and conveniently central.

Happyland
FAST FOOD €

(ul Lenina 52; mains R100-150; ☺10.30am-9.30pm, bar to 11pm) This Russian self-service canteen in the cinema foyer is the cheapest source of empty calories in the city centre. It has a popular bar with Baltika 7 and Carlsberg on tap.

Sputnik Supermarket
SUPERMARKET

(Супермаркет Спутник; ul Kommunisticheskaya 48; ☺24hr) A convenient but pricey supermarket stocking foreign groceries. Get there early for real freshly baked croissants.

Nikolayevsky Supermarket
SUPERMARKET

(ul Borsoeva 25; ☺9am-11pm) Another (cheaper) supermarket on the way to the train station from the city centre – handy for buying supplies for long Trans-Sib journeys.

Drinking

Bochka
BEER HALL

(ul Kommunisticheskaya 52; ☺10am-1am) Large timber beer hall serving a range of Russian and international brews to rinse down the succulently smoky shashlyk. The covered terrace is *the* place to do some elbow bending on sultry summer evenings.

Sky Bar
CAFE

(10th fl, Eurozone Centre, ul Baltakhinova; mains R175-360; ☺9am-midnight, to 2am Fri & Sat) Perched atop the new glass-and-steel Eurozone Centre (an unwise choice of name if ever there was one), this cafe-bar has the best views in all Ulan-Ude with stupendous vistas across the entire city and the hills beyond. Opened in May 2011, the owners were eventually planning to create a more upmarket restaurant here, but whatever the space becomes, the unrivalled views are guaranteed to draw punters.

Beer Mug
BAR

(pr 50-let Oktyabrya 8a; ☺5pm-6am) New and popular nightspot with cheap beer, cocktails, a dance floor but occasional face control.

Kofeynya Marco Polo
CAFE

(Кофейня Marco Polo; ul Kommunisticheskaya 46; ☺9am-10.30pm; ☎) This cosy coffee house has a touch of Central European character, great desserts, and wi-fi for R150 per 100MB. Main dishes are pricey.

Shopping

Ochir
SOUVENIRS

(Очир; ul Lenina 46; ☺10am-7pm) Authentic, beautifully hand-painted items such as plates with Buddhist and Buryat motifs, decorated wooden eggs, *matryoshka*/Buryat dolls and Chinggis Khaan key rings. Some items are painted on the premises by the owner.

Baikal Naran Tour souvenir kiosk
SOUVENIRS

(room 105, Hotel Buryatiya, ul Kommunisticheskaya 47a) This tiny kiosk in the Baikal Naran Tour office sells authentic Buryat souvenirs such as oriental costumed dolls, shaman drums and colourful felt hats.

Ekspeditsiya
OUTDOOR GEAR

(Экспедиция; ul Borsoeva 19; ☺9am-6pm) The Ulan-Ude branch of Ekspeditsiya offers

good-quality sleeping bags, tents and other essential outdoor kit.

Information

There are exchange bureaus and ATMs in the Geser and Buryatiya hotels.

Baikal Bank (Байкал Банк; pl Sovetov 1; ☺9am-8pm Mon-Fri, 9am-7pm Sat) Most central place for changing dollars and euros.

Post office (ul Lenina 61; ☺8am-10pm Mon-Fri, 9am-6pm Sat & Sun) Internet access.

UUModa (www.uumoda.ru) Heaps of city listings, all in Russian.

Getting There & Away

Train

Train tickets can be bought at the station, but it's much more convenient to book through the **Central Ticket Office** (ul Erbanova 14; ☺9am-1pm & 2-6pm), **Baikal Naran Tour** (p209) and upper-bracket hotels (where they offer this service).

You'll miss possibly the most photogenic section of the Trans-Sib trip if you take a night train to Irkutsk. The line skirts the southern shoreline of Lake Baikal affording wide-screen views of this vast body of water, obviously best appreciated when it's light. There are four handy overnight services to Chita, train 8 being the pick of the bunch. Otherwise Ulan-Ude has the following rail connections:

Běijīng *kupe* R6000, two days to two days 15 hours, two weekly

Chita *platskart* R970, *kupe* R1500 to R2500, 10 to 12 hours, up to six daily

Irkutsk *platskart* R810, *kupe* R1200 to R2000, seven hours, up to nine daily

Ulaanbaatar *kupe* R3000, 18 to 24 hours, up to two daily

Air

UU's ageing **Baikal Airport** (www.airportbaikal.ru), 11km from the city centre, handles surprisingly few flights. Buy tickets at **S7 Airlines** (ul Sukhe-Batora 63; ☺9am-7pm) or **Akbes Tur** (ul Kommunisticheskaya 46; ☺9am-8pm, from 9.30am Sun). Ulan-Ude has the following flight connections:

Irkutsk R2500, three weekly

Moscow R10,600 to R17,000, two daily

Nizhneangarsk R4700, four weekly

Bus

Ulan-Ude has three bus stations. The former **main bus station** (ul Sovetskaya), **Banzarova Station** (ul Banzarova), and the new and utterly inconvenient **North Station** (pr Avtomobilistov 3a) – take bus 30 from pl Sovetov. Buses to destinations on Baikal's eastern shore all take the same route via the resort villages of Grem-yachinsk, Turka, Goryachinsk and Maksimikha. The city has the following bus and *marshrutka* connections:

Barguzin R500, eight hours, daily (North Station)

Kurumkan R600, 10 hours, daily (North Station)

Ust-Barguzin R400, seven hours, daily (North Station)

Kyakhta R250, three hours, many daily (main station)

Arshan R610, 11 hours, five daily (main station)

Ivolga R30, 40 minutes, many daily (Banzarova Station, *marshrutka* number 130)

Additional *marshrutky* to Arshan (R600, six hours), Irkutsk (R700, eight hours) and Chita (R700, seven hours) run from the courtyard of the train station, departing throughout the day when full but mainly around 9pm.

ⓘ Getting Around

Ulan-Ude's Trans-Sib station is situated around 500m north of the main pl Sovetov. The vast majority of *marshrutky* leaving from in front of the building head into the city centre. If you prefer to walk, cross the footbridge at the end of the platform and head southeast along ul Borsoeva.

From pl Sovetov *marshrutky* 28 and 55 run a few times hourly to the airport while *marshrutka* 37 passes the hippodrome, Ethnographic Museum and Baatarai Urgöö restaurant. *Marshrutka* 97 climbs to the Rinpoche Bagsha Datsan. Any ride on public transport costs R14.

Around Ulan-Ude

IVOLGINSKY (IVOLGA) DATSAN
ИВОЛГИНСКИЙ ДАЦАН

Possibly the last person you might expect to have backed the building of a Buddhist temple was Stalin, but in 1946 permission came from the Kremlin to erect a *datsan* in Buryatiya, in gratitude to the locals for their sacrifices during WWII it's often claimed. But instead of reviving the erstwhile centre of Buryat Buddhism at Gusinoe Ozero, the authorities granted a plot of marshy land near the village of Ivolga, 35km from central Ulan-Ude, on which the temple was to be built. The first temple was a modest affair, but today the **datsan** has grown large and is expanding fast. The confident epicentre of Russian Buddhism attracts large numbers of the devout as well as tourists on half-day trips from the Buryat capital.

UU TO UB

There are now three ways to travel from the Buryat capital to Ulaanbaatar. The least comfortable way is by Trans-Mongolian **train**, which takes up to 24 hours to complete the 657km trip and can wait up to 11 hours on the border at Naushki. A much cheaper and convenient way to go is to hop aboard the daily **coach** (R1100, 10 hours) which leaves from a stop near the roundabout behind the Opera & Ballet Theatre. Tickets can be bought from Baikal Naran Tour and the Ulan-Ude Travellers House Hostel. If you've got the cash and/or are in a hurry, there are now three **flights** a week from UU to UB with **Eznis Airways** (www.eznisairways.com). One-way tickets cost in the region of R4000.

One of only two working Buddhist temples in Soviet days (the other was at Aginskoe) most of what you see today has been built in the last two decades. A clockwise walk around the complex takes in countless monastery faculties, administrative buildings, monks' quarters and temples, but the most elaborate of all is the **Itygel Khambin Temple** honouring the 12th Khambo Lama, whose body was exhumed in 2002. To general astonishment, seven decades after his death his flesh had still not decomposed. Some 'experts' have even attested that the corpse's hair is still growing, albeit extraordinarily slowly. The body is displayed six times a year, attracting pilgrims from across the Buddhist world.

To reach the monastery, first take *marshrutka* 130 (R30, 40 minutes, four hourly) from Ulan-Ude's Banzarova bus station to the last stop in uninteresting Ivolga. There another *marshrutka* (R15, no number, just a picture of the monastery pasted to the front windscreen) waits to shuttle visitors the last few kilometres to the monastery compound. Otherwise contact agencies in Ulan-Ude who offer private transfers and tours with well-informed guides.

Eastern Baikal

✒30144

Sparsely scattered beach villages of old-fashioned log cottages dot the pretty east Baikal coast. Further north is the dramatic

Barguzin Valley, from which Chinggis Khaan's mother, Oilun-Ehe, is said to have originated. Some of the area has been slated for mass-tourism development but little has appeared in the intervening years, save for a mirror-smooth new road which has cut journey times considerably. Ulan-Ude agencies can book basic accommodation along the eastern coast where summer *turbazy* (holiday camps) are popular among Russians seeking sand.

Access to the coast is across a forested pass from Ulan-Ude via tiny **Baturino** village with its elegantly renovated Sretenskaya Church.

After around 2½ hours' drive, the newly paved road first meets Lake Baikal at pretty little **Gremyachinsk** (Гремячинск), a popular trip out of Ulan-Ude for hurried Trans-Siberian travellers with a day to spare. Buses stop at a roadside cafe from which Gremyachinsk's sandy but litter-strewn beach is a 15-minute walk up ul Komsomolskaya. *Marshrutky* back to Ulan-Ude are often full so consider prebooking your return.

Approximately 5km from Gremyachinsk, at least 10 large tourist camps are strung around **Lake Kotokel**, whose thermal springs keep it warm year-round. At the northern end of the lake rises **Monastyrsky Island**, once home to an isolated hermitage and a church.

The main road offers surprisingly few Baikal views until the fishing port of **Turka**, from where there are pleasant walks to several secluded bays in either direction. Bigger **Goryachinsk** (Горячинск), around 3km from the lake, is centred on a typically institutional hot-springs **kurort** (spa) with cheap cottage homestays in the surrounding village.

Further north through the uninhabited taiga lies the quaint little fishing hamlet of **Maksimikha** (Максимиха) where picturesque Baikal beaches stretch northwest. From here the blacktop bends before zipping through the forest to Ust-Barguzin.

UST-BARGUZIN УСТЬ-БАРГУЗИН

☏30131 / POP 7100 / ⊙MOSCOW +5HR

Low-rise Ust-Barguzin has sandy streets of traditional log homes with blue-and-white carved window frames. These are most attractive towards the northern end of the main street, ul Lenina, where it reaches the Barguzin River **ferry** (8am to 11pm). From here, views are magical towards the high-ridged peaks of the Svyatoy Nos Peninsula.

Other than watching the rusting car ferry being towed by a fume-belching motorboat across the fast-flowing Barguzin River, the only other attraction here is the **Banya Museum** (☏91 574; per Bolnichny 9; ⊙by appointment only), displaying four traditional timber *bani* lovingly fashioned by national park ranger and guide, Alexander Beketov, who also runs a very comfortable **homestay** (full board per person R1500) at the same address. The Beketovs provide a superb base and run tours to the Barguzin Valley and the national park. Their welcome and home-cooked meals make Ust-Barguzin a preferable base to Barguzin.

Daily *marshrutky* to Ulan-Ude (R500, seven hours) depart around 8am and will pick you up from your accommodation if you book ahead. In July and August a daily hydrofoil links Ust-Barguzin with Irkutsk and Khuzhir on Olkhon Island; check out **VSRP** (www.vsrp.ru) for details. In February and March the ice drive across Lake Baikal to Severobaikalsk takes around five hours.

SVYATOY NOS (HOLY NOSE) PENINSULA

ПОЛУОСТРОВ СВЯТОЙ НОС

Rising almost vertically out of shimmering waters, dramatic Svyatoy Nos is one of Lake Baikal's most impressive features. It's within the mostly impenetrable **Zabaikalsky National Park** and joined to Ust-Barguzin by a muddy 20km sand bar that's possible but painful to drive along (there's also a toll). Guides can be hired at the **national park offices** (per Bolnichny 9) in Ust-Barguzin for all-day trek-climbs to the top of the peninsula, more than 1800m above Lake Baikal. The views from the summit are truly awe-inspiring.

Nerpa seals are particularly abundant off the peninsula's west coast around the **Ushkanny Islands**, accessible by charter boat from Ust-Barguzin. Contact Alexander Beketov at the national park headquarters. Prices begin at around R5000.

BARGUZIN & THE BARGUZIN VALLEY

БАРГУЗИН и БАРГУЗИНСКАЯ ДОЛИНА

The road north from Ust-Barguzin emerges from thick forests at Barguzin, a low-rise town of wooden cottages that dates back to 1648. Walking from the bus station you can see its handful of dilapidated historic buildings in about 20 minutes by heading along ul Krasnoarmeyskaya past the cursorily renovated old **church** to pl Lenina.

Opposite the quaint little post office, the wooden-colonnaded **former Uezdnogo Bank** (ul Krasnoarmeyskaya 54) was once the grand home of Decembrist Mikhail Kyukhelbeker. Other exiles to make a home in Barguzin were Jews from Poland and European Russia who arrived here in the 1830s and 1860s. The last signs of the Jewish community can be seen in the crumbling old **cemetery** (a block northeast of the church) where crooked Hebrew-inscribed graves stand to the left and orthodox headstones, including that of Kyukhelbeker himself, to the right.

Hidden in the village school and difficult to access, the small **museum** (☑8-924-391 3126; www.barguzinmuseum.ru; ul Kalinina 51a) has some interesting Decembrist-related exhibits as well as the usual dusty rocks and mammoth bones.

Barguzin's real interest is as a launch pad for visiting the stunningly beautiful Barguzin Valley as it opens out into wide lake-dotted grassland, gloriously edged by a vast Toblerone of mountain peaks. These are most accessibly viewed across the meandering river plain from **Uro** village. Similarly inspiring panoramas continue for miles towards the idyllic village of **Suvo**, overshadowed by rock towers of the **Suvo Saxony** (Suvinskaya Saksoniya), so-called for its similarity to rock formations on the Czech-Saxony border. A few kilometres beyond Suvo the roadside **Bukhe Shulun** (Byk), a huge boulder resembling a bull's hoof, is considered to have miraculous powers. Heading north you'll pass through widely scattered, old-fashioned villages where horse carts and sleighs outnumber cars. Way up on the valley's mountainous west side, **Kurumkan** (411km northeast of Ulan-Ude) has a small but photogenic peak-backed *datsan*. The valley tapers to a point 50km north of Kurumkan at **Alla** where a tiny *kurort* can accommodate guests in the summer months.

Buy tickets ahead for Ulan-Ude *marshrutky* (R500, eight hours), departing early morning. Other public transport to Ust-Barguzin, Uro and Kurumkan is rare, though there's usually at least one service early morning and in the afternoon. Hitchhike or arrange a tour through the Beketovs in Ust-Barguzin.

SELENGA DELTA

Some 300 waterways feed Lake Baikal, but none compare in size and volume to the Selenga River. One of only 80 rivers around the world to form a delta, the Selenga dumps its load of sand (and pollution from Mongolia) on Baikal's eastern shore in a huge fan of islands, reed beds and shallow channels measuring 35km across. Over 200 bird species draw spotters from all over the world; motorboat trips can be arranged through Ulan-Ude agencies. Between birdwatching sessions many bed down in the village of Posolskoe where the Western-standard **Sofiya Hotel** (s/d R1400/1800) shares a lakeside location right beside a beautifully renovated monastery.

Ulan-Ude to Vladivostok

Includes »

Route Info

» Distance: 3648km

» Duration: Two days, 13½ hours

» Time zones: Moscow +5 to Moscow +7

Best Places to Stay & Eat

» Boutique Hotel (p235)

» See You Hostel (p244)

» Hotel Vizit (p225)

» Zima bar (p246)

» Pyongyang restaurant (p245)

Why Go?

The Trans-Siberian's last leg covers 3648km – that's more than the Moscow–Ulan-Ude journey alone – as it rolls into Russia's 'wild east'. This region has always lived by its own rules. 'Moscow is far' runs the local mantra. The people, like the countryside, are a bit wilder and more rugged than their Western brethren. Travelling this way before the Trans-Siberian was built, Anton Chekhov wrote that it 'seethes with life in a way that you can have no conception of in Europe'. And that's still apt.

Out the window, the taiga and Stalin-era housing blocks may seem similar to back west, but off the tracks lurk surprises like Blagoveshchensk, a border town of tsar-era buildings on the Amur River; Birobidzhan, Stalin's failed 'Zion'; and the bustling riverside metropolis of Khabarovsk. The railway ends at the stunning mountains-meet-ocean setting of Vladivostok, a once-closed navy port that today is Asia's uniquely Russian rising powerhouse.

When to Go

Vladivostok

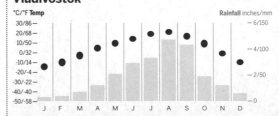

Feb & Mar Still the season for snowy delights, yet not too dark or too slushy.

Jun Essentially mid-spring, with all the beauty and climatic uncertainty that entails.

Sep & Oct Better weather, more square hectares of autumn foliage than anywhere on Earth.

The Route
Ulan-Ude to Chita

5655KM FROM MOSCOW Trans-Mongolian trains (p265) bid farewell to the main Trans-Sib route at **Zaudinsky**, virtually a suburb of Ulan-Ude. The main line then follows the wide Uda Valley with bare rolling hills visible across the plains. At an unmarked station about half an hour out of Ulan-Ude (before Onokhoi), a marshalling yard serves as a steam-loco graveyard. The scenery here is pretty, as the wide, flood-prone valleys continue, their rolling meadows backed distantly by trees on the north-facing slopes.

5771KM Quaint log-cabin settlements are scattered with patches of attractive woodland. You enter **Zabaikalsky Region** 20km beyond Novoilyinsky. Local time becomes Moscow time plus six hours.

5784KM Petrovsky-Zavod is the station for the mildly historic town of Petrovsk-Zabaikalsky. The station name (and the old name of the town) means 'Peter's Factory', so called for the huge ironworks you may spot from the train. Decembrists jailed here from 1830 to 1839 are commemorated in a large mural on the station building, worth getting off to take a snap of if there's time (although the *Rossiya* makes only a two-minute stop here). There's also a good Decembrist Museum not far from the station, and if you're on the Decembrist trail through Siberia the town could make a very off-the-beaten-track day trip from Ulan-Ude. A few minutes out of Petrovsk-Zabaikalsky look out for a cemetery to the right of the tracks where some Decembrists are buried.

5800-6300KM The tracks now head northeast following the Khilok Valley, with the **Yablonovy Mountains** forming blue shadows in the distance.

5884KM At the small airbase town of **Bada**, look up from your instant noodles to admire a MiG-fighter monument.

5925KM The train slows as it leaves the valley and climbs into the mountains, affording inspiring views of the winding river and fields filled with wildflowers.

5932KM The ever-so-slightly art deco station at **Khilok** is the next major stop, with some trains pausing for up to 20 minutes. There is a machine shop for repairing train engines here but little else, as the town is a product of the railway and even has a yellow Trans-Sib train hurtling across its coat of arms.

6130KM Soon after Mogzon the highest point (1040m) on the world's longest rail journey is reached at **Yablonovaya**, where trains pass through a slender gap in the rock.

6198KM Most trains loiter for 25 minutes at **Chita** (p223), long enough to explore the cathedral in the station forecourt. At the station, fans

ULAN-UDE TO VLADIVOSTOK ROUTE PLANNER

Here's a suggested itinerary for finishing up the Trans-Siberian from Ulan-Ude to Vladivostok:

Day 1: Take overnight train to Chita (10 hours); take share taxi to Aginskoe for night

Day 2: Share taxi back to Chita; night train to Blagoveshchensk (36 hours)

Day 3: On train to Blagoveshchensk

Day 4: Tour Blagoveshchensk and spend the night

Day 5: Take a morning *marshrutka* to Bureya, and pick up an eastbound train to Birobidzhan. Spend night in Birobidzhan. Alternatively, spend day in Blagoveshchensk and take night train 386 to Birobidzhan.

Day 6: In Birobidzhan; tour synagogue. Take a *marshrutka* or afternoon commuter train (three hours) to Khabarovsk.

Day 7: Tour Khabarovsk; overnight train to Vladivostok (13 hours)

Day 8: Arrive in Vladivostok

of the *Long Way Round* TV show will recognise the freight platform where Ewan McGregor et al struggled to heave their bikes aboard a Tynda-bound goods wagon.

Chita to Mogocha

6198-6450KM For the next 250km or so east the Trans-Siberian route follows the Ingoda and Shilka Rivers. Stay awake, as it's the most scenic part of this entire route. The best views are to the south, so if heading east grab an aisle seat in *platskart* for this part of the journey. But don't ignore the north side of the train with its rolling, colourful hills. Unfortunately, the *1/2 Rossiya* (and the identically timed *7/8* train) trundles this way by night, so consider other options, like train 133/134, or (when the days are long) 392 from Chita to Blagoveshchensk.

6264KM River views open up around **Darasun**.

6295KM You'll have 18 minutes at the platform in the industrial city of **Karymskaya** – enough time to quickly check out the brand-new Orthodox church on the north side of the tracks.

6312KM The picturesque village of **Tarskaya** is where the Trans-Manchurian peels off and heads south to the Chinese border; for details of this route, see p290.

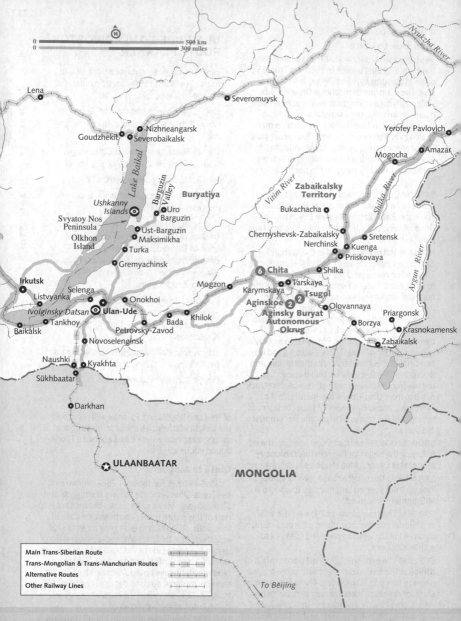

Ulan-Ude to Vladivostok Highlights

① Poking around for the best views of the bays, bridges and islands of mountain-spiked **Vladivostok** (p238)

② Spinning prayer wheels around Buddhist temples at

Tsugol (p227) and **Aginskoe** (p227)

③ Taking a party cruise on the Amur River before a night of clubbing in hip **Khabarovsk** (p231)

④ Taking in exquisite tsarist-era buildings along the legendary Amur River in **Blagoveshchensk** (p228)

Vestuzhevo
Tynda
Zeisk Reservoir
Khabarovsky Territory
Amur River
Amur Region
Komsomolsk-na-Amure
Amursk
Bamovskaya
Skovorodino
Magdagachi
Reynovo
Albazin
Zeya River
Ulegorsk
Svobodny
Belogorsk
Zavitaya
Novy Urgal
Tyrma
Litovko
Raychikhinsk
Bureya
Arkhara
Volochaevka
Khabarovsk 3
Blagoveshchensk 4
Hēihé
Poyarkovo
Obluche
Leninsk
Birobidzhan 5
Fuyuan
Jewish Autonomous Region
Vyazemskaya
Bikin
Primorsky Territory 7
Selemdzha River
CHINA
Dalnerechensk
Ruzhino
Lake Khanka
Sibirtsevo
Gaivoron
Spassk-Dalny
Hā'ěrbīn
Ussuriysk
Sanatornaya
Vladivostok 1
Slavyanka
NORTH KOREA
To Běijīng

5 Searching for the lost Jewish soul of 'Stalin's Zion', **Birobidzhan** (p229)

6 Hunting down banished aristocrats at Chita's delightful **Decembrist Museum** (p223)

7 Looking for Amur tiger tracks on a tour of the wildlife-infested nature reserves of the **Primorsky Territory** (p243)

Ulan-Ude to Vladivostok

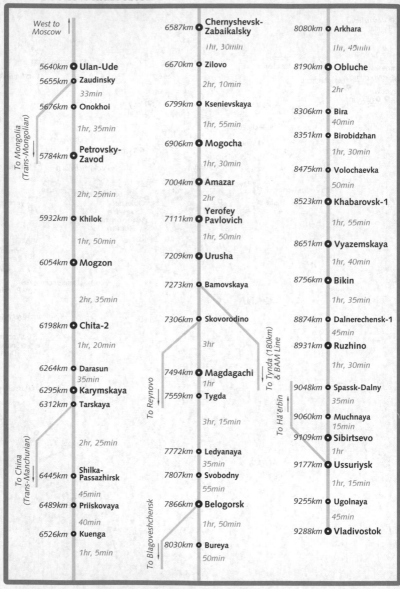

West to Moscow

To Mongolia (Trans-Mongolian)

5640km Ulan-Ude
5655km Zaudinsky
33min
5676km Onokhoi
1hr, 35min
5784km Petrovsky-Zavod
2hr, 25min
5932km Khilok
1hr, 50min
6054km Mogzon
2hr, 35min
6198km Chita-2
1hr, 20min
6264km Darasun
35min
6295km Karymskaya
6312km Tarskaya
2hr, 25min

To China (Trans-Manchurian)

6445km Shilka-Passazhirsk
45min
6489km Priiskovaya
40min
6526km Kuenga
1hr, 5min

6587km Chernyshevsk-Zabaikalsky
1hr, 30min
6670km Zilovo
2hr, 10min
6799km Ksenievskaya
1hr, 55min
6906km Mogocha
1hr, 30min
7004km Amazar
2hr
7111km Yerofey Pavlovich
1hr, 50min
7209km Urusha
7273km Bamovskaya
7306km Skovorodino
3hr

To Reynovo

7494km Magdagachi
1hr
7559km Tygda
3hr, 15min
7772km Ledyanaya
35min
7807km Svobodny
55min
7866km Belogorsk
1hr, 50min

To Blagoveshchensk

8030km Bureya
50min

To Tynda (180km) & BAM Line

To Hā'ěrbīn

8080km Arkhara
1hr, 45min
8190km Obluche
2hr
8306km Bira
40min
8351km Birobidzhan
1hr, 30min
8475km Volochaevka
50min
8523km Khabarovsk-1
1hr, 55min
8651km Vyazemskaya
1hr, 40min
8756km Bikin
1hr, 35min
8874km Dalnerechensk-1
45min
8931km Ruzhino
1hr, 30min
9048km Spassk-Dalny
35min
9060km Muchnaya
15min
9109km Sibirtsevo
1hr
9177km Ussuriysk
1hr, 15min
9255km Ugolnaya
45min
9288km Vladivostok

6312-6412KM For the next 100km or so the train rumbles along the Ingoda past a series of quaint villages strewn with classic Siberian *izby* (wooden houses) adorned with colourful, intricately carved shutters. Just east of Tarskaya station, spot the weather-beaten Orthodox church on the far (south) side of the Ingoda.

Come spring you'll see plenty of fishermen in the river.

6417KM East of **Onon** the Ingoda merges with the Onon River to become the Shilka River.

6445KM Look south to see piles of train wheels east of the station in **Shilka**, where some trains stop. The hills are pretty, as the route follows the Shilka River, marred by the derelict factories of **Kholbon** (6465km).

6489KM On most trains (but not the *Rossiya*), the brakes squeal again at **Priiskovaya**, from where a 10km branch line heads north to the old silver-mining town of **Nerchinsk** (p227). This is where the Treaty of Nerchinsk was signed in 1689, carving up Russian and Chinese spheres of influence in the Far East.

AROUND 6510KM Keep an eye out for the picturesque church in the Byankino Valley, as well as a few other buildings on the floodplain across the Shilka River.

6526KM Another renovated cube of a station meets the eye at **Kuenga**, after which the Trans-Sib route turns sharply north, while a 52km branch line heads to Sretensk, the eastern terminus of the Trans-Baikal Railway (see p331). Until the Amur Railway was completed in 1916, Trans-Sib passengers used to disembark from the train here to board Khabarovsk-bound steamers.

6587KM Most train services take a lengthy breather at **Chernyshevsk-Zabaikalsky**, giving you time to stock up from the food and drink sellers (unless it's 3am). It's named after the 19th-century exile Nikolai Chernyshevsky, whose silver-painted statue is on the platform.

AROUND 6660KM There are sweeping views to the north of the train across the Siberian plains.

6906KM Some trains stop for 15 minutes at **Mogocha**, a railway and gold-mining town of 12,000 souls who endure one of the harshest climates on Earth. Winter temperatures in this permafrost zone can plunge to a rail splitting -62ºC!

Mogocha to Magdagachi

7000-7600KM The tracks on this stretch of the line run only about 50km north of the Amur River, the border with China. At one time, strategic sensitivity meant that carriages containing foreigners had their window blinds fastened down during this stretch – so don't complain about the monotony of the scenery!

7004KM At the station in **Amazar**, you have about a 20-minute stop; there's a nearby graveyard of steam locomotives to see.

7079KM About two hours east of Amazar the train arrives at the **border between Zabaikalsky Territory and Amurskaya Region**, marking the end of Siberia and the beginning of the Russian Far East – you'll notice no difference whatsoever (geographically, most of the Far East is considered part of Siberia).

7111KM Settled in low-lying hills, **Yerofey Pavlovich** is named after the Siberian explorer Yerofey Pavlovich Khabarov (the remainder of his name went to the big city further down the line). The station building here must be one of the oddest on the line, with its curving steps up from the platform flanked by what look like two Lego dragons.

7273KM You'll be well into day six of your journey from Moscow by **Bamovskaya**, the southern terminus of the 'Little BAM', which runs north to connect with the BAM proper (the Baikal-Amur Mainline or Baikalo-Amurskaya Magistral) in Tynda. The Little BAM was built long before the BAM with slave labour in the 1930s (although much of it was dismantled in WWII and rebuilt in the 1970s). It constitutes the southern arm of the AYaM (Amur-Yakutsk Mainline, or Amuro-Yakutskaya Magistral), which extends to Yakutsk in the Sakha Republic (although passenger services only reach Tommot).

7306KM If you plan to head north on the Little BAM, do not get off in Bamovskaya, as few Tynda-bound trains stop there. Instead, connect in **Skovorodino**, where an impressive Soviet steam locomotive holds court in front of a pretty pink station.

From Skovorodino, a spur line follows the Bolshoi Never River south to Dzhalinda (station name: Reynovo) near **Albazin**, an important Russian outpost on the Amur River in the 17th century and the site of key battles between Cossacks and Manchurians. The final Manchurian siege of the Albazin fort in 1686–87 claimed nearly 800 Russian lives, with only 66 survivors, and led to the signing of the Treaty of Nerchinsk. Colin Thubron writes about the bloodbath and his search for the remnants of the fort in his book *In Siberia*.

7306-7450KM Heading east from Skovorodino, you'll get periodic views of a polished, unusually empty highway (look north at 7342km, just before entering a long tunnel). This is the **Amur Hwy** connecting Chita and Khabarovsk. Long the province of extreme adventurers only, its entire length is newly paved as of 2010. East of the tunnel you'll begin to see more pine trees mixing in with the taiga's birch and larch.

7494KM About three hours east of Skovorodino you pull into **Magdagachi**. The 15- to 25-minute stop here is time enough to walk down the tree-lined street south of the tracks to photograph the Lenin Statue (unless it's 1am). There's a post office next to the station and an ATM inside in case you need more vodka money.

Magdagachi to Khabarovsk

7772KM From little **Lednyanaya**, a short spur goes to Ulegorsk, where the giant new **Vostochny Cosmodrome** is being built. This new launch pad, scheduled for completion in 2018, will reduce Russian dependence on the Baikanor Cosmodrome in Kazakhstan. It's unclear whether the facility will be visible from the tracks, but surely someday lucky Trans-Siberian travellers will witness the odd spacecraft launch.

7807KM The train stops at **Svobodny** (pop 61,000), with its piano-like station, then crosses the Zeya River over the Trans-Siberian Railway's second-longest bridge.

7866KM At the key junction of **Belogorsk**, several trains peel off on a 110km spur line to **Blagoveshchensk** (p228), the administrative capital of Amurskaya Region with a ferry service to Hēihé, China. More than 150 years after the Russians were driven out of the Amur region at Albazin, Count Nikolai Muravyov-Amursky broke the treaty of Nerchinsk and regained the Left Bank of the Amur under a treaty signed in Argun (modern day Aihui, China), 30km south of Hēihé.

8080KM **Arkhara** marks the official end of the Trans-Baikal line and the beginning of the Far Eastern Line.

8140KM Here you spend about two minutes in the Trans-Siberian main line's **longest tunnel** (2km).

8190KM Turn your clocks to Moscow plus seven hours in **Obluche**, where you leave the Amurskaya region and enter the Jewish Autonomous Region. Most trains stop for about 15 minutes here, time enough to admire the art deco train station and stretch your legs in the leafy park next to the station. Fifteen minutes east of Obluche is another long tunnel.

8350-8450KM The area around **Bira** (8306km) is pretty as the train follows the Bira River, with some fairly substantial hills rising to the south.

8351KM There's a short stop in the Jewish Autonomous Region's capital, **Birobidzhan** (p229), where you can see the Hebrew letters of the station from your window. Depending on when your train arrives you may have time to spend a few hours looking around before boarding the next train through or the 6.15pm *elektrichka* (suburban train) to Khabarovsk.

8475KM Just east of the station in **Volochaevka**, you'll notice a distinct hill to the north. This is the site of the famous 1922 civil war battle glorified in the Birobidzhan and Khabarovsk regional museums. The man who orchestrated this victory, Marshal Vasily Blyukher, was elevated to hero status before falling victim to Stalin's purges in the late 1930s. The Military History Museum in Khabarovsk has a great portrait of Blyukher.

8514KM The train crosses the 2.6km **Khabarovsk Bridge** over the Amur River – the longest rail bridge in Russia. You can see this double-decker bridge, built in the early 1990s to replace one built by the tsar, on the back of the R5000 note. There's also a 7km tunnel under the Amur, secretly completed during WWII. You won't go through it, however, as it's used mostly by freight trains.

8523KM If you're not overnighting in pleasant **Khabarovsk**, you have a 30-minute stop on most trains – enough time to admire the Khabarov statue out front and the train station, which resembles the old duma (parliament) building on central ul Muravyova-Amurskogo. You can also switch for a train to connect with the BAM at **Komsomolsk-na-Amure** (p261).

Khabarovsk to Vladivostok

8523-9200KM All trains from Khabarovsk to Vladivostok depart during the evening, leaving you mostly in the dark for the final 13 hours of your Trans-Siberian odyssey. One reason for the cover of darkness is that the line, in places, comes within 10km of the sensitive Chinese border.

8606KM Here you cross the **Khor River**, which flows into the Ussuri River on the border of China. The train shadows the Ussuri all the way to Lesozavodsk (8938km).

8651KM Most trains stop for 15 minutes at **Vyazemskaya**, where there will be plenty of people selling bread, salmon caviar, dried fish and pickles. From here the forests are dominated by deciduous trees, such as maple and elm, which briefly blaze in a riot of autumn colours during September.

8756KM You'll probably be settling down for some sleep by the time the train makes a brief stop in **Bikin**. The line crosses the Bikin River here and follows it south to the **border between Khabarovsky and Primorsky Territories** (8780km). The southern forests of the 165,900-sq-km Primorsky Territory are the world's most northerly monsoon forests and home to black and brown bears, the rare Amur (Siberian) tiger and the virtually extinct Amur leopard.

8931KM There's a 15-minute stop in the dead of night at **Ruzhino**.

9010-9080KM About 30km either side of **Spassk-Dalny** (9048km), you may be able to make out Lake Khanka, a 4000-sq-km, lotus-covered lake that straddles the China–Russia border.

9177KM At **Ussuriysk**, you can contemplate changing to the branch line west to Hā'ěrbīn (Harbin) in China; the train goes only twice a week and is monotonously slow. Ussuriysk, formerly named Nikolskoe in honour of the tsarevich's 1891 visit, and home to a smattering of historic buildings, was once of greater size and importance than nearby Vladivostok.

9249KM After a week of travel from Moscow, you finally meet the **Pacific Ocean** – in the form of the **Amursky Gulf** – just south of the town of Prokhlodnaya. It should be dawn by now as the train travels south along the hilly peninsula that forms the eastern side of Amursky Gulf, passing a series of beach towns such as **Okeanskaya** (9266km), **Sanatornaya** (9269km) and **Sedanka** (9271km). Further south, Vladivostok rises in a series of concrete tower blocks on the hillsides.

9288KM Your epic journey ends (or begins) on the platform at the station in **Vladivostok** (p238). Before leaving, take a moment to admire the old locomotive on the platform beside the monument commemorating the completion of the great railroad you've just travelled along.

Chita
Чита

🚂 3022 / POP 324,000 / 🕓MOSCOW +6HR

Of all Eastern Siberia's major cities, Chita is the least prepared for visitors. Literally put on the map by the noble-blooded Decembrists, one of whom designed its street-grid layout, today there's nothing aristocratic about this regional capital where Soviet symbols still embellish Stalinist facades, shaven-headed conscripts guard pillared military headquarters and Chinese cross-border peddlers lug monster bales past a well-tended Lenin statue. Non-Chinese foreigners are still a rarity here, tourism a thing that happens elsewhere.

Echoes of the Decembrist chapter in Chita's history make the city just worth visiting, and a number of attractive old timber merchant's houses grace its arrow-straight streets. It's also the jumping-off point for two of Russia's best Buddhist temples at Aginskoe and Tsugol.

History

Founded in 1653, Chita developed as a rough-and-tumble silver-mining centre until it was force-fed a dose of urban culture in 1827 by the arrival of more than 80 exiled Decembrist gentlemen-rebels – or more precisely, by the arrival of their wives and lovers who followed, setting up homes on what became known as ul Damskaya (Women's St). That's now the southern end of ul Stolyarova, where sadly only a handful of rotting wooden cottages remain amid soulless concrete apartment towers.

As gateway to the new East Chinese Railway, Chita boomed in the early 20th century, despite flirting with socialism. Following the excitement of 1905, socialists set up a 'Chita Republic' which was brutally crushed within a year. After the 'real' revolutions of 1917, history gets even more exciting and complex. Bolsheviks took over, then lost control to Japanese forces who possibly intercepted part of Admiral Kolchak's famous 'gold train' before retreating east. By 1920 Chita was the capital of the short-lived Far Eastern Republic, a nominally independent, pro-Lenin buffer state whose parliament stood at ul Anokhina 63. The republic was absorbed into Soviet Russia in December 1922 once the Japanese had withdrawn from Russia's east coast. Closed and secretive for much of the Soviet era, today Chita is still very much a military city and once again flooded with Chinese traders.

👁 Sights

TOP CHOICE **Decembrist Museum** MUSEUM
(Музей Декабристов; ul Selenginskaya; admission R100; ⏰10am-6pm Tue-Sun) If you're on the Decembrist trail through Siberia, this small but comprehensive museum is one of the best, though there's not a word of English anywhere. It's housed in the 18th-century **Archangel Michael log church**, an unexpected

THE DECEMBRIST WOMEN

Having patently failed to topple Tsarist autocracy in December 1825, many prominent 'Decembrist' gentlemen-revolutionaries were exiled to Siberia. They're popularly credited with bringing civilisation to the rough-edged local pioneer-convict population. Yet the real heroes were their womenfolk, who cobbled together the vast carriage fares to get themselves to Siberia: in pre-railway 1827 the trip from St Petersburg to Irkutsk cost the equivalent of US$200 (about US$10,000 today).

And that was just the start. Pauline Annenkova, the French mistress of one aristocratic prisoner, spent so long awaiting permission to see her lover in Chita that she had time to set up a fashionable dressmakers' shop in Irkutsk. By constantly surveying the prisoners' conditions, the women eventually shamed guards into reducing the brutality of the jail regimes, while their food parcels meant that Decembrists had more hope of surviving the minimal rations of their imprisonment. The Decembrist women came to form a core of civil society and introduced 'European standards of behaviour'. As conditions eventually eased, this formed the basis for a liberal Siberian aristocracy, especially in Chita and Irkutsk where some Decembrists stayed on even after their formal banishment came to an end.

Chita

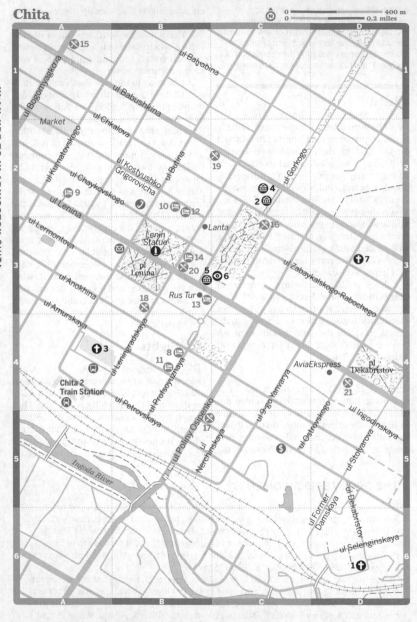

sight amid the neighbourhood's shambolic apartment blocks. Inextricably linked to the Decembrist story, this was where they came to pray, where Annenkov married his French mistress Pauline and where the Volkonskys buried their daughter Sofia.

The ground-level exhibition begins with the names of all the Decembrists picked out in gold on a green background, followed by interesting items such as the original imperial order sentencing the noble rebels to banishment in Siberia and oils show-

Chita

◎ Sights

⊟ Sleeping

⊗ Eating

⊘ Drinking

ing their leaders' executions. The 2nd floor looks at the wives who followed their menfolk into the Nerchinsk silver mines and the fates of all the Decembrists once they were allowed to settle where they pleased. It's fascinatingly detailed, but with no Russian you'll flounder.

Kuznetzov Regional Museum   MUSEUM
(Краеведческий Музей Кузнецова; ul Babushkina 113; admission R110; ◎10am-6pm Tue-Sun) The excellent and unusually lively Kuznetzov Regional Museum is housed in an early 20th-century mansion. Beyond the gratuitous stuffed elk, you'll find some pretty interesting local exhibits, including a very thorough examination of the heritage and architectural renaissance of the city and region. There's a decent cafe on the premises.

Military Museum   MUSEUM
(Музей История Войск ЗабВО; ul Lenina 86; admission R80; ◎9am-1pm & 2-5pm) This dry Russian-language-only museum is only for those with a passion for Eastern Siberia's

military history, though it does contain some semi-interesting exhibits on Beketov's Cossacks, the Soviet invasion of Afghanistan and communist repressions. Each of the six floors bristles with weapons, and the museum's collection of **tanks and artillery** can be seen by walking up the passage between the museum and the impressive **Officers' Club** (Дом Офицеров) building next door.

Cathedral   CHURCH
(Кафедральный собор; train station forecourt) The train station reflected in its gilt onion domes, Chita's turquoise cathedral is the city's most impressive building, though inside it's plain. The original pre-Stalin cathedral stood on the main square, right on the spot where Lenin now fingers his lapels.

Art Museum   GALLERY
(Картинная галерея; ul Chkalova 120a; admission R50; ◎10am-7pm Tue-Sat, to 6pm Sun) The Art Museum shows frequently changing exhibitions by school children and local artists.

Voskreseniya Church   CHURCH
(Свято-Воскресенский храм; ul 9-go Yanvarya) The recent-looking Voskreseniya Church is actually the city's oldest, but was almost burnt to the ground in 1996. Some of the original 19th-century icons are displayed inside.

🛏 Sleeping

Chita has little budget accommodation and homestays are nonexistent. Hotels are often full, meaning many travellers who fail to book ahead often have no choice but to check into top-end hotels.

Hotel Vizit   HOTEL €€€
(Гостиница Визит; ☑356 945; www.visit-hotel.ru; ul Lenina 93; s/tw R3190/5800; ❋🖰) Occupying the 5th floor of an ultramodern smoked-glass tower at the busy intersection of uls Lenina and Profsoyuznaya, this is Chita's best luxury offering with relaxing en suite rooms, English-speaking receptionists and sparkling bathrooms. Some doubles have baths and the air-con provides relief from Chita's superheated summers. It's half price for stays of between six and 12 hours.

Hotel Montblanc   HOTEL €€€
(☑357 272; www.eldonet.ru; ul Kostyushko Grigorovicha 5; s R3150-3450, d R3850-4650; ❋🖰) A block away from the main square, this purpose-built business hotel has immaculately snazzy rooms, though at these prices

the plumbing could be a touch more professional. The buffet breakfast is served in the Ukraine-themed restaurant and check-out time at reception provides an opportunity to witness just how badly Russian and Chinese businessmen can behave.

Hotel Zabaikale
HOTEL €€

(Гостиница Забайкалье; ☑359 819; www .zabaikalie.ru; ul Leningradskaya 36; s/tw from R1900/3800) Unbeatably located overlooking the main square, the cheaper renovated rooms at this huge complex are a fairly good deal. The hotel has a huge range of facilities including an air and rail ticket office, a spa, a children's playroom and a gym. Rates include ham-and-egg breakfast in the kitschily grand 2nd-floor restaurant.

Hotel Arkadia
HOTEL €€

(Гостиница Аркадия; ☑352 636; www.arkadia .chita.ru; ul Lenina 120; s R1800-2900, tw R2400-4500) The Arkadia is set back from ul Lenina and equipped with 35 bland but comfy rooms and some imaginative plumbing. The foyer has one of Chita's best caffeine halts and is a good place to grab breakfast.

Hotel Chitaavtotrans
HOTEL €€

(Гостиница Читаавтотранс; ☑355 011; ul Kostyushko Grigorovicha 7; s/tw R1500/1800) As just about Chita's cheapest digs, the cosmetically improved but cramped rooms here are usually full, so book ahead.

Hotel Dauria
HOTEL €€€

(Гостиница Даурия; ☑262 350; ul Profsoyuznaya 17; s/d from R2000/4000; ☎) Renovated, very comfortable en suite rooms with semi-stylish furniture make this a characterful choice. Breakfast is included but reservations are essential.

Hotel AChO
HOTEL €€

(Гостиница Управления делами Администрации Читинской Области; ☑351 968; ul Profsoyuznaya 19; dm R423-625, s R500-3000, tw R2000-2400) Occupying a fine 1906 brick mansion with many of its architectural features still in place, this hotel sadly sports bare, unlovely, overpriced rooms. Anyone turning up without a booking will be sent packing, even if the hotel is empty.

✖ Eating & Drinking

Eating out ain't high on the list of things to enjoy in Chita, but despite the lack of choice and unimaginative menus, you won't go hungry.

Khmelnaya Korchma
UKRAINIAN €€

(Хмельная Корчма; ul Amurskaya 69; mains R150-400; ☺noon-midnight Mon-Thu & Sun, noon-3am Fri & Sat; ✿) Plastic sunflowers, dangling onion strings, folksy embroidered tea towels and a menu of borsch, *salo* (pork fat), *vareniki* (sweet dumplings) and *holubtsi* (cabbage rolls stuffed with rice) teleport you to rural Ukraine. Live music, liberal helpings and a low-priced lunch menu (R150) arguably makes this Chita's best option.

Kafe Kollazh
INTERNATIONAL €€

(Кафе Коллаж; ul Bogomyagkova 24; mains R150-400; ☺noon-midnight; ✿) Unpromising from the outside, this mood-lit and cosy place adorned with spinning wheels, old samovars and dried flowers is one of Chita's better dining spots. The international-themed food is tasty but slightly overpriced.

Shokoladnitsa
CAFE

(ul Leningradskaya 36; ☺8am-11pm; ☎) This new central cafe is good for people-watching from the big windows while sipping a beer or coffee and making full use of the free wi-fi.

Kafe Traktyr
RUSSIAN €€

(Кафе Трактыр; ul Chkalova 93; mains R230-460; ☺noon-2am) Russian home-style cooking is served at heavy wooden tables in this rebuilt wooden-lace cottage, with a quietly upmarket Siberian-retro atmosphere. The summer beer-and-shashlyk tent is a popular drinking spot.

Tsiplyata Tabaka
CAFE €

(Цыплята Табака; ul Ostrovskogo 20; meals R250; ☺noon-5pm & 6pm-1am) Judging by the Socialist Realist reliefs and Brezhnev-era decor, this quirky eatery once had a previous life as something else. Roast chicken priced by weight (R47 per 100g) is the only main course.

Poznaya Altargana
BURYAT €

(Позная Алтаргана; ul Leningradskaya 5; pozi R30; ☺10am-midnight Mon-Thu & Sun, to 2am Fri & Sat) If *pozi* are your thing, Poznaya Altargana is your place, but the tasty *plov* and meatballs are an equally filling alternative. There's a larger branch at ul Babushkina 121.

Kofeynya Kofe Moll
CAFE

(Кафе Молл; Hotel Arkadia, ul Lenina 120; ☺24hr) Occupying half of a hotel lobby, this is one of the few places in town offering true solace to disciples of the bean. It also has a long list of cocktails.

ⓘ Information

Lanta (Ланта; ☑353 638; www.lanta-chita.
ru; ul Leningradskaya 56; ⊙9am-7pm Mon-Fri)
Runs limited tours of Chita and Zabaikalsky
Region. No English spoken.

Main post office (ul Butina 37; ⊙8am-10pm
Mon-Fri, 9am-6pm Sat & Sun) Quaintly spired
wooden building on pl Lenina.

Rus Tur (☑264 283; www.rustur.chita.ru; ul
Lenina 93, office 410) Can arrange tours to
Tsugol (R9000 per car); some English is spoken
in the office.

Telephone office (ul Chaykovskogo 22; ⊙8am-
8pm) Has an ATM.

VTB Bank (ВТБ Банк; ul Amurskaya 41;
⊙9am-6pm Mon-Fri) Changes US dollars,
euros, Chinese yuán and even British pounds.

ⓘ Getting There & Away

Train

Chita has the following rail connections:

Běijīng *kupe* R5500, two days five hours, weekly

Blagoveshchensk *platskart/kupe*
R1300/3050, one day 9½ to 13 hours, two daily

Khabarovsk *platskart* R2700, *kupe* R5500 to
R7300, one day 15½ to 17½ hours, up to three
daily

Tynda *platskart* R1700, *kupe* R2700 to R3800,
26½ hours, every other day

Ulan-Ude *platskart* R970, *kupe* R1480 to
R2570, 11 hours, up to seven daily

Zabaikalsk *platskart* R1170, *kupe* R2500 to
R3000, 11½ hours, daily

Air

Kadala Airport (www.aerochita.ru) is 15km west
of central Chita. Take *marshrutka* 12 or 14. **Avia-
Ekspress** (АвиаЭкспресс; ☑325 572; www
.aviaexpress.ru; ul Lenina 55; ⊙9am-10pm
Mon-Sat) sells tickets for the following flights:

Běijīng R10,500, two weekly

Moscow from R12,500, up to three daily

Bus

The only two services you're likely to need are
the *marshrutky* to Aginskoe (R250, two hours,
hourly) and the long-distance minivans to Ulan-
Ude (R700, seven hours). Both leave from a stop
on the train station forecourt.

Around Chita

AGINSKOE АГИНСКОЕ
☑30239 / POP 11,700 / ⊙MOSCOW +6HR

For an intriguing day trip from Chita, take a
marshrutka (R250, two hours, hourly) to the
spruced-up Buryat town of Aginskoe. Scenery
en route transforms from patchily forested
hills via river valleys into rolling grassy steppe.

Once in Aginskoe, hop straight into a taxi
(R100) to visit the beautiful old Buddhist
datsan (6km west of the centre), a large
complex of brightly decorated temples and
monastery faculties. Back on the central
square, the admirably well-curated **Tsybik-
ov Museum** (ul Komsomolskaya 11; admission
R100; ⊙10am-1pm & 2-5.30pm Mon-Fri) takes
an in-depth look at the local Buryat culture.
Opposite stands the custard-yellow 1905 **St
Nicholas Church**, whose reconstruction
was bankrolled by former Moscow mayor
Yury Luzhkov.

Self-service **Kafe Biznes Lanch** (ul Lenina
58; mains R15-50; ⊙9am-10pm Mon-Sat) on the
opposite side of the square from the museum
has an unpretentious Siberian menu. **Zaku-
sochnaya Yukhen Tug** (ul Tataurova 17A; mains
R20-50; ⊙9am-8pm) near the market is a no-
frills greasy spoon where tasty goulash, *plov*
and salad are piled tall on saucer-size plates.
There's a supermarket and an ATM nearby.

TSUGOL ЦУГОЛ

Set just 2km from the 'holy' Onon River,
Tsugol village is not particularly pretty but
the perfectly proportioned **Tsugol Datsan**
is surely the most memorable Buddhist
temple in Russia. Built in 1820, it is just four
years younger than Aginskoe Datsan and
even more photogenic, with gilded Mongolian script-panels, wooden upper facades
and tip-tilted roofs on each of its three sto-
reys. The interior is less colourful than the
Ivolginsky temple, but clinging to the front
is a unique, colourfully painted wrought-
iron staircase.

Getting to/from Tsugol is a pain – it lies
13km from Olovyannaya, reachable by a
single morning bus (R400, departs 8.30am)
from Chita. From Olovyannaya take a taxi
(at least R400, much more if asked to wait)
or hike along the river. On the return journey, you could ask around in Olovyannaya
for an unofficial *marshrutka* back to Chita
(or Aginskoe) – otherwise it's a long lonely
wait for the overnight train (this may be an
opportunity to test your hitchhiking skills).
Alternatively, contact tour companies in Chita who run (expensive) excursions to Tsugol
on request.

Nerchinsk Нерчинск

Anyone with a knowledge of Russian history will be familiar with the name Nerchinsk.
The 1689 Treaty of Nerchinsk recognising

Russia's claims to the trans-Baikal region was signed here and 130 years later the Decembrists were sent to work the silver mines around the village. Once one of Eastern Siberia's foremost towns but inexplicably bypassed by the Trans-Siberian Railway just 10km to the south, Nerchinsk leads a forgotten existence with just a few fading reminders of its rich past. If you're looking to break up the long 300km trip from Chita to Blagoveshchensk, hop off here. Most don't.

The only visitable attraction is the **Butin Palace Museum** (ul Sovetskaya 83; admission R100; ⏰10am-1pm & 2-5.30pm Tue-Sat). Mikhail Butin, the local silver baron, built himself this impressive crenellated palace, furnished with what were then claimed to be the world's largest mirrors. He'd bought the mirrors at the 1878 World Fair in Paris and miraculously managed to ship them unscathed all the way to Nerchinsk via the China Sea and up the Amur River. These four mammoth mirrors form the centrepiece of the collection, along with a delightful pair of hobbit-style chairs crafted from polished tangles of birch roots. Three-quarters of the palace, including the grand, triple-arched gateway (demolished in 1970), still stand in ruins.

A block from the museum, the active 1825 **Voskresensky Cathedral** (ul Pogodaeva 85) looks like an opera house from the outside; its interior is plain and whitewashed. Head around the sports pitch with its little silver Lenin to the imposing though now crumbling 1840 **Trading Arches**, slated for desperately needed renovation in the coming years. Nearby is a fine colonnaded pharmacy and the very grand facade of the pink former **Kolobovnikov Store** (ul Shilova 3), now a barnlike Torgovy Tsentr filled with some desultory stalls and kiosks.

About 1km south of the museum, just before the post office and bank, a little pink column-fronted building was once the **Dauriya Hotel** (Sovetskaya ul 32). As locals will proudly tell you, Chekhov stayed here in June 1890. Diagonally across the same junction, the Kozerog shop doubles as a minuscule bus station from where services to Priiskovaya depart.

To reach Nerchinsk, take any train from Chita to Priiskovaya (*platskart* R690, *kupe* R1000 to R1400, six hours) on the Trans-Siberian main line, 10km from Nerchinsk. Change there onto local *marshrutky*.

Blagoveshchensk
Благовещенск

📱4162 / POP 210,000 / ⏰MOSCOW +6HR

It's sometimes easy to forget where you are out here – in deepest Asia – until you find a place like this modest border town, 110km south of the Trans-Siberian and across the Amur River from China. The mix of scattered tsarist-era buildings and Chinese tourists walking past Lenin statues is fascinating. On hot days, locals share the river, jumping in from beaches on opposite shores.

The border is peaceful now, but once was tense. In 1900, Cossacks, seeking to avenge European deaths in the Chinese Boxer Rebellion, slaughtered thousands of Chinese people in the city. In the '60s and early '70s, Blagoveshchensk (meaning 'good news') endured round-the-clock propaganda being pumped over the river. One elderly local explained, 'It was awful. Their embankment was lined with pictures of Mao, and we listened to broadcasts – all in Chinese. We were scared.'

◉ Sights & Activities

A good starting point for a wander around is on the riverfront at pl Lenina, where teen skaters take over the Lenin statue steps and tots take over the fountains. From here a short walk west along the pleasant riverside promenade, or along parallel ul Lenina, takes you to yawning pl Pobedy.

Tsarist-Era Buildings   HISTORICAL BUILDINGS

At the regional museum, pick up the darling *Stary Blagoveshchensk* (Old Blagoveshchensk) map (R10, in Russian) to plot your own walking tour of the dozens of glorious tsarist-era buildings on shady backstreets around the centre. The most impressive buildings are on ul Lenina within a few blocks of the museum and on and around nearby pl Pobedy. Anton Chekhov came through Blagoveshchensk during his epic trip through the Far East in 1891 (and headed straight to a Japanese prostitute, as recounted luridly in his later-published letters). A **bust** commemorating Chekhov's visit is on the facade of the lovely Institute of Geology and Wildlife Management building on pl Pobedy.

Amur Regional Museum   MUSEUM

(Амурский Облотной Музей; ul Lenina 165; admission R120; ⏰10am-6pm Tue-Sun) A short walk northwest of pl Pobedy, this museum is housed in a former tsarist-era trading house and Soviet-era HQ for the Communist Youth League (Komsomol). Inside are 26 halls, with plenty of interesting photos, 1940s record players and a meteor that fell in 1991 near Tynda. Russian history buffs will enjoy the model of the 17th-century Cossack fortress in nearby Albazin and a painting depicting the Manchurian invasion of the fort in 1685. This battle swung control of the upper Amur to the Chinese for the next two centuries.

River Cruises
BOAT TRIPS

One-hour daytime river cruises (per person R150) and longer evening disco cruises (R240) leave from a pier just east of pl Lenina from mid-May through September.

Sleeping & Eating

Hotels include breakfast unless otherwise indicated.

Yubileynaya
HOTEL €€

(Юбилейная; 370 073; www.bighotel.ru; ul Lenina 108; s/d from R1700/2800;) This 150-room beast overlooking the river won't win any beauty contests, but the location near pl Lenina is absolutely ideal. Rooms are simple spruced-up Soviet fare, while the international restaurant (mains R150 to R500), festooned with old beer posters, is more 21st-century.

Amur Hotel
HOTEL €€

(Гостиница Амур; 251 113; www.hotelamur.ru; ul Lenina 122; s with/without shower R1500/800, d from R1500;) The lovely looking Amur, roughly opposite the Regional Museum, is tsarist on the outside but thoroughly Soviet on the inside, with shoebox-sized rooms, lino floors and narrow beds draped in gold satin. Fancier rooms include air-con and breakfast.

Zeya Hotel
HOTEL €€

(Гостиница Зея; 539 996; www.hotelzeya .ru; ul Kalinina 8; s/d from R1700/2100;) Zeya makes a valiant attempt to make Soviet rooms look cheery, but goes a bit over the top with the extra-frilly curtains and bedspreads. Twelve-hour rates available. It's near the river just west of pl Pobedy.

Tsentralnaya Pizzeria
PIZZA €

(Центральная Пиццерия; ul Lenina 115; pizzas R130-270;) If you can ignore the over-priced drinks, you'll be quite happy with the thin-crust pizza here, available by the half pie. Neighbouring sister Tsentalnaya Kofeynya focuses on coffee, cocktails and salads.

Khing An
CHINESE €€

(Хинг Ан; ul Shevchenko 11; mains R200-400; 10am-midnight;) Among the many Chinese restaurants in Blagoveshchensk, this one stands out. On warm days locals mass on the outdoor patio. It's 200m west of pl Lenina.

Getting There & Away

Blagoveshchensk is 110km off the Trans-Siberian, reached via the branch line from Belogorsk. The train station is 4km north of the river on ul 50 Let Oktyabrya, the main north–south artery.

Trains heading east backtrack to Belogorsk on their way to Vladivostok (platskart/kupe from R2000/2300, one day eight hours, odd-numbered days) and Khabarovsk (platskart/kupe R1000/2200, 16 hours, even-numbered days). Heading west, trains serve Chita (platskart/kupe R1850/3800, one day 13 hours, daily) and Tynda (platskart/kupe R1400/3400, 16 hours, odd-numbered days).

Additional options are available from Belogorsk to the north or Bureya to the east. Marshrutky connect Blagoveshchensk's **bus station** (cnr ul 50 let Oktyabrya & ul Krasnoarmeyska) with the train stations in Belogorsk (R250, two hours, almost hourly until early evening) and Bureya (R450, 3½ hours, five daily). Don't miss the awesome mosaic of Soviet sportsmeny (athletes) opposite the bus station.

The **River Terminal** (Речной Вокзал; ul Chaykovskogo 1), 500m east of the Druzhba Hotel, sends eight daily boats to Hēihé, China (one way/return R1075/1450, 15 minutes), where there's an evening train to Hā'ěrbīn. You'll need a Chinese visa and a multiple-entry Russian visa to return.

Birobidzhan   Биробиджан

42622 / POP 80,000 / MOSCOW +7HR

Quiet and shady, Birobidzhan is the capital of the 36,000-sq-km Jewish Autonomous Region and is a couple of hours shy of Khabarovsk on the Tran-Siberian line (if you're heading east). Its concept has always been a bit more interesting than its reality (as evidenced by the quick influx of Jews coming to 'Stalin's Zion' in the 1930s, then leaving the undeveloped swamp just as quickly). Still, its sleepy provincial feel and riverside setting make it worth a half-day visit – more if the weather's good or if you want to explore the city's Jewish heritage.

The town is quite walkable. The main streets ul Lenina and partially pedestrian ul Sholom-Aleykhema parallel the tracks just a five-minute walk south on ul Gorkogo from the train station. The Bira River is another five minutes along.

History

The Soviet authorities conceived the idea of a homeland for Jews in the Amur region in the late 1920s and founded the Jewish Autonomous Region in 1934 with its capital at Birobidzhan (named for the meeting place of the Bira and Bidzhan Rivers). Most of the Jews came from Belarus and Ukraine, but also from the US, Argentina and even Palestine. The Jewish population never rose above 32,000, and dropped to 17,500 by the end of the 1930s, when growing anti-Semitism led to the ban of Yiddish and synagogues. The Jewish population rose gradually to about 22,000 by 1991, when Russia's Jews began emigrating en masse to Israel. The Jewish population has levelled off at 3000 to 4000 these days.

⊙ Sights & Activities

Jewish Birobidzhan   CULTURAL HERITAGE
A few vestiges of Birobidzhan's Jewish heritage remain. Note the Hebrew signs on the **train station**, the lively **farmer's market** (ul Sholom-Aleykhema) and the **post office** on the riverfront at the southern terminus of ul Gorkogo. On the square in front of the train station a **statue** commemorates Birobidzhan's original Jewish settlers, and on the pedestrian stretch of ul Sholom-Aleykhema is a quirky **statue of Sholem Aleichem** (Памятник Шолом-Алейхему; *Fiddler on the Roof* was based on Aleichem's stories).

A five-minute walk west from the centre on ul Lenina is a complex containing Birobidzhan's Jewish culture centre, **Freid** (Общинный центр Фрейд; ☑41 531, 8-924-642 8731; ul Lenina; ◷9am-5pm Mon-Fri), and a synagogue with a small **Jewish history museum** (◷by appointment) inside. Call or ask around for Rabbi Roman Isakovich, who will give you a tour of the complex, talk local history or find you a souvenir yarmulke (skull cap).

Regional Museum   MUSEUM
(Краеведческий музей; ul Lenina 25; admission R100; ◷10am-6pm Wed-Thu, 9am-5pm Fri-Sun) Next door to Freid, this museum has an excellent exhibit on the arrival of Jewish settlers to Birobidzhan in the 1930s,

plus boars and bears and a minidiorama of the Volochaevka Civil War battle (akin to Khabarovsk's bigger one, but here blood pours from a 3-D dead guy's head).

🛏 Sleeping

For apartments in the R1500 to R2000 range, call one of the numbers advertising Квартиры (apartments) on the building opposite the train station.

Resting rooms   HOSTEL €
(комнаты отдыха, komnaty otdykha; ☑91 605; train station; dm/lyux R600/2000) The simple train station rooms are probably the best option for a quick visit. There are discounts for 12-hour stays and it's an easy walk from the centre.

Hotel Vostok   HOTEL €€
(Гостиница Восток; ☑65 330; ul Sholom-Aleykhema 1; s/d R1800/2600; ❋) Birobidzhan's central hotel has a good location next to the farmer's market.

✕ Eating & Drinking

Teatralny   SHASHLYK €
(Театральный; pr 60 let SSSR 14; mains R200-300; ❋) An average indoor Chinese restaurant during the cold months, in the warm months its vast outdoor patio near the river is *the* place to eat shashlyk and guzzle draft beer (R60). It's behind Birobidzhan's gargantuan Philharmonic Hall.

David Trade Centre   RUSSIAN €€
(Торговый Центр Давид; cnr pr 60 let SSSR & ul Gorkogo; mains R150-750) The best overall choice for a bite or a drink on its streetside patio, it offers fine dining, fast food and a happening nightclub (admission R200) all under one roof. It's kitty-corner from the Philharmonic.

Prime Internet Bar   BAR
(Прайм Интернет Бар; pr 60 let SSSR; ◷24hr; ❋ 🛜) Wi-fi and internet use here are free if you order a drink. It's in front of the Philharmonic.

ⓘ Getting There & Away

Coming from the west on the Trans-Siberian, you can easily stop off, have a look and grab a late train or bus for Khabarovsk.

All Trans-Siberian trains stop here, but if you're heading to Khabarovsk, it's cheaper on the *elektrichka* (suburban train; R300, three hours, three daily); a *platskart* seat on other trains runs to R500.

You can also catch *marshrutky* to Khabarovsk (R250, three hours, hourly until 6pm) from beside the train station.

Khabarovsk   Хабаровск

☏ 4212 / POP 590,000 / ⊘ MOSCOW +7HR

The Far East's most pleasant surprise – and a welcome break after days of relentless taiga on the train – Khabarovsk boasts a dreamy riverside setting, a vibrant nightlife and broad boulevards lined with pretty tsarist-era buildings. Unlike so many places, the city has shelled out funds to develop its riverside in the public interest. It has a great strolling area with multicoloured tiles, parks, monuments and walkways. A one-day stop is easily filled looking around.

It's hot in summer, but winter temperatures give it the unglamorous title of 'world's coldest city of over half a million people'. A dazzling display of **ice sculptures** occupies pl Lenina from January until the spring thaw. Khabarovsk's City Day is a good time to visit – it's 31 May, or the closest Saturday.

History

Khabarovsk was founded in 1858 as a military post by Eastern Siberia's governor-general, Count Nikolai Muravyov (later Muravyov-Amursky), during his campaign to take the Amur back from the Manchus. It was named after the man who got the Russians into trouble with the Manchus in the first place, 17th-century Russian explorer Yerofey Khabarov.

The Trans-Siberian Railway arrived from Vladivostok in 1897. During the Russian Civil War, the town was occupied by Japanese troops for most of 1920. The final Bolshevik victory in the Far East was at Volochaevka, 45km west.

In 1969, Soviet and Chinese soldiers fought a bloody hand-to-hand battle over little Damansky Island in the Ussuri River. Since 1984, tensions have eased. Damansky and several other islands have been handed back to the Chinese.

◉ Sights & Activities

Walking is the main activity in Khabarovsk. Three good spots are the **riverfront**, **Dinamo Park** and along **ulitsa Muravyova-Amurskogo** with its impressive turn-of-the-20th-century architecture. Some buildings to look out for on the latter are the striking red-and-black-brick **Far Eastern State Research Library** (Библиотека Дальне-Восточного Иследования; ul Muravyova-

Amurskogo 1), built from 1900 to 1902; the mint-green Style Moderne **Tsentralny Gastronom** (ul Muravyova-Amurskogo 9), built in 1895 and topped by a statue of Mercury; and the former **House of Pioneers** (Дом Пионеров, Dom Pionerov; ul Muravyova-Amurskogo 17).

No place in the Far East asks more for its museums, so it might be worth just sticking with its best – the newly expanded Territorial Museum.

Khabarovsk Territorial Museum   MUSEUM
(ul Shevchenko 11; admission R330; ⊘10am-6pm, closed Mon & last Fri of month) Located in an evocative 1894 red-brick building, this museum contains a far-better-than-average look into native cultures and a full-on panorama of the snowy 1922 Civil War battle at Volochaevka – look for the dead dude in a hut minus an arm and note the Trans-Siberian whizzing by to the south of the battle site on Volochaevka Hill. You can actually spot Volochaevka Hill from the train some 30km west of Khabarovsk. Also here is an iconic painting of Count Muravyov-Amursky signing the 1858 Treaty of Aigun, which gave the left bank of the Amur to the Russians. The **new building** has a wing dedicated to the Amur River, with lots of live fish in tanks and some impressive stuffed giant koluga sturgeon. There's no Gulag camp coverage, though the nearby prison population was bigger than the city's in the '30s.

Amur River Cruise   BOAT TRIPS
(river boat landing; day/evening cruise R250/350) Vital to Khabarovsk's rise, the Amur River can be seen on (at times rollicking) party boats. Cruises (one to 1½ hours) on the *Moskva-80* depart every two hours from 12.30pm to 12.30am, provided enough customers show up.

Military History Museum   MUSEUM
(Военно-исторический музей; ☏326 350; ul Shevchenko 20; admission R150; ⊘10am-5pm Tue-Sun) If you didn't get enough war history in the Territorial Museum, add a stop at this four-room frenzy of battle axes, guns, knives and busts and photos of moustached heroes of past conflicts. Lined up in the back courtyard are army trucks, cannons, tanks, rockets, a MiG-17 fighter plane and a luxury officers-only rail carriage dating from 1926.

Archaeology Museum   MUSEUM
(Музей Археологии; ul Turgeneva 86; admission R220; ⊘10am-6pm Tue-Sun) The highlights of

Khabarovsk

To Bus
Station (1km)

ul Serysheva

Chinese
Consulate

Old
Olympic
Pool

34

1

ul Serysheva

38

ul Frunze

14

ul Kalinina

5

ul Muravyova-Amurskogo

27

26

ul Istomina

2

17

per Arseneva

16

11

29

21

Intour-Khabarovsk

33

30

23

6   7

8

4

22

Count Nikolai
Maravyov-Amursky
Monument

3

Assumption
Cathedral

pl
Komsomolskaya

25

ul Komsomolskaya

City
Park

ul Turgeneva

ul Shevchenko

19

Japanese
Consulate

9

39

Amur River

10

WWII
Memorial

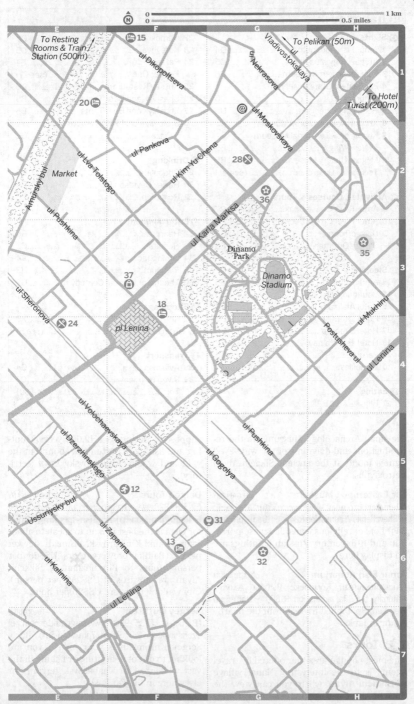

0   1 km
0   0.5 miles

To Resting
Rooms & Train
Station (500m)

To Pelikan (50m)

Vladivostokskaya

To Hotel
Turist (200m)

ul Dikopoltseva

ul Nekrasova

15

20

@   ul Moskovskaya

ul Pankova

ul Lva Tolstogo

ul Kim Yu Chena

28

Market

Amursky bul

ul Pushkina

ul Karla Marksa

36

35

Dinamo
Park

Dinamo
Stadium

37

ul Sheronova

24

pl Lenina

18

ul Mukhinu

Postysheva ul

ul Lenina

ul Volochaevskaya

ul Pushkina

ul Dzerzhinskogo

ul Gogolya

Ussuriysky bul

12

ul Zaparina

31

ul Kalinina

13

32

ul Lenina

Khabarovsk

the small Archaeology Museum are the reproductions and diagrams of the wide-eyed figures found at the ancient Sikachi-Alyan petroglyphs.

Far Eastern Art Museum ART GALLERY
(Дальневосточный Художественный музей; ul Shevchenko 7; admission R240; ☺10am-7pm Tue-Sun) Lots of religious icons, Japanese porcelain and 19th-century Russian paintings are on display here.

Amur Fish Aquarium AQUARIUM
(Аквариальный Комплекс Рыббы Амура; Amursky bul 13a; admission R180; ☺11am-5pm Wed-Sun) Spot gilled friends from the nearby Amur in tanks.

☞ Tours

The most popular area tour offered by travel agents is to the interesting Nanai village of **Sikachi-Alyan**, where you can view the Sikachi-Alyan petroglyphs – stone carvings supposedly dating back 12,000 years. Hunting and fishing opportunities abound in the wild and woolly Khabarovsky *kray* (territory).

Dalgeo Tours TOUR COMPANY
(☎318 829; www.dalgeo.com; ul Turgeneva 78; ☺10am-7pm Mon-Fri) English-speaking director Olga is the best person to speak to about tours around Khabarovsk, although they get pricey (Baltika brewery tours US$66 per person; tours to Birobidzhan or Sikachi-Alyan are upwards of US$250 per person). City walking tours are US$20 per hour.

Sergey Outfitter TOUR GUIDE
(Велком; ☎735 990; www.sergoutfitter.com; ul Dzerzhinskogo 24; ☺9am-7pm Mon-Sat) Burly Sergey Khromykh is your man if you are looking to do some hunting or fishing in the vast wilderness of Khabarovsk Territory or elsewhere in the Far East.

🛏 Sleeping

One knock against Khabarovsk is its poor-value hotels. Dalgeo Tourist's homestay service is worth considering for solo travellers (US$61 per person including breakfast). Apartments (R1500 and up) are also an option. Try calling apartment rental agency **Kvartira** (📞301 504, 8-909-823 4477).

TOP CHOICE ▶ Boutique Hotel   BOUTIQUE HOTEL €€€
(📞767 676; www.boutique-hotel.ru; ul Istomina 64; s/d incl breakfast from R4500/5100; ❄@⑤) By far Khabarovsk's most foreigner-friendly hotel, this relatively new offering has smiling receptionists and huge, beautifully furnished rooms adorned with classy black-and-white photos from a bygone era. Throw in gorgeous bathrooms, luxurious white bedspreads and the full complement of mod-cons, and it's the rare Khabarovsk hotel that won't leave you desperate to escape.

Versailles   HOTEL €€
(Версаль; 📞659 222; Amursky bul 46a; s/d incl breakfast from R2000/3000; ❄@⑤) This cheerful hotel, an easy walk from the train station, has pleasant red-carpeted rooms with fridge and small sitting area. It's set back from the street, fronted with seal lamp posts – just like back in France. Wi-fi costs extra and there's a 15% reservation fee.

Resting rooms   HOSTEL €
(комнаты отдыха, komnaty otdykha; 📞383 710; 3rd fl, train station; 4-bed dm 12/24hr R610/900, s R1250) The train station's nice resting rooms are really the only budget digs anywhere near the city centre.

Amur Hotel   HOTEL €€
(Гостиница Амур; 📞221 223; www.amurhotel.ru; ul Lenina 29; s/d incl breakfast from R2450/3400; ❄❄@⑤) An old standby, the Amur serves up clean rooms with plenty of space to sit and relax. English can be problematic and it's a long stroll to the riverfront action, but it's still an excellent choice in this price range. The booking fee is 22%.

Parus   HISTORICAL HOTEL €€€
(Парус; 📞327 270; www.hotel-parus.com; ul Shevchenko 5; s/d incl breakfast from R5200/6100; ❄@⑤) Part of a century-old brick building near the water, the 80-room Parus sure makes a grand entrance – with chandeliers, iron staircase and reading room. Rooms are also overdone, but plenty sizeable and come with expensive Italian furniture and flat-screen TVs.

Hotel Afalina   HOTEL €€
(Гостиница Афалина; 📞211 260; afalina-treld@rambler.ru; ul Dikopoltseva 80; s/d from R3400/3600, 12hr R2200/2500; ❄❄⑤) Twelve-hour rates and proximity to the train station make this a good choice if you are arriving late into Khabarovsk. Rooms are on the small side but stylish with flat-screen TVs and futuristic shower stalls in the bathroom. English spoken.

Hotel Tsentralnaya   HOTEL €€
(Гостиница Центральная; 📞303 300; ul Pushkina 52; s R1700-2300, d R1900-2500; ❄⑤) It's been years since the staff would let us see a room (maybe they were burned by Paul Theroux when he stayed here while researching *The Great Railway Bazaar*), but you can expect the standard diet of lightly renovated Soviet fare. Half the 200 rooms look over pl Lenina. A booking fee of 25% applies.

Hotel Intourist   HOTEL €€
(Гостиница Интурист; 📞312 313; Amursky bul 2; s/d from R2750/3050; ❄@⑤) Teeming with tour groups, this big Bolshevik still breathes as if it's 1975. Service is so-so and the cheaply renovated rooms are closet-sized (but do have remarkable river views on upper floors). You're paying for the prime location and, apparently, the two English TV channels. Wi-fi costs extra and the booking fee is 25%. The entrance is on per Arseneva.

Hotel Sapporo   HOTEL €€€
(Гостиница Саппоро; 📞304 290; www.sapporo-hotel.ru; ul Komsomolskaya 79; s/d incl breakfast from R4300/5000; ❄@⑤) The Sapporo is a Japanese-run midrange hotel with top-end prices.

Hotel Turist   HOTEL €€
(Гостиница Турист; 📞439 674; www.habtour.ru; ul Karla Marksa 67; s/d/tr incl breakfast R1860/2520/3000; ⑤) This Soviet special can often find a roommate for solo travellers looking to split costs; 25% booking fee.

Eating

On nice days, nothing beats the **shashlyk and beer tents** along Amursky bul and at the (unrenovated) northern end of the riverside promenade. Expect to pay R150 to R200 for a generous pork kebab and R60 to R80 for a beer. A 2011 law banned beer sales along the spruced-up southern portion of the promenade.

GETTING CHINESE VISAS IN THE FAR EAST

Foreigners can get Chinese visas at consulates in **Khabarovsk** (🖉4212-302 590; http://khabarovsk.china-consulate.org; Lenin Stadium 1, Southern Bldg; ⊙11am-1pm Mon, Wed & Fri) and **Vladivostok** (🖉4232-495 037; Hotel Gavan, ul Kyrgina 3; ⊙9.30am-12.30pm Mon, Wed & Thu).

A one-month tourist visa for Europeans costs R900/1500/1800 for five-/three-/one-day processing. Americans pay R4000 (10-day processing only). You'll need a letter of invitation, application form (available on the Khabarovsk Consulate website) and copies of your immigration card, latest hotel registration and Russian visa. Travel agencies in Vladivostok and Khabarovsk may be able to assist with Chinese visas.

TOP CHOICE **Stolovaya Lozhka & Tempo Pizza** RUSSIAN €

(Столовая Ложка и Темпо Пицца; ul Dikopoltseva 29; meals R200-300; ⊙stolovaya 9am-9pm, pizzeria 10am-midnight; ⊖🖤) One of a host of upscale *stolovye* (canteens) that have been cropping up all over Russia, this one boasts an outdoor beer patio and is twinned with a pizzeria selling pizza by the slice (R60 to R90).

Pepper One ITALIAN €

(ul Muravyova-Amurskogo 9; pizza for two R300-400; ⊙10am-2am; 🖤) Khabarovsk is famous for its pizzerias and this is one of the best. It has decent pasta and coffee too, plus groovy tunes.

Kofeynya CAFE €€

(Кофейня; ul Muravyova-Amurskogo 18; mains R120-350; ⊙8am-midnight; 🖤) A snappy little cafe with wonderful omelettes, bliny and other affordable breakfast fare, along with heartier mains and its trademark coffee.

Russky Restaurant RUSSIAN €€€

(Русский Ресторан; 🖉306 587; Ussuriysky bul 9; mains R300-750; ⊙noon-1am; 🖤) The kitsch factor at this Russian folk-themed restaurant is high but the food is tasty. Traditional music that plays most nights from 8pm cheekily costs R200 per head.

Demokratiya CAFE €€

(Демократия; ul Muravyova-Amurskogo 12; mains R150-400; ⊙noon-1am; 🖤) Join hipsters drinking home brew in this low-lit space. It has good salads and business lunches from R140.

Blin FAST FOOD €

(Блин; Lotus Shopping Centre basement, ul Muravyova-Amurskogo 5; bliny R50-75; ⊙10am-10pm) Locals queue up for the bliny here.

Pelikan SUPERMARKET

(Пеликан; ul Vladivostokskaya 61; ⊙24hr) There is another **branch** in the Dom Byta shopping centre at ul Sheronova 92.

🍷 Drinking

Harley Davidson Bar BAR

(ul Komsomolskaya 88; ⊙24hr; 🖤) Harley Bar features nightly live classic rock, 10 brews on tap, tattooed bartenders and a looooong wooden bar – the kind you can slide a beer mug down. Weekend after-hours parties are legion.

Pool Club PUB

(ul Lenina 33) More Irish pub than pool bar, this is a great place to warm up for a night out with an expansive menu of pub grub and suds.

Chocolate CAFE, LOUNGE BAR

(ul Turgeneva 74; mains R400-900; ⊙24hr; 🖤🖤) A cafe with a pricey menu of slick international snacks (fajitas, burgers, brownies) by day, it becomes a prime party spot after hours.

☆ Entertainment

Khabarovsk is most definitely a party town, with arguably the best clubs east of the Volga.

Hospital NIGHTCLUB

(Госпиталь; http://hospitalclub.ru; ul Komsomolskaya 79; cover R300-1000; ⊙Fri & Sat) One of Russia's top clubs, with several packed dance chambers and a consistent line-up of top DJ talent from Russia and abroad. YouTube has highlights.

Heart NIGHTCLUB

(ul Sheronova 7; cover R400-600 Fri & Sat, free Thu; ⊙Thu-Sat) Heart is not far behind Hospital in the Far East club hierarchy.

Platinum Arena ICE HOCKEY

(Платинум Арена; 🖉233 216; ul Dikopoltseva 12) This is the home arena for Khabarovsk's ice hockey team, the Amur Tigers, a hot ticket from October to March.

Lenin Stadium · FOOTBALL
(Стадион Ленина; Riverfront Sports Complex; tickets R150) Home to Khabarovsk's first division football team, SKA-Energiya.

Theatre of Musical Comedy · CONCERTS
(Театр Музыкальной Комедии; ☎211 196; ul Karla Marksa 64; tickets R80-800) Funny operettas run from November to April; big musical acts run from May to October. There's also the occasional heavy-metal concert (Ron-

nie James Frickin' Dio started his 2005 tour here).

Shopping

Tainy Remesla · SOUVENIRS
(Тайны Ремесла; ul Muravyova-Amurskogo 17; ☺10am-7pm) This is the best souvenir shop in town, located in the old House of Pioneers building.

Knizhny Mir · MAPS
(Книжный Мир; ul Karla Marksa 37; ☺9am-8pm) Stock up on your Far East maps here; it has

TRANSPORT CONNECTIONS FROM KHABAROVSK

DESTINATION	MAIN TRAINS SERVING DESTINATION* & FREQUENCY	RAIL PRICE (PLATSKART/ KUPE)	RAIL DURATION	AIRLINES SERVING DESTINATION	AIR PRICE	AIR DURATION & FREQUENCY
Běijīng	n/a	n/a	n/a	Vladivostok Air	from R5000	3hr, 2 weekly
Blagoveshchensk	**35 (odds**)**, 385 (evens***)	R1000/2200	16hr	Ir-Aero	from R5000	2hr, 3 weekly
Irkutsk	1 (odds), 7 (evens), **43 (odds)**, 133 (odds), 239 (odds, summer)	from R3100/7800	2 days 10 hours	Ir-Aero, Vladivostok Air	from R5000	3¾hr, almost daily
Komsomolsk	351 (daily), **667 (daily)**	from R925/1900	10hr	n/a	n/a	n/a
Moscow	1 (odds), **43 (odds)**, 239 (odds, summer)	from R5200/11,000	5½ days	Aeroflot, Transaero, VIM Airlines, Vladivostok Air	from R12,500	8½hr, several daily
Neryungri (via Tynda)	325 (daily)	R2000/4000	35hr	n/a	n/a	n/a
Seoul	n/a	n/a	n/a	Asiana, Vladivostok Air	from R8000	3hr, almost daily
Vladivostok	2 (odds), **6 (daily)**, 8 (evens), 134 (odds), 352 (daily), 386 (evens)	from R1000/2100	11-15hr	Vladivostok Air	from R2500	1¼hr, daily

Trains originating in Khabarovsk **in bold**

**Odd-numbered days

***Even-numbered days

the best selection outside of Yakutsk. A compact map of the city centre in English sells for R60.

ℹ️ Information

Internet Access & Post

Port@l (Порт@л; ul Moskovskaya 7; per hr R75; ⏰10am-10pm)

Post office (Главпочтамт; ul Muravyova-Amurskogo 28; internet per hr R100; ⏰internet 9am-8pm, post 8am-10pm Mon-Fri, 9am-6pm Sat & Sun)

Medical Services

The Hotel Intourist has a doctor in room 132.

Travel Agencies

Intour-Khabarovsk (Интур-Хабаровск; ☎312 119; www.intour-khabarovsk.com; Hotel Intourist, Amursky bul 2; ⏰10am-6pm Mon-Fri) Not recommended, but it hands out a good guide to the city in English and an OK free map.

ℹ️ Getting There & Away

Most travel agents book train or air tickets for a modest commission. The best booking agent is **Aviakassa** (bul Amursky 5; ⏰8.30am-8pm Mon-Sat, 9am-6pm Sun) because of its generous opening hours.

Train

Khabarovsk's train station is lovely but there is little in the area grocery-wise. See the transport table (p237) for train connections. Almost all trains to Vladivostok are overnight.

Note that the 1/2 *Rossiya* train between Moscow and Vladivostok is significantly more expensive than all other trains, and only slightly faster. The 7/8 train between Novosibirsk and Vladivostok is also relatively expensive.

For Birobidzhan, take any westbound train or a cheaper *elektrichka* (R300, three hours, three daily).

Air

The **airport** is 7km east of the train station. See the transport table for air connections.

Boat

Between late May and late October, hydrofoils leave five days a week at 7.30am from the **river station** (Ussuriysky bul; ⏰8am-7pm) for Komsomolsk-na-Amure (from R800, six hours) on the BAM train line.

ℹ️ Getting Around

From Khabarovsk's train station, about 3.5km northeast of the waterfront, bus 4 goes to pl Komsomolskaya (board opposite the station

and head southeast) and trams 1 and 2 go near pl Lenina.

From the **airport**, 9km east of the centre, trolleybus 1 goes to pl Komsomolskaya along ul Muravyova-Amurskogo and bus 35 goes to the train station (25 minutes) and bus station. A taxi to the centre from the airport is R500; usually R300 or R400 the other way.

Trolleybuses and trams cost R15, *marshrutky* R20 to R30.

Vladivostok Владивосток

☎4232 / POP 610,000 / ⏰MOSCOW +7HR

At first look, Vladivostok is something like 'Russia's San Francisco' – a real stunner, with pointed mountains springing up above a network of bays, most strikingly the crooked dock-lined Golden Horn Bay (named for its likeness to Istanbul's). Closer up, it can be a little grey, with Soviet housing blocks squeezed between new condos and century-old mansions. But it's a great place to kick off or finish a Trans-Siberian trip – however, be warned: leg muscles not used to the ups and downs of hilly streets will get more sore than a butt on the Trans-Siberian.

Big changes arrived in Vladivostok thanks to the 2012 Asian Pacific Economic Conference (APEC). Timing-wise, June can often be grey and wet, while September and October are the nicest, sunniest months (another thing Vladivostok has in common with San Francisco). Vladivostok's City Day is 2 July, or the closest Saturday to it.

History

Founded in 1860, Vladivostok (meaning 'To Rule the East') became a naval base in 1872. *Tsarevitch* Nicholas II turned up in 1891 to inaugurate the new Trans-Siberian rail line. By the early 20th century, Vladivostok teemed with merchants, speculators and sailors of every nation in a manner more akin to Shanghai or Hong Kong than to Moscow. Koreans and Chinese, many of whom had built the city, accounted for four out of every five of its citizens.

After the fall of Port Arthur in the Russo-Japanese War of 1904–5, Vladivostok took on an even more crucial strategic role, and when the Bolsheviks seized power in European Russia, Japanese, Americans, French and English poured ashore here to support the tsarist counterattack. Vladivostok held out until 25 October 1922, when Soviet forces finally marched in and took control – it was the last city to fall.

In the years to follow, Stalin deported or shot most of the city's foreign population. Closed from 1958 to 1992, Vladivostok opened up with a bang – literally (mafia shoot-outs were a part of early business deals) – in the '90s, and is only starting to settle down in recent years.

◉ Sights & Activities

CENTRAL VLADIVOSTOK
On tree-lined streets around the city centre you'll find plenty of tsarist-era buildings from Vladivostok's first crazy incarnation a century past. The main areas for locals to mill about is **ploshchad Bortsov Revolutsii** (on ul Svetlanskaya at the southern end of Okeansky pr) and **Sportivnaya Harbour,** near the west end of ul Fokina (aka 'the Arbat'). There you can find a popular beach and beer and shashlyk stands.

TOP CHOICE Funicular   FUNICULAR
(Фуникулёр; ul Pushkinskaya; ticket R6; ⊙7am-8pm) Vladivostok's favourite attraction may just be the smoothest-running operation in the Far East: the well-oiled **funicular railway,** which every few minutes makes a fun 60-second ride up a 100m hill. At the top, go under ul Sukhanova via the slummy underpass to a great **lookout** over the bay. It's next to a **statue of Saints Cyril and Methodius** (inventors of the Cyrillic alphabet) on the hilltop campus of DVGTU (Far Eastern State Technical University).

The base of the funicular is about a 15-minute walk from the centre. Bus 164 goes to/from the top of the funicular from the corner of ul Aleutskaya and ul Svetlanskaya.

Arsenev Regional Museum   MUSEUM
(Объединённый Краеведческий музей Арсеньева; ul Svetlanskaya 20; admission R150; ⊙9.30am-6pm Tue-Sun) Grey-haired ladies keep watch over every Russian museum in existence, but none do it more sweetly than at the interesting Arsenev Regional Museum, which dates from 1890. Exhibits are in Russian only, but it's still enjoyable for non-Russian speakers. On the 1st floor note the stuffed tiger and bear interlocked as if dancing; the 2nd floor is filled with great 19th-century photos of Vlad's early days, including a display of the Brynner family.

Primorsky Picture Gallery   ART GALLERY
(Приморская Картинная галерея; pr Partizanski 12; admission R50; ⊙9am-6pm) Vladivostok's bipolar art museum's original locale (ul Aleutskaya 12) has long been under renovation, but may be open by the time you read this. While most of the impressive collection is in storage, bits and pieces rotate through the annexe east of Park Provotsky. We saw the likes of da Vinci, Botticelli, Goya, Feshin, Kandinsky, and Chagall when we dropped by.

S-56 Submarine   MUSEUM
(Подводная Лодка С-56; Korabelnaya nab; admission R100; ⊙9am-8pm) The S-56 submarine is worth a look. The first half is a ho-hum exhibit of badges and photos of men with badges (all in Russian). Keep going: towards the back a periscope provides a green-tinted view of what's going on outside, and you walk through a bunk room with Christmas-coloured torpedoes and an officers' lounge with a framed portrait of Stalin. Outside note the '14', marking the WWII sub's 'kills'.

Vladivostok Fortress Museum   MUSEUM
(Музей Владивостокская Крепость; ul Batareynaya 4a; admission R120; ⊙10am-6pm) On the site of an old artillery battery overlooking Sportivnaya Harbour, this museum has cannons outside and a six-room indoor exhibit of photos and many, many guns. There are English explanations. Access is from ul Zapadnaya.

FREE Artetage   ART GALLERY
(4th fl, ul Aksakovskaya 12; ⊙10am-6pm Tue-Fri, 11am-5pm Sat & Sun) DVGTU's humble modern art showcase has a few intriguing pisstakes at the country's red past, such as a bust of Lenin as a *novy Russky* ('New Russian,' aka gangster).

FREE Arka Art Gallery   ART GALLERY
(ul Svetlanskaya 5; ⊙11am-6pm Tue-Sat) Often-interesting rotating exhibits down an alley with great graffiti.

OUTER VLADIVOSTOK
Much of the water facing Vladivostok is quite polluted but it gets cleaner as you go north. Sunbathers can get on a northbound *elektrichka* and hop off at any beach that looks good – try Sedanka, where there are a few resorts with services. You'll find better swimming on Popov or Russky Islands.

Russky Island   ISLAND
A fully militarised island for most of the past 150 years, this big island just offshore,

Vladivostok

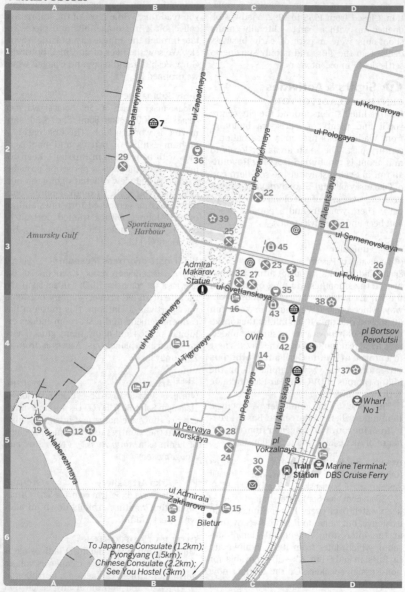

which only opened to foreigners in the early 2000s, has been completely reinvented as a business and – supposedly – tourism zone. The most obvious changes will have occurred near the new bridge's terminus on the island's eastern peninsula. The rest of

the island should remain relatively quiet for the time being, despite the newly paved ring road. Voroshilov Battery sells a good map of the island (R50).

One of the highlights has always been the trip out to the island by car ferry, which takes

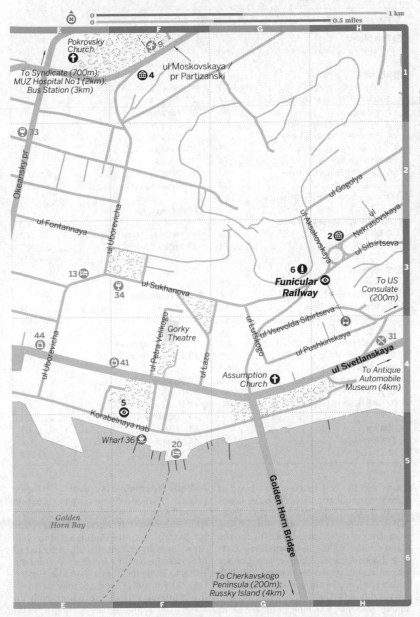

you past the icebreakers and automobile-packed container ports of **Golden Horn Bay**. While the new suspension bridge will allow vehicular access to Russky Island, we expect that these atmospheric ferries will continue to run. The ferries depart from Vladivostok's

Wharf No 1 *(pervy prichal)*, 100m north of the Marine Terminal, and land in the village of Podnozhne (R90 return, 50 minutes, six to eight daily).

Buses await the ferries in Podnozhne. One goes west to **Rynda**, which has a couple of

Vladivostok

resorts and the best beaches (just hop out when you see one you like). The other heads east to 'DOF' (Dom Ofitseya Flota). From DOF it's a pleasant 5km walk through the taiga along a newly paved road to Russky Island's main sight, the **Voroshilov Battery** (Ворошиловской Батарее, Voroshilovskoy Bataree; admission weekday/weekend R70/100; ⏱10am-6pm), where three massive cannons aim roughly at Hokkaido. The battery, now a military museum, was built in 1933–34 and housed 75 soldiers at its peak. Underground you can explore the guts of the battery, while above ground there are great views of the Pacific. Walk or hitch back to DOF, where buses to Podnozhe are timed for ferry departures. Podnozhe has an old **monastery** to explore.

Antique Automobile Museum MUSEUM
(Музей Автомотостарины; http://automoto museum.vl.ru; ul Sakhalinskaya 2a; admission R70; ⏱10am-6pm) If you're a bit of a car (or Soviet) nerd, the Antique Automobile Museum is an absolute classic. A room full of Sovietmobiles (motorcycles too) from the 1930s to 1970s includes a 1948 M&M-green GAZ-20 'Pobeda' (Victory). If they start selling reproductions of the poster with an acrobat on a motorcycle holding a Stalin flag, send us one, please! Take bus 31 along ul Svetlanskaya and exit after it reaches ul Borisenko's end.

Fort No 7 FORTRESS
(Форт 7; ☎8-950-282 7373; asomiw@mailru; admission 1/2-4/5+ people, per person R500/250/150; ⏱10am-6pm Tue-Sun) Attention

fort fans: Vladivostok teems with sprawling, rather unique subterranean forts built between the late 19th and early 20th century to ward off potential Japanese (or American) attacks. Sixteen protective forts (including four on Russky Island) and hundreds of artillery batteries and other military objects encircle Vladivostok. The best to visit is the hilltop Fort No 7, 14km north of the centre. It has 1.5km of tunnels, pretty much untouched since the last 400 soldiers stationed here left in 1923, although the NKVD later used it as an execution chamber. Views are good too. Admission includes a tour in Russian with eccentric 'fort commander' Grigory. To get here take bus 59 from the train station, get off at the last stop ('F Zarya'), and walk 20 minutes east on the road leading up the hill (you may have to ask directions). It's not a bad idea to let Grigory know you're coming before you arrive. This and other forts can be visited on a tour with Vladivostok Digger Club (see p244).

Popov Island   ISLAND

Just beyond Russky Island, Popov Island is better regarded for its beaches and filled with many guesthouses and dachas. You'll probably need to overnight if you head out here, as there is usually only one boat per day (R70, 1½ hours), departing from Vladivostok's first wharf. Ask at a travel agent if they can help with accommodation. Day trips are possible on days when there are two trips – check the schedule.

☞ Tours

Vladivostok travel agents run a variety of city and regional tours, but they can get pricey.

Heading outside of Vladivostok into Primorsky Territory, the most interesting tour is probably to **Sikhote-Alin Nature Reserve**, home to the Russian-American Siberian (Amur) Tiger project. It's a short flight or an 11-hour drive to Terney, where the 3440-sq-km forested reserve is headquartered. Chances of seeing a tiger are basically nonexistent, but the reserve is thick with birds, seals and other wildlife, and the scenery is incredible. Dalintourist and Lucky Tour run six-day trips here from about €1200 per person (including guide,

---

FACELIFT FOR VLAD

Vladivostok's infrastructure was torn asunder and rebuilt for the big APEC summit on Russky Island in 2012. A few new developments are sure to catch your eye, starting with two giant suspension bridges: one across Golden Horn Bay to the previously difficult-to-access Cherkavskogo Peninsula, the other spanning more than 1km over the Eastern Bosphorus Strait to Russky Island. They are among the highest suspension bridges in the world – the pylons of the Russky Island bridge are a whopping 321m high.

The Russky Island bridge was just part of a massive development plan for the island that was to continue well beyond APEC. The convention centre used for APEC was slated to become part of the campus of an ambitious new university. The rough ring road around this sleepy island was being paved and widened at the time of research. New resorts and other tourist facilities were slated to follow.

Critics have lambasted the billions being spent on the project, and the island's several thousand residents are generally lukewarm. 'Why do we need this, why are we spending all this money?' wondered Vladivostok resident Yury Shvets, who has family on the island. 'They kicked my aunt off her land to build the new road and gave her nothing in return – just a token. She didn't even have a choice.' Many worry about the toll increased traffic and tourism will have on the island's pristine environment.

Officials retort that upgrades of the city's dilapidated infrastructure will drive economic growth. Other major APEC-related infrastructure projects include the newly expanded airport and the new highway from the airport to the city centre.

Downtown Vladivostok has seen its share of changes, as well. The city's beloved 'Arbat' (walking street), ul Fokina, and the promenade along the waterfront at Sportivnaya Harbour were given flashy upgrades, and all city sidewalks were ripped up and replaced wholesale. Fortunately, this has all been done without detracting too much from the turn-of-the-20th-century elegance of streets such as ul Aleutskaya and ul Svetlanskaya. Indeed, the bridge to Cherkavskogo Peninsula, dubbed the Golden Horn Bridge, adds character to the city, a-la-San Francisco, with which Vladivostok is often compared.

transport, accommodation and meals) and can be combined with a stay at Lazovsky Nature Reserve east of Nakhodka, home to a population of about 20 tigers.

The Far East is all about its Amur tigers, and at **Gaivoron**, 235km north of Vladivostok, you can see a couple at the Russian Academy of Sciences biological research reserve, run by Dr Victor Yudin and his daughter. Tours by Vladivostok agents include about 90 minutes of tiger time, lunch and a four-hour ride each way. It's not possible to go independently.

Dalintourist TOURS
(☎410 903, 9-914-670 9109; www.dalintourist.ru; ul Fokina 8a; ⏲9am-7pm Mon-Fri, 10am-3pm Sat) Contact English-speaking Evgenya on the 2nd floor for help with area tours and info or to hire English-speaking guides (R450 per hour).

Lucky Tour TOURS
(☎449 944; www.luckytour.com; ul Moskovskaya 1; ⏲9.30am-6pm Mon-Fri) Interesting tour to Khasan on North Korean border; requires several weeks' notice.

Shamor.Info TOURS
(☎499 799; www.trans-siberian.su; ul Svetlanskaya 147; ⏲9am-6pm Mon-Fri) Formerly known as Vizit, covers the basics such as Sikhote-Alin and Gaivoron, and is generally responsive. You want Galina.

Vladivostok Digger Club TOURS
(☎552 086; www.vtc.ru/~vladdig; grom-2000@mail.ru) Club head Artur leads hour-long to full-day tours of Fort No 7 and other forts, batteries and the tunnels (some 3.5km long) that link them.

Sleeping

Two five-star **Hyatt hotels** were scheduled to open for APEC – one near the S-57 Submarine at Korabelnaya nab 6 and another on Cape Burny near the Amursky Zaliv hotel.

Apartments *(kvartiry)* and homestays are an option, although registration is usually not available if you go this route. **Dialog** (Диалог; ☎497 909; Marine Terminal, office 133; ⏲9am-8pm) offers studio apartments from R1000 per night and rooms from R500. **Vladivostok Guest House** (vladivostokhostel@yahoo.com) is really more of a homestay and you should get in touch in advance to arrange. **Lyudmila** (lyu-lomakina@yandex.ru) also runs a homestay.

TOP CHOICE **Hotel Primorye** HOTEL €€
(Гостиница Приморье; ☎411422/582; www.hotelprimorye.ru; ul Posetskaya 20; s/d incl breakfast from R3200/3400; @📶) Considering quality and location, this is Vladivostok's best. Don't be fooled by the 'economy' tag on the cheaper rooms; they are beautifully appointed and have playful details like funny artwork and a clock. The higher-priced superiors offer more space, bigger beds, air-con and views of the warships in Golden Horn Bay. One fuss: rock-hard beds.

Hotel Hyundai HOTEL €€€
(Гостиница Хюндай; ☎402 233; www.hotelhyundai.ru; ul Semenovskaya 29; s/d incl breakfast from R6500/7500; 🚭❄@📶🏊) Big with Asian business travellers, this 12-floor, 335-room tower is perfectly fine – big rooms with writing desk, satellite TV, modern bathroom and some sterling views on higher floors. Service can be clunky – surprising if you consider the room rates! There's a barber, Korean restaurant, sauna, gym and pool (non-guests R400).

See You Hostel HOSTEL €
(☎487 779; www.seeyouhostel.com; apt 133, ul Krygina 42a; dm R650; @📶) The Far East's only bona fide hostel is hidden in an apartment block near the southern end of the long peninsula running south from the train station. It features 16 beds in several rooms, free wi-fi and laundry at R100 per load. Check website for directions.

Hotel Moryak HOTEL €€
(Гостиница Моряк; ☎499 499; www.hotelm.ru; ul Posetskaya 38; s/d from R1500/1700; 🚭❄) Terrific value considering its perfect location, this grey-brick yet cheerful place has an endearing lobby with a stuffed version of the hotel namesake – a sea man. The colourful rooms are compact but ship-shape, with thin walls (and mattresses) and *tiny* bathrooms. Laundry is a reasonable R250 per bag. No lift. Pay for your wi-fi; a 25% booking fee applies.

Hotel Vladivostok HOTEL €€
(Гостиница Владивосток; ☎411 941; www.azimuthotels.ru; ul Naberezhnaya 10; d incl breakfast from R3000; ❄@📶) The Azimut group has taken over this 12-floor grey tower and turned it into a decent midrange business hotel. A few Soviet vestiges remain (notably the toilets and sinks) and rooms can be smoky, but they are bigger than expected and come with fresh wallpaper and qual-

ity linens. Pony up an extra R500 for water views.

Hotel Versailles
HOTEL €€€

(Гостиница Версаль; ☎264 201; www.versailles.vl.ru; ul Svetlanskaya 10; s/d incl breakfast R5300/6000; ✳@ ⓢ) The Versailles does a decent job of recapturing the pre-USSR grace of the century-old hotel that reopened in the '90s, despite enigmatic pairings in the lobby ('70s lounge seats, tsarist-style chandeliers). Quarters are plenty roomy with exquisite furniture and lovely bathrooms.

Hotel Amursky Zaliv
HOTEL €€

(Гостиница Амурский Залив; ☎462 090; www.azimuthotels.ru; ul Naberezhnaya 9; r unrenovated/renovated from R1800/2900; ⓢ) Hotel Vladivostok's poor step-sibling is gradually being renovated, so expect a price rise in some rooms. All rooms have balconies overlooking city beach.

Hotel Zhemchuzhina
HOTEL €€

(Гостиница Жемчужина; ☎414 387; www.gemhotel.ru; ul Bestuzheva 29; s/d from R1400/1800; ⓢ) Formerly the Chayka, this is a well-located but charmless cheapie. Registration costs R100. Pay extra for wi-fi.

Equator Hotel
HOTEL €€

(Гостиница Экватор; ☎300 110; www.hotelequator.ru; ul Naberezhnaya 20; dm in q R600, s/d with bathroom from R2300/2900; @ⓢ) This old-school Soviet hotel's grotty economy rooms are among Vlad's cheapest; fancier rooms are reasonably good value.

 Eating

Eating options coat the town, offering more class and types of cuisine than pretty much anywhere between here and Moscow or Alaska.

Some restaurants offer 'business lunches' from noon to 4pm for R200 to R300. In good weather, **open-air stands** sell beer (R70 to R100) and cook up sizzling shashlyk (R150) and *shawarma* (doner kebab; R80) on the waterfront north of Sportivnaya Harbour.

Healthy snacks like nuts and dried fruit are available at the **farmer's market** (ul Aleutskaya) that runs most days in the square opposite the train station.

TOP CHOICE Pyongyang
KOREAN €€

(Пхенян; Hotel Korona, ul Verkhneportovaya 68b; mains R300-400; ⊙noon-midnight; ✐) Staffed by female newcomers from North Korea who periodically break out in karaoke, this DPRK-sponsored establishment is just strange enough to be considered a must-visit. You can pick from a photo menu of excellent food such as *bibimbap* (rice mixed with fried egg, sliced meat, and other stuff) and spicy fried pork with kimchi. The beer is cheap (from R90) and pricier mains serve two.

Stolovaya No 1
CAFETERIA €

(Столовая 1; ul Svetlanskaya 1; meals R150-200; ⊙24hr; ⊜ⓢ✐) Defining 'stolovaya chic', this is the best cafeteria in all the Far East, with a hip soundtrack, plum location, snazzy bar serving coffee and booze

---

CAR CITY *ROBERT REID*

It's hard to walk around the centre's traffic-jammed streets without noticing that Vladivostok's gone Texas about cars. You have to have one, the bigger the better. One local with a Bentley stated he wouldn't go to a nearby cinema: 'No parking, and I don't want to walk.' The mass import of Japanese cars with right-hand steering causes some confusion on Russian streets, where cars stick to the right. But the city's so fanatic over the imports that when Yeltsin and later Putin tried to restrict the use of right-hand steering cars, officials in Vladivostok practically threatened revolution.

Not long ago, locals exchanged old cars in a sketchy park in eastern Vladivostok, but now just enter one of 50 'live auction houses' across town. The auction houses broadcast 30-second internet auctions to bid on used Japanese and Korean cars that arrive a week later. Many of the cars coming will be shipped across Russia; meanwhile, all can be seen, awaiting customs, in multi-level garages along Golden Horn Bay.

For fun, I stopped by an auction house at the Marine Terminal and asked about getting a 1977 Russian Lada. 'Oh, very bad,' the mulleted attendant protested. 'Can't we bid on a Toyota Corolla for you?' Three-year-old Corollas go for US$12,000, plus US$500 shipping and US$3000 customs. I passed. 'Yes,' he said, 'this is a very good business.'

and well-above-average *stolovaya* fare. It gets packed at meal times, but otherwise is a perfect place for a drink in front of the laptop.

Syndicate
AMERICAN €€€

(ul Komsomolskaya 11, Ignat Mal; mains R400-1600; ☻noon-2am; 🖥) Taking over Vladivostok in an Al Capone frenzy, this ultra-1930s themed restaurant – 'Chicago, New York, whatever', per one waitress – has seats next to faux storefronts and a stage that lights up with live music. The specialty is steaks – a 350g T-bone runs to R1600. Add R300 per person at weekends, when popular band Blues Line plays. It's north of the centre, reachable via any 'Vtornaya Rechna' bus.

Mauro Gianvanni
PIZZERIA €€

(Мауро Джанванни; ul Fokina 16; mains R240-650; ☻noon-midnight; 🖉🖥) This slick little brick-oven pizzeria – run by an Italian – pumps VH1 videos in the modern interior, though most sit out on the deck when weather behaves. The dozen-plus pizzas are crispy and tasty, probably the best pie east of the Urals.

Nostalgiya
RUSSIAN €€

(Ностальгия; ul Pervaya Morskaya 6/25; mains R200-500; ☻8am-11pm; 🖥) This compact, long-running restaurant offers hearty and tasty Russian meals with a little for-the-tsars pomp. Most visitors come for the souvenir shop (big collection of paintings and handicrafts) or a snack at the cafe.

Dva Gruzina
GEORGIAN €€

(Два Грузина; ul Pogranichnaya 12; mains R150-300; ☻10am-1am; 🖥) The Georgians are the Italians of the former Soviet Union for their love of wine and food. Sample trademark Georgian *khachapuri* (cheese bread) and rich stews like *chanakhi* and *kharcho,* washed down with wine by the glass (from R60) or beer (from R80). This stretch of ul Pogranichnaya is somewhat of a restaurant row.

Five O'Clock
CAFE €

(ul Fokina 6; snacks R60-100; ☻8am-9pm Mon-Sat, 11am-9pm Sun; ☻🖉🖥) Vladivostok, take note of this novel idea – coffee, brownies, cakes and quiche (R70), all made daily and sold for less than an espresso at most 'cafes'.

Gutov
GERMAN €€

(Гутов; ul Posetskaya 23; mains R300-500; ☻noon-midnight, to 2am Sat & Sun; 🖥) This snazzy beer hall with chunky wood tables serves Bavarian sausages and large Russian meals – mostly meats and fish fillets cooked up with a host of vegetable toppings. 'Business lunch' means gentler pricing of the same dishes.

Pizza M
PIZZERIA €€

(Пицца M; 🖉 delivery 413 430; Hotel Primorye, ul Posetskaya 20; medium pizzas R260-420; ☻24hr; ☻🖥) Classier than its name might suggest, the M (inside Hotel Primorye) is one of Vlad's coolest hang-outs, with two unique rooms setting their style-sights higher than the humble slice. The pizzas are quite good (note: a small is *not* enough for one).

Republic
CAFETERIA €

(Республика; meals R150-250; ☻9am-11pm Sun-Thu, 10am-midnight Fri & Sat; ☻🖉) These perfectly respectable twin *stolovye*, one located on ul Aleutskaya, the other on ul Svetlanskaya, draw more than a couple of cheap dates with their tasty Russian dishes, home brew (R80 for 500mL) and funky interiors. Both have bars on-site.

Mauro Gianvanni Café
ITALIAN €€

(Кафе Мауро Джанванни; Okeansky pr 9; mains R240-500; ☻11am-midnight, to 2am Fri & Sat; 🖥) No pizza like in the main restaurant, but perfectly cooked pasta served in a basement setting.

Myunkhen
GERMAN €€

(Мюнхен, Munich; ul Svetlanskaya 5; mains R180-800; 🖥) More meaty meals and towers of home brew in a beer-hall setting.

Clover Leaf
FAST FOOD €

(cnr ul Semenovskaya & ul Aleutskaya; ☻🖱🖉) A convenient mall housing a 24-hour supermarket with a deli, a top-floor beer bar and a food court with incredible views.

Supermarket
SUPERMARKET

(Супермаркет; ul Aleutskaya; ☻24hr) This grocery store is under the Republic restaurant across from the train station.

🍷 Drinking

Zima
LOUNGE BAR

(ul Fontannaya 2; drinks from R200, mains R200-500; ☻11am-2am, 24hr Fri & Sun; 🖱🖉🖥) You'd think a place this swanky would be snobby and grossly overpriced. Yet Zima dispenses with the *feiskontrol* and serves up mouthwatering mixed shashlyk and sushi at perfectly normal (for Russia) prices. Oh yeah, and you order on iPads. This all occurs in an elaborate but classy Angkor Wat–themed interior, replete with design surprises (check out the little boys' and girls' rooms). Cocktails and beer are expensive; Leffe on tap makes up for it.

Rock's Cocktail Bar   BAR
(ul Svetlanskaya) If you prefer a grungier crowd, this smoky basement dive is for you. Cool kids get dancing – and things often get sloppy – late night, as the DJ pays homage to Kurt, Layne, Zack and other '90s icons.

Moloko & Myod   LOUNGE BAR
(Молоко и Мёд; ul Sukhanova 6a; mains R270-320; ⊗noon-midnight Sun-Thu, to 3am Fri & Sat; ⊛📶📱) A busy spot with a trendy street-side terrace shaded by birch trees, 'Milk & Honey' has a daily brunch plus coffee, pricey cocktails and chic chow like crab risotto with asparagus. Blankets warm terrace dwellers on chilly evenings.

El Dorado   SPORTS BAR
(Okeansky pr 29; ⊗24hr) You're likely to get into weird conversations with harmless drunks playing online poker, but the 10 TV screens or so will be playing the sport you need (NBA, Premiership, NFL, maybe netball) – best is the viewing room with rows of old airplane seats.

Sky Bar   LOUNGE BAR
(12th fl, Hotel Hyundai, ul Semenovskaya 29; ⊗6pm-2am) It attracts its share of high rollers and those looking for their business, but the views are undeniably tremendous.

☆ Entertainment

Stadium Dinamo   SPORTS
(Стадион Динамо; ul Pogranichnaya; tickets R150-230) The popular local football team, Luch-Energiya, plays games at this bayside stadium from April to November. On other days you can pay R50 to jog on the track.

Zabriskie Point   LIVE MUSIC
(Забриский Пойнт; ul Naberezhnaya 9a; cover Tue-Thu & Sun R500, Fri & Sat R700; ⊗9pm-5am Tue-Sun) Attached to the rear of the Hotel Amursky Zaliv, Zabriskie is Vladivostok's main rock and jazz club, drawing an older crowd to view live music acts such as Blues Line. Pricey, but not without character.

Yellow Submarine   NIGHTCLUB
(ul Naberezhnaya 9a; cover R100-500) Right next to Zabriskie Point, this thumping club draws a younger crowd to hear a mix of live music and techno-spinning DJs.

Cukoo   NIGHTCLUB
(Ку-Ку; Okeansky pr 1a; cover R500; ⊗Fri & Sat) One of Vladivostok's poshest clubs, the dance floor here seethes at weekends. Dress to impress to get through the velvet rope.

Philharmonic Hall   CLASSICAL MUSIC
(Филармония; ul Svetlanskaya 15) Hosts classical music and jazz performances.

🛍 Shopping

And in other news, an explosion of modern malls! It's happened across Vladivostok – often with a confusing network of shops selling similar (but not quite the same) collections of imported clothing.

Magazin Kollektsionera   SOUVENIRS
(Магазин Коллекционера; ul Fokina 5/3; ⊗10am-6pm) A retired navy vet, now a spry octogenarian, opened this collection of (mostly) Soviet keepsakes about two decades ago. Super stuff: Soviet cameras, watches, toy soldiers, warship clocks, banners, Stalin paintings – all very reasonably priced.

Flotsky Univermag   OUTDOOR GEAR
(Флотский Универмаг; ul Svetlanskaya 11; ⊗10am-7pm Mon-Fri, to 6pm Sat & Sun) For unusual souvenir turf, follow the navy – this outfitter has those cute blue-and-white-striped navy undershirts (R140) and other navy gear, as well as useful travel gear like flashlights, 'Russia' bags, knives, maps and deodorant. Also has an OK map selection.

Nostalgiya   SOUVENIRS
(Ностальгия; ul Pervaya Morskaya 6/25; ⊗10am-8pm) Nostalgiya keeps a good range of pricey handicrafts (wood boats from R250 and way up) and many art pieces.

Dom Knigi   MAPS
(Дом Книги; ul Aleutskaya 23; ⊗10am-7pm) This store carries compact Vladivostok city-centre maps (R45) and bigger maps of greater Vladivostok and Primorsky Territory, along with postcards and a funny Vladivostok-photo matchbox set (R180). Another branch is at ul Svetlanskaya 43.

GUM   SOUVENIRS
(ГУМ; ul Svetlanskaya 35; ⊗10am-8pm Mon-Sat, 10am-7pm Sun) This Soviet-style department store is the Far East's most art deco elegant. Some traditional souvenirs on the 1st floor.

❶ Information

Internet Access, Post & Telephone

Interface (Интерфейс; ul Semenovskaya 8; per hr R70; ☺24hr)

OS (ОС; ul Fokina 6; per MB R2, per hr R40; ☺24hr)

Post office (Почта; ul Aleutskaya; per MB R30, per hr R0.80; ☺8am-10pm Mon-Fri, 9am-6pm Sun) Post, telephone and internet opposite the train station. Watch out – those per MB fees really add up.

Media

Guide to Vladivostok This free ad-based guidebook (half in English) has listings for most tourist-based services. Available at kiosks and bookstores around town.

Vibirai A free Russian-language biweekly entertainment mag available in hotel lobbies and many restaurants.

Vladivostok Guidebook Sound familiar? This English guidebook (R100), found at kiosks and some bookstores, has more listings than the same-named freebie.

Vladivostok News (www.vladivostoknews.com)

Vladivostok Times (www.vladivostoktimes.com)

Medical Services

MUZ Hospital No 1 (МУЗ Больница 1; ☎453 275; ul Sadovaya 22)

Money

There are currency exchange desks and ATMs all over town.

Sberbank (Сбербанк; ul Aleutskaya 12; ☺8.45am-8pm Mon-Sat, 10am-5pm Sun) Accepts travellers cheques (2% commission).

❶ Getting There & Away

See the transport table for air and rail connections. Ticket agents all over town can sell plane and train tickets, including **Biletur** (☎407 700; ul Posetskaya 17; ☺8am-7pm Mon-Sat, 9am-6pm Sun).

Train

Save money by avoiding the No 1 *Rossiya* train to Moscow.

The Hä'ĕrbīn train is an enigma, with many stops and a long border check. Departures are at 5.23pm on Monday and Thursday, but the first night you only go as far as Ussurinsk, where they detach your car from the 351. You overnight in Ussurinsk and depart the next day for the border and Hä'ĕrbīn. It's much quicker and easier to take a bus to Hä'ĕrbīn.

Air

Vladivostok's airport was undergoing a major expansion at research and should be ready to go by the time you read this, with additional international routes likely and budget flights from Moscow a possibility. Additional international destinations served by Vlad's flagship carrier, **Vladivostok Air**, include Hanoi (seasonal), Nha Trang, Tokyo, and Niigata, while Transaero runs seasonal flights to Bangkok.

Boat

DIY travellers can check out the schedule at **Wharf (Prichal) 36** (Korabelnaya nab), 100m east of the S-56 Submarine, where ferries shuttle locals to the port of Slavyanka, 50km south towards the (off-limits) North Korean border. There are usually a couple of hydrofoils per day (R400, one hour) and four weekly car ferries (R130, three hours).

DBS Cruise Ferry (☎302 704; www.parom .su; Marine Terminal, office 124) Sends a passenger-only ferry to Donghae, Korea (from US$185 one way, 20 hours), continuing on to Sakaiminato, Japan (from US$250 one way, 42 hours), every Wednesday at 3pm.

Bus

Buses to Hä'ĕrbīn, China, depart every morning at 6.20am (R2500, eight hours) from the **bus station** (ul Russkaya), 3km north of the centre. There are also frequent departures for Nakhodka (four hours) and other destinations in the Primorsky Territory. Some southbound destinations may be off-limits to foreigners without a permit.

❶ Getting Around

The train station is easy walking distance from most hotels listed. From in front of the train station, buses 23, 31 and 49 run north on ul Aleutskaya then swing east onto ul Svetlanskaya to the head of the bay.

For trips of more than 5km, you'll save money ordering a taxi by phone. Try **PrimTaxi** (☎555 555) or the curiously named **Cherepakha** (Turtle; ☎489 948).

To/From the Airport

A rail link to the airport (43km north in Artyom) should be ready by the time you read this. Meanwhile, bus 107 (R55) runs from the airport to the train station every 45 to 75 minutes from 8.25am to 8pm (return trips are 6.40am to 5.45pm). If it's not running, take bus 7 from the airport to Artyom's bus station and the frequent 106 from there to Vladivostok's train station.

A taxi booth in the arrivals area charges R1500 for trips to the centre. Outside taxis start higher (up to R2500) and end lower (R1000). Try sharing a ride to reduce costs. Allow at least 90 minutes, although the new highway linking Artyom with Vladivostok should cut that in half.

TRANSPORT CONNECTIONS FROM VLADIVOSTOK

DESTINA-TION	MAIN TRAINS SERVING DESTINA-TION & FREQUENCY	RAIL PRICE	RAIL DURATION	AIRLINES SERVING DESTINA-TION	AIR PRICE	AIR DURATION & FREQUENCY
Běijīng	351 to Ussurinsk (Mon & Thu)	*kupe* R4000 (to Hǎ'ěrbīn)	40hr (transfer in Hǎ'ěrbīn)	China Southern, S7, Vladivostok Air	from R4500	2½hr, almost daily
Hǎ'ěrbīn	351 to Ussurinsk (Mon & Thu)	*kupe* R4000	40hr	Vladivostok Air	from R3200	1¼hr, weekly
Irkutsk	1 (evens*), 7 (odds**), 133 (evens), 239 (evens, summer)	*platskart/ kupe* from R4000/9000	2 days 22hr	S7, Ural Airlines, Vladivostok Air	from R11,300	4hr, most weekdays
Khabarovsk	1 (evens), 5 (daily), 7 (odds), 133 (evens), 351 (daily), 385 (odds)	*platskart/ kupe* from R1000/2100	11-15hr	Vladivostok Air	from R2500	1¼hr, daily
Moscow	1 (odds), 239 (evens, summer)	*platskart/ kupe* from R6000/13,100	6 days	Aeroflot, Transaero, Vladivostok Air	from R4000	10hr, frequent
Seoul	n/a	n/a	n/a	Korean Air, Vladivostok Air	from R11,000	2½hr, daily

*Even-numbered days

**Odd-numbered days

Around Vladivostok

The broad, mountainous Primorsky Territory is beloved by locals with cars, who visit the beaches and mountains. You might consider renting a car and doing the same, but note that some areas near the Chinese border require permits. Those without their own wheels lean on pricey tours to get further away. One easy trip to do by public transport is to Nakhodka, where Primorsky's best beaches are a short bus or taxi ride away. Buses and trains to Nakhodka take three to four hours.

ARTYOM ΑΡΤËΜ

42337 / POP 102,600/ ☾MOSCOW +7HR

Vladivostok's distant airport is in Artyom, a mellow provincial town. Staying out here saves you time, money and sleep if you have an early-morning plane the next day. **Hotel Svetlana** (Гостиница Светлана; 307 603; ul Pushkina; 39, Artyom; s/d from R1500/2400) offers a very good deal right in the centre of town. **Venice Hotel** (307 603, www.venice.far-east.ru; ul Portovaya 39, Artyom; s/d R3500/4000) is a grossly overpriced hotel at the airport.

There are a couple of cafes near the main square in the centre. Bus 7 goes to/from the airport (10 minutes); catch it at the bus station or along the main drag, ul Pushkina.

The Baikal-Amur Mainline (BAM)

Route Info

» Distance: 4287km

» Duration: Four days one hour

» Time zones: Moscow +5 to Moscow +7

Best Places to Stay

» Baikal Trail Hostel (p257)

» Biznestsentr (p263)

» Zolotaya Rybka (p257)

» Hotel Taiga (p255)

» Hotel Olymp (p257)

Why Go?

Most people know the Trans-Siberian Railway, but how many can say they've heard of the 'other' Trans-Sib, its poor country cousin, the BAM (Baikal-Amur Mainline, or Baikalo-Amurskaya Magistral)? The branch line to end all branch lines, the BAM begins as a set of points at Tayshet, and ends over 4200 lonely kilometres further east at Sovetskaya Gavan, passing through some jaw-slackeningly off-the-map places en route. As great railway journeys go, this is a Soviet epic, a rail-clanging odyssey you'll never forget.

But it's a miracle the BAM was ever built at all. Costing billions of dollars and declared a 'Hero Project of the Century', construction was fraught with seemingly insurmountable difficulties. The line opened fully in 1991, just as the USSR collapsed. Today only a handful of trains ply the route.

Riding the BAM's snail-paced trains takes you to some very out-of-the-way places. Only Severobaikalsk on Lake Baikal is geared up for visitors.

When to Go

Tynda

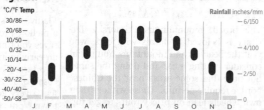

Mar Ponder the weird shapes into which Lake Baikal freezes from the shore at Severobaikalsk.

Sep–Nov Avoid the crowds and ticket shortages of summer by taking an autumn trip along the BAM.

Sep & Oct Watch larch trees around Lake Baikal's north fill the landscape with autumnal gold.

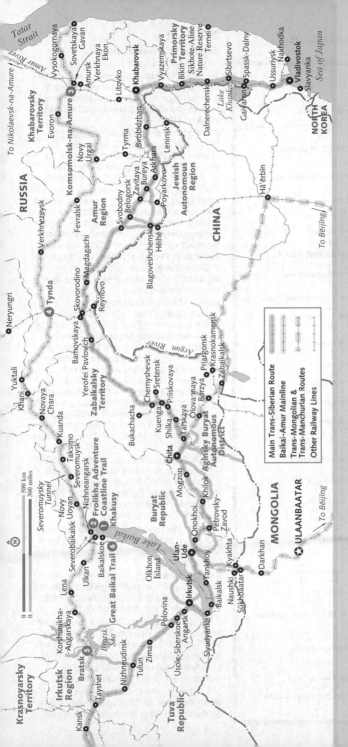

BAM Highlights

1 Getting into hot water at **northern Baikal's mini-spas** (p260) for a spot of R&R Siberian-style

2 Bagging up your boots for the **Frolikha Adventure Coastline Trail** (p258), one of Siberia's most exhilarating long-distance hiking routes

3 Touring the BAM's nicest town, St Petersburg-styled **Komsomolsk-na-Amure** (p261), with Soviet monuments and nearby Nanai villages

4 Soaking up all things BAM at the varied and welcoming **BAM Museum** (p260) in the BAM capital, Tynda

5 Looking out across the Bratsk Sea from a BAM train window as you trundle across the top of the **Bratsk Dam** (p254)

6 Trekking a rugged section of the **Great Baikal Trail** (p259) between Baikalskoe and Echo Turbaza

Baikal-Amur Mainline by BAM

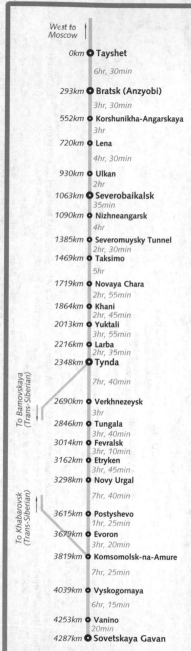

West to Moscow

0km	**Tayshet**
	6hr, 30min
293km	**Bratsk (Anzyobi)**
	3hr, 30min
552km	**Korshunikha-Angarskaya**
	3hr
720km	**Lena**
	4hr, 30min
930km	**Ulkan**
	2hr
1063km	**Severobaikalsk**
	35min
1090km	**Nizhneangarsk**
	4hr
1385km	**Severomuysky Tunnel**
	2hr, 30min
1469km	**Taksimo**
	5hr
1719km	**Novaya Chara**
	2hr, 55min
1864km	**Khani**
	2hr, 45min
2013km	**Yuktali**
	3hr, 55min
2216km	**Larba**
	2hr, 35min
2348km	**Tynda**
	7hr, 40min
2690km	**Verkhnezeysk**
	3hr
2846km	**Tungala**
	3hr, 40min
3014km	**Fevralsk**
	3hr, 10min
3162km	**Etryken**
	3hr, 45min
3298km	**Novy Urgal**
	7hr, 40min
3615km	**Postyshevo**
	1hr, 25min
3679km	**Evoron**
	3hr, 20min
3819km	**Komsomolsk-na-Amure**
	7hr, 25min
4039km	**Vyskogornaya**
	6hr, 15min
4253km	**Vanino**
	20min
4287km	**Sovetskaya Gavan**

To Bamovskaya (Trans-Siberian)

To Khabarovsk (Trans-Siberian)

The Route

Tayshet to Severobaikalsk

0KM FROM TAYSHET The junction with the Trans-Sib at **Tayshet** is the official start of the BAM, but only hardcore purists would begin in this uninspiring railway town. Most connect through on daily services from livelier **Krasnoyarsk** (p180).

293–339KM The first major stops along the BAM are for **Bratsk** (p254), a sprawling city of almost 250,000 people on the edge of the Bratsk 'Sea', an artificial lake created in the 1960s by the building of the Bratsk Hydroelectric Station. The railway line actually crosses the top of the gigantic 1km-long dam at the 330km mark, presenting wide views on both sides. If you get off you must choose between three Bratsk stations: **Anzyobi** (293km from Tayshet) for the crushingly dreary central (Tsentralny) area, **Padunskiye Porogiye** (326km) for Energetik, or **Gidrostroitel** (339km) for the dam. Bratsk's biggest attraction is the Angara Village open-air ethnographical museum.

552KM The taiga closes in on the line as you travel the next 600km towards the jagged mountains hemming in the northern end of Lake Baikal. **Korshunikha-Angarskaya** is the train station for the claustrophobic 1960s iron-ore processing town of **Zheleznogorsk-Ilimsky**. A 2km walk diagonally uphill to your right as you leave the station brings you to the town's one modest attraction, the **Yangel Museum** (⊘9am-4pm Mon-Fri), which not only celebrates a local astroscientist friend of Yury Gagarin, but also has a well-arranged exhibition on local wildlife, an art gallery and a section on ZI's twin town in Japan.

573KM One of the few branch lines off the BAM veers north from Khrebtovaya to **Ust-Ilimsk**, a town of almost 100,000 people on the Angara River 215km away. The historic town of Ilimsk lies drowned at the bottom of the reservoir created by the Ust-Ilimsk Dam.

720KM A few kilometres after **Lena** the line swings across the Lena River on a single-track bridge with views down onto a large timber port to the north.

930KM At **Ulkan** halt, a small but eye-catching metallic Lenin relief stands against a bright red 'flag' on the east end of the platform, but you'll only have three minutes to admire it.

982KM After **Kunerma** the track performs a full 180-degree loop. Hurry for the camera before you disappear into the 6km-long Daban tunnel.

1028KM Around half an hour before reaching Lake Baikal, some trains make a brief stop at picturesque mini-spa **Goudzhekit** (p260).

1063KM Though architecturally dull, **Severobaikalsk** (p255) is by far the most interesting stop on the entire route. The surrounding area, which takes in the northern part of Lake Baikal, is beautiful and offers lots of opportunities for outdoor adventure. The *Thunderbirds*-style station, inspired, it is said, by the mayor's love of ski jumping, is one of the most striking along the line. Outside there's a steam train and a statue commemorating the workers from across the USSR who toiled on the BAM.

Severobaikalsk to Tynda

1090KM This is where the BAM get serious. From Severobaikalsk to the fishing village of **Nizhneangarsk** (p258), 30km north, the line skirts Lake Baikal, though views are often better from the road (unencumbered by tunnels). At **Nizhneangarsk 2** station, look out for the small airport, from where there are flights to Ulan-Ude and Irkutsk.

1105KM Only local *elektrichki* (suburban trains) stop at the Evenk village of **Kholodnaya** by the Verkhnaya Angara River delta.

1142KM The tiny hot-springs spa at **Dzelinda** (p260) is also served by local slow trains only.

1150–2500KM The next 1300km or so gives you ample time to appreciate the truly massive engineering achievement of the BAM. Many consider this the most interesting section of the line, as it climbs over densely forested, mountainous terrain along switchbacks and through several tunnels. But despite the region's remoteness, the train stops at least once an hour at communities established by BAM construction workers and their families in the 1970s and 1980s.

1242KM The first major halt on this section of the line is the low-rise ferroconcrete station belonging to **Novy Uoyan**, though there's no reason to get off here save to stretch your legs. Trains then snake across the flood plain of the Verkhnaya Angara River until the line slams into the mountains again.

1385KM The 15.3km-long **Severomuysky tunnel** is the longest in Russia and was only completed in 2004 after years of severe technical difficulties with the permafrost. The tunnel replaced over 50km of track, which had steep gradients and was prone to avalanches.

1469KM The born-of-the-BAM town of **Taksimo** provides the next opportunity to escape the muggy air of *platskart* and take on a few provisions at the station kiosks. Get some much-needed exercise during the 30-minute stop by running to see the BAM Pioneer Monument. There are wilderness hiking possibilities in the surrounding mountains and along the River Muya, and flights operate south to Ulan-Ude from the tiny airport.

1535KM Local time becomes Moscow time plus six hours.

1561KM At **Kuanda** look out for the Golden Link Monument commemorating the uniting of the two sections of the BAM in 1984.

BAM ROUTE PLANNER

Here's a suggested itinerary for the BAM:

Day 1: Take an overnight train from Krasnoyarsk to Bratsk to see the dam holding back the Bratsk 'Sea'

Day 2: Overnight hop to Severobaikalsk

Day 3: Take a dip in Lake Baikal or a boat trip; chill out at the Baikal Trail Hostel

Day 4: Excursion from Severobaikalsk to Baikalskoe, Nizhneangarsk or one of the mini-spas at Dzelinda or Goudzhekit. Catch the night-day train to Tynda.

Day 5: After spending most of the day on the train, wash off in the town's *banya* (bathhouse)

Day 6: Explore Tynda's BAM Museum before catching a sleeper to Komsomolsk-na-Amure

Day 7: Arrive Komsomolsk-na-Amure, spend the day exploring this surprisingly attractive city. Overnight train to Sovetskaya Gavan.

Day 8: Arrive at BAM's end on the Tatar Strait

1850–1950KM Shortly before **Khani** (1864km) you enter the Sakha Republic and continue along its border with Zabaikalsky Territory and Amur Region. Shortly beyond **Olyokma** (1918km) the train veers southeast and follows the Olyokma River into Tynda Region.

2000–2210KM The train leaves the Olyokma River, veers due east and rumbles into **Yuktali** (2013km), where there's a 35-minute stop. The next four hours are very scenic as you follow the Nyukzha River southeast until just before **Larba** (2216km).

2348KM Finally you roll into **Tynda** (p259), the unofficial BAM 'capital,' with a '70s train station that looks like a science-fiction film set. If you're coming straight from Moscow, you've been travelling for almost five days. The main BAM trains all terminate in Tynda, so you'll have a layover if you are continuing east to Komsomolsk or west to Severobaikalsk or Moscow.

In the TV series *Long Way Round*, Ewan McGregor went north by motorcycle from here on the AYaM (Amur-Yakutsk Mainline or Amuro-Yakutskaya Magistral) highway, bound for Yakutsk in the Sakha Republic. There's also an AYaM train line that goes north into Sakha and south to Bamovskaya on the Trans-Siberian (for details on the train-jeep combo trip north to Yakutsk, see p263).

Tynda to Sovetskaya Gavan

2348-2690KM Heading east on the BAM, the 364 train to Komsomolsk pulls out at 5.26pm and crosses the mighty Gulyuy River twice (at 2364km and 2409km). Night falls as you cross several more rivers and enter the swamps leading into **Verkhnezeysk** (2690km) on the Zeysk Reservoir.

2779-2894KM The stretch from Ogoron to Dugda is about the prettiest the eastern BAM has to offer, with a range of snow-capped mountains to the northeast and patches of thick taiga near the tracks, but eastbound travellers will need to get up early. The eastbound stretch is 10km either side of **Tungala** (2846km).

3015KM In **Fevralsk** (3014km) on the Byssa River, you get 35 minutes to contemplate the permafrost below, or gold mines and pulp mills outside town. It's a two-minute walk south to the little town centre, with food shops and a post office with internet access. The train station has an ATM.

3155KM You leave Amurskaya Region and enter Khabarovsky Territory between the station stops of Ulma (3149km) and Etryken (3162km).

3298KM After crossing the Bureya River (3292km), the train stops for 35 minutes in **Novy Urgal**, a coal-mining town near green hills and the white waters of the Akisma River. If you are having one of those rare macabre instincts for an authentic, fading pocket of '70s Sovietlandia, stop. Otherwise, move on. You can switch to the 663 here for a short cut to the Trans-Siberian line and Khabarovsk.

3382KM A couple hours away, the train passes through the 2km **Dusse-Alin Tunnel**. Gulag camp labourers toiled (and died) over this during Stalin's watch, but it was only completed and put into use in 1982.

3615KM In **Postyshevo**, locals sell the town's famous red *ikra* (caviar) on the platform in late summer and autumn. The interesting station has socialist-realist bas-reliefs over both entrances, and a psychedelic, copper-toned, honeycombed ceiling inside.

3819KM Five hours east of Postyshevo, the 364 terminates in the BAM's loveliest city, **Komsomolsk-na-Amure** (p261), with direct links with Khabarovsk on the Trans-Siberian, by bus or by boat.

3819-4253KM While most people get off in Komsomolsk, the BAM still has another 468km to go. Two night trains tackle this final 12-hour stretch. Some train mates may joke you're on an 'international route' as the train clanks through a couple of ho-hum villages passed on the way – **Kenada** (4080km) and **Toki** (4243km); they

liken them phonetically with 'Canada' and 'Tokyo' (it's OK to fake a chuckle).

The BAM then pulls into view of a snaking Pacific bay lined with shipyards at **Vanino** (4253km; population 18,500), where boats leave for Sakhalin Island (p264). Vanino's often foggy bay, looked over by two lighthouses, sees some 20 million tonnes of goods shipped in/out each year (including coal, lumber and gas).

4287KM The BAM terminates at **Sovetskaya Gavan-Sortirovochny** ('SovGavan' on train timetables; not to be confused with the city of Sovetskaya Gavan, about 25km further south).

Bratsk Братск

☑ 3953 / POP 246,000 / ⊙ MOSCOW +5HR

Unless you're a fan of BAM or dam, it's perhaps not worth leaving the 'comfort' of your carriage bunk for Bratsk, though it does neatly break up the journey from both Irkutsk and Krasnoyarsk to Severobaikalsk. The city's *raison d'être* is a gigantic dam, which drowned the original historic town in the 1960s. New Bratsk is an unnavigable string of disconnected concrete 'subcities' and belching industrial zones, with the spirit-crushingly dull Tsentralny area at its heart.

⊙ Sights & Activities

Bratsk Dam
LANDMARK

(Братская ГЭС) A ferroconcrete symbol of the USSR's efforts to harness the might of Siberia's natural assets, between 1967 and 1971 the Bratsk hydroelectric power station was the world's largest single electricity producer. Slung between high cliffs and somehow holding back the mammoth Bratsk Sea, no one can deny it's a striking spectacle, especially from the window of the BAM trains that pass right across the top.

Take any *marshrutka* from Tsentralny to Gidrostroitel, the closet slab of Bratsk to the dam. The only way to access the turbine rooms is through a local tour agency.

Angara Village
OPEN-AIR MUSEUM

(admission R100; ⊙ 10am-5pm Wed-Sun) Some 12km from Tsentralny, this impressive open-air ethnographic museum contains a rare 17th-century wooden watchtower and buildings rescued from submerged old Bratsk. A series of shaman sites and Evenki *chum* (tepee-shaped conical dwellings) lie in the woods behind. Take a taxi or arrange a visit through Taiga Tours.

🛏 Sleeping

The following hotels are both in Tsentralny.

Hotel Taiga HOTEL €€
(Гостиница Тайга; ☑413 979; www.hotel-taiga
.ru; ul Mira 35; s R1750-3550, d R2500-5250) The
flashiest in town, this renovated Soviet hulk
has cramped rooms packed with tasteless
furniture but clean 21st-century bathrooms.
Some staff speak English, guest visas are
registered and there's a decent hotel restaurant. Breakfast is extra.

Hotel Shvedka HOTEL €
(Гостиница Шведка; ☑412 520; www.hotel
-shvedka.ru; ul Mira 25; dm R500, s R700-3000,
d R1000-2500) Rooms here range from battered and cheap to well kept and reasonably
priced. Ask to see which you're getting before you commit. On-site tour agency offering Bratsk tours. No breakfast.

ℹ Information

Lovely Tour (☑459 909; www.lovelytour.ru;
ul Sovetskaya 3, Tsentralny) Bratsk tours plus
plane and train tickets.
Taiga Tours (☑416 513; www.taiga-tours.ru;
2nd fl, Hotel Taiga) Permits and guides to visit
the dam's turbine rooms.

ℹ Getting There & Away

For Tsentralny, get off BAM trains at the Anzyobi
(Анзеби) station and transfer by bus or *elek-trichka* (suburban train). Bratsk has the following
rail connections:

Irkutsk *platskart* R1330, *kupe* R2000 to
R3000, 17 hours, daily
Krasnoyarsk *platskart* R1130, *kupe* R1750 to
R2500, 13 hours, up to four daily
Moscow *platskart* R4650, *kupe* R7600 to
R10,800, five days five hours, even days only
Severobaikalsk *platskart* R1050, *kupe* R1600
to R2260, 14 to 17 hours, up to four daily

Irkutsk can also be reached by Western-
standard coach (R900, 11 hours) from the Tsentralny **bus station** (ul Yuzhnaya) and summer
hydrofoil from a river station in southeast Tsentralny. Check **VSRP** (www.vsrp.ru) for details of
the latter.

Severobaikalsk
Северобайкальск

☑30130 / POP 25,500 / ⊙MOSCOW +5HR
Founded as a shack camp for railway workers in the mid-1970s, Severobaikalsk (SB)
has grown into the most engaging halt on

WORKING THE BAM

As you gaze from your carriage window
at the wall of pine and birch passing
slowly by, spare a thought for the poor
BAM workers whose orange Russian
Railways jackets occasionally punctuate the green. Dispatched for a month
at a time to impossibly remote locations and armed with only rudimentary
tools, this army of workers somehow
keep the tracks straight and level in the
harshest of conditions. Their accommodation and food are basic, and bear
attacks are not unknown.

the BAM, where travellers vacate stuffy railway compartments to stretch legs in the
taiga or cool off in Lake Baikal. The town
itself is a grid of soulless, earthquake-proof
apartment blocks with little in between, but
the mountainscape and nameless wilder-
nesses backing the lake quickly lure hikers
and adventurers away from the concrete.
They discover a land more remote, less peo-
pled and generally more spectacular than
Baikal's south, a place where lazy bears and
reindeer-herding Evenkis still rule in timeless peace, despite the best efforts of *Homo
sovieticus*.

◎ Sights & Activities

BAM Museum MUSEUM
(Музей БАМа; ul Mira 2; admission R50; ⊙10am-
1pm & 2-6pm Tue-Sat) The town's friendly little
museum has exhibits on BAM railway history (workers' medals, grainy black-and-white
photos, 'old' BAM tickets), some Buryat artefacts and a few mammoth bones. Around
the corner is a small art gallery where local
artists display their works.

Railway Station NOTABLE BUILDING
(pr 60 let SSSR; ⊙5am-midnight) The epicentre
of SB's world is a striking construction with
a nostalgically stranded steam locomotive
standing guard to the right. The sweeping
architectural design of the brave-new-world
station resembles a ski-jump – thanks to a
previous mayor's love of the sport, locals
claim.

Orthodox Church CHURCH
(Leningradsky pr) SB's newest Orthodox church
sports two impressive onion domes in
gleaming gold and a monster chandelier

Severobaikalsk

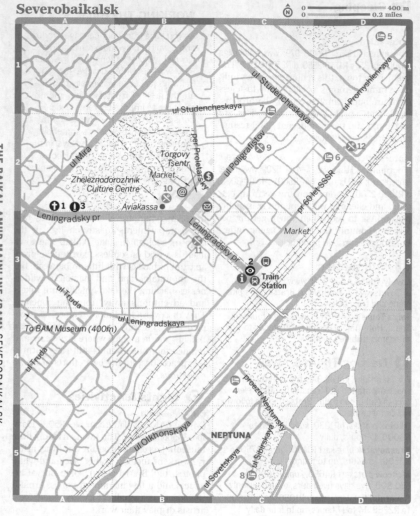

inside. It stands just beyond the town's gun-toting grey-concrete **war memorial**.

👉 Tours

The following agencies and individuals can help arrange accommodation and back-country excursions.

Ecoland　　　　　　　　TOUR COMPANY
(📞22 506; www.ecoland-tour.ru) This award-winning tour agency specialises in horse-riding trips, Baikal boat excursions and trekking.

Maryasov Family　　　　　TOUR GUIDE
(📞8-924-391 4514; baikalinfo@gmail.com) The English-speaking Maryasov family (Yevgeny and daughters Alyona and Anna) run Severobaikalsk's hostel, information centre and tourism association as well as organising guided treks to Baikalskoe and Lake Frolikha, seal-spotting trips to Ayaya Bay and Evenki-themed excursions to the village of Kholodnoe.

Rashit Yakhin/BAM Tour　　TOUR GUIDE
(📞21 560; www.gobaikal.com, ul Oktyabrya 16/2) This experienced full-time travel-fixer, guide and ex-BAM worker suffered an

Severobaikalsk

◎ Sights
1 Orthodox Church A2
2 Railway Station C3
3 War Memorial A2

🛏 Sleeping
4 Baikal Resort C4
5 Baikal Service D1
6 Baikal Trail Hostel D2
7 Hotel Olymp C1
8 Zolotaya Rybka C5

⊗ Eating
9 Anyuta C2
10 TiC B2
11 VIST Supermarket B3
12 VIST Supermarket D2

immobilising stroke in the mid-1990s rendering his spoken English somewhat hard to follow. Nonetheless, he is quick to reply to emails and is always keen to please. He rents out a brilliant central apartment (R600, negotiable).

🛏 Sleeping

TOP CHOICE Baikal Trail Hostel HOSTEL €
(☑23 860; www.baikaltrailhostel.com; baikalinfo@gmail.com; ul Studencheskaya 12, apt 16; dm R500; @📶) Initially set up to house Great Baikal Trail volunteers working in the North Baikal area, this spacious eight-bed apartment-hostel is well equipped with essential backpacker facilities such as kitchen, washing machine and communal climbing frame. It's one of the best places in town to arrange backcountry treks and trips into the wilds around the northern end of Lake Baikal.

Zolotaya Rybka GUESTHOUSE €€
(Золотая Рыбка; ☑21 134; www.baikalgoldenfish.ru; ul Sibirskaya 14; tw R1200-3500) Well signposted from ul Olkhonskaya, SB's best guesthouse maintains immaculate and imaginatively designed rooms in three buildings, providing glimpses of Lake Baikal through the trees. There are spotless toilets and showers throughout, guests have access to kitchens and a cook prepares a restaurant-standard breakfast on request (R300 extra). The owner, Oleg, runs intriguing taiga trips to visit a self-sufficient family who survive unsupported in the forest north of SB.

Hotel Olymp HOTEL €€
(Гостиница Олимп; ☑239 80; www.hotelolymp.ru; ul Poligrafistov 2b; s & d R1300-2500; 📶) Severobaikalsk's smartest sleep has spotless, cool, airy rooms though the plumbing could be more professionally screwed down. For this price you might expect breakfast and free wi-fi – you get neither. Despite the name you'll be disappointed/relieved to find no Greek theme inside.

Baikal Service GUESTHOUSE €€
(Байкал Сервис; ☑23 912; www.baikaltour.irkutsk.ru; ul Promyshlennaya 19; cottage R3800, s/d R1400/2800) Hidden in a peaceful pine grove at the otherwise unpromising northeast end of town, Baikal Service has three very comfy pine cottages sleeping up to five, and less-exciting but well-appointed singles and doubles in a separate guesthouse. Breakfast is included in the rates for the guesthouse but not for the cottages.

Baikal Resort GUESTHOUSE €€
(Дом у Байкала; ☑23 950; www.baikal-kruiz.narod.ru; proezd Neptunsky 3; tw R700-1800) This 'resort' is really just a house and a row of basic cabins in a quiet area, walking distance from the lake. Rooms are spacious and have a clean shower and toilet, but summer-only huts are a bit cramped.

✕ Eating & Drinking

For quick eats (*pozi*, shashlyk, *plov* and beer), try the **fast-food row** east of the station on pr 60 let SSSR or the greasy spoons around the Torgovy Tsentr. Otherwise, pickings are meagre indeed.

TiC CAFE €
(ТиЦ; Railway Culture Centre, Tsentralny pl; mains R40-70; ◷11am-5pm & 6pm-1am). Climb the gloss-painted stairs for a return to Soviet-style 1980s dining. The food is basic and cheap, the dinner ladies belligerently unsmiling, the alcohol plentiful and the hand-scrawled menu a challenge even to Russian speakers.

Anyuta CAFE €
(Анюта; ul Poligrafistov 3a; mains R90-180; ◷6pm-2am Tue-Sun) Evening dinner nook housed in a red-brick building amid high-rise blocks at the northern end of town.

VIST Supermarket SUPERMARKET
(ВИСТ) Leningradsky pr 5 (◷8.30am-9pm) ul Studencheskaya (◷8.30am-8pm) The town's

FROLIKHA ADVENTURE COASTLINE TRAIL

The latest instalment in the Great Baikal Trail saga is this incredible, relatively demanding 100km adventure trekking route between the delta of the Verkhnyaya Angara River and the spa hamlet of Khakusy on Baikal's eastern shore. You'll need a boat to find the start of the trail at the mouth of the river, from where it takes eight days to reach the spa village of Khakusy via countless lonely capes and bays, wild camping by the lake all the way. Exhilarating river crossings (including a biggie – the River Frolikha), deserted beaches and show-stopping Baikal vistas punctuate the trail, and from Ayaya Bay a there-back hike to remote Lake Frolikha beckons.

For more information and trail maps, contact Severobaikalsk tour agencies, the Baikal Trail Hostel or Dresden-based **Baikalplan** (www.baikalplan.de) predeparture.

VIST supermarkets stock a limited range of groceries.

ℹ Information

There are ATMs at the railway station, in the Zheleznodorozhnik Culture Centre and at the Leningradsky pr branch of the VIST Supermarket.

Library (Библиотека; Zheleznodorozhnik Culture Centre; ☺11am-7pm Mon-Thu, to 6pm Fri) Cheap internet access.

Post office (Почта; Leningradsky pr 6; ☺9am-2pm & 3-7pm Mon-Fri, 9am-2pm Sat).

Sberbank (Сбербанк; per Proletarsky; ☺9am-6.30pm Mon-Fri, 10am-3pm Sat) ATM and currency exchange counter.

Tourist office (train station forecourt; ☺9am-6pm Jun-Aug) Yellow-blue kiosk on the train station forecourt providing information on the North Baikal area.

Warm North of Baikal (www.privet-baikal.ru) Website belonging to the local tourism association with tons of information and listings.

ℹ Getting There & Away

Train

Tickets can be bought from the station or the Zheleznodorozhnik Culture Centre. The station is within walking distance of the town centre

and most places to stay. Severobaikalsk has the following rail connections:

Bratsk *platskart* R1050 to R1140, *kupe* R1600 to R2450, 15 to 17 hours, up to four daily

Irkutsk *platskart* R2090, *kupe* R3320 to R4700, 32 to 37 hours, daily

Krasnoyarsk *platskart* R2600 to R4860, *kupe* R1660 to R1800, 26 to 36½ hours, three daily

Moscow *platskart* R8300 to R12,900, *kupe* R5080, three days 20½ hours, daily

Tynda *platskart* R1600, *kupe* R3600 to R4400, 26 hours, daily

Air

The **Aviakassa** (Tsentralny pl; ☺9am-noon & 1-4pm) in the Dom Kultury Zheleznodorozhnik sells tickets for flights to Irkutsk and Ulan-Ude from Nizhneangarsk, 30km northeast. These short air hops are a quick way to link from the BAM to the main Trans-Sib line.

Boat

From late June to late August a hydrofoil service runs the length of Lake Baikal between Nizhneangarsk, Severobaikalsk and Irkutsk via Olkhon Island. Check **VSRP** (www.vsrp.ru) for times and ticket prices.

Bus

From outside Severobaikalsk's train station *marshrutky* run to:

Baikalskoe R60, 45 minutes, two daily

Goudzhekit R100, 45 minutes, three daily

Nizhneangarsk Airport R37, 50 minutes, half-hourly

Around Severobaikalsk

NIZHNEANGARSK НИЖНЕАНГАРСК
📞30130 / POP 5500 / ☺MOSCOW +5HR

Until the BAM clunked into town, Nizhneangarsk had led an isolated existence for over 300 years, cobbling together its long streets of wooden houses and harvesting Baikal's rich *omul* (a type of fish) stocks. If truth be told, not much changed when the railway arrived, but despite the appearance of now larger Severobaikalsk 30km away, the 5km-long village remains the administrative centre of northern Baikal.

The town's **tourist office** (☐8-924-354 5092, 47 883; www.sbvizit.ru; ul Rabochaya 125, office 10) is housed in the regional administration building.

The recently relocated **Regional Museum** (ul Pobedy 37; admission R100; ☺10am-6pm Mon-Fri) chases the history of the region back to the 17th century and includes several Evenki exhibits.

To the east of the town a long spit of land known as **Yarki Island** caps the most northerly point of Lake Baikal and keeps powerful currents and waves out of the fragile habitat of the Verkhnaya Angara delta. You can walk along its length.

Friendly tour agency **109 Meridian** (⤳8-914-050 5909; sb109m@yandex.ru) runs reasonably priced summer coach excursions to Evenki villages and Baikalskoe, as well as multiday boat trips on Lake Baikal and up the Verkhnaya Angara River. Staff can arrange permits to land on Baikal's eastern shore and book accommodation in Dzelinda, Goudzhekit and Severobaikalsk. The company also produces a detailed, annually updated Russian-language guidebook to the region *(Poputchik)*.

Few choose to stay over in Nizhneangarsk, but if you do, the timber **Severny Baikal** (⤳47 280; ul Rabochaya 10; tw R1800) has well-appointed standard rooms with attached bathrooms and views across the mudflats towards Baikal. Basic **Baikalsky Bereg** (ul Pobedy 55a; meals R100; ☺8am-5pm, to 1am summer) has an attractive lakeside location and a hand-written menu of borscht, meatballs and *pelmeni*, while the **airport snack bar** stays open even when there are no flights (which is most of the time).

Scenic low-altitude flights cross Lake Baikal to Ulan-Ude (R5000, four per week) and Irkutsk (R5000, weekly summer only) when weather conditions allow.

Marshrutky (R37, 50 minutes) from Severobaikalsk run every 30 minutes along ul Pobedy then continue along the coast road (ul Rabochaya) to the airport. The last service back to Severobaikalsk is at 6.50pm, and 5.50pm at weekends.

BAIKALSKOE БАЙКАЛЬСКОЕ

This timeless little fishing village of log-built houses 45km south of Severobaikalsk has a jaw-droppingly picturesque lakeside location backed by wooded hills and snow-dusted peaks. Your first stop should be the small, informal **school museum** (admission R100; ☺10am-4pm) where hands-on exhibits tell the story of the village from the Stone Age to the seal hunts of the 20th century. The only other sight is the wooden **Church of St Innocent**, which strikes a scenic lakeside pose.

Most come to Baikalskoe on a day trip from Severobaikalsk, but if you do want to stay the night, arrange a homestay through helpers in Severobaikalsk. There's no cafe, just a couple of shops selling basic foodstuffs.

Marshrutky (R60, 45 minutes) leave from outside Severobaikalsk train station every day at 8am and 5pm, returning an hour or so later.

A section of the Great Baikal Trail heads north from the fishing port 20 minutes up a cliff-side path towards the radio mast, from which there are particularly superb views looking back towards the village. Beyond that, Baikalskoe's shamanic **petroglyphs** hide in awkward-to-reach cliff-side locations and can only be found with the help of a knowledgeable local. The well-maintained trail continues another 18 scenic kilometres through beautiful cedar and spruce forests and past photogenic **Boguchan Island** to chilly **Lake Slyudyanskoe**, next to which stands the small Echo *turbaza* (holiday camp) – book through the Maryasov family in Severobaikalsk (p256).

The hike makes for a rewarding day trip and, with the path hugging the lake most of the way, there's little chance of getting lost. From the Echo *turbaza* head along a dirt track through the forest to the Severobaikalsk–Baikalskoe road to hitch a lift, or prearrange transport back to Severobaikalsk. Alternatively some hikers tackle the day the other way round, catching the morning *marshrutka* to Echo *turbaza* then timing the hike to make the 6pm *marshrutka* back to Severobaikalsk.

Tynda Тында

⤳41656 / POP 35,500 / ☺MOSCOW +6HR

The king of the BAM, Tynda is a nondescript BAM HQ flanked by low-lying pine-covered hills. Many stop here, as it's a hub for trains between Severobaikalsk, Komsomolsk-na-Amure and, on the 'Little BAM', Blagoveshchensk to the south, or, on the in-progress AYaM (Amur-Yakutsk Mainline, or Amuro-Yakutskaya Magistral), Neryungri and Tommot to the north.

Don't expect quaint. Tynda's fully Soviet – it was nothing but a few shacks before the BAM centralised its efforts here in 1974. Liven up your visit by arriving during a festival. The **Bakaldin Festival** rotates between several nearby Evenki villages in late May or early June, with traditional song, dance, reindeer rides and plenty of reindeer shashlyk and other native delicacies. March sees the **Reindeer Hunter and Herder Festival**.

NORTHERN BAIKAL'S MINI-SPAS

Seismic activity in the northern Baikal area shakes free lots of thermal springs around which tiny spas have sprouted. These are great places to soothe aching muscles after days of contortion in your BAM carriage bunk, though facilities are pretty basic.

Goudzhekit Гоуджекит

Goudzhekit's lonely BAM station is beautifully situated between bald, high peaks that stay dusted with snow until early June. Five minutes' walk to the right, the tiny timber **spa** (☉7am-3am) has two pools fed by thermal springs whose waters gurgle a soothing 40°C.

There are two basic hotels at the spa, but most just come for the day. Take the *marshrutka* which leaves from in front of Severobaikalsk train station at 9am, noon and 3pm, returning around an hour later.

Dzelinda Дзелинда

Tiny timber Dzelinda is another hot-springs spa on the BAM railway but with a much more appealing forest location than Goudzhekit. Thermal springs keep the outdoor pools at a toasty 44°C even in winter, and when the surrounding hills are thick with snow and the temperature plunges to -35°C, a warm swim can be exhilarating. Guests stay in timber houses, one of which has an intricately carved gable. All meals are provided. Book through Severobaikalsk helpers and tour companies.

Elektrichka 5608 leaves Severobaikalsk at 6.10am, arriving at the Dzelinda halt 92km later at 8.10am. The return service leaves at 7pm. The spa is a short walk from the halt along a newly paved road through the forest.

Khakusy Хакусы

To land at this idyllically isolated hot-spring **turbaza** (holiday camp; www.sbkhakusy.ru) requires permits in summer but these are waived in February and March, when it takes about an hour to drive across the ice from Severobaikalsk. Bathing is fun in the snow and frozen steam creates curious ice patterns on the wooden spa buildings. Make sure you book the ferry well in advance as it's a popular trip among Russian holidaymakers in summer. An alternative way to reach Khakusy is along the 100km Frolikha Adventure Coastline Trail (see p258).

◉ Sights & Activities

BAM Museum   MUSEUM
(Музей БАМа; ul Sportivnaya 22; admission R100; ☉10am-2pm & 3-6pm, to 7pm Sat, closed Sun, Mon & last Thu of month) Tynda's pride and joy has four rooms of BAM relics and photos (no English), but also covers native Evenki culture, WWII, local art, regional wildlife, and medicine (including jarred human organs and foetuses). One section covers the Little BAM and the Gulag camp prisoners who built it in the 1930s. They lived (and died) in 24 BAM *lagery* ('*bamlag*', or labour camps) between Tynda and Bamovskaya. Photos chronicle the extreme hardships these prisoners endured. Two rooms are dedicated to the big BAM, sections of which were built in the 1930s, 1940s and 1950s before Stalin died and the project was mothballed. Displays cover the period between its relaunch in 1974 and completion in 1984 (although it wasn't made fully operational until 1991). The museum is hard to find: From the Orthodox cathedral walk 400m west, turn left just before the blue building at ul Krasnaya Presnaya 6, and proceed 200m or so.

About the only other thing worth checking out in Tynda is the dramatic sledgehammer-wielding **BAM worker statue** at the far eastern end of central ul Krasnaya Presnaya. **Zarya** is a native Evenki village nearby. Bus 105 from the train station goes eight times daily (30 minutes).

Contact feisty adventurer **Alexey Podprugin** (☎8-914-552 1455; bamland@mail.ru) for kayaking, hiking and cross-country skiing trips.

⊨ Sleeping

Resting rooms   HOSTEL €
(комнаты отдыха, komnaty otdykha; ☎73 297; bed per 6/12/24hr from R350/600/1100) Comfy and clean dorm rooms in the train station.

Shower available (R100 for guests and non-guests alike).

Hotel Yunost HOTEL €
(Гостиница Юность; ☑43 534; ul Krasnaya Presnaya 49; 4-bed dm R700, s/d from R820/2400) Faded but fine option in centre; Dervla Murphy recuperated here as related in her book *Through Siberia by Accident*.

ℹ Information

Internet access is at **Disly Club** (ul Krasnaya Presnaya 55; per hr R50; ⊘9am-6pm Mon-Sat), in the Rostelekom office between Hotel Yunost and the post office. The train station has an ATM.

ℹ Getting There & Away

The train station – the city's most striking landmark – is across the Tynda River. A pedestrian bridge leads 1km north to ul Krasnaya Presnaya.

Train 75 heads via BAM to Moscow (*platskart/kupe* R4250/11,000, five days) on even-numbered days, stopping in Severobaikalsk (R1400/3100, 26 hours), while train 77 to Novosibirsk (R2900/7450, 67 hours) takes the Little BAM south on odd-numbered days to connect with the Trans-Siberian line at Skovorodino.

For Neryungri (from R520, 5½ hours) take the nightly 326 at 11.52pm, or the 658 at 6.13pm. Train 364 trundles to Komsomolsk daily at 11.26am (*platskart/kupe* R1400/3110, 37 hours), and 325 heads daily to Khabarovsk at 8.13pm via Skovorodino (R1450/3140, 28½ hours, daily).

An adventurous alternative route to Khabarovsk is to take the BAM east to Novy Urgal (arrival at 5.13pm) and take the 663 south through Tyrma and Izvestkovaya (departure from Novy Urgal daily at 7.16pm, 23 hours to Khabarovsk).

Komsomolsk-na-Amure
Комсомольск-на-Амуре
☑4217 / POP 280,000 / ⊘MOSCOW +7HR

After days of taiga and grey Soviet towns, Komsomolsk-na-Amure hits the BAM adventurer like a mini St Petersburg. Komsomolsk was built virtually from scratch by Stalin in the 1930s as a vital cog in the Soviet Union's military industrial complex.

The location was no accident: the city was far removed from potential prying eyes along the Pacific Coast and Chinese border, yet its position along the Amur allowed for relatively easy transport of goods. Imitating the tsars, Stalin erected elaborate neo-Renaissance and neoclassical buildings in the city centre, only festooned with stars, crescents and statues of model Soviet citizens instead of the usual angels and goblins. To build the city he enlisted volunteers from the Communist Youth League (Komsomol – hence the city's name) as well as Gulag camp labourers. Around town, factories sprouted up to produce ships, weapons, electricity and, most famously, Sukhoi (Su) fighter jets in a factory that still works today.

Set along a few grand boulevards, the city is worth a night or more if you are getting on or off the BAM. Nearby attractions include ski slopes, Nanai villages and rafting. Just east of the river terminal is a beach, which is well attended on nice days.

⊙ Sights

Soviet Mosaics STREET ART
Komsomolsk has a wealth of wonderful murals adorning the sides of apartment blocks and factories. Most were the creation of

THE BAIKAL-AMUR MAINLINE (BAM) KOMSOMOLSK-NA-AMURE

WHAM BAM, IT'S THE RED ELVIS! *ROBERT REID*

One of the more bizarre tours of all time rolled through Tynda in August 1979 when the 'Red Elvis' – Dean Reed, an American singer turned Marxist – did a 19-day tour on BAM, immortalised in his song 'BAM' ('Everybody sing along… the towns are here to stay, it's the future of our day!').

His show at Tynda's Festivalnaya Hill drew 25,000 spectators, but didn't kick off the way he wanted: according to one story, told on the priceless website www.deanreed.de, a local refused to let the American use his horse for a dramatic cowboy entrance.

Reed remains virtually unknown in the West – not surprising with songs like 'Wake Up America' and photos of him chumming around with Central American revolutionaries. He died under mysterious circumstances in East Germany in 1986.

Tip: Hours – and hours – of enjoyment can be had YouTubing Dean's videos. You can read more about him in *Comrade Rockstar* by Reggie Nadelson.

Komsomolsk-na-Amure

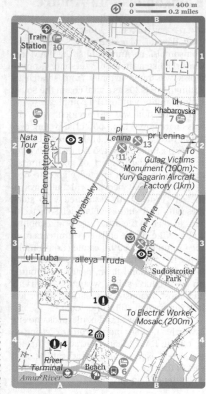

Komsomolsk-na-Amure

Khabarovsk-based artist Nikolai Dolbilkin, who lived here in the '50s and '60s. Among the best are the double triptych **WWII mosaic** (2nd fl, pr Mira & ul Truba) in the central grey *dom kultura* building at Sudostroitel Park, the **nauka (science) mosaic** (pr Lenina) at the Polytechnic Institute, a block east of Hotel Voskhod; and the stunning **electric worker mosaic** (alleya Truda) on the side of the TETs electric station.

Municipal Museum of
Regional Studies   MUSEUM
(pr Mira 8; admission R100; ⊙9.30am-5pm Tue-Fri, 10am-5pm Sat & Sun) The several rooms of old photos and knick-knacks show how Komsomolsk rose from the tent camps of original pioneers in 1932 to an industrial Soviet city. It also contains some stylish old fish-skin jackets and other Nanai artefacts.

Memorials   MONUMENT
Just northwest of the river terminal is the impressive **WWII memorial**, which features stoic faces chipped from stone, with nearby pillars marking the years of WWII. Other memorials include a tiny **Gulag victims monument** – an unremarkable jagged piece of rock – in a tiny park next to the city court building on pr Lenina and a simple **Japanese POW memorial** off pr Mira.

👉 Tours

Nata Tour   TOUR COMPANY
(Hara Typ; ☏201 067, 8-914-189 1784; www.komsomolsknata.ru; office 110, ul Vasyanina 12; ⊙10am-6pm Mon-Fri) Located in the big grey building in back, this experienced travel service arranges three- to five-hour 'Stalin tours' of city communist sites (including a Gulag camp; R800 to R1500 per person); adventure tours involving fishing, rafting or skiing; and day trips and/or homestays at Verkhnyaya Ekon. White-water rafting trips involve a train ride to Novy Urgal on the BAM. Slower one- to several-day floats can be done closer to KNA. Tours of the **Yury Gagarin Aircraft Factory**, where the Su jets are built, can also be arranged.

🛏 Sleeping

Nata Tour can arrange homestays (R1000 per person including breakfast). Wi-fi requires bling and a booking charge applies unless otherwise stated.

TOP CHOICE **Biznestsentr** HOTEL €€

(Бизнесцентр; ☎521 522; bc@etc.kna.ru; ul Dzerzhinskogo 3; s/d R2000-4000; ❇@☎) This place is an anomaly in that it's both KNA's most modern, business-oriented hotel and its cheapest. The rooms are plenty spacious, bathrooms are fresh and English rolls off the tongues of the friendly receptionists. The massive suites, with flat-screen TVs, are fit for Count Muravyov-Amursky himself. No booking charge.

Hotel Amur HOTEL €

(Гостиница Амур; ☎590 984; ruma@kmscom.ru; pr Mira 15; s R500-2350, d R860-2600; ❇☎) A rare budget hotel in the Far East, the Amur has 15 old-fashioned rooms (many with shared toilet and shower) in a lovely 1932 building.

Dacha Krushcheva GUESTHOUSE €€

(Дача Хрущёва; ☎540 659; ul Khabarovska 47; r R2360-3400; ❇) Built for Nikita Khrushchev, this back-street dacha is a step back in time. The suites could fit a Young Pioneers troupe and all six rooms have 1970s easy chairs to kick back in. Basically, it's the polar opposite of the renovated but cramped Hotel Voskhod.

Hotel Voskhod HOTEL €€

(Гостиница Восход; ☎535 131; pr Pervostroiteley 31; s/d from R2600/3600; ❂@☎) Eight-storey grey beast with bog standard Soviet rooms.

Resting rooms HOSTEL €

(комнаты отдыха, komnaty otdykha; ☎284 193; train station; s with shared bathroom R1100, dm in d/tr R910/810) Showers cost R75 at these sparkling clean resting rooms.

🍴 Eating

Kofeynya CAFE €€

(Кофейня; ul Oktyabrsky 48; snacks R60-130; ⏱24hr; ❂☎) Salads and light snacks are on the menu here, along with a diverse coffee selection. There's a built-in internet cafe (per hr R30).

SSSR RUSSIAN €€

(СССР; alleya Truda 22; mains R150-200; ⏱10am-1am) It's only appropriate that there's an honest-to-Lenin retro-Soviet cafe in a place like Komsomolsk, innit? All the Russian staples are on the menu, some with names like 'partizan chicken', and the walls are festooned with every type of Soviet kitsch imaginable.

OVERLAND FROM TYNDA TO YAKUTSK

Travellers in Tynda often have their sights on the vast Sakha Republic, where you can track down reindeer herders, search for abandoned Gulag camps and experience some of the coldest temperatures on Earth. Yakutsk, the capital, is the world's coldest city of any decent size, while in Oymyakon, a remote village 650km north of Yakutsk, temperatures have dropped as low as -71°C.

To get to Yakutsk you must first take a train to Neryungri, 5½ hours north. From there you embark on one of the Far East's classic overland journeys: 15 to 20 bumpy hours in a Russian UAZ jeep or van to cover 810km on the AYaM (Amur-Yakutsk Mainline or Amuro-Yakutskaya Magistral) highway.

Daily departures from the Neryungri train station are timed for the 6.22am arrival of train 658 from Khabarovsk. Trips are in 11-passenger vans or four-passenger jeeps. The price varies with the season; it cost us R3500 in early June. It's a pretty trip that cuts over a mountain pass and through tracts of virgin taiga before traversing the Lena River by *parom* (car ferry) an hour south of Yakutsk.

Passenger services on the AYaM train line run further north to Aldan (six hours) and Tommot (eight hours), but you'll keep well ahead of the train (and avoid a possible overnight in either Aldan or Tommot) if you get a head start from Neryungri. There is a notoriously rickety bus from Aldan to Yakutsk that departs at 8am on Wednesday (R2200, at least 16 hours), but this requires a night in Aldan.

The AYaM train line is being extended north to Nizhny Bestyakh (opposite Yakutsk on the Lena River), and plans are to open the entire route to passenger services. This may happen within the lifetime of this book, but we're not taking bets.

Purchase the Russian Far East chapter of Lonely Planet's *Russia* guidebook through www.lonelyplanet.com for more detail on this region.

BAM ENDS, SAKHALIN BECKONS

For an adventurous route to Sakhalin Island, take the BAM to nearly the end of the line in Vanino, where in theory a daily (in reality leave-when-full-and-when-weather-allows) boat leaves at 4pm to Kholmsk (tickets R1710 to R2850, 18 hours). The information numbers are 8233-66 098 or 8233-66 516 (in Russian). Call the day before to reserve a seat – they should have a reasonable idea of whether the next day's ship will sail. But no guarantees. Or just go and take your chances. From June to September, determined mariners can then make their way by ferry to Wakkanai, Japan, from the Sakhalin port of Korsakov (from R8700, five hours).

Purchase the Russian Far East chapter of Lonely Planet's *Russia* guidebook, or the Sapporo & Hokkaido chapter of Lonely Planet's *Japan* guidebook through www.lonelyplanet.com for more detail on this region.

U City Pizza   FAST FOOD €
(pr Lenina 19; meals from R150; ☺10am-11pm)
Load up for your BAM ride with pizza by the slice (R70 to R90), bliny, burgers, burritos, salads and other quick eats. It's attached to a one-screen cinema (hence the popcorn smell).

ℹ Information

The best internet point is Kofeynya (p263).
Dalsvyaz (Дальсвязь; pr Mira 27; per hr R45; ☺8am-8.30pm) Internet access in the post office building.

Post office (Почта; pr Mira 27; ☺8am-10pm Mon-Fri, to 6pm Sat & Sun)

ℹ Getting There & Around

From Komsomolsk's pink **train station** (pr Pervostroiteley) the excruciatingly slow train 352 leaves daily for Vladivostok (*platskart/kupe* R1240/2720, 24½ hours); see p237 for connections to Khabarovsk.

On the BAM, train 363 heads west to Tynda (*platskart/kupe* R1400/3110, 37 hours, daily); to reach Severobaikalsk, change in Tynda. The daily train 351 heads east to Vanino (*platskart/kupe* R700/1435, 11 hours). For information on boats from Vanino to Sakhalin, see p264.

A hydrofoil to Khabarovsk leaves five days a week from the river terminal (from R800, six hours), and there are regular buses to Khabarovsk as well (R600, six hours) from the **bus station** (☺6am-10.30pm) near the river.

Within the city, handy tram 2 runs from the train station along ul Lenina and pr Mira to the river terminal (R13).

Around Komsomolsk-na-Amure

VERKHNYAYA EKON ВЕРХНЯЯ ЭКОНЬ
Tucked between the Amur River and bear-inhabited hills, this village of 500 (of which half are Nanai) makes a fun day trip from Komsomolsk across the river. Its school has a small **Nanai Museum** (Музей Нанай), with old shaman costumes and plenty of Nanai traditional pieces. It's possible to hike up the mountain.

Three daily buses come from Komsomolsk (R30, 30 minutes), but if you arrange for a taxi you can visit an eerie, unfinished 800m-long BAM tunnel at nearby **Pivan** village (north of the Amur Bridge), with rusted pieces left from the project that was abandoned after WWII broke out.

The Trans-Mongolian Route

Includes »

Route Info

» Distance: 2217km

» Duration: Two days six hours

» Time zones: Ulan-Ude: Moscow +5; Ulaanbaatar and Dàtóng: Moscow +4

Best Places to Stay & Eat

» Lotus Guesthouse (p277)

» Zaya Backpacker Hostel (p277)

» Ulaanbaatar Hotel (p277)

» Tóngtiě Bīnguǎn hotel (p289)

» Millie's Espresso cafe (p278)

» Mongolians restaurant (p278)

Why Go?

The Trans-Mongolian route is the most diverse leg of the cross-continental journey, cutting across three distinct cultures, landscapes and languages. It includes some of the most awe-inspiring sights of the long journey, not the least of which is the Great Wall of China, but also the Gobi Desert and the vast Mongolian steppes, still the domain of horsebound nomads. The major jumping-off point is Ulaanbaatar. Many travellers plan their visit around the colourful Naadam Festival, but a visit any time of year reveals a surprisingly fast-paced city with great cultural attractions and heady nightlife. Before heading for Mongolia from Russia, pause to explore Ulan-Ude, where you could leave the train briefly for a minibus ride to the border, taking in the historic towns of Novoseleginsk and Kyakhta. The China leg is a relatively short hop but has its own unique character, highlighted by the beguiling Yungang Caves near Dàtóng.

When to Go
Ulaanbaatar

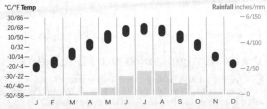

mid-Jul Naadam grinds Ulaanbaatar to a halt to make way for wrestling, archery and horse racing.

Aug Prime time for lounging in Ulaanbaatar's open-air cafes, swapping travel stories.

Sep Autumn brings changing colours in forested areas and smaller tourist crowds.

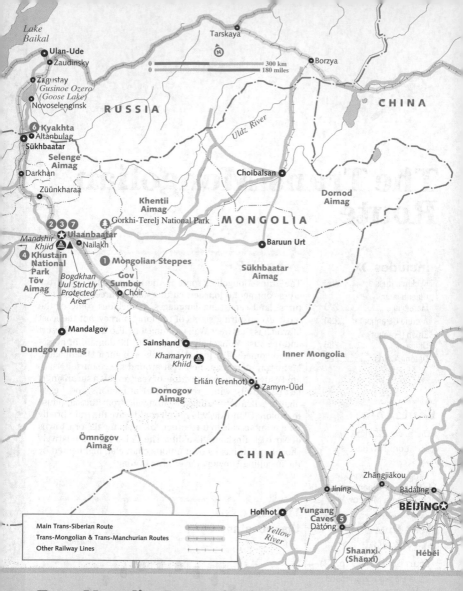

Trans-Mongolian Route Highlights

❶ Enjoying a meal of boiled mutton and fermented mare's milk in a ger (yurt) on the vast **Mongolian steppes** (p285)

❷ Attending a mystical ceremony at the country's largest monastery, Ulaan-baatar's **Gandan Khiid** (p272)

❸ Browsing through the collection of stuffed animals,

curios and artefacts at Ulaanbaatar's **Winter Palace of the Bogd Khan** (p272)

❹ Spotting rare wild horses at **Khustain National Park** (p285)

❺ Staring in wonder at the 51,000 Buddhist statues inside the **Yungang Caves** (p288) near Dàtóng

❻ Exploring the antiquated town of **Kyakhta** (p269) on the Mongolian–Russian border, once home to a thriving trading post on the ancient tea route

❼ Celebrating **Naadam** (p280), Mongolia's mid-summer festival that features the country's best wrestlers, archers and race horses

The Route

The Trans-Mongolian line branches off from the main Trans-Siberian route at Zaudinsky, about 13km east of Ulan-Ude. Mongolia and China each have their own kilometre markers. In Mongolia, the markers measure the distance to the Russian–Mongolian border, so 0km is the border town of Naushki. Once in China, the markers measure the distance to Běijīng.

Zaudinsky to Naushki

5655KM FROM MOSCOW At **Zaudinsky** the branch line turns south and continues to follow the Selenga River, crossing at around 5701km. Here you'll see herds of cattle grazing across low green hills beside a wide, lazy river, and villages of wooden houses with brightly painted window shutters and flourishing gardens that explode with fruits and flowers in summer.

5769KM After you pass the town of **Zagustay** the train follows the shoreline of Gusinoe Ozero (Goose Lake), surrounded by thick woods of pine and birch that are usually prevalent further north.

5885KM Another crossing over the Selenga River.

5902KM The train arrives at **Naushki** (5902km in Russia but 0km for Mongolia), a small, uneventful town that serves as the Russian border post. If you haven't gotten to the end of War and Peace by now you'll certainly have the chance here as the train hangs around the border for several hours for customs and passport checks.

Sükhbaatar to Ulaanbaatar

21KM FROM NAUSHKI Mongolia's chief border town, **Sükhbaatar** (population 19,700), is set at the junction of the Selenga and Orkhon Rivers. Founded in the 1940s, it's named after the revolutionary hero Damdin Sükhbaatar, who in 1921 famously rode his horse to Russia to enlist the aid of the Bolsheviks after Mongolia was invaded by White Russian troops. The train stops for an hour or two (depending on which train you're on), giving you time to stretch your legs and perhaps head across the street to grab a meal in one of the small Mongolian restaurants.

63KM When you cross the **Eröö River** look out for cranes, herons and other waterfowl in the marshy areas on the west side of the train. Having entered Mongolia you'll also sense a change of scenery: the forests thin out into the lush green pastures of the fertile Selenga River basin. You may also notice new scents (in the form of mutton) as the Mongolian dining car is attached after the train crosses the border.

123KM The rolling green hills of northern Mongolia break momentarily as the train pulls into **Darkhan** (population 73,500), Mongolia's third-largest city. Darkhan, which means 'blacksmith', was built from scratch in 1961 as a model

socialist city, complete with wide boulevards, factories and uniform housing blocks. Of cultural interest is Kharaagiin Khiid, an active monastery housed in a pretty log cabin. The train stops for about 20 minutes. You can buy some *buuz* (mutton-filled dumplings) from the ladies who sell them out of plastic containers.

Should you venture off the rails, the most interesting sight in the area is **Amarbayasgalant Khiid**, the best-preserved Buddhist monastery in Mongolia. The three- to four-hour drive from Darkhan can be made in a taxi for around T100,000 return.

274-290KM This is the most scenic stretch of the Trans-Mongolian route, a 15km ride through a pretty valley and alongside the Kharaa River.

355-365KM The train passes the area of **Hui Doloon Khutag**, where the Naadam horse races are held from 10 to 12 July. In the days before Naadam locals move out here en masse, creating a city of scattered gers. After another 20km the train curves around a valley towards **Ulaanbaatar** (p270), where you'll get your first glimpse of the smokestacks and urban sprawl of the Mongolian capital.

404KM After a long march through the industrial outskirts the train pulls into Ulaanbaatar for 30 minutes. If stopping off here, expect throngs of people on the platform offering tours, taxi rides or a bunk in a local guesthouse.

Ulaanbaatar to Zamyn-Üüd

415-440KM South of Ulaanbaatar, the line winds through the gently swelling hills of the **Bogdkhan Uul** mountain range. Trees eventually disappear and the landscape becomes a 180-degree panorama of steppe, the only interruptions being grazing horses and the occasional ger.

649KM There's a 15-minute stop at **Choir**, where a statue of the first Mongolian cosmonaut stands in front of the station. During the Soviet era this grim town of 13,000 people was home to Mongolia's biggest Soviet air base. After the Russians left, many of the buildings sat empty and were vandalised. Despite having declared itself a free trade zone, Choir continues to languish.

South of Choir, the train enters the flat, arid and sparsely populated **Gobi Desert**. In a good year, the desert sprouts short grass, which sustains a limited number of sheep, goats and camels for their ethnic Khalkh owners. In a bad year, the wells go dry, the grass turns brown and the animals die. From the train, the view of this desolate landscape is impressive. Any small bodies of water attract livestock, and you'll probably spot horses, camels, sheep and goats (sorry, no yaks in this part of the country).

876KM The train stops for around 20 minutes at **Sainshand** (Good Pond). The *buuz* vendors on the platform sell out of their product quickly, so

Ulan-Ude to Běijīng

West to Moscow ↑

5640km ● Ulan-Ude

5655km ● Zaudinsky

4hr, 45min

5902km ● Naushki

RUSSIA

MONGOLIA

21km ● Sükhbaatar

1hr, 50min

123km ● Darkhan

2hr

235km ● Züünkharaa

3hr

404km ● Ulaanbaatar

4hr, 15min

649km ● Choir

3hr, 45min

876km ● Sainshand

3hr, 20min

1113km ● Zamyn-Üüd

MONGOLIA

CHINA

842km to Běijīng ● Èrlián (Erenhot)

4hr, 15min

498km ● Jíníng

1hr, 50min

371km ● Dàtóng

3hr, 10min

193km ● Zhāngjiākou

2hr, 30min

73km ● Bādálíng

1hr, 30min

0km ● BĚIJĪNG

To Vladivostok (Trans-Siberian) & Běijīng (Trans-Manchurian)

THE TRANS-MONGOLIAN ROUTE

you'll need to act fast. As the capital of the Dornogov province, Sainshand sports a couple of museums, a modern monastery and several hotels and ger camps, should you feel the urge to jump the train and get closer to the Gobi. About one hour drive south of Sainshand is **Khamaryn Khiid**, one of the most important Buddhist monasteries in the Gobi and former home of the poet-monk Danzan Ravjaa (1803–56), a mystic whose writings about nature, ethics and Buddhism are still beloved by the locals.

1113KM The bleak, dusty landscape continues to the border town of **Zamyn-Üüd**. Travel writer Paul Theroux visited the town in the mid-1980s and commented that Zamyn-Üüd was 'a wreck of a town set on glaring sands and so lacking in events that when a camel went by everyone watched it'. Sadly, not much has changed since then. From here you can cross by road or rail over the border to China. If you're coming from China you'll have to wait around for the next local train heading north. While there isn't much happening in town you can kill some time at the internet cafe, located in the Telecom office.

Zamyn-Üüd to Běijīng

842KM (FROM BĚIJĪNG) Compared to Zamyn-Üüd, the Chinese side of the border, **Èrlián** (p286), is a veritable megalopolis. From here it takes about 13 hours to get to Běijīng by direct train.

For the first several hours the train continues through the Gobi, now in the ostensibly autonomous region of **Inner Mongolia**. Mongolians make up only about 15% of the population here, and since 1949 China has done its best to assimilate their nomadic lifestyle, even though they have been permitted to keep their written and spoken language. Further south, the desert slowly gives way to grasslands and you'll spot Mongol shepherds tending their flocks.

It's a long journey between Ulaanbaatar and Běijīng, so if you're getting a little antsy go to the dining car, where most of the train's socialising takes place. The Chinese dining car is arguably the best on the entire Trans-Siberian route – but we'll let you be the judge of that.

498KM There is a stop at the main rail junction of **Jíníng**, where vendors sell drinks, snacks and colourful balloons on the platform. This is where the Ulaanbaatar–Hohhot train breaks off the main line and heads west.

371KM The train creaks into **Dàtóng** (p286), where it halts for 25 minutes. Dàtóng is a Chinese version of England's Newcastle – the region is hugely dependent on coal mining and everybody seems to have a little coal dust behind the ears. For the locals, coal has been both a burden and curse. While the mines provide work opportunities, they also have damaged the local environment, created enormous traffic jams on the highways (some of them 100km long) and contributed to the already high levels of air pollution. Despite its current challenges, the region remains an important centre of Chinese history and was the powerbase for the Tang dynasty (618–907).

300KM From Dàtóng the line turns east, entering Héběi province. Héběi is characterised by its mountainous tableland where the Great Wall runs. There are good views of the Wall on the northern side of the tracks between 295km and 275km. In addition, keep your eyes peeled for the occasional walled villages, typically composed of thick rammed-earth walls with traditional homes stuffed into their small interior. One example can be seen between the 264km and 263km markers on the south side of the tracks.

193KM The train stops for 10 minutes in the industrial city of **Zhāngjiākou**. Formerly known as Khaalga, which means 'door' or 'gate' in Mongolian, this town was where the ancient tea caravans crossed the Great Wall. From here the terrain becomes increasingly hilly and the scenery is quite dramatic as the train travels across a plateau punctuated by cropland and tree-filled gullies.

85KM From here the train begins its final approach to Běijīng, swiftly entering a mountainous zone that separates the Chinese capital from the northern plains. There are some 60 tunnels to pass through and while it can be difficult to spot the kilometre markers you can easily count down (or count up if you're heading north) the tunnel numbers, painted at the entrance of the tunnels (on the right side). The first number is the tunnel number, the second is the kilometre marker and the third is the length of the tunnel. Each time the train emerges from a tunnel there are stunning scenes of canyons, rivers and soaring rock towers.

0KM Make a toast with any leftover Russian vodka; you've reached **Běijīng**, the end of the line. If you're starting your journey in Běijīng, take a moment to wipe down the windows with a dust cloth; the photo opportunities are excellent outside Běijīng and you'll want a clear shot (heading north the best views are out the left side of the train).

Kyakhta, Russia   Кяхта

📱30142 / POP 18,400 / ⊙MOSCOW +5HR

Tight against the Mongolian border, the intriguing, if somewhat sad, town of Kyakhta was formerly called Troitskosavsk. Kyakhta's fortunes boomed with the Chinese tea trade and by the mid-19th century up to 5000 cases of tea were arriving daily on a stream of horse or camel caravans. The caravans

TRANS-MONGOLIAN ROUTE PLANNER

The following is a suggested itinerary for covering the main sites along the Trans-Mongolian route:

Day 1: Leave Ulan-Ude and take a six-hour train trip to Naushki, cross border, overnight on train

Day 2: Arrive in, and tour, Ulaanbaatar

Day 3: Tour Ulaanbaatar and around

Day 4: Half-day in Ulaanbaatar, overnight train to the Chinese–Mongolian border (15 hours)

Day 5: Travel to and overnight in Dàtóng

Day 6: Tour Dàtóng

Day 7: Train to Běijīng (seven hours)

returned loaded with furs. This all came to an abrupt end with the completion of the Trans-Mongolian Railway, after which Kyakhta withered into a remote border garrison town.

The town's centre is around ul Lenina, where you'll find the bus terminus next to the 1853 trading arches (Ryady Gostinye) and the central park. The border post is in Kyakhta's smaller Sloboda district, 4km south of the commercial centre.

The impressive shell of the 1817 Troitsky Cathedral lies at the heart of the overgrown central park. Northeast is the delightfully eccentric **museum** (ul Lenina 49; admission R200; ⊙10am-6pm Tue-Sun), with its imaginative displays of treasures salvaged from Soviet-plundered churches and *datsani* (Buddhist temples). It houses a great collection of photographs and memorabilia from Kyakhta's heyday, including a rich collection of Chinese furniture and art. Running parallel to ul Lenina is ul Krupskaya, along which you'll find several attractive wooden buildings, including No 37, where the first meeting of the Mongolian People's Revolutionary Party was held in 1921.

In Sloboda a dwarfish Lenin glares condescendingly at the extraordinarily grand **Resurrection Church** (1838), with its splendid Italianate cupola. The church was undergoing extensive renovation in 2011. Behind Lenin is the big but rather mutilated 1842 Zdaniye Gostinogo Dvora (Historic Customs Warehouse), with an appended

THE TRANS-MONGOLIAN ROUTE KYAKHTA, RUSSIA

RUSSIA–MONGOLIA BORDER CROSSINGS

Naushki–Sükhbaatar

Russia and Mongolia use the same rail gauge, so no bogie-changing is required. However, the time saved is eaten up in customs procedures and general hanging around – it can last six to 11 hours!

Southbound travellers fill out customs forms in duplicate, then Russian border guards collect their passports. When you get your passport back, you can get off the train. There usually are no moneychangers here, but you can change roubles to tögrög when you arrive in Sükhbaatar (or Ulaanbaatar).

Train 4 from Moscow arrives at night, so most travellers stay on or near the train. Train 362 from Irkutsk arrives in daytime and hangs around the station for five hours, so there's plenty of time to get off and wander around Naushki. The station also has a shower block where you can get a hot shower for R100. There's a farmers market just outside the station (walk to the southern end of the platform and cross the street). There's also a small park and a little hill to climb for the view. Just make sure to ask the *provodnitsa* (carriage attendant) about departure times so you know when to return.

The customs and immigration process is repeated by Mongolian officials in Sükhbaatar where, if you need it, there should be no problem buying a ticket for the 9pm train to Ulaanbaatar. The trip takes nine hours and costs T6300 *obshchiy* (hard seat), T11,800 *platskart* (hard sleeper) or T18,900 *kupe* (soft sleeper). *Marshrutky* (fixed-route minibuses; T12,000, six hours) to Ulaanbaatar depart when full from a lot outside the station; these are a good bet in daylight hours.

There are some cafes near Sükhbaatar station, plus some ATMs and moneychangers at the station itself.

Northbound travellers can expect to spend a few hours at Sükhbaatar station. Train 3 from Běijīng arrives at 8.50pm, but train 361 (Ulaanbaatar–Irkutsk) goes through during the day. The daily Sükhbaatar–Ulan-Ude train leaves at 10.45am and, if you can score a ticket, costs T31,700.

At Naushki station a couple of ATMs dispense roubles. The local Naushki–Ulan-Ude train ride, for R320 *platskart* (3rd class, open carriage), is an attractive but excruciat-

communist-era spire. Directly behind is the frontier post for crossing into Mongolia.

Beside the Assumption Church, **Hotel Druzhba** (📞91 321; ul Krupskaya 8; dm from R280, ste R560), about 10 minutes' walk south of Kyakhta's main centre, has good-value suites with hot water, sitting room and king-sized bed.

There are hourly *marshrutky* connections between and Ulan-Ude and Kyakhta (R250, 3½ hours). For details of crossing to/from Mongolia, see p270.

Ulaanbaatar, Mongolia
Улаанбаатар

📞011 / POP 1,112,300 / ⊘MOSCOW + 4HR

After several days of travelling across the Eurasian landmass, approaching Ulaanbaatar by train can feel otherworldly. Rolling green hills covered in pine trees harbour the occasional ger, and horsemen can be seen galloping alongside the train tracks. But any romantic expectations of a frontier outpost are rapidly quashed as the train bends into the Tuul River valley and the breadth of the Mongolian capital unfolds before your eyes.

Ulaanbaatar is a bizarre cocktail of crumbling Soviet-built apartment blocks, satanic smokestacks, the odd glass tower and derelict suburbs of gers that sprawl for 25km across an otherwise lovely valley. But don't allow the city's harsh appearance to put you off. The chaotic capital bursts with activity and will delight you with its friendly locals, quirky sights and live-for-the-moment buzz.

UB, as it's known among expats, has several excellent museums and a lively Buddhist monastery in Gandan Khiid. International cuisine is surprisingly varied and brew pubs overflow onto bright patios. If the city gets too hot you can go for a hike up Bogdkhan Uul, the forested holy peak to the south of the city. Beautiful countryside, ingly slow ride (six hours). The more frequent *marshrutky* from Kyakhta are faster (three hours, R250).

Kyakhta–Altanbulag

You can avoid the extreme tedium of the direct train crossing by taking this alternative road route into or out of Mongolia. There's a daily bus (R1100, 12 hours) to Ulaanbaatar departing at 7.30am from a stop near the Opera House roundabout in Ulan-Ude. Contact Baikal Naran Tour in Ulan-Ude (see p209) for tickets. In Ulaanbaatar, contact **Vostok Trans** (☎7011 0696), which has a ticket office inside the Discovery Mongolia Centre, near Peace Bridge. Buses leave from outside the Discovery Mongolia Centre, also known as Avto Teveriin Gazar, the vehicle registration office. Tickets cost T45,600.

More interesting, though, is to take a minibus to the Mongolian border at Kyakhta. Going the other way, shared taxis for Sükhbaatar leave from a parking lot next to the Ulaanbaatar train station. In Sükhbaatar there are shared taxis to the border.

The **Russia–Mongolia border** (☉9am-8pm Russian side, 8am-7pm Mongolian side) is open to bicycles and vehicles, and some officials speak English. You can't walk across, so pedestrians need to negotiate passage with private drivers. Start as close as possible to the front of the chaotic queue: processing takes about two hours, with only a handful of vehicles allowed through at any one time. The going rate is R150 (or T5000) per passenger across no-man's-land. The Mongolian side has a small bank where you can change money and there are also private moneychangers in Altanbulag (they hang out near the border). There are no moneychangers on the Russian side, so if you're coming from Mongolia it's a good idea to have a few roubles on hand to get you into Kyakhta, where you can change more.

The Mongolian border town Altanbulag has been decimated by vandals who have carted away bricks from its old Soviet buildings. From here it's another 26km to Sükhbaatar train station. Rides here in a shared vehicle should cost R50 or T2500.

Going from Mongolia to Russia, your driver will probably drop you in Kyakhta's Sloboda district, near the Voskresenskaya Church. From here you can take a *marshrutka* (R10) into the town centre and the bus stand.

national parks and nomadic culture can be found a short drive in any direction.

Most of the city spreads east–west along the main road, Enkh Taivny Örgön Chölöö (Peace Ave). At the centre is Sükhbaatar Sq.

History

Ulaanbaatar traces its roots back to the old capital, Örgöö, which was established in 1639 at the Da Khuree Khiid, about 420km from Ulaanbaatar. The monastery was the residence of the five-year-old Zanabazar, who had been proclaimed the head of Buddhism in Mongolia. In keeping with the nomadic lifestyle, the capital was moved frequently to various locations along the Orkhon, Selenga and Tuul Rivers (with a name change accompanying each move).

The capital was finally established in its present location in 1778 and grew quickly as a religious, commercial and administrative centre. Its architecture remained predominantly gers. Further name changes accompanied invasions by the Russians and the Chinese. In 1924 the city was renamed Ulaanbaatar (Red Hero) in honour of the communist triumph, and declared the official capital of an 'independent' Mongolia (independent from China, not the USSR).

From the 1930s the Soviets built the city in typical Russian style: lots of uniform apartment blocks, large brightly coloured theatres and cavernous government buildings. Tragically, the Soviets also destroyed almost all of the monasteries and temples.

A large influx of rural migrants has put tremendous strain on the city's basic infrastructure. Housing is inadequate, roads are jammed and the city's power grid is stretched to the limit. But private investment has also poured in, causing a miniboom in glass towers, shopping malls and the like.

Dangers & Annoyances

Pickpockets are a problem in Ulaanbaatar, especially on Peace Ave between Sükhbaatar

Sq and the State Department Store. Leave valuables in your hotel and carry your backpack on your chest. Be careful when walking out of upscale restaurants and nightclubs. Don't become paranoid; but don't let your guard down either. When taking a taxi from the train station into town, don't leave your bags in the trunk of the car as the driver may hold them for ransom. There are also increasing reports of random acts of violence against foreigners in Ulaanbaatar, sometimes in broad daylight. These may be just a few isolated cases but take care in any case.

Maps

The 1:10,000 *Ulaanbaatar City Map* is updated yearly. It's available at hotels, souvenir shops and the Central Post Office (CPO). See also Seven Summits (p281) and the Map Shop (p281).

◉ Sights

Sükhbaatar Square   PUBLIC SQUARE

The heart of Ulaanbaatar is Sükhbaatar Sq, named after the 1921 revolutionary hero who ushered in the era of communism. A **statue of Damdin Sükhbaatar** straddling a horse, hand aloft, stands in the centre of the square. At the northern end of the square is a marble portico housing an enormous bronze **statue of Chinggis Khaan**. His son Ögedei and grandson Kublai flank him on the west and east sides respectively. Behind the portico is Government House (Parliament).

The Palace of Culture and the Opera House flank the east side of the square. The 17-storey silver-coloured modern building next to the Opera House is the Central Tower, which contains offices, luxury shops and restaurants. A short walk west of the Central Tower is the Ulaanbaatar Hotel and a statue of Lenin.

Ulaanbaatar's City Hall, the Mongolian Stock Exchange and the Central Post Office are located on the west side of the square.

Gandan Khiid   MONASTERY

(Gandantegchinlen Khiid; www.gandan.mn; Öndör Geegen Zanabazaryn Gudamj; admission T3500, camera T5000, video T10,000; ☺8.30am-7pm) The largest and most important monastery in Ulaanbaatar, Gandan Khiid is home to the spiritual head of Mongolia, the Khamba Lama. The name translates roughly as 'the great place of complete joy'.

The monastery was built in 1838 by the second Bogd Gegeen and even served as home to the 13th Dalai Lama for a few years after he fled Lhasa in 1904. It survived the communist purges of the 1930s and was reopened in 1944 as a stage monastery to show to foreign dignitaries. Today there are over 600 monks in residence and in its main building, the **Migjid Janraisig Süm**, you can view the 26.5m-tall gilded statue of Buddha, a replacement for one moved to St Petersburg in 1937.

The courtyard on the right of the main entrance contains two temples, the **Ochirdary Süm** and the smaller **Golden Dedenpovaran Süm**. If you come in the morning you can witness the fascinating ceremonies that take place here.

Winter Palace of the Bogd Khaan   MUSEUM

(Chingisiin Örgön Chölöö; admission T2500, camera T10,000, video T15,000; ☺9.30am-5.30pm 15 May-15 Sep, 9am-5.30pm Fri-Tue Oct-Apr) Mongolia's eighth living Buddha and last king, Jebtzun Damba Hutagt VIII, lived for 20 years in this palace. The grounds house six ornate temples; the white building on the right is the palace itself. It contains an eclectic collection of gifts received from foreign dignitaries and an extraordinary array of stuffed animals. Take bus 7 or 19 (from near the Bayangol Hotel).

Choijin Lama Temple Museum   MUSEUM

(admission T2500; ☺9am-5pm Jun-Oct, 10am-5pm Nov-May) This museum is also known as the

---

CHANGING THE BOGIES

As in Russia, Mongolia's trains run on a 5ft (1.5m) gauge, which is slightly wider than the standard gauge used in much of the rest of the world. Before the train can continue its journey, it must make a stop at the bogie-changing shed, where the carriages are raised and the bogies are replaced with the appropriate size. The bogies are changed with the passengers still on board the train and you can see the operations happening around you. To get a better look, get off the train at the platform (after your passport has been checked) and walk back to the shed, where you can watch the operations at ground level. It's a 10-minute walk from the platform to the shed. Bring a flashlight for the walk and follow the leftmost tracks (about halfway along a sidewalk will appear on your left).

ULAANBAATAR IN...

Two Days

Ulaanbaatar's main sights can be seen in a couple of days. On your first morning in town pay a visit to the **National Museum of Mongolia**, then take a turn around **Sükhbaatar Square**. Grab lunch at **Millie's** and then visit the nearby **Choijin Lama Monastery Museum**. Watch a Mongolian cultural show in the evening. The following day get up early for hot apple pastries at **Michele's French Bakery** and then head up to **Gandan Khiid** in time to catch the monks chanting. Next visit the **Museum of Natural History** and later in the day head south to the **Winter Palace of Bogd Khan**. Finally, climb the steps to the **Zaisan Memorial** to watch the sun set over the city.

Four Days

On day three visit the **Zanabazar Museum of Fine Arts** and then head over to **Naran Tuul Market**. In the evening down a pint or two on the deck of the **Grand Khaan Irish Pub** and then hit **Metropolis Nightclub** after midnight. On day four take a day trip out of town, either to **Terelj** or **Mandshir Khiid**. Have dinner at **Mongolians** then listen to live music at **River Sounds**.

Museum of Religion and hasn't operated as a monastery since 1938. There are five temples within the tranquil grounds and a concrete ger with a good selection of souvenirs and books about Buddhism and Mongolia. Sadly, a forest of glass-and-steel office towers are shooting up around the ancient complex, giving the place a less than pleasant backdrop.

Museum of Natural History   MUSEUM
(cnr Sükhbaataryn Gudamj & Sambugiin Örgön Chölöö; adult/student T2500/1000; ⏰10am-4.30pm, closed Mon & Tue mid-Sep–mid-May) The best reason to visit this old and rambling museum is to see the massive dinosaur fossils and skeletons dug up in the Gobi. The museum houses two impressive complete skeletons of a *Tarbosaurus* and a *Saurolophus*, as well as petrified dinosaur eggs and fossils.

Zanabazar Museum of Fine Arts   MUSEUM
(Juulchin Gudamj; adult/student T2500/1000; ⏰10am-6pm May-Sep, to 5pm Oct-Apr) This art museum has an excellent collection of paintings, carvings and sculptures, including many by the revered sculptor and artist Zanabazar. It also contains other rare religious exhibits such as *thangka* (scroll paintings) and Buddhist statues, representing the best display of its kind in Mongolia.

**National Museum of
Mongolian History**   MUSEUM
(www.nationalmuseum.mn; Juulchin Gudamj; adult/student T2500/1200; ⏰9.30am-6pm daily 15 May-31 Aug, 9.30am-5.30pm Tue-Sat 1 Sep-14 May) Mongolia's national museum has been revamped and is not to be missed. The 1st floor has an excellent collection of Stone Age and Bronze Age sites, including a remarkable trove of gold artefacts found in 2001 by archaeologists in central Mongolia. The 2nd floor contains a collection of costumes, hats and jewellery representing most of Mongolia's ethnic groups. The 3rd floor is a must-see for fans of the Mongol horde, with displays of ancient Mongol armour and weapons.

FREE **Zaisan Memorial &
Buddha Park**   MONUMENT
This memorial is the tall, thin landmark on top of Zaisan hill, south of the city. Built by the Russians to commemorate 'unknown soldiers and heroes' from various wars, this masterpiece of socialist realism offers sweeping views of the city and surrounding hills, as well as a workout on the climb up. Next to the hill is a small park containing a 16m-tall standing image of Sakyamuni (historical Buddha). Below the statue is a small room containing *thangkas*, sutras (religious books) and images of the Buddha and his disciples. Bus 7 from Bayangol Hotel will get you here.

National Amusement Park   AMUSEMENT PARK
(Children's Park; admission T1000, rides T2500-4000; ⏰10am-9pm) The only amusement park in Mongolia is a good diversion if you're travelling with small kids.

Central Ulaanbaatar

Enebish Örgön Chölöö

Damdin Gudamj

Gandan Khiid

Freedom Sq

Sambugiin Örgön Chölöö
Самбуугын Өргөн Чөлөө

Zanabazar Museum of Fine Arts

Builder's Sq

Juulchin Gudamj

Urt Tsagaan Mall

Ikh Toiruu Их тойруу

Öndör Gegeen Öндөр Гэгээн

Zanabazaryn Gudamj Занабазарын Гудамж

Tömörchiin Gudamj Төмөрчийн Гудамж

35

24

Choimbolyn Gudamj Чоймболын Гудамж

39

13

Baruun Selbe Gudamj Баруун Сэлбэ Гудамж

6
3
4

20
37

State Department Store

41
16

Khaddorjiin Gudamj

7

8

36

Enkh Taivny Örgön Chölöö 18
Энх Тайвны Өргөн Чөлөө

Enkh Taivny Örgön Chölöö (Peace Ave)

Partizan Gudamj Партизан Гудамж

Namnansurengiin Gudamj Намнансүрэнгийн Гудамж

Tserendorjiin Gudamj Цэрэндоржийн Гудамж

@

15

50

Seoul St Соүл Гудамж

Undsen Khuulin Gudamj Үндсэн Хуулийн Гудамж

17

33

28

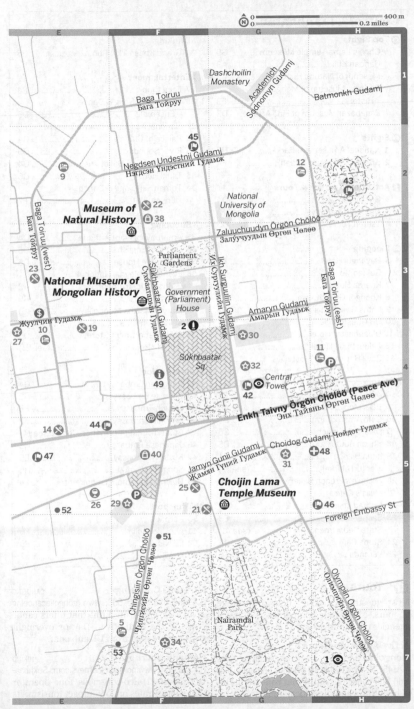

N 0 —————— 400 m
0 —————— 0.2 miles

Dashchoilin
Monastery

Academich
Sodnomyn Gudamj

Batmonkh Gudamj

Baga Toiruu
Бага Тойруу

Negdsen Undestnii Gudamj
Нэгдсэн Үндэстний Гудамж

45

12

9

43

National
University of
Mongolia

22

Museum of
Natural History

38

Zaluuchuudyn Örgön Chölöö
Залуучуудын Өргөн Чөлөө

Baga Toiruu (west)
Бага Тойруу

Parliament
Gardens

23

National Museum of
Mongolian History

Government
(Parliament)
House

Ikh Surguuliin Gudamj
Их Сургуулийн Гудамж

Amaryn Gudamj
Амарын Гудамж

Baga Toiruu (east)
Бага Тойруу

Sükhbaataryn Gudamj
Сүхбаатарын Гудамж

Жуулчин Гудамж

10

19

30

2

11

27

Sükhbaatar
Sq

32

49

42

Central
Tower

Enkh Taivny Örgön Chölöö (Peace Ave)
Энх Тайвны Өргөн Чөлөө

14

44

@

47

40

Jamyn Gunii Gudamj
Жамян Гүний Гудамж

Choidog Gudamj Чойдог Гудамж

48

31

25

Choijin Lama
Temple Museum

46

Chingisiin Örgön Chölöö
Чингисийн Өргөн Чөлөө

26

29

21

Foreign Embassy St

52

51

Olympiin Örgön Chölöö
Олимпийн Өргөн Чөлөө

5

53

Nairamdal
Park

34

1

Central Ulaanbaatar

◉ Top Sights
Choijin Lama Temple Museum............ G5
Gandan Khiid.. A3
Museum of Natural History F3
National Museum of Mongolian
    History.. F3
Zanabazar Museum of Fine Arts.......... D3

◉ Sights
1 National Amusement Park H7
2 Statue of Chinggis Khaan F4

◉ Activities, Courses & Tours
3 Ger to Ger... D4
    Nomadic Journeys .... (see 38)
4 Tseren Tours... D5

◉ Sleeping
5 Bayangol Hotel F7
6 Golden Gobi D4
7 Kharaa Hotel B5
8 Khongor Guesthouse C5
9 Lotus Guesthouse E2
10 UB Guesthouse...................................... E4
11 Ulaanbaatar Hotel H4
12 Zaluuchuud Hotel G2
13 Zaya Backpacker Hostel...................... B5

◉ Eating
14 40K E5
15 BD's Mongolian Barbeque A6
16 Café Amsterdam D5
17 Dalai Eej Market C6
18 Khaan Buuz D5
19 Luna Blanca E4
    Merkuri Market .... (see 17)
20 Michele's French Bakery...................... D5
21 Millie's Cafe F5
22 Nomad Legends F2
23 Sacher's Café.. E3
    State Department Store .... (see 41)
24 Stupa Café D4
25 Veranda..F5

◉ Drinking
26 Grand Khaan Irish Pub............................ E5

◉ Entertainment
27 Face Club E4
28 Moonstone Song & Dance
    Ensemble D6
29 National Academic Drama Theatre...... F5
30 Palace of Culture................................... G4
31 River Sounds G5
32 State Opera & Ballet Theatre.............. G4
33 Tsuki House D6
34 Tumen Ekh Song & Dance
    Ensemble F7

◉ Shopping
35 Amarbayasgalant Antique....................D4
36 Books in English C5
37 Cashmere House D5
38 Egshiglen Magnai National
    Musical Instrument Shop F2
39 Map Shop...B5
    Mary & Martha Mongolia .... (see 16)
40 Seven Summits F5
41 State Department Store........................D5
    Xanadu Books .... (see 21)

◉ Information
42 Canadian Embassy G4
43 Chinese Embassy...................................H2
44 French Embassy...................................... E5
45 German Embassy.................................... F2
    Guide Tourist Information Centre (see 14)
46 Japanese Embassy.................................H5
47 Russian Embassy.................................... E5
48 Songdo Hospital.....................................H5
49 Ulaanbaatar Information Centre.......... F4

◉ Transport
50 Aeroflot B6
51 AeroMongolia F6
52 EZ Nis E5
53 MIAT F7

☞ Tours

Most guesthouses offer their own range of tours. Many tour companies and travel agencies offer tours to gers.

Active Adventure Tours
Mongolia   CYCLING, HORSERIDING
(☏345 662; www.tourmongolia.com; Erkhugiin Gudamj) Eco-conscious outfit that runs traditional homestays and hires local guides.

Mongolia Canoeing   CANOEING
(☏9982 6883, 685 503; www.mongoliacanoeing.com) A German-run outfit that offers canoe trips on the Tuul River. Day or overnight trips are possible from Ulaanbaatar.

Nomadic Journeys   HIKING
(☏328 737; www.nomadicjourneys.com; Sükhbaataryn Gudamj 1) Eco-conscious tour operator that concentrates on low-impact tourism. Its

camp at Jalman Meadows is less than two hours' drive from UB.

Stone Horse HORSERIDING
(☑95921167; www.stonehorsemongolia.com; Jamyn Gunii Gudamj 5-1, Viva Bldg, room 104) Offers horse treks in the Khan Khentii Mountains (trips start just one hour out of UB).

Tseren Tours SIGHTSEEING, CYCLING
(☑99111832,327083; www.tserentours.com; Baruun Selbe Gudamj 14/1) Dutch- and Mongolian-run outfit that does countrywide family tours and biking trips.

✪ Festivals & Events

Tsagaan Sar LUNAR NEW YEAR FESTIVAL
Held sometime between late January and early March depending on the lunar calendar.

Naadam SPORTS FESTIVAL
Mongolia's No 1 festival draws the multitudes to Ulaanbaatar on 11 and 12 July (see also p280).

🛏 Sleeping

All room rates following include breakfast, although at the budget places this may just be tea, coffee and some bread and jam. Expect 15% value-added tax (VAT) to be tacked onto your bill at top-end places.

WEST OF SÜKHBAATAR SQUARE

TOP CHOICE Lotus Guesthouse GUESTHOUSE $
(☑325 967, 9909 4943; www.lotuschild.org; Baga Toiruu West, Apt 6; dm/s/d US$5/10/14; @☎) This homey place feels more like a boutique hotel than a guesthouse. Rooms are individually styled, some with traditional Mongolian furniture. It's located on a quiet bend of the Little Ring Rd, away from the bustle of Peace Ave. It's run by the Lotus Children's Centre and the staff are young Mongolians that once lived at the Lotus orphanage.

TOP CHOICE Zaya Backpacker Hostel GUESTHOUSE $
(☑331 575; www.zayahostel.com; Peace Ave; dm/s/d/tr US$12/25/30/36; @☎) The plushest guesthouse in the downtown area, Zaya has hardwood floors, modern bathrooms and a comfy lounge. It's set off Peace Ave in an orange eight-storey apartment block (on the 3rd floor), just past the Seoul Hotel. There are two separate locations, but the one in the orange apartment block is definitely best.

Khongor Guesthouse GUESTHOUSE $
(☑316 415, 9925 2599; www.khongor-expedition .com; Peace Ave 15, Apt 6; dm/s/d US$5/10/14; @☎) This well-established guesthouse is clean and friendly with a big lounge, kitchen facilities and a central location. The countryside tours run by the owners get rave reviews from readers. The entrance is around the back of the third building west of the State Department Store.

Golden Gobi GUESTHOUSE $
(☑322 632, 9665 4496; www.goldengobi.com; dm US$6, d with/without bathroom US$23/19; @☎) You'll probably hear about this funky place and its eccentric owners long before your train arrives in UB. It has two lounges, clean dorms and doubles and a party vibe. It's in the courtyard just east of the State Department Store.

UB Guesthouse GUESTHOUSE $
(☑311 037, 9119 9859; www.ubguest.com; cnr Baga Toiruu & Juulchin Gudamj; dm/s/d US$6/16/20; @☎) A popular guesthouse with clean rooms and a good travellers' vibe. The Korean-Mongolian management has plenty of experience in helping backpackers with logistics and trip planning. It's centrally located above Golomt Bank on Baga Toiruu west; the entrance is around the back.

Kharaa Hotel HOTEL $$
(☑313 717; Choimbolyn Gudamj 6; s/d US$65/75; P@) The Kharaa is nothing spectacular, but the rooms are comfortable enough, the service is friendly and it's within walking distance of the city centre. Views are better on the street side of the hotel.

EAST OF SÜKHBAATAR SQUARE

Zaluuchuud Hotel HOTEL $$
(☑324 594; www.zh.mn; Baga Toiruu 43; s/d/ste incl breakfast US$35/65/90; @) The spiffy rooms here have been renovated with a modern, simple design and are equipped with TV, fridge and kettle. It's not the fanciest in town, but it's reliable and fairly priced and has a nice location near the Chinese embassy.

Ulaanbaatar Hotel HOTEL $$$
(☑320 620; www.ubhotel.mn; Baga Toiruu East; s/d T150,000/180,000; @☎) A throwback to socialist Mongolia, this Soviet-built hotel has a big marble staircase, creaky hallways and decent rooms, although some are a tad small. Facilities include sauna, billiards room, business centre, travel agency, coffee shop and two restaurants.

Kempinski Hotel Khan Palace   HOTEL $$$
(463 463; www.khanpalace.com/en/ulaanbaatar; East Cross Rd; s/d from US$98/120; P✻@) This Kempinski-managed hotel is one of the best in the city. Facilities include free internet, sauna and a fitness centre. Expats rave about the breakfasts. The hotel is located at the 'East Cross Road', about 2km east of Sükhbaatar Sq.

SOUTH OF SÜKHBAATAR SQUARE

Bayangol Hotel   HOTEL $$$
(328 869; www.bayangolhotel.mn; Chingisiin Örgön Chölöö 5; s/d T145,000/180,000; P☺@) Reliable and centrally located hotel with a couple of good restaurants and a bar. Bathrooms are small but otherwise rooms have contemporary furnishings and come with a computer with internet access.

TRAIN STATION AREA

LG Guest House   GUESTHOUSE $
(328 243, 9989 4672; www.lghostel.com; Narny Gudamj; dm US$6-8, s/d US$16/20; @☎) With 12 rooms this is one of the largest guesthouses in the city. It has clean dorms and private rooms with attached bathroom, a common area, a kitchen where you can cook your own meals and a restaurant on the ground level.

Voyage Hotel   HOTEL $$
(327 213; www.voyagehotel.mn; Narny Gudamj; s/d US$30/50; @) Good-value midrange place with friendly service and well-maintained rooms. 'Half-lux' rooms (renovated deluxe doubles with new furniture) are US$65; 'lux' accommodation (with an extra room, like a small apartment) is US$90.

✗ Eating

Ulaanbaatar's restaurants offer a surprisingly decent variety of cuisines and atmospheres. There's great international fare and an infinite number of Mongolian places.

[TOP CHOICE] **Mongolians**   MONGOLIAN $$
(www.mongolians.mn; Ikh Toiruu 93, Barilga Mega Store; meals T6000-8000; ☺11am-midnight; ▯) Part museum, part restaurant, this place sports great atmosphere, the walls lined with Mongolian antiques and old photos. The menu is contemporary Mongolian, with stir-fried meats, dumplings and boiled mutton with some Russian and European influence. If you want to go all out, order the *khorkhog* (meat chunks cooked in a metal steamer with scalding hot rocks added to

the pot to aid in cooking), enough for six to eight people (you must call six hours in advance). Two nights a week a traditional Mongolian band plays here at 8pm (usually Monday and Tuesday). Mongolians is 600m east of the US embassy.

Millie's Espresso   AMERICAN, LATIN $$
(Marco Polo Bldg; mains T7000-9500; ☺8am-8pm Mon-Sat; ☎▯) The preferred lunch spot for consultants, diplomats, expat businessmen and the occasional member of parliament. Great options include the steak sandwich, lasagne, lemon pie and fruit smoothie. Cuban chef Daniel and Ethiopian owner Millie are always around for a pleasant chat.

Luna Blanca   VEGETARIAN $$
(M-100 Bldg, Juulchin Gudamj; meals T5000-10,000; ☺10am-9pm; ☺▱▯) Better-than-average vegetarian restaurant serving kebabs, soups, salads, smoothies and vegie twists on Mongolian dishes. The owners are three English-speaking sisters who learned to cook vegie food while studying in India.

Veranda   FRENCH, ITALIAN $$
(Jamyn Gunii Gudamj; mains T6000-8000; ☺noon-midnight) This place has seating on comfortable sofas or at tables looking over the mystical monastery-museum of Choijin Lama. The French-Italian cuisine is superb and the prices reasonable. Note that it's on the 2nd floor, above Silk Road restaurant.

40K   WESTERN $$
(cnr Peace Ave & Baga Toiruu; meals T6000-9000; ☺noon-11pm; ☎▯) In a central spot on Peace Ave, this chic little restaurant prepares excellent salads, soups, pizzas and other Western fare. In the lobby you'll also find a toddlers' playroom and a tourist information desk.

BD's Mongolian Barbeque   MONGOLIAN $$$
(Seoul St; all-you-can-eat T10,500; ☺noon-midnight) This is more like an Americanised version of Mongolian barbecue, but it's tasty nonetheless. Choose your ingredients and allow the chefs to grill up your meal before your eyes. It's a good place to go after a long train ride as you can eat as much as you like (within 90 minutes). The kid-friendly atmosphere makes it good for families.

Nomad Legends   MONGOLIAN $$
(Sükhbaataryn Gudamj 1; meals T6000-8000; ☺noon-midnight; ▯) This tiny nook is a good place to try some Mongolian food in a somewhat upscale atmosphere. There are lots of soups and meat dishes on the menu and the

brave can try the sheep's head – crack open the skull for some tasty sheep offal.

Khan Buuz
MONGOLIAN $$
(Peace Ave; meals T5000-10,000; ⊘10am-9pm) Reliable cafeteria-style Mongolian place opposite the State Department Store. Good for sampling Mongolian traditional soups and *buuz*.

Stupa Café
VEGETARIAN $
(Juulchin Gudamj, Builder's Sq; snack & drink T4500; ⊘10am-8pm Mon-Fri, 9am-7pm Sat & Sun; ⊜) Attached to a Buddhist cultural centre, this very appealing cafe is ideal for a quiet pit stop and has some great handmade souvenirs as well as newspapers and a free English library.

Michele's French Bakery
BAKERY $
(off Peace Ave; snacks from T900; ⊘8am-7pm) Take away croissants and apple strudels or sit down with a panini or crepe. A popular haunt for expats.

Café Amsterdam
CAFE $$
(www.amsterdam.mn; Peace Ave; lunch T5000; ⊘7am-10pm; ⊜) A literary cafe of sorts, this place attracts journalists, writers and other creative folk. It sometimes puts on cultural events, so check the noticeboard. Menu items include soups, sandwiches, teas, coffees and light European breakfasts. Some of the vegetables come from a local women's co-op.

Sacher's Café
BAKERY $
(Baga Toiruu west; snacks T500-2000; ⊘8am-10pm) A German-run place with an excellent selection of cakes, pretzels and breads; perfect snack food for the train.

Self-Catering
Stock up for your train ride or a trip to the countryside by visiting the 1st floor of the **State Department Store** (Peace Ave), or for a better selection try **Dalai Eej Market** (⊘10am-8pm) and **Merkuri Market** (⊘10am-8pm).

Drinking
Locally brewed beers have taken off in UB. Most bars are open 11am to midnight daily and all serve food of the meat-and-potatoes variety.

Grand Khaan Irish Pub
PUB
(Seoul St; meal with beer T7000; ⊘11am-midnight; ⊝⊚) Big crowds, lots of smoke, free-flowing beer and loud music set the scene for Ulaanbaatar's most popular nightspot. Drink some beer and have a meal on the patio overlooking the only tree-lined street in the city.

Hennessy Restbar
PUB
(East Cross, ⊘11am-midnight) Of the six or seven Irish pubs in UB, this is the only one that is run by a real live Irishman. The purveyor, Sean Hennessy (a distant relative of the founder of Hennessy brandy), serves up some fantastic pub grub (meals T10,000 to T18,000) and a great Sunday roast brunch. Thursday is quiz night and on Tuesday in summer they host a pub crawl (meet in front of the State Department Store at 7pm). The bar is behind the Kempinski Khan Palace Hotel.

☆ Entertainment
Check the English-language weeklies for info on coming events. The **Arts Council of Mongolia** (www.artscouncil.mn) produces a monthly cultural-events calendar that covers most theatres, galleries and museums.

Tumen Ekh Song & Dance Ensemble
THEATRE
(⊠9665 0711; www.tumen-ekh.mn; Nairamdal Park; admission T12,000; ⊘6pm May-Oct) Puts on a nightly cultural show in summer, complete with traditional song, dance, *khöömii* (throat singing) and contortionists.

Moonstone Song & Dance Ensemble
THEATRE
(⊠318 802; admission US$7; ⊘4pm, 6pm & 8pm May-Oct) At the Tsuki House next to the State Circus, Moonstone puts on a similar show to Tumen Ekh's in cabaret fashion. One drink is included with admission and food is available.

State Opera & Ballet Theatre
THEATRE
(⊠70110389; Sükhbaatar Sq; admission T5000-8000; ⊘closed Aug) Stages productions in Mongolian of many of the classics, as well as works by Mongolia's most famous poet and playwright, Natsagdorj.

National Academic Drama Theatre
THEATRE
(⊠324 621; cnr Seoul St & Chingisiin Örgön Chölöö; admission T7000; ⊘6pm May-Sep) Cultural shows.

Palace of Culture
THEATRE
(⊠321 444) On the northeastern corner of Sükhbaatar Sq. Puts on cultural shows.

THE NAADAM FESTIVAL

The high point of the Mongolian year is the Naadam Festival, held on 11 and 12 July. Part family reunion, part fair and part nomad Olympics, Naadam (meaning 'games') has its roots in the nomad assemblies and hunting extravaganzas of the Mongol armies.

Smaller Naadams are held throughout the country and are well worth attending if you want to get close to the action and have a more authentic experience. The Naadam in Ulaanbaatar does have all the traditional events, but it's typically crowded and somewhat exhausting as you end up having to do a lot of driving and walking about. Perhaps the best part of the Ulaanbaatar Naadam is the extravagant opening ceremony, which features some great costumes and performances.

To find out what's going on during the festival, look for the events program in the two English-language newspapers (see p282); there are often sports matches and other events in the lead-up to the main two days.

The Tournament

The wrestling starts at the stadium immediately after the opening ceremony. The final rounds on day two, just before the closing ceremony, are the most exciting matches. Mongolian wrestling has no time limits; a match ends only when a wrestler falls (or any body part other than feet or hands touches the ground).

Archery is held in an open stadium next to the main stadium. Archers use a bent composite bow made of layered horn, bark and wood. Arrows are usually made from willow branches and vulture feathers.

Horse racing is held about 28km west of the city at Hui Doloon Khutag. Buses and minivans travel here from the parking lot outside the stadium (T2000). It is also possible to take the train (T1200). Tour operators can organise vehicles or you could take a taxi (about T25,000 return). The racing, which takes place not on a track but on the open steppe, has six categories, based on the age of the horse and the distance of the race (either 15km or 30km). Jockeys are children aged five to 12. Note that traffic to/ from the race track is one way, depending on whether a race is starting or ending. To avoid getting caught in a back-up it's best to go very early in the morning (before 8am). Alternatively, go in the early evening and camp out.

The smallest event, anklebone shooting, is held in a large tent next to the archery stadium. This entails flicking a small, wedge-shaped piece (made from reindeer horn) at a small target (made from sheep anklebones) about 3m away. Apart from providing some shade, the tent has an electric atmosphere as competitors are spurred on by the yodelling of spectators.

Tickets

Admission to the archery and horse racing is free, but you'll need a ticket to enter the stadium for the opening/closing ceremonies and wrestling matches. Ticket costs vary per section; the north side of the stadium (which is protected from the sun and rain by an overhang and has the best view of the opening event) is more expensive, with tickets going for T30,000. Tickets are distributed via the tour operators and hotels. It's also possible to buy tickets at the Naadam stadium or from a window on the north side of the Cultural Palace. Small batches of tickets are sold each day and lines to buy them are long, so the best way to get a ticket is through your hotel or guesthouse. If you're desperate, some locals try to sell their extra tickets at the stadium, but you'll need to pay more than face value.

River Sounds LIVE MUSIC
(Olympiin Örgön Chölöö; admission T5000; ⊗8pm-3am) Dedicated live-music venue that usually hosts jazz and occasionally rock bands.

Metropolis NIGHTCLUB
(Sky Shopping Centre; admission T5000; ⊗10pm-4am) UB's biggest, baddest discotheque pumps disco, techno, pop and salsa well into the night. Locals call it 'Metro Police'; it's behind the Chinggis Khaan Hotel.

Face Club NIGHTCLUB
(Juulchin Gudamj; admission T3000; ⊙7pm-3am)
This lively little place with a Tahitian theme
has a central location, near many of the
hostels.

🛍 Shopping

UB abounds with shops selling tacky tourist souvenirs as well as locally produced
cashmere clothing and blankets. A few of
the better places for that special Mongolian
keepsake are below.

Amarbayasgalant Antique ANTIQUES
(Juulchin Gudamj 37/31) Quality antique shop
for the serious buyer. Some items are crea-
tions of Zanabazar (Mongolia's first Bogd
Gegeen and the country's greatest sculptor)
and are not for sale. Great for browsing.

**Egshiglen Magnai National Musical
Instrument Shop** MUSICAL INSTRUMENTS
(Sükhbaataryn Gudamj) It sells *morin khuur*
(horsehead fiddles) with prices ranging from
T150,000 to T700,000. *Yattag* (zithers) and
two-string Chinese fiddles are also available.

Cashmere House CASHMERE
(Peace Ave) High-quality cashmere products;
located opposite the Russian embassy.

State Department Store SHOPPING CENTRE
(Peace Ave 44; ⊙9am-8pm Mon-Sat, 10am-7pm
Sun) Numerous departments sell clothing,
electronics, camping gear and more. The 5th
floor has souvenirs and traditional clothing.

Mary & Martha Mongolia SOUVENIRS
(www.mmmongolia.com; Peace Ave) Fair-trade
shop selling handicrafts, felt products and
modern Kazakh wall hangings.

Books in English BOOKS
(Peace Ave) Buys and sells used books including guidebooks. It's a tiny shop buried in a
basement, about 70m west of Khaan Buuz
restaurant.

Xanadu BOOKSTORE
(Marco Polo Bldg; ⊙10am-6pm Mon-Sat) Sells
mostly Lonely Planet titles.

Map Shop MAPS
(Ikh Toiruu; ⊙9am-1pm & 2-6pm Mon-Fri, 10am-
4pm Sat) Near the Elba Electronics shop. Has
a good selection of maps for parts of Mongolia beyond the capital.

Seven Summits OUTDOOR GEAR
(www.activemongolia.com/7summits; btwn Peace
Ave & Seoul St) Stocks German-made Vaude
gear, GPS units, maps, stoves and gas, travel
books and accessories. It also hires out gear,
including tents, sleeping bags, gas stoves,
mountain bikes and inflatable kayaks. It's
opposite the Central Post Office (CPO).

ℹ Information

Head to **Lonely Planet** (www.lonelyplanet.com/
mongolia) for planning advice, author recommendations, traveller reviews and insider tips.

Emergency
It may take a few minutes to get an English-
speaker on these numbers.
Emergency aid and ambulance (☏103)
Police emergency (☏102)
Robbery Unit (☏318 783)

Internet Access
There's a growing number of wireless hotspots
in Ulaanbaatar. Your hotel may offer free wi-fi, or
you can get easily get online at cafes including
Café Amsterdam, Michele's French Bakery or
Sacher's Cafe.
Internet Cafe (Peace Ave; per hr T600;
⊙24hr) Inside the CPO.
Internet Centre (Tserendorjiin Gudamj 65; per
hr T800; ⊙9am-midnight) One of the largest
internet cafes.

ROCK 'N' ROLL MONGOL STYLE

There's a thriving contemporary-music
scene in Ulaanbaatar – try to catch a
live performance while you're in town.
Grand Khaan Irish Pub usually stages
local talent. Popular genres include
pop, rap and hip hop, as well as a
totally Mongolian brand of folklore-
rock fusion music that includes drums
and guitars along with traditional
instruments. Folklore bands include
Altan Urag (www.altanurag.mn) and
Khusugtun (www.khusugtun.com). If
you're into hip hop look out for upcom-
ing artists **Opozit, Quiza, Tatar** and
Tsetse. Rock bands include the
Lemons, the **Pips** and **Nisvanis**.
Many of these outfits portray a Western image, but the lyrics are pure
Mongol, with frequent references to
the blue sky, grasslands and mothers.
You can hear most of these artists on
YouTube, or buy their CDs in Ulaanbaa-
tar's many souvenir and music shops.

Media

Pick up English-language weekly newspapers the *Mongol Messenger* (www.mongolmessenger.mn; T500) and the *UB Post* (http://ubpost.mongol news.mn; T600) for local news and entertainment information.

Medical Services

The best place for most of your health-care needs is the SOS clinic, but life-or-death emergencies are evacuated to Seoul or Běijīng.

SOS Medica Mongolia Clinic (☎464 325, after hours 9911 0335; 4a Bldg, Big Ring Rd; ☺9am-6pm Mon-Fri) Staffed by Western doctors on call 24 hours. Services are pricey (examinations start at around US$195), but it's the best place to go in an emergency.

Songdo Hospital (☎7012 9000; Peace Ave; ☺8.30am-5pm Mon-Fri, 8am-noon Sat) Modern, South Korean–run hospital with examinations starting at T6000.

Money

Banks, ATMs and moneychangers are widespread. ATMs (you'll find them in department stores, hotel lobbies and the CPO) dispense tögrögs. You can get dollars from a bank teller with your debit card and passport (fees from your home bank will apply). There's a handy moneychanger on the 1st floor of the State Department Store.

Trade & Development Bank (Juulchin Gudamj; ☺9am-4pm Mon-Fri) Will change travellers cheques into tögrögs (1% fee) or dollars (2% fee). Will also replace lost Amex travellers cheques.

Valiut Arjiljaa (Moneychangers; Baga Toiruu West btwn Peace Ave & Juulchin Gudamj; ☺8.30am-9pm) The square next to the Ard bus stop has several private moneychangers with the best rates in town.

Post

Central Post Office (CPO; Töv Shuudangiin Salbar; Peace Ave; ☺7.30am-9pm Mon-Fri, 9am-8pm Sat & Sun)

Tourist Information

Ulaanbaatar Information Centre (☎7011 8083; www.ubtourism.mn; Sükhbaataryn Gudamj; ☺9am-6pm) Located on the west side of Sükhbaatar Sq, this office has free city maps but the staff seem pretty indifferent to visitors.

Guide Tourist Information Centre (☎7010 1011; cnr Baga Toiruu West & Peace Ave; ☺9am-9pm May-Sep, 10am-7pm Oct-Apr) Located inside Erel Bank; the staff here are better informed compared to those at the one on the square.

Travel Agencies

Ulaanbaatar has no shortage of travel agents and tour operators (see p276) who can help organise ger visits and other excursions or obtain train tickets.

Air Market (☎305 050; www.airmarket.mn) Opposite the CPO. Good for flight tickets.

Legend Tour (☎315 158, 9984 2999; www .legendtour.ru; Seoul St, Mongol Nom Bldg, 2nd fl) On the 2nd floor of a building opposite Master Food Supermarket, this outfit offers Russian visa support for some Western nationals. But it's still best to get your Russian visa in your home country.

ⓘ Getting There & Away

Train

Ulaanbaatar's train station is in the city's southwestern corner around 2km from the centre. It has an ATM, a small cafe and some basic shops. The domestic ticketing office is in a separate building to the left of the entrance to the platform. Give yourself plenty of time because traffic to the station can be bad during much of the day.

The yellow **International Railway Ticketing Office** is 200m northwest of the train station. Inside the office, specific rooms sell tickets for direct trains heading to destinations in Russia and China. The easiest place to book a ticket is in the **foreigners' booking office** (☎21-24133, enquiries 21-243 848; Zamchdyn Gudamj; ☺8am-8pm Mon-Fri). It's upstairs and the staff speak some English. On weekends you can use the downstairs booking desk. Tickets for international trains can be booked up to one month in advance. However, the Moscow–Běijīng through trains don't go on sale until the day before departure because they need to wait for seat availability from their counterparts in either China or Russia.

For China, most travellers book an international train ticket all the way to Běijīng. If you want to save some money (and don't mind an adventure), take a local train to the border, cross into China by jeep, and then continue to Běijīng or Dàtóng by local train.

For Russia, most travellers take the daily bus to Ulan-Ude as it's faster than the local train (12 hours versus 31 hours). The express Moscow–Ulaanbaatar or Moscow–Běijīng trains are little better, completing the journey in about 18 hours.

Air

Chinggis Khaan International Airport is 18km southwest of the city. The airport has ATMs and banking services. There's also a post office and internet access for T50 per minute. A tourist booth opens when planes arrive.

The domestic routes are covered by Aero-Mongolia and EZ Nis. On domestic routes

INTERNATIONAL TRAINS DEPARTING ULAANBAATAR

DESTINATION	TRAIN NUMBER	DEPARTURE DAY	DEPARTURE TIME	DURATION
Běijīng	24 (year-round)*	Thu or Mon**	1.50pm	30hr
Běijīng	24 (summer only extra train)*	Mon or Wed***	1.50pm	30hr
Běijīng (originates in Moscow)	4	Sun	7.15am	30hr
Hohhot	34	Mon, Fri	8pm	24hr
Irkutsk	263	daily	9.10pm	36hr
Moscow	5	Tue, Fri	1.50pm	70hr
Moscow (originates in Běijīng)	3	Thu	1.50pm	70hr

*Train 24 departs Zamyn-Üüd at 8.35pm, Èrlián at 12.55am Jíníng at 6.37am and Dàtóng at 8.35am. Note that this train changes its departure day each year (depending on whether it's run by China or Mongolia railway).

**The Chinese train typically leaves Ulaanbaatar on Thursday, while the Mongolian typically leaves Ulaanbaatar on Monday. In addition, the Chinese and Mongolians swap operating duties in May.

***The 24 summer train is an extra train put on for the summer holiday season (it usually runs June to September). When operated by Mongolia it will most likely depart Ulaanbaatar on Wednesday, when run by China it will mostly likely run on Monday.

Ulaanbaatar–China Train Fares

The costs (in tögrög) for destinations in China from Ulaanbaatar:

DESTINATION	HARD SLEEPER	SOFT SLEEPER	DELUXE
Běijīng	130,050	217,750	184,550
Dàtóng	113,250	188,450	160,250
Èrlián	80,050	131,350	111,650
Hohhot	118,150	166,650	

Ulaanbaatar–Russia Train Fares

The costs (in tögrög) for destinations in Russia from Ulaanbaatar:

DESTINATION	2ND CLASS	1ST CLASS
Naushki	42,250	66,750
Ulan-Ude	64,150	99,050
Irkutsk	97,850	146,950
Krasnoyarsk	142,750	220,350
Omsk	183,450	301,650
Yekaterinburg	216,350	359,950
Perm	226,350	373,950
Moscow	266,250	445,050

DOMESTIC TRAINS DEPARTING ULAANBAATAR

TRAIN (NUMBER)	FREQUENCY	DEPARTURE	DURATION (HR)	FARE (T)*
Sükhbaatar (263)	daily	9.10pm	7¾	6300/11,800/18,900
Sükhbaatar (271)	daily	10.30am	7¾	6300/11,800/18,900
Zamyn-Üüd (276)	daily	4.30pm	15½	9600/16,800/27,300
Zamyn-Üüd (34; fast)	Mon, Wed, Fri	8pm	12	-/22,100/39,200
Sainshand (285)	daily	10.15am	10	7400/13,200/21,500
Darkhan 211 (fast)	daily	3.50pm	5	5000/10,000/15,300

*seat/hard sleeper/soft sleeper

AeroMongolia allows you 15kg for luggage but EZ Nis allows 20kg (and they weigh your hand bags too). You'll pay around T1500 per kilogram over the limit. Flight days always change so check updated schedules.

AeroMongolia (☑330 373; www.aeromongolia .mn; Monnis Bldg, 1st fl) International routes include two flights per week to Irkutsk (Russia) and three flights per week to Hohhot (China).

EZ Nis (☑333 311; www.eznis.com; 8 Zovkhis Bldg, Seoul St) International routes include three flights per week to Ulan-Ude (Russia) and a twice-weekly flight to Hailar (China, via Choibalsan). Plan well ahead for the Hailar flight because your passport details will need to be confirmed by immigration several days in advance.

MIAT (☑333 999; www.miat.com; Chingisiin Örgön Chölöö; ☉9am-6pm Mon-Sat, to 3pm Sun) Has flights to Běijīng, Berlin, Irkutsk, Moscow, Osaka, Seoul, Tokyo and Hong Kong. The office is in a glass building south of the Bayangol Hotel.

Foreign airline offices include the following:
Aeroflot (☑320 720; www.aeroflot.ru; Seoul St 15) Two weekly flights to Moscow.
Air China (☑452 548; www.fly-airchina .com; Ikh Toiruu, Bldg 47) Six weekly flights to Běijīng.
Korean Air (☑317 100; www.koreanair.com; 2nd fl, Chinggis Khaan Hotel) Four weekly flights to Seoul.

Bus & 4WD

Minivans heading for destinations in the north and west leave from the **Dragon Bus Stand** (☑7017 4902) on Peace Ave 7km west of Sükhbaatar Sq. The **Bayanzürkh Avto Vaksal** (☑7015 3386), 6km east of Sükhbaatar Sq, has buses leaving to eastern cities and Dalanzadgad. Most buses depart between 7.30am and 8am; it's best to buy a ticket one or two days in

advance. Shared vans and 4WDs also depart from these bus stations, leaving when full.

ⓘ Getting Around

A taxi from the airport should be around US$12 to US$15. Bus 11 or 22 runs from the airport every 20 minutes to the Bayangol Hotel (T300, 25 minutes). However, it doesn't come to the terminal; it stops on the highway outside the airport. It's much better to organise a pick-up from your hotel.

From the train station to the city centre it's about a 25-minute walk (about 2km). Alternatively, metered taxis charge a standard T500 per kilometre (check the current rate as this increases regularly); most taxi drivers are honest and will use their meters. If there's no meter, make sure the driver sets the odometer to zero. Expect to pay around T4000 from the station to Sükhbaatar Sq. This price will be lower if you walk away from the station and hail a cab on the street.

Around Ulaanbaatar

Mongolia's real attraction lies in the untouched beauty of the countryside, its exhilarating wide open spaces and rich nomadic culture. Fortunately, these aspects are within reach on day trips or overnights from Ulaanbaatar. See p276 for details on tours.

MANDSHIR KHIID   МАНДШИР ХИЙД
Just over 50km south of Ulaanbaatar, Mandshir Khiid was a monastery – established in 1733 – that once contained more than 20 temples and housed 350 monks. Destroyed during the 1930s, the main temple has been restored and now functions as a museum, but the other temples remain in ruins.

The monastery itself is not as impressive as Gandan Khiid in Ulaanbaatar, but the setting is exquisite. Hidden away in the **Bogdkhan Uul Strictly Protected Area** (admission T5000), the monastery overlooks a beautiful valley of pine, birch and cedar trees, dotted with granite boulders. Behind the main temple, climb up the rocks to discover some **Buddhist rock paintings**.

You can catch a taxi straight to Mandshir Khiid from Ulaanbaatar. Alternatively, take one of the hourly minibuses to the nearby town of Zuunmod (T1500, one hour) and then walk the 5km to the monastery or take a taxi.

There's a popular hike from Mandshir Khiid, over the Bogdkhan Mountain and back to Ulaanbaatar. The hike takes eight to 10 hours; with a very early start you could do it in a day but otherwise plan on camping on the mountain. The trail starts from the left side of the monastery. It is marked with paint on the trees but the markers can be hard to follow so bring a compass or GPS. In 2010 an American hiker died here after getting stranded overnight on the mountain during a fierce rainstorm. Be well prepared with extra food, warm clothing and rain gear. Let someone in UB know where you are going and when you will be back.

TERELJ   ТЭРЭЛЖ

Although it's fast becoming developed, Terelj, about 80km northeast of UB and part of the **Gorkhi-Terelj National Park** (admission T3000), is still a beautiful and relaxing place to head to. There are many opportunities for hiking, rock climbing, swimming (in icy water), rafting and horse riding (T12,000 to T20,000 per day) in the alpine hills.

The most popular destination for hiking or horseriding is the appropriately named **Turtle Rock**, easily spotted along the main road through the park. From here it's less than an hour's hike up to the picturesque Buddhist meditation retreat of Aryapala.

Terelj is a great place to go camping, or guesthouses can arrange accommodation in the park – sometimes staying in real gers with local families. Most of the tourist ger camps in Terelj offer similar facilities and prices – about US$30 per person, including three hearty meals, or US$15 without food. Among the better ones are **Buuveit** (☑322 870; www.tsolmontravel.com), which has a beautifully secluded location, and the friendly **Miraj** (☑325 188), 14km along the main road from the park entrance.

For the slightly more adventurous, there is the **Ecotourism Ger Camp** (☑9973 4710; bergoo@hotmail.com; with/without meals US$35/14), run by a Dutchman named Bert. It's a 30-minute horse ride from the Terelj-Juulchin hotel, across the river. Bert can organise horse-riding trips of the area and can show you his cheese-making operation.

A bus (T2300) for Terelj village (passing Turtle Rock) leaves at 11am and 4pm in summer or 3pm in winter (1 October to 15 May) from Peace Ave in Ulaanbaatar, opposite the Narantuul Hotel. They may charge you T5000 but this includes the park entry fee. Otherwise, hire a taxi for about US$35 one way.

KHUSTAIN NATIONAL PARK
ХУСТАЙН НУРУУ

Also known as Khustain Nuruu (Birch Mountain Range), this park was set up to protect the reintroduced *takhi* or Przewalski's horse. The horse (a separate species from domesticated horses) had become extinct in the wild by the late 1960s, but the animals had been preserved in the zoos of

GER TO GER TREKKING

Seeing Mongolia's beautiful nature from the train window will probably entice you to get off the rails. One of the best active-adventure options is offered by **Ger to Ger** (☑313 336; www.gertoger.org; Arizona Plaza, Suite 11, Baruun Selbe Gudamj 5/3, Ulaanbaatar), a local nonprofit organisation that combines the great outdoors with a dose of traditional culture.

Trekkers travel by foot, horse and even yak cart between gers, with distances ranging from 5km to 20km. The gers act like warming huts, and once you've arrived the host family will introduce various aspects of Mongolian culture, such as archery, cooking or horse training. Ger to Ger also provides a seminar on language and culture before you set off.

You can choose from routes in the desert, mountains or steppe, as well as levels of difficulty and duration. The closest route to Ulaanbaatar is a one-hour drive away in Gorkhi-Terelj National Park. Profits from the project go back to the local communities for small-scale development projects.

DON'T MISS

CHINGGIS KHAAN STATUE

The 40m-tall **Chinggis Khaan Statue** (☏11-328 960, www.genco-tour.mn; admission foreigner/Mongolian T10,000/5000; ☉9am-sunset) is a new local landmark and popular day trip for people from Ulaanbaatar. The statue features an enormous silver-plated Chinggis on horseback, holding his famed golden whip. There is an elevator rising up the tail with steps to the horse's head.

The complex includes a museum and six-minute film that describes how the statue was built. For an extra T1000 you can dress up in Mongol battle gear and pose for photos near a giant Mongol boot. The statue is located by the main eastern highway, 23km east of Nalaikh.

Europe and Australia. A reintroduction program in the 1990s brought some back to Mongolia and they have been thriving in Khustain Nuruu. There's a wildlife-safari feel to the place as you drive around looking for horses to photograph. The park is also home to wolves, steppe gazelles, boars and lynxes.

You can stay at a small **ger camp** (per person without meals US$20, tent US$5; ☏) near the park entrance or at the **Moilt camp** (per person US$15) inside the park. For reservations contact the **Hustai National Park Trust** (☏021-245 087; www.hustai.mn). Food at the camp is overpriced, so bring your own supplies.

To get to the park, travel 100km west of Ulaanbaatar and then 13km up a road off the main highway. Guesthouses and tour operators offer trips here, or contact the Park Trust for transport options.

Èrlián (Erenhot), China

二连

☏0479 / POP 400,000 / ☉MOSCOW +5HR

This small city (by Chinese standards) owes its entire existence to its position on the China–Mongolia frontier. Twenty years ago it was little more than a dusty outpost in the Gobi. Today it's a thriving commercial centre with an economy based almost entirely on trade with Mongolia. Vast markets all around town exist solely to feed the needs of Mongolian traders, who load up their Russian trucks and lumber back over the border. Many hotels and restaurants here display signboards with Mongolian Cyrillic to cater for the traders.

A number of important dinosaur fossils have been discovered in the desert areas around town, and city authorities are promoting Èrlián as a sort of dinosaur capital of China. The highway that leads into the city is lined with an impressive, somewhat bizarre collection of dinosaur statues, including a pair of brontosauruses, whose long necks stretch over the highway, their faces meeting in a kiss.

If you're heading for Mongolia and need a visa, there's a **Mongolian consulate** (Měnggǔ Lǐngshìguǎn; ☏151-6497-1992; Weijian Binguan, 206 Youyi Beilu; ☉8.30am-4.30pm Mon-Fri) in Èrlián. To find the consulate from the train station, walk west one block and at the first intersection turn right. Walk north along this road (Youyi Beilu) for 1.2km (15 to 20 minutes) until you see the red, blue and yellow Mongolian flags on your left. A 30-day rush tourist visa (Y495) can be issued the same day you drop off your application; you'll need one passport-size photo. A taxi can take you there for Y5.

If you've just come from Mongolia, change any remaining tögrög here or you'll be keeping it as a souvenir.

The **Hǎifēng Dàjiǔdiàn** (海丰大酒店; Xinghua Dajie; ☏751 5555; d incl breakfast Y328; ☏) is a reliable midrange hotel; you'll see it to the left as you walk out of the train station. There are some cheapies directly across the street from the station, with rooms for about Y100.

Èrlián's new airport is located 25km south of the city. Air China has one daily flight to/from Běijīng (Y540), departing Èrlián at 9.30am. At the time of writing there were plans to add a flight from Ulaanbaatar to Èrlián. Tickets can be purchased online at www.elong.com (note that the website spells Èrlián 'Erlianhaote').

The bus station is halfway between the consulate and the train station. For bus info see p287.

Dàtóng, China

大同

☏0352 / POP 1.1 MILLION / ☉MOSCOW +4HR

Coal-dusted Dàtóng was ripped apart in the 1950s to make way for a new era of socialist greatness and industrial power, but the

MONGOLIA–CHINA BORDER CROSSINGS

This border crossing takes about five hours no matter which direction you are travelling in. Most trains cross the border at night, which guarantees that you won't get much sleep. In Zamyn-Üüd, Mongolian customs officials board the train and collect paperwork from passengers. In Èrlián, Chinese customs and passport officials repeat the process (or start it, if you're travelling west). You must fill out customs forms and departure/ arrival cards.

You'll spend about an hour on the Mongolian side and about three hours on the Chinese side; it's on the Chinese side where the bogies are changed. The Èrlián station is usually quite lively, even at night. Once your passport is returned, catch some fresh air and explore the station and surroundings where you can change money or get something to eat. If you do get off, you will not have a chance to get back on the train for about two hours while the bogies are changed.

Alternative Routes to/from Běijīng

In the week leading up to Naadam, with thousands of visitors heading to Mongolia, it's practically impossible to score last-minute reservations on the direct trains and flights to Ulaanbaatar. After Naadam there is a reverse migration and it can be difficult to get tickets out of the country. If you haven't booked well in advance, all is not lost as there are alternatives.

Train tickets are often available on the twice-weekly service between Ulaanbaatar and Hohhot (China). For Běijīng, buy a ticket as far as the main junction at Jíníng (kupe T85,730), where you can connect with a nightly train to Běijīng (hard sleeper Y160). To be sure of getting a ticket for this connection contact **CC Inter Tour Company** (☎245 380, 9665 8367) on the ground level of UB's International Railway Ticketing Office (see p282), which can make the arrangements. It charges the tögrög equivalent of Y230 for the same hard-sleeper ticket from Jíníng to Běijīng; you'll be met at Jíníng by its local agent, who will have your ticket.

Another option is to take local transport to the border (Zamyn-Üüd on the Mongolian side and Èrlián on the Chinese side), cross the border, then continue by local bus or train to your destination.

If you're headed south, the daily Ulaanbaatar to Zamyn-Üüd train arrives in the early morning and there is a scramble to get into a 4WD (T8000) to cross the border. Once you reach Èrlián you can quickly move on by bus. (There are only a handful of trains each week and most leave late at night.) There is one morning bus to Dàtóng (Y90, five hours), three afternoon buses to Běijīng (Y180, 10 hours) and five buses to Hohhot (Y88, six hours), the first at 8am.

For those headed north, there are two daily buses to Zamyn-Üüd (Y40) at 1.30pm and 3pm. Some travellers have tried taking a local taxi to the border and then changing to a Mongolian 4WD for a ride across the border. This almost never works because all the 4WDs heading to the border are full to capacity. Most people that tried this ended up taking the same taxi back to the city (and paying for the ride) to look for a cross-border 4WD. Cross-border 4WDs and vans load up with cargo and then wait for passengers in different parts of town, charging around Y50. Some 4WDs will trawl for passengers at the bus station, but if there no vehicles here you'll need to ask for the nearest pick-up spot. Taxi drivers in Èrlián are notorious for overcharging foreigners, so always agree on a price beforehand, or better yet, use the meter.

Once you reach Zamyn-Üüd you'll have to wait for the 5.30pm train to Ulaanbaatar. Three times a week there is also an evening train. Tickets for Ulaanbaatar usually sell out so it's best to get over the border early in the morning to get in line. If you're in a hurry (and don't mind spending more for your transport), its usually possible to buy a ticket at the station in Èrlián for Ulaanbaatar-bound trains; prices are Y537/687/792 for hard sleeper/soft sleeper/deluxe.

Whichever way you're travelling, you have to cross the border in a vehicle. The border is open daily from 8.30am to 5.30pm.

past decade has seen a revitalisation of the city, with a restored old quarter and spruced up public spaces. Besides marvelling at the facelift under way, the main reason to stop here is to visit the magnificent Yungang Caves, on the outskirts of the city.

Dàtóng has long been recognised as important regional centre. It first rose to greatness as the capital of Tuoba, a federation of Turkic-speaking nomads who united northern China (AD 386–534), converted to Buddhism and, like most other invaders, were eventually assimilated into Chinese culture. Tuoba's outstanding legacy is the Yungang Caves and sublime 5th-century Buddhist carvings.

◉ Sights

The city centre is where you'll find Dàtóng's few remaining *hútòng* (narrow alleys) and the city's old core. The alleys are concentrated on either side of Huayan Jie, just south of Golou Xijie. Take bus 4 (Y1) from the train station to reach downtown, from where most sights are within walking distance.

Nine Dragon Screen   MONUMENT
(九龙壁; Jiǔlóng Bì; admission Y10; ⊙8am-6pm) Using the Bell Tower as a reference point, walk 300m northeast to this stunning Ming-era screen, erected in 1392. The multicoloured wall of coiling dragons is 45.5m long, 8m high and 2m thick, making it the largest glazed-tile wall in China.

Huáyán Temple   TEMPLE
(华严寺; Huáyán Sì; ⊙8am-6pm summer, to 5.30pm winter) About 600m west of the Nine Dragon Screen is this sprawling complex, erected during the Liao dynasty (AD 907–1125). The main hall of the upper temple (admission Y20) is one of the largest Buddhist halls in China, with Ming-era statues and Qing murals. The rear hall of the lower temple (admission Y20) is the oldest building in Dàtóng (1038) and contains some remarkable Liao-dynasty wooden sculptures.

Yungang Caves   HISTORIC SITE
(云冈石窟; Yúngāng Shíkū; admission Y10; ⊙8am-6pm) The main reason to stop in Dàtóng is the opportunity to visit this spectacular 5th-century trove of Buddhist art, which contains some 51,000 ancient statues. Carved by the Turkic-speaking Tuoba, the caves draw their designs from the Indian, Persian and even Greek influences that swept along the Silk Road. Work began in AD 460, continuing for 60 years before all 252 caves had been completed, making this the oldest collection of Buddhist carvings in China. The largest Buddha statue is located in Cave 5, a 17m-high seated effigy of Sakyamuni with a gilded face. The caves are just 16km west of Dàtóng, but road construction and traffic can slow progress to a crawl. From Dàtóng train station take bus 3-2 (Y2.50, 50 minutes, from 6am to 6pm).

Dàtóng

Dàtóng

◉ **Sights**

◉ **Sleeping**

THE GOBI DESERT

The world's northernmost desert straddles the border between Mongolia and China, an immense, barren plateau the size of Western Europe. The Mongolians say that there are 33 different types of Gobi, but only about 2% of it is *Lawrence of Arabia*–style sand dunes. Most of the land is dry gravel plains, an occasional mountain range, and some sandstone cliffs.

The harsh climate sees the temperature shift from minus 30°C in winter to above 40°C in summer. Still, some hardy nomads manage to eke out an existence here, raising camels, goats and other livestock. They have recently been joined by an army of entrepreneurs, prospectors, geologists and others seeking to cash in on Mongolia's booming mining sector, based largely in the south Gobi.

The Gobi was brought into the consciousness of the Western world thanks largely to the explorations of Roy Chapman, the head of New York's Museum of Natural History. In the 1920s Andrews made five trips into the Gobi (with both camels and Dodge trucks sent across the Pacific), where he collected an enormous amount of dinosaur skeletons, fossils and dinosaur eggs.

Contrary to popular belief, the Gobi is home to a significant amount of wildlife, including *khavtgai* (wild camels), *hulan* (wild asses), *zeer* (gazelles), *argal* (argali sheep), *yangir* (ibex), *irbis* (snow leopards) and *mazaalai* (Gobi bears).

In the Gobi the locals have a lot of time on their hands, and can spin yarns about other legendary beasts of the desert, including the *allegorhoi horhoi* ('death worm'), which sprays poisonous venom from its mouth and discharges a powerful electric shock from its tail. Another Gobi resident is the Almas, a sort of Bigfoot or Yeti that locals describe as a 'marmot-eating half-ape.' Both creatures have inspired National Geographic–style search expeditions in recent years. So far both have remained elusive.

🛏 Sleeping

Tóngtiě Bīnguǎn HOTEL $$
(同铁宾馆; ☑713 0768; 15 Zhanbei Jie; 站北街15号; s/d/ste Y280/280/398, discounts of 30%; 🆒) Offers excellent, spacious and modern rooms with traditional furnishings and elegant touches. Rooms are clean and well maintained. It is located about 500m north of the train station.

Fēitiān Bīnguǎn HOTEL $
(飞天宾馆; ☑281 5117; 1 Zhanqian Jie; 站前街1号; dm/tw/tr Y35/160/280, discounts of 30%; 🆒) Across the street from the train station, this old favourite is a comfortable budget choice with remodelled rooms.

❶ Information

Bank of China (Zhōngguó Yínháng; Xiao Nanjie) Has an ATM; from the train station walk straight ahead for 250m.

China International Travel Service (CITS; 中国国际旅行社; Zhōngguó Guójì Lǚxíngshè; ☑510 1111, 13934758077; Tàijiā Hotel) Helpful tourist-information branch in the Tàijiā Hotel, just north of the train station.

Internet cafe (网吧; wǎngbā; Xinjian Beilu; per hr Y2; ☺24hr) West of Fēitiān hotel.

❶ Getting There & Away

There are frequent services between Dàtóng and Běijīng (Y105 to Y159, six to 7½ hours), but sleeper cars tend to sell out fast so you still need to book ahead. If you're continuing on to Mongolia your options are the K3 or K23 (running three days a week in summer), which can be purchased at the train station in Dàtóng. It's best if you can buy this ticket ahead of time at the CITS office in Běijīng (p319), so that you can be assured of a ticket. If tickets are unavailable in Dàtóng, take a daily bus to Èrlián, cross the border and continue by rail to Ulaanbaatar.

The Trans-Manchurian Route

Includes »

Route Info

» Distance: 2790km

» Duration: Two days, eight hours

» Time zones: Chita: Moscow +6; Hā'ěrbīn and Běijīng: Moscow +4

Best Places to Stay & Eat

» Fēngzéyuán Lǚdiàn guesthouse (p295)

» Modern Hotel (p299)

» Zhōngdà Dàjiǔdiàn hotel (p299)

» Kazy International Youth Hostel (p299)

» Cafe Russia 1914 (p299)

» Barguuzin restaurant (p295)

Why Go?

For connoisseurs of obscure rail routes, the Trans-Manchurian Railway ranks high on the wish list. It's not on the main line to Vladivostok, nor does it take the 'tourist route' via Mongolia; rather, the weekly *Vostok* (19/20) chugs through China's rust belt, where foreign faces are few and far between. From Chita the railway heads toward the Chinese border at Mǎnzhōulǐ, sweeps through the grasslands of Inner Mongolia and passes through Hā'ěrbīn (Harbin) before carrying on towards the megalopolis that is Běijīng. The highlight is fascinating Hā'ěrbīn, where elements of turn-of-the-century Russia still poke through the surface of a thoroughly modern Chinese city. Bullet trains speed south from Hā'ěrbīn to Běijīng, but there's plenty to see along the way. Jumping-off points include Chángchūn, one-time capital of Japanese-occupied Manchukuo; Shěnyáng, with well-preserved relics of the Manchu era; and Shānhǎiguān, where the Great Wall meets the sea.

When to Go

Hā'ěrbīn

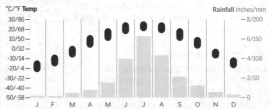

Jan Hā'ěrbīn hosts the dazzling Ice & Snow Festival.

Apr & May Avoid the summer crush of tourists and the hot weather by visiting in the shoulder season.

Sep & Oct Another good time to visit, after peak summer season and before the cold sets in.

The Route

In Russia, the kilometre markers show the distance from Moscow. Once in China, they show the distance to Hā'ĕrbīn (Harbin); south of Hā'ĕrbīn, they show the distance to Bĕijīng.

Chita to Zabaikalsk

6199KM FROM MOSCOW There's a 20-minute stop at **Chita** (p223), where you can stagger off the train and forage for snacks at the small shops near the platform.

6293KM The next major stop is **Karymskaya**, from where it's 12km down the line to Tarskaya, the official start of the Trans-Manchurian route; here the train crosses the Ingoda River and heads southeast.

6444KM There's a short stop at **Olovyannaya**, then the train crosses the Onon River, a tributary of the Ingoda. This area is said to be the birthplace of Chinggis (Genghis) Khaan.

6543KM The train makes another 10-minute stop at **Borzya**. A little-known spur line heads south from here to Mongolia; it was built to move military equipment into eastern Mongolia during the Japanese invasion of 1939.

6666KM The bogies are changed in the Russian border town of **Zabaikalsk** before the train can travel into China. Passably edible meals are available at a cafe across from the station (take the bridge over the tracks and turn left). An ATM inside the station dispenses roubles.

Mănzhōulĭ to Hā'ĕrbīn

935KM (TO HĀ'ĔRBĪN) Chinese border town **Mănzhōulĭ** (p294), established in 1901 as a stop for the train, is booming thanks to cross-border trade.

749KM Next along the line is **Hăilāĕr**, the northernmost major town in Inner Mongolia, where the train stops for about 10 minutes. Should you choose to linger longer, a great option is to go to the **Jinzanghan Grassland** (金帐汗草原), just 40km north of Hăilāĕr, where you can eat mutton stew, sleep in a yurt (per person Y80) and ride horses (per hour Y150). There's also a **grasslands ger camp** (☎133 2700 0919). A taxi here from Hăilāĕr is Y120 return.

650-560KM The train enters the Greater Hinggan Mountains. Some trains make stops at towns such as **Mianduhe** (634km), **Yilick Ede** (574km) and **Xinganling** (564km). From here the train descends on the eastern side of the range.

539KM Shortly after the 15-minute halt at **Boketu**, the train leaves Inner Mongolia and enters the province of Hēilóngjiāng, meaning Black Dragon River. Known in Russian as the Amur River, Hēilóngjiāng's namesake river marks the border with Russia in northeastern China. At this point you can sense a changing climatic and

Chita to Bĕijīng

West to Moscow

6199km	**Chita**
	5hr
6444km	**Olovyannaya**
	2hr
6543km	**Borzya**
	2hr, 30min
RUSSIA 6666km	**Zabaikalsk**
CHINA	
935km to Hā'ĕrbīn	**Mănzhōulĭ**
	2hr, 15min
749km	**Hăilāĕr**
	1hr, 30min
634km	**Mianduhe**
	1hr
564km	**Xinganling**
	30min
539km	**Boketu**
	3hr, 30min
270km	**Angangxi**
	40min
159km	**Dàqìng**
	40min
0km, 1388km to Bĕijīng	**Hā'ĕrbīn**
	5hr
1146km	**Chángchūn**
	3hr, 25min
841km	**Shĕnyáng**
	2hr, 30min
599km	**Jĭnzhōu**
	2hr
415km	**Shānhăiguān**
	3hr, 35min
133km	**Tiānjīn**
	2hr
0km	**BĔIJĪNG**

To Vladivostok (Trans-Siberian)

THE TRANS-MANCHURIAN ROUTE

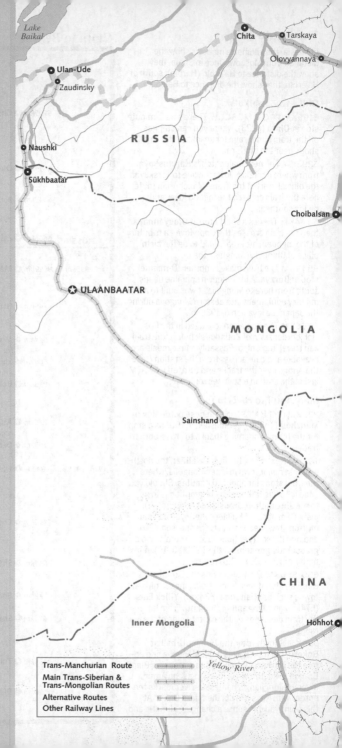

Trans-Manchurian Route Highlights

1 Hanging out with Russian traders in the prosperous border town of **Mǎnzhōulǐ** (p294)

2 Experiencing the unique fusion of historic Russia and modern-day China on the cobblestone streets of Hā'ěrbīn's **Dàolǐqū district** (p296)

3 Viewing some majestic felines at the **Siberian Tiger Park** (p297), just outside Hā'ěrbīn

4 Delving into Hā'ěrbīn's unique Semitic past at **Hā'ěrbīn New Synagogue** (p296), which recounts the experience of 20,000 Jews on Chinese soil

5 Braving the cold to see the spectacular ice sculptures carved at Hā'ěrbīn's legendary **Ice & Snow Festival** (p298)

6 Going on the trail of Puyi, the last emperor of China, at the **Imperial Palace of the Manchu State** (p300) in Chángchūn

7 Following the **Great Wall** (p300) to where it meets the sea at the tourist town of Shānhǎiguān

TRANS-MANCHURIAN ROUTE PLANNER

The following is a suggested itinerary for covering the main sights along the Trans-Manchurian route in this chapter:

Day 1: Leave Chita; overnight train to Zabaikalsk (10 hours); cross border, explore Mǎnzhōulǐ

Day 2: Cross border to Mǎnzhōulǐ, overnight train to Hā'ěrbīn

Day 3: Explore Hā'ěrbīn and overnight

Day 4: See more of Hā'ěrbīn, then train to Chángchūn

Day 5: Explore Chángchūn, then train to Shěnyáng

Day 6: Tour Shěnyáng, then continue to Shānhǎiguān

Day 7: Enjoy Shānhǎiguān, then travel to Běijīng

topographic shift as you leave the steppes behind and enter the steamy Manchurian lowlands.

159KM The train makes a brief stop in **Dàqìng** at the centre of a large oilfield; look out for the 'nodding donkeys' pumping crude oil out of the ground.

1388KM (TO BĚIJĪNG) The final stretch before Hā'ěrbīn, the capital of Hēilóngjiāng province, offers excellent views, especially as you cross the 1km-long bridge over the Songhua river.

Hā'ěrbīn to Běijīng

1146KM (TO BĚIJĪNG) The train stops for 10 minutes in the industrial city of **Chángchūn** (p300), capital of Jílín province.

841KM Heading south, the train plies China's blighted rust belt towards **Shěnyáng** (841km), where the *Vostok* halts for 15 minutes. This industrial city of 3.5 million people was a Mongol trading centre from the 11th century, becoming the capital of the Manchu empire in the 17th century. The founder of the Qing dynasty, Huang Taiji, is buried here in an impressive tomb. Another reason to stop is a chance to visit Shěnyáng's Imperial Palace, which resembles a small-scale Forbidden City.

841-500KM The outskirts of Shěnyáng continue for what seems like an eternity and for a while you'll be travelling over the morass on an elevated train track. At around the 545km marker the train passes through an area of rice paddies and natural wetlands. Then at 528km there are some picturesque low mountains flanked by cornfields and small villages. The *Vostok* passes

through this area at night, but if you are on a local day train you can watch the scenery pass by and grab some lunch. Cabin attendants push food carts up and down the aisles; a box lunch includes rice, chopped meat and cold vegies.

415KM The train passes the Great Wall about 4km north of **Shānhǎiguān**, where the Wall meets the sea. The small town has been tarted up for Běijīng day-trippers and there are a number of sights worth visiting should you decide to alight.

133KM The last stop before Běijīng is **Tiānjīn**, a sprawling metropolis of 9.6 million people. During the 19th century this port city attracted the interest of almost every European nation with a ship to put to sea. The evidence is that Tiānjīn is a living museum of early-20th-century European architecture. Note that many local trains will bypass Tiānjīn and travel direct between Běijīng and Shānhǎiguān.

0KM Blink into the glaring light of **Běijīng** as the masses pour off the train and into the chaotic Chinese capital.

Mǎnzhōulǐ 满洲里

☑0470 / POP 55,400 / ◷MOSCOW +5HR

This laissez-faire border city, where the Trans-Siberian Railway crosses from China to Russia, is a pastel-painted boomtown of shops, hotels and restaurants catering to the Russian market. Unless you look Asian, expect shopkeepers to greet you in Russian.

Getting around is easy; it's a 10-minute walk from the train station to the town centre. Turn right immediately as you exit the station, then right again to cross the footbridge over the train tracks. On the other side of the footbridge is a statue of Zhou Enlai and the start of Zhongsu Lu, which you can walk along to reach the International Hotel and the town centre. From Běifāng Guǎngchǎng (北方广场; North Sq) it's 2km to the bus station or 10km to the border.

Mǎnzhōulǐ is pleasantly walkable and packed with every variety of shop, restaurant and hotel; coming over from dreary Zabaikalsk it feels like another world. The town has modernised at lightning speed, but a few **Russian-built log houses** still line Yidao Jie (and some have been converted to hotels). On the pedestrianised streets look out for the odd collection of **bronze statues**, including hip-hop artists and sauntering tourists.

Halfway between the city and the Russian border is a bizarre outdoor **park** filled with giant Russian *matryoshka* dolls, many with portraits of famous historical figures from Albert Einstein to Michael Jordan. The largest doll is a five-storey restaurant and souvenir shop. Next to the park is a **Russian Art Museum** (admission Y50; ⏱8.30am-9pm) with some 19th- and 20th-century landscape paintings and sculptures.

🛏 Sleeping & Eating

There must be a hundred hotels and guesthouses in Mǎnzhōulǐ, all within walking distance of each other. Signs are in Russian – гостиница (*gostinitsa*) is Russian for 'hotel'. Likewise, there are plenty of restaurants, so just wander around and see what takes your fancy.

TOP CHOICE / Fēngzéyuán Lǔdiàn GUESTHOUSE $ (丰泽源旅馆; ☎225 4099, 139 4709 3443; Yidao Jie; 一道街; d Y100; @) Located inside a restored Russian log cabin (painted yellow and green), this friendly guesthouse has clean rooms and modern bathrooms. As you come off the pedestrian bridge from the train station it's the first building in front of you, near the statue of Zhou Enlai.

Wéi duōlìyà Jiǔdiàn HOTEL $$ (维多利亚酒店; ☎391 9999; 116 Erdao Jie; 二道街116号; d Y480; 🖥) The Victoria Hotel is a 28-storey tower with an impressive glass elevator, sweeping views of the city and modern rooms. Outside the peak summer months you might be able to bargain the price down to Y200. It's opposite the Guójì Fàndiàn (International Hotel).

Barguuzin MONGOLIAN, RUSSIAN $ (巴图敖其尔; ☎622 0121; cnr Erdao Jie & Zhongsu Lu; dishes Y10-30; ⏱6.30am-midnight) Run by Buriat Mongols from Hǎilǎěr, this place is located about 50m west of the Guójì Fàndiàn on Zhongsu Lu.

ℹ Information

Bank of China (中国银行; Zhōngguó Yínháng; Yidao Jie) Near the junction with Haiguan Lu.
China International Travel Service (CITS; 中国国际旅行社; Zhōngguó Guójì Lǚxíngshè; ☎624 7759; 38 Erdao Jie; ⏱8.30am-noon & 2.30-5pm Mon-Fri) This CITS office attached to the Kǒu Àn Dàjiǔdiàn (Port Hotel) sells train tickets for Chita. The CITS office in the Guójì Fàndiàn (International Hotel) is pretty unhelpful.
Internet cafe (网吧; wǎngbā; Yidao Jie; per hr Y3; ⏱24hr) About 50m east of the Jǐxiáng

Lǚguǎn. You can use wi-fi in the lobby of the Guójì Fàndiàn.

ℹ Getting There & Around

There are frequent trains to Hǎilǎěr (Y29, three to 3½ hours) and Hā'ěrbīn (hard sleeper Y222, 13 hours). Note that some trains to Hā'ěrbīn won't have soft sleeper carriages.

Taxis charge Y10 from the station to the centre or the bus station. Otherwise, most trips around town are Y7. The bus station is 2km out of town on the road to the border. Buses leave all day for Hǎilǎěr (Y41, 3½ hours).

For details about crossing into Russia, see p298.

Hā'ěrbīn 哈尔滨

🚂0451 / POP 3.29 MILLION / ⏱MOSCOW +5HR
Hā'ěrbīn (Harbin) feels quite unlike the cookie-cutter cities found all over China. Zhongyang Dajie, the main drag of the historic Dàolǐqū district, is pleasantly car-free and sports architecture that wouldn't look out of place in Russian Sīběria.

The European-style streets in the old town owe their influence to Hā'ěrbīn's days as a sort of Russian enclave in Manchuria during the construction of the Chinese Eastern Railway line (1897–1901), when thousands of Russians were sent here to work on the railroads.

Hā'ěrbīn's relaxed feel is most evident along its riverfront promenade, where locals stroll in summer or wade knee-deep into the Songhua River. Despite its quirky Russian architecture, Hā'ěrbīn is even more famous for its bitterly cold winters and the legendary Ice & Snow Festival. A Siberian-tiger sanctuary and the grim remains of a WWII germ-warfare base are other places of interest.

The main train station is in the centre of Hā'ěrbīn, surrounded by a cluster of hotels. The Dàolǐqū area, with a few hotels and many of the city's attractions, is about 2km northwest of the train station. At the northern end of Zhongyang Dajie, Stalin Park is on the river's shores. Across the river lies Sun Island Park and the Siberian Tiger Park.

History

At the end of the 19th century, Hā'ěrbīn was a quiet village. However, when the Russians negotiated the contract to construct the Chinese Eastern Railway line through Manchuria, Hā'ěrbīn's role was changed forever. Although the Japanese gained control of the new railway because of Russia's defeat in

Hā'ěrbīn

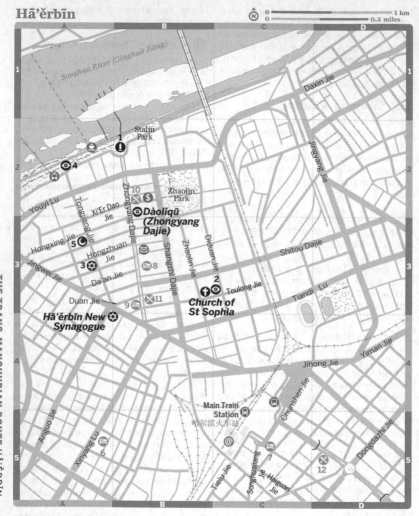

THE TRANS-MANCHURIAN ROUTE HĀ'ĚRBĪN

the Russo-Japanese War, Russian refugees flocked to Hā'ěrbīn in 1917, fleeing the Bolsheviks. The Russians continued to influence the town's development until the end of WWII, when the region was finally handed over to the Kuomintang (China's Nationalist Party).

⊙ Sights

Church of St Sophia
CHURCH

(圣索非亚教堂; Shèng Suǒfēiyà Jiàotáng; cnr Zhaolin Jie & Toulong Jie; admission Y20; ⊙8.30am-5.30pm) Most of Hā'ěrbīn's Orthodox churches were ransacked during the Cultural Revolution and have since fallen into disrepair. But the majestic Church of St Sophia, built by the Russians in 1907 in the Dàolǐqū district, has been beautifully restored. It now houses the **Hā'ěrbīn Architecture Arts Centre**, which displays black-and-white photographs of the city from the early 1900s, as well as some icons from the Russian era.

Hā'ěrbīn New Synagogue
MUSEUM

(哈尔滨犹太新会堂; Hā'ěrbīn Yóutài Xīnhuìtáng; 162 Jingwei Jie; admission Y25; ⊙8.30am-5pm) In the 1920s, Hā'ěrbīn was home to some 20,000 Jews, the largest Jewish community in the Far East at the time (the vast majority

Hā'ěrbīn

of its members had emigrated from Russia). Built in 1921, and restored and converted to a museum in 2004, the synagogue houses art galleries, photos and exhibits that tell the story of the history and cultural life of Hā'ěrbīn's Jews.

Dàolíqū NEIGHBOURHOOD
The cobblestone street of Zhongyang Dajie is the most obvious legacy of Russia's involvement in Hā'ěrbīn. Now a pedestrian-only zone, this street and those nearby (collectively known as Dàolíqū) are lined with buildings that date back to the early 20th century.

Siberian Tiger Park ANIMAL PARK
(东北虎林园; Dōngběi Hǔ Línyuán; www.dongbeihu.net.cn, in Chinese; 88 Songbei Jie; admission Y65; ⊙8am-4.30pm, last tour 4pm) The mission of the Siberian Tiger Park is to study, breed, release and ultimately save the Manchurian (aka Siberian) tiger from extinction (see p374).

The park houses some 400 of these magnificent animals, as well as a pride of African lions, a leopard, a panther and a pair of rare white tigers. Visitors are driven around safari-like through the fenced-off fields, and the minibus drivers encourage passengers to buy live animals (chickens, ducks and even cows!) to throw to the tigers. So if you're not into the animal-kingdom version of *Gladiator*, maybe give this one a miss.

The park is located roughly 15km north of the city. From Zhongyang Dajie, walk down Hongzhuan Jie for five minutes to Gaoyi Jie and catch bus 67 to the Gonglu Da Qiao stop just before the bridge over the river. Change to bus 54, which drops you at the entrance to the park (look for the statue of a tiger). Alternatively, a taxi from the city centre is about Y40 one way.

Stalin Park PARK
(斯大林公园; Sīdàlín Gōngyuán) This park, a pleasant tree-lined promenade with statues, playgrounds and a cafe in a brightly painted historic **Russian wooden chalet**, is strung along the 42km embankment built to curb the unruly Songhua River. At the end of Zhongyang Dajie, the **Flood Control Monument** (防洪胜利纪念塔), built in 1958, commemorates the thousands who died in the floods up to that time.

A resort feel holds sway in summer, with ice-cream stands, photo booths and boating trips (Y30) along the river and across to **Sun Island Park** (太阳岛公园; Tàiyángdǎo Gōngyuán), which features landscaped gardens, forested areas and water parks. Buy ferry tickets for Y10 from the dock directly north of the Flood Control Monument. You can also take a **cable car** (览车; 1 way/return Y50/100) from the foot of Tongjiang Jie, one block west.

FREE **Germ Warfare Base – 731 Division** MUSEUM
(侵华日军第731部队遗址; Qīnhuá Rìjūn Dì 731 Bùduì Yízhǐ; Xinjiang Dajie; ⊙9am-11am & 1-3.30pm, last entry 4pm) The extreme horrors of war are on display at this museum, 20km south of the city.

During 1939 the Japanese army set up this top-secret research centre, where Japanese medical experts experimented on prisoners of war. More than 4000 people were infected with bubonic plague, injected with syphilis or roasted alive in furnaces. When the Soviets took Hā'ěrbīn in 1945, the Japanese blew the place up, but a tenacious Japanese journalist dug up the story in the 1980s. The main building of the base is now a museum, with photos and sculptures and exhibits of

CROSSING THE RUSSIA–CHINA BORDER

Rail

Expect to spend at least half a day crossing from Zabaikalsk to Mǎnzhōulǐ and vice versa, with time eaten up by customs procedures on the Russian side, and the need to change the bogies on the train to match the narrower gauge used in China. This will likely be the case for travellers on the *Vostok* (19/20) or the Mǎnzhōulǐ–Chita train (Friday and Sunday from Mǎnzhōulǐ, Thursday and Saturday from Chita). If you arrive in Zabaikalsk on the train from Irkutsk and it's Friday or Sunday morning, it may be possible to buy a ticket (R80) for the Chita–Mǎnzhōulǐ train. However, this train is usually full by the time it gets to Zabaikalsk so scoring a ticket at the station may be difficult.

In Mǎnzhōulǐ the international terminal is the yellow building next to the main station. This is where international travellers heading to Russia go through customs and passport control. However, international tickets are not sold here: you'll need to go to the China International Travel Service (CITS) branch at the Port Hotel. Services to Chita leave on Monday at 7pm, Friday at 2pm and Sunday at 2pm; *platskart* (3rd-class) tickets may only be available (Y608).

There are daily overnight trains connecting Zabaikalsk and Chita (*platskart/kupe* R1200/2221, 12 hours); if these are full you can also take a train to Borzya and connect with a slower train to Zabaikalsk from there. Hǎ'ěrbīn and Mǎnzhōulǐ are also connected by four overnight trains (hard/soft sleeper Y202/222, 13 hours), departing between 6pm and 9pm.

The train ride between Zabaikalsk and Mǎnzhōulǐ takes about 10 minutes. There's a sort of rivalry at the border: each country has built an enormous arch over the railway line as if they were trying to outdo each other. You'll need to be quick with your camera as the train does not linger on the border for long.

Bus

There are frequent buses travelling between the Zabaikalsk bus station and the Mǎnzhōulǐ bus station. From Zabaikalsk to China it costs R350 and from Mǎnzhōulǐ to Russia it's Y72. The first buses leave at 7.50am. There's also one daily bus from Mǎnzhōulǐ to Chita (Y330), departing at 6.40pm.

The crossing in either direction is slow, taking up to five hours. Going from China to Russia usually takes longer because the Russian border guards spend a lot of time checking travellers for contraband. Private vehicles driven by Russians tend to get through faster, so one option is to negotiate a ride with a Russian driver either in town or at the border.

At the Chinese border post you'll have to pay Y10 departure tax: do this at the door left of the entrance and then give the receipt to the immigration officials as they stamp you out of the country.

There's an exchange office in the Russian customs hall where your immigration card will be registered.

the equipment used by the Japanese. There are extensive English captions.

The base is a one-hour trip on bus 343 (Y2) from the train station (catch it from a stop near the post office on Tielu Jie). Get off at the stop called Xinjiang Dajie and walk back for about five minutes. The base is on the left-hand side of the road.

Huangshan Jewish Cemetery CEMETERY
(黄山犹太墓地; Huángshān Yóutài Mùdì) In the far eastern suburbs of Hǎ'ěrbīn is the largest Jewish cemetery in the Far East. There are over 600 graves here, all very well maintained. A taxi (Y50) takes around 45 minutes.

Old Main Synagogue NOTABLE BUILDING
(82 Tongjiang Jie) The former main synagogue has now been converted to a guesthouse but still has some Star of David symbols in its windows.

Turkish Mosque NOTABLE BUILDING
(Tongjiang Jie) Built in 1906, the mosque, with its distinctive minarets, is no longer operating and is closed to visitors.

✳ Festivals & Events

Ice & Snow Festival WINTER FESTIVAL
(Bīngxuě Jié; ✆8625 0068; admission to main area Y200, other prices vary; ◷8am-10pm) Hǎ'ěrbīn's

peak tourist season is during this festival, held in Zhaolin Park and along the Songhua River, where elaborate ice sculptures sparkle in the frigid air. Past sculptures have included a miniature Great Wall of China and scaled-down Forbidden City. At night the sculptures are illuminated with coloured lights, turning the area into a fantasy world. Figure-skating shows, hockey tournaments and other events round out the calendar. Officially, the festival runs from 5 January to 15 February, although it frequently starts a week earlier and glistens into March.

Sleeping

During the Ice & Snow Festival, prices are at least 20% higher than those listed here. The most convenient places to stay are along Zhongyang Dajie in Dàolǐqū or in one of the many hotels that surround the train station.

TOP CHOICE Zhōngdà Dàjiǔdiàn HOTEL $$
(中大大酒店; ✆8463 8888; 32-40 Zhongyang Dajie; 中央大街32-40号; d & tw Y198-298; ✳@) With a prime location on Zhongyang Dajie and comfortable rooms flooded with light, this heritage hotel is your best midrange choice in Hā'ěrbīn. All rooms include free broadband and a Chinese-style breakfast.

Lóngyùn Hotel HOTEL $$
(龙运宾馆; Lóngyùn Bīnguǎn; ✆8283 0102; Huochezhan Zhanqian Guangchang; 火车站站前广场; s with shared bathroom Y158, d & tw Y308-328; ✳) This tower is next to the bus station (in the same building as the KFC), and opposite the train station. It's a busy place, but fairly clean and comfortable inside, making this a convenient escape from the hectic train-station area.

Modern Hotel HOTEL $$$
(马达尔宾馆; Mǎdié'er Bīnguǎn; ✆8488 4199; http://hotel.hrbmodern.com; 89 Zhongyang Dajie, 中央大街89号; s/d from Y680/980; ✳@✉) This hotel defies its name, as it's housed in a historic Dàolǐqū building dating from 1906. Rooms are comfortable, rates include a buffet breakfast and the location is unbeatable. The entrance is around the back. Discounts of up to 50% are often available.

Kazy International Youth Hostel HOSTEL $
(卡兹国际青年旅舍; Kǎzī Guójì Qīngnián Lǚshè; ✆8765 4211; www.snowtour.cn; dm/s/d shared bathroom Y40/60/100, d with bathroom Y120; @✆) This hostel has taken over the lower floors of the old Main Synagogue. Rooms are well maintained but can feel a little cramped when the place is busy. The unique double rooms still have Star of David frame windows. There is no air-con, so it gets very stuffy in summer, but there are nice bonuses like laundry and free wi-fi.

Harbin Northern International Hostel HOSTEL $
(哈尔滨北方国际青年旅舍; Hā'ěrbīn Běifāng Guójì Qīngnián Lǚshè; ✆8451 0081; Dàolǐ Qū 65 Dìjié Jiē, 道里区地节街65号; dm Y45-55; @✆) Popular with Chinese travellers, this place has a spacious lounge and fan-cooled rooms with either four or six bunks. YHA members get a slight discount. It's not located near any main landmarks, so it's probably best to take a taxi there the first time.

✗ Eating

Dōngfāng Jiǎozi Wáng DUMPLINGS $
(东方饺子王; Kingdom of Eastern Dumplings; 51 Zhongyang Dajie; dumpling plate Y2-20; ◷10.30am-9.30pm; ◻) Serves royal helpings of *jiǎozi* (dumplings) with a large choice of fillings; try the pork with coriander or the vegie with egg. A second location is next to the Overseas Chinese Hotel.

Bì Fēng Táng CHINESE $
(避风塘; 185 Zhongyang Dajie; dishes Y9-49; ◷7am-2am) Bright and lively Chinese place that serves delicate, southern-style dumplings, as well as rice noodles, drunken chicken and great desserts. Good for late-night munchies.

Cafe Russia 1914 RUSSIAN $
(露西亚咖啡西餐厅; Lùxīyà kāfēi Xīcān Tīng; ✆8456 3207; 57 Xitoudao Jie; dishes Y10-80, coffees Y18-25, teas Y8-15; ◷9am-midnight) Housed in a historic building (from 1914), this quaint restaurant serves faux-Russian food and drink.

❶ Information

Head to **Lonely Planet** (www.lonelyplanet.com/china) for planning advice, author recommendations, traveller reviews and insider tips.

There are many banks and ATMs along Zhongyang Dajie in the Dàolǐqū district. The train station has a left-luggage room (Y30 per day) near the entrance.

Harbin Modern Travel Company (✆8488 4433; www.hrbmodern.com; 89 Zhongyang Dajie) This office at the Modern Hotel can arrange ski trips to Yabuli.

Internet bar (网吧; wǎngbā; Tielu Jie; per hr Y6; ◷24hr) West of the train station.

Public Security Bureau (PSB; 公安局; Gōng'ānjú; 26 Duan Jie; ◷8.40am-noon & 1.30-4.30pm Mon-Fri)

❶ Getting There & Away

For Vladivostok, train N23 departs the **main train station** (哈尔滨火车站) on Wednesday and Sunday at 9.26pm and takes 36 hours. A soft-sleeper ticket costs Y908. These tickets are available at the **Harbin Railway International Tourist Agency** (Hā'ěrbīn Tiědào Guójì Lüxíngshè; ☎5366 4450; 7th fl, Kunlun Hotel, 8 Tielu Jie), 100m southwest of the train station. However, it's much faster to take the train as far as Suífēnhé, cross the border and then take a bus to Vladivostok (see p248).

For Blagoveshchensk, take a Hēihé-bound train. K7033 (hard/soft sleeper Y148/220) departs nightly at 10.57pm.

The *Vostok* (19/20) passes once a week in each direction, on Thursday heading to Běijīng and on Sunday to Moscow. If you want to buy a ticket on this train for Russia, go to the **Heilongjiang Travel Service** (☎5367 9485; Harbin Overseas Chinese Hotel, 72 Hongjin Jie). A ticket for a four-bed berth costs Y1654 to Ulan-Ude, Y1824 to Irkutsk and Y3601 to Moscow.

There are frequent connections between Hā'ěrbīn and Běijīng, but services vary widely. The best overnight connection is the very comfortable Z15/16 sleeper service (Y429 soft sleeper only). During the day there are high-speed D-class trains (Y281 seat only) that resemble Japanese bullet trains (they reach 160km per hour). Sleeper tickets sell out days in advance in summer, but it's usually not a problem to get a seat on a D-class train.

The following table presents the costs for trains out of Hā'ěrbīn:

DESTINA-TION	FRE-QUENCY (DAILY)	COST HARD/ SOFT SLEEPER (Y)	DURATION (HR)
Běijīng	13	281/429	8-18
Hēihé	2	157/250	12
Mǎnzhōulǐ	6	134/352	12-16
Suífēnhé	2	157/250	10

❶ Getting Around

For now, the easiest way to get around Hā'ěrbīn is by taxi. Flag fall is Y7. Buses 101 and 103 (Y1) regularly travel between Stalin Park and the train station. A subway is under construction, with the first line expected to open by 2013.

Chángchūn 长春

☎0431 / POP 3.2 MILLION / ⏱MOSCOW +5HR

The Japanese capital of Manchukuo between 1933 and 1945, Chángchūn is today an industrial city and the heart of China's car-manufacturing business. The main reason to stop here is to visit the **Imperial Palace of the Manchu State** (伪满皇宫博物院; Wěimǎn Huánggōng Bówùyuàn; 5 Guangfu Lu; admission Y80; ⏱8.30am-4.20pm, last entry 40min before closing), the former residence of Puyi, the Qing dynasty's final emperor. His story was the basis for the 1987 Bernardo Bertolucci film *The Last Emperor*. There are dozens of rooms to wander through, most of them still with the original furnishings. The site also has an interesting museum that chronicles of the life of Puyi, and a second museum that describes in graphic detail the Japanese occupation of Manchuria. A taxi to the palace from the train station costs Y12.

Shānhǎiguān 山海关

☎0335 / POP 19,500 / ⏱MOSCOW +5HR

The drowsy, walled town of Shānhǎiguān is where the Great Wall snakes out of the hills to greet the sea. The town has recently undergone a massive renovation project, which entailed ripping down all the old buildings, only to replace them with faux-traditional buildings. While the town does have the look and feel of an outdoor theme park, with tour buses almost outnumbering local cars, Shānhǎiguān is an essential stop for travellers wanting to see the unofficial 'start' of the Great Wall.

Old Dragon Head (老龙头; Lǎolóngtou; admission Y50; ⏱7.30am-5.30pm), where the wall begins, is essentially a 1980s reconstruction, the original wall having crumbled away long ago. Buses 25 and 21 come here from Shānhǎiguān's South Gate. While Old Dragon Head makes for a nice photo opportunity, there's no hiking to be done here. If you want to hike, take a taxi 3km north of Shānhǎiguān to Jiǎo Shān (角山; admission Y50; ⏱7.30am-5.30pm), the Wall's first high peak. It's a 20-minute hike to the top or you can take a chairlift for Y20.

Yùlín Shānhǎi Jiǔdiàn (御临山海酒店; ☎505 8811; r Y200; ❇@) is a reliable budget hotel near the train station (walk one block straight ahead, then turn left and walk two blocks).

There are frequent train connections to Běijīng (Y47 to 118), but you'll still need to endure some long queues at the station; try to buy your ticket the night before departure. The station has a left-luggage room (Y5 per bag).

Běijīng

Best Places to Stay

» Red Capital Residence (p313)

» Lusongyuan Hotel (p313)

» Peking International Youth Hostel (p311)

» Beijing Downtown Backpackers Accommodation (p311)

Best Places to Eat

» Xiao Wang's Home Restaurant (p313)

» Quanjude Roast Duck Restaurant (p314)

» Ghost Street (p315)

» Bellagio (p314)

Why Go?

For weary Trans-Siberian travellers, Běijīng (北京) will feel like the figurative pot of gold at the end of the rainbow. The 2008 Olympics were instrumental in transforming the Chinese capital and for the first time since the Mongol invasion, Běijīng feels like an international city, brimming with overseas business, cuisine of every kind, daring modern architecture and a thriving arts scene. Despite its headlong rush into the future, the best of Běijīng lies in its past. Sights such as the Forbidden City, Tiananmen Sq, the Temple of Heaven, the Great Wall and the Summer Palace will keep you busy for days. Duck into the fast disappearing *hútòng* (narrow alleyway) neighbourhoods and discover Běijīng at its most intimate. Come evening, choose from a million or so drinking spots and celebrate the end (or beginning) of your epic cross-continental journey.

When to Go
Běijīng

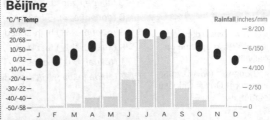

Sep–early Nov The best time weather-wise, with blue skies, pleasant temperatures and fewer tourists.

Apr Temperatures are pleasant and flowers are blooming but be prepared for dust storms.

MEDIA

Pick up the free monthly listings magazines the *Beijinger* (www.thebeijinger.com), *Agenda* (www.agendabeijing.com) and *City Weekend* (www.cityweekend.com.cn) from expat bars and restaurants in the Sānlǐtún and Qianhai Lake areas. *China Daily* is the main English-language newspaper.

Běijīng Basic Costs

» Bus ticket: Y1
» Subway ticket: Y2
» Local SIM card: Y45
» Taxi rate (first 3km): Y10
» Great Wall T-shirt: from Y15
» Bed in a hostel: Y70

Fast Facts

» Telephone code: ☑010
» Population: 15.6 million
» Time zone: Moscow +4

Resources

» Ctrip (www.english.ctrip.com) Hotel and flight bookings.
» Danwei (www.danwei.com) Web magazine on daily life.
» Zhongwen (www.zhongwen.com) Online Chinese dictionary.

Getting Around

To/from the train station Beijing station, one block south of Jianguomenwai Dajie, is 3km southeast of the Forbidden City. To reach the station by subway take the circle line (Line 2) to Beijing Train Station. When leaving the subway, use Exit C to reach the station. From the airport, the best way to reach the station is with airport bus line 1.

To/from the airport Běijīng's Capital Airport is 27km from the centre of town, about 30 minutes to one hour by car depending on traffic. The 30-minute Airport Express (机场快轨; Jīchǎng Kuàiguǐ) runs every 15 minutes, connecting Capital Airport with Line 2 of the underground system at Dongzhimen and connecting with Line 10 at Sanyuanqiao. A taxi from the city centre to the airport will cost around Y85.

CLIMATE & HOLIDAYS

In deciding when to visit, consider the following:

Winter travel has its pros and cons. On the plus side you can get deep discounts on hotel and flights; on the downside it's glacial outside (dipping as low as -20°C) and the northern winds cut like a knife through bean curd.

In summer, temperatures can surge over 35°C and the humidity is intense. Additionally, summer is when hotels typically raise their rates and the Great Wall nearly collapses under the weight of marching tourists.

Air pollution can be very harsh in both summer and winter.

During major holidays, such as May Day (1–3 May), National Day (1–7 October) and the spring festival (late January or February), be prepared for intense crowds at tourist sites, airports and train stations.

Train Categories in China

» C (*chéngjì gāosù;* 城际高速) ultra-high-speed express
» D (*dòngchē;* 动车, *héxiè hào;* 和谐号) high-speed express
» G (*gāotiě;* 高铁) high-speed
» K (*kuàisù;* 快速) fast train
» T (*tèkuài;* 特快) express
» Z (*zhídá tèkuài;* 直达特快) direct express

Běijīng Highlights

1 Romping through the seemingly endless courtyards of the **Forbidden City** (p304)

2 Standing in **Tiananmen Sq** (p304), centre of the Chinese universe and the scene of jubilation and strife since the founding of modern China

3 Hiring a bike to skirt through the dense **hútòng**

(p317), Běijīng's traditional alleyways

4 Ascending the heights of the **Great Wall** (p321) and looking back towards Mongolia

5 Celebrating the end (or beginning) of your Trans-Siberian journey at one of Běijīng's rocking **nightclubs** (p315)

6 Feasting on **Peking duck** (p313) and China's myriad other speciality foods

7 Strolling around the gorgeous grounds of the **Temple of Heaven** (p311)

8 Checking into a courtyard hotel then dining and partying in Běijīng's most famous alley, **Nanluogu Xiang** (p315)

History

Běijīng (Northern Capital) – affectionately called Peking by diplomats, nostalgic journalists and wistful academics – emerged as the preeminent cultural and political force with the 13th-century Mongol occupation of China, when Chinggis (Genghis) Khaan descended on the city. His grandson, Kublai Khaan (c 1216–94), renamed the city Khanbalik (Khan's town). From here, Kublai ruled the largest empire in world history.

Although the capital was moved for a brief period, Emperor Yongle (of the Ming dynasty) reestablished Běijīng as the capital in the 1400s and spent millions of taels of silver to refurbish the city. Yongle is known as the architect of modern Běijīng, building the Forbidden City and the Temple of Heaven, as well as developing the bustling commercial streets outside the inner city. The Qing dynasty expanded the construction of temples, palaces and pagodas.

In January 1949, the People's Liberation Army (PLA) entered the city. On 1 October of that year Mao Zedong proclaimed a 'People's Republic' to an audience of some 500,000 citizens in Tiananmen Sq.

Like the emperors before them, the communists significantly altered the face of Běijīng to suit their own image. Whole city blocks were reduced to rubble to widen major boulevards. From 1950 to 1952, the city's magnificent outer walls were levelled in the interests of traffic circulation. Before the Sino-Soviet split of the 1960s, Russian experts and technicians poured in, leaving their own Stalinesque touches.

The capitalist-style reforms of the past 25 years have transformed Běijīng into a modern city, with skyscrapers, slick shopping malls and freeways cutting right through the city. The 2008 Olympics thrust Běijīng into the limelight and forced it to address some of its major issues, such as the appalling air pollution and heaving traffic. While many problems persist, the city is cleaner and greener than it was before, with some world-class sporting venues to boot.

Maps

English-language maps of Běijīng can be bought at the airport, train station newspaper kiosks, and the Foreign Languages Bookstore (p317). They can also be picked up for free at most big hotels and, for Y8, branches of the Běijīng Tourist Information Center (p318).

◉ Sights

FORBIDDEN CITY 紫禁城

The largest and best-preserved cluster of ancient buildings in China is the **Forbidden City** (Zǐjìn Chéng; Map p306; admission high/low season Y60/40; ◷8.30am-4pm May-Sep, to 3.30pm Oct-Apr; Ⓜ Tiananmen Xi, Tiananmen Dong). It was home to two dynasties of emperors, the Ming and the Qing, who rarely strayed from this pleasure dome, although it was off limits to everyone else (hence, the name).

Renting the self-guided tour (available in several languages) is worth the extra Y40. Tickets and audio-guide rental are available at the Forbidden City's south gate, not to be confused with the Gate of Heavenly Peace (Tiānānmén) facing onto the square of the same name. Continue through Tiānānmén and go northward until you can't proceed without paying. (The booth in the centre of the first plaza sells tickets to climb Tiānānmén, *not* to the Forbidden City.) A second ticket booth is located at the North Gate.

The palace is huge (800 buildings, 9000 rooms) and under constant renovation. The main **ceremonial buildings** lie along the north-south axis in the centre. Despite its vast scale, this area is frequently crowded; you may prefer to explore the **courtyards** and **pavilions** (and mini-museums within them) on either side of the main drag.

TIANANMEN SQUARE & AROUND 天安门广场

As the focal point for the history of communist China, **Tiananmen Square** (Tiānānmén Guǎngchǎng; Map p306; Ⓜ Tiananmen Xi, Tiananmen Dong, Qianmen) is sure to inspire a mix of emotions. This is where Mao's student armies waved his 'Little Red Book' in surges of nationalism and where dissidents faced down tanks in the summer of 1989. Today it's largely the domain of young kite flyers and photographers snapping pictures of Chinese families in from the hinterlands. For Trans-Sib travellers having just crossed the continent, a visit here is a ritual of sorts – it's fascinating to size up Tiananmen against your experience in Moscow's Red Square, thousands of kilometres distant.

If you get up early you can watch the **flag-raising ceremony** at sunrise, performed by a troop of PLA soldiers drilled to march at precisely 108 paces per minute, 75cm per pace. The same ceremony in reverse is performed at sunset.

BĚIJĪNG IN THREE DAYS...

Start your exploration at the city centre, visiting the **Forbidden City** and sights around **Tiananmen Square**. Grab lunch at **Quanjude Roast Duck Restaurant** or **Wangfujing Snack Street**, then jump in a taxi to the **Temple of Heaven** or spend the afternoon exploring the **hútòng** (narrow alleyways) by bicycle, especially around mellow Qianhai Lake. After dinner hit the bars along **Nanluogu Xiang**.

Rise early on day two for a journey to the **Great Wall**, and spend the evening enjoying a performance of **Chinese acrobatics** before rounding off the day wining and dining in Sanlitun.

On day three take an early morning visit to the **Lama Temple** before checking out the ultramodern **National Stadium** and **Water Cube** in north Běijīng, built for the 2008 Olympics. Browse the bric-a-brac shops of **Liulichang** or bargain like mad at the **Sanlitun Yashou Clothing Market**. In the afternoon, make an expedition to the **Summer Palace**. At night, dine at **Ghost Street** or spend the evening enjoying **Běijīng opera** at one of the city's numerous theatres.

Although the square is the symbolic centre of the Chinese universe, what you see today is a modern reconception by Mao to project the enormity of the Communist Party. His giant portrait still hangs over the **Gate of Heavenly Peace** (天安门; Tiānānmén; Map p306; admission Y15, bag storage Y1-6; ☺8.30am-4.30pm) at the northern end of the square, flanked by the slogans 'Long Live the People's Republic of China' (left) and 'Long Live the Unity of the Peoples of the World' (right).

At the square's southern end, **Front Gate** (前门; Qián Mén; Map p306; admission Y20; ☺8.30am-4pm; ⓜQianmen) is a remnant of the wall that guarded the ancient Inner City as early as the 15th century. It actually consists of two gates: the Arrow Tower to the south and the Main Gate to the north.

On the site of the old Outer Palace Gate, the **Monument to the People's Heroes** is a 36m obelisk that bears bas-relief depictions of key revolutionary events. Just behind this monument is **Chairman Mao's Mausoleum** (毛主席纪念堂; Máo Zhǔxí Jìniàntáng; Map p306; admission free, bag storage Y2-10; ☺8am-noon Tue-Sun). Most Chinese continue to respect and revere Mao, who died in 1976, despite the atrocities carried out during his rule (Western historians say the Chairman was responsible for 40 to 70 million peacetime deaths). Expect long queues and only the briefest glimpse of the body as impatient guards shuffle the hoi polloi towards other rooms packed with Mao memorabilia. Bags must be left in a building east of the Mausoleum.

The National People's Congress, China's rubber-stamp legislature, sits on the western side of the square in the monolithic and intimidating **Great Hall of the People** (人民大会堂; Rénmín Dàhuìtáng; Map p306; admission Y30, bag storage Y2-5; ☺9am-3pm, closed when Congress is in session). Further to the west, the bulbous, titanium-and-glass **National Grand Theatre** (国家大剧院; Guójiā Dàjùyuàn; Map p306; www.chncpa.org; admission Y30; ☺1.30-5pm Tue-Fri, 9.30am-5pm Sat & Sun) could be mistaken for an alien mothership that has landed to refuel. A tour of the interior includes a fascinating exhibition of designs short-listed for the theatre, before the massive mercury bead concept eventually topped them all.

A slight detour east of the square bring you to the unique **Foreign Legation Quarter** (Map p306), a classy cluster of elegantly restored legation buildings towards the west end of Dongjiaomin Xiang (东交民巷), once called Foreign Legation Street (and renamed 'Anti-Imperialism Road' during the Cultural Revolution). A few of the iconic buildings on this road include the **Dutch Legation** (number 40), the **French Post Office** (number 19) and **St Michael's Church** (number 11).

Běijīng Police Museum   MUSEUM
(北京警察博物馆; Běijīng Jǐngchá Bówùguǎn; Map p306; 36 Dongjiaomin Xiang; admission Y5-Y20; ☺9am-4pm Tue-Sun; ⓜQianmen) An insightful peek into the history of the Běijīng police force. The 'through ticket' includes laser shooting practice and a souvenir.

FREE **China National Museum**   MUSEUM
(中国国家博物馆; Zhōngguó Guójiā Bówùguǎn; Map p306; 16 Dongchang'an Jie; ☺8.30am-4.30pm; ⓜTiananmen Dong) A 7.9m statue of

BĚIJĪNG SIGHTS

BĚIJĪNG

Dōngchéng

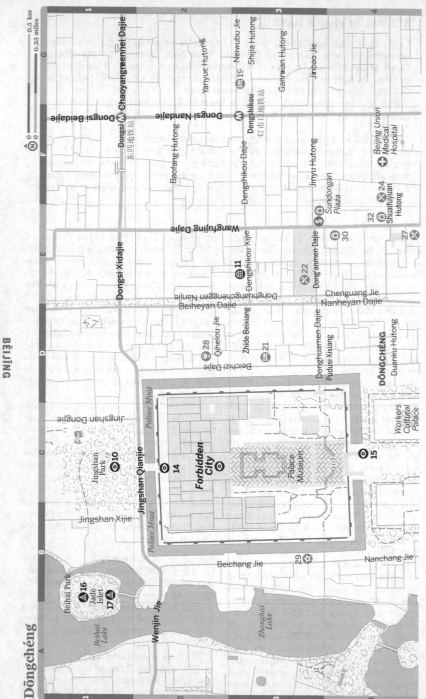

0.5 km
0.25 miles

Beihai Park
Beihai Lake
16
Jade Islet
17

Jingshan Xijie

Jingshan Park
Jingshan Dōngjie
10

Palace Moat

Jingshan Qianjie

Wenjin Jie

Palace Moat

Zhongnhai Lake

Beichang Jie
29

Nanchang Jie

Dongsi Xidajie

Dongsi Beidajie
Dongsi ⓜ Chaoyangmennei Dajie
东四地铁站

Yanyue Hutong

Baofang Hutong

Neiwubu Jie
Shijia Hutong
Dengshikou
灯市口地铁站 ⓜ

Dongsi Nandajie

Gamian Hutong

Jinbao Jie

Wangfujing Dajie

Dengshikou Dajie

Dengshikou Xijie
Dongan anmen Dajie

Dengshikou Nanjie
Dongfuangchengean Nanjie
Beiheyan Dajie

Chenguang Jie
Nanheyan Dajie

Qihelou Jie
Zhide Beixiang

Beichizi Dajie

Donghuanmen Dajie
Pudusi Xixiang
Chenguang Jie

Jinyu Hutong

Sundongan Plaza

Shuaifuyuan Hutong

Beijing Union Medical Hospital

$
30
32
24

22
11

28
21

14
Forbidden City
Palace Museum

15

DŌNGCHÉNG

Workers Cultural Palace

Duanku Hutong

27

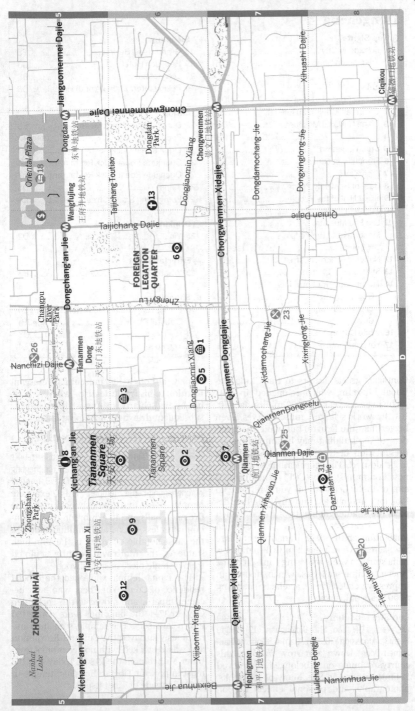

Dōngchéng

Confucius greets visitors to the China National Museum, which re-opened in 2011 following a six-year US$400 million facelift. It's the world's largest museum (yes, even bigger than the Louvre) but while the grandeur of the building may be impressive, its presentation of the past leaves something to be desired. The glorification of the Chinese Communist Party (CCP) is the unstated aim of the collection and you will need to look long and hard to find anything that depicts the shadier moments of its past, such as the Great Leap Forward, the Cultural Revolution or the 1989 Tiananmen Square massacre. If your interest in CCP paraphernalia starts to wane try losing yourself in the 'Ancient China' galleries, which houses an impressive collection of artefacts spanning 5000 years of history.

Lao She Museum　　　　　MUSEUM
(老舍纪念馆; Lǎo Shě Jìniànguǎn; 19 Fengfu Hutong; admission Y10; ⊘8.30am-4.30pm; MTiananmen Dong) Down a narrow *hútòng*, this courtyard home once belonged to beloved Běijīng author Lǎo Shě. Many of his books, photographs and personal effects are on display, although the museum gives scant mention to his tragic demise – a severe beating by Red Guards in August 1966 and his subsequent drowning in Taiping Lake.

NORTH OF THE FORBIDDEN CITY

TOP CHOICE **Lama Temple**　　　BUDDHIST TEMPLE
(雍和宫; Yōnghé Gōng; Map p318; 28 Yonghegong Dajie; admission Y25, audio guide Y20; ⊘9am-4pm; MYonghegong-Lama Temple) This exquisite temple is vast and riotously colourful. The five main halls and 10 exhibition rooms contain countless serene and smiling Buddhas, the most notable of which is the 18m-high statue of the **Maitreya Buddha** sculpted from a single piece of sandalwood.

The Lama Temple was once the official residence of Count Yin Zhen, who later became emperor and moved to the Forbidden City. In 1744 the buildings were converted into a lamasery. The temple somehow miraculously survived the Cultural Revolution and was 'restocked' with novice monks from Inner Mongolia in the 1980s. Today it is the most important Tibetan Buddhist temple in China (outside of Tibet itself).

Poly Art Museum MUSEUM
(保利艺术博物馆; Bǎolì Yìshù Bówùguǎn; www
.polymuseum.com; 14 Dongzhimen Nandajie; admission Y20; MDongsishitiao) Recently rehoused
in the new Poly Plaza, this wonderful museum of Chinese art and antiquities is not
to be missed. The exhibits range from Shang
dynasty bronze pieces and Tang dynasty
bodhisattvas to Western-style bronze work
plundered from the Old Summer Palace.

Confucian Temple &
Imperial College CONFUCIAN TEMPLE
(孔庙, 国子监; Kǒng Miào & Guózǐjiàn; 13
Guozijian Jie; admission Y20; ⊙8.30am-5pm;
MYonghegong-Lama Temple) Just a short distance down the *hútòng* opposite the entrance to the Lama Temple is the Confucian
Temple & Imperial College. The unkempt
grounds and undisturbed peace are a pleasant contrast to just about every other sight
in Běijīng. The **stelae** in the temple courtyard record the names of those successful in
the civil-service examinations (possibly the
world's first) of the imperial court. The Imperial College was where the emperor annually expounded the Confucian classics to an
audience of thousands of kneeling students
and professors.

Beihai Park PARK
(北海公园; Běihǎi Gōngyuán; Map p306; admission high season/low season Y10/5, Jade Islet Y10;
⊙6.30am-8pm, buildings open to 4pm; MTiananmen Xi, then bus 5) A relaxing place for a stroll
is Beihai Park, northwest of the Forbidden
City. There are four gates to the park, which
is formed around Beihai Lake.

The site is associated with Kublai Khaan's
palace, the navel of Běijīng before the creation of the Forbidden City. Dominating **Jade
Islet** (Map p306) on the lake, the 36m-high
White Dagoba (白塔; Map p306) as originally
built in 1651 for a visit by the Dalai Lama,
and was rebuilt in 1741. You can reach the
dagoba (stupa) through the **Yongan Temple** (永安寺; Map p306), with its halls decorated with statues of Buddhist figures and
past lamas, as well as a bamboo grove. The
pretty **Xitian Fanjing** (西天梵境; Western Paradise; Map p318) temple and the **Nine Dragon
Screen** (九龙壁; Map p318), a 5m-high and
27m-long wall of coloured glazed tiles, are
also worth searching out within the park.

Jingshan Park PARK
(景山公园; Jǐngshān Gōngyuán; Map p306; admission Y2; ⊙6am-9.30pm; MTiananmen Xi, then bus
5) This park is worth visiting for its priceless
views over the Forbidden City immediately
to its south. Its central hill, shaped from the

BĚIJĪNG'S DARING NEW ARCHITECTURE

The 2008 Summer Olympics did more than bring the world's greatest athletes to Běijīng: it also lifted the curtain on some of the most daring achievements in modern architecture. First and foremost among them is the US$423 million, 91,000-seat, 'Bird's Nest' **National Stadium** (北京国家体育场; Běijīng Guójiā Tǐyùchǎng; admission Y50; MOlympic Green), the world's largest steel structure. Right next door is the futuristic **Water Cube** (水立方; Shuǐ lìfāng; admission Y30) where the swimming events were held. The stadium is now used for sporting events and concerts, while the pool is used for competitions (a water park is planned).

Another unique design in Běijīng is the new National Grand Theatre (p305) also known as the 'Egg' for its instantly recognisable titanium dome shape. The 6500-seat theatre is surrounded by an artificial lake and looks impossible to enter (until you realise access is through a tunnel). It's a short walk west of Tiananmen Sq.

The most mind-boggling piece of modern architecture in Běijīng is the US$600 million **China Central Television (CCTV) Headquarters** (中央电视台总部大楼; Zhōngyāng Diànshìtái Zǒngbù Dàlóu; off Map p318; 32 Dongsanhuan Zhonglu; MJintaixizhao). The 51-floor building consists of five continuously linked sections that defy the laws of physics. Locals have given it a variety of nicknames, including the 'big underpants', the 'twisted donut' and, ominously, 'dangerous building'. It's located in Chaoyang District.

As if all these projects weren't enough, Běijīng had to go and build the world's largest airport (the new Terminal 3) and the world's largest train station (the new South Train Station). Unfortunately, international trains from Russia and Mongolia arrive at Běijīng train station but you can use the south station if you are continuing your rail journey to Shànghǎi.

earth excavated to create the palace moat, supposedly protects the palace from the evil spirits – or dust storms – from the north (the billowing dust clouds in the spring have to be seen to be believed). Clamber to the top of this regal pleasure garden for a magnificent panorama of the capital.

Drum Tower & Bell Tower   HISTORIC SITE

(Map p318) Repeatedly destroyed and restored, the **Drum Tower** (鼓楼; Gǔlóu; Gulou Dongdajie; admission Y20; ◎9am-5pm) originally marked the centre of the old Mongol capital. Stagger up the incredibly steep steps for impressive views over Běijīng's *hútòng* rooftops. Drum performances are given every half hour from 9am to 11.30am and 1.30pm to 5pm. Fronted by a Qing-dynasty stele, the **Bell Tower** (钟楼; Zhōnglóu; Zhonglouwan Hutong; admission Y15; ◎9am-5pm) originally dates from Ming times and the current edifice dates to the 18th century. Both the Drum and Bell Towers can be reached on bus 5, 58 or 107; get off at the namesake Gǔlóu stop.

FREE 798 Art District   ART GALLERIES

(798 艺术新区; cnr Jiuxianqiao Lu & Jiuxianqiao Beilu) This disused and sprawling electronics factory found a new lease of life several years ago as the focus of Běijīng's feisty art community. Wander the former factory workshops and peruse the artwork on view at its highlight galleries, **Long March Space** (www.longmarchspace.com; ◎11am-7pm Tue-Sun) and **Chinese Contemporary Běijīng** (www.chinesecontemporary.com; ◎11am-7pm), or admire the photographic stills at **798 Photo Gallery** (Bǎinián Yìnxiàng; www.798photogallery.cn). Ride the subway to Dongzhimen station, then jump on bus 909 (Y1, 25 minutes) and get off at Dashanzi Lukounan (大山子路口南).

China Train Museum   MUSEUM

(中国铁道博物馆; Zhōngguó Tiědào Bówùguǎn; Jiuxianqiao North Rd, Chaoyang District; admission Y20) This museum houses several retired steam engines from China, the US, Russia and the UK, including the locomotive used to tote around Mao's train. It's great for railway enthusiasts of all ages, especially kids, as they let you climb all over the trains and fiddle with the instruments. The museum is located near the East Fifth Ring Rd about 2km northeast of the 798 Art District.

Ancient Observatory   HISTORIC SITE

(古观象台; Gǔ Guānxiàngtái; Map p312; admission Y10; ◎9.30am-4.30pm Tue-Sun; Ⓜ Jianguomen) Běijīng's ancient observatory, mounted on the battlements of a watchtower lying along the line of the old Ming city wall, originally dates back to Kublai Khaan's days when it lay north of the present site.

Within the courtyard is a reproduction-looking **armillary sphere** (1439), supported by four dragons. At the rear is an attractive garden with grass, sundials and another armillary sphere. Climb the steps to the roof and an array of Jesuit-designed astronomical instruments, embellished with sculptured bronze dragons and other Chinese flourishes, making a unique combination of East and West.

During the Boxer Rebellion, the instruments disappeared into the hands of the French and Germans. Some were returned in 1902 and others were returned after WWI.

Summer Palace   HISTORIC SITE

(颐和园; Yíhé Yuán; 19 Xinjian Gongmen; admission Y40-50, audio guides Y30; ◎8.30am-5pm) The immense park of the Summer Palace requires at least half a day of your time. Nowadays teeming with tour groups, this complex, dominated by **Kunming Lake**, was once a playground for the imperial court. Royalty came here to elude the summer heat that roasted the Forbidden City. Empress Dowager Cixi rebuilt the park in 1888 with money supposedly intended for the creation of a modern navy. (At least the empress restored the still-immobile marble boat for lakeside dining.)

The palace's main building is the **Hall of Benevolence & Longevity**, near the lake towards the eastern gate, which is where the emperor handled state affairs and received visitors. The 700m **Long Corridor** along the northern shore is decorated with mythical scenes. Visitors can also see exhibitions specific to the Empress Dowager Cixi, including her furniture and memorabilia.

Towards the North Palace Gate, **Suzhou Street** is an entertaining and light-hearted diversion of riverside walkways, shops and eateries designed to mimic the famous Jiāngsū canal town. **Row boats** are available for hire.

The park is about 12km northwest of the city centre; get there by taking the subway to Xizhimen station, then a minibus or bus 375.

TOP CHOICE **Temple of Heaven Park** PARK

(天坛公园; Tiāntán Gōngyuán; Tiantan Donglu; admission low season Y10-30, high season Y15-35, audio tour Y40; ☺park 6am-9pm, sights 8am-6pm; MChongwenmen, Tiantandongmen) China's finest example of Ming architecture is the **Temple of Heaven**. This complex, set in a 267-hectare park, functioned as a stage for the solemn rites performed by the Son of Heaven, who came here to pray for good harvests, seek divine clearance and atone for the sins of the people.

The design and position of the park, as well as the shape and colour of structures within, have symbolic significance for the ancient interplay between heaven and earth. The **Round Altar**, for example, possesses an obsessive symmetry revolving around the heavenly number nine (nine rings of stone, each ring composed of multiples of nine stones etc). The altar's most mystifying feature is its ability to amplify voices emanating from the centre of the upper terrace.

Just north of the Round Altar is the **Imperial Vault of Heaven**, which is surrounded by the **Echo Wall**. Sixty-five metres in diameter, the wall allows a whisper to travel clearly from one end to the other.

The crown of the whole complex is the **Hall of Prayer for Good Harvests**. Amazingly, this temple's wooden pillars support the ceiling without nails or cement!

🛏 Sleeping

Běijīng has a tremendous range of places to stay, from hostels to five-star luxury. The most atmospheric hotels are those built in the courtyards of the *hútòng* neighbourhoods. Hotels are subject to a 10% to 15% service charge (on top of the prices quoted here), but many cheaper hotels don't bother to charge it. Dorms and the cheapest budget rooms are without a private bathroom.

TOP CHOICE **Peking International Youth Hostel** HOSTEL $

(北平国际青年旅社; Běipíng Guójì Qīngnián Lǚshè; Map p306; ✆6526 8855; www.peking .hostel.com; 5 Beichizi Ertiao; 北池子二条5号; 4-/8-/12-bed dm Y100/100/90, d Y400-500; ✳@☂; MTiananmen Dong) This hostel is hidden away in a *hútòng* a dumpling's throw from the Forbidden City. The interior offers a homey lounge, leafy courtyard, good dorms and intimate ambiance (singles and doubles are small though). Book ahead.

BĚIJĪNG MUSEUM PASS

This pass (博物馆通票; Bówùguǎn Tōngpiào) is a fantastic investment that will save you both money and queuing for tickets. For Y80 you get either complimentary access or discounted admission (typically 50%) to almost 100 museums, temples and tourist sights in and around Běijīng. Not all museums are worth visiting, but you only have to visit a small selection of museums to get your money back. The pass is effective from 1 January to 31 December in any one year and can be picked up from participating museums and sights. If you can't find one, call ✆6222 3793 or ✆6221 3256 to locate stocks. Alternatively, try the Chinese-only website www.bowuguan.com.cn.

Leo Hostel HOSTEL $

(广聚元饭店; Guǎngjùyuán Fàndiàn; Map p306; ✆8660 8923; www.leohostel.com; 52 Dazhalan Xijie; 大栅栏西街52号; dm Y50-60, d Y180-240, tr Y210-300; ✳@☂; MQianmen) It's popular and ever-busy, so it's best to phone ahead to book a room at this bargain hostel tucked away down Dazhalan Xijie. It has an attractive interior courtyard decked out with plastic plants, OK dorm rooms (pricier dorms with bathroom), simple but passable doubles, a lively bar and a fine location.

Beijing Downtown Backpackers Accommodation HOSTEL $

(东堂客栈; Dōngtáng Kèzhàn; Map p318; ✆8400 2429; www.backpackingchina.com; 85 Nanluogu Xiang; 南锣鼓巷85号; dm Y75-90, s/d/tr Y150/200/300; ✳@; MAndingmen) This hostel's central *hútòng* location on teeming Nanluogu Xiang is hard to beat. It's close enough to the bars to crawl (or be carried) home. Free breakfast, bike rental (Y20 per day, Y400 deposit) and internet access (Y6 per hour).

Beijing Saga International Youth Hostel HOSTEL $

(北京实佳国际青年旅社; Běijīng Shíjiā Guójì Qīngnián Lǚshè; Map p312; ✆6527 2773; www.sagayouthhostelbeijing.cn; 9 Shijia Hutong; 史家胡同9号; dm Y65, d Y218-238, tr Y258, courtyard r Y268; ✳@☂; MDengshikou) Enjoying a top location on historic Shijia Hutong, this popular hostel has well-kept rooms, a spacious seating area in the main lobby, laundry and internet

South Cháoyáng

South Cháoyáng

access (Y8 per hour). The three small courtyard rooms are at the back. Free breakfast with some rooms.

Lusongyuan Hotel
HUTONG HOTEL $$$
(侣松园宾馆; Lǔsōngyuán Bīnguǎn; Map p318; ✒6404 0436; 22 Banchang Hutong; 板厂胡同22号; s/d Y658/1188; ✦@; ⓜAndingmen) Built by a Mongolian general during the Qing dynasty, this popular courtyard hotel has pocket-sized singles with pea-sized baths and just one suite. Courtyard-facing rooms are slightly dearer. The bikes (half/full day Y15/30) are pretty ancient. Taichi demonstrations are on offer, and there is internet (open 7.30am to 11pm; Y30 per hour). Rooms are typically discounted by around 40%.

Sanlitun Youth Hostel
HOSTEL $
(三里屯青年酒店; Sānlǐtún Qīng Nián Jiǔdiàn; Map p318; ✒5190 9288; www.sanlitun.hostel.com; 1 Chunxiu Lu; 春秀路1号; dm/s/d Y70/200/320; ✦@☎; ⓜDongsishitiao) Despite touting itself as a youth hostel this place feels more like a budget hotel. There are a couple of dorm rooms but most rooms are pod-sized singles and doubles. Cheaper rooms lack windows. Services include laundry, wi-fi and a travel desk. It's on a leafy side street within walking distance of the Sānlǐtún bar area.

Haoyuan Hotel
HUTONG HOTEL $$
(好园宾馆; Hǎoyuán Bīnguǎn; Map p306; ✒6512 5557; www.haoyuanhotel.com; 53 Shijia Hutong; 史家胡同53号; d standard/deluxe Y760/930, ste Y1080-1380; ✦@; ⓜDengshikou) This delightful Qing courtyard hotel has pleasant staff and a handful of tastefully finished rooms. Laid out with trees, the courtyard at the rear is gorgeous. There is a restaurant as well as bike rental, and rates include breakfast.

Red Capital Residence
HERITAGE HOTEL $$$
(新红资客栈; Xīnhóngzī Kèzhàn; Map p318; ✒6402 7150; www.redcapitalclub.com.cn; 9 Dongsi Liutiao; 东四六条9号; d from US$148; ⓜDongsishitiao) An unusual guesthouse that carries you back to Běijīng, c 1962. The five rooms are decked out with stuff that wouldn't look out of place in a museum. Enjoy wine and cigars in the bomb shelter bar. For a real treat, take a swing through town in the Red Flag limo, once the property of Mao's inner circle.

Holiday Inn Express
HOTEL $$
(智选假日酒店; Zhìxuǎn Jiàrì Jiǔdiàn; Map p318; ✒6416 9999; www.holidayinnexpress.com.cn; 1 Chunxiu Lu; 春秀路1号; d Y498-536; ✦@☎; ⓜDongsishitiao) A welcome addition to the Sānlǐtún area, this hotel offers the efficient service, reasonable rates and a substantial Western/Chinese breakfast buffet.

Grand Hyatt Beijing
HOTEL $$$
(北京东方君悦大酒店; Běijīng Dōngfāng Jūnyuè Dàjiǔdiàn; Map p306; ✒8518 1234; www.hyatt.com; 1 Dongchang'an Jie; 东长安街1号; d US$443; ✦@☎; ⓜWangfujing) Bang in the midst of the Wangfujing shopping district, this contemporary and opulent hotel offers a great location and sizable rooms.

NEAR BĚIJĪNG TRAIN STATION

Paragon Hotel
HOTEL $$
(宝辰饭店; Bǎochén Fàndiàn; Map p312; ✒6526 6688; www.hojo.com; 18A Jianguomennei Dajie; 建国门内大街18号; r from Y598; ✦@; ⓜBeijing Train Station) This 280-room midrange hotel is located across the street from the Běijīng train station (the entrance to the hotel is around the west side of the building). Rooms are clean and well appointed but those that face the station can be a bit noisy.

Beijing City Central Youth Hostel
HOSTEL $
(北京城市国际青年旅社; Běijīng Chéngshì Guójì Qīngnián Lǚshè; Map p312; ✒8511 5050; www.centralhostel.com; 1 Beijingzhan Qianjie; 北京站前街1号; dm Y60, s with bathroom Y298-328, without bathroom Y120-160, tw with/without bathroom Y328/160; ✦@☎; ⓜBeijing Train Station) Good for budget train travellers wanting to stay near the station, this hostel has reasonably clean rooms and a bar on the 3rd floor but is otherwise charmless. Due to its busy location it's a revolving door of humanity and the three or four receptionists are constantly preoccupied with other guests.

✗ Eating

Some of your best memories of Běijīng are likely to be those involving eating. The best areas to look for restaurants, cafes and bars include Sanlitun and around Qianhai and Houhai Lakes. Unless stated otherwise, restaurants and cafes are open from 11am to 11pm.

TOP CHOICE Xiao Wang's Home Restaurant
CHINESE $$
(小王府; Xiǎowáng Fǔ; Map p312; 2 Guanghua Dongli; meals Y70; ⓜYong'anli) Treat yourself to home-style Běijīng cuisine from this excellent restaurant. Recommended dishes

include deep-fried spare ribs, lemon chicken or sautéed asparagus. Another very attractive branch with outdoor seating can be found in **Ritan Park** (Map p312).

Quanjude Roast Duck Restaurant
PEKING DUCK **$$$**

(全聚德烤鸭店; Quànjùdé Kǎoyādiàn; Map p306; 9 Shuaifuyuan Hutong; half/whole duck Y84/168; M Wangfujing) Quanjude, first established in 1864, is a world renowned restaurant that has served meals to kings, queens and presidents from dozens of countries. Peking duck is the signature dish but there are specialist dishes such as duck feet with mustard sauce, salted duck's liver or deep-fried duck heart. There's also a more famous and touristy branch at **Qianmen** (32 Qianmen Dajie; M Qianmen).

Bāguó Bùyī
SICHUAN **$$**

(八国布衣; Map p318; 89-3 Di'anmen Dongdajie; dishes from Y16; M Zhangzizhong Lu) Spicy Sichuān cuisine is served in a marvellous Chinese inn-style restaurant setting. There's a range of good value dishes, including Chóngqìng hot pepper chicken and chilli fish slices. As a bonus, short opera performances are staged as you dine.

Bellagio
TAIWANESE **$$**

(鹿港小镇; Lùgǎng Xiǎozhèn; Map p312; 35 Xiaoyun Lu; dishes from Y70; ⊙24hr; M Chaoyangmen) This authentic Taiwanese restaurant with an Italian name is one of the more popular places in town for hipsters, actors, models, clubbers and poets. Try a delicious Hakka stir-fry or kung pao chicken, topped off with their signature shaved-ice dessert.

Liqun Roast Duck Restaurant
PEKING DUCK **$$$**

(利群烤鸭店; Lìqún Kǎoyādiàn; Map p306; ☑6702 5681; 11 Beixiangfeng Hutong; roast duck Y68; M Qianmen) Book a table before arriving at this tiny, busy Peking-duck restaurant buried in a maze of *hútòng* in east Qianmen. No medals for service but the duck is excellent.

Le Little Saigon
FRENCH, VIETNAMESE **$$$**

(西贡在巴黎; Xī Gòng Zài Bā Lí; Map p318; 141 Jiugulou Dajie; meals Y100-150; M Gulou Dajie) This French-Vietnamese fusion restaurant has the look and feel of a Parisian brasserie and a diverse menu that spans the continents. Try the pork and spring rolls and the tasty Hanoi noodle soup. Linger a while; this is a relaxing place where you could easily spend an evening over wine.

Purple Haze
THAI **$$$**

(紫苏庭; Zǐsūtíng; Map p318; meals Y100-150; M Dongsishitiao) A great neighbourhood restaurant with a loyal following, Purple Haze offers some of the best Thai cuisine in the city. Try the red curry chicken or the signature dish, duck salad. It's along the small lane opposite the Workers' Stadium's north gate.

Tiāndì Yījiā
CHINESE **$$$**

(天地一家; Map p306; 140 Nanchizi Dajie; meals around Y300; M Tiananmen Dong) This refined Chinese courtyard-style restaurant is decked out with traditional furniture, water features and side rooms for snug hotpot dinners. Graze on Cantonese dim sum (served from 11am to 2pm and 5pm to 9.30pm).

Makye Ame
TIBETAN **$$**

(玛吉阿米; Mǎjí Āmǐ; Map p312; 2nd fl, A11 Xiushui Nanjie; dishes from Y20; M Jianguomen) Behind the Friendship Store, this is one of Běijīng's few Tibetan restaurants, where you can sample boiled yak with chilli and *tsampa* (roasted barley meal). There's a comfy upper room decorated with a generous crop of Tibetan ornaments.

⌜TOP CHOICE⌝ Bookworm
CAFE **$**

(书虫; Shūcóng; Map p318; www.beijingbookworm.com; Bldg 4 Nansanlitun Lu; ⊙8am-1am; ☎; M Tuanjiehu) The Bookworm is a great stop for breakfast, light lunch, a solo coffee or a serious reading binge. It has a library and bookstore.

Wangfujing Snack Street
STREET FOOD **$**

(王府井小吃街; Wángfǔjǐng Xiǎochījiē; Map p306; west off Wangfujing Dajie; kebabs from Y3, dishes from Y5; M Wangfujing) Fronted by an ornate archway, here you'll find a good selection of small restaurants and stalls overhung with colourful banners and bursting with character and flavour. Try Xinjiāng or Muslim Uighur cuisine such as lamb kebabs and flat bread. There's plenty of exotic stuff on offer too – daredevil gastronomes can sample scorpion, seahorse-on-a-stick and various other deep-fried creepy crawlers.

Donghuamen Night Market
STREET FOOD **$**

(东华门夜市; Dōnghuāmén Yèshì; Map p306; Dong'anmen Dajie; ⊙3-10pm, closed Chinese New Year; M Dengshikou) A sight in itself is this bustling night market near Wangfujing Dajie. It's for tourists, so expect to pay around Y5 for a lamb kebab (much more than you would pay for one from a *hútòng* vendor).

GHOST STREET

Decades ago this small street was an all-night vegetable market where local farmers would gather to sell their produce by the light of their lanterns. When viewed from afar the gently illuminated farmers looked like ghosts huddled in the dark. The 'Ghost Street' moniker stuck. The vegetable stands eventually gave way to restaurants and today Ghost Street (鬼街; Guǐ Jiē; Map p318; Ⓜ Beixinqiao) is a non-touristy strip of cheap hotpot places, each with homey, convivial atmosphere. Many of the restaurants are open 24/7 but it's most attractive at night, when the street is lit with red lanterns. Because hotpot is standard fare here, it's a particularly popular place to visit in the cold months. A stove will be placed on your table, broth is prepared and you choose the vegetables you want to add. To get here, take the subway to Beixinqiao, head east along Dongzhimennei Dajie until you reach Ghost Street.

Food Court ASIAN CUISINE $
(Map p306; Basement, Oriental Plaza, 1 Dongchang'an Jie; dishes from Y10; Ⓜ Wangfujing) This spacious, hygienic food court offers a world of Chinese cuisine, plus other Asian dishes. You can eat very well for around Y20. Buy a prepaid card at the kiosk at the entrance; credits are deducted with each dish ordered.

Sequoia Café CAFE $
(美洲杉咖啡屋; Měizhōu Shān Kāfēiwū; Map p312; 44 Guanghua Lu; sandwiches Y23-35; ⊙8am-8pm; Ⓜ Jianguomen) For a taste from home, Sequoia offers excellent coffee and deservedly popular sandwiches, including vegetarian options.

Self-Catering
At Běijīng's supermarkets you'll find everything you need for long train journeys. Some options:

April Gourmet DELI
(绿叶子食品店; Lûyèzi Shípǐndiàn; Map p318; 1 Sanlitun Beixiaojie; ⊙8am-9pm; Ⓜ Dongzhimen) An expat-oriented deli with wines, cheese and other imported goodies.

Yansha Supermarket SUPERMARKET
(燕莎超市; Yànshā Chāoshì; Map p312; basement, Henderson Center, Jianguomennei Dajie; ⊙10am-8pm; Ⓜ Jianguomen) Convenient for the train station.

🍷 Drinking

Sānlìtún is a good place for a wild night out as it combines bars and mini-nightclubs. The streets around Qianhai and Houhai Lakes are atmospheric but quieter, while Nanluogu Xiang can be downright mellow. Most bars and clubs are open daily from about noon until the last customer leaves,

unless otherwise specified. Expect to pay Y15-18 for a beer at the following places.

TOP CHOICE Passby Bar BAR
(过客; Guòkè; Map p318; 108 Nanluogu Xiang; ⊙9am-2am; Ⓜ Andingmen) One of the original bars on cafe-bar strip Nanluogu Xiang and still one of the best, with travel-oriented bar staff, a winning courtyard ambience, shelves of books and mags, and a funky feel.

Drum & Bell Bar BAR
(鼓钟咖啡倌; Gǔzhōng Kāfēiguǎn; Map p318; 41 Zhonglouwan Hutong; Ⓜ Gulou Dajie) Clamber to the roof terrace of this bar slung between its namesake towers and enjoy drinks amid an idyllic panorama of low-rise Běijīng rooftops.

Bed Bar BAR
(床吧; Chuángbā; Map p318; 17 Zhangwang Hutong; Ⓜ Gulou Dajie) Catering to folk who simply can't stand up after a few drinks, this place has seating on traditional *kang* (Chinese-style beds). It also plays great music and has a small dance floor.

Yǐn BAR
(饮; Map p306; 33 Qihelou; Ⓜ Dongsi) Celebrate your arrival in Běijīng with a tipple in this well-heeled bar atop the Emperor Hotel. The bar overlooks the Forbidden City and views are best around sunset.

⭐ Entertainment

Nightclubs

MixBeijing NIGHTCLUB
(梅克斯; Méikèsī; Map p318; inside Workers' Stadium north gate; ⊙8pm-late; Ⓜ Dongsishitiao) Major hip-hop and R&B club west of Sānlìtún, with regular crowd-pulling foreign DJs.

WANT MORE?

For in-depth information, reviews and recommendations at your fingertips, head to the Apple App Store to purchase Lonely Planet's Beijing City Guide iPhone app.

GT Banana
NIGHTCLUB

(吧那那; Bānànà; Map p312; Scitech Hotel, 22 Jianguomenwai Dajie; cover Y20-50; ⊗8.30pm-4am Sun-Thu, to 5am Fri & Sat; Ⓜ Jianguomen) A mainstay of Běijīng's club land, Banana is loud and to the point. Select from techno, acid jazz and chill-out sections according to your energy levels or the waning of the night.

Destination
NIGHTCLUB

(目的地; Mùdìdì; www.bjdestination.com; 7 Gongrentiyuchang Xilu; admission free weekdays, weekend admission incl drink Y60; ⊗8pm-late; Ⓜ Dongsishitiao) Běijīng's premier gay dance bar is a stylish, lively place with a mixed crowd. It hosts the occasional lesbian night.

Opera

Běijīng opera is the most famous of the many forms of performance art on offer in the city. You can catch performances at the following theatres:

Chang'an Grand Theatre
CHINESE OPERA

(长按大戏院; Chángān Dàjùchǎng; Map p312; Chang'an Bldg, 7 Jianguomennei Dajie; tickets Y80-800; ⊗performances 7.30pm; Ⓜ Jianguomen)

Huguang Guild Hall
CHINESE OPERA

(湖广会馆; Húguǎng Huìguǎn; 3 Hufang Lu; tickets Y160-680; ⊗performances 7.30pm; Ⓜ Caishikou) Built in 1807, this historic theatre has an intimate feel and is a fine place to see traditional Peking opera.

Acrobatics

Chaoyang Theatre
ACROBATICS

(朝阳剧场; Cháoyáng Jùchǎng; off Map p318; 36 Dongsanhuan Beilu; tickets Y180-380; ⊗performances 5.15pm & 7.30pm; Ⓜ Hujialou) The Chaoyang Theatre is the venue for visiting acrobatic troupes, who fill the stage with plate-spinning and hoop-jumping.

Tianqiao Acrobatics Theatre
ACROBATICS

(天桥杂技剧场; Tiānqiáo Zájì Jùchǎng; Beiwei Lu, Xuanwu District; tickets Y100-200; ⊗performances 7.15-8.45pm; Ⓜ Qianmen) West of the Temple of Heaven, this is one of Běijīng's most popular venues.

Live Music

East Shore Bar
LIVE MUSIC

(东岸; Dōngàn; Map p318; 2nd fl, 2 Shishahai Nanyan; ⊗4pm-3am) With views out over Qianhai Lake, this excellent bar hits all the right notes with its low-light, candlelit mood and live jazz sounds from 9.30pm (Thursday to Sunday).

What Bar?
LIVE MUSIC

(什么吧; Shénme Bā; 72 Beichang Jie; cover on live-music nights incl 1 beer Y30; ⊗3pm-late, live music from 9pm Fri & Sat) Microsized and slightly deranged, this broom cupboard of a bar stages regular, rotating, grittily named bands to an enthusiastic audience. It's north of the Forbidden City's west gate.

🛍 Shopping

In Běijīng, the best bargains include silk, cashmere and brand-name clothing (often fake). Pirated CDs and DVDs abound. While prices are fixed in the department stores, bargaining is expected everywhere else. Items at places like Sanlitun Yashou may not even have price tags; sellers will simply size you up and state an opening price. With a good game plan you should be able to get around 80% off their starting price. Shop around for the best price, as many stalls sell the same items.

Wangfujing Dajie is a lively shop-lined pedestrianised street, two blocks east of the Forbidden City. Its name, meaning 'Well of Princely Palaces', dates to the 15th century, when this area was the site of several royal palaces. The mammoth **Oriental Plaza** (东方新天地; Dōngfāng Xīntiāndì; Map p306; 1 Dongchang'an Jie; Ⓜ Wangfujing) shopping mall anchors the southern end of the street, while elsewhere along it you'll find tea emporium **Ten Fu's Tea** (天福茗茶; Tiānfú Míngchá; Map p306; www.tenfu.com; 88 Wangfujing Dajie; Ⓜ Wangfujing).

Dashilar (Ⓜ Qianmen), a colourful hútòng off Qianmen Dajie, is a jumble of silk shops, tea and herbal-medicine shops, theatres and restaurants. Also known as 'Silk Street', it is a hangover from when specialised products were sold in particular areas. **Ruifúxiáng** (瑞蚨祥; Map p306; 5 Dazhalan Jie) is a good place to buy silk near Dashilar.

Běijīng's premier antique street is tree-lined **Liulichang** (Ⓜ Hepingmen), west of Dashilar. Designed to look like an ancient Chinese village, it's a nice place to stroll even if you don't want to buy Chinese paintings, calligraphy materials, art books or ceramics.

Panjiayuan Market (潘家园古玩市场; Pānjiāyuán Gǔwán Shìchǎng; ⊗dawn-around 3pm

Sat & Sun; ⓂGuomao) Located off Dongsanhuan Nanlu, it's hands-down the best place to shop for arts, crafts and antiques – everything from Cultural Revolution memorabilia to Buddha heads. Come early and bargain hard.

Sanlitun Yashou Clothing Market (三里屯雅秀服装市场; Sānlǐtún Yǎxiù Fúzhuāng Shìchǎng; Map p318; 58 Gongrentiyuchang Beilu; ⓂTuanjiehu) Offers five floors of all the clothing you may need.

If you are shopping for books, check out Bookworm (p314) and **Le Petit Gourmand** (小美食家; Xiǎo Měishíjiā; Map p318; Tongli Studio, Sanlitun Beilu; ⓂTuanjiehu) – both are Sānlǐtún cafes that sell books. The **Foreign Languages Bookstore** (外文书店; Wàiwén Shūdiàn; Map p306; 235 Wangfujing Dajie; ⓂWangfujing), also has a good selection of novels and travel books.

Information

Emergency
Ambulance (☏120)
Fire (☏119)
Police (☏110)

Internet Access

Internet cafes (网吧; wǎngbā) have become harder to find in Běijīng over the past few years. Many cheaper hotels and youth hostels provide internet at around Y10 per hour. Free wi-fi is often available at hostels and cafes.

Internet Cafe (网吧; wǎngbā; per hr Y4; ☺24hr; ⓂTuanjiehu) You'll find this cafe on the 2nd floor (up a fire escape) just east of the Bookworm cafe (p314).

Internet Cafe (网吧; wǎngbā; Map p312; 2nd fl, Beijing City Central Youth Hostel, 1 Beijingzhan Qianjie; per hr Y5; ☺24hr; ⓂBeijing Train Station)

Songjie Internet Cafe (松杰网吧; Sōngjié Wǎngbā; Map p318; 140-7Jiaodaokou Nandajie; per hr Y2; ☺24hr; ⓂZhangzizhong Lu)

Medical Services

Běijīng has some of the best medical facilities and services in China. If you need to purchase medicine, note that pharmacies will be cheaper than what you will pay at a clinic.

Beijing Union Medical Hospital (北京协和医院; Běijīng Xiéhé Yīyuàn; Map p306; ☏6529 6114, emergencies ☏6529 5284; 53 Dongdan Beidajie; ☺24hr;

BĚIJĪNG'S HÚTÒNG

Běijīng's homely interior lies waiting to be discovered in the city's *hútòng* (narrow alleyways). Criss-crossing east to west through the city, these alleyways link to create a huge, enchanting warren of one-storey, ramshackle dwellings and historic courtyard homes.

After Chinggis (Genghis) Khaan's army reduced Běijīng to rubble, the city was redesigned with *hútòng*. By the Qing dynasty there were over 2000 such passageways riddling the city, leaping to around 6000 by the 1950s; now the figure has dwindled again to around 2000, home to about a quarter of Běijīng's residents. Marked with white plaques, historic homes are protected, but for many others a way of life is being ruthlessly bulldozed at a rate of over 10,000 dwellings a year.

Hútòng land is a hodgepodge of the old and the new; Qing-dynasty courtyards are riddled with modern brick outhouses and socialist-era conversions, cruelly overlooked by grim apartment blocks.

Old walled *sìhéyuàn* (courtyard homes) are the building blocks of this delightful world. More venerable courtyards are fronted by large, thick, red doors, outside of which perch either a pair of Chinese lions or drum stones.

Hútòng nearly all run east to west, ensuring that the main gate faces south to satisfy the requirements of feng shui. This south-facing aspect guarantees a lot of sunshine and protection from more negative forces from the north. This positioning also mirrors the layout of all Chinese temples, nourishing the *yáng* (the male and light aspect), while checking the *yīn* (the female and dark aspect). Little connecting alleyways that run north to south link the main alleys.

The best way to see *hútòng* is just to wander or cycle around the centre of Běijīng, as the alleyways riddle the town within the Second Ring Rd. Otherwise, limit yourself to historic areas, such as around the Drum Tower or the area around Nanluogu Xiang. If you want to join a tour, the **China Culture Center** (☏6432 9341; www.chinaculturecenter .org) operates a rewarding *hútòng* and *sìhéyuàn* tour. Any number of other pedicab tour operators infest the roads around Qianhai Lake – they will circle you like hyenas, baying '*hútòng, hútòng*'.

Cháoyáng & Sānlǐtún

Ⓜ Dongdan) Foreigners' and VIP wing in the back building.

International SOS (北京亚洲国际紧急救援医疗中心; Běijīng Yàzhōu Guójì Jǐnjí Jiùyuán Yīliáo Zhōngxīn; Map p318; clinic appointments ☏ 6462 9112, dental appointments ☏ 6462 0333, emergencies ☏ 6462 9100; www.internationalsos.com; Suite 105, Wing 1 Kunsha Bldg, No 16 Xinyuanli, Chaoyang District; ⊙ 9am-6pm Mon-Fri; Ⓜ Liangmaqiao) Expensive, high-quality clinic with English-speaking staff.

Money

Foreign currency and travellers cheques can be changed at large branches of the Bank of China, Citic Industrial Bank, the airport and hotel money-changing counters, and at several department stores (including the Friendship Store), as long as you have your passport. Changing currency at a bank usually involves filling out a form with personal details and the process can be a bit tedious; change a good amount when you first arrive to avoid multiple visits to the bank. Foreign ATM cards won't work at all banks, but the Bank of China is reliable, so we have included Bank of China locations below.

Bank of China (中国银行; Zhōngguó Yínháng) Lufthansa Center Youyi Shopping City (Map p318; 1st fl, 50 Liangmaqiao Lu; Ⓜ Liangmaqiao); Oriental Plaza (Map p306; cnr Wangfujing Dajie & Dongchang'an Jie; Ⓜ Wangfujing);

Sundongan Plaza (Map p306; Ⓜ Wangfujing) The ATM at Sundongan Plaza is next to the main plaza entrance on Wangfujing Dajie. Also ATMs in the Capital Airport arrivals hall and at the train station.

Post

There are convenient post offices in the Citic building next to the Friendship Store and in the basement of the China World Trade Center. Large post offices are generally open from 9am to 5pm daily.

International Post Office (国际邮电局; Guójì Yóudiànjú; Map p312; Jianguomen Beidajie; ⊙ 8am-7pm Mon-Sat; Ⓜ Jianguomen)

Tourist Information

Běijīng Tourism Hotline (☏ 6513 0828; ⊙ 24hr) English-speaking operators available to answer questions and hear complaints.

Běijīng Tourist Information Center (北京旅游咨询服务中心; Běijīng Lǚyóu Zīxún Fúwù Zhōngxīn; ⊙ 8.30am-6pm) airport (☏ 6459 8148); Beijingzhan (Map p312; ☏ 6528 8448; www.bjta.gov.cn, in Chinese; 16 Beijingzhan Jie; Ⓜ Beijing Train Station); Chaoyang (Map p318; ☏ 6417 6627; 27 Sanlitun Beilu; Ⓜ Dongsishitiao) The Beijingzhan office is a one-minute walk north of Běijīng train station; Chaoyang is west of the Sanlitun Yashou Clothing Market. The Chaoyang office also sells train tickets.

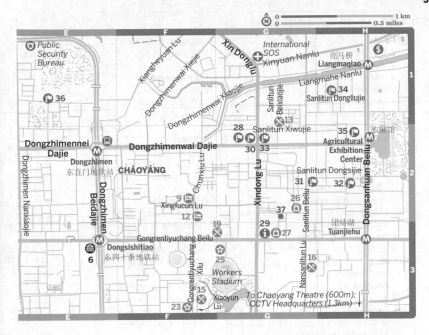

Visa Extensions

The Foreign Affairs branch of the **Public Security Bureau** (PSB; 公安局; Gōng'ānjú; Map p318; ☑8402 0101, 8401 5292; 2 Andingmen Dongdajie; ◷8.30am-4.30pm Mon-Sat; Ⓜ Yonghegong Lama Temple) handles visa extensions. The visa office is on the 2nd floor on the east side of the building. First-time extensions of 30 days are generally issued on any tourist visa, but further extensions are harder to get and you might only end up with a further week. Expect to wait up to five days for your visa extension to be processed; extensions cost Y150 to Y200 depending on your nationality. You can also get passport photographs here (Y30 for five).

❶ Getting There & Away

Train

INTERNATIONAL TICKETS

Moscow, Ulaanbaatar and Hā'ěrbīn (Harbin) trains depart from and arrive at **Běijīng Railway Station** (北京火车站; Běijīng Huǒchēzhàn; Map p312; ☑5101 9999; Ⓜ Beijing Train Station), southeast of the Forbidden City. **Běijīng West train station** (北京西站; Běijīng Xīzhàn; ☑5182 6273; Ⓜ Junshibowuguan), near Lianhuachi Park, has trains for Hong Kong and Vietnam. Buses 122 and 721 connect Běijīng train station with Běijīng west train station.

International tickets to Ulaanbaatar and Moscow are sold at the **CITS International Train Ticket Center** (中国国际旅行社; Map p312; ☑6512 0507; 1st fl, Běijīng International Hotel, 9 Jianguomenwai Dajie; ◷8.30am-noon & 1.30-5pm; Ⓜ Beijing Train Station). Note that you can get a discount if you have a group of eight or more people.

If you want to stop in Dàtóng on the way to Ulaanbaatar, it is possible to buy a Dàtóng–Ulaanbaatar ticket from CITS, then go to the Běijīng train station and buy a separate ticket for Běijīng to Dàtóng. However, in summer it's just about impossible to book a sleeper ticket to Dàtóng on short notice (you should buy at least one week in advance). It is possible to buy a hard seat to Dàtóng on short notice but the carriage will be packed, as hundreds of others will board with standing-room-only tickets.

If you want to avoid the headache of buying multiple rail tickets, contact experienced travel agent **Monkey Business** (Map p318; ☑6591 6519; www.monkeyshrine.com; Room 305, Youyi Poachers Inn, 43 Beisanlitun Nan; Ⓜ Dongshishitiao) which specialises in Trans-Siberian journeys and can arrange tickets if you plan to make the journey in stages. For example, they can purchase you tickets for trains leaving from Ulaanbaatar or Irkutsk. They can also provide visa support and tours to Mongolia.

DOMESTIC TICKETS

Tickets for domestic trains are available from Běijīng train station. Window 16 has an English-speaking ticket seller (but the window

Cháoyáng & Sānlǐtún

number may shift during the lifetime of this book).

The crowds in the ticketing hall can be overwhelmingly long so it's far easier to buy a ticket from a **ticketing office** (◷8am-10pm) in the city, such as **Qianhai Lake** (Di'anmen Xidajie), at the southern end of the lake, or **Sanlitun** (☎5166 6464; 11 Gongrentiyuchang Beilu; Ⓜ Tuanjiehu). They charge a commission of Y5 to Y30. However, these offices only have a limited number of tickets so if they say your train is sold out, it may still be possible to get a ticket from the station.

Note that the Běijīng railway station can only sell tickets for trains that originate (or pass through) Běijīng. This complicates matters if you want to make a rail journey in stages – you have to buy tickets as you go. Having said this, it is still possible to buy such a ticket if you go through a tour operator. This involves the tour operator contacting their agents in other cities, who then buy the ticket on your behalf (with a small mark-up).

Air
Běijīng's **Capital Airport** has direct air connections to most major cities in the world and every major city in China. For more information about international flights to Běijīng, see p394.

Bus
No international buses depart from Běijīng but you can take a bus to the Mongolian border town Èrlián, then switch to a second bus that crosses the border to Zamyn-Üüd. Daily sleeper buses for Èrlián leave from **Mùxīyuán bus station** (木樨园汽车站; ☎6729 7149) at 6pm and take between nine and 14 hours. A ticket costs Y178. Mùxīyuán is located on the Third Ring Rd, in the southern part of the city. From Qianmen subway station, take bus 826, 639 or 17 and get off at Mùxīyuán bridge. There are buses to Èrlián from two other stations, but Mùxīyuán is considered to be the most convenient of the three.

ⓘ Getting Around
To/From the Airport
The airport is 27km from the city centre. The **Airport Express** (机场快轨; Jīchǎng Kuàiguǐ; Y25, 30 minutes; ◷first/last train to airport 6.30am/10.30pm, from airport 6.30am/11.05pm) light-rail link runs every 15

minutes, connecting Capital Airport with Line 2 of the underground system at Dongzhimen.

Express buses (Y16) also run along several routes. Line 3 (first/last bus from Capital Airport 7.30am/last flight, from Běijīng train station 5.30am/9pm) is the most popular with travellers, running to the Běijīng International Hotel and Běijīng train station via Chaoyangmen. A taxi should cost only about Y85 from the airport to the centre (including the Y15 road toll); make sure the driver uses the meter. Join the taxi ranks and ignore approaches from drivers, as scams are common.

Bicycle

To get around the city in true Běijīng style, consider riding a bicycle, which can be rented from many hotels, especially those in the budget range. **Universal Bicycle Rental Outlet** (双人驿站; Shuāngrén Yìzhàn; Map p318; Qianhai Lake; single/tandem bike per hr Y10/20, deposit Y500; Ⓜ Gulou Dajie) has two outlets in the vicinity of Qianhai Lake.

Public Transport

Given the frequently appalling traffic, the **subway** (地铁; dìtiě) is a hassle-free way to get around the centre of Běijīng. Currently nine lines are operating, with two more under construction, including Line 9, which will link Běijīng West train station with Line 1 and Line 4. It operates from 5am to 11pm and the fare is a flat Y2. Signs are in English and easy to understand. Stations are marked by a blue sign with a capital 'D'. Běijīng Train Station is a stop on the circle subway line.

Taxi

Taxis are cheap and plentiful: the standard per-kilometre charge starts from Y2, with a Y10 minimum. Make sure your driver turns on the meter, especially coming from the airport or the train station. Between 11pm and 6am there is a 20% surcharge added to the flag-fall metered fare. Drivers will rarely speak English so have a map handy to point out your destination; better still, have somebody write down your destination and address in Chinese characters so you can show it to the driver.

AROUND BĚIJĪNG

Great Wall of China   长城

Stretching 7200km from the Bo Sea in the east to the Gobi Desert in the west, the Great Wall of China is truly a wonder, due to both its breathtaking beauty and its ancient architectural achievement. Several sections of the Great Wall, particularly at Bādálǐng, have been recently revamped for the benefit of tourists. Also renovated but less touristed are the sections at Sīmǎtái and Jīnshānlǐng.

History

The 'original' construction of the Great Wall is credited to Emperor Qin Shihuang (221–207 BC), China's first sovereign emperor. He accomplished this feat by reconstructing and linking the ruins of older walls, which had been built by the vassal states under the Zhou dynasty in the 7th century BC. The result was a magnificent 4800km stretch of wall, which was meant to keep out the marauding nomads in the north (Huns, Turks and Mongols). The effort required hundreds of thousands of workers, most of them prisoners. Over the course of 10 years, an estimated one million people died; legend has it

---

VISAS FOR ONWARD TRAVEL

Mongolia

At the Mongolian embassy in Běijīng (see p383) you can purchase a visa for Y270 (available in five working days) or Y495 (available in one working day). The embassy is open for visa drop-off Monday, Wednesday, Friday from 9am to noon and Tuesday and Thursday from 2 to 4pm. Visa pick-up is 4 to 5pm. To pay for the visa, you will need to go to a nearby bank (the embassy will provide instructions). Note that between June and September the embassy is very busy, it's best to line up around one to two hours before the embassy opens (or even earlier at peak times).

Russia

Only permanent or temporary residents of China can obtain Russian tourist visas in Beijing. Visitors with a tourist visa can get a Russian transit visa in Beijing but will have to provide tickets for the entire journey into and out of Russia. If at all possible, apply in your home country.

Consular hours are 9am to noon Monday to Friday. Get there by 8am to avoid the rush.

INTERNATIONAL TRAINS DEPARTING BĚIJĪNG

DESTINATION	TRAIN NUMBER	DEPARTURE DAY	DEPARTURE TIME	DURATION
Moscow (via Ulaanbaatar)	K3	Wed	7.47am****	100hr (arrives Monday 2.04pm)
Moscow (via Ha'ěrbīn)	K19	Sat	10.56pm	120hr (arrives Friday 5.57pm)
Pyongyang	K27	Mon, Wed, Thu, Sat	5.55pm	26hr
Ulaanbaatar	K23 (year round)*	Tue or Sat**	8.03am	30hr
Ulaanbaatar	K23 (summer only extra train)*	Mon or Sat***	8.03am	30hr
Hanoi	T5	Thu & Sun	6.08pm	40hr

*Train 23 passes through Dàtóng at approximately 2.15pm, Jíníng at 4.15pm, Èrlián at 8.45pm and Zamyn-Üüd at 11.45pm.

**The K23 changes its departure day each year (depending on whether its run by China or Mongolia railway). The Chinese train typically departs Běijīng on Tuesday, while the Mongolian typically departs Běijīng on Saturday. Note that the Chinese and Mongolians switch off operating duties in May.

***The K23 summer train is an extra train put on for the summer holiday season (it usually runs June to September). When operated by Mongolia it will most likely departs Běijīng on a Monday, when run by China it will mostly likely departs Běijīng on Saturday.

****Departure time from Běijīng varies slightly in some years.

International Train Fares from Běijīng

The costs (in yuán) for international destinations from Běijīng:

DESTINATION	HARD SLEEPER (4-BERTH)	SOFT SLEEPER (4-BERTH)	DELUXE (2-BERTH)
Moscow (K3)	3732	5493	6013
Moscow (K19)	4122	-	6405
Pyongyang	1122	-	1604
Ulaanbaatar	1321	1897	2068
Hanoi	-	1604	1122

that the bodies of deceased workers weren't buried but simply stuffed into the Wall.

By the collapse of the Qin, the Great Wall had already started to crumble due to years of neglect. Emperor Han Wu-Di once again undertook the task of rebuilding the existing wall, and extending it 480km further west into the Gobi Desert. During this period, the wall served mainly as an elevated highway, along which men and equipment could be transported across mountainous terrain. Furthermore, the Hans established a system of smoke signals, by which they could warn each other of enemy attacks. Thus, the wall protected traders and explorers who were travelling the ancient caravan routes between China and Europe.

The wall that you see today is largely a product of the Ming dynasty (1368–1644). The Ming wall was taller, longer and more ornate than any earlier incarnations. It was also stronger, due in part to the advanced brick technology the Ming workers used.

BĀDÁLǏNG 八达岭

Most visitors see the Great Wall at **Bādálǐng** (Bādálǐng Chángchéng; admission Y45; ⊘6am-10pm summer, 7am-6pm winter), 70km northwest of Běijīng, at an elevation of 1000m. The section of masonry at Bādálǐng was first built during the Ming dynasty, and was heavily restored in the 1950s and the 1980s. Punctuated with watchtowers, the 6m-wide wall is clad in brick, typical of the stonework employed by the Ming when they restored and expanded the fortification.

The surrounding scenery is raw and impressive and this is the place to come to see the wall snaking off over the undulating hills. Also come here for guard rails, souvenir stalls, a fairground feel and the companionship of squads of tourists surging over the ramparts. Try to avoid summer weekends when the place is a crush of humanity. Come during the week instead, and if possible, during the colder months when it's covered in snow.

Cable cars exist for the weary (round-trip Y60).

The admission fee also includes a 15-minute film about the Great Wall at the **Great Wall Circle Vision Theatre** (⊘9am-5.45pm), a 360-degree amphitheatre, and the **China Great Wall Museum** (⊘9am-4pm).

On the road to Bādálǐng (50km out of Běijīng) you will pass another section of the Wall called **Jūyōngguān** (居庸关), an over-restored section with an admission price of Y45.

❶ Getting There & Away

The cheapest and easiest way to get to Bādálǐng is to take bus 919 (Y12, 1½ hours) from just north of the old gate of Déshèngmén, about 500m east of the Jishuitan subway stop. In summer, the first bus from Běijīng leaves at 6.30am and the last bus from Bādálǐng departs at 8.30pm (but confirm this).

CITS (☑6512 3075; www.cits.com.cn, in Chinese), the Běijīng Tourist Information Center, big hotels and everyone else in the tourist business does a tour to Bādálǐng. Watch out for high-priced hotel tours (up to Y300 per person).

A taxi to the wall and back will cost a minimum of Y400 for an eight-hour hire with a maximum of four passengers.

MÙTIÁNYÙ 慕田峪

The 2250m-long granite section of wall at **Mùtiányù** (admission Y45; ⊘6.30am-6pm), 90km northeast of Běijīng, was developed as a decoy alternative to Bādálǐng and is, on the whole, a less commercial experience. Despite some motivated hawking and tourist clutter, the stretch of wall is notable for its numerous Ming dynasty guard towers and stirring views. The wall is also equipped with a **cable car** (round-trip Y50; ⊘8.30am-4.30pm). October is the best month to visit, for the autumn colours of the trees that envelop the surrounding countryside.

❶ Getting There & Away

From **Dōngzhímén Transport Hub Station** (东直门枢纽站; Dōngzhímén Shūniǔzhàn; Map p318) you can take either bus 916 (Y8, one hour) or 936 (Y5) to Huáiróu (怀柔) then change for a minibus to Mùtiányù (Y25).

Tour bus 6 (☑6601 8285) runs to Mùtiányù (Y50) from outside the South Cathedral at Xuānwǔmén, operating between 6.30am and 8.30am on Saturday, Sunday and public holidays from April to October.

SĪMǍTÁI 司马台

The stirring remains at **Sīmǎtái** (admission Y40; ⊘8am-5pm), 110km northeast of Běijīng, make for a more exhilarating Great Wall experience. Built during the reign of Ming-dynasty emperor Hongwu, the 19km stretch is marked by watchtowers, steep plunges and scrambling ascents.

NORTHBOUND DOMESTIC TRAINS DEPARTING BĚIJĪNG

DESTINATION	DEPARTURE TIME	DURATION (HR)	FARE
Èrlián (K23)	7.47am, Mon, Tue	13	Y202
Èrlián (K3)	7.47am, Wed	13	Y202
Dàtóng	15 daily	6-7	Y64-105
Ha'ěrbīn	16 daily	8-12	Y281-429
Mǎnzhōulǐ (1301)	10.49am, daily	32	Y413-675

Not for the faint-hearted, this rough section of the wall is very steep. A few slopes have a 70-degree incline and you need both hands free, so bring a rucksack to hold your camera and other essentials. The **cable car** (round-trip Y50) could be an alternative to a sprained ankle. Take strong shoes with a good grip.

Sīmǎtái has some unusual features, such as 'obstacle walls' – walls-within-walls used for defending against enemies who had already scaled the Great Wall. There's also a **toboggan ride** (Y30), and, unfazed by the dizzying terrain, hawkers make an unavoidable appearance.

❶ Getting There & Away

To get here on local transport, take fast bus 980 (Y15, regular services 5.50am to 8pm) to Mìyún (密云) from the **Dōngzhímén Transport Hub Station** (东直门枢纽站; Dōngzhímén Shūniǔzhàn; Map p318) from 6am (Y20) and change to a minibus to Sīmǎtái, or a taxi (round-trip Y120).

Weekend tour bus 12 (☑ 6601 8285) leaves from outside the South Cathedral at Xuānwǔmén for Sīmǎtái (Y50) between 6.30am and 8.30am Saturday, Sunday and public holidays. Backpacker hotels often run morning trips by minibus for around Y60 (not including entrance fee). A taxi from Běijīng for the day costs about Y400.

JĪNSHĀNLĬNG 金山岭

Though not as steep (and therefore not as impressive) as Sīmǎtái, the Great Wall at **Jīnshānlǐng** (Jīnshānlǐng Chángchéng; admission Y40), near the town of Gǔběikǒu, has 24 watchtowers and is considerably less developed (and therefore much quieter) than any of the sites previously mentioned, despite undergoing some restoration work.

Perhaps the most interesting thing about Jīnshānlǐng is that it's the starting point for a 10km hike to Sīmǎtái. It takes nearly four hours because the trail is steep and stony. Parts of the wall along the route are in a state of ruin, but it can be traversed without too much difficulty. Upon arrival at Sīmǎtái, however, you may have to buy another ticket.

You can do the walk in the opposite direction, but getting a ride back to Běijīng from Sīmǎtái is easier than from Jīnshānlǐng. Of course, getting a ride should be no problem if you've made arrangements with your driver to pick you up (and didn't pay in advance).

❶ Getting There & Away

To get to Jīnshānlǐng from **Dōngzhímén Transport Hub Station** (东直门枢纽站; Dōngzhímén Shūniǔzhàn; Map p318), take a minibus to Mìyún (密云; Y10, 1¼ hours), and then hire a minivan to drop you off at Jīnshānlǐng.

Understand
Your Journey

History of the Railway

In the second half of the 19th century, the more advanced industrial states contested with each other for strategic advantage, economic fortune and imperial expansion. The stakes were high – no less than continental conquest and, in Russia's case, claim over the still undeveloped and even undiscovered natural wealth of Inner Eurasia. Up until this time, the distance between St Petersburg and the Pacific was measured in an arduous overland trek or a hazardous sea voyage. Russia's solution was to construct the world's longest railroad – the great Siberian railway.

Russia's Railways & Visionaries

A latecomer to the Industrial Revolution, Russia had long been dominated by a bloated autocratic state tied to an obsolete, landowning aristocracy. By the mid-19th century, Russia was slipping from the ranks of Europe's great powers. In 1857, Tsar Alexander II issued a railway decree, through which the state determined to reinvigorate the economy's pre-industrial infrastructure with modern railway routes.

Worth tracking down is the out-of-print *To the Great Ocean* by Harmon Tupper, a well-researched, lively and interesting take on the construction of the Trans-Siberian Railway.

The new railroads connected the central industrial region to the raw materials of the Urals and the agricultural products of the Black Earth region. Moscow became the hub of the national rail system, as the terminus of nine different lines. This spurt of construction was mostly confined to European Russia, but fear of British encroachment from the Indian subcontinent prompted the construction of a trans-Caspian line, which penetrated deep into Central Asia in the 1880s. Much to the chagrin of Siberian nationalists, some of whom believed that forces in the capital were even deliberately trying to hinder their region's development,

TIMELINE

Early 1580s	1601	1619
Yermak Timofeevich and his Cossack brigands capture Isker, the capital of the Turkic khanate Sibir abandoned by Khan Kuchum as the Cossacks approach, beginning Russia's expansion into Siberia.	A customs house is erected at Verkhotu-rye in the Urals, and this town becomes the only legal entry and exit point for those crossing the Urals to and from Siberia.	The Northern Sea Route along Siberia's north coast is closed completely to hinder the British and Dutch, whose search for a new sea route to Asia rouses territorial concerns.

RUSSIA'S EARLY RAILS

In 1833, inspired by newfangled steam technology from overseas, EA Cherepanov and his son ME Cherepanov invented Russia's first steam railway locomotive at Nizhny Tagil in the Urals (there's a model of it in Yekaterinburg, opposite the railway station). The locomotive and first Russian rail line, just 2km long, were built to support the Urals' mining industry, although the Cherepanovs also sent one of their engines to Tsar Nicholas I in St Petersburg.

It was here in St Petersburg that Russia's first public railway opened, in 1836. Built by Austrian engineer Franz Anton von Gerstner and operating with British-built locomotives, it was a 24km line connecting the imperial capital to the tsar's summer residence, Tsarskoe Selo. Nicholas I was so impressed with this new form of transport that plans were quickly made to roll out a rail network across European Russia.

Legend has it that in 1850, when the tsar commanded that a 650km rail line be built between Moscow and St Petersburg, he accidentally drew around his own finger on the ruler as he traced out a straight line between the cities. Engineers, too afraid to point out the error, duly incorporated the kink into the plans, which became a 17km bend near the town of Novgorod.

The truth is somewhat more prosaic. The curve was actually built to circumvent a steep gradient that Russian steam locomotives of the time were not powerful enough to climb. In 2001, the line was closed for 24 hours so that workers could finally straighten it out.

Siberia remained a distant, exotic land whose potential was not being fully realised.

The Dream of a Siberian Railway

In the 1840s, a geological expedition discovered that the Chinese had left the Amur River region unsettled and unfortified. Shortly thereafter, Tsar Nicholas I appointed the ambitious and able Nikolai Muravyov as the governor-general of Eastern Siberia. Unlike his predecessors, Muravyov was not another corrupt official, but a strong advocate of developing the Siberian Far East. With the tsar's approval, he collected some Cossacks and cruised the Amur, establishing towns for Russia and provoking fights with China. Preoccupied with foreign encroachment along the eastern seaboard, China was in no mood for hassles over Siberian forests. Thus, without bloodshed, Muravyov was able to redraw the border with China along the Amur River in the north and the Ussuri River in the east in exchange for some cash and a promise of mutual security. At the tsar's request, Muravyov henceforth attached the sobriquet 'Amursky' to his name.

1628–39	1649–51	1689	1730
Russian pioneers reach the Lena River in 1628, establish the fort of Yakutsk in 1637 and, two years later, sail out of the Ulya River into the Sea of Okhotsk.	Siberian explorer Yerofei Khabarov leads 150 men from Yakutsk towards the Amur River, which he reaches in the winter of 1650, ruthlessly subduing Daur tribes and encroaching on Chinese territory.	Russia and China sign the Treaty of Nerchinsk, defining the Sino-Siberian frontier and halting Russia's expansion east of the Amur. Russia gains right of passage to Běijīng for its traders.	Work begins on a full-scale Siberian Post Road, the only means of travel across Siberia to the Mongolian border. Over the centuries the route is gradually redirected south to Yekaterinburg.

Muravyov-Amursky continued to pursue his vision of Siberian colonisation, becoming a leading advocate of a railway that would connect European Russia to the Far East. He attracted a long line of suitors from Russia, England and the USA, offering their own proposals for a railroad to the Pacific, including Howard Duff, a British gent who came up with the somewhat bizarre idea of using wild Siberian horses to pull trains across Siberia until steam engines could be afforded.

Nothing came of the proposals, however, until circumstances in the late 19th century brought a change of heart. First, the economy in European Russia deteriorated in the 1880s, with overcrowding in villages, failed harvests, famine and peasant unrest. One solution would be peasant migration to the uncultivated lands of Western and Southern Siberia.

Second, Siberia was at risk of being lost altogether. In the late 19th century the region was turning into a political hotbed where well-educated Siberian autonomists had begun carving out their own regional identity as a resource-rich, multi-ethnic frontier society not unlike the USA. Ruling circles back in European Russia concluded that Siberia's radicals needed to be reined in.

Third, a weakened China was enabling foreign powers such as the British and French to become more influential in the Far East.

Finally, Alexander III replaced his reformist father Alexander II in 1881 – his father had abolished serfdom and taken steps belatedly to liberalise and modernise Russian society – and Russia again had a reactionary on its throne. Centralism, the prestige of territorial possessions and a nationalist spirit that infused the Age of the Industrial Empire became cornerstones of the new tsar's policies.

In March 1891 the tsar officially proclaimed the building of a Trans-Siberian Railway, from the Urals to the Pacific, and dispatched his son and heir apparent, Nicholas, to lay the first stone at Vladivostok.

Witte's State Within a State

The task of building the Trans-Siberian Railway fell to one of imperial Russia's most industrious and talented statesmen, Sergei Witte (1849–1915). Son of a colonial bureaucrat in the Caucasus and a graduate in mathematics, Witte had risen from lowly ticket-seller in Odesa's Southwest Railway Company to stationmaster and then company director. His power grew so strong that even the foreign minister of the day remarked that Witte had built his own 'state within a state'.

Witte's only problem was finding the cash for his 'state'. He implemented a host of financial policies and did some sharp manoeuvring, including issuing bonds, raising taxes and taking out foreign loans. Finally, he triggered a wave of inflation by resorting to the printing presses

One of the most interesting and readable accounts of the BAM railway is *Brezhnev's Folly* by Christopher Ward. The author goes against the grain of most researchers and believes, despite political stagnation, the Brezhnev era can also be seen as a dynamic period.

For general histories of Russia, China and Mongolia flick through the following: Nicholas Riasanovsky's *A History of Russia*, Stephen Haw's *A Traveller's History of China* and Charles Bawden's *The Modern History of Mongolia*.

1833–35	1837	1851	1857
Father and son mechanics EA and ME Cherepanov construct Russia's first steam locomotives, based on British technical knowledge. One of the engines is sent to St Petersburg.	On 30 October, Russia's first passenger railway, the 24km Tsarskoe Selo line connecting St Petersburg with Pavlovsk, is opened in order to illustrate the value of railways to the country.	On 1 November the first passenger train on the 649.7km St Petersburg–Moscow railway, Russia's second such transport line, departs on a journey of 21 hours and 45 minutes to Moscow.	Tsar Alexander II issues a railway decree to build a Russian rail network, the same year in which American Perry McDonough Collins proposes an Amur Railroad between Chita and Irkutsk.

to produce extra roubles to cover the soaring costs. 'Better to lose money than prestige', he explained to the concurring tsar.

The Trans-Siberian Railway also provided Witte with the opportunity to play diplomat, when he proposed to build a 560km shortcut across Manchuria, rather than follow the northern bend in the Amur to Vladivostok. Already besieged with foreigners, the Chinese emperor rejected the proposal.

A determined Witte changed tactics. He bought the influence of senior Chinese statesmen, offered a generous loan to the close-to-bankrupt Chinese government and repackaged his proposal to look like a Chinese-Russian joint venture. The result was an 80-year lease agreement over a corridor of territory for the railway. The Manchurian diversion led to the formation of the East Chinese Railway Company and the Russo-Chinese Bank, which were both in fact fronts for the Russian Ministry of Finance.

In 1898 Witte negotiated further territorial concessions, allowing Russia to build a Southern Manchurian line to a warm-water outlet at Port Arthur (Dàlián), located on the southern tip of the Liaodong Peninsula (west of the Korean Peninsula). The minister of finance, in effect, became the tsar's chief envoy to the Far East.

Building the Railroads

Construction on the railway got under way almost immediately after the tsar's decree was issued in 1891. Beginning at Chelyabinsk, in the southern Urals, it was decided the line would run parallel to the old post road as far as Irkutsk. Then it would blaze an iron trail eastward through the untamed Baikal, Amur and Ussuri regions to Vladivostok, the eastern terminus on the Pacific.

This route was selected out of consideration for the south's warmer weather conditions and more arable lands, which would hopefully encourage new agricultural settlements. But it didn't please local industrialists and merchants, since it bypassed many larger mining colonies and river towns in the north. The line was later altered to accommodate these influential economic lobbies by including Perm, Yekaterinburg and Tyumen.

Building the railroad across a formidable landscape posed ongoing challenges of engineering, supply and labour. The railroad cut through thick forests, crossed countless rivers, scaled rocky mountains and traversed soggy quagmires. Work brigades were poorly outfitted. The heavy work was carried out using shovels and picks, while horses and humans did the hauling.

Workers were recruited, or conscripted, from all over the empire as well as from abroad. Some of these were imprisoned exiles being held in Siberia, others labour recruits from China or Italian stonemasons, who

Russia's Frozen Frontier by Alan Wood takes you through the history of Siberia until 1991. The definitive book on Russian expansion into Siberia and the native Siberians is *A History of the Peoples of Siberia* by James Forsyth.

Before the Trans-Siberian Railway was built, it was quicker to travel from St Petersburg to Vladivostok by crossing the Atlantic, North America and the Pacific than by going overland.

1860	1876	1886–89
The Treaty of Peking sees China cede all territory east of the Ussuri and as far south as the Korean border to Japan. Russia loses Vladivostok, the newly founded port.	China's first railroad, the Woosung Railway, connects Shànghǎi with Woosung (now Baoshan District). However, the private project, constructed without government approval, is demolished the following year.	Following Tsar Alexander III's approval of the idea of a Trans-Siberian Railway, topographical surveys are taken along part of the proposed route between Tomsk and Sretensk, and around Vladivostok.

» Tsar Alexander III

worked on the tunnels. They toiled from dawn to dusk in the sweltering heat and freezing cold, and were preyed on by deadly diseases, forest bandits and hungry tigers. The construction work was divided into territorial segments, starting simultaneously from the eastern and western terminus points.

Western Siberian: 1892–96

From Chelyabinsk in the west (which is no longer part of the official Trans-Siberian route), the railway ran through Omsk and on to the Ob River, the site of present-day Novosibirsk. The Western Siberian section was 1440km long and the easiest to build. For the engineers, the main challenge was spanning the many rivers that fed the Ob Basin. The crossings for the Irtysh and Ob Rivers both required the building of bridges that were almost 1km long.

Ussuri: 1891–97

An exquisite miniature version of a Trans-Siberian train, with luxury carriages and church car, was created in 1900 to go inside one of the jewelled eggs made by Fabergé for the tsar; today it's at the Armoury of Moscow's Kremlin.

Meanwhile, construction was under way in the east on the Ussuri section of the railway. Beginning in Vladivostok, the line ran northward through the Ussuri River valley to Khabarovsk, a distance of about 800km. The forest terrain was more difficult for the engineers. Moreover, after the first tracks had been laid, it was discovered that the Amur rose as much as 10m during the spring, which meant redrawing the route and starting again. The builders faced severe labour shortages in this remote corner of the Far East. Despite initial misgivings, the construction brigades recruited over 8000 workers from the local Korean population and migrant Chinese labourers, over one-half of the total workforce for this section. They received lower wages than the Russian workers because, the foremen said, their work was inferior (though it may have been because they did not run tabs in the company canteen).

The builders of the Ussuri line introduced convict labour to the railroad, when 600 prisoners destined for incarceration on Sakhalin Island were instead ordered to start digging. Some prisoners escaped from their inexperienced handlers and went on a local crime spree. The project as a whole eventually employed nearly 15,000 convicts and exiles, with far better results. Convicts could work time off their sentences, and the living conditions were a small improvement on the tsar's prisons.

Central Siberian: 1893–98

The Central Siberian section covered a distance of 1920km from the Ob through Krasnoyarsk and on to Irkutsk, west of Lake Baikal. The work of the engineers became more complicated on this leg, because of the mountainous terrain and the steep river valleys. The Yenisey River

Early 1890s	1891	1892–96	1893–99
Russian playwright Anton Chekhov and American journalist George Kennan travel along the Trakt, the rough road across Siberia and the Far East, inspecting the penal colonies of the region.	Following a grand tour of Greece, Egypt, India, Indo-China and Japan (where he escapes assassination), Nicholas II lays the first stone in Vladivostok for the Ussuri line to Khabarovsk.	Almost at the same time, construction of the Western Siberian segment from the tea-trading city of Chelyabinsk in the Southern Urals to the Ob River (present-day Novosibirsk) is under way.	Mountainous terrain and the steep river valleys of Central Siberia prove the chief challenges for the construction of the segment from the Ob River to Lake Baikal, via Krasnoyarsk.

required a steel bridge nearly 1km in length. The earth – frozen until July and then swampy after the thaw – was less than ideal for digging. Water from the drained bogs collected in stagnant pools, which bred swarms of bloodthirsty mosquitoes around work sites.

Supply and labour became chronic. Unlike on the plains, there were few settlements to tap for workers (particularly those skilled with stone) or provisions. The builders advertised throughout the empire, offering higher wages and bonuses to entice fresh forces. In August 1898, the first train rolled into the station at Irkutsk.

Trans-Baikal: 1895–1900

The Trans-Baikal section ran from the eastern shore of Lake Baikal past Ulan-Ude and Chita, then on to Sretensk on the Shilka River. For the engineers, this section of 1072km of dense forest was nearly as daunting as the Circumbaikal section was a few years later, and would prove more frustrating. The railroad had to scale the Yablonovy Mountains, rising 5630m above sea level. The rivers were not so wide, but they ran in torrents and cut steep valley walls. The tracks were laid on narrow beds along high mountain ledges. Harsh weather, including summer droughts and heavy rains, exacerbated the difficulties. The great flood of 1897 washed away over 300km of laid track and 15 completed bridges.

East Chinese: 1897–1901

In 1894 Russia secured an agreement from the weakened Chinese that allowed for a Manchurian section of the Trans-Siberian Railway. From Chita, the 1440km-long East Chinese Railway turned southeast, crossing the Argun River and rolling through Hā'ĕrbīn (Harbin) to Vladivostok. It sliced over 600km off the journey and, after a one-sided negotiation, the Russian wide gauge was laid across the terrain of flat steppe lands, broad mountain passes and fertile river valleys.

In 1898–1901 the East Chinese Railway was extended in a branch line south from Hā'ĕrbīn to the ice-free harbour of Port Arthur, which Russia was leasing from China. Sergei Witte vehemently opposed building this branch, saying it would inflame Chinese nationalism. He was right. In 1899 Chinese nationalism mobilised into a rancorous antiforeigner movement, the self-proclaimed 'Fists of Higher Justice'. Better known as the Boxer Rebellion, the movement quickly spread to Manchuria and the Russian-controlled railway. Stations and depots were set ablaze, 480km of track were torn up and besieged railroad workers took flight. The main East Chinese line was only able to return to service after the Russian military intervened, and in 1901 the entire main line and branch to

VIRTUAL JOURNEY

Ride the virtual Trans-Sib from Moscow to Vladivostok replete with a choice of audio – rolling wheels, Russian radio (ubiquitous on any Russian train) or Russian literary classics: www.google.ru/intl/ru/landing/transsib/en.html.

HISTORY OF THE RAILWAY RUSSIA'S RAILWAYS & VISIONARIES

1896	**1895**	**1898**	**1900**
China grants Russia a concession to build the Chinese Eastern Railway (the Manchurian line) from Chita to Vladivostok via Hā'ĕrbīn in Manchuria, avoiding the difficult terrain of Russia's Amur region.	Construction starts on the Trans-Baikal line from Lake Baikal to Sretensk. Two years later torrential flooding washes away over 300km of the track and 15 bridges, wrecking another two irreparably.	Work begins on the South Manchurian Railway 550km from Hā'ĕrbīn to the ice-free, deep-water port at Lüshun (Port Arthur, the present-day Dàlián) near the tip of the Liaodong Peninsula.	The first Trans-Siberian services go into operation, using the train-ferry *Baikal* to transport passengers across Lake Baikal. It's later supplemented by the *Angara* ferry, transporting passengers and freight only.

Port Arthur came into service. Both were later integrated into the fully-fledged Trans-Manchurian Railway used today.

Circumbaikal: 1901–04

The Circumbaikal consumed four times as much stone as the entire Trans-Baikal section. Workers chiselled 39 tunnels into the lake's craggy capes and erected over 100 bridges and viaducts.

Heading east from Irkutsk, the builders encountered their most formidable obstacle: Lake Baikal. No previous experience prepared the engineers for the frigid lake's steep and rocky cliffs, which dominated the shoreline.

Engineers initially decided that construction of a railroad line around the lake would be impossibly expensive. Instead, the steamship *Baikal*, strong enough to smash through ice and big enough to carry train carriages, was commissioned from Britain. From April 1900, it transported trains and passengers between Port Baikal and Mysovaya (now Babushkin), while more passengers followed on the *Angara* – now moored in Irkutsk. However, the ships proved less than efficient, being prey to severe storms and sometimes impassable ice. This hindrance became a national security threat in 1904 – when Russia needed to transport troops and supplies to the front during the Russo-Japanese War, temporary tracks were actually laid across the ice in an attempt to expedite the military movement. Tragically, the first train to attempt this crossing sank through the cracked ice into Baikal's depths.

The decision was made in 1901 to construct a railway line that would skirt the southern edge of the lake, connecting Port Baikal and Mysovaya. The cliffs around the lake made this the most challenging section of all to build. Tsar Alexander III brought in Armenian and Italian masons to design the portals and arched bridges. The pride of Mother Russia at the time, this section was nicknamed 'the Tsar's Jewelled Buckle'.

It's believed that Russia adopted the wider 5ft gauge track for its railways, as opposed to the 4ft 8.5in track favoured by the rest of Europe and American railways, to stop foreign invaders being able to use standard-width rolling stock.

In the 1950s the Angara River was dammed, raising the level of Lake Baikal by about 1.5m and submerging the railway line between Irkutsk and Port Baikal. A shortcut bypassing this flooded section was built between Irkutsk and Slyudyanka – today's Trans-Siberian main line. The remaining 94km of the Circumbaikal became a neglected branch line, along which a few weekly minitrains still chug, much to the delight of train buffs; see p203 for details.

Amur: 1907–16

The 2080km-long Amur section presented similar engineering, supply and labour challenges. The Amur required some of the longest and most complicated bridges, including a span of almost 2km across the Amur. The builders relied heavily on convict labour, supplemented by army units and Chinese migrants. Building materials, including iron rails, had to be imported from British and North American suppliers.

1901	1904	1905	1906
With ferries proving a less than successful solution to crossing Baikal, the decision is taken to construct the Circumbaikal line along the southwestern shore of the lake.	Port Arthur comes under attack from the Japanese, provoking the Russo-Japanese War. The Trans-Siberian Railway buckles under the strain of transporting troop reinforcements to the Far East.	The Russian fleet is annihilated in the Tsushima Straits in May and Russia signs the Treaty of Portsmouth, turning Southern Manchuria over to Japan; Russia keeps the East Chinese Railway.	Japan founds the South Manchurian Railway Company within Japanese-controlled southern Manchuria. The railway runs to Hā'ěrbīn where it connects to the Chinese Eastern Railway.

The Amur was the last section of the Trans-Siberian Railway built, going into operation in 1916. The railway's first travellers transferred into boats at Sretensk for a long river voyage down the Amur to Khabarovsk, where they reboarded. The completion of the East Chinese Railway in 1898 bypassed the Amur, diverting passengers through northern China.

The Promise of Luxury

At the dawn of the 20th century, Russia was ready to launch its engineering achievement to the world. Prince Mikhail Khilkov, the communication minister, made arrangements with a Belgian company to create 'an ambulant palace of luxury' and had promotional brochures printed up in four languages proclaiming how it would now only 'take 10 days to cover the 5500 miles between Moscow and Vladivostok, or Port Arthur'.

To further press home the Trans-Siberian Railway's advantages a 'Palace of Russian Asia' pavilion was constructed at the Exposition Universelle in Paris in 1900. Inside the pavilion, visitors were treated to images of Siberia's pristine rugged landscape and exotic native cultures – including, incongruously, stuffed polar bears clinging to papier mâché icebergs. Luxurious, mock 1st-class sleepers offered comfortable and commodious compartments decorated with French Empire and Chinese-style furnishings.

It's estimated that by the time the Trans-Siberian Railway was completed in 1916 it had cost around R1400 million, over four times its original estimated cost of R300 million.

HISTORY OF THE RAILWAY THE PROMISE OF LUXURY

THE 'TRACK OF THE CAMEL'

The completion of the Trans-Siberian Railway and its glamorous unveiling at the Paris Exhibition lured many a curious traveller onto the rails to Siberia. Among Russians it became known as the 'track of the camel', because it wound and bypassed so many towns and ran through the middle of nowhere. A principal goal of the railway, however, was not to satisfy a craving for luxury among a travelling elite intent on sipping champagne in a spectacular wilderness. It was to facilitate the resettlement of Russian peasants to Siberia.

Restrictions on internal migration had been lifted in the 1800s, but a modest 500,000 people resettled to Siberia between 1860 and 1890. Once the train came on line, this turned into a raging torrent. Between 1891 and 1914, over five million new immigrants sought a better future there. Station halls were packed with hundreds of waiting peasants sleeping on the floor. One could travel for more than 3200km on the Trans-Siberian for less than R20 in 3rd class. These wagons dispensed with any pretension of style or comfort. A 1st-class rider observed: 'The 3rd-class passengers are packed like sardines. Their cars hold nothing save wooden bunks, two tiers thereof, and each has four and sometimes six. One's health would certainly be jeopardised by a passage through them. I notice that our car is constantly guarded. I am not surprised, and do not object in the least.'

1907

To protect Russia's Pacific access and territory in the Far East, Russia decides to construct the Amur line from Sretensk to Khabarovsk, the final portion of the Trans-Siberian Railway.

1908

China's last emperor, two-year-old Puyi, ascends the throne. As new railways are financed and built in Chinese territory by foreigners, an anti-Qing dynasty Railway Protection Movement is born.

STRINGER COLLECTION / GETTY IMAGES ©

» Trans-Siberian Railway under construction c 1903

RELIGION ON THE RAILS

The original pre-1917 Trans-Siberian trains included a Russian Orthodox church car, complete with icons, bells and a travelling priest. At stations along the route where a church had yet to be built the church car was used to hold services for the locals, railway workers and any interested passengers.

Jump forward a century to April 2005 and the Russian Orthodox Church signed an agreement with Russian Railways to cooperate on, among other things, restoring chapels and mobile carriage chapels to the railway transport system.

The imitation dining car served caviar, sturgeon and other Russian delicacies, while allowing visitors to admire moving Siberian scenery through the window, as recreated by a complex, multilayered painted panorama. The exhibit also featured a handsome smoking car, a music salon with piano, a well-stocked library, a fully equipped gymnasium and a marble and brass bath.

Travel along the early Trans-Siberian Railway, however, did not live up to its luxurious billing. East of Baikal, the train routinely ran out of food. 'Today we did not eat until 3pm, and then it was vile', wrote one cranky American traveller in 1902. 'There was one wretched little eating room filled with Russians. You may stand around and starve for all they care.'

Nor did the hastily constructed Trans-Siberian succeed in providing a more expeditious route to the Far East. Travellers experienced frequent delays, sometimes lasting days. The Trans-Siberian had the highest accident rate of any line in the empire. Ties splintered, bridges buckled and rails warped. The locomotives chugged along at no more than 25km/h because of the risk of derailment. One passenger bound for Běijīng scribbled in resignation: 'A traveller in these far eastern lands gradually loses his impatience and finally ceases to care whether his train goes fast or slowly, or does not go at all. Certainly we have been two hours at this station for no apparent reason.'

Trains buffs can flick through evocative historic and more contemporary images of past Trans-Siberian locos and carriages at Trains-World Expresses (http://trains-worldexpresses.com).

War & Revolution

Alexander III saw the Trans-Siberian Railway as the means for Russia to become a Far East power. Under his less able successor, Nicholas II, the construction of the railway instead provoked confrontations that exposed the many weaknesses of imperial Russia.

The Russo-Japanese War

The East Chinese Railway involved Russia in the multilateral dismemberment of the Chinese empire. In the subsequent grab for territorial

1914–21	1915	1916	1918
About 60% of Russia's railway network, 90% of its locomotives and 80% of the country's railway carriages are destroyed either during WWI or in the civil war	Having declared its independence from the dying Manchu empire in 1911, Mongolia signs the Treaty of Kyakhta with China and Russia, and is granted limited autonomy.	The completion of the 2.6km Khabarovsk bridge (the longest Trans-Siberian bridge) over the Amur River allows the opening of the 1920km Amur line, establishing the modern-day Trans-Siberian route.	Following the October Revolution, Lenin pulls Russia out of WWI and moves the capital to Moscow. Civil War. The tsar and family are executed in Yekaterinburg.

and commercial concessions in Manchuria, Russia came into direct conflict with imperial Japan. Witte was always inclined towards diplomacy in Russia's Far Eastern policy, but Nicholas was poorly advised: 'What Russia really needs,' the minister of interior opined, 'is a small victorious war'.

The tsar's aggressive stance in the Far East provoked Japan to attack Port Arthur in February 1904. The overconfident Nicholas was dazed by the rapid string of defeats. Japanese forces quickly seized the advantage over Russia's outnumbered troops, while the reinforcements remained stalled at Lake Baikal. The single-track, light-rail Trans-Siberian was simply inadequate. The tsar dispatched his prized Baltic fleet. In May 1905 the war concluded when – upon reaching the Tsushima Straits – the fleet was annihilated in just one afternoon.

Nicholas summoned Witte to salvage Russia's dignity in the peace negotiations. Under the Treaty of Portsmouth, Russia vacated southern Manchuria, but managed to hold on to the main East Chinese Railway line. Almost all of the branch line south to Port Arthur fell to the Japanese and was upgraded into the so-called South Manchurian Railway.

The 1905 Revolution

Russia's woeful performance in war unleashed a wave of anti-tsarist protest at home that culminated in the 1905 revolution. Railroad workers were quick to join the protest movement, with 27 different lines experiencing strikes in the first two months of 1905. In April, they coordinated their efforts by forming an All-Russia Union of Railroad Workers. At first, they demanded economic concessions, such as higher wages and shorter hours, but soon their demands became more political, such as the rights to organise and strike.

The government attempted to impose martial law over the railway system, and striking rail workers sparked a nationwide general strike.

The Bolshevik Revolution

Radical railroad workers also played a crucial role in the Bolshevik Revolution of 1917. Exhausted by its involvement in WWI, the tsarist regime fell to street demonstrators in February 1917. Nicholas' abdication created a power vacuum in the capital. The liberal provisional government was hesitant in dealing with the war issue, which swung public sentiment towards the more radical political parties.

In an attempt to restore order, General Kornilov ordered his troops at the front to march on St Petersburg, with the intention of declaring martial law. Radicals and liberals alike took cover. But Kornilov's men never made it. Railroad workers went on strike, refusing to transport them, and the putsch petered out. Within weeks, Vladimir Ilych Lenin and the

Published in 1897, *Roughing it in Siberia* by Robert Louis Jefferson is an amusing account of the eccentric English adventurer's journey on the Trans-Siberian as far as Krasnoyarsk and then by road to Minusinsk.

Robert Service is the author of both a biography of Vladimir Ilych Lenin and the *History of Twentieth Century Russia*, both excellent introductions to the dawn and progress of the Soviet era.

HISTORY OF THE RAILWAY WAR & REVOLUTION

1918–20	1920	1926	1929
The Czechoslovak Legion, a volunteer army who fought with Britain, France and Russia in WWI, seizes control of large parts of the Trans-Siberian Railway.	Admiral Kolchak, leading the counter-revolutionary White Army, is defeated by the Red Army at Omsk. He retreats to Irkutsk where he's executed. The civil war ends two years later.	US correspondent Junius B Wood reports that the railway is falling apart and rarely punctual. In the dining car he finds 'pre-cooked cauliflower warmed with a sauce of unknown texture'.	Electrification of the Trans-Siberian line begins as part of the first of Stalin's Five-Year Plans, designed to centralise the economy, boost heavy industry and make the USSR a superpower.

Bolsheviks staged a palace coup, deposed the provisional government and declared themselves rulers of Russia.

The Russian Civil War

The Bolsheviks' claim on power was soon challenged. In the spring of 1918, as the war in Europe continued without Russia, a legion of Czech POWs tried to return home to rejoin the fighting. Unable to cross the front line in the west, they headed east. Along the way, they provoked a confrontation with the Bolsheviks. When the White Army, hostile to the Bolsheviks, came to support the Czechs, the Russian Civil War began.

The Czech legion seized control of the western half of the Trans-Siberian Railway; in the meantime, the Japanese, who had landed in Vladivostok, took control of the railway east of Baikal. A separatist Siberian Republic was formed in Omsk, that is, until tsarist naval officer Admiral Kolchak overthrew the Omsk government and was declared supreme ruler of Siberia. Another former tsarist general reigned over the East Chinese Railway in Manchuria. Cossacks menaced the Trans-Baikal and Amur regions. Siberia had returned to the era of warlords.

It took the Bolsheviks more than three years to secure complete control over the Trans-Siberian Railway and to establish Soviet power across Siberia. Kolchak was arrested, tried and shot in Irkutsk.

WWII

In WWII, Nazi Germany's blitzkrieg invasion was an unintended impetus for Siberia's industrial development, when the industrial stock of European Russia was hastily evacuated to safer interior locations. Cities like Yekaterinburg, Tyumen, Novosibirsk, Barnaul (south of the Trans-Siberian) and Krasnoyarsk received an industrial boost, and Lenin's body was removed from its mausoleum in Moscow and freighted to Tyumen for safe-keeping. During the German occupation, the Trans-Siberian Railway served as a lifeline, furnishing the front with the reinforcements and equipment.

Development of Siberia

While the Trans-Siberian Railway had brought Russia's peasants flocking to Siberia to share in a better life, it also meant increased demand for materials to feed the railway and helped spur a period of tremendous optimism on the subcontinent. A second track was built alongside the original single line and the light rails were replaced with heavier, more durable rails. Wooden bridges and supports were replaced with iron and steel.

From the late 1920s, the Soviet leader Josef Stalin (1878–1953) abandoned the New Economic Policy (NEP) begun by Lenin – who before his death in 1924 had set about liberalising sectors to bolster a stagnating

MOMENTS IN TIME

Seventeen Moments in Soviet History (www.soviethistory.org) is a well-designed and highly informative site that covers all the major events that occurred during the life of the USSR.

1930s	1931	1934	1935
Slave labour from Siberia's Gulag system is used to start constructing the Baikal-Amur Mainline (BAM), an ambitious project to provide a backup Trans-Siberian Railway, should the other become incapacitated.	A turn-of-the-century proposal to connect the Trans-Siberian Railway with the tsarist-built Trans-Caspian Railway is realised with the opening of the Turkestan-Siberian line from Novosibirsk to Lugovoi, in Kazakhstan.	The Asia Express plies the South Manchurian Railway between Dàlián and Hsinking, capital of Japanese-controlled Manchuria. Reaching a speed of 134km/h, it's the world's fastest scheduled train of its day.	Russia sells the East Chinese Railway in Manchuria to Japan for ¥170 million (around US$48.3 million), the year Mao Zedong is recognised as the head of the Chinese Communist Party.

SIBERIA & THE EXILES

Siberia's reputation as a 'House of the Dead' for exiles and convicts has its beginnings in the mid-17th century, when a formal system of exile to Siberia was introduced, but even before that political exiles and criminals had been dispatched across the Urals. Siberians often call the Uglich Bell Siberia's first exile – a bell that was publicly flogged and dispatched to Siberia during a 16th-century uprising in the town of Uglich. Often, being exiled was the soft part of the punishment, and beforehand you might be flogged or mutilated, like having the septum of your nose ripped out for illegally using snuff. Gradually, though, Siberia itself and performing various degrees of hard labour came to be seen as punishment enough.

Nineteenth-century political reformists like the Decembrists (exiled after an uprising in 1825) or the Petrashevsky Circle (Russia's famous writer Fyodor Dostoevsky was exiled for being a member of this group) were among the best-known waves of exiles, and the Decembrists and the wives who followed their husbands into exile did much for Siberia's cultural and academic life.

By the time the US author George Kennan travelled Siberia to write a series of damning articles about the exile system, the main types of exiles were *katorzhniki* (the ones serving hard labour), *poselentsy* (someone in a penal colony), *ssylny* (banished but they were able to return afterwards), and those who went voluntarily to be with their exiled spouse or relative. Communist revolutionaries such as Lenin, Stalin and Sverdlov were all exiled in Siberia along different stretches of the Yenisey River.

After a brief respite following the Russian Revolution of 1917, a new system of exile took shape under Stalin: the Gulag camp. This 'archipelago' of brutal forced labour camps strung across the country – but in Siberia in particular – exploded in number during Stalin's purges and drive to industrialise in the 1930s and 1940s, continuing to exist until just after his death in 1953, when the camps were slowly disbanded. Today the best-preserved memorial is the Perm-36 Gulag camp located in the Urals.

economy – and Stalin put economic control firmly back into state hands with his First Five Year Plan. This was aimed at industrialising Russia's regions, especially Siberia, but it also foresaw collectivisation of agriculture, the breaking down of what it saw as 'backward' indigenous lifestyles by shifting children of the small nationalities of the north into boarding schools, and resulted in political paranoia and purges.

Stalin's drive for industrialisation was enormously successful, but it was also to a large extent achieved on the backs of prisoners of the Gulag camps, who were worked to death in slave labour camps (see p338).

In the 1950s and 1960s, oil and gas discoveries energised Siberia. While these deposits were in the north, they promoted development in the cities along the railway.

1937

Russia's railways, including the Trans-Siberian, are revived. The largest plant east of the Urals for building and repairing locomotives and rolling stock goes into operation in Ulan-Ude.

1939

Japan invades Mongolia from Manchuria in May. With help from the Soviet Union, and after heavy fighting, the Mongols defeat Japan by September – just as WWII starts in Europe.

1941

In June, Hitler invades the Soviet Union in Operation Barbarossa, beginning the 'Great Patriotic War'. During WWII, much Russian industry is transferred to Siberia.

» Retired 1930s locomotive

Stalin's reform-minded successor, Nikita Khrushchev, denounced his former boss and liberated millions of labour-camp inmates. Meanwhile, incentive-laden offers lured new workers to the region, and the Siberian population became highly skilled. A uniquely planned academic community was created near Novosibirsk. Military industry flourished in secret cities, sheltering well-tended scientists and technicians. By 1970, 13 Siberian cities had populations of 250,000 or more.

During this time, Siberia's native populations were increasingly assimilated into the lifestyle and culture of Soviet Russian society. In 1900 native peoples accounted for more than 15% of Siberia's total population but, by 1970, this number was less than 4%. Simultaneously, Siberia's development was having detrimental effects on the environment.

The Pulitzer Prize–winning *Gulag: A History* by Anne Applebaum is the definitive account of the forced labour camps of Russia's most desolate regions.

Branching Out

The Soviet regime continued to develop overland rail access to the Eurasian continent so that travellers could reach ever more remote corners of the Far East. The construction and operation of branch lines throughout the Far East were entangled in the politics of the region for most of the 20th century.

The Trans-Manchurian

The Trans-Manchurian line connects Běijīng to the Trans-Siberian at Chita, via the Russian-built East Chinese Railway and also the section leading down to Port Arthur later known as the South Manchurian Railway. The South Manchurian, however, had fallen to Japan as spoils of war in 1905. At this time, American railroad baron EH Harriman made several generous bids to buy these routes from their respective operators.

THE RAILROAD OF DEATH

It's impossible to tally the human toll of building railways across Siberia's wilderness, but one section of track in the far north of the region was so perilous that it was known as the Railroad of Death. The 1297km railway between Salekhard and Igarka was planned under Stalin's rule for three reasons: to aid the export of nickel from Norilsk; to connect the ports of Salekhard and Igarka with Russia's railway network; and as work for the thousands of prisoners herded into the Gulag system of forced-labour camps.

Construction started in 1949 but was immediately hampered by terrible weather and permafrost. Poorly treated workers died in droves. Only Stalin's death in 1953 put a halt to the railway's construction, by which time 699km of track had been laid, at a cost of nearly R42 billion. After construction ceased, the elements quickly finished off what was left of the railway. All that remains today is the ghostly presence of abandoned villages, rusting rails and machinery and rotting sleepers amid dense forests.

1945	1947–49	1950–52	1956
The USSR declares war against Japan. Soviet troops occupy Manchuria. When Japan surrenders, the Manchurian railway is placed under Sino-Russian administration.	Construction of the Trans-Mongolian line begins in 1947, with an extension from Ulan-Ude south towards the border town of Naushki. In 1949 the line reaches Mongolia's capital of Ulaanbaatar.	In 1950 the USSR signs a treaty with the People's Republic of China, shifting its support from the Nationalists to Mao's Communists. In 1952 China receives Manchuria's East Chinese Railway.	The Gobi Desert is spanned; the Trans-Mongolian Railway connecting Moscow with Běijīng via Ulaanbaatar is completed. Due to different gauges, bogies have to be changed at the China–Mongolia border.

He saw a rare opportunity to realise his ambition of building a railroad line that circumnavigated the globe. Harriman's offers, however, were rebuffed.

From 1917 until the early 1920s, revolution and civil war had thrown the Soviet Union into chaos. Gradually, however, the country recovered. Although Russia was good to its promises to renounce its privileges in Manchuria, it baulked at handing over its main-line segment of the East Chinese Railway across northern Manchuria. Instead it negotiated a temporary joint custody of the line, stacked positions with its own people and stalled all attempts by China to get it back.

The Russians had to continuously defend their (partial) claim to the railway line. During the 1920s the Russian managers were arrested by a Manchurian warlord and again by Chiang Kaishek (leader of the Kuomintang, the Chinese Nationalist Party), both of whom seized control of the railroad. In each case the aggressors were forced to relinquish their prizes and prisoners. In 1932 the Japanese took control of Manchuria, renaming it Manchukuo and installing the last Manchu emperor, Puyi, as a puppet ruler. Under pressure, Russia sold her interest in the main-line segment of the East Chinese Railway to the new rulers in 1935.

This was not the proverbial end of the line, however. According to the secret protocols negotiated at Yalta, Winston Churchill and Franklin D Roosevelt conceded back to Stalin the East Chinese and South Manchurian rail lines as part of the price of Soviet entry into the Pacific War. The lines were given back to China in 1952 as a Soviet goodwill gesture to the new Chinese communist regime.

By the mid-1960s relations between China and Russia had soured and the border was closed, thus stopping the Trans-Manchurian service. The low point was reached in 1969 when armed clashes occurred over Damansky Island in the Ussuri River, part of the border between the two communist neighbours. The so-called Sino-Soviet Split lasted until the early 1980s, and since this time Russian-Chinese relations have warmed considerably, allowing the Trans-Siberian to be reconnected to the Trans-Manchurian, giving us the route you follow today.

The Trans-Mongolian

The 2080km Trans-Mongolian line was built along the route travelled by the ancient tea caravans, from Běijīng through Mongolia to Ulan-Ude. The line was built piecemeal, a direct result of fluctuations in the relationship between Russia and China.

During the late 19th century, Mongolia was formally part of the Chinese Manchu empire. After centuries of neglect, China's officials became more interested in the region, much to the irritation of the Mongolians.

For a very personal history of China through the 20th century read *Wild Swans* by Jung Chang. She followed this epic tale in 2005 with her collaborative warts-and-all portrait of Mao Zedong, *Mao: The Unknown Story*, cowritten with Jon Halliday.

Bernardo Bertolucci's *The Last Emperor* (1988) is a lavish, epic-scale story of Puyi, China's last imperial ruler. The film tells the story through the eyes of Puyi, using flashbacks to his childhood and days heading a Japanese puppet regime.

1961	1961–63	1965	1969
Mongolia is admitted to the UN as an independent country, but the Soviet Union continues to occupy Mongolia with troops and run it as a satellite state.	The Trans-Siberian Railway is used to transport cosmonaut hardware to Baikonur (in present-day Kazakhstan). The first man in space, Yury Gagarin, blasts off in 1961.	Oil begins to flow in Siberia as Prime Minister Alexey Kosygin tries to shift the Soviet economy over to light industry and consumer goods. Under Brezhnev's opposition brings economic stagnation.	Political relations between China and Russia deteriorate and armed clashes erupt along the Ussuri River. The Trans-Mongolian and Trans-Manchurian routes into China are suspended.

In 1999 a 2612m combined road and rail bridge over the Amur River replaced the original 18 span, 2568m-long construction – the longest such bridge on the Trans-Siberian Railway.

Plans were made to construct a railroad from Běijīng to Örgöö (Ulaanbaatar). Instead, the Chinese empire collapsed in 1911.

Mongolia was very eager to be rid of its Chinese overlord but was too weak to fend for itself. Russia emerged conveniently as a protective patron of Mongolian independence. The Soviet Union consolidated its influence in 'independent' Mongolia and in 1936 a short rail route was announced, linking Mongolia and Soviet Buryatiya, whose peoples shared close ethnic ties. This new line between Ulan-Ude and Naushki was completed in 1940, and in 1949, it was extended to the capital, Ulaanbaatar.

In the early 1950s, relations between the Soviet Union and communist China relaxed somewhat, allowing the Chinese to finally begin work on the long-planned railroad connecting Běijīng with Ulaanbaatar. Although train service began on this line in 1956, the Sino-Soviet Split in the 1960s closed the border. Like the Trans-Manchurian, the Trans-Mongolian line was reopened in the 1980s.

The Baikal-Amur Mainline

In 2005 China and Russia settled a post-WWII dispute over 2% of their 4300km common border. For the first time, the whole border was legally defined.

The 4234km Baikalo-Amurskaya Magistral (Baikal-Amur Mainline, or BAM) begins west of Irkutsk and passes north of Lake Baikal on its way east to the Pacific coast. The route was first considered as an option for the Trans-Siberian line in the 1880s, but it would not be until the 1930s that work actually started on its construction, beginning at Tayshet.

Although parts of the far-eastern end of the line were built from 1944 (partly using Japanese and German POWs as labour), the project was put on indefinite hold in 1953 after the death of Stalin. Its resumption, amid much fanfare, came in 1974, when Leonid Brezhnev hailed it the 'Hero Project of the Century'. The call went out to the youth of the Soviet Union to rally to the challenge of constructing the BAM.

DERVLA MURPHY – ON THE BAM

Among intrepid foreign travellers, BAM has somewhat of a cult following, led by Irish octogenarian travel writer Dervla Murphy, who wrote two contemporary books on her travels on and around the BAM (*Through Siberia by Accident* and *Silverland*). *Platskart* was the only way to roll for the famously frugal 'Irish babushka,' as she dubbed herself. Travelling alone and speaking not a word of Russian, Murphy brought out the best in Siberian people, whose hospitality she describes as nothing short of legendary.

Dedicated to a carbon-friendly, organic lifestyle, ferociously anti-war and an avowed technophobe and critic of today's gadget-obsessed world, she mixes colourful vignettes about her travels with evocative landscape descriptions and riveting historical asides about the BAM and Siberia in general. She also excels at bringing to life the Cossack 'heroes' who conquered and ruled these unforgiving lands centuries ago.

1974	1980s	1990	1991
As work resumes on the long-abandoned BAM, the railroad is styled by party general secretary Leonid Brezhnev as a huge Komsomol (Communist youth league) project with completion scheduled for 1982.	Following a thaw in international relations between Russia and China, the Trans-Mongolian and Trans-Manchurian lines reopen for business and travellers begin writing about the routes again.	Democracy demonstrations occur in Ulaanbaatar. Soviet troops begin withdrawing, and in the first free, multiparty elections the Mongolian People's Revolutionary Party wins 85% of the vote.	The BAM's official opening is overshadowed by an attempted coup against USSR president Mikhail Gorbachev, and the demise of the Soviet Union. Boris Yeltsin becomes Russia's president.

The BAM, however, was poorly coordinated and badly mismanaged. The project employed 100,000 workers, including 20,000 communist youth league 'volunteers'. Lacking housing and electricity, few workers reenlisted and others simply deserted.

The BAM blazed a trail through inhospitable climate and terrain, providing access to the region's mineral-rich basins. The BAM towns expanded with the new railway, which was being forced through virgin wilderness. Overcoming Siberia's swamps, its seven mountain ranges, its seemingly infinite number of rivers and, in particular, its vast swath of permafrost, pushed the cost of the project to a staggering US$25 billion.

The line was officially opened in 1991, when it became possible to travel the whole length from Tayshet to Sovetskaya Gavan on the Pacific coast. However, the BAM's 15.34km Severomuysky tunnel, the longest in Russia, was only completed in 2003. Work continues very slowly on the AYaM (Amur-Yakutsk Mainline or Amuro-Yakutskaya Magistral), a branch line that already extends south from Tynda on the BAM to Bamovskaya on the Trans-Siberian line, and will eventually terminate in the north at Yakutsk, capital of the Republic of Sakha. At the time of research passenger trains stopped at the coal mining town of Neryungri on the AYaM, and the entire line is expected to open in 2013.

> The Russian railway system, covering 85,500km of track, is the second-largest in the world after the USA's 228,464km of track.

1992	2002	2005
A third route from Russia to China is established via a railway from Ürümqi to the border of Kazakhstan, connecting with a line completed in 1960 to Aktogay, between Almaty and Semey.	The electrification of the Trans-Siberian line, started in 1929, is finally completed. Train weights can be doubled to 6000 tonnes on this route covering one-sixth of the globe.	The private *Golden Eagle* luxury train service begins service between Vladivostok and Moscow, making a detour on some services to Ulaanbaatar in Mongolia, complementing the private Tsar's Gold service.

SAVERKIN ALEXANDER / ITAR-TASS / CORBIS ©

» *Golden Eagle* dining car

Siberian Travellers

Siberia's Great Post Road, along with the Trans-Siberian, Trans-Mongolian and the Trans-Manchurian railways of Russia, Mongolia and China, have been plied by many a famous or notorious traveller and writer. Frostbitten and broken by a mock execution in St Petersburg, the Russian realist writer Fyodor Dostoevsky (1821–1881) shuffled across the subcontinent in shackles in the mid-19th century and reworked his hardships into the novel *The House of the Dead* (1862). The American George Kennan (1845–1924) gave us poignant descriptions of Siberia's prison system in the late 1880s, and shortly afterwards the Russian playwright Anton Chekhov (1860–1904) followed, on a journey to Sakhalin Island to describe prison conditions there.

The Real Siberia, together with an Account of a Dash Through Manchuria (1902) by John Foster Fraser describes Siberia during its boom years and avoids many of the prejudices of the period.

Zhang Qian & the Silk Road

Although he travelled only to Siberia's fringes, Chinese explorer Zhang Qian (195–114 BC) was the most influential of the early explorers of northern and central Asia. He brought back to China the first descriptions of Central Asia, leading to the development of ancient trading routes into the Silk Road.

The northern Silk Road through Samarkand would have a considerable impact on Siberia; even prior to Russian colonisation, traders from Bukhara (in modern-day Uzbekistan) provided a trade lifeline between the towns of the khanate of Sibir and the Silk Road. The Bukharans also conducted the religious education of the Tartar khans of Sibir. Once the Russians arrived, the Bukharan trade caravans and their wares were a common sight at Siberian markets and in the Tartar quarters of towns such as Tobolsk.

In 138 BC Zhang Qian set out on his famous journey to negotiate an alliance against the Xiongnu nomadic tribes controlling much of the steppes of northern and central Asia. He was taken prisoner by the Xiongnu and spent 10 years in captivity, returning to China with his reports 13 years after his departure. He wrote of the Ferghana Valley (a valley crossing through Uzbekistan, Kyrgyzstan and Tajikistan) and told of an unusual breed of horses, which the Chinese later adopted to improve their cavalry.

Roy Chapman Andrews (1884–1960), who was director of New York's Museum of Natural History, explored the Gobi Desert in the 1920s and 1930s using cars and camels. For more, see www .roychapman andrewssociety .org.

Chekhov Unplugged

As contemporary author Ian Frazier notes in his *Travels in Siberia,* critics are puzzled about why Chekhov decided to cross Siberia to visit Sakhalin Island. Soviet authorities, meanwhile, preferred to give us a Chekhov without the spice and did not publish some of the juiciest passages from the letters he wrote home from Siberia.

In one remarkable missive he writes about a visit to a brothel in Blagoveshchensk. This begins with descriptions of a Japanese prostitute's room – 'A Japanese girl's room is small and clean, sentimental in that Asian way, and laden with knick-knacks ... neither basins nor natural rubbers or portraits of generals' – continues with comparison of the act with an 'equestrian school of the highest order' and culminates with possibly the most bizarre lines ever written about the Trans-Sib: 'The road back from Sakhalin leads through Ceylon, where heaven is found. Here, in this Paradise, I covered more than 100 versts by rail and was up to the neck in palm leaves and bronzed women. When I have children, then I will tell them not without some pride, "Sons of bitches, in my lifetime I had intercourse with a black-eyed Hindu ... and where? In the coconut forest on a moonlit night!"'

Although Chekhov's letters during this period make interesting reading in themselves, his classic work arising from the journey across Siberia is *Sakhalin Island*, an account of the time he spent on the island visiting the prison colonies.

A Fine Place for a Freak

Siberia has long attracted freak travellers. One of the more unusual was the Briton James Holman (1786–1857), who edged across Siberia as blind as a proverbial badger and recorded his journey, writing with mechanical help, in *Travels through Russia, Siberia, Poland, Austria, Saxony, Prussia, Hanover, etc. undertaken during the years 1822, 1823, and 1824, while suffering from total blindness, and comprising an account of the author being conducted a state prisoner from the eastern parts of Siberia* (1825).

In a very different way from Chekhov, Holman proved to be a ladies' man, spending a suspiciously long time in Irkutsk, probably philandering with the Cockney-born widow of a deceased British adventurer, who even led him to the tomb of St Innocent of Irkutsk and had tincture rubbed into Holman's eyes in an attempt to cure his blindness. While awaiting near-impossible permission to exit Siberia at the Mongolian border, Holman was arrested and expelled as a spy (explaining his moniker 'the Blind Spy').

The American John Ledyard (1751–89) was a completely different type of Siberian traveller. He had been on Captain James Cook's third voyage of the Pacific in the late 1770s (the one that ended with Cook being eaten in Hawaii), and his aim in Siberia was to walk and sail to North America via Asia. He kept a journal of the trip from 1787, sprinkled with dubious theories about Siberia's native peoples, published in selected form by Jared Sparks in 1828 as *The Life of John Ledyard, the American Traveller*.

In *Strange Siberia, Along the Trans-Siberian Railway* (1911), Marcus Lorenzo Taft (1850–1936) mentions arriving in Glasgow, located across the Angara River in Irkutsk. Russia adopted many British names in the railway age; even the word for station *(vokzal)* comes from London's Vauxhall station, once the last word in stations.

THE SIBERIAN POST ROAD

The Sibirsky Trakt, the post road leading across Siberia, was the main route across the subcontinent before the advent of today's Trans-Siberian Railway. In George Kennan's day (the late 19th century) it connected Yekaterinburg with the Amur River, petering out on the border to Mongolia almost 5000km away. Siberia had been colonised by its rivers, with short portages between them, but once construction of a post road was stepped up in the 1730s, travellers, explorers and settlers often followed routes between isolated post stations set about 30km to 40km apart and housing a postmaster, his family, and the *yamshchiki,* the drivers you hired along with horses and a *telega* (a rudimentary one-horse cart without suspension) .

George Kennan says he used to feel ashamed waking up a driver in the dead of night to be driven across dangerous country for a pittance. Sometimes the drivers were so drunk or tired that they toppled off the carts, and travelling in a *telega* often meant holding on tight with your legs dangling over the sides.

Travellers could also use the hired horses – usually a *troika* (group of three) and driver for their own vehicles. Anton Chekhov travelled to Sakhalin Island in his own *tarantass* – the most comfortable vehicle because it was fully enclosed and had suspension – and another option was the *kibitka*, which resembled a baby's rocking cradle on wheels and had struts jutting out on each side to prevent a complete capsize. In winter, the *kibitka* and *tarantass* were adapted into sleds.

While sailing with Cook on the third voyage of discovery, he was the first American to encounter Russians in the Pacific. Now he was freeloading his way across Siberia. On reaching Irkutsk Ledyard encountered the Third Kamchatka Expedition, led by another crew member of Cook's, Joseph Billings, who took Ledyard under his wing. According to one expedition member, Ledyard repaid the kindness by abusing everyone. Eventually, back in Irkutsk, Russian authorities solved everybody's problem with Ledyard by arresting him on the pretence of being a French spy and deporting him.

Early Travellers of Siberia & the East

Some of the best travel writing is from the early 18th century, a time when travellers were less susceptible to nationalist prejudices. Standing out among the early crop is the Scottish-born physician John Bell (1691–1780), who travelled with an embassy to Běijīng in 1719. Bell's embassy was typically large, consisting of guards, valets, footmen, interpreters, clerks and even musicians – anything between 60 and 100 people. His recollections, published in 1763 as *Travels from St. Petersburg in Russia to Diverse Parts of Asia,* are refreshing and interesting.

The retinue received camels on the Mongolian border to complement their horses and, later, once in China itself, Bell describes the turreted post houses, set about 2.5 miles apart within sight of each other. These, he explains, were guarded by several soldiers, who were part of a network of stations for running messages across the Manchu Empire and who also kept highway robbers at bay. He passes through the Great Wall and is met by a former Chinese ambassador, Túlǐshēn (see below). Once in Běijīng, the Russian ambassador and Bell meet the ageing Emperor Kangxi (Kāngxīdì; 1654–1722), who receives gifts in the name of Peter the Great – furs, clocks, watches set in diamonds, mirrors.

Túlǐshēn – China's First Embassy to Russia

The first full-scale embassy from Manchu China through Mongolia to Russia took place in 1712, when the ambassador of the Qing dynasty, Túlǐshēn (1667–1741), travelled on a roundabout route through Russia to negotiate with the Kalmyks on the Volga. Túlǐshēn records the journey in his *Yìyùlù*, first published in English translation by George Thomas Staunton as *Narrative of the Chinese Embassy to the Khan of the Tourgouth Tartars, in the years 1712, 13, 14, and 15, by the Chinese Ambassador, and published by the Emperor's Authority, at Peking* (1821).

After crossing the Russia–Mongolia border, Túlǐshēn and his attendants meet a messenger sent by the governor of the Selenga district, who was taking an active interest in the (self-proclaimed) 'imperial ambassadors and heavenly messengers of his most excellent majesty, emperor of China'. The governor arranged accompaniment and the embassy was taken in boats on the Selenga River to Lake Baikal, where Túlǐshēn writes: 'The Baykale Lake is surrounded by mountains; its banks are overgrown with reeds, and upon its surface thick fogs and noxious vapours collect from the vast forests and deserts in the vicinity. It is a great expanse of waters, extending further than the eye can reach, and its waves are like those in the ocean.'

Trans-Siberian Railway Travellers

The advent of the Trans-Siberian Railway generated enormous interest in Siberia and produced a flood of books about rail travel. The best are insightful, the worst are culturally jaundiced or xenophobic. Mrs John Clarence Lee's *Across Siberia Alone: An American Woman's Adventures* (1913) is both, but interesting for a take on the Trans-Manchurian.

The New York politician and engineer Lindon Bates Jr (1883–1915) had the misfortune to perish in 1915 on the *Lusitania,* a British passenger ship, but his *The Russian Road to China* (1910) remains a nice

In *A Ribbon of Iron,* Annette Meakin, the first Englishwoman to circumnavigate the globe by rail in 1900, recounts her generally favourable impression of the early Trans-Siberian services.

The Swede Sven Hedin (1865–1952) spent much of his life exploring Central Asia. Read about his journeys in *My Life as an Explorer,* including explorations of the Gobi Desert, Xīnjiāng in Western China, the Silk Road and on by rail by Dodge from Běijīng to Ulan-Ude and on by rail to Moscow.

In *Xanadu* (1989) by William Dalrymple is the best of a bunch of books following in the footsteps of Marco Polo, who travelled from Jerusalem to Shàngdū (about 280km north of Běijīng), better known in the West as Xanadu, the summer residence of the Kublai Khan.

IAN FRAZIER – 'SIBERIA IS BIGGER SKY COUNTRY'

In 2010 Ian Frazier's highly acclaimed *Travels in Siberia* appeared. Almost immediately it took its place among the best of the travel writing about Siberia. The book recounts the author's travels during several visits to Russia.

What does Siberia mean for you personally? I'd done a book about my family, who come from Norwalk in Ohio, and the most famous man in that town was the traveller George Kennan. In 1866 Kennan travelled to Siberia and wrote *Tent Life in Siberia,* and later he returned and wrote about the prisons. When *Siberia and the Exile System* appeared in the 1890s everybody read it – people like Tolstoy and Chekhov. The personal connection is that when Kennan went to Siberia the first time he wrote letters back to the local newspaper, which was edited by my great-great-great grandfather. So an ancestor was Kennan's first publisher. I wanted to retrace George Kennan's route as much as I could.

What was it like travelling through the contemporary Siberian landscape? The landscape was overwhelmingly big, and quite monotonous. There's a wonderful phrase from the French traveller Marquis de Custine, who I think wrote the best book on Russia by a foreigner [de Custine's *Empire of the Czar: A Journey through Eternal Russia*]. He said monotony is the divinity of Russia – it's really true. I love the American West 'big sky country'. Well this is 'bigger sky country', scenery beyond conception.

Does it strike you as being like the New World? I feel like I'm in the New World back when wilderness was terrifying. Today we're very solicitous of wilderness. We feel we've got to preserve it. But wilderness used to be overwhelming; people had the feeling there was plenty of it – they didn't want more. I understand why we chop it up and put roads and fences in it, because it's almost like looking at the eternity of the cosmos or something – so overwhelming that you can't think. That was a lot of the appeal of Siberia, and still is today.

Much of the time you travelled by road, with Russians as guides. How do you find travelling with guides? Oh, it's awful. If you read de Custine's *Empire of the Czar* you see that somebody was sent with him. He had the same vexed relationship as I did. You feel manipulated by them, condescended to, pushed around, and later I realised I was wounding my guides in the same way with my arrogance and my will. It's a clash of wills.

How was it different writing 'Travels in Siberia' and one of your earlier books, 'Great Plains'? The big difference was that I knew the American West and I didn't know Russia, so I had to do a huge amount just to get to the point where I didn't feel like a complete newcomer. And in *Great Plains,* reading books, I noticed that many authors talked about the Native Americans as 'the finest light cavalry in the world'. To me, that's utter bullshit. I was doing a genre but I was writing *against* this genre in terms of style and what I wrote about. In Siberia, I was straightforwardly admiring George Kennan and hoping to do a 21st-century version of what he had done in the 19th century.

What's your experience of the Trans-Siberian? I haven't had good experience of the Trans-Siberian. I was in a railway car with no windows and sat in our vehicle [inside a vehicle transport carriage between Chernyshevsk and Magdagachi on the Moscow to Vladivostok line]. It was a passenger railway car with all the seats taken out – dim, there were little cracks at the tops where the windows used to be, and at night it was totally dark. Still, it was pretty. You would go out in the space between the railroad cars and see the landscape.

blend of history, railway description and travel with occasional literary glimpses of life on the train ('Darkness may be ahead, behind, and beside, but within there is light – enjoy it!').

In the 1896 title *The New Siberia* (partly about the penal colonies), traveller Harry de Windt (1856–1933), a rail as well as a road traveller, journeyed much of the way on a *telega* (an open cart without any suspension). De Windt reckoned he could hardly keep a cigarette between his teeth because of the jolting, adding that he had blisters from trying to hold on.

Among the modern-day train travellers, Paul Theroux's *Riding the Iron Rooster* (1988) is an enthralling classic of travel in China. Colin Thubron captures Siberia with poetic force in his *In Siberia* (1999).

population per sq km

RUSSIA   UK   USA

♦ ≈ 8 people

Russia Today

The Ruling Tandem

Russia is ruled by the tandem of prime minister Vladimir Putin and president Dmitry Medvedev, who have benefited greatly from some forthcoming high-profile events and relative economic stability. Sports fans have their eyes on the country as it prepares for, first, the Winter Olympics in Sochi in 2014 and, four years later, the soccer World Cup. Economic growth was steady at 4% in 2010 and resources have filled the state coffers with international reserves.

In June 2011 the average Russian lived on a monthly salary of R24,137 (US$775), with some 20 million or so subsisting on less than R5000 (US$160) a month.

If You've Got the Cash...

Moscow has more billionaires than any other city in the world. A good way to stay one is to play by the rules of Russian society and politics that became established after 2000, the year Vladimir Putin came to power. Arguably, Mikhail Khodorkovsky is a case in point. Khodorkovsky was found guilty of tax evasion and fraud in 2005 and sentenced to prison. He and his supporters (including many Western governments) claim the conviction is political. On the other hand, the European Court of Human Rights ruled in 2011 that Khodorovsky had not proved this sufficiently.

Crooks & Thieves

Corruption is a major problem daily life in Russia, and Medvedev and Putin have declared verbal war on it. But it's 34-year-old lawyer and blogger Alexey Navalny who has become Russia's leading anti-corruption crusader. In 2011, three months after he launched RosPil (http://rospil.info/), a site dedicated to exposing state corruption, suspicious government contracts worth nearly US$7 million were annulled.

Speaking out this way against the system in Russia has consequences. Reporters Without Borders lists many cases of harassment – judicial and

Top Docos

Russia – A Journey with Jonathan Dimbleby (www.dimblebys-russia.co.uk) The veteran British journalist covers 16,000km in the five episodes of this BBC series, giving a snapshot of the nation.

My Perestroika (http://myperestroika.com) Robin Hessman's film focuses on five ordinary Russians and how their lives were affected by the tumultuous last 20 years of Russian history.

Raconteurs

Russians love anecdotes with a twist, and they're masters of irony and wordplay, all of which is difficult to understand for foreigners. Jokes played a special role under communism. See www.prospectmagazine.co.uk/2006/05/communist-jokes.

belief systems
(% of population)

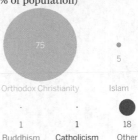

75 — Orthodox Christianity
5 — Islam
1 — Buddhism
1 — Catholicism
18 — Other

if Russia were 100 people

80 would be Russian
4 would be Tatar
2 would be Ukrainian
1 would be Bashkir
1 would be Chuvash
12 would be other

---

otherwise – that the Russian authorities use to intimidate bloggers and those who dare to speak their mind. Suspicious deaths include that of Anna Politkovskaya, the human-rights activist and writer gunned down on her doorstep in 2006.

Russia for Russians!

A major issue in Russia is the rise in extreme nationalism, pungently illustrated in 2010 when 5000 soccer supporters rampaged through central Moscow in late 2010 shouting 'Russia for Russians!' and attacking people assumed to be foreigners because of the colour of their skin.

Russia has anything between seven and 12 million immigrants, many from the North Caucasus or former Soviet republics in Central Asia.

While attacks on foreigners are not unique to Russia, this is a multi-ethnic country, and any widespread rise in ultranationalism that glorifies the Slavic, Orthodox identity is not only a threat to foreigners but might also threaten the unity of the country.

The Elections

National legislative (Duma) elections were held in December 2011 and a presidential election will be held in March 2012. United Russia, headed by Vladimir Putin, is the dominant party and endorsed Dmitry Medvedev in the 2008 presidential elections. United Russia won the Duma elections with less than 50% of the vote, with strong allegations of electoral fraud and nationwide anti-government protests.

United Russia's dominance is partly fuelled by a lack of effective parliamentary opposition. Right-wing liberal Right Cause (Pravoe Delo), headed by billionaire oligarch Mikhail Prokhorov, saw itself as an opposition party. But commentators, such as *The Economist*, speculated that

In 2011 the film *Generation P* was released, based on the bestselling book of the same name, written in the 1990s by Victor Pelevin. It describes the often bizarre lifestyle of a generation during the Yeltsin years of the 1990s (http://en.wikipedia.org/wiki/Generation_P).

Choice Fiction

Moscow Noir Fourteen short stories by contemporary authors.
The Master and Margarita (Mikhail Bulgakov) A satirical masterpiece.
Snowdrops (AD Miller) An edgy thriller about dark deeds in modern Russia.

Top Playlist

Leningrad (www.sosimc.ru) Punk rock, Latino, polka and Tom Waits with a strong brass section.
Markscheider Kunst (www.mkunst.ru) Afro-beat-infused music.
Deti Picasso (www.myspace.com/detipicasso) Armenian-Russian folk-rock band.

Zemphira (www.zemfira.ru) Jazz-rock muso is Russia's Alanis Morissette.
Leonid Fedorov (www.leonidfedorov.ru) Semi-absurd poetry with melodies.

it was little more than a convenient sparring partner for the Kremlin and a lightning rod to catch people's anger. It didn't. Prokhorov was ousted, and the party failed miserably in the 2011 elections. It's unclear whether Prokhorov will be a serious contender in Russian politics in future.

More predictable but more nebulous is the All-Russia People's Front, a catch-all group organised by Putin to generate new ideas among those sharing the broad political goals of the ruling United Russia. Meanwhile, Medvedev has set out his idea of a 'broad government' – a platform upon which local governments, NGOs and civil institutions might complement the state cabinet in decision-making.

Seats were also won in the Duma by the Communist Party of Russia, led by Gennardy Zhuganov; and firebrand nationalist Vladimir Zhirinovsky's Liberal Democratic Party of Russia.

Against this background, one party strongly critical of Russia's political system, the liberal Party of People's Freedom (led by Mikhail Kasyanov, a former prime minister, and Boris Nemtsov, a former deputy prime minister) was denied registration by the Russian Justice Ministry.

In late 2011 Putin accepted a nomination to run for president in 2012. Potentially, he could remain president until 2024. Medvedev will probably seek election as prime minister.

Most Russians relish individual expression and the freedom to travel. Russia has a cultural groundswell – whether that's high, low, experimental or everyday culture – that makes it exciting like few other countries. Politically, however, many Russians see *zastoy* (stagnation) looming. One question that Russia's 'old-new-next' president is likely to face is how to cope if Russia's strongest, most independent or best-qualified minds seek more politically liberal pastures abroad.

Newsweek, in an article published in August 2011, reported that many organisers of extreme nationalist groups started off and learned their skills in Kremlin-sponsored youth groups such as Nashi.

Good Reads

Lost and Found in Russia
Susan Richards describes how events from 1992 to 2008 affect a group of people from provincial southern Russia.

Black Earth: A Journey Through Russia After the Fall
In dispatches from Chechnya, Moscow, Norilsk, Sakhalin and St Petersburg, Journalist Andrew Meier paints an insightful, if sometimes bleak, picture of the country.

Hospitality

Russians are among the most genuinely hospitable, interested and empathetic people in the world. They love to converse, and if conversation strikes a language barrier, offering food, drink or help with baggage are great communication alternatives.

Russia

The Russian People

Russia is a multiethnic country with over 160 different 'nationalities' and ethnic groups, making it one of the world's most heterogeneous nations.

In Russia, 'nationality' refers not to a person's national passport but to their ethnicity. The country's multiethnic society is the result of imperial expansion, forced movements, migration and the mingling of ethnic groups over many thousands of years.

The overwhelming majority of Russia's population – about 80% – have Slavic European-Russian roots. Almost 4% are Tartars who descend from the Mongol armies of Chinggis (Genghis) Khaan, his successors and from earlier Hunnic, Turkic and mostly Finno-Ugric settlers. The remainder of Russia's population consists of smaller ethnic groups such as Ukrainians (2%), Muslim Bashkirs (1.2%) and Orthodox Christian Chuvash (about 1.15%). In Siberia, the largest ethnic groups are the ethnic Mongol Buryats (445,000), who speak a language closely related to Mongolian, and the peoples who speak languages with Turkic roots or Turkic influences: Yakuts or Sakha (444,000), Tuvans (243,000), Khakass (76,000) and Altai (67,000). As well as these are the so-called 'small-numbered peoples of the North' – Siberians mostly spread across Siberia's northern regions.

In *Arctic Mirrors,* the historian Yuri Slezkine gives a detailed account of relations between European Russians and the 'small-numbered peoples of the North' since colonisation. *The Reindeer People* by Piers Vitebsky is a poetic and informative description of life among reindeer herders of the north.

Indigenous Peoples of Siberia

Russians who ventured across the Urals before the 16th century returned with colourful reports of an endless forest rich in fur-bearing sable, but also told of bizarre people who didn't stop short of hacking up their own children to feed a guest (which would be an unusual take on hospitality)

YERMAK'S CONQUEST OF SIBERIA

The person at the forefront of Russia's concerted expansion into Siberia was the Volga brigand and Cossack Yermak Timofeevich, who was later glorified in a series of religious stories known as the *Siberian Chronicles,* compiled over later centuries. Some historians liked to colour him as a Russian Hernán Cortés, the conquistador of South America.

From 1563, Sibir began raiding what were then Russia's easternmost flanks on the cusp of the Urals. Funded and given firearms by the Stroganov industrial family, Yermak led his group of 840 Cossacks into the khanate of Sibir. He marched and sailed the rivers into Siberia, probably armed only with the tacit agreement of Ivan the Terrible, taking Tyumen (on the Trans-Siberian line today) as his first major possession. In late 1582 or 1583 (dates are conflicting) Yermak reached an abandoned Isker (the capital of Sibir, buried in the river meadows near today's Tobolsk), triggering what would later become Russia's extraordinary drive across Siberia to the Pacific, culminating in Russians reaching Alaska by the 1730s.

A good book about the conquest of Siberia is *Russia's Frozen Frontier: A History of Siberia and the Russian Far East 1581–1991,* by Alan Wood.

TOP SACRED VISITS

» **St Petersburg** Church of the Saviour on Spilled Blood
» **Moscow** Assumption, Archangel, St Basil's cathedrals
» **Kazan** Kul Sharif Mosque
» **Yekaterinburg** Church of the Blood
» **Tyumen** Trinity Monastery
» **Tobolsk** St Sofia & Intercession cathedrals
» **Irkutsk** Znamensky Monastery
» **Around Ulan-Ude** Ivolginsky Datsan

Three Recent Siberia Films

» *How I Ended this Summer (Kak ya provyol etim letom;* 2010)

» *Sibir. Monamur* (2011)

» *The Edge (Krai;* 2010)

or who died each winter because water trickled out of their noses and caused their feet to freeze to the ground.

The rumours were fanciful; the reality, however, was that Orthodox Russians had begun to weave themselves into a complex cultural region and dominate it. This region included the Turkic-speaking Tartars (but also other Turkic-speaking groups, such as the peoples of Altai), Mongol-speaking Buryats, as well as Khanty and Mansi peoples who inhabited the plains and taiga of Western Siberia, spoke a Finno-Ugric language and lived from hunting, fishing and sometimes reindeer herding.

In the north of Siberia, Orthodox Russians encountered clans of Samoyeds along a vast stretch of tundra and taiga from the Urals region to the Lena River in Eastern Siberia. So-called Samoyeds included Nenets (today centred on the capital, Salekhard, in Western Siberia), Enets, Nganasans and other tundra peoples who hunted and fished and whose lifestyle was often based around reindeer herding. Small related groups of Selkups (earlier known as Yenisey Ostyaks or Ostyak Samoyeds) lived south in forests around the Yenisey River, and even further south Russians met upon descendents of the Kets, some of whom even lived on houseboats similar to the sampans of China.

Further east across the north of Siberia were peoples such as the reindeer-herding Chukchi, seafaring Aleuts, reindeer-herding Koryaks, and Koryaks and Itelmeni of Kamchatka who mostly hunted and fished. In the southern regions of the Far East lived over half a dozen ethnic groups of fishing or hunting peoples such as the Nivkhi of Sakhalin Island.

In terms of land area, the most widespread ethnic group in Siberia comprised the Evenki (and Evens, together often called Tungusi), who populated pockets of Western Siberia, a vast heartland of Central Siberia and the north that took in Central Siberia, a large swath of Yakutia and even parts of the Pacific seaboard. In the south, Tungusi populated large portions of the Lake Baikal and Amur River regions, and even the northern fringes of Mongolia and China, where they adopted Mongolian equestrian culture. Most Tungusi, however, were forest people who hunted and fished. Many were reindeer people; they revered bears and practised shamanism like almost all of the Siberian peoples, and they lived in groups of a couple of families, or up to a dozen in summer. Today there are about 35,000 Evenki, mostly living in Russia.

Many of these peoples make up the 'small-numbered people of the North', 40 indigenous groups throughout Russia's taiga and tundra whose ethnicity and traditional lifestyle have survived today, who number less than 50,000 and who live either in the north or under conditions similar to those in the north (see http://raipon.info/en/history/populations.html for more information). Among these groups, 17 have fewer than 1500 people. On top of these 'small-numbered peoples of the North' are another five groups that are viewed as indigenous but have more than 50,000 – notably, the Yakuts.

Peoples of the Borderlands

For the Trans-Siberian traveller, the Lake Baikal and Amur regions are especially interesting as it's here that one enters a historical and contemporary conflux of Russian, Mongolian and Chinese cultures.

While Russia was expanding eastwards, Manchu China, ruled by the Qing dynasty (Qīng Cháo or the Manchu dynasty), was gradually expanding into present-day Mongolia. As James Forsyth wryly notes in his *A History of the Peoples of Siberia*, when Russia and China encountered each other in the Amur region, the arrogance of the 'Great Lord, Tsar and Grand Duke of All Russia' met upon Manchu China's 'son of Heaven' and 'Celestial Emperor of the Middle Kingdom'.

With the Treaty of Kyakhta in 1727, many Khalkh Mongolians – a tribe that makes up about 86% of all Mongolians today – were stranded on the Russian side, became integrated into Buryat culture and had an enormous influence on Buryatiya.

The Amur region was traditionally inhabited by Mongol-speaking Daurs, and further east of the Daurs were Juchers, a group related to the Tungusi and to the Manchus. Beyond these were various other Manchu-Tungusi peoples, including the predecessors of today's 16,000-strong community of Nanai (also known as Goldi) who live around both the Amur and the Ussuri rivers and across the Amur in Hēilóngjiāng province in China. In China, the Amur is known as the Black Dragon River.

Religion

One of the most noticeable phenomena in Russia since the end of the atheist Soviet Union is the resurgence of religion.

Orthodox & Islamic Faiths

Since 1997 the Russian Orthodox Church has been legally recognised as the leading faith, but Russia also has anything between six and 20 million Muslims (depending on whether you define this by practice or ethnicity), 250,000 Jews and about 1.5 million Buddhists, as well as various smaller groups that adhere to shamanism.

The Orthodox Church flourished until 1653, when it was split by reforms of Patriarch Nikon (1605–81), who insisted on a new translation of the Bible to bring it closer to the Greek original and that the sign of the cross be made with three fingers. This led to a schism, with many of the persecuted Starovery (Old Believers) fleeing. A large number settled in remote pockets of Siberia and Central Asia.

Mostly, Soviet leaders dealt blow after blow to the Church, but today about 90% of Russians identify with the Orthodox Church, if only about 15% to 20% practise Orthodoxy.

862
The legendary Scandinavian Rurik of Jutland gains control of the village Staraya Ladoga near Novgorod and Rus, the infant version of Russia, is born.

10th–11th Centuries
Oleg of Novgorod shifts the centre of Rus to Kyiv (Kiev) in the early 10th century, where the powerful Kyivan Rus reach their zenith, eventually uniting Kyiv with the Novgorod principality.

1223
Chinggis Khaan's defeat of the Russian princes at the Battle of Kalka River sparks Mongol incursions into Rus territory, followed by Batu Khaan's massive invasion from 1236 to 1240.

1552–56
Ivan IV (aka 'the Terrible' for his fearsome temper) defeats the splinter khanates of Kazan (once Batu's headquarters) and Astrakhan. The Volga region also falls to Russia; Siberia beckons.

Early 1580s–1613
Yermak Timofeevich and his Cossacks cross the Urals and capture Tyumen and Isker, the capital of the surviving khanate of Sibir based in Western Siberia. Romanov dynasty begins in 1613.

1660
Nikon, Patriarch of the Orthodox Church, enacts reforms and creates a schism, leading to his being deposed. Many 'Old Believers', who reject the reforms, flee to Siberia and form communities.

THE TRADITIONS OF THE BANYA

For centuries, travellers to Russia have commented on the particular (in many people's eyes, peculiar) traditions of the *banya* (bathhouse). To this day, Russians make it an important part of their week and you can't say you've really been to Russia unless you've visited a *banya*.

The main element of the *banya* is the *parilka* (steam room). Here, rocks are heated by a furnace, with water poured onto them using a long-handled ladle. A few drops of eucalyptus or pine oils (sometimes even beer) are often added to the water, creating a scent in the burst of scalding steam that's released into the room. You'll note that even though people are naked in the *banya*, some wear a *chapka* (felt cap) to protect their hair from the effects of the heat.

As they sweat it out, some bathers grab hold of a *venik* (a tied bundle of birch branches) and beat themselves or each other with it. Though it can be painful, the effect can also be pleasant and cleansing: the birch leaves (sometimes oak or, agonisingly, juniper branches) and their secretions are supposed to help rid the skin of toxins. After the birch-branch thrashing, bathers run outside and, depending on their nerve, plunge into the *basseyn* (ice-cold pool) or take a cooling shower. The whole process is then repeated several times for anything up to two hours.

Many city *bani* are rundown and unappealing (a classy exception is Moscow's splendid Sanduny Baths; p72). Grab any chance to try a traditional countryside *banya*: nearly all the guesthouses on Olkhon Island (p202) in Lake Baikal have them.

Muslim history dates back about 1000 years in Russia, but like all other religions it suffered under Soviet rule. The majority of Muslims live in the Caucasus region. Kazan, situated on the Volga River, is the capital of the Tatarstan Republic, where about 48% of the population is Tatar and 43% Russian. Other cities on the middle Volga with large Muslim populations are Ulyanovsk, Samara and Nizhny Novgorod, while significant communities also live in Moscow and St Petersburg. In Siberia, Tyumen, Tobolsk, the Baraba Steppe and Tomsk have significant Muslim Tartar populations.

Buddhism

Russia has about 1.5 million Buddhists, a figure that has steadily grown since the *glasnost* (openness) reforms of Mikhail Gorbachev in the late 1980s, when Buddhist organisations were free to reopen temples and monasteries. The Kalmyks (from the Republic of Kalmykia north of the Caspian Sea) form the largest group. These are Gelugpa or 'Yellow Hat' Buddhists, as in Tibet. The Gelugpa sect reached eastern Buryatiya via Mongolia in the 18th century, but only in the 19th century did it really take root. Stalin's ideologues and henchmen destroyed hundreds of *datsani* (Buddhist temples) in the 1930s, and executed or exiled thousands of peaceable lamas. At the end of WWII two *datsani* were opened – a new one at Ivolginsk near Ulan-Ude, which houses Russia's largest collection of Buddhist texts, and another at Aginskoe (southeast of Chita). The glorious 1820 Tsugol Datsan is the only other Siberian *datsan* to survive virtually intact.

One of the best books about shamanism is *The Shaman's Coat* by Anna Reid. This combines journeys to native communities with histories and accounts of shaman practices in traditional and modern life.

Shamanism & Animism

Many cultures, from the Finno-Ugric Mari and Udmurts to the nominally Buddhist Mongol Buryats, retain varying degrees of animism. This is often submerged beneath, or accepted in parallel with, other religions. Animism is a primal belief in the presence of spirits or spiritual qualities in objects of the natural world. Peaks and springs are especially revered and their spirits are thanked with token offerings. This explains (especially in Tuva and Altai) the coins, stone cairns, vodka bottles and abundant prayer ribbons that you'll commonly find around holy trees and mountain passes.

Spiritual guidance is through a medium or shaman – a high priest, prophet and doctor in one. Animal skins, trance dances and a special type of drum are typical shamanic tools, though different shamans have different spiritual and medical gifts. Siberian museums exhibit many shamanic outfits.

The Arts

With 19th-century composers such as Modest Mussorgsky (1839–81) and Pyotr Tchaikovsky (1840–93), later greats like Sergei Rachmaninov (1873–1943) and Dmitry Shostakovich (1906–75), and the contemporary soprano star Anna Netrebko (b 1971), Russia has a lot to offer the classical-music buff. Understandably, Moscow and St Petersburg take the lead role in stage, music and theatre in Russia, and galleries like the Tretyakov Gallery or the Pushkin Museum of Fine Arts in Moscow and the Hermitage in St Petersburg are absolute highlights.

Moscow's Rerikh Museum contains works by the artist and spiritualist Nikolai Rerikh (known internationally as Nicholas Roerich). The Tretyakov has a large collection of paintings by the Krasnoyarsk-born painter Vasily Surikov (1848–1916), including details of his *The Conquest of Siberia by Yermak*. The full-scale painting is in the Russian Museum in St Petersburg.

In Siberia itself, Surikov's house in Krasnoyarsk is a splendid inner-city retreat, and there are Rerikh works in the State Art Museum in Novosibirsk. In Irkutsk's Art Gallery are a couple of works by Ilya Repin (1844–1930) and Ivan Shishkin (1832–98). Both are closely tied to the Peredvizhniki (Wanderers) movement, a 19th-century breakaway group that began staging exhibitions at temporary locations and focused on national and Slavic themes in its paintings.

The regional museums across Siberia are excellent places to learn about indigenous arts and crafts.

Near Irkutsk, the Taltsy Museum of Wooden Architecture is excellent for traditional Russian-European wooden designs, including original 17th-century structures from the Ilimsk fort. Further east, just outside Ulan-Ude, the Ethnographic Museum has Old Believer houses and Buryat artefacts. In Listvyanka, check out the small artists colony with a picture gallery *(kartinaya galeriya)* in the side valley at Chapaeva 76 (a sign points to it).

In literature, Valentin Rasputin (b 1937) has written some evocative and thought-provoking works about Siberia and was associated early on with the Village Prose movement, which focused on traditional Russian values. Siberia, with its abundance of villages, was a perfect locus for the movement. Another Siberian of national and international acclaim is Vasily Shukshin (1929–74), who wrote *Stories from a Siberian Village*. Shukshin was a famous Soviet-era director, screenwriter and writer who hailed from the Altai region.

1689
Russia and China sign the Treaty of Nerchinsk. Russia withdraws from the Amur basin; it retains the Transbaikal and trade caravans receive rights of passage to travel to Beijing.

1696–1725
Peter I ('the Great') becomes sole tsar after a period co-ruling with his half-brother. Under Peter the Great, St Petersburg is founded and Russia modernises and becomes more European.

1812–14
Napoleon's invasion of Russia (1812) culminates in his ill-fated march on Moscow, when Muscovites burn two-thirds of the capital rather than see it occupied. Russians briefly occupy Paris in 1814.

1904–05
The Russo-Japanese War results in Russia's defeat. Abysmal social and political conditions lead to the revolution of 1905, when Russia nominally becomes a constitutional monarchy, but reform remains patchy.

1914–18
WWI rages. In February 1917 Nicholas II abdicates; in October Bolsheviks seize power. In 1918 Lenin pulls Russia out of WWI and Nicholas II is murdered during Russia's civil war.

1922–53
Stalin rules over an era that brings brutal collectivisation, purges and Gulag camps. Russia industrialises and liberates parts of Europe in WWII, but it establishes a stifling hegemony over Eastern Europe.

Russian Cuisine

Russia has a great food heritage enriched by influences from the Baltic to the Far East as well as pan-European trends. One of the healthiest culinary highlights of a rail journey through Russia will be the freshwater fish of Lake Baikal, and in Moscow don't forgo a meal in a good Georgian restaurant.

Russians like to eat till late, and they also like to enjoy a crossover of eating, drinking, dancing and entertainment (often karaoke these days) in one session. So while the traditional Slavic kitchen might lack the culinary peaks of, say, French or Italian cooking, a night out in a restaurant in Russia can be a splendid 'universal' experience.

In *A Year of Russian Feasts*, Catherine Cheremeteff-Jones recounts how Russia's finest dishes have been preserved and passed down through the feast days of the Russian Orthodox Church.

Staples

Most hotels in Russia include breakfast in their prices, and a typical *zavtrak* (breakfast) will include bliny (pancakes) with savoury or sweet fillings, various types of *kasha* (porridge), and *syrniki* (cottage-cheese fritters), delicious with jam, sugar and the universal Russian condiment, *smetana* (sour cream). Russians excel in dairy products such as *tvorog* (soft curd) and dairy drinks, so make sure you explore these.

A meal starts with *zakuski* (appetisers), progresses to soup such as borsch, made with beetroot and mostly beef; *lapsha* (chicken noodle) and *solyanka* (a thick broth with meat, fish and a host of vegetables) – often served with piles of bread and a thick dollop of sour cream. *Ukho* (fish soup) and *shchi* (cabbage soup) can be very good.

Main dishes often come with a small salad garnish, and side dishes are almost always ordered separately on the menu as *garniry*. Lamb from the steppes of Kalmykia and beef from Altai are excellent. *Pelmeni* (ravioli) has been elevated to an art form in Siberia; it has various fillings and is commonly eaten in a broth or fried in butter.

During summer, outdoor pizza and shashlyk (kebab) stalls pop up all over the place – in Krasnoyarsk you will find an enormous row of shashlyk stands and beer tents along the Yenisey River. Not to be missed are *pirozhki* (pies) with a range of fillings.

In most Russian cities it's common to find restaurants serving set three-course *biznes* lunches from noon to 4pm Monday to Friday; these cost as little as R200 (up to R400 in Moscow and St Petersburg).

Sweet-toothed Russians adore *morozhenoe* (ice cream) and gooey *torty* (cream cakes), often decorated in lurid colours. *Pecheniye* (pastries) are eaten at tea time in the traditional English style and are available at any *bulochnaya* (bakery). Locally made chocolate and *konfetki* (sweets) are also excellent and, with their colourful wrappings, make great presents.

THE SOVIET SUN GOD

Soviet authorities liked to depict shamans in propaganda as forces of evil. In practice, shamans were simply a threat to the Soviet ideologists' own influence over the native peoples. But in an interesting turn of events, the ideologists even tried to win hearts and minds by depicting Lenin and Stalin as *über*-shamans who battled evil spirits.

In his book *The Peoples of the Soviet Far East*, Walter Kolarz mentions a 'Nanai' tale in which Lenin is depicted as a kind of sun god who resides far away and spreads light into the darkness and upon the oppressed of the land. With the death of Lenin, evil seems to triumph, but no, along comes an omniscient Stalin, Lenin's great friend, who sees and hears everything (the propagandists were almost right about that): 'Nobody can equal the strength of that hero. He sees everything that goes on on Earth. His ears hear everything people say. His brain knows all that people think.'

Specialities

The following are among the variety of regional food specialities you'll find along the rail routes.

kasylyk (dried horsemeat sausages) and *zur balish* (meat pies) – both from Tatarstan, where *chek chek* (honey-drenched, macaroni-shaped pieces of fried dough) are also an essential part of celebrations.

manti (steamed, palm-sized dumplings) – known as *pozy, buuz* or *buuzy* in Buryatiya and *pyan-se* (a peppery version) in the Russian Far East.

oblyoma (dried, salty fish found in the Volga) – most often eaten as a snack food with beer.

omul (a cousin of salmon and trout) – endemic to Lake Baikal and considered a great delicacy. *Kharius* (grayling) is also delicious.

Vegetarians & Vegans

Russia restaurants are tough on vegetarians, Georgian ones less so. Salmon is widespread for those who eat fish. *Zakuski* include quite a lot of meatless ingredients, such as eggs and mushrooms. Failing that, a Greek salad with fetta cheese is fairly widespread in cities. If you're travelling during Lent, you'll find that many restaurants have special nonmeat menus.

Drinks

Russia produces hundreds of different brands of vodka, including ones that you'll certainly have heard of such as Stolichnaya and Smirnoff. Also look out for Moskovskaya, Flagman and Gzhelka. As well as 'plain' vodka you'll find *klyukovka* (cranberry vodka, one of the most popular kinds), *pertsovka* (pepper vodka), *starka* (vodka flavoured with apple and pear leaves), *limonnaya* (vodka with lemon), and *okhotnichya* (meaning 'hunter's vodka', with about a dozen ingredients, including peppers, juniper berries, ginger and cloves).

The local market leader in beer is Baltika, making 10 brews; No 3, the most common, is a very quaffable lager.

Most wines drunk in Russia are foreign, and although you will find some decent ones, there will be little unique about drinking wine in Russia. The word for 'dry' is *sukhoe*. Russian *konyak* (brandy) from the Caucasus is generally a very pleasant surprise. *Kvas* is fermented rye-bread water, and in summer is dispensed on the street from big, wheeled tanks. It tastes not unlike ginger beer, and is a wonderfully cool and refreshing drink. *Mors,* a fruit drink made from cranberries and other fruits, is popular in summer.

Russians are world-class tea drinkers, and this partly explains the samovars at the end of every railway carriage. In Russian homes, the traditional brewing method is to make an extremely strong pot, pour small shots of it into glasses and fill the glasses with hot water from the kettle. Putting jam, instead of sugar, in tea is quite common.

Coffee comes in small cups, and unless you buy it at kiosks or stand-up eateries, it's usually quite good. There's been an explosion of Starbucks-style cafes all across Russia's bigger cities – cappuccino, espresso, latte and mocha are now as much a part of the average Russian lexicon as elsewhere.

Other drinks, apart from the ubiquitous canned soft drinks, include *sok* (juice) and *kefir* (yogurt-like sour milk).

1953–82

Nikita Khrushchev becomes first secretary and condemns Stalin's brutal policies. The years from 1964 under successor Leonid Brezhnev are marked by stagnation. Siberian oil discoveries hide Soviet economic flaws.

1985–91

Mikhail Gorbachev is elected first secretary and initiates *perestroika* and *glasnost* reforms. A failed coup in August 1991 causes the collapse of the USSR and the rise of Boris Yeltsin.

1990s

Yeltsin uses force in 1993 to crush dissenters in parliament; the decade brings civil freedoms but also powerful oligarchs, crime, poverty, and war in breakaway Chechnya. Yeltsin resigns in 1999.

2000–12

A 'tandem' of Vladimir Putin and Dmitry Medvedev ruling variously as president and prime minister oversee relative re-stabilisation of Russia. Power is re-centralised, but many Russians seek greater civil freedoms.

RUSSIA RUSSIAN CUISINE

population per sq km

MONGOLIA CHINA USA

🧍 ≈ 2 people

Mongolia Today

The New Mongol Horde

Mongolia may be just a little fish in the big pond of globalisation, but its importance on the world stage is growing. Pundits have dubbed the country 'Mine-golia' in a nod to its enormous mineral wealth, the sector that Mongolians hope to ride to economic prosperity. The country is rich in copper, gold, coal and other resources and the government is being wooed by international firms hoping to grab a piece of the pie. Mongolians are proceeding cautiously, aware that other natural resource–rich countries have been plagued by corruption and mismanagement. All the talk now is of what path the government will take: rapid development and poverty reduction, or corruption and a greater split between rich and poor.

The hot topic of conversation is Tavan Tolgoi (TT), the world's largest undeveloped coal field. In an immense socio-economic project, the government has set aside 10% of TT's shares for public distribution, making every Mongolian a shareholder in this potentially lucrative company.

China is a ready market for Mongolia's raw materials and the government is trying to build up its infrastructure to deliver the goods. New rail and road links to China are being planned, and in a bid to diversify its markets Mongolia is also planning a 1000km railway from Ömnögov all the way to Russia (via Choibalsan).

Mongolia's political leaders seem keenly aware of the need to invest their newfound wealth back into the country. An industrial complex planned for Sainshand envisions a copper smelter, oil refinery and coal-washing plant, while in Nalaikh the government is hoping to build a sparkling new university and IT complex. Money is also being poured into Ulaanbaatar, where new roads, bridges, schools, apartment blocks, hospitals and power plants are all desperately needed.

» GDP: US$3100 per capita (135th out of 182 listed countries)

» Leading 2011 exports: copper, wool, gold, cashmere, leather

» Literacy rate: 98%

» Average life expectancy: 68 years

Ger Dos & Don'ts

» Do accept a snuff bottle with your right hand (as if you were shaking hands). If you don't take the snuff, at least sniff the top part of the bottle. But don't grab the bottle from the top.

» If you step on anyone, or kick their feet, shake their hand.

» Don't point your feet at the hearth, at the altar or at another person. Sleep with your feet pointing towards the door.

» Don't stand on or lean over the threshold.

» Don't touch another person's hat.

Top Books

» **When Things Get Dark** (Matthew Davis)

» **Dateline Mongolia** (Michael Kohn)

» **Wild East** (Jill Lawless)

» **The Secret History of the Mongol Queens** (Jack Weatherford)

belief systems
(% of population)

80
Mahayana Buddhism

5
Islam

5
Christianity

10
Atheism

if Mongolia were 100 people

95 would be Mongol (mostly Khalkh)
5 would be Turkic (mostly Kazakh)

Forging a New Future

On the political front, Mongolia has largely overcome the strife of 2008, when four died and hundreds were arrested in the wake of disputed elections. Although the Mongolian People's Revolutionary Party (MPRP; now called the Mongolian People's Party) was declared winner of the election, it offered an olive branch to the Democrats, giving several senior Democrats positions in the government.

The ability of Mongolia's political parties to cooperate is unique in Central Asia and may provide lessons for neighbours. Even China has sent election observers to Mongolia.

For Mongolia, the challenge lies largely in the task of nation building. From a cultural point of view, Mongolia has moved on from the Soviet period and has established a new path of strong nationalism fused with Western influences. One only needs to look at Ulaanbaatar's urban youth – tattooed with the *soyombo* (the national symbol) and rapping about the blue skies and other traditional Mongolian themes – to realise that the country is forging a unique new identity.

But on the ground life is still hard. Poverty stalks the urban fringe as rural folk crowd into Ulaanbaatar in search of work. Some struggle for jobs, housing, food and education, while others are rocketing to riches. Double-digit inflation makes it harder for the poor to keep up.

Despite the challenges ahead, surveys show widespread support for the path the government has taken, with only 10% of people still hoping for a return to communism. There is strong optimism among most of the population, but the country has a long way to go before it can claim success.

» Population: 2,754,000 (2010)

» Horse-to-human ratio: 13 to 1

» Head of livestock: 44 million

Top Films

» **The Story of the Weeping Camel** (2003)

» **The Cave of the Yellow Dog** (2005)

» **Mongol** (2007)

» **Tracking the White Reindeer** (2008)

Top Phrases

» Hold the dog! *Nokhoi khorio!*

» May we camp near your ger? *Tanaa khajuud maihantaigaa honogloj boloh uu?*

» I would like to ride a calm (non-aggressive) horse. *Bi nomkhon mori unmaar baina.*

» Not too much [food, tea, vodka], please. *Dunduur*. Or, *jaakhan, jaakhan.*

» Please write down your address and I will send your photo later. *Ta nadad hayagaa bichij ogno uu. Bi tand zurag ilgeene.*

Mongolia

The Mongolian People

Mongolians, no matter how long they may have lived in a city, are nomads at heart. The nomadic way of life was born out of necessity, as herders were forced to move their animals over the harsh landscape in search of fresh pasture. This lifestyle has shaped Mongolians' psyche, worldview, philosophy, ethics and relationship with their neighbours.

Livestock, especially horses, play a crucial role in Mongolian culture. It was the horse that allowed ancient tribesman to spread across the steppes and cover great distances as they tended their animals. Later it was the horse that carried Mongol warriors across Asia as they built their empire. An old Mongolian proverb says: 'A man without a horse is like a bird without wings'.

Nomadic peoples are greatly affected by the climate and other natural forces. Because good pastures are a requirement for the survival of the herds (and therefore the people), traditional beliefs eschew mining, construction or other development of the land. Down the ages, Mongolians have believed that nature is not something to be tamed or dominated but something that's better left untouched. These traditional beliefs are now giving way to other considerations as politicians and businesspeople seek to develop mines and other infrastructure.

Seasons also shape Mongolian life. Spring in particular is a crucial time. Because the country's rainy season comes towards the end of summer, spring is dry, dusty, windy and unforgiving. This is the time when

The 2010 documentary *Babies* featured four newborns from different corners of the globe: Namibia, San Francisco, Tokyo and Mongolia. Watching the film gives unique insight into the life of a typical Mongolian rural family.

THE MAD BARON

Throughout their history the disparate countries of Mongolia, Russia and China have had few agreements. It was only in 1920 that the three found themselves facing a common enemy – one Baron Roman Nikolaus Fyodirovich von Ungern-Sternberg, aka the Mad Baron.

A renegade White Russian officer who believed he was the reincarnation of Chinggis (Genghis) Khaan, the Baron was described by his contemporaries as a psychotic killer whose army consisted of escaped convicts and bandits.

In the summer of 1920 the Baron led his 6000-strong army on an assault of Ulaanbaatar, chasing out the Chinese army that occupied the city. The Baron declared himself emperor of Mongolia and Russia, and then sent his men on a three-day orgy of looting, burning and killing.

After only a few months, the Bolshevik advance across Siberia forced the Baron to abandon Urga. Out on the steppes, his own followers tried to kill him by shooting him in his tent, but he managed to escape. He was eventually captured by the Bolsheviks, deported to Novosibirsk and shot on 15 September 1921.

The Mad Baron (2010) by Stephen Palmer is a vivid account of the rise and fall of this legendary character.

the weaker animals die and, it is said, when people die. Despite the severe temperatures, it's during winter that Mongolians feel most comfortable. After a difficult summer filled with chores and moving around the herds, winter is a time to relax inside a ger (yurt) and fatten up against the cold.

Mongolia's vast, open steppes and great distances have made hospitality a matter of sheer necessity rather than simply a social obligation. It would be difficult for anyone to travel across this vast, sparsely populated country without the hospitality that has developed, as each ger is able to serve travellers as a hotel, restaurant, pub and repair shop. As a result, Mongolians are able to travel rapidly over long distances without the weight of provisions.

Life on the steppes is by no means easy or idyllic. Constant work is required to care for the animals, cook food and collect dung and water. It's also a precarious life: a harsh winter can kill millions of head of livestock, as happened in 2009. The government can resupply some herders who lose animals in a severe storm, but many herders have ended up jobless in the sprawling suburbs around Ulaanbaatar.

In the capital, urban Mongolians have developed their own unique blend of Mongolian and Western lifestyles. You'll see young people wearing the latest European or American fashions, sporting mohawks, hoop earrings, gangsta garb and iPhones. Materialism is apparent in all the flashy SUVs bounding around the city. But talk to some young locals and you'll soon realise that their hopes and dreams lie not only in the West but also in the future of Mongolia, its success and prosperity and the continuation of its unique culture.

Religion

Spirituality in Mongolia comes in many forms, with many day-to-day rituals rooted in Mongolia's shamanic past. The ancient animist beliefs of the Siberian and steppe tribes who worshipped the sun, earth and sky are still very much alive, woven intimately into the fabric of modern Mongolia.

Shamanism

Mongolians have long believed in the spirit world as their shamans described it to them. Their cosmic view of the universe did not differentiate between the worlds of the living and the dead, nor did they consider themselves any greater than other creatures in this or other worlds. Any imbalance between the human and natural worlds could cause calamity.

Shamanism centres on the shaman – called a *bo* if a man or *udgan* if a woman – who has special medical and religious powers. One of a shaman's main functions is to cure any sickness caused by the soul straying, and to accompany the soul of a dead person into the afterlife. Shamans act as intermediaries between the human and spirit worlds, and communicate with spirits during trances, which can last up to six hours.

MONGOLIAN HISTORY

209–174 BC
Reign of Modun, as *shanyu* of the Huns; the first great steppe empire of Mongolia stretches from Korea to Lake Baikal in Siberia and south into northern China.

AD 552–744
Succession of two Turkic empires; greatest ruler is Bilge Khan. Following his death in 734 a monument is erected near Lake Ögii.

744–840
The Uighur empire occupies central Mongolia until expelled by the Kyrgyz tribe; the Uighur move south into western China and control the Silk Road for nearly 1000 years.

1162
Birth of Temujin, the child destined to become Chinggis Khaan, near the Onon River. According to legend, Temujin emerges with a blood clot clutched in his fist.

1206
Chinggis Khaan calls a massive conclave at Kherlen Gol and creates his empire, to which he gives the name Great Mongol Nation.

1368
Yuan dynasty collapses in China but the Mongol government returns to Mongolia refusing to submit to the newly created Ming dynasty. They continue ruling as the 'Northern Yuan'.

1585
Founding of Erdene Zuu, first Buddhist monastery in Mongolia, at the site of the Mongol capital, Karakorum (modern Kharkhorin).

Sky worship is another integral part of shamanism and you'll see Mongolians leaving blue scarves (representing the sky) on *ovoos* (piles of stones built to honour earth spirits). Sky gods are likewise honoured by flicking droplets of vodka into the air before drinking.

Buddhism

The Mongols had limited contact with organised religion before their great empire of the 13th century. It was Kublai Khaan who first found himself with a court in which all philosophies of his empire were represented, but it was a Tibetan Buddhist, Phagpa, who wielded the greatest influence on the khaan.

In 1578 Altan Khaan, a descendant of Chinggis Khaan, met the Tibetan leader Sonam Gyatso, was converted, and subsequently bestowed on Sonam Gyatso the title Dalai Lama (*dalai* means 'ocean' in Mongolian). Sonam Gyatso was named as the third Dalai Lama and his two predecessors were named posthumously.

Mass conversions occurred under Altan Khaan. As Mongolian males were conscripted to monasteries, rather than the army, the centuries of constant fighting seemed to wane (much to the relief of China, which subsequently funded more monasteries in Mongolia).

Buddhist opposition to needless killing reinforced strict hunting laws already set in place by shamanism. Today, Buddhist monks are still influential in convincing local populations to protect their environment and wildlife.

Buddhism in Mongolia was nearly destroyed in 1937 when the young communist government, fearing competition, launched a purge that wiped out nearly all of the country's 700 monasteries. Up to 30,000 monks were massacred and thousands more sent to Siberian labour camps. Freedom of religion was only restored in 1990 following Mongolia's peaceful democratic revolution.

Restoring Buddhism has been no easy task, as two generations had been essentially raised atheist. While many will make the occasional visit to their local temple, the Buddhist rituals and meanings are not well understood. Despite this, numbers swell at Ulaanbaatar's Gandan monastery when well-known Buddhist monks from Tibet or India (or even Western countries) visit Mongolia.

Ovoos, the large piles of rocks found on mountain passes, are repositories of offerings for local spirits. Upon arriving at an *ovoo*, walk around it clockwise three times, toss an offering onto the pile (another rock should suffice) and make a wish.

CHINGGIS KHAAN

Known to the world as a bloodthirsty conqueror, Chinggis (Genghis) Khaan is remembered by Mongolians as the great lawgiver and they proudly refer to him as the Man of the Millennium (a title bestowed on him by the *Washington Post* in 1995). His laws derived from practical considerations more than ideology or religion.

After the abduction of his wife Borte, Chinggis Khaan recognised the role of kidnapping in perpetuating feuds among clans and outlawed it. Similarly, he perceived religious intolerance as being a source of violence in sedentary society and so decreed religious freedom for everyone and exempted religious scholars and priests from taxes.

To promote trade and communications, Chinggis Khaan built an international network of postal stations that also served as hostels for merchants. He decreased and standardised taxes on goods so that they would not be repeatedly taxed. Under these laws the Mongol empire formed the first intercontinental free-trade zone.

In an era when ambassadors served as hostages to be publicly tortured or killed during times of hostilities, Chinggis Khaan ordered that every ambassador be considered an envoy of peace. This law marked the beginning of diplomatic immunity and international law. Today nearly every country accepts and promotes, at least in theory, the ideas and policies behind the 'Great Law of Chinggis Khaan'.

Islam

The country has a significant minority of Sunni Muslims, most of them ethnic Kazakhs who live primarily in Bayan-Ölgii. Because of Mongolia's great isolation and distance from the major Islamic centres of the Middle East, Islam has never been a major force in Bayan-Ölgii. However, most villages have a mosque and contacts have been established with Islamic groups in Turkey. Several prominent figures in the community have been on a hajj to Mecca. A small population of Kazakhs live in the city of Nalaikh, 35km southeast of Ulaanbaatar.

Christianity

The fastest-growing religion in Mongolia is Christianity. A whole spectrum of mainstream and fundamentalist sects have set up shop in Ulaanbaatar, each of them competing to convert a nation whose native faith is not well supported. In 1990 the number of Christians was negligible. Today there are an estimated 65,000 Christians and more than 150 churches.

Nestorian Christianity was part of the Mongol empire long before Western missionaries arrived. The Nestorians followed the doctrine of Nestorious (358–451), patriarch of Constantinople (428–31), who proclaimed that Jesus exists as two separate persons: the man Jesus and the divine son of God.

The Arts

From prehistoric oral epics to the latest movie from MongolKino film studios in Ulaanbaatar, the many arts of Mongolia convey the flavour of nomadic life and the spirit of the land.

Music

Traditional Mongolian music, which can be heard at concerts in Ulaanbaatar, is usually played on a *morin khuur* (horsehead fiddle), a two-stringed vertical violin, and a lute. These instruments are also used by some of Mongolia's popular rock bands, including Altan Urag and Boerte Ensemble.

There are also several unique traditional singing styles. The enigmatic *khöömii* – throat singing – has the remarkable effect of producing two notes simultaneously – one low growl and the other an ethereal whistling. Translated as 'long songs', *urtyn-duu* use long trills to relate traditional stories about love and the countryside.

Today a new brand of Mongolian sound fuses traditional music with Western rock. Well-known fusion bands include Altan Urag, Boerte Ensemble and Khusugtun. They can often be heard in clubs and restaurants in Ulaanbaatar.

Theatre & Film

Mongolia's best-known modern poet and playwright is Dashdorjiin Natsagdorj (1906–37), regarded as the founder of Mongolian literature. His dramatic

1639

Zanabazar, a direct descendent of Chinggis Khaan and the greatest artist in Mongolian history, is recognised as the first Jebtzun Damba, the supreme religious leader of Mongolia.

1696

The Manchus defeat Galdan Khaan of Zungaria and claim western Mongolia for the Qing dynasty, but some western Mongolians continue to resist foreign rule for several generations.

1911

Mongolia declares independence from the dying Manchu empire and sets up religious leader Bogd Khan as the head of state.

1915

Treaty of Khyakhta is signed by Mongolia, China and Russia, granting Mongolia limited autonomy.

1921

The Mad Baron, Ungern von Sternberg, briefly conquers Mongolia, but the Red Army and Mongolian forces under D Sükhbaatar defeat him.

1924

The Bogd Khan, the eighth reincarnation of the Jebtzun Damba, dies; the People's Republic of Mongolia is created on 26 November.

1937

Choibalsan's Buddhist purge leaves 700 monasteries destroyed and 27,000 monks and civilians dead. Purge victims include former prime minister P Genden.

WHAT'S YOUR DRINK?

Mongolians are big tea drinkers and will almost never start a meal until they've had a cup of tea, as it's thought to aid digestion.

Süütei tsai, a classic Mongolian drink, is milk tea with salt. If you can't get used to the salty brew, try asking for *khar tsai* (black tea), which is like European tea, with sugar and no milk.

Alcoholic drinks are readily available and Mongolians can drink you under the table if you challenge them. There is much social pressure to drink, especially on males – those who refuse to drink *arkhi* (vodka) are considered wimps.

Locally produced beer labels include Mongol, Chinggis, Borigo and Khan Brau. Popular vodkas include the very smooth Chinggis black label, which costs just US$8 a bottle.

While it may not seem obvious at first, every countryside ger doubles as a tiny distillery. One corner of the ger usually contains a tall, thin jug with a plunger that is used for fermenting mares' milk. The drink, known as *airag* or *koumiss,* has an alcohol content of about 3%. Go easy on the *airag* from the start or your guts will pay for it later.

nationalist poems and plays are still performed in Mongolian theatres today. There's also been a revival in Mongolian cinema, its brightest star being director Byambasuren Davaa. Her best-known films, *The Story of the Weeping Camel* (2003) and *The Cave of the Yellow Dog* (2005), depict nomadic life, the simplicity of the steppes and Mongolia's transition into the 21st century.

Visual Arts

Many of Mongolia's visual arts are religious in nature. Religious scroll paintings, depicting deities and their enlightened qualities, can be found on family altars in many homes. Another traditional style of painting is *zurag* – landscape storytelling. These landscapes include intricate sketches depicting every aspect of Mongolian life. Balduugiyn Sharav (1869–1939) is Mongolia's best-known painter in this style. The sculptor Zanabazar (1635–1723) is one of Mongolia's most revered artists, as well as a religious and political leader. He is known primarily for his cast-bronze statues, which are now on display in monasteries and museums around Ulaanbaatar.

Ulaanbaatar has a vibrant modern-art scene. The best place to see contemporary art is in the Tsagandarium Art Gallery, near Zaisan Monument.

Nearly all nomadic families have a short-wave radio to get national and world news. Some can receive satellite TV and certainly everyone reads newspapers when they're available (98% of Mongolians are literate).

Mongolian Cuisine

Mongolian cuisine evolved from nomadic traditions and the types of food available on Mongolia's barren steppes. Livestock (which offer meat and milk) have long been in plentiful supply. Fruit, vegetables, nuts, herbs and spices are mostly absent, due to the fact that nomadic people move frequently and crops do not. Mongolians have long traded for goods such as rice and flour, but more perishable products rarely made it north of the Gobi.

Mongolian food tends to be seasonal. In the summer months, when animals provide milk, dairy products become the staple. Meat (and fat) takes over in winter, supplemented with flour (in some form) and potatoes or rice if these are available.

Almost any Mongolian dish can be created with meat, rice, flour and potatoes. Most meals consist of *talkh* (bread) in the towns and cities and *bortzig* (fried unleavened bread) in the gers, and the uncomplicated *shölte khool* (literally, soup with food) – a meal involving hot broth, pasta

Because of his failing health, Ögedei Khaan (a son of Chinggis) was advised to halve the number of cups of alcohol he drank per day. Ögedei readily agreed, then promptly ordered that his cups be doubled in size.

slivers, boiled mutton and a few potato chunks. Nowadays, you can find plenty of international cuisine in the capital.

Buuz (steamed meat dumplings) and *khuushuur* (deep-fried meat pancakes) are two of the most popular menu options you'll find in restaurants. Miniature *buuz*, known as *bansh*, are usually dunked in milk tea. If you are travelling north from Běijīng, *buuz* may seem familiar – they are distant cousins of Chinese *bāozi*.

The classic Mongolian dinner staple is referred to simply as *makh* (meat) and consists of boiled sheep bits (bones, fat, various organs and the head) with some sliced potato, served in a plastic bucket. This meal does not require silverware; just trawl around the bucket of bones until a slab catches your fancy. There'll be a knife to slice off larger chunks.

The other main highlight of Mongolian cuisine is *khorkhog*, made by placing hot stones from an open fire into a pot or urn with chopped mutton, some water and sometimes vodka. The container is then sealed and left on the fire. When eating this meal, it's customary to pass the hot, greasy rocks from hand to hand, as this is thought to be good for your health.

In summer you can subsist as Mongolians do on *tsagaan idee* (dairy products; literally 'white foods'): yoghurt, milk, delicious fresh cream, cheese and fermented milk drinks. When you visit a ger you will be offered dairy snacks such as *aaruul* (dried milk curds), which are as hard as a rock and often about as tasty.

Finally, if you get a chance, don't miss the opportunity to try blowtorched marmot (prairie dog), a delicacy of the steppes.

Meals are occasionally interrupted for a round of vodka. Before taking a swig, a short ritual is employed to honour the sky gods and the four cardinal directions. There is no one way of doing this, but it usually involves dipping the left ring finger into the vodka and flicking droplets into the air four times before wiping your finger across your forehead.

1939

Japan invades Mongolia from Manchuria in May. With help from the Soviet Union, and after heavy fighting along the Khalkh Gol, the Mongols defeat Japan by September.

1956

Trans-Siberian railroad through Mongolia is completed, connecting Beijing with Moscow; Chinese and Russian trains operate on different gauges, requiring the bogies to be swapped at the border.

1961

Mongolia admitted to the UN as an independent country, but the Soviet Union continues to occupy Mongolia with troops and run the country as a satellite state.

1990

Democracy demonstrations break out in Ulaanbaatar. In June the first free, multiparty elections are held, with the Mongolian People's Revolutionary Party (MPRP) winning 85% of the vote.

1996

The Democratic Coalition becomes the first non-communist government to win an election (although a series of scandals causes the fall of four successive governments).

1998

S Zorig, the leader of the 1990 democratic revolution, is assassinated in his apartment on 2 October. The killers are never found and the murder never solved.

2008

In hotly contested parliamentary elections the MPRP narrowly defeats the Democratic Coalition. Protestors allege vote rigging, and subsequent riots end with four people shot dead and hundreds arrested.

population per sq km

SHÀNGHÀI   KŪNMÍNG   HONG KONG

≈ 320 people

China Today

An Economic Superpower

For decades, the world has been awestruck by China's potential. Gazing into the statistics of growth, it's all too easy to fall in with those who perceive the country as an emergent superpower. Books such as *When China Rules the World* by Martin Jacques triumphantly declare the establishment of a new world order.

China's apparent ability to shrug off the global financial crisis (despite a downturn in its exports) by means of a massive stimulus package revealed a robust determination to ride out the worst. Despite a slowing in the rate of economic growth, the Chinese economy continues to expand at a rate of around 9% per year and the growing middle classes are upbeat.

The pace of change is staggering. Year by year China churns out some of the world's biggest infrastructure projects as it upgrades its airports, train stations, high-speed rail links and bridges. Naysayers discern a coming crash, initiated perhaps by the pricking of a property-market bubble like Japan's in the 1990s. Already there are large 'ghost towns' in Inner Mongolia and elsewhere, planned cities built from scratch that remain void of humanity. Yet just as many pundits say the only way is up and point to the fact that China will soon overtake the US as the world's largest economy.

A more balanced view is that China remains a developing country. Despite its giant economy, its per-capita income is just US$6600, comparable to that of Namibia. Inequality in China is among the most extreme in the world, with billionaire businessmen walking the same streets as peasant farmers shouldering all their worldly possessions.

» Population: 1.34 billion

» GDP (purchasing power parity): US$8.75 trillion

» GDP per capita: US$6600

» Labour force: 813 million

Dos

» Do take your shoes off, or offer to, when visiting a Chinese person's home.

» Do tuck your feet underneath you or cross your legs when sitting down – avoid pointing the bottoms of your feet at anyone.

Don'ts

» Don't fight over the bill at a restaurant if your host is determined to pay the bill.

» Never give a clock as a gift (it has morbid overtones). White-, blue- or black-coloured gifts are also bad omens.

» Don't beckon to people with upturned fingers (keep your fingers pointed down).

» Don't leave your chopsticks stuck in a bowl of rice; this would be a curse on the owner of the restaurant. Also, don't point your chopsticks at anyone.

belief systems
(% of population)

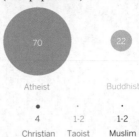

70
Atheist

22
Buddhist

•
4
Christian

·
1-2
Taoist

·
1-2
Muslim

if China were 100 people

92 would be Han Chinese
8 would be ethnic minorities, eg Zhuang, Manchu, Uighur etc

Prickly Politics

China is a growing political and military power and in 2011 launched its first aircraft carrier. But the government is tentative about assuming a leadership role on the world stage, partly because China is focused on maintaining a tight grip on border areas like Tibet and Xīnjiāng, and keeping its sights on Taiwan. But what China lacks in overseas military operations it makes up for in soft power positions in Africa, Central Asia and South America, requiring vast natural resources to fuel its booming industrial sector.

Chinese history is a revolving door of revolutions and revolt. Even today the government anticipates the next mass uprising, hence its often severe response to anything resembling a protest or dissident gathering. China's Communist Party, under the direction of Hu Jintao, has tried appealing to the masses for 'harmony' as part of the formula for China's 'peaceful rise'. The 'harmonious' theme is bandied about in the media without end, but the 'harmony' China espouses only goes as far as its political agenda will allow: Nobel Prize winners such as the Dalai Lama and Liu Xiaobo are perceived as enemies of the state for their 'unharmonious' sentiments.

Ethnic tensions are also prickly. The underlying problems that ignited deadly riots in Tibet in 2008 and Xīnjiāng in 2009 are perhaps yet to be fully addressed.

A certain fragility exists in China's growing sense of confidence. Some of this feeds into a kind of nationalism that is particularly appealing to young Chinese who perhaps lack other ideologies they can believe in.

» Number of Mao badges cast during the Cultural Revolution: 2.2 billion

» Length of China's longest river, the Yangzi: 6300km

» Percentage of university students that are female: 44

Travel Reads

» **Iron & Silk** (Mark Salzman)
» **The Travels** (Marco Polo)
» **China Road** (Rob Gifford)
» **River Town** (Peter Hessler)
» **Fried Eggs with Chopsticks** (Polly Evans)
» **Riding the Iron Rooster** (Paul Theroux)

Top Films

» **Still Life** (2005) directed by Zhang Ke Jia
» **The Last Emperor** (1987) directed by Bernardo Bertolucci
» **Raise the Red Lantern** (1991) directed by Zhang Yimou
» **The Painted Veil** (2007) directed by John Curran

Websites

» **Ctrip** (www.english.ctrip.com) Hotel- and flight-booking website.
» **Danwei** (www.danwei.org) Informative perspectives and handy links.
» **Zhongwen** (www.zhongwen .com) Includes online dictionary of Chinese characters.

China

The Chinese People

Ethnic Groups

When we think of China, we think of the world's most populous nation, dominated by the Han Chinese. While 92% of the population is Han, China is also home to 55 other ethnic minorities, including Tibetans, Uighurs and Mongols, plus smaller groups such as the Hui, Miao and Li. Most of the minorities live on China's borderlands, in the remote hill villages of the southwest or the distant deserts of western China. In the northeast, near Hǎilāěr, there are small pockets of Evenki (reindeer herders) and even ethnic Russians who speak Mandarin as their native tongue.

But it is indeed the Han Chinese who dominate, not only in the population figures but in every aspect of life in China – including writing, the arts, literature, sport and politics. For the minorities, the ability to operate comfortably in Han culture and language is essential for moving ahead in society.

The Han are distributed throughout the country but predominantly concentrate along the Yellow River, Yangzi River and Pearl River basins. These core areas are but a small fraction of the total area of China – the colossal areas of Tibet, Qinghai, Xīnjiāng, Inner Mongolia and the northeast (Manchuria) are historically non-Han areas but were slowly brought into the motherland following centuries of warfare and occupation.

The Chinese Character

Shaped by Confucian principles, the Han Chinese tend to be thoughtful and discreet but also very pragmatic. Self-sufficiency has been a guiding principle among villagers for centuries.

A 2011 poll reported in *China Daily* said that only 6% of Chinese people consider themselves happy. In another poll, 40% of respondents said that more money would make them happier.

CHINA'S ONE-CHILD POLICY

The 'one-child policy' (actually a misnomer) came into effect in 1979 in a bid to keep China's population to one billion by the year 2000; the latest government estimate is that the population will peak at 1.5 billion in 2033. The policy was originally harshly implemented, but rural revolt led to a softer stance; nonetheless, it has generated much bad feeling between local officials and the rural population. All non-Han minorities are exempt from the one-child policy.

Rural families are now allowed two children if the first child is a girl, but some have upwards of three or four kids. Additional offspring can result in fines and families having to shoulder the cost of education themselves, without government assistance. Official stated policy opposes forced abortion or sterilisation, but allegations of coercion continue as local officials strive to meet population quotas. Families who do abide by the one-child policy often go to great lengths to make sure their child is male, which has resulted in a lopsided male-to-female ratio of 111 boys to 100 girls.

Chinese people are very generous. Don't be surprised if a Chinese person you have met on the train invites you for a meal in the dining carriage. They will probably insist on paying, in which case do not attempt to thwart their efforts. The Chinese also simply adore children and are particularly warm to them.

The Chinese are an exceptionally proud people. They are proud of their civilisation and history, their written language and their inventions and achievements. Pride in the nation seeps through in almost everything the Chinese put their minds to; whether it be missions to the moon or the regimental training of Olympic athletes, the Chinese strive to be the best.

But in a country with a billion people, the Chinese have developed a take-no-prisoners attitude when it comes to fighting through crowds at shopping malls, train stations or any other assemblage of humanity. The large population also means greater competition for skilled work. Parents encourage their children to be competitive in order to get ahead in their careers, which is perhaps why the Chinese excel in the fields of maths and science. According to 2009 OECD rankings, students from China ranked first in reading, maths and science, in a survey of 34 countries.

Recent political realities have also influenced the Chinese character. While the Chinese people have always been reserved, in today's China they may appear even more circumspect. While the Chinese are very open about certain subjects (asking your age or how much money you earn, or expressing their dislike for Japan), they will often shy away from certain political issues (such as freedom of speech in the context of China). A rigid and controlled local media that filters out information deemed offensive to the regime has helped shape the Chinese worldview, so dissenting viewpoints about the status of Tibet or other political issues are largely unknown.

The rift between rural and urban Chinese is wide and continues to grow. Inhabitants of China's major cities can enjoy all the benefits of (nearly) first-world infrastructure, health care and education, while life for those in some rural areas may not have changed in three decades. Another divide in China is the distinct generation gap. The worldview of older Chinese who so fervently waved Mao's *Little Red Book* as they united in spirited communism is colliding against that of siblingless 'little emperors' struggling to climb the corporate ladder in the ruthless world of capitalist China.

Religion

Religion in China has been influenced by three streams of thought: Taoism, Confucianism and Buddhism. All three have been inextricably entwined in popular Chinese religion along with ancient animist beliefs. The founders of these traditions have been deified; the Chinese worship them and their disciples as fervently as they worship their own ancestors and a pantheon of gods and spirits.

CHINESE HISTORY

c 4000 BC

Archaeological evidence for the first settlements along the Yellow River (Huáng Hé). Even today the river remains a central cultural reference point for the Chinese.

551 BC

Birth of Confucius. Collected in the *Analects*, his ideas of an ethical, ordered society that operated through hierarchy and self-development would dominate Chinese culture until the early 20th century.

214 BC

Emperor Qin indentures thousands of labourers to link existing city walls into one Great Wall, in hopes of reducing attacks on his country by nomadic warriors from Mongolia.

c 100 BC

Buddhism arrives in China from India. This religious system ends up thoroughly assimilated into the culture and is now more powerful in China than in its country of origin.

1215

Chinggis Khaan conquers Běijīng as part of his creation of a massive Eurasian empire under Mongol rule.

1368

Zhu Yuanzhang founds the Ming dynasty and tries to impose a rigid Confucian social order on the population. However, China is too commercialised for the policy to work.

1644

Běijīng falls to peasant rebel Li Zicheng and the last Ming emperor, Chongzhen, hangs himself in Jǐngshān Park; the Qing dynasty is established.

ANCESTORS, GHOSTS & KITCHEN GODS

Beliefs about ancestor worship permeate almost every aspect of Chinese philosophy. Many homes have their own altar, where family members pay their respects to deceased relatives by burning spirit money and providing offerings. It's believed that a person possesses two 'souls' – a *guǐ*, which is yin and represents everything dark, damp and earthly, and a *shén*, which is yang, and represents light, goodness and strength. When a person dies the two souls go in separate directions – the *shén* to heaven and the *guǐ* to the underworld. If a person has suffered a tragic death or if the body is neglected the *guǐ* lingers on earth, often seeking revenge.

Closely tied to ancestor worship is popular religion, which consists of an immense celestial bureaucracy of gods and spirits, from the lowly but all-important kitchen god (*zào jun*) to the celestial emperor himself (*tiāndì*). Each god has a particular role to fulfil and can be either promoted or demoted depending on his or her performance. Lower-ranking gods who protect homes, doors and neighbourhoods from evil spirits (*guǐ*) are of particular interest, and in pre-communist China tiny altars and shrines were a ubiquitous sight. Offerings to the gods consisted not only of food and incense but also opera performances, birthday parties (to which the other local gods were invited) and the occasional procession around town.

China likes to present itself as a 'harmonious society', but dissent is still widespread. Some 180,000 large and small demonstrations were recorded in 2010, double the number recorded in 2005.

The Chinese communist government professes atheism. It considers religion to be base superstition, a remnant of old China used by the ruling classes to maintain power. Nevertheless, in an effort to improve relations with the Muslim, Buddhist and Lamaist minorities, in 1982 the Chinese government amended its constitution to allow freedom of religion. However, only atheists are permitted to be members of the Chinese Communist Party (CCP). Since almost all of China's 55 minority groups adhere to one religion or another, this rule precludes most of them from party membership.

Muslims and Christians are believed to be the largest identifiable religious groups still active in China today, each numbering perhaps 3% to 5% of the nation's population. The government has not published official figures of the number of Buddhists – hardly surprising given the ideological battle it has been waging with Tibetan Buddhists, who have been fighting for decades to preserve their culture and their nation. It's impossible to determine the number of Taoists, but the number of Taoist priests is very small.

Traditional Chinese religious beliefs took a battering during the Cultural Revolution when monasteries were disbanded, temples were destroyed and the monks were sometimes killed or sent to the fields to labour. Since Mao's death, the Chinese government has allowed many temples (sometimes with their own contingent of monks and novices) to reopen as active places of worship. All religious activity is firmly under state control and many of the monks are caretakers within renovated shells of monasteries, which serve principally as tourist attractions and are pale shadows of their former selves.

China Demographics

» Population: 1.34 billion

» Birth rate: 12.17 births per 1000 people

» Percentage of people over 65 years of age: 8.6%

» Urbanisation rate: 2.7%

» Life expectancy: 74.5 years

The Arts

China is the custodian of one of the world's richest cultural and artistic legacies. Until the 20th century, China's arts were deeply conservative and resistant to change; in the last hundred years revolutions in technique and content have fashioned a dramatic transformation. Despite this evolution, China's arts – whatever the period – remain united by a common aesthetic that taps into the very soul of the nation.

In reflection of the Chinese character, Chinese aesthetics have traditionally been marked by restraint and understatement, a preference for oblique references over direct explanation, vagueness in place of specificity. These guiding principles compellingly find their way into virtually every Chinese art form.

Calligraphy

Perhaps the most iconic of China's arts is calligraphy. However, it can be tricky for Westerners to comprehend calligraphy as an art form, unless they have a sound understanding of written Chinese. This is because the characters represent both an image of beauty as well as a description or concept. Less 'insider' knowledge is needed, however, to appreciate Chinese traditional painting. There may be subtle meanings behind the work, but in general Chinese landscapes are accessible to any eye and have long been treasured in the West for their beauty.

Visual Arts

China turned an artistic corner of sorts after 1949, when artists eschewed washes on silk in favour of oil on canvas. The Chinese obsession with the mysterious and the ineffable made way for attention to detail and realism. By the 1970s, Chinese artists aspired to master the skill of socialist-realism. Saturated with political symbolism and propaganda, the blunt artistic style was produced on an industrial scale. Traditional Taoist and Buddhist philosophy was overturned; humans were now the masters of nature, which would bend to their will.

Mao's death ended the era of 'art for the masses' and a new school of artists began exploring a variety of themes, largely influenced by the Western art world. After the Tiananmen protests in 1989 the Chinese art world turned cynical, with many works mocking Chinese consumerism and political ideology. Today there is a vast array of subjects as Chinese artists have moved away from overtly political work towards more universal concerns.

Ceramics

One of China's biggest art exports is ceramics, for which it has been developing techniques for thousands of years. Some of the best pieces date from the Yuan dynasty, when the 'blue-and-white' (qīnghuā) porcelain, made with cobalt-blue paint from Persia, was developed. The porcelain became famous the world over, eventually acquiring the name 'Chinaware' whether the pieces were produced in China or not.

Sculpture

Sculpture in China reached its zenith after the arrival of Buddhism, when artists across the land were commissioned to carve enormous statues of the Buddha. Early concepts for Buddhist sculpture came from India, so it's not surprising that some of China's most spectacular Buddhist statues are found along the Silk Road west of Xī'ān. The Poly Art Museum in Běijīng contains an impressive collection of Chinese statuary.

1842
The treaty of Nanjing concludes the first Opium War. China is forced to hand over Hong Kong island to the British and open up five Chinese ports to foreign trade.

1898
The New Territories adjoining Kowloon in Hong Kong are leased to the British for 99 years, eventually being returned, along with the rest of Hong Kong, in 1997.

1904–05
The Russo-Japanese War is fought entirely on Chinese territory. The victory of Japan is the triumph by an Asian power over a European one.

1911
Revolution spreads across China as local governments withdraw support for the dynasty, and instead support a republic under the presidency of Sun Yatsen.

1931
Japan invades Manchuria (northeast China), provoking an international crisis and forcing Kuomintang leader Chiang Kaishek to consider anti-Japanese as well as anti-communist strategies.

1949
Mao Zedong stands on top of the Gate of Heavenly Peace in Běijīng on 1 October and announces the formation of the People's Republic of China, saying 'The Chinese people have stood up.'

1962
Mao initiates the Great Leap Forward; at least 20 million people starve when his plan to industrialise the country causes a collapse in the agricultural sector.

Architecture

Along the Trans-Manchurian route the architecture stands out from the rest of China, primarily as a result of foreign influences in the region. At the turn of the 20th century, much of Manchuria was occupied – either economically or militarily – by Russia, Japan and various European powers, all of whom left their mark on the cities in this region. The best example is Tiānjīn, which contains quarters once dominated by Austro-Hungarians, Belgians, Germans, Italians and Japanese. In Dàolǐqū, the oldest part of Hā'ěrbīn (Harbin), onion domes and ornamental facades reveal the city's Russian roots.

Zhang Xiaogang's 1988 triptych oil work, *Forever Lasting Love*, sold for US$10.1 million, a record amount for a piece of contemporary Chinese art.

Contemporary Music

Zhōngguó Yáogǔn yīnyuè (literally 'Chinese shaking and rolling music') has seen spectacular growth since the pioneering sound of Northwest Wind (xīběi fēng) first shook up the local music scene in the 1980s. The Northwest Wind genre appealed to young, progressive audiences with its fast-tempo music and lyrics that drew from traditional folk music.

The first Chinese rock bands emerged in the mid- and late 1980s, led by Cui Jian, who released 'Nothing to My Name', a popular Northwest Wind song recognised as China's first rock ballad. The lyrics describe lost love and desire but have been interpreted as a metaphor for a lack of political freedoms in China. The song later became an anthem played to rally demonstrators at Tiananmen Sq in 1989.

Chinese rock entered the mainstream in the early 1990s, with bands like Black Panther filling up concert halls and selling records by the millions in both China and other Asian markets. The music was largely Běijīng based, but by the mid-1990s there was much competition from more established canto-rock bands from Hong Kong. New crossover bands like Brain Failure emerged, singing in both Mandarin and English.

Major art festivals in Běijīng include the 798 International Art Festival (May), the Běijīng Biennale (October 2013), and the China International Gallery Exposition (October).

Punk and punk-pop is the latest trend and numerous bands perform in every imaginable venue, from seedy underground clubs to outdoor rock festivals. In Běijīng the most popular place to hear grungy-punk sounds is D-22 (www.d22beijing.com.cn), where you can check out the latest from bands like PK-14, Joyside, Demerit Carsick Cars and Lonely China Day.

HALLMARK NORTHERN DISHES

PINYIN	SCRIPT	ENGLISH
Běijīng kǎoyā	北京烤鸭	Peking duck
jiāo zhá yángròu	憔炸羊肉	deep-fried mutton
qīng xiāng shāo jī	清香烧鸡	chicken wrapped in lotus leaf
shuàn yángròu	涮羊肉	lamb hotpot
mántou	馒头	steamed buns
jiǎozi	饺子	dumplings
ròu bāozi	肉包子	steamed meat buns
sān měi dòufu	三美豆腐	sliced bean curd with Chinese cabbage
yuán bào lǐ jí	芫爆里脊	stir-fried pork tenderloin with coriander
zào liū sān bái	糟溜三白	stir-fried chicken, fish and bamboo shoots

Chinese Cuisine

China is a gastronome's paradise. Cooking is a way of life here and first-time visitors will find a world of culinary delights, far greater than what is on offer in Chinatowns the world over. Food plays a prominent role in the national psyche – work, play, romance, business and family life all revolve around it. When people meet, a common greeting is 'Nǐ chīfàn le ma?' ('Have you eaten yet?')

The food in China varies greatly by region and is influenced by the topographical and climatic disparities that exist across this vast nation. Naturally, seafood is plentiful near the coast and meat dominates in interior regions like Inner Mongolia. Likewise, grains are more prevalent in the north, while rice is the staple in the south.

The Northern School

The northern school of cooking is what you'll experience when travelling along the Trans-Mongolian and Trans-Manchurian railway lines, although big cities like Běijīng and Hā'ěrbīn will have restaurants that represent the southern, eastern and western schools.

The northern school has a reputation for being bland and unsophisticated, but it's filling, appetizing and particularly well suited to the harsh winter climate. There's a particular accent on millet, sorghum, maize, barley and wheat rather than rice (which requires a lot of water). The spectrum of flavours is somewhat muted compared to southern cooking, as salt is preferred to spice.

Roasting meat is also more common in the north than in other parts of China. Meats in northern China are braised until they're falling off the bone, or brushed with spices and barbequed until smoky. Pungent garlic, chives and spring onions are used with abandon and are also used raw.

Culinary Influences

The influence of Manchurian cooking and the cold climate of the northeastern provinces have left a legacy of rich and hearty stews, dense breads and dumplings. The cooking of the nomadic Mongolians has also left a pronounced mark on northern meat cooking, especially in the development of northern hotpot. Milk from nomadic herds of cattle, goats and horses has also made its way into northern cuisine, as yoghurts for example. In Běijīng it's common to spot small clay jars of Mongolian yoghurt selling in snack stalls.

1966
The Cultural Revolution breaks out, and Red Guards demonstrate in cities across China. The movement is marked by a fetish for violence as a catalyst for transforming society.

1976
Mao Zedong dies, aged 83. The Gang of Four (faction led by Mao's wife Jiang Qing) are arrested by his successor and put on trial, where they are blamed for all the disasters of the Cultural Revolution.

1980
The one-child policy is enforced. The state adopts it as a means of reducing the population but at the same time imposes unprecedented control over women's personal liberty.

1989
Hundreds of civilians are killed by Chinese troops in the streets around Tiananmen Sq. No official reassessment has been made, but rumours persist of deep internal conflict within the party.

2008
Běijīng hosts the 2008 Summer Olympic Games and Paralympics. The Games go smoothly and are widely considered to be a great success in burnishing China's image overseas.

2008–09
Violent riots erupt in Tibet and Xīnjiāng, evidence that Beijing's policy of development in Western regions is not enough to quell local demands for greater autonomy and limited Han migration.

Landscapes & Wildlife

One of the attractions of the Trans-Siberian routes is the ability to experience the changes in landscape across the three countries. Much of the wildlife is naturally shy, hidden from view or too distant to be observed well, so the best way to appreciate nature in Russia, Mongolia and China is to alight and spend a few days exploring the countryside.

The Lie of the Land

The most prevalent of the vegetation zones traversed by the railway is the iconic Russian taiga, a dense forest belt running from Scandinavia across Siberia to the Pacific coast. Hints of the vast taiga lying ahead can be found even as Trans-Siberian trains crawl across European Russia, but train travellers get a sense of what writer Anton Chekhov called the true Siberian taiga once they have crossed the Yenisey River at Krasnoyarsk. The BAM route (from Tayshet) is wall-to-wall taiga for days on end.

True taiga is coniferous forest, particularly Siberian pine *(Pinus sibirica)*, but you will often find mixed conifer and deciduous forest, and in some places completely deciduous forest. Silver firs, spruce, larch and birch often mingle with maple and aspen, while willows and poplars dominate the innumerable rivers, lakes and ponds. Typically, as you cross Siberia, the mixed and coniferous forest is broken by clearings or farmland, which in turn are punctuated by Siberian towns, villages and settlements. In Eastern Siberia and the Far East the landscape folds and rises in parts into forested mountains, such as the Barguzin Mountains that flank the eastern shore of Lake Baikal.

As the Trans-Mongolian Railway crosses Mongolia, it passes through the pastures of the Selenga Gol (Selenga River) valley. Gradually, however, the landscape changes to steppe. The steppe (some of it mountain forest steppe) spans the continent from the plains north of the Black Sea across Central Asia through Mongolia to the western edge of China. This gently rolling and – in its driest form – semiarid grassland is often unsuitable for cultivation, but it provides sufficient vegetation to support large herds of grazing animals.

To the south, the steppe becomes arid and gives way to the deserts of central Asia. The Gobi Desert in Mongolia and China retains a thin grass cover that sustains some of the hardier herbivores. The section traversed by the Trans-Mongolian south of Choir gets grass in a good year.

Rivers & Lakes on the Routes

Russia has six of the world's 20 longest rivers. Forming the China–Russia border, the east-flowing Amur (4416km) is the longest, along with the Lena (4400km), Yenisey (4090km), Irtysh (4245km) and Ob (3680km), all of which flow north across Siberia ending up in the Arctic Ocean.

GOBI DESERT

The Gobi Desert is encroaching on Beijing at a rate of 2km per year, and to stop it the Chinese government is trying to create a 5700km long 'green wall' by paying farmers to plant trees.

Beautiful Lake Baikal itself is the world's deepest lake, holding nearly one-fifth of all the globe's unfrozen fresh water. Formed by rifting tectonic plates, Baikal is also the world's oldest lake, dating back 25 million years. The rift, which widens by about 2cm per year, is thought to be 9km deep, of which 7km of depth is covered by sediment.

Europe's longest river, the Volga (3690km), rises northwest of Moscow and flows via Nizhny Novgorod and Kazan into the Caspian Sea.

National Parks & Reserves

Along or close by the Trans-Siberian routes you'll find easily reached national parks and reserves.

» Perm (p137), Kungur (p142) and Yekaterinburg (p148) are good springboards into the Urals landscapes and parks.

» Irkutsk (Listvyanka; p200) provides access to spectacular walking trails, whereas Ulan-Ude is best for the Barguzin National Reserve (p214) within the Zabaikalsky National Park.

» Krasnoyarsk has the unusual Stolby Nature Reserve (p180)

» Close to Ulaanbaatar, you'll find the Gorkhi-Terelj National Park (p285) and the Khustain National Park (p285)

One of the best places to spot waterfowl is on the Baraba Steppe between Omsk and Novosibirsk. Part of this is an outlier of the Vasyugian Swamp, the largest swamp in the northern hemisphere.

SIBERIAN LANDSCAPES & BELIEFS

Landscapes, perhaps more than anything else, shape the lives and beliefs of human beings.

In Russia, the countryside is imbued with aspects of both Christian and traditional lifestyles. After the Cossack Yermak drowned in the Irtysh River near Tobolsk during a Tatar ambush, his corpse was described in the early semi-religious *Siberian Chronicles* as being too miraculous to be touched even by birds. Almost a century later, the exiled Old Believer Archpriest Avvakum (1621–82) was flogged and tormented across Siberia and on reaching Lake Baikal he described it as a paradise on earth, where everything was larger than life. Later still, in 17th-century Russia, the Daur region in the Amur Basin was widely seen by Cossacks as a land of milk and honey to which they could flee and where they might find refuge from brutal masters. For Russian peasants as a whole, Siberia stood for freedom from serfdom.

In the 18th century, a bizarre castrati sect (called Skoptsy in Russian) established itself in Siberia and several other regions, according to which males were (as the name suggests) castrated. Even today, sects and gurus are attracted to Siberia, the most famous being the neo-Jesus, Vissarion, aka Sergei Torop, whose Abode of Dawn community is tucked away in forest near the town of Abakan, south of Krasnoyarsk. If one religious movement would seem to be without a future, however, it was the castrati. Bizarrely, it later spawned an offshoot 'neo-castrati' sect in the Balkans.

South of the Trans-Siberian at Novosibirsk, in the Altai Republic, the Russian painter and mystic Nikolai Rerikh (known internationally as Nicholas Roerich) sought the mythical, heavenly kingdom of Shambhala, and today ordinary Russians popularly perceive the picturesque Altai as a 'sacred' place imbued with spiritual energy.

The tie between landscape and shamanism among Buryats of the regions around Lake Baikal is very similar to those of Mongolians across the border. The sky is an integral aspect of shamanist belief, and in Mongolia blue scarves are placed on *ovoos* (stone cairns) to represent it. Mongolians also flick droplets of vodka into the air before they drink, in order to honour the sky gods. For a deeper insight into this, see p359.

In China a special role is played by its sacred mountains. Beyond Tibet, there are four sacred Buddhist mountains, each one the home of a specific bodhisattva, an enlightened being or source of enlightenment. The two most famous mountains are Wǔtái Shān and Éméi Shān, respectively ruled over by Wenshu and Puxiang. See p368 for more on ancestor worship.

Wildlife

Wildlife flourishes in the taiga; the indigenous cast includes squirrels, chipmunks (which dine well on pine-cone seeds), voles and lemmings, as well as small carnivores such as polecats, foxes, wolverines and, less commonly, the sable – a weasel-like creature whose luxuriant pelt played such a great role in the early exploration of Siberia.

The most common species of large mammal in the taiga is the elk, a large deer that can measure over 2m at the shoulder and weighs almost as much as a bear. The brown bear itself is also a Siberian inhabitant that you may come across, despite the Russian penchant for hunting it. Other taiga-dwelling animals include deer, wolves, lynx and foxes.

Mongolia's Wild Heritage by Christopher Finch, written in collaboration with the Mongolian Ministry of Nature and Environment, is an outstanding book on Mongolia's fragile ecology, and has excellent photos.

Lake Baikal

Lake Baikal's wildlife is unique. Thanks to warm water entering from vents in the bottom of the lake, and the filtering action of countless millions of minute crustaceans called epishura, the water is exceptionally clear and pure. Over 1700 species of plants and animals live in the lake (nearly all endemic), including over 200 types of shrimp and 80 of flatworm; one species of flatworm is the world's largest and eats fish.

The many kinds of fish include the endemic *omul*, Baikal's main commercial fish. A remarkable species, the *omul* (a white fish of the salmon family) is reputed to emit a shrill cry when caught. It spawns in the Selenga River, but its main food source is the endemic Baikal alga, *melosira*, which has declined drastically because of pollution.

The *golomyanka* – a pink, translucent oilfish with large pectoral fins – is endemic to Baikal. It's unusual in having no scales and being viviparous – giving birth to live young, about 2000 at a time. It is the lake's most common fish, although its numbers have been depleted by pollution. By day it lives in the deep, dark depths, rising at night to near the surface.

Golomyanka is the preferred food of the *nerpa* (Baikal seal, *Phoca siberica*), the world's only freshwater seal, with no relatives nearer than the ringed seal of the Arctic. The *nerpa* is an attractive, gentle creature with unusually large eyes set in a round, flat face, enabling it to hunt down to at least 1500m below the surface – even at night. Despite their size (less than 1.5m, making them the world's smallest seal), they have particularly strong claws for forcing their way through winter ice and keeping their breathing holes open. Pups are born in late winter. At the

SPECIES UNDER THREAT

The largest of all wild cats, the Siberian tiger can measure up to 3.5m in length. There are currently estimated to be only about 500 tigers in Russia's Ussuriland, but their genetic diversity is so low that the effective number is just 14 animals. Across the border in China the situation is even less rosy – there is thought to be no more than 50 or 60 Siberian tigers living there freely. Though protected by Chinese law and recognised as one of the world's most endangered species, the animals' survival hangs by a thread due to urban encroachment on its territory and a lucrative poaching industry. Tiger bones are prized in traditional Chinese medicine, while tiger skins also fetch a hefty price on the black market.

In response to the tigers' plight, the Chinese government set up a number of breeding centres, including the Siberian Tiger Park (p297) outside Hā'ěrbīn (Harbin). The centres aim to restore the natural tiger population by breeding and reintroducing them into the wild. While this might seem like a good idea in theory, in practice the need for minimal human contact and 'natural' conditions is at odds with the busloads of tourists snapping photos of big cats munching on cows and chickens at the park.

top of the food chain, Baikal seals have been greatly affected by pollution and are still harvested by local people. According to research by Greenpeace, the seal population hovers around the 60,000 mark – not sufficient for the animal to be endangered but meaning it could be in the future as its under threat from excessive hunting.

There is plenty of other wildlife around the lake. The huge delta, nearly 40km wide, formed by the sediment brought down to the lake by the Selenga River, is a great attraction to wild fowl and wading birds. In summer such beautiful and rare species as the Asiatic dowitcher and white-winged black tern nest in the delta, while in autumn vast numbers of waterfowl from the north use the mudflats and marshes to rest and feed on their migration south. It's a sort of international bird airport, with many birds overwintering there, too.

Vast numbers of caddis flies and other insects hatch and swarm on the lake in summer, providing a rich and vital food source for all kinds of wildlife from fish to birds. Despite their lack of visual impact for the Trans-Siberian traveller, these tiny insects, along with the microscopic plant and animal organisms, form the base of the pyramid of wildlife that graces this unique area.

China has an incredibly diverse range of natural escapes scattered across the country. Since the first nature reserve was established in 1956, around 2000 more parks have joined the ranks, protecting about 14% of China's land area, and offering the traveller a wonderful variety of landscapes and diversity of wildlife.

Survival Guide

Directory A–Z

Accommodation

For much of your Trans-Siberian journey your bed will be on the train, but at either end of your journey and most likely at points along it you'll be looking for more traditional accommodation.

The prices listed in this book are for a standard twin or double room in the high season (summer), including breakfast, and with a private bathroom unless otherwise stated.

Russia

Russia offers everything from cosy homestays to five-star luxury hotels. You can generally stay where you like, though a few of the cheapest hotels won't want to register your visa (p45).

It's a good idea to book a few nights in advance for big cities, but elsewhere it's usually not necessary. Big discounts on rack rates (the ones we list in this guide) can be had for online bookings on sites such as www.booking .com.

Make bookings by email or fax rather than telephone so you get a written copy of your reservation. Some hotels charge a booking surcharge

(bron) which can be up to 50% of the first night's accommodation rate.

If you're looking for cheaper places to stay, head for the smaller towns or consider a homestay or serviced apartment; many travel agencies can arrange these. Occasionally, twin rooms are cheaper than singles, but you may end up sharing with a stranger unless you make it clear that you'd prefer single occupancy.

HOTELS

Budget hotel rooms may have their own toilet, washbasin or shower, or you may have to use facilities shared by the whole corridor. Take care with security in some. They will cost up to R2000 (R3000 in Moscow) for a twin. In midrange hotels you can still often find cheaper unrenovated rooms at budget prices.

Midrange hotels are the most common hotels in cities and you'll pay R2000 to R4000 for a twin (except in Moscow and St Petersburg, where the midrange prices start above R3000).

The definition of 'luxury hotel' varies according to whether you are in a major city or in a smaller town. In large cities, expect Western standards, but in the country the top end sometimes means a spruced-up Soviet monolith.

CAMPING & TOURIST BASES

Kempingi (organised camping grounds) are rare and, usually, only open from June to September. Camping is generally not allowed in the wild – check with locals if you're in doubt. Turbazy, tourist bases with shared bungalows or sometimes space for tents, are good alternatives.

B&B, HOSTELS, HOMESTAYS AND APARTMENTS

Especially common around Lake Baikal but available in most places in Russia, homestays are a good way to get a glimpse of how Russians live. Prices depend on proximity to the centre, whether meals are included or whether the owners speak English. St Petersburg, Moscow, Irkutsk and Vladivostok have good hostels. In larger cities apartments are also good value.

RESTING ROOMS

Resting rooms (komnaty otdykha) are found at all major train stations and several of the smaller ones as well as at a few larger bus stations. Generally, they have basic (but usually clean) shared accommodation, mostly with communal facilities. The beds

BOOK YOUR STAY ONLINE

For more accommodation reviews by Lonely Planet authors, check out hotels.lonelyplanet.com/Russia. You'll find independent reviews, as well as recommendations on the best places to stay. Best of all, you can book online.

can be rented by the hour (from R100), for a half day (from R500) or for a 24-hour (from R1000) period. Some will ask to see your train ticket before allowing you to stay.

China

In China you will find rustic homesteads, homestays, youth hostels, student dormitories, guesthouses, courtyard lodgings, boutique hotels or five-star towers. The choices are twins (common in China), singles, doubles, and suites that are available at most midrange and top-end hotels. Dorms are usually, but not always, available at youth hostels. Booking online can secure good prices on rooms, and should be the first place you look. Dorms in hostels usually cost between Y50 and Y100 around the centre of Běijīng. Doubles or twin rooms in Běijīng hostels start at around Y200 with a shared bathroom.

Useful accommodation websites:

Asia Hotels (www.asia -hotels.com)
Ctrip (www.english.ctrip.com)
China Hotels (www.china -hotelguide.com)
Redflag (www.redflag.info)
SinoHotel (www.sinohotel .com)

Once in China, book discounted rooms on the following sites:
Ctrip (☎800 820 6666; www.english.ctrip.com)
Elong (☎800 810 1010; www.elong.com)

Mongolia

It's always advisable to book ahead in Mongolia, especially in the guesthouses of Ulaanbaatar.

Mongolia has excellent camp sites everywhere, even near Ulaanbaatar in places such as Terelj, and camping is the better option if you are travelling in the countryside, considering the lack of hotels and the expense of ger (yurt) camps.

A tourist ger camp is a 'camping ground' with traditional ger, a separate building for toilets and showers, and a restaurant-bar. The gers are furnished with two to four beds. Toilets and bathrooms, which are shared, are usually clean. Most ger camps in Terelj are open from June to September. In the Gobi Desert, they are open from May to October.

Ulaanbaatar has an abundant range of guesthouses targeting foreign backpackers. Most guesthouses are in apartment blocks and have dorm beds as well as private rooms.

At US$20 to US$30 per day, an apartment is much better value than Ulaanbaatar's hotels, which are decent but overpriced. Comfortable and clean, guesthouse and apartment rooms usually have hot water and satellite TV, and maybe even English-speaking staff.

Dorm beds at Ulaanbaatar guesthouses cost around US$5, private rooms around US$10. You will be hard-pressed to find a double room at a midrange hotel for less than US$40.

Ger camps typically charge US$20 to US$40 per person per night, including three hearty meals, but prices are negotiable, and they may drop considerably if you bring your own food. Tour agencies (p282) and travel agencies (p282) in Ulaanbaatar can arrange visits.

Activities

See p17, Ulaanbaatar (p282) and the index for activities options. Below is a brief overview of when a permit is required.

Parks, Reserves & Protected Areas

Places covered in this book can be entered without special permits, but you will usually have to pay an admission/permit fee at the entrance.

HOMESTAY AGENCIES

The following agencies can arrange homestays mainly in Moscow and St Petersburg (as can some travel agencies; see individual city listings for details) from as little as US$15 a day but more commonly €30 to €60, depending on location and quality of accommodation.

International Homestay Agency (www .homestayagency.com/ homestay/russia.html)

Host Families Association (HOFA; ☎8-901-305 8874; www .hofa.ru)

Worldwide Homestay (www.worldwide homestay.com/Russia .htm)

Fishing

Russia and Mongolia are the two places you are likely to go fishing.

Russia Fishermen will take you out onto the waters (or the winter ice) of Lake Baikal. Rules on when you can fish, how and for what species vary from region to region and the time of year; the local boat operator or tour company can take care of permits where required.

Mongolia The situation with permits is very strict. If you fish illegally you risk a fine of about US$40 (or jail, depending on the mood of the ranger). While it's relatively easy to get a fishing permit in a national park in Mongolia, buying one for other areas is much more difficult. Anglers must have a special permit authorised by the **Ministry of Nature & Environment and Tourism** (☎051-266 286; www.mne.mn; Negdsen Undestnii Gudamj 5/2, Government Bldg II, Ulaanbaatar), which costs US$120 a week.

ACCOMMODATION PRICES

SYMBOL	MAJOR RUSSIAN CITIES	REST OF RUSSIA	MONGOLIA	CHINA
€ or $	<R3000	<R1500	<T48,000 (US$40)	<Y400
€€ or $$	R3000–10,000	R1500–4000	T48,000–T108,000 (US$40–90)	Y400–1000
€€€ or $$$	>R10,000	>R4000	>T108,000 (US$90)	>Y1000

Activities in Border Regions

Russia Designated border zones throughout Russia can only be entered with a permit from the local Federalnaya Sluzhba Bezopasnosti (FSB), the Russian Federal Security Service (formerly known as the KGB). No special permits are required for the rail routes and the border crossings mentioned in this book. Nor do you usually need one if you are transiting on a main road, but for side-trips or deeper exploration inside border regions, such as the Mongolia–Russia border zone in the Altai Republic or Tuva, you certainly will require one. When required, a permit is usually a formality, but you will need a tour operator to help arrange it (this will usually be done free of charge), and the process takes about five days locally, sometimes longer.

China Much of the northeastern border between China and Siberia follows the Black Dragon River (Hēilóng Jiāng), known to the Russians as the Amur River. At the time of writing, you didn't need permits to visit any areas along the border but it would be good to check with the PSB in Hā'ěrbīn nonetheless, at the **Public Security Bureau** (PSB; 公安局; Gōng'ānjú; 26 Duan Jie; ⊙8.40am-noon & 1.30-4.30pm Mon-Fri).

Mongolia If you are travelling to border areas such as Altai Tavan Bogd National Park in Bayan-Ölgii, the **General Office of Border Protection** (Border Defence Bldg, in Ulaanbaatar; ⊙10am-12.30pm & 2-5pm Mon-Fri), in the east of the city, is the place to go for permits. Permits are free but you must send a Mongolian on your behalf to apply. The office requires a passport photocopy and a map showing your route.

Business Hours

Exceptions to business hours have been noted in individual listings in this book.

Russia

Museum hours are not uniform. They close one day a week and there will be one extra 'sanitary' day per month when the facility is closed for cleaning.

Banks	9am-6pm Mon-Fri, some open 9am-5pm Sat
Restaurants & bars	noon-midnight
Businesses & shops	10am-9pm Mon-Fri, 10am-7pm Sat & Sun

Mongolia

Many museums and tourist attractions have shorter hours and more days off in winter.

Banks	9am-6pm Mon-Fri, 10am-3pm Sat
Government offices	9am-5pm Mon-Fri
Restaurants	10am-10pm
Shops	10am-8pm

China

Banks	9am-noon & 2-5pm Mon-Fri
Restaurants	10.30am-11pm
Shops	10am-10pm

Children

Travelling in Russia, China or Mongolia with children can be a breeze as long as you come well prepared with the right attitudes, equipment and patience.

Practicalities

» Baby-changing rooms are uncommon.

» Public toilets are in poor condition.

» Nappies, powdered milk and baby food widely available except in rural areas.

» Finding English-language kids' publications is difficult; toy shops are plentiful.

» Some Russian *firmeny* (premium) trains (including the 1/2 and 9/10) have a staff carriage for children in which the *provodnitsa* (carriage attendant) is also a child-minder and there is a shower, as well as films and toys for children. Staff in the restaurant of some trains will also prepare children's dishes on demand.

» If you are travelling alone with a child on trains,

carriage attendants will briefly watch over children while you use the toilet.

» Lonely Planet's *Travel with Children* contains useful advice on how to cope with kids on the road and what to bring to make things go more smoothly.

Customs Regulations

» If you declared foreign currency when you entered Russia (see p381), make sure you are carrying less when leaving, otherwise you may have to change the excess into roubles.

Russia

Even though searches beyond the perfunctory are quite rare, clearing customs, especially when you leave Russia by a land border, can be lengthy. Currently, visitors are allowed to bring in and take out under US$3000 (or its equivalent) in currency, and goods in value under R65,000, weighing less than 50kg, without making a customs declaration.

The only time it's worth filling in a customs declaration form is if you're bringing into the country any major equipment, antique, art work or musical instrument (including a guitar) that you plan to take out with you – get it stamped (in the red channel at airports) to avoid any problems on leaving Russia with the same goods.

If you plan to export anything vaguely 'arty' – manuscripts, instruments, coins, jewellery, antiques, antiquarian books (anything published pre-1975) – it must be assessed by the **RosOkhranKultura** (Moscow ☑495-628 5089; Kitaygorodsky proezd 7, bldg 2; ☺10am-5pm Mon-Fri; Ⓜ Kitay-Gorod; St Petersburg ☑812-571 0302; Malaya Morskaya ul 17; Ⓜ Nevsky Prospekt). Bring your item (or a photograph, if the item is large) and your

receipt. The bureaucrats will issue a receipt for tax paid, which you show to customs officers on your way out of the country.

China

Chinese customs officers generally pay tourists little attention. There are no restrictions on foreign currency, but you should declare any cash exceeding US$5000 (or its equivalent in another currency).

Objects considered to be antiques require a certificate and red seal to clear customs. To get these, your antiques must be inspected by the **Relics Bureau** (Wénwù Jiàndīng; ☑010-6401 9714, no English spoken). Basically anything made before 1949 is considered an antique and needs a certificate, and if it was made before 1795 it

cannot legally be taken out of the country.

Mongolia

The main issue for foreign travellers is the export of antiques. You must have a receipt and customs certificate from the place you bought them; most reliable shops in Ulaanbaatar provide this, otherwise you'll need one from the **Centre of Cultural Heritage** (☑7011 0877) in the Palace of Culture in Ulaanbaatar. You'll need to fill in a form giving your passport number, details of where the antique was purchased and two photos of the antique itself. If you have anything that even *looks* old, it is a good idea to get a document to indicate that it is not an antique. That goes for Buddha images and statues as well.

RUSSIAN STREET NAMES

We use the Russian names of all streets and squares in this book to help you when deciphering Cyrillic signs and asking locals the way. To save space, the following abbreviations are used:

bul – bulvar бульвар – boulevard

nab – naberezhnaya набережная -embankment

per – pereulok переулок – side street

pl – ploshchad площадь – square

pr – prospekt проспект – avenue

sh – shosse шоссе – road

ul – ulitsa улица – street

Please also note that some of the Soviet-era names for streets and places have been changed back to their prerevolutionary names or to new names.

Discount Cards

Full-time students and people aged under 26 can sometimes (but not always) get a substantial discount on admissions – flash your student card or International Student Identity Card (ISIC) before paying. If you're not a student but are under 26, ask a student agency at home for an ISIC Youth Card. Check the ISIC website (www.isic card.com) for updates.

Senior citizens also *might* get a discount, but no promises: carry your pension card or passport anyway.

Electricity

Electrical power in Russia, China and Mongolia is 220V, 50Hz. Sockets in Russia and Mongolia are designed to accommodate two round prongs in the European style. Chinese plugs come in at least four designs: three-pronged angled pins as used in Australia; three-pronged round pins as in Hong Kong; two-pronged flat pins as in the USA; or two narrow round pins as in Europe. For more information, check www.kropla.com.

Embassies & Consulates

Russia

IRKUTSK

Mongolia (☑3952-342 145; www.irconsul.angara.ru; ul Lapina 11)

KHABAROVSK

China (☑4212-302 353, fax 302 432; Lenin Stadium 1)

Japan (☑4212-326 418; ul Pushkina 38a)

MOSCOW

Australia (Посольство Австралии; ☑495-956 6070; www.russia.embassy.gov .au; Podkolokolny per 10a/2; ⓂKitay Gorod)

Belarus (Консульство Белорусии; ☑495-624 7095; www.embassybel.ru; Maroseyka ul 17/6; ⓂKitay Gorod)

Canada (Посольство Канады; Map p84; ☑495-925 6000; www.russia.gc.ca; Starokony-ushenny per 23; ⓂKropotkin-skaya)

China (Посольство Китая; ☑499-783 0867; consu-lar 499-143 1540; http:// ru.chineseembassy.org; ul Druzhby 6; ⓂUniversitet)

Finland (Посольство Финляндии; Map p84; ☑495-787 4174; www.finland .org.ru; Kropotkinsky per 15/17; ⓂPark Kultury)

France (Посольство Франции; Map p84; ☑495-937 1500; www.ambafrance-ru .org; ul Bolshaya Yakimanka 45; ⓂOktyabrskaya)

Germany (Посольство Германии; ☑495-937 9500; www.moskau.diplo.de; Mosfil-movskaya ul 56; ⓂUniversitet, then bus 119)

Ireland (Посольство Ирландии; ☑495-937 5911; www.embassyofireland.ru; Grokholsky per 5; ⓂProspekt Mira)

Japan (Посольство Японии; ☑495-229 2550; www.ru.emb -japan.go.jp; Grokholsky per 27; ⓂArbatskaya)

Mongolia (Посольство Монголии; Map p78; ☑495-290 6792; Spasopeskovsky per 7/1; ⓂSmolenskaya)

Netherlands (Посольство Голландии; Map p78; ☑495-797 2900; www.netherlands -embassy.ru; Kalashny per 6; ⓂArbatskaya)

New Zealand (Посольство Новой Зеландии; Map p78; ☑495-956 3579; www.nz embassy.com/russia; Pov-arskaya ul 44; ⓂArbatskaya)

UK (Посольство Великобритании; Map p78; ☑495-956 7200; http://ukin russia.fco.gov.uk; Smolenskaya nab 10; ⓂSmolenskaya)

Ukraine (Посольство Украины; Map p78; ☑495-629 9742; www.ukremb.ru; Leontevsky per 18, Moscow; ⓂPushkinskaya)

USA (Посольство США; Map p78; ☑495-728 5000; http://moscow.usembassy.gov; Bol Devyatinsky per 8; ⓂBarrikadnaya)

NOVOSIBIRSK

Germany (☑383-231 0020; www.nowosibirsk.diplo.de; Krasny pr 28)

ST PETERSBURG

Australia (☑812-315 1100; ul Italyanskaya 1; ⓂNevsky pr)

Belarus (☑812-274 7212; ul Bonch-Bruevicha 3a; ⓂChernyshevskaya)

China (☎812-713 7605; nab kanala Griboedova 134; Ⓜ Sadovaya, Sennaya Ploshchad)

Finland (☎812-331 7600; Preobrazhenskaya pl 4; Ⓜ Chernyshevskaya)

France (☎812-332 2270; nab reki Moyki 15; Ⓜ Nevsky Pr)

Germany (☎812-320 2400; Furshtatskaya ul 39; Ⓜ Chernyshevskaya)

Japan (☎812-314 1434; nab reki Moyki 29; Ⓜ Nevsky Pr)

UK (☎812-320 3200; pl Proletarskoy Diktatury 5; Ⓜ Chernyshevskaya)

USA (☎812-331 2600; ul Furshtatskaya 15; Ⓜ Chernyshevskaya)

ULAN-UDE

Mongolia (☎3012-211 078; ul Profsoyuznaya 6)

VLADIVOSTOK

Australia (☎4232-427 464; ul Krasnogo Znameni 42)

China (☎4232-497204; Hotel Gavan, ul Krygina 3)

Japan (☎4232-267 481, 267 502; ul Verkhneportovaya 46)

Korea (☎4232-402 222; ul Pologaya 19)

UK (☎4232-411312; ul Svetlanskaya 5)

USA (☎4232-300 070; ul Pushkinskaya 32)

YEKATERINBURG

Germany (☎343-359 6399; ul Kuybysheva 44)

USA (☎343-379 4691; http://russian.yekaterinburg.usconsulate.gov; ul Gogolya 15)

China
BĚIJĪNG

There are two main embassy compounds in Bĕijīng: Jiànguóménwài and Sānlǐtún. Embassies are open from 9am to noon and 1.30pm to 4pm Monday to Friday, but visa departments are usually only open in the morning.

Australia (澳大利亚大使馆; Map p318; ☎010-5140 4111; www.china.embassy.gov.au; 21 Dongzhimenwai Dajie)

Canada (加拿大大使馆; Map p318; ☎010-5139 4000; www.china.gc.ca; 19 Dongzhimenwai Dajie)

France (法国大使馆; Map p318; ☎010-8532 8080; www.ambafrance-cn.org; 3 Sanlitun Dongsanjie)

Germany (德国大使馆; Map p318; ☎010-8532 9000; www.peking.diplo.de; 17 Dongzhimenwai Dajie)

India (Map p312; ☎010-6532 1908; www.indianembassy.org.cn; 1 Ritan Donglu)

Ireland (爱尔兰大使馆; Map p312; ☎010-6532 2691; www.embassyofireland.cn; 3 Ritan Donglu)

Kazakhstan (Map p318; ☎010-6532 6182; 9 Sanlitun Dongliujie)

Mongolia (蒙古大使馆; Map p312; ☎010-6532 1203; www.mongolembassychina.org; 2 Xiushui Beijie)

Netherlands (荷兰大使馆; Map p318; ☎010-8532 0200; www.hollandinchina.org; 4 Liangmahe Nanlu)

New Zealand (新西兰大使馆; Map p312; ☎010-8532 7000; www.nzembassy.com/china; 1 Ritan Dong Erjie)

North Korea (Map p312; ☎010-6532 1186; 11 Ritan Beilu)

Pakistan (Map p318; ☎010-6532 2504/2558; 1 Dongzhimenwai Dajie)

Russia (俄罗斯大使馆; Map p318; ☎010-6532 1381; www.russia.org.cn; 4 Dongzhimen Beizhongjie)

UK (英国大使馆; Map p312; ☎010-5192 4000; http://ukinchina.fco.gov.uk; 11 Guanghua Lu)

USA (美国大使馆; Map p312; ☎010-8531 3000; fax 010-8531 4200; http://beijing.usembassy-china.org.cn; 55 Anjialou Lu)

Vietnam (Map p312; ☎010-6532 1155; www.vnemba.org.cn; 32 Guanghua Lu)

HOHHOT

Mongolia (Měnggǔ Lǐngshìguǎn; 5 Dongying Nanjie; ◷8.30am-12.30pm Mon, Tue & Thu) Most travellers can get a 30-day visa, although some are only given 21 days. The visa costs Y260 and takes four days to process. A rush visa (Y446) can be given on the same day. A letter of invitation from a travel agency is sometimes demanded.

ÉRLIÀN

Mongolia (Měnggǔ Lǐngshìguǎn; ☎151-6497-1992; Bldg 1206 Youyi Beilu; ◷8.30am-4.30pm Mon-Fri)

Mongolia

Note that the German embassy also looks after the interests of Dutch, Belgian, Greek and Portuguese citizens. The British embassy handles normal consular duties for most Commonwealth countries.

ULAANBAATAR

Canada (☎328 285; www.mongolia.gc.ca; Central Tower 6th fl, Peace Ave)

China (☎323 940; http://mn.china-embassy.org; Zaluuchuudyn Örgön Chölöö 5) The consular section is actually on Baga Toiruu.

France (☎324 519; www.ambafrance-mn.org; Peace Ave 3)

Germany (☎323 325; www.ulan-bator.diplo.de; Negdsen Undestnii Gudamj 7)

Japan (☎320 777; www.mn.emb-japan.go.jp; Olympiin Gudamj 6)

Kazakhstan (☎345 408; www.kazembassy.mn; Zaisan Gudamj, Khan Uul District)

Russia (☎327 191, 312 851; www.mongolia.mid.ru; Peace Ave A6)

UK (☎458 133; fax 458 036; http://ukinmongolia.fco.gov.uk; Peace Ave 30)

US (☎329 095; http://ulaanbaatar.usembassy.gov; Ikh Toiruu 59/1)

Food

See p354 for info on Russian cuisine, p362 for Mongolian food and p371 for the low-down on Chinese dishes and eating in China. See p50 for eating options on the train journey. Restaurant hours:

» China: 10am to 10pm
» Mongolia: 10am to 10pm
» Russia: noon to midnight

Gay & Lesbian Travellers

Spartacus International Gay Guide (Bruno Gmunder Verlag) is the best-selling guide for gay travellers.

Russia

Young Russian urban sophisticates couldn't give a hoot who you love, but this is sadly not true for the broader population except in Moscow, St Petersburg and a couple of the larger cities along the line. Note that in otherwise quite homophobic Russia, the pastime of men flogging each other with birch twigs in the *banya* (bathhouse) is par for the course, so don't be surprised if, as a male traveller, a Russian invites you to his *banya* for some heavy twigging. Mostly, this is hospitality. Resources include:

Moscow Times (www .themoscowtimes.com) and **St Petersburg Times** (www.sptimes.ru) Articles and some listings.

Gay.ru (http://english.gay.ru)
Krilija (Wings; ✆812-312 3180; www.krilija.sp.ru) Russia's oldest officially

registered gay and lesbian community organisation.

China

Despite China's florid homosexual traditions, the puritanical overseers of the Chinese Communist Party (CCP) have worked tirelessly to suppress gays. Even in urban areas, gay and lesbian visitors should not be too open about their sexual orientation in public.

Utopia (www.utopia-asia .com/tipschin.htm) Tips on travelling in China and a complete listing of gay bars nationwide.

Mongolia

Mongolia is not a gay-friendly place, nor one to test local attitudes towards homosexuality. Ulaanbaatar has a small gay community that will occasionally convene at a tolerant restaurant or bar, but it moves around every few months, so you'll need to quietly tap into the scene and ask. Insight can be found at www.globalgayz.com/ g-mongolia.html and www. gay.mn.

Insurance

It's wise to take out travel insurance to cover theft, loss and medical problems. There are many policies available, so check the small print for things such as ambulance cover or an emergency flight home. For more details,

see p403. Worldwide travel insurance is available at www.lonelyplanet.com/ travel_services. You can buy, extend and claim online any time – even if you're already on the road.

Internet Access

Most hotels in big cities along the Trans-Siberian routes have in-room broadband or wi-fi connections. Throughout this book the internet icon @ and the wi-fi icon 🛜 are used in hotel, restaurant, cafe or bar reviews to indicate where you can get online.

Russia

Internet access is cheapest at the main post office or telephone office (typically around R30 to R40 an hour). Wi-fi is common, particularly in Moscow and St Petersburg and other large cities, where many bars, cafes, restaurants and hotels have it. Often access is free but you may have to ask for a password (*parol*) to get online. A few hotels have high-speed link via broadband cables; if so they can usually provide the connection cords if you don't have one.

China

Despite massive usage, China's clumsy tango with the internet continues to raise eyebrows abroad. The number of internet cafe licences is strictly controlled, users need to show ID before going online (in the big cities) and periodic police raids keep surfers twitchy as records are kept of what was viewed by whom. Some internet cafes even digitally photograph you before you are allowed online. Rules are rigorously enforced in Běijīng, but in small towns you are rarely asked for ID.

Up to 10% of websites are traditionally inaccessible in China due to draconian censorship. But for checking email, reading foreign news-

---

MEAL PRICES

In this book meal prices are for two courses plus a non-alcoholic drink:

SYMBOL	RUSSIA	MONGOLIA	CHINA
€ or $	<R500	<T5000 (US$4)	<Y40
€€ or $$	R500–1000	T5000–T10,000 (US$4-8)	Y40–100
€€€ or $$$	>R1000	>T10,000 (US$8)	>Y100

papers online and chatting with friends, China's internet cafes are generally trouble free, even though access to some newspapers can suddenly vanish. Video-sharing sights have also come under control.

When looking for an internet cafe (wǎngbā), look for the characters 网吧. Rates should be around Y5 per hour for a standard, no-frills outlet, but comfier and smarter options naturally charge more. Deposits of Y10 are sometimes required or you may be asked for ID. Slow connections are frequent, especially on congested sites.

Youth hostels and other backpacker accommodation options should have internet access in common areas; if not gratis, rates will be around Y5 per hour.

Mongolia

You'll find internet cafes on nearly every street in downtown Ulaanbaatar. Expect to pay between T400 to T800 per hour for online access, double or triple that for hotel business centres.

Wi-fi access is widespread in Ulaanbaatar. Wi-fi in rural areas is still uncommon. Many apartment rentals offer internet access of some kind, either wi-fi or with a cable hook-up. If you don't mind a slow connection you can even use dial-up – a card that will last for 10 hours is available from the Central Post Office for T3000.

Legal Matters

In Russia, and to a lesser extent in Mongolia, it's generally best to avoid contact with the police. It's not uncommon for Russian police to bolster their puny incomes by extracting sham 'fines' from the unaware; you always have the right to insist to be taken to a police station (we don't recommend this) or that the 'fine' be paid the legal way through Sber-

bank. If you do need police assistance (ie you've been the victim of a robbery or an assault) go to a station with a Russian for both language and moral support.

If you are arrested, the police in all three countries are obliged to inform your embassy or consulate immediately and allow you to communicate with it without delay. Although you can insist on seeing an embassy or consular official straight away, you can't count on the rules being followed, so be polite and respectful towards officials and hopefully things will go far more smoothly for you.

Maps

Maps of all the major cities covered in this guide are on sale in each city.

» **Russia** City and regional maps for Russia are available from bookshops and map shops in Moscow or St Petersburg. Magazine kiosks at larger Russian train stations usually sell city maps.

» **China** In Běijīng, English-language maps of the city are available for free at most big hotels and branches of the Běijīng Tourist Information Center.

» **Mongolia Conservation Ink** (www.conservationink.org) produces maps (US$8) using satellite images combined with useful information on culture, wildlife and tourist facilities. The national park series includes Gorkhi-Terelj and Khustain Nuruu.

Money

For information on train-ticket costs, see p36.

The unit of Russian currency is the rouble (ru-bl), which is written as 'рубль' or abbreviated as 'ру' or 'р'. The rouble is made up of 100 kopecks. Kopecks come in coin denominations of one (rarely seen), five, 10 and 50. Also issued in coins, roubles come

in amounts of one, two and five, with banknotes in values of 10, 50, 100, 500, 1000 and 5000 roubles. Notes above R500 can be inconvenient to change sometimes, specially on the trains.

In Russia, it is illegal to make purchases in any currency other than roubles. When you run into prices quoted in dollars (or the pseudonym 'units', often written as 'ye' – the abbreviation for uslovnye yedenitsy, conventional units) or euros in expensive restaurants and hotels, you will still be presented with a final bill in roubles. In this guide we list whichever currency is quoted on the ground.

The Chinese currency is the Renminbi (RMB), or 'People's Money'. Formally the basic unit of RMB is the yuán, which is divided into 10 jiǎo, which is again divided into 10 fēn. Colloquially, the yuán is referred to as kuài and jiǎo as máo. The fēn has so little value these days that it is rarely used.

The Bank of China issues RMB bills in denominations of one, two, five, 10, 20, 50 and 100 yuán. Coins come in denominations of one yuán, five jiǎo, one jiǎo and five fēn.

The Mongolian unit of currency is the tögrög (T), which comes in notes of T5, T10, T20, T50, T100, T500, T1000, T5000, T10,000 and T20,000 (T1 notes are basically souvenirs).

See p14 for exchange rates and costs.

ATMs

Russia Using a credit card or the debit card you use in ATMs at home, you can obtain cash as you need it – usually in roubles, but sometimes in dollars or euros, too. You're rarely a block or so from an ATM: look for signs that say bankomat (БАНКОМАТ).

China Bank of China and the Industrial & Commercial Bank of China (ICBC) 24-hour ATMs are plentiful, and you can use Visa, Master-Card, Cirrus, Maestro Plus and American Express to withdraw cash. All ATMs accepting international cards have dual language ability.

Mongolia Golomt, Trade & Development Bank, Khan Bank and Khas Bank all have ATMs in their Ulaanbaatar and countryside branches. These ATMs accept Visa and MasterCard and work most of the time, allowing you to withdraw up to T600,000 per day.

Cash

Any currency you bring should be in pristine condition: banks and exchange bureaus do not accept old, tatty bills with rips or tears. Wrap notes in plastic if you're carrying them anywhere sweaty.

There are no official facilities for exchanging money on the train but some *provodnitsas* or the restaurant staff will accept foreign cash at very poor exchange rates – don't count on this. Stock up at your major stops, where you should find ATMs. There are usually exchange places at border-town train stations.

Get rid of your tögrög before you leave Mongolia, as almost no one will want to touch them once you are outside.

Credit Cards

Credit cards are accepted in large Russian cities, less so in smaller centres. When using a credit card at Russian stations to buy tickets, say so early on by showing it. Cash is usually required for train tickets in China and Mongolia.

Most sizable cities in Russia have banks or exchange bureaus that will give you a cash advance on your credit card, but be prepared for paperwork in the local language. Always carry enough cash for a night in a hotel – hand-held card machines in Russian hotels often suffer communication breakdown.

In Mongolia credit cards are often accepted at top-end hotels, the expensive souvenir shops, airline offices and travel agencies, but usually with an additional 3% charge. Banks can give cash advances off credit cards, often for no charge if you have Visa, but as much as 4% with MasterCard.

In China credit cards are useful for drawing money at ATMs but are much less useful for buying goods and services.

Tipping

» **Russia** Common in upmarket restaurants – about 10% is good; elsewhere, 10% is also fine if service warrants it. Tip your guide, if you have one, a similar amount of their daily rate; a small gift is appropriate if service is especially good.

» **China** Neither required nor expected, except in the case of porters in upmarket hotels.

» **Mongolia** Optional; if you round up the bill, then your server will be satisfied.

Travellers Cheques

These are worth taking as back up or if you are going to be getting off the train in large cities. In descending order of acceptance, the favourites are American Express, Thomas Cook and Visa; you'll have little or no luck with other brands.

Photography

For more professional tips on taking some decent photos, read Lonely Planet's *Travel Photography*, by Richard I'Anson.

Equipment & Back Up All major towns have photographic shops for digital burning to CD, printing and film purchases. Slide film is not widely sold.

Photographing People Always ask before photographing someone, especially on the train (including the *provodnitsa*). In Russian, 'May I take a photograph of you?' is *'Mozhno vas sfotografirovat?'*, and in Mongolian it is *'Bi tany zurgiig avch bolokh uu?'*. Remember that many people will be touchy if you photograph 'embarrassments' such as drunks, run-down housing and other signs of social decay.

Restrictions

Sensitive Infrastructure In all three countries (but especially in Russia), be particularly careful about taking photographs of stations, official-looking buildings and any type of military/security structure. Sometimes overeager police in Russia will stop you taking a platform photo.

Museums and Galleries Many forbid flash pictures, some ban all photos and most will charge you extra to snap away. Some caretakers in historical buildings and churches charge mercilessly for the privilege of using a still or video camera.

Religious Buildings Taking photos inside churches and in monasteries and temples is discourteous or, in the case of the latter in Mongolia, forbidden; you may photograph building exteriors and monastery grounds.

Post

The postal service in all three countries is generally reliable, although Russia can still be a problem zone. Allow at least a couple of weeks for letters and postcards to arrive home from Mongolia, more like four or five from Russia (although it can be quicker), and about five to 10 days from China. The major Russian cities, plus Běijīng and Ulaanbaatar, have international private courier firms such as **FedEx** (www.fedex .com), **UPS** (www.ups.com), **DHL** (www.dhl.com) and **TNT Skypak** (www.tnt.com).

For receiving post along the Trans-Mongolian, Běijīng and Ulaanbaatar central post offices are useful for poste restante (in Russia there's no poste restante, and embassies and consulates won't hold mail for transient visitors):

Ulaanbaatar Central Post Office ('Poste Restante, Central Post Office Ulaanbaatar') seems to work quite well; bring along your passport as proof of identification. Don't even think about using poste restante anywhere else in the country.

Běijīng International Post Office ('Poste Restante GPO, Beijing') Costs Y3 and letters are held for a maximum one month. Take your passport for collection.

Public Holidays

Russia

Many businesses are closed from 1 to 7 January. Another widely celebrated holiday is Easter Monday.

New Year's Day 1 January

Russian Orthodox Christmas Day 7 January

Defender of the Fatherland Day 23 February

International Women's Day 8 March

International Labour Day/Spring Festival 1 May

Victory Day (1945) 9 May

Russian Independence Day (when the Russian republic of the USSR proclaimed its sovereignty in 1991) 12 June

Unity Day 4 November

China

The 1 May holiday kicks off a three-day holiday, while National Day marks a week-long holiday from 1 October, and the Chinese New Year is also a week-long holiday for many. It's not a great idea to arrive in China or go travelling during these holidays as things tend to grind to a halt. Hotel prices in China rapidly shoot up during these holiday periods.

New Year's Day 1 January

Chinese New Year (Spring Festival) Usually February

International Women's Day 8 March

International Labour Day 1 May

Youth Day 4 May

International Children's Day 1 June

Birthday of the Chinese Communist Party 1 July

Anniversary of the Founding of the People's Liberation Army 1 August

National Day 1 October

Mongolia

Note that Constitution Day, Women's Day and Mongolian Republic Day are generally normal working days.

Shin Jil (New Year's Day) 1 January

Constitution Day 13 January

Tsagaan Sar January/February; a three-day holiday celebrating the Mongolian New Year

Women's Day 8 March

Mother & Children's Day 1 June; a great time to visit parks

National Day Celebrations (Naadam Festival) 11–12 July

Mongolian Republic Day 26 November

Safe Travel

Russia, China and Mongolia are generally safe countries and crime against foreigners is rare.

Trains On the whole the trains are reasonably safe, but it always pays to take simple precautions with your luggage. If you've got the compartment to yourself, ask the carriage attendant to lock it when you leave for the restaurant car or get out at the station platforms. See Life on the Rails for further tips (p48).

Traffic Your biggest danger in all three countries –

always keep your wits about you.

Stray Dogs A problem especially in rural areas in Russia and Mongolia. An often effective defence against dogs (and potential muggers) is a loud whistle.

Pickpockets Exercise caution, especially in Ulaanbaatar on Peace Ave, between the post office and the State Department Store.

Alcoholism A problem in Mongolia and Russia; you are bound to encounter drunks in both the city and countryside. On the trains, the carriage attendant can sort out difficulties.

Hotels Generally, hotels are quite safe, but leaving valuables lying around your room is tempting providence. Always take precautions at youth hostels and guesthouses, where other travellers may be trying to subsidise their journeys.

Taxis Use an official taxi – as opposed to a private vehicle – late at night in Ulaanbaatar. The same goes for Russia, and even with official taxis in Russia it's usually better to agree on a price before you get in; whenever possible, store your luggage on the back seat, where you can easily retrieve it, not in the boot. While the risk is greater outside of cities, even in Běijīng taxi drivers have been known to take passengers to remote areas and rob them.

Manipulation of ATMs Use ATMs in carefully guarded public places such as at banks, major hotels and restaurants as manipulation that allows thieves to read credit card and PIN details is common.

Mosquitoes & Ticks These are the great bane of summer throughout the region. Mostly, they're an annoyance, but in rural areas of Siberia they can be a grave health threat. For some precautions to take against them, see p406. From May to July, tick-borne encephalitis and lyme disease are problems in Russia. See Health for more information (p405).

Scams

Russian police They want to see your documents, find fault (such as not being registered, even when it's not necessary) and want you to pay a 'fine' to get the documents back. It's ransom, and fortunately it's happening less often these days. The only course of action is to remain calm, polite and stand your ground. Show copies, not originals, whenever possible. Try to enlist the help of a passer-by to translate for you (or at least witness what is going on).

Běijīng airport taxis A well-established illegal taxi operation at the airport attempts to lure weary travellers into a Y300-plus ride to the city, so be on your guard. If anyone approaches you offering a taxi ride, ignore them and insist on joining the queue for a taxi outside.

Pretty-woman scam On Běijīng's Wangfujing Dajie well-dressed girls flock to drag single men to expensive cafes or Chinese teahouses, leaving them to foot monstrous bills.

Racism & Discrimination

Sadly, racism is a problem in Russia. Frightening reports of racial violence appear from time to time in the media, and it's a sure thing that if you are non-Caucasian you'll be targeted with suspicion by many (the police, in particular). In the lead-up to Victory Day (9 May), a nasty, alcohol-charged nationalist edge can develop.

GOVERNMENT TRAVEL ADVICE

The following government websites offer travel advisories and information on current hot spots.

» **Australian Department of Foreign Affairs** (www.smart traveller.gov.au)

» **British Foreign Office** (www.fco.gov.uk)

» **Canadian Department of Foreign Affairs** (www.dfait -maeci.gc.ca)

» **US State Department** (http://travel .state.gov)

Telephone & Fax

City codes are listed in this book under the relevant section headings. In all three countries faxes can be sent from most post offices and upmarket hotels.

Russian authorities have an annoying habit of frequently changing telephone numbers, particularly in cities. We've listed the correct phone number as at the time of research, but it's likely that some will change during the lifetime of this book, particularly in cities such as Moscow.

Russia

» The country code for Russia is ☑7.

» Local calls from homes and most hotels are free.

» To make a long-distance call from most phones first dial ☑8, wait for a second dial tone, then dial the city code and number.

» To make an international call dial ☑8, wait for a second dial tone, then dial 10, then the country code etc. Some phones are for local

calls only and won't give you that second dial tone. From mobile phones, just dial + followed by the country code to place an international call.

MOBILE PHONES

There are several major networks, all offering pay-as-you-go deals, including the following:

Beeline (www.beeline.ru/ index.wbp)

Megafon (www.megafon.ru)

MTS (www.mts.ru)

Skylink (http://skylink.ru)

Reception is available right along the Trans-Siberian Railway and increasingly in rural areas. MTS probably has the widest network. Our researchers found Beeline to be pretty reliable.

To call a mobile phone from a landline, the line must be enabled to make paid (ie nonlocal) calls. SIMs and phone call-credit top-up cards, available at any mobile phone shop and kiosks across cities and towns (you'll usually find them in the airport arrival areas and train stations) and costing as little as R300, can be slotted into your regular mobile phone handset during your stay. Call prices are very low within local networks, but charges for roaming larger regions can mount up; cost-conscious locals switch SIM cards when crossing regional boundaries.

Topping up your credit can be done either via prepaid credit cards bought from kiosks or mobile phone shops or, more commonly, via certain ATMs (look for phone logos on the options panel) and the brightly coloured QIWI Cash-in paypoint machines found in all shopping centres, metro and train stations and the like. Choose your network, input your telephone number and the amount of credit you'd like to top up by, insert the cash and it's done, minus a small fee for the transaction. Confirmation of the top-up comes via a text message to your phone.

PAY PHONES

Taksofon (pay phones, ТАКСОФОН) are located throughout most cities. They're usually in working order but don't rely on them. Most take prepaid phonecards. There are several types of card-only phones, and not all cards are interchangeable. Card phones can be used for either local and domestic calls, or for international calls.

PHONECARDS & CALL CENTRES

Local phonecards (телефонная карта) in a variety of units are available from shops and kiosks – they can be used to make local, national and international calls.

Sometimes a call centre is better value for international calls – you give the clerk the number you want to call, pay a deposit and then go to the booth you are assigned to make the call. Afterwards, you either pay the difference or collect your change. Such call centres are common in Russian cities and towns – ask for *mezhdunarodny telefon* (международний телефон).

China

» The country code for China is ☑86.

» To call internationally from China, drop the first zero of the area or city code after dialling the international access code, and then dial the number you wish to call.

» Local calls from hotel-room phones are generally cheap (and sometimes free), although international phone calls are expensive; it's best to use a phonecard.

MOBILE PHONES

If you have a GMS phone, you can use it with a SIM card from China Mobile, which will cost from Y45 to Y100

depending on the phone number (Chinese avoid the number four as it sounds like the word for death) and will include a small amount of credit. When this runs out, you can top up the number by buying a credit-charging card (*chōngzhí kǎ*) from China Mobile outlets and some newspaper stands.

PAY PHONES

If making a domestic call, look out for very cheap public phones at newspaper stands (报刊亭; *bàokāntíng*) and hole-in-the-wall shops (小卖部; *xiǎomàibù*); you make your call and then pay the owner. Domestic and international long-distance phone calls can also be made from main telecommunications offices and 'phone bars' (话吧; *huàbā*). Cardless international calls are expensive and it's far cheaper to use an IP card.

PHONECARDS

If you wish to make international calls, it is much cheaper to use an IP card. You dial a local number, then punch in your account number, followed by a pin number and finally the number you wish to call. English-language service is usually available. IP cards can be found at newspaper kiosks, hole-in-the-wall shops, internet cafes and from any China Telecom office, although in some cities they can be hard to find. Some IP cards can only be used locally, while others can be used nationwide, so it is important to buy the right card (and check the expiry date).

Mongolia

» The country code for Mongolia is ☑976.

» Ulaanbaatar has several area codes. 11 is the most widely used. If a phone number begins with a 23, 24 or 25, then the area code is 21. If the phone number begins with a 26, the code is 51.

» If you are calling out of Mongolia, and are using an international direct dial (IDD) phone, just dial ☑00 and then your international country code. On non-IDD phones you can make direct long-distance calls by dialling the international operator (☑106), who may know enough English to make the right connection (but don't count on it).

The cost of calls from the central Telecom offices in any city are reasonable: T560 per minute to the USA and UK, T820 per minute to Australia. To make the call, you need to pay a deposit in advance (a minimum equivalent of three minutes). A couple of the top-end hotels have Home Country Direct dialling, where the push of a button gets you through to international operators in the USA, Japan and Singapore. You can then make a credit-card, charge-card or reverse-charge (collect) call.

MOBILE PHONES

If you bring a GSM phone, it will work with the SIM cards from the main companies Mobicom and Unitel. (Make sure you buy a SIM card appropriate for your phone, as the companies G-Mobile and Skytel are both on the CDMA network). The process is simple – just go to a mobile-phone office (a good one is the Tedy Centre on Baruun Selbe Gudamj), buy a SIM card (around T7000), and top up with units as needed.

If abroad, to call a mobile-phone number in Mongolia, just dial the country code (☑976) without the area code. Note that you drop the '0' off the area code if dialling an Ulaanbaatar number *from* a mobile phone but you retain the '0' if using other area codes.

PHONECARDS

Pre-paid, international phone cards are available at the Central Post Office, starting from T3000. You can use these when calling from a landline.

Time

No one on the train knew what time it was. Some people said the train travelled on Moscow time but operated on local time, if you can figure that out. But half the people were on Beijing time and one diplomat said he was on Tokyo time, which was the same for some reason as Ulaanbaatar time. Our Chinese porter changed his watch 15 minutes every few hours or so but this was a system of his own devising.

Mary Morris, Wall to Wall

One of the most disorienting aspects of a Trans-Siberian trip is working out what time it is. The important thing to remember is that all long-distance trains run on Moscow time – so check carefully when you buy a ticket exactly what time *locally* you should be at the station. Once inside the station and on the train all clocks are set to Moscow time. Bizarrely, there are villages in Russia (Berdyaush in the Urals is one) that have nothing of note except the train station, and therefore exist as islands on Moscow time in a sea of local time beyond the village fences.

In 2011 Russia adopted summer time (four hours ahead of GMT/UTC) as its year-round time.

Mongolia is divided into two time zones: the three western aimags of Bayan-Ölgii, Uvs and Khovd are one hour behind Ulaanbaatar and the rest of the country. Since 1949, China has had only one time zone, which is the same as the time in Ulaanbaatar. Russia, China and Mongolia do not change clocks to daylight-saving time.

In the guide we list how far major cities and towns are ahead of Moscow time, eg 'Moscow + 5hr' means five hours ahead.

Toilets

It's rare that paper will actually be available in the stalls of public toilets, so always bring a supply of toilet paper or tissue with you. Plumbing systems in all three countries often have problems digesting toilet paper. If there is a rubbish basket next to the toilet, this is where the paper should go.

Russia

Pay toilets are identified by the words платный туалет *(platny tualet)*. In any toilet Ж *(zhensky)* stands for women's, while M *(muzhskoy)* stands for men's.

In cities, you'll now find clusters of temporary plastic toilet cubicles in popular public places, although other public toilets are rare and often dingy and uninviting. A much better option are the loos in major hotels or in modern food outlets. In all public toilets, the attendant who you pay your R10 to can provide miserly rations of toilet paper.

China & Mongolia

Public toilets in hotels, ger camps and restaurants are usually European-style, moderately clean facilities. On the other hand, public facilities in parks, stores and train stations usually require that you squat over a smelly hole. In China you'll also come across toilets without doors and separated only by a low partition, making it easy to strike up a conversation with the person squatting next to you.

Toilets along the Route

» On Russian and Mongolian trains the toilets are the

TIMES

Moscow	Noon	(GMT/UTC +4 hours)
London	8am	(GMT/UTC +0 hours)
New York	3am	(GMT/UTC -5 hours)
San Francisco	midnight	(GMT/UTC -8 hours)
Perth	4pm	(GMT/UTC +8 hours)
Sydney	6pm	(GMT/UTC +10 hours)
Krasnoyarsk, Tuva, Ulaanbaatar, Běijīng	4pm	(GMT/UTC +8 hours)
Vladivostok	7pm	(GMT/UTC +11 hours)
Helsinki	10am	(GMT/UTC +2 hours)
Paris, Berlin	9am	(GMT/UTC +1 hour)
Irkutsk, Ulan-Ude	5pm	(GMT/UTC +9 hours)

Western variety. The bowl on older toilets is designed to allow you to squat. The carriage attendants generally do a good job of keeping them clean, particularly on the more prestigious class of trains.

» Before and after any major stops, and along any densely populated stretches of the line, the toilets will be locked on most trains; a timetable for this is usually posted on the toilet door.

» On Chinese trains (but not train 3/4) toilets are often of the squat variety.

Tourist Information

Russia

Tourist offices like you may be used to elsewhere are few and far between in Russia. Along the Trans-Siberian routes the only places we've found them are St Petersburg, Perm, Kazan and Irkutsk. Elsewhere you're mainly dependent for information on the moods of hotel receptionists and administrators, service bureaus and travel firms. The latter two exist primarily to sell accommodation, excursions and transport – if you don't look like you want to book something, staff may or may not answer questions.

Overseas, travel agencies specialising in Russian travel are your best bet.

China

While Běijīng's tourist information structure is improving, on the whole tourist information facilities in China are rudimentary and of little use for travellers. The fallback position is the China International Travel Service (CITS), with branches in all major towns and cities. There is usually a member of staff who can speak English who may be able to answer questions and offer some travel advice, but the main purpose of CITS is to sell you an expensive tour.

Mongolia

Ulaanbaatar has a reasonably good tourist information centre.

Travellers with Disabilities

Russia, China and Mongolia can be difficult places for disabled travellers. Most buildings, buses and trains are not wheelchair accessible. In China and Russia, crossing busy streets often requires using underground walkways with many steps. Uneven pavements in the cities and rough roads in the countryside make for uncomfortable and potentially dangerous travel.

Russian Railways has over 300 carriages designated for passengers with disabilities (see Russian Railways at http://eng.rzd.ru – click on 'Passengers'). These allow you to be hoisted into the carriage in a wheelchair, have two-berth compartments and toilets that are larger than usual and equipped with easily accessible controls. Failing these, travellers in wheelchairs will have to be carried on and off the train and into their compartments and will have difficulty with the toilets, which are utterly unfriendly for wheelchairs.

Some useful organisations are:

Australia

Nican (✆02-6241 1220, 1800-806 769; www.nican.com.au; Unit 5, 48 Brookes St, Mitchell, ACT 2911)

Germany

Mare Nostrum (✆030-4502 6454; www.mare-nostrum.de; Oudenarder Strasse 7, Berlin 13347)

UK

Tourism For All (✆0845-124 9971; www.tourismforall .org.uk; Vitalise, Shap Rd

Industrial Estate, Shap Rd, Kendal, Cumbria LA9 6NZ)

USA

Accessible Journeys (✆800-846 4537; www.disa bilitytravel.com; 35 West Sellers Ave, Ridley Park, PA 19078)

Mobility International USA (✆541-343 1284; www .miusa.org; 132 East Broadway, Suite 343, Eugene, Oregon, 97401)

Visas

For information about obtaining visas for Russia, China and Mongolia, see p42. Following is supplementary information to be read in conjunction with that section.

Russia

In addition to tourist, business and transit visas, it is possible to get a private visa in order to visit family or friend. These are valid for up to three months and can be issued for single or double entry. To get one you'll need an official invitation certificate from the relatives or friends you will be staying with, which is a big hassle for them to get; applying for a regular tourist or business visa is far simpler.

REGISTRATION & EXTENSIONS

You need to register within seven working days of arrival, and it is imperative that you are registered at least once. You therefore need to build time into your itinerary after arrival for the first registration. If you are catching the train the following day (or if the following day is a Wednesday, when the UFMS doesn't process registrations), check with the hotel beforehand that it is able to register you immediately. Some hotels are not authorised to do this immediately and require a day or more.

Whenever you change towns, you need to register again within seven working days. However, after your first registration, if you move on within seven working days, you do not need to register. (It used to be three days, and some police and hotel staff are unaware of the change.) To avoid exposure to corrupt police and officials, keep your train and bus tickets so you can prove that you didn't need to register.

If you are not staying in a hotel (some hostels and homestays register you, but most don't), your options are to register yourself at a post office (see http://way torussia.net/RussianVisa/Registration.html for the steps), which can be difficult at the best of times or nearly impossible in remote places, or seek the help of an agency. See the www.realrussia.com for some agents who may be able to assist.

Extensions are time consuming and difficult; tourist visas can't be extended at all. Try to avoid the need for an extension by initially arranging a longer visa than you might need.

China
LONGER VISAS & EXTENSIONS
To get a visa for China your passport must be valid for at least six months after the expiry date of your visa and you'll need at least one entire blank page in your passport for the visa. As well as the standard 30-day visa, it is possible to obtain double entry, which is fairly straight forward but – depending on the consulate – 60-day and 90-day visas of any type can be more difficult to obtain.

The Foreign Affairs Branch of the local Public Security Bureau (PSB) deals with visa extensions, which can easily be obtained a first time on single entry tourist visa. In Běijīng go to the **PSB** (公安局; Gōng'ānjú; ☏8402 0101, 8401 5292; 2 Andingmen Dongdajie; ◷8.30am-4.30pm

Mon-Sat). It takes about five days. See p319.

There is no individual registration requirement when you enter China. Remember, if you go to Hong Kong or Macau (which are visa-free for many nationalities), you need a new visa or a double entry to return to the mainland.

Mongolia
VISAS & REGISTRATION
As well as 30-day single entry visas, it is possible to get a transit visa for Mongolia, but these are only valid for 72 hours from the date of entry. This will only allow you to get off the Trans-Mongolian train in Ulaanbaatar for a very short time before catching another train to Russia or China. A single-entry/exit transit visa costs between US$25 and US$60 depending on where you apply for it, but cannot be extended. You will need to show the train or plane ticket and a visa for the next country (Russia or China).

If you stay less than 30 days, you don't need to register. All visitors who plan to stay more than 30 days *must* be registered within seven days of their arrival. This applies to everyone, including US citizens.

EXTENSIONS
If you have a 30-day tourist visa, you can extend it by another 30 days. For extensions, registration and exit visas, go to the **Office of Immigration, Naturalization & Foreign Citizens** (INFC; ☏011-1882; ◷9am-1pm & 2-6pm Mon-Fri). This office is located about 1.8km east of the airport (next to the large sports arena); an inconvenient 15km trek from the city centre. The office is usually quite busy so you should expect to spend an hour or two here. If you have already registered, you should apply for an extension about a week before your visa ex-

pires. It costs US$2 per day but the minimum extension is seven days. You will need a passport-sized photo and must pay a T5000 processing fee. The extension will be issued on the same day. Bring cash.

Several guesthouses in Ulaanbaatar will take care of visa extensions (and registration) for a small fee. If you don't have a letter of support you can write your own (handwritten is OK); the letter should state the date of your arrival, the date of extension and the reason for travel.

Getting a visa extension outside of Ulaanbaatar is difficult, as they would need to send your passport back to Ulaanbaatar.

Women Travellers

You need to be wary; a woman alone should certainly avoid private taxis at night. Never get in any taxi with more than one person – the driver – already in it. You're unlikely to experience sexual harassment on the streets in most parts of Russia, though sexual stereotyping remains strong. In rural areas, revealing clothing will probably attract unwanted attention (whereas on hot days in Moscow women wear as little as possible).

When journeying by train, women might consider buying a *platskart* ticket (*platskartny*; open carriage) rather than one in a *kupe* (*kupeyny*; compartmentalised carriage), to avoid the risk of getting stuck in a closed compartment with three shady characters. On some Russian trains you can choose to be in a female (*zhensky*) compartment. If you travel *kupe* and don't like your cabin mates, tell the conductor, who will more than likely find you a new place. If a drunk starts accosting you, especially on trains or in minibus taxis, simply do what Russian women do: ignore him and avoid eye contact.

China is probably among the safest places in the world for foreign women to travel alone. Women are generally treated respectfully, because principles of decorum are ingrained deeply in the culture.

Mongolia doesn't present too many problems for foreign women travelling independently. The majority of Mongolian men behave in a friendly and respectful manner, without ulterior motives. However, you may come across an annoying drunk or the occasional macho idiot. The phrase for 'Go away!' is 'Sasha be!'.

There are occasional incidents of solo female travellers reporting being harassed by their male guide. If your guide is male, it is best to keep in touch with your tour agency in Ulaanbaatar, perhaps making contingency plans with them if things go awry. Better yet, take a female guide whenever possible.

Transport

GETTING THERE & AWAY

Most travellers will start their Trans-Siberian or Trans-Mongolian trip in either Moscow or Běijīng. It's also possible to fly into or out of other major gateways, such as St Petersburg (see p116), Irkutsk (p196), Vladivostok (p248) or Ulaanbaatar (p282).

Flights, tours and rail tickets can be booked online at lonelyplanet.com/bookings.

See p42 for details about entry requirements for Russia, China and Mongolia.

Air

Airports & Airlines

Moscow's **Sheremetyevo-2** (www.sheremetyevo-airport .ru) and **Domodedovo** (www .domodedovo.ru) airports host the bulk of Russia's international flights. There are also many daily international services to St Petersburg's **Pulkovo-2** (www.pulkovoair port.ru/eng) airport.

Plenty of other cities have direct international connections, including Irkutsk, Kazan, Khabarovsk, Nizhny Novgorod, Novosibirsk, Perm, Yekaterinburg and Yuzhno-Sakhalinsk.

Běijīng's **Capital Airport** (http://en.bcia.com.cn) is served by both international and domestic connections, as is Ulaanbaatar's **Chinggis Khaan Airport** (www.airport .mn).

Airlines flying internationally to/from Mongolia are Aeroflot, Aero Mongolia, Air China, Korean Air and MIAT; see p282 for details. From continental Europe, the best connection is MIAT's Berlin–Ulaanbaatar twice-weekly flights via Moscow for one-way/return US$899/1237 (at the time of research).

The choice of airlines for Russia and China is much greater, and tickets are usually cheaper.

Tickets

Use the fares quoted in this book as a guide only. Quoted airfares do not necessarily constitute a recommendation for the carrier. See p396 for a list of agencies that specialise in tours: some may offer discount fares.

The peculiarity about flying to and from the railheads for travel on the Trans-Siberian routes is that you will probably be flying in and out of two different cities on one-way tickets, and perhaps using two different airlines.

The cheapest tickets to Hồng Kông and China can often be found in discount agencies in Chinatowns around the world.

Land

Train fares for trips to/from Russia listed under individual countries in this section are for a 2nd-class *kupe* ticket in a four-berth compartment. Most routes also offer cheaper *platskart* (3rd-class open carriage) fares. See Russian Railways for a complete list of international services (http://eng.rzd.ru – click on 'Passengers').

Border Crossings

RUSSIA–MONGOLIA

The border crossed by the Trans-Mongolian trains is at Naushki (Russia) and Sükhbaatar (Mongolia). It's also possible to cross borders by minivan or local train. In addition, there are three road crossings between Russia and Mongolia: Tashanta–Tsagaannuur in Bayan-Ölgii aimag; Kyakhta–Altanbulag in Selenge; and Solovyevsk–Ereentsav in Dornod. As a rule, crossings are open from 9am to noon and 2pm to 6pm daily except holidays. The Mondy–Khankh border in northern Khövsgöl is not open to third-country nationals. For more about crossing the Russia–Mongolia border, see p270.

MONGOLIA–CHINA

The border crossing is at Zamyn-Üüd and Ereen (Érliàn or Erenhot in Chinese). Don't be concerned if you get off at Ereen (on the Chinese side of the border) and the train disappears from the platform. About an hour is spent changing the bogies (wheel assemblies) because the Russians (and, therefore, the Mongolians) and the Chinese use different railway gauges.

CLIMATE CHANGE & TRAVEL

Every form of transport that relies on carbon-based fuel generates CO_2, the main cause of human-induced climate change. Modern travel is dependent on aeroplanes, which might use less fuel per kilometre per person than most cars but travel much greater distances. The altitude at which aircraft emit gases (including CO_2) and particles also contributes to their climate change impact. Many websites offer 'carbon calculators' that allow people to estimate the carbon emissions generated by their journey and, for those who wish to do so, to offset the impact of the greenhouse gases emitted with contributions to portfolios of climate-friendly initiatives throughout the world. Lonely Planet offsets the carbon footprint of all staff and author travel.

For more information on crossings, see p287.

RUSSIA–CHINA

The Trans-Manchurian train crosses the border at Zabaikalsk (Russia) and Mǎnzhōulǐ (China). The bogies are changed here to account for the different rail gauges.

Buses to/from Zabaikalsk (Y65), on the Russian side of the border, depart eight times daily between 7.50am and 1.30pm, but they tend to be much slower than the private cars (because the Chinese traders on your bus will take ages to get through customs). In Mǎnzhōulǐ you could ask around for a ride from a Russian trader (Russians get through faster). Otherwise, take a taxi to the border (Y20), 9km from town, and get a ride across from there with a Russian driver.

See p298 for more.

Belarus

TRAIN

Minsk is well connected by train with Kaliningrad (from R3700, two daily, 13 hours), Moscow (R3170, 20 daily, 11 hours), Smolensk (from R2700, 15 daily, four hours) and St Petersburg (R3900, three daily, 15 hours).

BUS

At least two buses a week from Minsk to Moscow and one a week to St Petersburg.

CAR & MOTORCYCLE

There are six main road routes into Russia from Belarus, the recommended one being the E30 highway that connects Brest and Minsk with Smolensk and finishes up in Moscow.

Estonia

Between Russia and Estonia, the nearest border crossing from Tallinn is at Narva (Estonia) and Ivangorod (Russia). Daily trains run between Tallinn and Moscow (R6500, 15 hours). By bus you can connect to/from Tallinn with St Petersburg (from R850, seven daily, 7½ hours) and Kaliningrad (R1715, daily, 14 hours).

Finland

See Getting There & Away in the St Petersburg chapter (p115) for other suggestions, including ferries and buses.

High speed Allegro trains (R4100; four daily; 3½ hours) connect St Petersburg and Helsinki. The daily 31/34 *Leo Tolstoy* service between Moscow and Helsinki (R5320, 13½ hours) also passes through St Petersburg (R3550, 6½ hours).

Highways cross at the Finnish border posts of Nuijamaa and Vaalimaa

FLIGHTS TO/FROM ULAANBAATAR

FROM	AIRLINE	FREQUENCY	ONE-WAY/ RETURN FARE
Běijīng	Air China	6 weekly	US$220/410
Běijīng	MIAT	6 weekly	US$218/481
Berlin	MIAT	2 weekly (via Moscow)	US$899/1237
Hailar (via Choibalsan)	EZ Nis	2 weekly	US$198/396
Hohhot	Aero Mongolia	3 weekly	US$215/430
Hong Kong	Aero Mongolia	2 weekly	US$355/608
Irkutsk	Aero Mongolia	2 weekly	US$205/370
Moscow	Aeroflot	2 weekly	US$639/892
Moscow	MIAT	2 weekly	US$593/815
Seoul	Korean	4 weekly	US$415/510
Seoul	MIAT	6 weekly	US$446/666
Tokyo	MIAT	1 weekly	US$792/1087
Ulan-Ude	EZ Nis	3 weekly	US$154/308

Note: Flights are high (summer) season, midweek.

(Brusnichnoe and Torfya-novka, respectively, on the Russian side).

Kazakhstan

There are trains on even days between Moscow and Almaty (R10,300, three dasy seven hours) in addition to several services from Siberia. Roads into Kazakhstan include those south from Chelyab-insk and Omsk.

Latvia

Overnight trains run daily between Rīga and Moscow (R6300, 16 hours) and St Petersburg (R6300, 13 hours). Rīga is connected by bus to St Petersburg (from R1000, 11 hours). The M9 Rīga–Moscow road crosses the border east of Rezekne (Latvia). The A212 road from Rīga leads to Pskov, crossing a corner of Estonia en route.

Lithuania

Train services link Vilnius with Moscow (R5000, three daily, 15 hours) and St Petersburg (from R3800, two daily, 15¼ hours). The St Petersburg trains cross Latvia, and the Moscow ones cross Belarus, for which you'll need a Belarus visa or transit visa.

Poland

Warsaw is connected with Moscow (R5850, 18 to 21 hours, two daily) and St Petersburg (R6825, 29 hours, daily). The Moscow trains enter Belarus near Brest. The St Petersburg trains leave Poland at Kuzni-ca, which is near Hrodna (Grodno in Russian) in Bela-rus. Changing the wheels to/from Russia's wider gauge adds three hours to the journey. You'll need a Belarus visa or transit visa. To avoid the hassle of getting a visa, you can take a daily connec-tion between St Petersburg and Warsaw (€160, 25½ hours), with changes of train in Vilnius and Šeštokai (both in Lithuania).

UK & Western Europe

Travelling overland by train from the UK or Western Eu-rope takes a minimum of two days and nights. See Choos-ing Your Route (p27) for sug-gestions. There are no direct trains from the UK to Russia. The most straightforward route you can take from Lon-don is on the **Eurostar** (www .eurostar.com) to Brussels, and then a two-night direct train to Moscow via Warsaw and Minsk (Belarus). The total cost can be as low as £165 one way. See www .seat61.com/Russia.htm for details of this and other train services to Moscow.

From Moscow and St Petersburg there are also regular international services to European cities including Amsterdam, Berlin, Buda-pest, Nice, Paris, Prague and Vienna.

For European rail time-tables check www.railfan europe.net, which has links to all of Europe's national railways.

Ukraine

Most major Ukrainian cities have daily train services to Moscow, with two border crossings: one used by trains heading to Kyiv, the other by trains passing through Kharkiv.

Trains from Kyiv to Mos-cow (9½ hours, 18 daily) cross at the Ukrainian border town of Seredyna-Buda. The best trains to take (numbers are southbound/north-bound) between Moscow and Kyiv are the 1/2 (R7800) and 3/4 (R4500). The best train between Moscow and Lviv is 73/74 (R4700, 23 hours, daily via Kyiv). Between Mos-cow and Odesa (R4900, 23 hours, daily via Kyiv) there's 23/24 *Odessa*. There are also daily trains to/from St Petersburg, Kyiv (R5300, 24 hours), Lviv (R5400, 37½ hours) and Odesa (R6000, 35 hours).

Services between Kharkiv and Moscow (13 hours, about 14 daily via Tula, Oryol and Kursk) include the night train, the *Kharkiv*, 19/20 (R4500). Between Moscow and Simferopol (R5700, 26 hours, daily via Kharkiv), the best train is 67/68, the *Sim-feropol*. Trains between Mos-cow and Donetsk (R4300, 21 hours, two daily), Dnipro-petrovsk (R4700, 18 hours, twice daily), Zaporizhzhya (R4900, 18 hours, 19 daily) and Sevastopol (R5300, 25½ hours, four daily) all go through Kharkiv.

Many trains travelling between Moscow and the Caucasus go through Kharkiv, including a daily service to Rostov-on-Don (12 hours). There are also daily international trains passing through Ukraine to/from Moscow's Kyivsky vokzal (station). These include the 15/16 Kyiv–Lviv–Chop–Budapest–Belgrade train, with a carriage to Zagreb three times a week.

River & Sea

Between early April and late September, international passenger ferries connect Stockholm, Helsinki and Tallinn with St Petersburg, and Vladivostok has connec-tions with Donghae, Korea (from US$185 one way, 20 hours), continuing on to Sakaiminato, Japan (from US$250 one way, 42 hours). China has good ferry connec-tions with Japan.

Travel Agencies & Organised Tours

The following information supplements those agencies listed in Booking Your Tickets (p33).

STA USA (☎1-800 781 4040; www.statravel.com); UK (☎0800 819 9339; www.sta travel.co.uk); Australia (☎134 782; www.statravel.com.au) Mainly organises packages, some of them for the Vodka Train (see Sundowners).

Sundowners (www.sun downersoverland.com, www

.vodkatrain.com) Sundowner's 'Vodka Train' is in semi-independent groups of up to 15 people (18 to 35 years of age) on the Trans-Mongolian and other routes. A local guide meets the group at stopovers. A St Petersburg–Běijīng route in either direction starts at €2300. A through ticket to the Trans-Mongolian with time in Moscow and Běijīng starts at €1220.

Australia & New Zealand

Eastern Europe/Russian Travel Centre (☏02 9262 1144; www.eetbtravel.com) In Australia; they also have a New Zealand office. Mostly Russia.

Passport Travel (☏03 9500 0444, www.travelcentre.com.au; Lvl 1, 12-14 Glenferrie Rd, Malvern, Victoria, Australia) Package and individual trips. Strong on China.

Russian Gateway Tours (☏02 9745 3333; www.russian-gateway.com.au) Mostly Russia.

Travel Directors (☏08 9242 4200; www.traveldirectors.com.au) Upmarket Trans-Siberian tour operator.

Travman Tours (☏1800 338 007; www.travman.com.au) CITS representative in Australia and cheapest place to book westward rail tickets from Australia. Also does tours.

Canada

Trek Escapes (☏866-338 8735; www.trekescapes.com) Handles bookings for other companies as well, such as Sundowners.

China

See Booking Your Tickets (p39) for suggestions.

Germany

Lernidee Reisen (☏030-786 0000; www.lernidee-reisen.de, www.transsibirische-eisenbahn.de, in German; Eisenacher Straße 11, Berlin) Very knowledgeable, sells tickets in conjunction with transfers and accommodation. Excellent value.

Gleisnost (☏0761-383 033; www.gleisnost.de; Bertoldstraße 44, Freiburg) Knowledgeable and good value.

Pulexpress (☏030-887 1470; www.pulexpress.de, in German; Meinekestraße 5, Berlin) Official agent of the Russian Railways, with online booking and delivery.

Japan

MO Tourist CIS Russian Centre (☏03-5296 5783; www.mo-tourist.co.jp) Tours and can help arrange ferries and flights to Russia.

Netherlands

Trans-Sputnik Nederland (070-388 27 57; www.trans-sputnik.nl; Parkstraat 99, Den Haag)

UK

Go Russia (☏020 3355 7717; www.justgorussia.co.uk) Cultural and adventure holiday specialist. Russia, China and Mongolia.

GW Travel Ltd (☏0161 928 9410; www.gwtravel.co.uk) Luxury Trans-Siberian tours on the *Golden Eagle* (see p41).

Imaginative Traveller (☏01473 667337; www.imaginative-traveller.com) Worldwide tours.

Intourist UK (☏0844 875 4026; www.intouristuk.com; 7 Wellington Tce, London W2 4LW) A 2nd-class ticket on the Trans-Mongolian from Moscow to Běijīng without a stopover cost £720 at the time of research. If you're already in Moscow, a ticket costs R18,000 (£400) in person at the Novy Arbat office (see p36).

Real Russia (☏020 7100 7370; www.realrussia.com; 3 The Ivories, Northampton St, London N1 2HY) Train tickets, package tours and full visa services. The **Moscow affiliate** (☏495-616 8086; ul Bolshaya Mariinskaya 9, office 313) has very professional and helpful staff who can also register visas for the full length of a stay.

Regent Holidays (☏0845 277 3317; www.regent-holidays.co.uk; Froomsgate House, Rupert St, Bristol BS1 2QJ) Specialises in individual and group tours on standard as well as luxury trains. From £1300 for the Trans-Mongolian with stopovers in Irkutsk (accommodation in Listvyanka) and accommodation in a ger in Mongolia's Terelj National Park.

Russia Experience (☏020 8566 8846; www.trans-siberian.co.uk) Specialising in packages with accommodation.

Russian Gateway (☏08704 46 1812; www.russian gateway.co.uk) Small specialist agency that offers mainly city-break packages and river cruises. Good visa invitation service for Russia (UK residents).

Russian National Tourist Office (☏020 7495 7570; http://visitrussia.org.uk) Offers tours across Russia.

Scott's Tours (☏020 7383 5353; www.scottstours.co.uk) Russia, China, Central Asia.

Steppes East (☏01285 880 980; www.steppeseast.co.uk) Russia, Mongolia and China.

Voyages Jules Verne (☏0845 166 7003; www.vjv.co.uk) Luxury Trans-Mongolian and other upmarket tours in Russia, China and Mongolia.

USA

East Russia Travel Market (☏206-282 0824; www.traveleastrussia.com) Eco-adventure tour company specialising in Far East Russia and Siberia.

Go To Russia Travel (☏404-827 0099; www.gotorussia.com) Has offices in Atlanta, San Francisco and Moscow; offers tours and a full range of travel and visa services for Russia.

Mir Corporation (☏20 6-624 7289; www.mircorp.com) Books individual and group

FROM LONDON TO NEW YORK BY TRAIN

It's billed as the 'trip of a lifetime', and if it ever leaves the drawing board it would certainly be worth the trip: London to New York by train via a tunnel beneath the Bering Strait.

It's an old idea, almost as old as the Trans-Siberian Railway itself, but now engineers believe it's possible. Today, the cost is reckoned to be around US$100 billion for the Russian side and tunnel alone, which would be about 103km, twice the length of the Channel Tunnel linking Britain with continental Europe.

It might take a while before the transcontinental tunnel grows legs, but in the meantime Russia is certainly continuing to expand its high-speed services – for an overview, see Russian Railways ((http://eng.rzd.ru – click on 'Passengers', then 'Trains'). According to Russia Today, it's even dreaming of a super-super fast train that would link Moscow and Vladivostok in seven hours. Ticket bookings are unlikely to open on that for a while, though (see Russia Today's report on YouTube:'Need for speed: Russian Railways is to defy physics').

Down south, China is looking at a railway that might eventually connect Běijīng with Singapore. An idea that dates back to colonial times, this one will at least in part eventuate in the foreseeable future; although the construction of a 421km stretch of track between Kūnmíng (China) and Vientiane in Laos was delayed in 2011 due to environmental considerations.

journeys on regular and luxury private trains.

Sokol Tours (☑724-935 5373; www.sokoltours.com) Rail trips covering Russia, Mongolia and China.

GETTING AROUND

For most, if not all, of your Trans-Siberian journey you're going to be getting around on the train, but sometimes you might need or want to take an internal flight, a boat or a bus.

Air

Unless you plan to explore destinations off the main Trans-Mongolian and Trans-Manchurian railways in China and Mongolia, it is unlikely you will need to fly within those countries. Russia is a different matter, as flights can shorten a route or may be necessary to return from, say, Vladivostok to Moscow.

Russia

Major Russian airlines allow you to book over the internet (see the boxed text, p399). Otherwise it's no problem buying a ticket at ubiquitous *aviakassa* (ticket offices). Generally speaking, you'll

do better booking internal flights once you arrive in Russia, where more flights and flight information are available, and where prices may be lower.

Most internal flights in Moscow use either Domodedovo or Vnukovo airports; if you're connecting to Moscow's Sheremetyevo-2 international airport, allow a few hours to cross town. It's a good idea to reconfirm your flight at least 24 hours before take-off.

China & Mongolia

The Civil Aviation Administration of China (CAAC; Zhōngguó Mínháng) is the authority for numerous airlines, including **Air China** (www.airchina.com.cn), **China Eastern Airlines** (www.ce-air.com) and **China Southern Airlines** (www.cs-air.com). Check timetables at www.ctrip.com and www.elong.net.

In Mongolia, dirt airstrips are the norm, and almost all destinations are served from Ulaanbaatar. If you plan to fly in one direction and travel overland in another, try to book and fly from Ulaanbaatar, as flying from rural towns can mean waiting several days for a seat, especially in summer. See http://eznis.mn

and www.aeromongolia.mn for inland routes and ticket purchases.

Train

Russia

Information here complements the Plan Your Trip features at the front of this book. For train classes in Russia, see p51. Also see Lonely Planet's *Mongolia* and *China* guides.

The trains of **Russian Railways** (RZD or РЖД; http://eng.rzd.ru) are generally comfortable and punctual. Bookings open 45 days before the date of departure, but on the Trans-Siberian main line try to book at least a few days ahead for the cheapest places. Tickets for key trains on the busy Moscow-St Petersburg route can be difficult to come by at short notice if you are not flexible.

If you speak Russian, the nationwide free information service on ☑8-800 775 0000 can be useful.

At the station you'll be confronted by several ticket windows. Some are special windows reserved exclusively for use by the elderly or infirm, heroes of the Great Patriotic War or members of the armed forces. All will have different operating hours and generally non-English-speaking staff.

The sensible option, especially if there are long queues, is to use the service centre (сервис центр) found at most major stations. Here you'll encounter helpful, sometimes English-speaking staff who, for a small fee (typically around R200), can book your ticket.

Tickets for suburban trains are often sold at separate windows or from an automatic ticket machine (автомат). A table beside the machine tells you which price zone your destination is in.

LEFT LUGGAGE
Many train stations have a left-luggage room (камера хранения, *kamera khranenia*) or left-luggage lockers (автоматические камеры хранения, *avtomaticheskiye kamery khranenia*). These are generally secure, but make sure you note down the room's opening and closing hours and, if in doubt, establish how long you can leave your stuff for. Typical costs are around R100 per bag per day (according to size) or R100 per locker.

Here is how to work the left-luggage lockers (they're generally the same everywhere). Be suspicious of people who offer to help you work them, above all when it comes to selecting your combination.

1 Put your stuff in an empty locker.
2 Decide on a combination of one Russian letter and three numbers and write it down or remember it.
3 Set the combination on the inside of the locker door.
4 Close the locker.
5 Pay the attendant the fee.

To open the locker, set your combination on the outside of your locker door. Note that even though it seems as if the knobs on the outside of the door should correspond directly with those on the inside, the letter is always the left-most knob, followed by three numbers, on both the inside and the outside. After you've set your combination, wait a second or two for the electrical humming sound and then pull open the locker.

China
Although carriages can be crowded, trains are the best way to get around the country in reasonable speed and comfort. For the categories of Chinese trains, see p302.

The following classes are available on Chinese trains:
Hard seat (硬座; *yìngzuò*) Generally padded, but this class can still be hard on one's sanity – it can be dirty, noisy and crowded. You may or may not have a seat reservation.

Soft seat (软座; *ruǎnzuò*) Less crowded, on some shorter routes.

Hard sleeper (硬卧; *yìngwò*) Doorless compartments with half a dozen bunks in three tiers, and sheets, pillows and blankets are provided.

Soft sleeper (软卧; *ruǎnwò*) Four comfortable bunks in a closed compartment; on Z-class trains (the best) you'll also have your own TV. Z-class trains also have luxury two-berth compartments with their own shower and toilet facilities. It does very nicely as an overnight hotel.

Once you are on the train, the conductor may be able to upgrade your ticket if space is available in other carriages. The cost of the upgraded ticket is pro rata to the distance travelled in the higher class.

For more info on China's railways and trains, consult the following sites:
Duncan Peattie's Chinese Railways Home Page (www.chinatt.org) English-language timetable information for trains in China.

Man in Seat 61 (www.seat61.com/china.htm)

Railways of China (www.railwaysofchina.com)

For tips on reading tickets, see http://cnvol.com/read-china-train-ticket.htm.

Mongolia
Note that you can't use the Trans-Mongolian Railway for domestic transport. If you're travelling from Ulaanbaatar, it is important to book a soft seat well in advance – this can be done up to 10 days before departure. There may be a small booking fee. In general, booking ahead is a good idea for any class, though there will always be hard-seat tickets available.

AIR TICKETS VIA THE WEB

Online agencies with English-language websites specialising in Russian air tickets include **Anyway-anyday** (☑495-363 6164; www.anywayanyday.com) and **Pososhok.ru** (☑495-234 8000; www.pososhok.ru).

Using modern 737s, **Sky Express** (☑495-580 9360; www.skyexpress.ru/en) is a Russian low-cost carrier with services between Moscow and Kaliningrad, Kazan, Murmansk, Perm, Rostov-on-Don, Sochi, St Petersburg, Tyumen and Yekaterinburg.

Primorsky AirAgency (☑4232-407 707; www.airagency.ru), a Vladivostok-based agency with branches in Moscow and St Petersburg, as well as across the Russian Far East, can also quote fares and has English-speaking agents.

READING A TRAIN TIMETABLE

Russian train timetables vary from place to place but generally list a destination, train number, category of train, frequency of service, and time of departure and arrival, in Moscow time unless otherwise noted (see following).

Trains in smaller city stations generally begin somewhere else, so you'll see a starting point and a destination on the timetable. For example, when catching a train from Yekaterinburg to Irkutsk, the timetable may list Moscow as the point of origin and Irkutsk as the destination. The following are a few key points to look out for.

Number

Номер (nomer). The higher the number of a train, the slower it is; anything over 900 is likely to be a mail train.

Category

Скорый (Skory), Пассажирский (Passazhirsky), Почтово-багажный (Pochtovo-bagazhny), Пригородный (Prigorodny) – and various abbreviations thereof. These are train categories and refer, respectively, to fast, passenger, post-cargo and suburban trains. There may also be the name of the train, usually in Russian quotation marks, eg 'Россия' (Rossiya).

Frequency

Ежедневно (yezhednevno, daily); чётные (chyotnye, even-numbered dates); нечётные (nechyotnye, odd-numbered dates); отменён (otmenyon, cancelled). All of these, as well, can appear in various abbreviations, notably еж, ч, не, and отмен.

Days of the week are listed usually as numbers (where 1 is Monday and 7 Sunday) or as abbreviations of the name of the day (Пон, Вт, Ср, Чт, Пт, С and Вск are, respectively, Monday to Sunday). Remember that time-zone differences can affect these days. So in Chita (Moscow +6hr) a train timetabled at 23.20 on Tuesday actually leaves 5.20am on Wednesday.

In months with an odd number of days, two odd days follow one another (eg 31 May, 1 June). This throws out trains working on an alternate-day cycle so if travelling near month's end pay special attention to the hard-to-decipher footnotes on a timetable. For example, '27/V – 3/VI Ч' means that from 27 May to 3 June the train runs on even dates. On some trains, frequency depends on the time of year, in which case details are usually given in similar abbreviated small print: eg '27/VI – 31/VIII Ч; 1/IX – 25/VI 2, 5' means that from 27 June to 31 August the train runs on even dates, while from 1 September to 25 June it runs on Tuesday and Friday.

Arrival & Departure Times

Corresponding trains running in opposite directions on the same route may appear on the same line of the timetable. In this case you may find route entries such as время отправления с конечного пункта (vremya otpravlenia s konechnogo punkta), or the time the return train leaves its station of origin. Most train times are given in a 24-hour time format, and almost always in Moscow time (Московское время, Moskovskoye vremya). But suburban trains are usually marked in local time (местное время, mestnoe vremya). From here on it gets tricky (as though the rest wasn't), so don't confuse the following:

» время отправления (vremya otpravleniya) Time of departure.

» время отправления с начального пункта (vremya otpravleniya s nachalnogo punkta) Time of departure from the train's starting point.

» время прибытия (vremya pribytiya) Time of arrival at the station you're in.

» время прибытия на конечный пункт (vremya pribytiya v konechny punkt) Time of arrival at the destination.

» время в пути (vremya v puti) Duration of the journey.

Distance

You may sometimes see the расстояние (rastoyaniye) – distance in kilometres from the point of departure – on the timetable as well. These are rarely accurate and usually refer to the kilometre distance used to calculate the fare.

There are usually three classes on domestic passenger trains:

Hard seat Padded bunks but there are no assigned bunks, nor any limit to the amount of tickets sold; carriages are always crowded and dirty.

Hard sleeper (platzkartnuu) Looks just like the hard seat but everyone gets their own bunk and optional sheets and a blanket (T1000). Upgrades available to soft seat.

Soft seat Compartments with four assigned beds. If you travel at night, clean sheets are provided for about T1100; a wise investment since some of the quilts smell of mutton.

Boat

Russia

In summer it's possible to travel long distances across Russia on passenger boats. You can do this either by taking a cruise, which you can book through agencies at home or in Russia, or by using scheduled river passenger services. The season runs from late May through to mid-October, but is shorter on some routes.

Numerous boats ply routes between Moscow and St Petersburg, many stopping at some of the Golden Ring cities on the way; and along the Volga River from Moscow to other Trans-Siberian cities such as Nizhny Novgorod and Kazan. In Siberia and the Russian Far East there are services along the Ob and Irtysh Rivers (between Omsk and Tobolsk), the Yenisey from Krasnoyarsk, the Lena from Ust-Kut via Lensk to Yakutsk, the Amur from Khabarovsk to Komsomolsk, as well as across Lake Baikal from Irkutsk to Nizhneangarsk.

Beware that boat schedules can change radically from year to year (especially on Lake Baikal) and are only published infuriatingly close to the first sailing of each season.

Bus

Long-distance buses generally serve areas with no railway or routes on which trains are slow, infrequent or overloaded.

Russia

Most cities have a main intercity *avtovokzal* (автовокзал; bus station). Tickets are sold at the station or on the bus. Fares are normally listed on the timetable and posted on a wall. As often as not you'll get a ticket with a seat assignment, scribbled almost illegibly on a till receipt. Buses are cheaper than trains and often faster. You need to pay a baggage fee for items that are too large for racks.

Marshrutky (just a diminutive form of *marshrutnoye taksi*, meaning a fixed-route taxi) are minibuses that are quicker than the rusty old buses and rarely cost much more. Where roads are good and villages frequent, *marshrutky* can be twice as fast as buses, and well worth the double fare.

China

Chángtú gōnggòngqìchē (long-distance buses) are one of the best means of getting around China. On popular long-haul routes, *wòpù qìchē* (sleeper buses) may cost around double the price of a normal bus service. Some have comfortable reclining seats, while others have two-tier bunks. Watch out for your belongings on them, however.

In many cities, the train station forecourt doubles as a bus station. Tickets are easy to purchase and often you can just turn up at the bus station and buy them. Booking in advance, however, can secure you a better seat, as many buses have numbered seats; the earlier you buy your ticket, the closer to the front of the bus you will sit.

Car & Motorcycle

If you are going to be travelling a lot by car or motorcycle in Russia, China or Mongolia, download the Transport chapter of the respective country guide from lonelyplanet.com.

A useful general site for motorcyclists, with some information on Russian road conditions, is www.horizonsunlimited.com.

In all countries, vehicles are driven on the right-hand side of the road, in theory. In practice, a Russian, for instance, will drive on footpaths whenever the need arises.

Russia

Siberian roads are atrocious, with potholes large enough to consume an entire vehicle – which is why vehicle workshops with puncture-repair services (шиномонтаж; *shinomontazh*) are everywhere in cities. If you are driving, this will be the most useful word to learn.

You'll need to be 18 years old and have an International Driving Permit with a Russian translation of your licence, or a certified Russian translation of your full licence (you can certify translations at a Russian embassy or consulate).

Don't forget your vehicle's registration papers, proof of insurance (be sure it covers you in Russia) and a customs declaration promising that you will take your vehicle with you when you leave. To get the exact details on all this it's best to contact your automobile association (eg the AA or RAC in the UK) at least three months before your trip.

See the US consulate website in Vladivostok (http://vladivostok.usconsulate.gov/acsdriving.html) for some useful tips.

Mongolia

Travellers can use an International Driving Permit to drive any vehicle in Mongolia. The roads are worse than atrocious. Accidents occur frequently. Try to avoid travelling at night, when unseen potholes, drunk drivers and wildlife can wreak havoc. Driving in the dark is also a great way to get completely and utterly lost in Mongolia.

What look like main roads on the map are often little more than tyre tracks in the dirt, sand or mud, and there is hardly a signpost in the whole country. Remote tracks quickly turn into eight-lane dirt highways devoid of any traffic, making navigation tricky – some drivers follow the telephone lines when there are any, or else ask for directions at gers along the way. Towns with food and water are few and far between, and very few people in the countryside will speak anything but Mongolian or, if you are lucky, Russian.

China

Road conditions in China should abolish any remaining desire to drive. Bilingual road signs are making a slow appearance along some highways, but much remains to confuse would-be drivers from abroad.

Both Běijīng's Capital Airport or Shànghǎi's Pǔdōng International Airport have a Vehicle Administration Office (车管所; chēguǎnsuǒ) where you can have a temporary three-month driving licence issued. This involves checking your driving licence and a simple medical exam (including an eyesight test). You will need this licence before you can hire a car from reputable companies.

Wikitravel (http://wikitravel.org/en/Driving_in_China) has useful information.

Hitching

Hitching is never entirely safe in any country in the world, and Lonely Planet doesn't recommend it. Travellers who hitch should understand that they are taking a small but potentially serious risk.

Russia

Hitching in Russia is a very common method of getting around. Hitching in cities in private vehicles is becoming less of a necessity these days but in the countryside, especially in remote areas not well served by public transport, it's a major mode of transport. You are expected to pitch in for petrol; paying what would be the normal bus fare for a long-haul ride is appropriate.

China

Hitching in China is more difficult. Sometimes even a moderate, agreed-upon price can be inflated by the driver on arrival. Unless you travel into extremely remote regions, there is little reason to hitch, as it's neither cost-saving nor necessary.

Mongolia

Because the country is so vast, public transport so limited and the people so poor, hitching (usually on trucks) is a recognised – and, often, the only – form of transport in the countryside. Hitching is seldom free and often no different from just waiting for public transport to turn up. It is *always* slow – with stops, a truck can take 48 hours to cover 200km.

Hitching is not generally dangerous personally, but it is still hazardous and often extremely uncomfortable. Don't expect much traffic in remote rural areas; you might see one or two vehicles a day on many roads, and sometimes nobody at all for several days. The best place to wait is at a petrol station on the outskirts of town, where most vehicles stop before any journey. Pay truck drivers about T3000 per hour travelled.

Local Transport

For details of local trains see p398. Also see the Getting Around sections of the various destinations for details of local bus, metro, tram and boat services.

China

Navigation on buses can be tricky for non-Chinese speakers as Chinese without Pinyin appears on stops. Taxis (出租汽车; chūzū qìchē) are cheap, plentiful and easy to find. Taxi drivers rarely speak any English so have your destination written down in characters. To use the same driver again, ask for his card (名片; míngpiàn). Taxi rates per kilometre are clearly marked on a sticker on the rear side window of the taxi, and there's a flagfall. China also has motorcycles, motor tricycles and pedal powered tricycles, all mustering outside train and bus stations. Agree on prices first for these.

Russia & Mongolia

In Russia and Mongolia, using buses and minibuses is easier than in China. For a taxi in Ulaanbaatar, just flag down any driver and agree on a price – T400 per kilometre was the rate at the time of writing.

In Russia, flagging down any driver and agreeing on a price is still a method in some cities, but official taxis are common. Some drivers use meters (the number on the meter must be multiplied by the multiplier listed on a sign that should be on the dashboard or somewhere visible), but generally it's better to haggle a price. Depending on your haggling skills and the city, this will be about R200 to R500 for a city ride.

Most Russians book taxis. Normally, the dispatcher will ring you back or send a text message within a few minutes to provide a description and licence number of the car. If you don't have a phone or speak Russian, duck into the nearest large hotel and ask them to order for you. Restaurant staff will often help if you eat there.

In Russia and Mongolia, whenever possible avoid putting luggage in the trunk of the taxi, as the driver can hold it for ransom.

Health

Russia, Mongolia and China present few serious health problems. If you are dependent upon strong or finely dosed medication, you should consult your doctor about dosages due to the changes in time zones. Apart from injury due to a traffic accident on the busy streets and bad drivers, the main dangers are ticks in some regions, bacteria in drinking water (especially in St Petersburg) and coping with heat or cold. HIV infection is a serious problem, especially in Siberia – *always* take precautions. This chapter offers basic advice on traveller health precautions.

BEFORE YOU GO

» Pack medications in their original, clearly labelled containers.

» Double your vital medication needs in case of loss or theft.

» Western medicine can be in short supply in Mongolia; bring whatever you think you might need from home.

» Take a signed and dated letter from your physician describing any medical conditions and medications (using generic names).

» If carrying syringes or needles, ensure you have a physician's letter documenting their medical necessity.

» If you have a heart condition, bring a copy of your ECG taken just prior to travelling.

» Get your teeth checked before you travel.

» If you wear corrective lenses, take a spare pair and your prescription.

Insurance

Make sure you are covered for all regions and activities and find out in advance what is excluded and how payment is arranged. If your health insurance does not cover you for medical expenses abroad, consider supplemental insurance. (Check the Lonely Planet website at lonely planet.com/travel_services for more information.) Make copies of your policy (a digital photograph uploaded into an email account is useful for all documentation). Declare any pre-existing conditions.

Medical Checklist

Following is a list of items you should consider including in your medical kit – consult your pharmacist for brands available in your country.

» Antibacterial cream (eg Muciprocin)

» Antibiotics (prescription only) – for travel well off the beaten track; carry the prescription with you in case you need it refilled

» Antifungal cream or powder (eg Clotrimazole) – for fungal skin infections and thrush

» Anti-nausea medication (eg Prochlorperazine)

» Antiseptic (such as povidone-iodine) – for cuts and grazes

» Aspirin or paracetamol (acetaminophen in the USA) – for pain or fever

» Bandages, Band-Aids (plasters) and other wound dressings

» Calamine lotion, sting-relief spray or aloe vera – to ease irritation from sunburn and insect bites or stings

» Cold and flu tablets, throat lozenges and nasal decongestant

» Insect repellent (DEET-based)

» Loperamide or diphenoxy-late – 'blockers' for diarrhoea

» Multivitamins – consider them for long trips, when dietary vitamin intake may be inadequate

» Rehydration mixture (eg Gastrolyte) – to prevent dehydration, which may occur during bouts of diarrhoea (particularly important when travelling with children)

» Scissors, tweezers and a thermometer – note that mercury thermometers are prohibited by airlines

» Sunscreen, lip balm, face cream against cold, and eye drops

» Water purification tablets or iodine (iodine is not to be used by pregnant women or people with thyroid problems)

REQUIRED & RECOMMENDED VACCINATIONS

Ask your doctor for an International Certificate of Vaccination (otherwise known as the yellow booklet), which will list all of the vaccinations you have received, and take it with you. If travelling from a yellow fever zone within six days of entering China, proof of vaccination is required. The following vaccinations are recommended.

Adult Diphtheria & Tetanus

Hepatitis A

Hepatitis B Today routine for most travellers.

Measles, Mumps & Rubella (MMR) Two doses are recommended unless you have had the diseases.

Typhoid

Varicella If you haven't had chickenpox, discuss this vaccination with your doctor.

Depending on circumstances and age, the following are worth keeping in mind.

Influenza A Especially for those over 65 years of age or with underlying medical conditions.

Pneumonia A single injection with a booster after five years is recommended for all travellers over 65 years of age or with underlying medical conditions that compromise immunity.

Rabies Three injections are required. A booster after one year will then provide 10 years' protection.

Tuberculosis (TB) A complex issue. It's usually recommended that high-risk adult long-term travellers have a TB skin test before and after travel, rather than a vaccination. Only one vaccine is given in a lifetime.

Japanese B Encephalitis Consider vaccination if spending a month or longer in parts of the Russian Far East and Siberia, in China, or if making repeated trips to at-risk areas.

Websites

Centers for Disease Control & Prevention (CDC; www.cdc.gov)

Lonely Planet (www.lonely planet.com)

MD Travel Health (www .mdtravelhealth.com) Provides complete travel health recommendations for every country; updated daily.

World Health Organization (WHO; www.who.int/ith) Publishes the excellent *International Travel & Health*, revised annually and available online at no cost.

Further Reading

Lonely Planet's Healthy Travel – Asia & India is a handy pocket size, and is packed with useful information. Also recommended is *Traveller's Health*, by Dr Richard Dawood, and *Travelling Well* (www. travellingwell .com.au), by Dr Deborah Mills.

IN RUSSIA, CHINA & MONGOLIA

Availability & Cost of Health Care

Medical care is readily available across Russia but the quality can vary enormously. The biggest cities and towns have the widest choice of places, with both Moscow and St Petersburg well served by international-style clinics. In remote areas, the standard of care is lower and care should always be taken to avoid the risk of hepatitis B and HIV transmission via poorly sterilised equipment.

Good clinics catering to travellers can be found in major cities of China. They are more expensive than local facilities. These clinics usually have a good understanding of the best local hospital facilities and close contacts with insurance companies.

Mongolia suffers from a serious lack of medical facilities. Health care is readily available in Ulaanbaatar, but choose your hospital and doctor carefully. Ordinary Mongolians won't know the best place to go, but a reputable travel agency or top-end hotel might. The best advice will come from your embassy. In the countryside the availability of health services is generally poor. You may be better off travelling on to Běijīng.

Apart from the chief *provodnitsa* (carriage attendant) probably having a first-aid box, there is no medical assistance available on the train itself.

Infectious Diseases

Rabies

This is a problem in all three countries. It is spread through bites or licks on broken skin from an infected animal. It's always fatal unless treated promptly. Vaccination is advisable for those travelling to remote areas where a reliable source of postbite vaccine is not available within 24 hours. A simple precaution against dog attack is to carry a high-pitched whistle.

Tick-borne Encephalitis & Japanese B Encephalitis

Tick-borne encephalitis is spread by tick bites and is a serious infection of the brain; vaccination is advised for those in risk areas who are unable to avoid tick bites (such as campers, forestry workers and walkers). The risk is highest in spring and summer, when ticks are active. The Ural Mountains, Siberia and the Far East and China's north are particular problem zones. Two doses of vaccine will give a year's protection, three doses will last up to three years.

Typhoid & Hepatitis A

Spread through contaminated food (particularly shellfish) and water, typhoid can cause septicaemia (blood poisoning); hepatitis A causes liver inflammation and jaundice. Neither is usually fatal but recovery can be delayed if you don't see your doctor immediately.

Traveller's Diarrhoea

Diarrhoea on a train is not much fun, and off the trains it leaves much to be desired as well. Treatment consists of staying well hydrated; rehydration solutions such as Gastrolyte are best. Antibiotics such as norfloxacin, ciprofloxacin or azithromycin will kill the bacteria quickly. Loperamide is just a 'stopper' and doesn't cure the problem; it can be helpful, however, for long rides. Don't take loperamide if you have a fever, or blood in your stools. Seek medical attention quickly if you do not respond to an appropriate antibiotic.

» Don't drink the tap water on the trains or in any of the countries unless it's been boiled (eg in the samovar).

» Brush your teeth using bottled mineral water.

» In all three countries avoid ice and unpeeled fruit and vegetables that have been washed in it tap water.

» Check use-by dates of food sold on train platforms.

» If a restaurant is full of locals, the food is probably safe.

Environmental Hazards

The temperatures on the trains are generally kept at a comfortable level, but once out in the wide open spaces of Russia, Mongolia and China the main environmental hazards to be careful of are heat exhaustion in summer and frostbite in winter.

Heat Exhaustion & Heatstroke

Heat exhaustion is best avoided by drinking water on a constant basis. Train carriages can get hot in summer and be overheated in winter, so make sure you have sufficient bottled water with you.

Heat stroke is much more serious, resulting in irrational and hyperactive behaviour and eventually loss of consciousness and death. Rapid cooling by spraying the body with water and fanning is ideal. Emergency fluid and electrolyte replacement by intravenous drip is recommended.

DRINKING WATER

The quality of drinking water varies greatly from region to region, so it's best to play it safe:

» Never drink tap water.

» Check that the seal on bottled water is intact on purchase.

» Avoid ice and fresh juices if you suspect they have been watered down.

» Boiling water is the most efficient method of purifying it. Trains have a samovar (hot-water heater) in every carriage. (Never use the tap in the train toilet for drinking water or washing vegetables.)

» The best chemical purifier is iodine. It should not be used by pregnant women or those with thyroid problems.

» Water filters should also filter out viruses. Ensure your filter has a chemical barrier such as iodine and a small pore size, eg less than four microns.

Hypothermia & Frostbite

Winters are cold on the Trans-Siberian routes and proper clothing will reduce the risks of getting hypothermia. Make sure you have a heavy coat ready for station stops. Don't overdo outdoor sightseeing if you are not well-prepared against the cold.

Frostbite is caused by freezing and subsequent damage to bodily extremities. As it develops, the skin blisters and then becomes black. Adequate clothing, staying dry, keeping well hydrated and ensuring adequate calorie intake will help prevent frostbite. Treatment involves rapid rewarming. Avoid refreezing and rubbing the affected areas.

Ticks & Mosquitoes

Ticks can transmit Lyme disease, an infection that may be acquired throughout the region. The illness usually begins with a spreading rash at the site of the tick bite, accompanied by fever, headache, extreme fatigue, aching joints and muscles, and mild neck stiffness. It is essential that you receive medical treatment as serious long-term complications can arise.

Always check all over your body after hiking or outdoor activities. The best way to remove a tick is to use dedicated plastic or metal tweezers designed to grip the head of the tick. Rotate it out of the skin. Ordinary tweezers can also be used.

Mosquitoes are a problem in summer all across Russia. From May to September in the rural areas bordering Mongolia, China and North Korea, take extra-special care as mosquito bites can cause Japanese encephalitis. If visiting rural areas you should consider being immunised.

Travelling with Children

Travelling the Trans-Siberian routes with children is relatively easy, and some carriages have play areas. Off the trains, children should be encouraged to avoid and mistrust any dogs or other mammals because of the risk of rabies and other diseases. Any bite, scratch or lick from a warm-blooded, furry animal should immediately be thoroughly cleaned. If there is any possibility that the animal is infected with rabies, immediate medical assistance should be sought.

Women's Health

Emotional stress, exhaustion and travelling through different time zones can all contribute to an upset in the menstrual cycle.

Travelling along the Trans-Siberia routes while pregnant is possible but not really advisable because emergency treatment can be patchy in remote segments. Always consult your doctor before planning your trip. The most risky times for travel are during the first 12 weeks of pregnancy and after 30 weeks.

Language

WANT MORE?

For in-depth language information and handy phrases, check out Lonely Planet's *Mandarin*, *Russian*, *Mongolian* or *China Phrasebooks*. You'll find them at **shop.lonelyplanet .com**, or you can buy Lonely Planet's iPhone phrasebooks at the Apple App Store.

In this chapter, we're providing some basic travel words and phrases in Mandarin, Mongolian and Russian that might come in handy during your travels.

MANDARIN

Pinyin & Pronunciation

In 1958 the Chinese adopted a system of writing their language using the Roman alphabet. It's known as Pinyin. The original idea was to eventually do away with Chinese characters. However, tradition dies hard, and the idea has been abandoned. Pinyin, which we've provided alongside the Mandarin script in this chapter, is often used on shop fronts, street signs and advertising billboards. Don't expect all Chinese people to be able to use Pinyin, however. In the countryside and the smaller towns you may not see a single Pinyin sign anywhere, just Chinese characters. Below are some basic guidelines as to how to pronounce Pinyin sounds (in blue in this chapter):

a	as in 'father'
ai	as in 'aisle'
ao	as the 'ow' in 'cow'
e	as in 'her', without audible 'r' sound
ei	as in 'weigh'
i	as the 'ee' in 'meet' (or like a light 'r' as in 'Grrr!' after c, ch, r, s, sh, z, zh)
ian	as the word 'yen'
ie	as the English word 'yeah'
o	as in 'or', without audible 'r' sound
ou	as the 'oa' in 'boat'
u	as in 'flute'
ui	as the word 'way'
uo	like a 'w' followed by 'o'
yu/ü	like 'ee' with lips pursed

c	as the 'ts' in 'bits'
ch	as in 'chop' *
h	as in 'hay', but articulated from further back in the throat
q	as the 'ch' in 'cheese'
sh	as in 'ship' *
x	as in 'ship'
z	as the 'ds' in 'suds'
zh	as the 'j' in 'judge'*

* but with the tongue curled up and back

In Pinyin, the only consonant sounds that occur at the end of a syllable are n, ng and r. Also, apostrophes are occasionally used to separate syllables in order to prevent ambiguity, eg the word píng'ān can be written with an apostrophe after the 'g' to prevent it being pronounced as pín'gān.

Finally, Mandarin is a language with a large number of words with the same pronunciation but a different meaning. The only thing that distinguishes these words are tones – the raising and the lowering of pitch on certain syllables. Mandarin has four tones (high, rising, falling-rising and falling), indicated by accent marks over the vowels. The word ma, for example, has four different meanings according to tone:

high tone	mā (mother)
rising tone	má (hemp, numb)
falling-rising tone	mǎ (horse)
falling tone	mà (scold, swear)

There's a fifth 'neutral' tone (without accent mark) that you can all but ignore.

Basics

When asking a question it is polite to start with qǐng wèn – literally, 'may I ask?'.

Hello.	你好。	Nǐhǎo.
Goodbye.	再见。	Zàijiàn.
Excuse me.		
(to get attention)	劳驾。	Láojià.
(to get past)	借光。	Jièguāng.
Sorry.	对不起。	Duìbùqǐ.
Yes./No.	是。/不是。	Shì./Bùshì.
Please ...	请……	Qǐng ...
Thank you.	谢谢你。	Xièxie nǐ.
You're welcome.	不客气。	Bù kèqi.

What's your name?
你叫什么名字？ Nǐ jiào shénme míngzi?

My name is ...
我叫…… Wǒ jiào ...

Do you speak English?
你会说英文吗？ Nǐ huìshuō Yīngwén ma?

I don't understand.
我不明白。 Wǒ bù míngbái.

Accommodation

Do you have a single/double room?
有没有（单人/ Yǒuméiyǒu (dānrén/
套）房？ tào) fáng?

How much is it per night/person?
每天/人多少钱？ Měi tiān/rén duōshǎo qián?

air-con	空调	kōngtiáo
bathroom	浴室	yùshì
bed	床	chuáng
campsite	露营地	lùyíngdì
guesthouse	宾馆	bīnguǎn
hostel	招待所	zhāodàisuǒ
hotel	酒店	jiǔdiàn
window	窗	chuāng

Directions

Where's (a bank)?
（银行）在哪儿？ (Yínháng) zài nǎr?

What's the address?
地址在哪儿？ Dìzhǐ zài nǎr?

Could you write the address, please?
能不能请你 Néngbunéng qǐng nǐ
把地址写下来？ bǎ dìzhǐ xiě xiàlái?

Please show me on the map where it is.
请带我找它在 Qǐng bāngwǒ zhǎo tā zài
地图上的位置。 dìtú shàng de wèizhi.

behind	背面	bèimiàn
far	远	yuǎn
in front of ...	……的前面	... de qiánmian
near	近	jìn
next to	旁边	pángbiān
opposite	对面	duìmiàn
Turn left.	左转。	Zuǒ zhuǎn.
Turn right.	右转。	Yòu zhuǎn.

Eating & Drinking

What would you recommend?
有什么菜可以 Yǒu shénme cài kěyǐ
推荐的？ tuījiàn de?

What's in that dish?
这道菜用什么 Zhèdào cài yòng shénme
东西做的？ dōngxi zuòde?

I don't eat (read meat).
我不吃(牛羊肉)。 Wǒ bùchī (niúyángròu)

Cheers!
干杯！ Gānbēi!

That was delicious!
真好吃！ Zhēn hǎochī!

The bill, please.
买单！ Mǎidān!

Key Words

appetisers	凉菜	liángcài
bar	酒吧	jiǔbā
bottle	瓶子	píngzi
bowl	碗	wǎn
bread	面包	miànbāo
breakfast	早饭	zǎofàn
butter	黄油	huángyóu
cafe	咖啡屋	kāfēiwū
children's menu	儿童菜单	értóng càidān
(too) cold	(太)凉	(tài) liáng
dinner	晚饭	wǎnfàn
dish (food)	盘	pán
egg	蛋	dàn
food	食品	shípǐn
fork	叉子	chāzi
glass	杯子	bēizi
halal	清真	qīngzhēn
herbs/spices	香料	xiāngliào
highchair	高凳	gāodèng
hot (warm)	热	rè
knife	刀	dāo
kosher	犹太	yóutài
local specialties	地方小吃	dìfāng xiǎochī

lunch	午饭	wǔfàn
main courses	主菜	zhǔ cài
market	菜市	càishì
menu (in English)	(英文)菜单	(Yīngwén) càidān
noodles	面条	miàntiáo
nuts	果仁	guǒrén
pepper	胡椒粉	hújiāo fěn
plate	碟子	diézi
restaurant	餐馆	cānguǎn
rice (raw/cooked)	大米/米饭	dàmǐ/mǐfàn
salt	盐	yán
soy sauce	酱油	jiàngyóu
(too) spicy	(太)辣	(tài) là
spoon	勺	sháo
sugar	砂糖	shātáng
tofu	豆腐	dòufu
vegetable oil	菜油	càiyóu
vegetarian food	素食食品	sùshí shípǐn
vinegar	醋	cù
yoghurt	酸奶	suānnǎi

Meat & Fish

beef	牛肉	niúròu
chicken	鸡肉	jīròu
duck	鸭	yā
fish	鱼	yú
lamb	羊肉	yángròu
pork	猪肉	zhūròu
poultry	家禽	jiāqín
seafood	海鲜	hǎixiān

Fruit & Vegetables

apple	苹果	píngguǒ
banana	香蕉	xiāngjiāo
bok choy	小白菜	xiǎo báicài
carrot	胡萝卜	húluóbo
cucumber	黄瓜	huángguā
'dragon eyes'	龙眼	lóngyǎn
fruit	水果	shuǐguǒ
grape	葡萄	pútáo
green beans	扁豆	biǎndòu
guava	石榴	shíliu
lychee	荔枝	lìzhī
mango	芒果	mángguǒ
mushroom	蘑菇	mógū
onion	洋葱	yáng cōng
orange	橙子	chéngzi
pear	梨	lí

pineapple	凤梨	fènglí
plum	梅子	méizi
potato	土豆	tǔdòu
radish	萝卜	luóbo
spring onion	小葱	xiǎo cōng
sweet potato	地瓜	dìguā
vegetable	蔬菜	shūcài

Drinks

beer	啤酒	píjiǔ
Chinese spirits	白酒	báijiǔ
coffee	咖啡	kāfēi
(orange) juice	(橙)汁	(chéng) zhī
milk	牛奶	niúnǎi
mineral water	矿泉水	kuàngquán shuǐ
red wine	红葡萄酒	hóng pútáo jiǔ
rice wine	米酒	mǐjiǔ
soft drink	汽水	qìshuǐ
tea	茶	chá
(boiled) water	(开)水	(kāi) shuǐ
white wine	白葡萄酒	bái pútáo jiǔ

Emergencies

Help!	救命！	Jiùmìng!
Go away!	走开！	Zǒukai!
I'm lost.	我迷路了。	Wǒ mílù le.

There's been an accident! 出事了！		Chūshì le!
Call a doctor! 请叫医生来！		Qǐng jiào yīshēng lái!
Call the police! 请叫警察！		Qǐng jiào jǐngchá!
I'm ill. 我生病了。		Wǒ shēngbìng le.
It hurts here. 这里痛。		Zhèlǐ tòng.
Where are the toilets? 厕所在哪儿？		Cèsuǒ zài nǎr?

Signs – Mandarin

入口	Rùkǒu	**Entrance**
出口	Chūkǒu	**Exit**
问讯处	Wènxùnchù	**Information**
开	Kāi	**Open**
关	Guān	**Closed**
禁止	Jìnzhǐ	**Prohibited**
厕所	Cèsuǒ	**Toilets**
男	Nán	**Men**
女	Nǚ	**Women**

Shopping & Services

I'd like to buy ...
我想买……　Wǒ xiǎng mǎi ...

How much is it?
多少钱？　Duōshǎo qián?

Can you lower the price?
能便宜一点吗？　Néng piányi yīdiǎn ma?

There's a mistake in the bill.
帐单上有问题。　Zhàngdān shàng yǒu wèntí.

ATM	自动取款机	zìdòng qǔkuǎn jī
credit card	信用卡	xìnyòng kǎ
internet cafe	网吧	wǎngbā
market	市场	shìchǎng
post office	邮局	yóujú
supermarket	超市	chāoshì
tourist office	旅行店	lǚxíng diàn

Time, Dates & Numbers

What time is it?
现在几点钟？　Xiànzài jǐdiǎn zhōng?

morning	早上	zǎoshang
afternoon	下午	xiàwǔ
evening	晚上	wǎnshàng
yesterday	昨天	zuótiān
today	今天	jīntiān
tomorrow	明天	míngtiān
Monday	星期一	xīngqī yī
Tuesday	星期二	xīngqī èr
Wednesday	星期三	xīngqī sān
Thursday	星期四	xīngqī sì
Friday	星期五	xīngqī wǔ
Saturday	星期六	xīngqī liù
Sunday	星期天	xīngqī tiān
January	一月	yīyuè
February	二月	èryuè
March	三月	sānyuè
April	四月	sìyuè
May	五月	wǔyuè
June	六月	liùyuè
July	七月	qīyuè
August	八月	bāyuè
September	九月	jiǔyuè
October	十月	shíyuè
November	十一月	shíyīyuè
December	十二月	shí'èryuè

1	一	yī
2	二／两	èr/liǎng
3	三	sān
4	四	sì
5	五	wǔ
6	六	liù
7	七	qī
8	八	bā
9	九	jiǔ
10	十	shí
100	一百	yībǎi
1000	一千	yīqiān

Transport

boat	船	chuán
bus (city)	大巴	dàbā
bus (intercity)	长途车	chángtú chē
plane	飞机	fēijī
taxi	出租车	chūzū chē
train	火车	huǒchē
tram	电车	diànchē

I want to go to ...
我要去……　Wǒ yào qù ...

Does it stop at (Hāěrbīn)?
在(哈尔滨)能下车吗？　Zài (Hā'ěrbīn) néng xià chē ma?

What time does it leave?
几点钟出发？　Jǐdiǎnzhōng chūfā?

What time does it get to (Hángzhōu)?
几点钟到(杭州)？　Jǐdiǎnzhōng dào (Hángzhōu)?

Can you tell me when we get to (Hángzhōu)?
到了(杭州)请叫我, 好吗？　Dàole (Hángzhōu) qǐng jiào wǒ, hǎoma?

I want to get off here.
我想这儿下车。　Wǒ xiǎng zhèr xiàchē.

When's the ... (bus)?	……(车) 几点走？	... (chē) jǐdiǎn zǒu?
first	首趟	Shǒutàng
last	末趟	Mòtàng
next	下一趟	Xià yītàng
A ... ticket to (Dàlián).	一张到 (大连)的 ……票。	Yīzhāng dào (Dàlián) de ... piào.
1st-class	头等	tóuděng
2nd-class	二等	èrděng
one-way	单程	dānchéng
return	双程	shuāngchéng

aisle seat	走廊的座位	zǒuláng de zuòwèi
buy a ticket	买票	mǎi piào
cancelled	取消	qǔxiāo
delayed	晚点	wǎndiǎn
hard-seat	硬席/硬座	yìngxí/yìngzuò
hard-sleeper	硬卧	yìngwò
one ticket	一张票	yìzhāng piào
platform	站台	zhàntái
soft-seat	软席/软座	ruǎnxí/ruǎnzuò
soft-sleeper	软卧	ruǎnwò
ticket office	售票处	shòupiàochù
timetable	时刻表	shíkè biǎo
train station	火车站	huǒchēzhàn
two tickets	两张票	liǎngzhāng piào
window seat	窗户的座位	chuānghu de zuòwèi

MONGOLIAN

Mongolian is a member of the Ural-Altaic family of languages, and as such it is distantly related to Turkish, Kazakh, Uzbek and Korean. It has around 10 million speakers worldwide. The traditional Mongolian script (cursive, vertical and read from left to right) is still used by the Mongolians living in the Inner Mongolia Autonomous Region of China. In 1944 the Cyrillic alphabet was adopted and is in use in Mongolia and two autonomous regions of Russia (Buryatiya and Kalmykia). We've used the Cyrillic script in this chapter. The only difference between Mongolian and Russian Cyrillic is that the Mongolian version has two added characters (ө and ү).

It's well worth the effort to familiarise yourself with the Cyrillic alphabet so that you can read maps and street signs. Mongolian pronunciation is also explained in the Cyrillic alphabet table, but if you just read the coloured pronunciation guides given next to each word below as if they were English, you'll be understood.

Just remember to pronounce double vowel letters as long sounds, because vowel length can affect meaning. In our pronunciation guides the stressed syllables are in italics.

Basics

Hello.	Сайн байна уу?	sain bai·na uu
Goodbye.	Баяртай.	ba·yar·tai
Excuse me.	Уучлаарай.	uuch·laa·rai
Sorry.	Уучлаарай.	uuch·laa·rai
Yes.	Тийм.	tiim
No.	Үгүй.	ü·güi

Thank you.	Баярлалаа.	ba·yar·la·laa
You're welcome.	Зугээр.	zü·geer

What's your name?
Таны нэрийг хэн гэдэг вэ? — ta·ny ne·riig khen ge·deg ve

My name is ...
Миний нэрийг ... гэдэг. — mi·nii ne·riig ... ge·deg

Do you speak English?
Та англиар ярьдаг уу? — ta an·gliar yair·dag uu

I don't understand.
Би ойлгохгүй байна. — bi oil·gokh·güi bai·na

CYRILLIC ALPHABET

Cyrillic	Sound (Mongolian)	
А а	a	as the 'u' in 'but'
Г г	g	as in 'get'
Ё ё	yo	as in 'yonder'
И и	i	as in 'tin'
Л л	l	as in 'lamp'
О о	o	as in 'hot'
Р р	r	as in 'rub'
У у	u	as in 'rude'
Х х	kh	as the 'ch' in the Scottish *loch*
Ш ш	sh	as in 'shoe'
Ы ы	y	as the 'i' in 'ill'
Ю ю	yu	as the 'yo' in 'yoyo'
	yü	long, as the word 'you'
Б б	b	as in 'but'
Д д	d	as in 'dog'
Ж ж	j	as in 'jewel'
Й й	i	as in 'tin'
М м	m	as in 'mat'
Ө ө	ö	long, as the 'u' in 'fur'
С с	s	as in 'sun'
Ү ү	ü	long, as the 'o' in 'who'
Ц ц	ts	as in 'cats'
Щ щ	shch	as in 'fresh chips'
Ь ь		'soft sign' meaning the preceding consonant is pronounced with a faint y after it.
Я я	ya	as in 'yard'
В в	v	as in 'van'
Е е	ye	as in 'yet'
	yö	as the 'yea' in 'yearn'
З з	z	as the 'ds' in 'suds'
К к	k	as in 'kit'
Н н	n	as in 'neat'
П п	p	as in 'pat'
Т т	t	as in 'tin'
Ф ф	f	as in 'five'
Ч ч	ch	as in 'chat'
Ъ ъ		'hard sign' meaning the preceding consonant is pronounced without a faint y after it.
Э э	e	as in 'den'

Accommodation

I'd like a single/double room.
Би нэг/хоёр хүний bi neg/*kho*·yor khü·*nii*
өрөө авмаар байна. ö·*röö* av·*maar bai*·na

How much is it per night/week?
Энэ өрөө хоногт/ e·ne ö·*röö* kho·nogt/
долоо хоногт ямар do·*loo* kho·nogt ya·mar
үнэтэй вэ? ün·*tei* ve

air-con	агааржуулалт	a·gaar·*juul*·alt
bathroom	угаалгын өрөө	u·*gaal*·gyn ö·*röö*
cot	хүүхдийн ор	khüükh·*diin* or
dormitory	нийтийн байр	*nii*·tiin bair
hotel	зочид буудал	zo·chid *buu*·dal
window	цонх	tsonkh
youth hostel	залуучуудын байр	za·*luu*·chuu·dyn bair

Directions

Where's ...?
... хаана байна вэ? ... khaan *bai*·na ve

How can I get to ...?
... руу би яаж очих вэ? ... ruu bi yaj o·chikh ve

Can you show me on the map?
Та газрын зураг ta gaz·*ryn* zu·rag
дээр зааж өгнө үү? deer zaaj ög·nö üü

address	хаяг	*kha*·yag
after	ард	ard
before	урд	urd
behind	хойно	*khoi*·no
in front of	өмнө	*öm*·nö
straight ahead	чигээрээ урагшаа	chi·*gee*·ree u·rag·*shaa*
to the left	зүүн тийш	züün tiish
to the right	баруун тийш	ba·*ruun* tiish

Eating & Drinking

Can I have a menu, please?
Би хоолны цэс авч bi *khool*·nii tses avch
болох уу? bo·lokh uu

What food do you have today?
Өнөөдөр ямар хоол ö·*nöö*·dör ya·mar khool
байна вэ? *bai*·na ve

I'd like to have this.
Би энэ хоолыг авья. bi en *khoo*·lyg a·*vi*

I don't eat (meat).
Би (мах) иддэггүй. bi (makh) id·deg·gui

We'd like to drink some koumiss.
Бид айраг уух bid *ai*·rag uukh
гэсэн юм. ge·sen yum

Cheers!
Эрүүл мэндийн төлөө! e·*rüül* men·*diin* tö·*löö*

The bill, please.
Тооцоогоо бодуулья. too·*tsoo*·goo bo·*duu*·li

ГАРЦ	Exit
ЛАВЛАГАА	Information
ОРЦ	Entrance
ХААСАН	Closed
ХАДГАЛСАН	Reserved/Engaged
ЭРЭГТЭЙН	Men
ЭМЭГТЭЙН	Women

Key Words

appetisers	хүйтэн зууш	*khüi*·ten zuush
bottle	шил	shil
bread	талх	talkh
breakfast	өглөөний хоол	ög·*löö*·nii khool
butter	цөцгийн тос	tsöts·*giin* tos
cake	бялуу	bya·*luu*
camel yogurt	хоормог	*khoor*·mog
canteen	гуанз	guanz
cold	хүйтэн	*khüi*·ten
cheese	бяслаг	byas·lag
cream	өрөм	ö·*röm*
cup	аяга	a·*yag*
(dried) curds	ааруул	*aa*·ruul
dairy	цагаан-идээ	tsa·*gaan* i·*dee*
dessert	амтат зууш	*am*·tat zuush
dinner	оройн хоол	o·*roin* khool
dining room	зоогийн газар	*zoo*·giin ga·zar
dumplings	банштай	*ban*·shtai
egg	өндөг	ön·dög
food	хоол	khool
fork	сэрээ	se·*ree*
fried	шарсан	*shar*·san
fried food	хуураг	*khuu*·rag
glass	шилэн аяга	*shi*·len a·yag
honey	зөгийн бал	zö·*giin* bal
hot	халуун	kha·*luun*
ice cream	зайрмаг	*zair*·mag
jam	жимсний чанамал	*jims*·nii *cha*·na·mal
knife	хутга	*khu*·tag
lunch	үдийн хоол	ü·*diin* khool
market	зах	zakh
menu	хоолны цэс	*khool*·ny tses
noodle soup	гоймонтой шөл	*goi*·mon·toi shöl
pasta	хөндий гоймон	khön·*diin* *goi*·mon
pepper	поваарь	po·*vaair*
plate	таваг	*ta*·vag
restaurant	ресторан	res·to·*ran*

rice	цагаан будаа	tsa·*gaan* bu·*daa*
salad	ногоон зууш	no·*goon* zuush
salt	давс	davs
set dish	бэлэн хоол	be·len khool
soup	шөл	shöl
sour cream	тараг/цөггий	ta·rag/tsöts·*gii*
spoon	халбага	khal·bag
tea shop	цайны газар	tsai·ny ga·zar
sugar	чихэр	chi·kher
vegetarian	ногоон хоолтон	no·*goon* khool·ton
with rice	будаатай	bu·*daa*·tai

Meat & Fish

antelope	цагаан зээр	tsa·*gaan* zeer
beef	үхрийн мах	ü·khriin makh
carp	булуу цагаан	bu·*luu* tsa·*gaan*
chicken	тахианы мах	ta·khia·ny makh
duck	нугас	nu·gas
fillet	гол мах	gol makh
fish	загас	za·gas
goat	ямаа	ya·*maa*
kebab	шорлог	shor·log
marmot	тарваг	tar·vag
meat	мах	makh
(fried) meat pancake	хуушуур	khuu·shuur
meat with rice	будаатай хуураг	bu·*daa*·tai khuu·rag
mutton	хонины мах	kho·ni·ny makh
mutton dumplings	бууз	buuz
patty	бифштекс	bif·shteks
perch	алгана	al·gan
pike	цурхай	tsurh·kai
pork	гахайн мах	ga·khain makh
salmon	омуль	o·mul
sausage	хиам/зайдас/ сосик	khiam/zai·das/ so·sisk
sturgeon	хилэм	khi·lem
antevenison	бугын мах	bu·gyn makh
wild boar	бодон гахай	bo·don ga·khai

Fruit & Vegetables

apple	алим	a·lim
cabbage	байцаа	bai·tsaa
carrot	шар лууван	shar luu·van
cucumber	өргөст хэмэх	ör·göst khe·mekh
fruit	жимс	jims
onion	сонгино	son·gin
potato	төмс	töms
radish	улаан лууван	u·*laan* luu·van
salad	салат	sa·lad

tomato	улаан лооль	u·*laan* loo·il
turnip	манжин	man·jin
vegetable	ногоо	no·*goo*

Drinks

beer	пиво	piv
coffee	кофе	ko·fi
(buckthorn) juice	(чацарганы) шүүс	(cha·tsar·ga·ny) shüüs
koumiss	айраг	ai·rag
lemonade	нимбэгний ундаа	nim·beg·nii un·daa
milk	сүү	süü
milk tea	сүүтэй цай	süü·tei tsai
milk with rice	сүүтэй будаа	süü·tei bu·daa
mineral water	рашаан ус	ra·shaan us
tea	цай	tsai
vodka	архи	a·rikh
wine	дарс	dars

Emergencies

Help!	Туслаарай!	tus·*laa*·rai
Go away!	Зайл!	zail
I'm lost.	Би төөрчихлөө.	bi töör·chikh·*löö*

There's been an accident.
Осол гарчээ. — o·sol gar·*chee*

Call a doctor/the police!
Эмч/Цагдаа дуудаарай! — emch/tsag·*daa* duu·*daa*·rai

I'm ill.
Би өвчтэй байна. — bi övch·tei bai·na

It hurts here.
Энд өвдөж байна. — end öv·döj bai·na

Where is the toilet?
хорлон хаана байна вэ? — jor·long khaan bai·na ve

Shopping & Services

I'd like to buy ...
Би ... авмаар байна. — bi ... av·*maar* bai·na

How much is it?
Энэ ямар үнэтэй вэ? — en ya·mar ün·tei ve

Can you reduce the price?
Та үнэ буулгах уу? — ta ün *buul*·gakh uu

exchange rate	мөнгөний ханш	möng·*nii* khansh
post office	шуудан	shuu·dan
public phone	нийтийн утас	nii·tiin u·tas
signature	гарын үсэг	ga·ryn ü·seg
travellers check	жуулчны чек	*juulch*·ny chek

Time, Dates & Numbers

What time is it?

Хэдэн цаг болж байна?		*khe·den tsag bolj bai·na*

morning	өглөө	*ög·löö*
afternoon	өдөр	*ö·dör*
evening	орой	*o·roi*
yesterday	өчигдөр	*ö·chig·dör*
today	өнөөдөр	*ö·nöö·dör*
tomorrow	маргааш	*mar·gaash*
Monday	даваа	*da·vaa*
Tuesday	мягмар	*myag·mar*
Wednesday	лхагва	*lkha·vag*
Thursday	пүрэв	*pü·rev*
Friday	баасан	*baa·sang*
Saturday	бямба	*byamb*
Sunday	ням	*nyam*

Remember to add the word cap sar (literally 'month', 'moon') after the following words:

January	нэгдүгээр	*neg·dü·geer*
February	хоёрдугаар	*kho·yor·du·gaar*
March	гуравдугаар	*gu·rav·du·gaar*
April	дөрөвдүгээр	*dö·röv·dü·geer*
May	тавдугаар	*tav·du·gaar*
June	зургадугаар	*zur·ga·du·gaar*
July	долдугаар	*dol·du·gaar*
August	наймдугаар	*naim·du·gaar*
September	есдүгээр	*yes·dü·geer*
October	аравдугаар	*a·rav·du·gaar*
November	арваннэг-дүгээр	*ar·van·neg·dü·geer*
December	арванхоёр-дугаар	*ar·van·kho·yor·du·gaar*

1	нэг	*neg*
2	хоёр	*kho·yor*
3	гурав	*gu·rav*
4	дөрөв	*dö·röv*
5	тав	*tav*
6	зургаа	*zur·gaa*
7	долоо	*do·loo*
8	найм	*naim*
9	ес	*yös*
10	арав	*ar·av*
100	зуу	*zuu*
1000	мянга	*myang·ga*

Transport

What times does the ... leave/arrive?

	... хэдэн цагт явдаг/ирдэг вэ?	*... khe·den tsagt yav·dag/ir·deg ve*
bus	Автобус	*av·to·bus*
plane	Нисэх онгоц	*ni·seh on·gots*
train	Галт тэрэг	*galt te·reg*
trolleybus	Троллейбус	*trol·lei·bus*

I want to go to ...

Би ... руу явмаар байна.	*bi ... ruu yav·maar bai·na*

Can you tell me when we get to ...?

Бид хэзээ ... хүрэхийг хэлж өгнө үү?	*bid khe·zee ... khu·re·hiig helj ög·nö uu*

I want to get off!

Би буумаар байна!	*bi buu·maar bai·na*

1st class	нэгдүгээр зэрэг	*neg·dü·geer ze·reg*
2nd class	хоёрдугаар зэрэг	*kho·yor·du·gaar ze·reg*
one-way ticket	нэг талын билет	*neg ta·lyn bi·let*
return ticket	хоёр талын билет	*kho·yor ta·lyn bi·let*
first	анхны	*ankh·ny*
next	дараа	*da·raa*
last	сүүлийн	*süü·liin*
airport	нисэх онгоцны буудал	*ni·sekh on·gots·ny buu·dal*
bus stop	автобусны зогсоол	*av·to·bus·ny zog·sool*
platform	давцан	*dav·tsan*
ticket office	билетийн касс	*bi·le·tiin kass*
timetable	цагийн хуваарь	*tsa·giin khu·vaair*
train station	галт тэрэгний буудал	*galt te·re·ge·nii buu·dal*

RUSSIAN

Russian belongs to the Slavonic language family and is closely related to Belarusian and Ukrainian. It has more than 150 million speakers within the Russian Federation and is used as a second language in the former republics of the USSR, with a total number of speakers of more than 270 million.

Russian is written in the Cyrillic alphabet (see the next page), and it's well worth the effort familiarising yourself with it so that you can read maps, timetables, menus and street signs. Otherwise, just read the coloured pronunciation guides given next to each Russian phrase in this chapter as if they were English, and you'll be understood. Most sounds are the same as in English, and the few differences in pronunciation are explained in the alphabet table. The stressed syllables are indicated with italics.

Basics

Hello.	Здравствуйте.	zdrast·vuy·tye
Goodbye.	До свидания.	da svi·da·nya
Excuse me.	Простите.	pras·ti·tye
Sorry.	Извините.	iz·vi·ni·tye
Yes./No.	Да./Нет.	da/nyet
Please.	Пожалуйста.	pa·zhal·sta
Thank you.	Спасибо.	spa·si·ba
You're welcome.	Пожалуйста.	pa·zhal·sta

What's your name?
Как вас зовут?   kak vas za·vut

My name is ...
Меня зовут ...   mi·nya za·vut ...

Do you speak English?
Вы говорите   vi ga·va·ri·tye
по-английски?   pa·an·gli·ski

I don't understand.
Я не понимаю.   ya nye pa·ni·ma·yu

Accommodation

Do you have a ... room?	У вас есть ...?	u vas yest' ...
single	одноместный номер	ad·na·myest·nih no·mir
double	номер с двуспальней кроватью	no·mir z dvu·spal'·nyey kra·va·tyu

How much is it for ...?	Сколько стоит за ...?	skol'·ka sto·it za ...
a night	ночь	noch'
two people	двоих	dva·ikh

boarding house	пансионат	pan·si·a·nat
campsite	кемпинг	kyem·ping
heating	отопление	a·ta·plye·ni·ye
hot water	горячая вода	ga·rya·cha·ya va·da
hotel	гостиница	ga·sti·ni·tsa
youth hostel	общежитие	ap·shi·zhih·ti·ye
light	свет	svyet

Cyrillic	Sound (Russian)	
А а	a	as in 'father' (in a stressed syllable); as in 'ago' (in an unstressed syllable)
Б б	b	as in 'but'
В в	v	as in 'van'
Г г	g	as in 'get'
Д д	d	as in 'dog'
Е е	ye	as in 'yet' (in a stressed syllable and at the end of a word);
	i	as in 'tin' (in an unstressed syllable)
Ё ё	yo	as in 'yore' (often printed without dots)
Ж ж	zh	as the 's' in 'measure'
З з	z	as in 'zoo'
И и	i	as the 'ee' in 'meet'
Й й	y	as in 'boy' (not transliterated after ы or и)
К к	k	as in 'kind'
Л л	l	as in 'lamp'
М м	m	as in 'mad'
Н н	n	as in 'not'
О о	o	as in 'more' (in a stressed syllable);
	a	as in 'hard' (in an unstressed syllable)
П п	p	as in 'pig'
Р р	r	as in 'rub' (rolled)
С с	s	as in 'sing'
Т т	t	as in 'ten'
У у	u	as the 'oo' in 'fool'
Ф ф	f	as in 'fan'
Х х	kh	as the 'ch' in 'Bach'
Ц ц	ts	as in 'bits'
Ч ч	ch	as in 'chin'
Ш ш	sh	as in 'shop'
Щ щ	shch	as 'sh-ch' in 'fresh chips'
Ъ ъ	–	'hard sign' meaning the preceding consonant is pronounced as it's written
Ы ы	ih	as the 'y' in 'any'
Ь ь	'	'soft sign' meaning the preceding consonant is pronounced like a faint y
Э э	e	as in 'end'
Ю ю	yu	as the 'u' in 'use'
Я я	ya	as in 'yard' (in a stressed syllable);
	ye	as in 'yearn' (in an unstressed syllable)

Directions

Where is ...?
Где ...?   gdye ...

What's the address?
Какой адрес?   ka·koy a·dris

Could you write it down, please?
Запишите, za·pi·*shih*·tye
пожалуйста. pa·*zhal*·sta

Can you show me (on the map)?
Покажите мне, pa·ka·*zhih*·tye mnye
пожалуйста pa·*zhal*·sta
(на карте). (na *kar*·tye)

behind ...	за ...	za ...
far	далеко	da·li·*ko*
in front of ...	перед ...	*pye*·rit ...
near	близко	*blis*·ka
next to ...	рядом с ...	*rya*·dam s ...
opposite ...	напротив ...	na·*pro*·tif ...
straight ahead	прямо	*prya*·ma

Eating & Drinking

What would you recommend?
Что вы рекомендуете? shto vih ri·ka·min·*du*·it·ye

What's in that dish?
Что входит в это shto *fkho*·dit v e·ta
блюдо? *blyu*·da

I don't eat (meat).
Я не ем (мяса). ya nye yem (*mya*·sa)

To your health!
За ваше здоровье! za va·shih zda·*rov*·ye

That was delicious!
Было очень вкусно! *bih*·la o·chin' *fkus*·na

Please bring the bill.
Принесите, pri·ni·*sit*·ye
пожалуйста счёт. pa·*zhal*·sta shot

Key Words

bottle	бутылка	bu·*tihl*·ka
bowl	миска	*mis*·ka
bread	хлеб	khlyep
breakfast	завтрак	*zaf*·trak
cheese	сыр	sihr
cold	холодный	kha·*lod*·nih
dinner	ужин	*u*·zhihn
dish	блюдо	*blyu*·da
egg	яйцо	yeyt·*so*
fork	вилка	*vil*·ka
glass	стакан	sta·*kan*
honey	мёд	myot
hot (warm)	жаркий	*zhar*·ki
knife	нож	nosh
lunch	обед	ab·*yet*
menu	меню	min·*yu*
nut	орех	ar·*yekh*

oil	масло	*mas*·la
pasta	паста	*pa*·sta
pepper	перец	*pye*·rits
plate	тарелка	tar·*yel*·ka
restaurant	ресторан	ris·ta·*ran*
rice	рис	ris
salt	соль	sol'
spoon	ложка	*losh*·ka
sugar	сахар	*sa*·khar
vinegar	уксус	*uk*·sus
with	с	s
without	без	byez

Meat & Fish

beef	говядина	gav·*ya*·di·na
caviar	икра	i·*kra*
chicken	курица	*ku*·rit·sa
duck	утка	*ut*·ka
fish	рыба	*rih*·ba
herring	сельдь	syelt'
lamb	баранина	ba·*ra*·ni·na
meat	мяса	*mya*·sa
oyster	устрица	*ust*·rit·sa
pork	свинина	svi·*ni*·na
prawn	креветка	kriv·*yet*·ka
salmon	лососина	la·sa·*si*·na
veal	телятина	til·*ya*·ti·na
turkey	индейка	ind·*yey*·ka

Fruit & Vegetables

apple	яблоко	*yab*·la·ka
bean	фасоль	fa·*sol'*
cabbage	капуста	ka·*pu*·sta
capsicum	перец	*pye*·rits
carrot	морковь	mar·*kof'*
cauliflower	цветная капуста	tsvit·*na*·ya ka·*pu*·sta
cucumber	огурец	a·gur·*yets*
fruit	фрукты	*fruk*·tih
mushroom	гриб	grip
onion	лук	luk
orange	апельсин	a·*pil'*·sin
peach	персик	*pyer*·sik
pear	груша	*gru*·sha
plum	слива	*sli*·va
potato	картошка	kar·*tosh*·ka
spinach	шпинат	shpi·*nat*
tomato	помидор	pa·mi·*dor*
vegetable	овощ	*o*·vash

Drinks

beer	пиво	*pi*·va
'soviet-brand' champagne	советское шампанское	sav·*yet*·ska·ye sham·*pan*·ska·ye
coffee	кофе	*kof*·ye
(orange) juice	(апельсин-овый) сок	(a·*pil'*·*si*·na·vih) sok
milk	молоко	ma·la·*ko*
tea	чай	chey
(mineral) water	(минеральная) вода	(mi·ni·*ral'*·na·ya) va·*da*
vodka	водка	*vot*·ka
(home-made) vodka	самогон	sa·ma·*gon*
wine	вино	vi·*no*

Emergencies

Help!
Помогите! — pa·ma·*gi*·tye

Leave me alone!
Приваливай! — pri·*va*·li·vai

I'm lost.
Я заблудился/ заблудилась. (m/f) — ya za·blu·*dil*·sa/ za·blu·*di*·las'

There's been an accident.
Произошёл несчастный случай. — pra·i·za·*shol* ne·*shas*·nih *slu*·chai

Call a doctor!
Вызовите врача! — *vih*·za·vi·tye vra·*cha*

Call the police!
Вызовите милицию! — *vih*·za·vi·tye mi·*li*·tsih·yu

I'm ill.
Я болен/больна. (m/f) — ya bo·lin/bal'·*na*

It hurts here.
Здесь болит. — zdyes' ba·*lit*

Where are the toilets?
Где здесь туалет? — gdye zdyes' tu·al·*yet*

Shopping & Services

I need ...
Мне нужно ... — mnye *nuzh*·na ...

How much is it?
Сколько стоит? — *skol'*·ka *sto*·it

That's too expensive.
Это очень дорого. — e·ta o·chen' *do*·ra·ga

There's a mistake in the bill.
Меня обсчитали. — min·*ya* ap·shi·*ta*·li

bank	банк	bank
market	рынок	*rih*·nak
post office	почта	*poch*·ta
telephone office	телефонный пункт	ti·li·*fo*·nih punkt

Signs – Russian	
Вход	Entrance
Выход	Exit
Открыт	Open
Закрыт	Closed
Справки	Information
Запрещено	Prohibited
Туалет	Toilets
Мужской (М)	Men
Женский (Ж)	Women

Time, Dates & Numbers

What time is it?
Который час? — ka·*to*·rih chas

Is this Moscow time?
Это московское время? — e·ta ma·*skof*·ska·ye *vryem*·ya

Is this local time?
Это местное время? — e·ta *myes*·na·ye *vryem*·ya

morning	утро	*ut*·ra
afternoon	после обеда	*pos*·lye ab·*ye*·da
evening	вечер	*vye*·chir
yesterday	вчера	vchi·*ra*
today	сегодня	si·*vod*·nya
tomorrow	завтра	*zaft*·ra
Monday	понедельник	pa·ni·*dyel'*·nik
Tuesday	вторник	*ftor*·nik
Wednesday	среда	sri·*da*
Thursday	четверг	chit·*vyerk*
Friday	пятница	*pyat*·ni·tsa
Saturday	суббота	su·*bo*·ta
Sunday	воскресенье	vas·kri·*syen*·ye
January	январь	yan·*var'*
February	февраль	fiv·*ral'*
March	март	mart
April	апрель	ap·*ryel'*
May	май	mai
June	июнь	i·*yun'*
July	июль	i·*yul'*
August	август	*av*·gust
September	сентябрь	sin·*tyabr'*
October	октябрь	ak·*tyabr'*
November	ноябрь	na·*yabr'*
December	декабрь	di·*kabr'*

1	один	a·din
2	два	dva
3	три	tri
4	четыре	chi·tih·ri
5	пять	pyat'
6	шесть	shest'
7	семь	syem'
8	восемь	vo·sim'
9	девять	dye·vyat'
10	десять	dye·syat'
100	сто	sto
1000	тысяча	tih·si·cha

Transport

A ... ticket (to Novgorod).	Билет ... (на Новгород).	bil·yet ... (na nov·ga·rat)
one-way	в один конец	v a·din kan·yets
return	в оба конца	v o·ba kan·tsa
arrival	прибытие	pri·bih·ti·ye
baggage	багаж	ba·gash
bus	автобус	af·to·bus
conductor/ carriage attendant	проводник	pra·vad·nik
departure	отправление	at·prav·lye·ni·ye
first	первый	pyer·vih
last	последний	pas·lyed·ni
map	карта	kar·ta
metro token	жетон	zhi·ton
platform	платформа	plat·for·ma
(bus) stop	остановка	a·sta·nof·ka
ticket	билет	bil·yet
ticket office	билетная касса	bil·yet·na·ya ka·sa
timetable	расписание	ras·pi·sa·ni·ye
train	поезд	po·ist
tram	трамвай	tram·vai
trolleybus	троллейбус	tra·lyey·bus

I want to go to ...
Я хочу ехать в ...   ya kha·chu ye·khat' v ...

Does it stop at ...?
Поезд останав-   po·yist a·sta·nav·
ливается в ...?   li·va·yit·sa v ...

When does it leave?
Когда отправляется?   kag·da at·prav·lya·it·sa

When is the next train?
Когда следующий   kag·da slye·du·yu·shi
поезд?   po·ist

Which platform does the train leave from?
С какой платформы   s ka·koy plat·for·mih
отходит поезд?   at·kho·dit po·ist

How long does it take to get to ...?
Сколько времени   skol'·ka vrye·mi·ni
нужно ехать до ...?   nuzh·na ye·khat' da ...

What station is this?
Какая эта станция?   ka·ka·ya e·ta stant·sih·ya

What's the next station?
Какая следующая   ka·ka·ya slye·du·yu·sha·ya
станция?   stant·sih·ya

Please stop here.
Остановитесь здесь,   a·sta·na·vit·yes' zdyes'
пожалуйста!   pa·zhal·sta

I need (assistance).
Мне нужна   mnye nuzh·na
(помощь).   (po·mash)

I'd like to buy an SV/kupe/platstkartny ticket for train number ... to ...
Я хотел/хотела   ya kha·tyel/kha·tye·la
бы купить билет   bih ku·pit' bil·yet
для СВ/для купе/   dlya es ve/dlya ku·pe/
в плацкарте   f plats·kar·tye
на поезд номер ...   na po·ist no·mir ...
до ... (m/f)   na ...

GLOSSARY

This glossary is a list of Russian (R), Chinese (C) and Mongolian (M) terms you may come across during your Trans-Siberian journey. See p354, p362 and p371 for words that will help you while dining.

aimag (M) – province or state within Mongolia

airag (M) – fermented mare's milk

apteka (R) – pharmacy

arkhi (M) – the common term for homemade vodka

aviakassa (R) – air-ticket office

avtomat (R) – automatic ticket machine

avtovokzal (R) – bus terminal

AYaM (R) – Amur-Yakutsk Mainline, in Russian Amuro-Yakutskaya Magistral

babushka (R) – grandmother

BAM (R) – Baikal-Amur Mainline, in Russian Baikalo-Amurskaya Magistral

bankomat (R) – ATM

banya (R) – bathhouse

bei (C) – north

bilet (R) – ticket

bīnguǎn (C) – tourist hotel

bolnitsa (R) – hospital

bulvar (R) – boulevard

CAAC (C) – Civil Aviation Administration of China, which controls most of China's domestic and foreign airlines

CCP (C) – Chinese Communist Party

Chángtú gōnggōngqìchē (C) – long-distance buses

CIS (R) – Commonwealth of a Independent States; an alliance of independent states comprising the former USSR republics, with the exception of the three Baltic countries

CITS (C) – China International Travel Service

CTS (C) – China Travel Service

dacha (R) – country cottage, summer house

dajie (C) – avenue

datsan (R) – Buddhist monastery

detsky (R) – child's, children's

dom (R) – house

dong (C) – east

duma (R) – parliament

dvorets (R) – palace

elektrichka (R) – also *prigorodny poezd*; suburban train

fen (C) – a 10th of a *jiao*, in Chinese currency (which makes it minuscule)

firmeny poezda (R) – trains with names (eg *Rossiya*); these are usually of a higher standard

FSB (R) – Federalnaya Sluzhba Bezopasnosti, the Federal Security Service, the successor to the KGB

gavan (R) – harbour

ger (M) – traditional, circular felt *yurt*

gol (M) – river

gorod (R) – city, town

gostiny dvor (R) – trading arcade

gudamj (M) – street

Gulag (R) – Glavnoe Upravlenie Lagerey (Main Administration for Camps); the Soviet network of concentration camps

hú (C) – lake

hútòng (C) – narrow alleyway

Inner Mongolia (M) – a separate province within China

Intourist (R) – the old Soviet State Committee for Tourism, now hived off, split up and in competition with hundreds of other travel agencies

izba (R & M) – traditional wooden cottage

jiao (C) – a 10th of a *yuán*, in Chinese currency

jie (C) – street

kassa (R) – ticket office, cashier's desk

Kazakh (M) – Turkic ethnic group from Central Asia, also found in the west of Mongolia; people from Kazakhstan

KGB (R) – Komitet Gosydarstvennoy Bezopasnosti; Committee of State Security; now the *FSB*

khaan (M) – a king or chief

Khalkh (M) – the major ethnic group living in Mongolia

khiid (M) – Buddhist monastery

khram (R) – church

kino (R) – cinema

kladbishche (R) – cemetery

komnaty otdykha (R) – literally 'resting rooms'; cheap lodgings in Siberian train stations

kray (R) – territory

kreml (R) – kremlin, a town's fortified stronghold

Kuomintang (C) – Chiang Kaishek's Nationalist Party, the dominant political force after the fall of the Qing dynasty; now Taiwan's major political party

kupeyny (R) – *kupe*; compartmentalised carriage

lama (M) – Tibetan Buddhist monk or priest

lavra (R) – senior monastery

living Buddha (M) – common term for reincarnations of Buddhas; Buddhist spiritual leader in Mongolia

lu (C) – road

lyux (R) – a *lyux* room in a hotel is a kind of suite, with a sitting room in addition to the bedroom and bathroom

Mafia (R) – anyone who has anything to do with crime, from genuine gangsters to petty criminals

magazin (R) – shop

Manchus (C) – non-Chinese ethnic group from Manchuria (present-day northeast China) that took over China and established the Qing dynasty

manezh (R) – riding school

marshrutky (R) – minibus that runs along a fixed route

matryoshka (R) – set of stacking, painted wooden dolls

mestnoe vremya (R) – local time

militsia (R) – police

more (R) – sea

morin khuur (M) – horsehead fiddle

most (R) – bridge

MPRP (M) – Mongolian People's Revolutionary Party, now called the Mongolian People's Party

muzey (R) – museum; also some palaces, art galleries and nonworking churches

muzhskoy (R) – men's (toilet)

naadam (M) – game

naberezhnaya (R) – embankment

nan (C) – south

novy (R) – new

nuruu (M) – mountain range

oblast (R) – region

obshchiy (R) – 4th-class train compartment

okrug (R) – district

örgön chölöö (M) – avenue

ovoo (M) – shamanistic collection of stones, wood or other offerings to the gods, usually placed in high places

ozero (R) – lake

Paskha (R) – Easter

pereryv (R) – break (when shops, ticket offices, restaurants etc close for an hour or two during the day)

pereulok (R) – lane or side street

Pinyin (C) – the system of writing the Chinese language in the Roman alphabet, adopted by the Communist Party in 1958

PLA (C) – People's Liberation Army

platskartny (R) – *platskart*, also *zhyosky*; 3rd class (or hard seat) in an open carriage of a train

ploshchad (R) – square

poezd (R) – train

posolstvo (R) – embassy

PRC (C) – People's Republic of China

prichal (R) – landing, pier

prigorodny poezd (R) – also *elektrichka*; suburban train

prospekt (R) – avenue

provodnik/provodnitsa (R) – male/female carriage attendant on a train

PSB (C) – Public Security Bureau; the arm of the police force that deals with foreigners

rayon (R) – district

rechnoy vokzal (R) – river terminal

Renminbi (C) – literally 'people's money', the formal name for the currency of China; shortened to RMB

Rozhdestvo (R) – Christmas

sad (R) – garden

samovar (R) – urn with an inner tube filled with hot charcoal, used for heating water for tea

selo (R) – village

sever (R) – north

shosse (R) – highway

siheyuan (C) – traditional house with courtyard

skory (R) – fast

spalny vagon (R) – also SV; sleeping wagon

stupa (M) – Buddhist religious monument composed of a solid hemisphere topped by a spire, containing relics of the Buddha; also known as a pagoda, or *suburgan* in Mongolian

süm (M) – Buddhist temple

taiga (R) – northern pine, fir, spruce and larch forest

teatr (R) – theatre

tögrög (M) – unit of currency in Mongolia

troika (R) – vehicle drawn by three horses

Tsagaan Sar (M) – 'White Moon' or 'White Month'; a festival to celebrate the start of the lunar year

tualet (R) – toilet

UFMS (R) – Upravleniye Federalnoy Migratsionnoy Slyzhby (Federal Migration Service) often shortened to UFMS or FMS. It's likely you'll hear the old acronyms PVU and OVIR used for this office.

ulitsa (R) – street

urtyn-duu (M) – traditional singing style

uul (M) – mountain

vokzal (R) – station

vostok (R) – east

xi (C) – west

yezhednevno (R) – daily

yuán (C) – the Chinese unit of currency, also referred to as RMB

yurt (R) – nomad's portable, round tent-house made of felt or skins stretched over a collapsible frame of wood slats

zheton (R) – token (for metro etc)

behind the scenes

SEND US YOUR FEEDBACK

We love to hear from travellers – your comments keep us on our toes and help make our books better. Our well-travelled team reads every word on what you loved or loathed about this book. Although we cannot reply individually to postal submissions, we always guarantee that your feedback goes straight to the appropriate authors, in time for the next edition. Each person who sends us information is thanked in the next edition – and the most useful submissions are rewarded with a free book.

Visit **lonelyplanet.com/contact** to submit your updates and suggestions or to ask for help. Our award-winning website also features inspirational travel stories, news and discussions.

Note: We may edit, reproduce and incorporate your comments in Lonely Planet products such as guidebooks, websites and digital products, so let us know if you don't want your comments reproduced or your name acknowledged. For a copy of our privacy policy visit lonelyplanet.com/privacy.

OUR READERS

Many thanks to the travellers who used the last edition and wrote to us with helpful hints, useful advice and interesting anecdotes:

Jenia, Konstanze, Francesca Broom, Nicola Butt, Rene Cabos, Cora De Koning, Roberto De Leon, Sien Deroo, Veronika Doblhoff-dier, Kieran Drake & Rachael Clapson, Thelma Gower, Reijo Härkönen, Basia Jozwiak, Suzanne Klein, Magnus Kohler, Francis Lafortune, Simo Laitinen, Neil Matthews, Amar Nanda, Emma Palios, Jiri Preclik & Andrea Votavova, Torben Prokscha, Fleur S Gittinger & Rico Czaja, Christopher Sexton, Suvi Tossavainen, Hanna Van Egmond, Tobias Welte, Ekaterina Zaytseva

AUTHOR THANKS

Anthony Haywood

Much of this new edition of the Trans-Sib guide was researched parallel to the Russia guide. I'd like to thank Simon Richmond in particular for valuable input that flowed into this book from his Russia original research. I'd also like to thank all authors and LP staff for doing such a professional job, fellow author Michael Kohn in particular for his expertise on Mongolia and China. Thanks to

Herr Fink from Lernidee-Erlebnisreisen and Herr Hahn at Gleisnost for their assistance; staff at Intourist's railway booking office who, without knowing the reason, patiently answered my questions; and staff at the information centres in Perm and Kazan. I'm also grateful to Tanya Ryabukhina in Moscow, Tamara Ryabukhina and Gennardy Doronin in Krasnoarmeysk, Katya Putina in Perm. Special thanks to Lyuba Suslyakova in Yekaterinburg, Mark Smith of 'Man in Seat 61' fame and author Ian Frazier for finding time to be interviewed.

Marc Bennetts

Thanks and love to Tanya Nevinskaya and Mariya Bennetts, who have been on many train journeys with me. Greetings to everyone who helped me on my travels.

Greg Bloom

The biggest thanks go to Pop, who rolled with me (literally) for four weeks, taking many vodka shots for the team. Dad, you asked for an adventure; you got it! Thanks to predecessor Robert Reid for engaging and passing along many tips. On the road, shouts go out to Daria and Bryan in Khabarovsk, to Leo for various tips, to Misha in Komsomolsk, to Lera and Alyona in Kamchatka and, of course, to my homeboy Christian in Yakutsk.

Marc Di Duca

A huge 'dyakuyu' to my Kyiv parents-in-law, Mykola and Vira, for taking care of my son Taras while I was on the road. Huge thanks also to Denis and Marina in Ulan-Ude, Svetlana and Naran in Ulan-Ude, Zhenya in Irkutsk, Maria from the Irkutsk tourist office, Yulia of Listvyanka tourist office, Svetlana in Irkutsk, Nikita and Natalia in Khuzhir, Anatoly and Oksana in Krasnoyarsk, and Russian Railways and S7 Airlines for getting me everywhere on time. Last, to my wife, Tanya: thank you for all your support both during my travels and while I was writing up. You were great.

Michael Kohn

Many thanks to fellow authors and editors, especially Anthony Haywood, Anna Tyler, Marc Di Duca and Damian Harper. In Mongolia, special thanks to travellers Kirk Olson, Oyuna and Toroo (Khongor Guesthouse). In China, thanks to Coco (Golden Pineapple Hostel) and Andy (Monkey Business). In Russia, thanks to Denis (Ulan-Ude Travellers House) and to Andrey the friendly customs official who smuggled me on the cross-border train to China. Special thanks to Baigal and Molly who joined me for part of the journey.

Tom Masters

Big thanks to my best friend in St Petersburg, Simon Patterson, for his good-humoured, vodka-soaked company on every trip I make to the city. Thanks also to Grégory Strub, Anna Knutson, Sergey Chernov, Tobin Auber, Dima Dzhafarov, Veronika Altukhova, Jessica Moroz, Chinawoman & Gang, Anthony Haywood, Simon Richmond, Mara Vorhees, Anna Tyler and all the in-house team in Melbourne for their continued hard work and support.

Leonid Ragozin

I would like to thank my wife, Masha Makeeva, for enduring my absences and accompanying me on some of my Golden Ring expeditions. Also, many thanks to Anna Tyler for taking me on board, and Anthony Haywood for guidance and a couple of great chats over shashlyk and beer in Moscow.

Mara Vorhees

Moscow with one-year-old twins requires an extra set of thank-yous to everyone who helped the monkeys settle into life in the Russian capital. Our awesome babysitter tops that list – Спасиба дорогоя Маша! My regular crew of Muscovite contacts was ever helpful, especially Tim O'Brien and Mirjana Vinsentin. Special thanks to Laura Bridge and Campbell Bethwaite for the 'local knowledge'. And a million kisses to Jerry, Shay and Van for coming along for the ride.

ACKNOWLEDGMENTS

Climate map data adapted from Peel MC, Finlayson BL & McMahon TA (2007) 'Updated World Map of the Köppen-Geiger Climate Classification', Hydrology and Earth System Sciences, 11, 163344.

Illustrations pp64-5 and pp98-9 by Javier Zarracina.

Cover photograph: Trans-Siberian, Irkutsk, Russia, Martin Moos, Lonely Planet Images. Many of the images in this guide are available for licensing from Lonely Planet Images: www.lonelyplanetimages.com.

This Book

This 4th edition of Lonely Planet's Trans-Siberian Railway guidebook was coordinated by Anthony Haywood. The following authors assisted with the research and writing of the book: Marc Bennetts, Greg Bloom, Marc Di Duca, Michael Kohn, Tom Masters, Leonid Ragozin and Mara Vorhees. Simon Richmond coordinated the previous two editions, and Mark Elliott and Robert Reid also contributed to them.

This guidebook was commissioned in Lonely Planet's London office, and produced by the following:

Commissioning Editors Anna Tyler, Emily K Wolman

Coordinating Editors Sarah Bailey, Carolyn Bain

Coordinating Cartographer Valentina Kremenchutskaya

Coordinating Layout Designer Nicholas Colicchia

Managing Editors Imogen Bannister, Tasmin Waby McNaughtan

Senior Editors Susan Paterson, Angela Tinson

Managing Cartographers Adrian Persoglia, Amanda Sierp

Managing Layout Designer Chris Girdler

Assisting Editors Andrew Bain, Jessica Crouch, Beth Hall, Briohny Hooper, Evan Jones, Kate Kiely

Assisting Cartographers Mick Garrett, James Leversha

Cover Research Naomi Parker

Internal Image Research Rebecca Skinner

Illustrator Javier Zarracina

Language Content Annelies Mertens

Thanks to Jo Cooke, Ryan Evans, Will Gourlay, Victoria Harrison, Laura Jane, Andi Jones, Yvonne Kirk, Shawn Low, Katie O'Connell, Trent Paton, Gerard Walker

NOTES

index

how to use this book

These symbols will help you find the listings you want:

- 👁 Sights
- 🐾 Beaches
- 🏃 Activities
- 🎓 Courses
- 👉 Tours
- 🎊 Festivals & Events
- 🛏 Sleeping
- 🍴 Eating
- 🍷 Drinking
- ☆ Entertainment
- 🛍 Shopping
- ℹ Information/Transport

These symbols give you the vital information for each listing:

- 📞 Telephone Numbers
- ⊙ Opening Hours
- Ⓟ Parking
- ⊖ Nonsmoking
- ✳ Air-Conditioning
- @ Internet Access
- 📶 Wi-Fi Access
- 🏊 Swimming Pool
- 🍃 Vegetarian Selection
- 📖 English-Language Menu
- 👪 Family-Friendly
- 🐾 Pet-Friendly
- 🚌 Bus
- ⛴ Ferry
- Ⓜ Metro
- Ⓢ Subway
- ⊖ London Tube
- 🚊 Tram
- 🚆 Train

Reviews are organised by author preference.

Look out for these icons:

- TOP CHOICE — Our author's recommendation
- FREE — No payment required
- 🌿 — A green or sustainable option

Our authors have nominated these places as demonstrating a strong commitment to sustainability – for example by supporting local communities and producers, operating in an environmentally friendly way, or supporting conservation projects.

Map Legend

Sights
- Beach
- Buddhist
- Castle
- Christian
- Hindu
- Islamic
- Jewish
- Monument
- Museum/Gallery
- Ruin
- Winery/Vineyard
- Zoo
- Other Sight

Activities, Courses & Tours
- Diving/Snorkelling
- Canoeing/Kayaking
- Skiing
- Surfing
- Swimming/Pool
- Walking
- Windsurfing
- Other Activity/Course/Tour

Sleeping
- Sleeping
- Camping

Eating
- Eating

Drinking
- Drinking
- Cafe

Entertainment
- Entertainment

Shopping
- Shopping

Information
- Bank
- Embassy/Consulate
- Hospital/Medical
- Internet
- Police
- Post Office
- Telephone
- Toilet
- Tourist Information
- Other Information

Transport
- Airport
- Border Crossing
- Bus
- Cable Car/Funicular
- Cycling
- Ferry
- Metro
- Monorail
- Parking
- Petrol Station
- Taxi
- Train/Railway
- Tram
- Other Transport

Routes
- Tollway
- Freeway
- Primary
- Secondary
- Tertiary
- Lane
- Unsealed Road
- Plaza/Mall
- Steps
- Tunnel
- Pedestrian Overpass
- Walking Tour
- Walking Tour Detour
- Path

Geographic
- Hut/Shelter
- Lighthouse
- Lookout
- Mountain/Volcano
- Oasis
- Park
- Pass
- Picnic Area
- Waterfall

Population
- Capital (National)
- Capital (State/Province)
- City/Large Town
- Town/Village

Boundaries
- International
- State/Province
- Disputed
- Regional/Suburb
- Marine Park
- Cliff
- Wall

Hydrography
- River, Creek
- Intermittent River
- Swamp/Mangrove
- Reef
- Canal
- Water
- Dry/Salt/Intermittent Lake
- Glacier

Areas
- Beach/Desert
- Cemetery (Christian)
- Cemetery (Other)
- Park/Forest
- Sportsground
- Sight (Building)
- Top Sight (Building)

Michael Kohn

The Trans-Mongolian Route, The Trans-Manchurian Route, Běijīng Michael first rode the Trans-Mongolian Railway in 1997, stepping off the train in Ulaanbaatar on a chilly -30°C December day. That was the start of an extended stay in Mongolia, where he worked for an English-language newspaper and various international media. He has since chugged along most of northeast Asia's rail routes, including the remote train journey from Choibalsan to the Russian border. Michael has updated three editions of Lonely Planet's *Mongolia* guide, and two editions of Lonely Planet's *China*. He is currently based in Ulaanbaatar.

Tom Masters

St Petersburg Tom first came to St Petersburg in 1996 while studying Russian at the School of Slavonic & East European Studies in London. He loved the city so much that he came back after graduating and worked as a writer and editor at the *St Petersburg Times*. Since then he's been based in London and Berlin but returns regularly to 'Piter' to take on documentary work and write freelance articles and Lonely Planet guides.

Leonid Ragozin

Moscow, Moscow to Yekaterinburg Leonid devoted himself to beach dynamics when he studied geology in Moscow. But, for want of really nice beaches in Russia, he helped gold miners in Siberia and sold InterRail tickets before embarking on a journalist career. After eight years with the BBC he became a foreign correspondent for Russian *Newsweek* – a job that took him to such unlikely destinations as Bhutan and Ecuador. Back at the BBC he plunged into the turbulent sea of TV news.

Mara Vorhees

Moscow Mara has been travelling to Moscow since it was the capital of a different country. The pen-wielding traveller has worked on dozens of Lonely Planet titles, including *Moscow* and *St Petersburg*. When not roaming around Russia, Mara lives in a pink house in Somerville, Massachusetts, with her husband, two kiddies and two kitties.

OUR STORY

A beat-up old car, a few dollars in the pocket and a sense of adventure. In 1972 that's all Tony and Maureen Wheeler needed for the trip of a lifetime – across Europe and Asia overland to Australia. It took several months, and at the end – broke but inspired – they sat at their kitchen table writing and stapling together their first travel guide, *Across Asia on the Cheap*. Within a week they'd sold 1500 copies. Lonely Planet was born. Today, Lonely Planet has offices in Melbourne, London and Oakland, with more than 600 staff and writers. We share Tony's belief that 'a great guidebook should do three things: inform, educate and amuse'.

OUR WRITERS

Anthony Haywood

Coordinating author; Moscow to Yekaterinburg, Yekaterinburg to Krasnoyarsk
Anthony was born in the port city of Fremantle, Western Australia, and pulled anchor early on to mostly hitchhike through Europe and the USA. Aberystwyth in Wales and Ealing in London were his wintering grounds at the time. He later studied comparative literature in Perth and Russian language in Melbourne. In the 1990s, fresh from a spell in post-Soviet, pre-anything Moscow, he moved to Germany. Today he works as a German-based freelance writer and journalist and divides his time between Göttingen (Lower Saxony) and Berlin. His book, *Siberia, A Cultural History*, was published in 2010.

Marc Bennetts

Yekaterinburg to Krasnoyarsk Marc moved to Russia in 1997 and immediately fell in love with the country's pirate-CD markets. Since then, he has written about Russian spies, Chechen football and Soviet psychics for a variety of national newspapers, including the *Guardian* and the *Times*. In 2008 his book *Football Dynamo: Modern Russia and the People's Game* was released. He is currently working on a book about Russia's fascination with the occult.

Greg Bloom

Ulan-Ude to Vladivostok, The Baikal-Amur Mainline (BAM) Greg cut his teeth in the former Soviet Union as a journalist and later editor-in-chief of the *Kyiv Post*. He left Ukraine in 2003, but returns frequently to the region. In the service of Lonely Planet he has been detained in Uzbekistan, taken a *shlagbaum* to the head in Kyiv, swum in the dying Aral Sea, snowboarded down volcanoes in Kamchatka, and hit 100km/h in a Latvian bobsled. These days Greg lives in Cambodia.

Read more about Greg at:
lonelyplanet.com/members/gbloom4

Marc Di Duca

Lake Baikal: Krasnoyarsk to Ulan-Ude, Ulan-Ude to Vladivostok, The Baikal-Amur Mainline (BAM) Marc has spent nigh on two decades crisscrossing the former communist world, the last seven years of them as a travel-guide author. Stints on previous editions of LP's *Russia* and *Trans-Siberian Railway* were preceded by other guides to Moscow, St Petersburg and Lake Baikal. During research on his stretch of the Trans-Sib this time around, Marc somehow found himself freezing extremities in Lake Baikal, attending Ulan-Ude opera in hiking gear and facing a starter of frozen horse liver.

Read more about Marc at:
lonelyplanet.com/members/madidu

OVER MORE
PAGE WRITERS

Published by Lonely Planet Publications Pty Ltd
ABN 36 005 607 983
4th edition – Apr 2012
ISBN 978 1 74179 565 3
© Lonely Planet 2012   Photographs © as indicated 2012
10 9 8 7 6 5 4 3 2 1
Printed in Singapore